Prismatic Translation

LEGENDA

LEGENDA is the Modern Humanities Research Association's book imprint for new research in the Humanities. Founded in 1995 by Malcolm Bowie and others within the University of Oxford, Legenda has always been a collaborative publishing enterprise, directly governed by scholars. The Modern Humanities Research Association (MHRA) joined this collaboration in 1998, became half-owner in 2004, in partnership with Maney Publishing and then Routledge, and has since 2016 been sole owner. Titles range from medieval texts to contemporary cinema and form a widely comparative view of the modern humanities, including works on Arabic, Catalan, English, French, German, Greek, Italian, Portuguese, Russian, Spanish, and Yiddish literature. Editorial boards and committees of more than 60 leading academic specialists work in collaboration with bodies such as the Society for French Studies, the British Comparative Literature Association and the Association of Hispanists of Great Britain & Ireland.

The MHRA encourages and promotes advanced study and research in the field of the modern humanities, especially modern European languages and literature, including English, and also cinema. It aims to break down the barriers between scholars working in different disciplines and to maintain the unity of humanistic scholarship. The Association fulfils this purpose through the publication of journals, bibliographies, monographs, critical editions, and the MHRA Style Guide, and by making grants in support of research. Membership is open to all who work in the Humanities, whether independent or in a University post, and the participation of younger colleagues entering the field is especially welcomed.

ALSO PUBLISHED BY THE ASSOCIATION

Critical Texts
Tudor and Stuart Translations • New Translations • European Translations
MHRA Library of Medieval Welsh Literature

MHRA Bibliographies
Publications of the Modern Humanities Research Association

The Annual Bibliography of English Language & Literature
Austrian Studies
Modern Language Review
Portuguese Studies
The Slavonic and East European Review
Working Papers in the Humanities
The Yearbook of English Studies

www.mhra.org.uk
www.legendabooks.com

TRANSCRIPT

Transcript publishes books about all kinds of imagining across languages, media and cultures: translations and versions, inter-cultural and multi-lingual writing, illustrations and musical settings, adaptation for theatre, film, TV and new media, creative and critical responses. We are open to studies of any combination of languages and media, in any historical moments, and are keen to reach beyond Legenda's traditional focus on modern European languages to embrace anglophone and world cultures and the classics. We are interested in innovative critical approaches: we welcome not only the most rigorous scholarship and sharpest theory, but also modes of writing that stretch or cross the boundaries of those discourses.

Editorial Committee
Chair: Matthew Reynolds (Oxford)
Robin Kirkpatrick (Cambridge)
Laura Marcus (Oxford)
Patrick McGuinness (Oxford)
Ben Morgan (Oxford)
Mohamed-Salah Omri (Oxford)
Tanya Pollard (CUNY)
Yopie Prins (Michigan)

Advisory Board
Jason Gaiger (Oxford)
Alessandro Grilli (Pisa)
Marina Grishakova (Tartu)
Martyn Harry (Oxford)
Linda Hutcheon (Toronto)
Calin-Andrei Mihailescu (London, Ontario)
Wen-Chin Ouyang (SOAS)
Clive Scott (UEA)
Ali Smith
Marina Warner (Birkbeck)
Shane Weller (Kent)
Stefan Willer (Berlin)

Managing Editor
Dr Graham Nelson
41 Wellington Square, Oxford OX1 2JF, UK

www.legendabooks.com/series/transcript

TRANSCRIPT

1. *Adapting the Canon: Translation, Visualisation, Interpretation*, edited by Ann Lewis and Silke Arnold-de Simine
2. *Adapted Voices: Transpositions of Céline's Voyage au bout de la nuit and Queneau's Zazie dans le métro*, by Armelle Blin-Rolland
3. *Zola and the Art of Television: Adaptation, Recreation, Translation*, by Kate Griffiths
4. *Comparative Encounters between Artaud, Michaux and the Zhuangzi: Rationality, Cosmology and Ethics*, by Xiaofan Amy Li
5. *Minding Borders: Resilient Divisions in Literature, the Body and the Academy*, edited by Nicola Gardini, Adriana Jacobs, Ben Morgan, Mohamed-Salah Omri and Matthew Reynolds
6. *Memory Across Borders: Nabokov, Perec, Chamoiseau*, by Sara-Louise Cooper
7. *Erotic Literature in Adaptation and Translation*, edited by Johannes D. Kaminski
8. *Translating Petrarch's Poetry: L'Aura del Petrarca from the Quattrocento to the 21st Century*, edited by Carole Birkan-Berz, Guillaume Coatalen and Thomas Vuong
9. *Making Masud Khan: Psychoanalysis, Empire and Modernist Culture*, by Benjamin Poore
10. *Prismatic Translation*, edited by Matthew Reynolds
11. *The Patient, the Impostor and the Seducer: Medieval European Literature in Hebrew*, by Tovi Bibring
12. *Reading Dante and Proust by Analogy*, by Julia Caterina Hartley
13. *The First English Translations of Molière: Drama in Flux 1663-1732*, by Suzanne Jones
14. *After Clarice: Reading Lispector's Legacy in the Twenty-First Century*, edited by Adriana X. Jacobs and Claire Williams
15. *Uruguayan Theatre in Translation: Theory and Practice*, by Sophie Stevens
16. *Hamlet Translations: Prisms of Cultural Encounters across the Globe*, edited by Márta Minier and Lily Kahn
17. *The Foreign Connection: Writings on Poetry, Art and Translation*, by Jamie McKendrick
18. *Poetics, Performance and Politics in French and Italian Renaissance Comedy*, by Lucy Rayfield

Prismatic Translation

Edited by Matthew Reynolds

Transcript 10
Modern Humanities Research Association
2019

Published by Legenda
an imprint of the Modern Humanities Research Association
Salisbury House, Station Road, Cambridge CB1 2LA

ISBN 978-1-78188-725-7 (HB)
ISBN 978-1-78188-726-4 (PB)

First published 2019
Paperback edition 2021

All rights reserved. No part of this publication may be reproduced or disseminated or transmitted in any form or by any means, electronic, mechanical, photocopying, recording or otherwise, or stored in any retrieval system, or otherwise used in any manner whatsoever without written permission of the copyright owner, except in accordance with the provisions of the Copyright, Designs and Patents Act 1988, or under the terms of a licence permitting restricted copying issued in the UK by the Copyright Licensing Agency Ltd, Saffron House, 6–10 Kirby Street, London EC1N 8TS, England, or in the USA by the Copyright Clearance Center, 222 Rosewood Drive, Danvers MA 01923. Application for the written permission of the copyright owner to reproduce any part of this publication must be made by email to legenda@mhra.org.uk.

Disclaimer: Statements of fact and opinion contained in this book are those of the author and not of the editors or the Modern Humanities Research Association. The publisher makes no representation, express or implied, in respect of the accuracy of the material in this book and cannot accept any legal responsibility or liability for any errors or omissions that may be made.

Trademark notice: Product or corporate names may be trademarks or registered trademarks, and are used only for identification and explanation without intent to infringe.

© Modern Humanities Research Association 2019

Copy-Editor: Dr Birgit Mikus

CONTENTS

	Acknowledgements	ix
	Notes on the Contributors	x
	Introduction MATTHEW REYNOLDS	1
	PART I: FRAMES	
1	Prismatic Agon, Prismatic Harmony: Translation, Literature, Language MATTHEW REYNOLDS	21
	PART II: LANGUAGES	
2	Poetic Traffic in a Multilingual Literary Culture: Equivalence, Parallel Aesthetics, and Language-Stretching in North India FRANCESCA ORSINI	51
3	'Annihilation is atop the lake': the Visual Untranslatability of an Ancient Egyptian Short Story HANY RASHWAN	72
4	[Mirroring] Events at the Sense Horizon: Translation over Time JOHN CAYLEY	96
	PART III: CULTURES	
5	Through a Prism, Translated: Culture and Change in Russia YVONNE HOWELL	121
6	Literary Metatranslations: when Translation Multiples Tell their own Story KASIA SZYMANSKA	140
7	Extreme Translation ADRIANA X. JACOBS	156
8	Translation Poetry: the Poetics of Noise in Hsia Yü's *Pink Noise* COSIMA BRUNO	173
9	Cultural Translation, or, the Political Logic of Prismatic Translation JERNEJ HABJAN	189
	PART IV: PRACTICES	
10	The Literary Translator as Dispersive Prism: Refracting and Recomposing Cultures JEAN ANDERSON	207

11	In Words and Colours: Lingo-Visual Translations of the Poetry of Shafii Kadkani PARI AZARM MOTAMEDI	221
12	T is for Translation(s): Translating Nonsense Alphabets into French AUDREY COUSSY	243
13	Algorithmic Translation: New Challenges for Translation in the Age of Algorithms ERAN HADAS	262
14	Du Bellay in the Modern University PHILIP TERRY	286

PART V: READINGS

15	Coleridge Diffracted: on the Opening Lines of *Kubla Khan* PATRICK HERSANT	297
16	The Hungarian Spectrum of Petronius's *Satyricon* PÉTER HAJDU	312
17	The Schizophrenic Prism: Louis Wolfson's Translation Practice ALEXANDRA LUKES	331
18	Less than Paper-Thin: Pseudotranslations, Absent Fathers and Harry Mathews's *Armenian Papers* DENNIS DUNCAN	346
19	Original-esque: Diderot and Goethe in Back-Translation STEFAN WILLER	359
	Index	369

ACKNOWLEDGEMENTS

Work towards this volume began at a conference hosted by the Oxford Comparative Criticism and Translation research centre (OCCT) in 2015: I am grateful to my co-organisers Maria Crosta, Adriana X. Jacobs, Xiaofan Amy Li, Ben Morgan, Mohamed-Salah Omri, Sowon S. Park and Philip Rothwell for their collaborative energy, as well as to the European Humanities Research Centre for its support. Investigations continued the following year in Vienna, at the AILC/ICLA Research Committee on Literary Theory, where Walid Hamarneh and Stefan Willer joined Sowon S. Park and myself in framing the discussion. Since 2016, the ongoing Prismatic Translation project has been supported by the AHRC as part of its Open World Research Initiative research programme in Creative Multilingualism, led by Katrin Kohl, and it continues to find a home in OCCT, which is itself supported by The Oxford Research Centre in the Humanities (TORCH) and St Anne's College. I am extremely grateful both to the AHRC and to OCCT's benefactors, Maria Ferreras Willetts, Jane and Peter Aitken, Celia Atkin, Fiona Lindblom and Arabella van Niekerk. Without their generosity, the contributors to this volume would not have been brought together for the searching conversations that have helped us all extend and deepen our ideas. The book has benefited from the publishing skills of Graham Nelson, Legenda's managing editor, and from the comments of a very helpful anonymous peer reviewer. Daniele Nunziata made the index.

M.R., Oxford, August 2019

NOTES ON THE CONTRIBUTORS

Jean Anderson is Associate Professor / Reader in French at Victoria University of Wellington, where she founded the Postgraduate Programme in Literary Translation Studies and Te Tumu Whakawhiti Tuhinga o Aotearoa / New Zealand Centre for Literary Translation in 2007. She has published a dozen books of Pacific fiction (translated from French to English or co-translated from English to French) and over 100 short pieces in anthologies and reviews. Her critical work in the field focuses on allusions and cultural ellipses, on the translation of transgeneric fiction, and on the translator as reader and mediator, particularly with regard to the work of postcolonial indigenous authors.

Cosima Bruno is Senior Lecturer in China Studies at the School of Oriental and African Studies, University of London. Her main research interests are in contemporary Chinese and Sinophone poetry, intermedial poetics, transculturation, and language art. Her publications include *Between the Lines: Yang Lian's Poetry through Translation* (Brill, 2012), translations, and articles in *Journal of Modern Literature in Chinese*, *Concentric*, *Life Writing*, *Target*, *Intervention*, *Shi tansuo*, *In forma di parole*, and in the collected volumes *Translating Others* (St Jerome, 2006) and *China and Its Others* (Rodopi, 2012).

John Cayley is a writer, theorist, and pioneering maker of language art in programmable media. Apart from more or less conventional poetry and translation, he has explored dynamic and ambient poetics, text generation, transliteral morphing, aestheticized vectors of reading, and transactive synthetic language. Today, he composes as much for reading in aurality as in visuality. *Grammalepsy: essays on digital language art* was published in 2018. Professor of Literary Arts at Brown University, he directs a graduate program in Digital Language Arts.

Audrey Coussy is Assistant Professor of Translation Studies and Literary Translation at the Department of French Language and Literature at McGill University. She completed a PhD in Translation Studies and Children's Literature at the Sorbonne Nouvelle Paris 3. Her dissertation focused on the way children's literature enables both the reader and the translator to experience non-reified language, orality, identity and alterity — these questions are central to her research in translation studies (general literature and children's literature). She is also a literary translator of contemporary fiction, working from English to French, and has translated the works of Patrick McCabe, Richard Milward and Danielle Teller, among others.

Dennis Duncan is a Lecturer in English Literature at UCL. His publications include *The Oulipo and Modern Thought* (2019) and *Tom McCarthy: Critical Essays*

(2016), while another monograph, *Index, A History of the*, is due out with Penguin in 2020. Recent academic articles have looked at Italo Calvino and writing machines, Mallarmé and jugs, and James Joyce's influence on mid-century French pornography. He has published translations of Michel Foucault, Boris Vian, and Alfred Jarry, among others, and was one of the curators of the exhibition *Babel: Adventures in Translation* at the Bodleian Library in Oxford.

Jernej Habjan is Research Fellow and Assistant Professor at the Research Centre of the Slovenian Academy of Sciences and Arts. He has a PhD in Sociology from the University of Ljubljana, and has held a postdoctoral position at the University of Munich and a research fellowship at the International Research Centre for Cultural Studies (IFK) in Vienna. He sits on the Research Committee on Literary Theory at the International Comparative Literature Association. His articles on contemporary literary theory have appeared in the *Canadian Review of Comparative Literature*, *CLCWeb*, *Journal of World Literature*, *Neohelicon*, and *South Atlantic Quarterly*.

Eran Hadas is an Israeli poet, software developer and new media artist. He is the author of eight books, creates hypermedia poetry and develops software based text generators. Among his collaborative projects are a headset that generates poems from brainwaves, a documentarian robot who interviews people about humanity, and an AI art curator. Hadas was the 2017 Schusterman Artist-in-Residence at Caltech. His projects have been exhibited at science museums (Heinz Nixdorf, Paderborn), art museums (Tel-Aviv Museum of Art), new media festivals (Ars-Electronica, Linz) and literature festivals (Tata Literature Live, Mumbai). He teaches interactive storytelling in the New Media Program at Tel-Aviv University.

Péter Hajdu is at Shenzhen University, and also works for the Research Centre for the Humanities, Budapest, Hungary, as research advisor. He received his M.A. in literature and classical philology from ELTE, Budapest, and his CSc degree from the Hungarian Academy of Sciences. He conducts research in ancient literature, literary theory, translation studies, comparative literature and *fin-de-siècle* Hungarian literature. He is the editor-in-chief of *Neohelicon*, a major journal on comparative literature.

Patrick Hersant is Associate Professor of English Literature and Translation Studies at Université Paris 8, and a researcher at the Institute for Modern Texts and Manuscripts (CNRS-ENS). Recent publications include a book (co-edited with Esa Hartmann) on translators' views on translation, *Au miroir de la traduction: Avant-texte, intertexte, paratexte* (Paris: Archives contemporaines, 2019), several papers on the genetics of translation, and *Traduire avec l'auteur* (Paris: Sorbonne Université Presses, 2019), an edited collection devoted to author-translator collaboration. As a translator, he has published French versions of British poets such as Philip Sidney, R.L. Stevenson, Edward Lear and Seamus Heaney.

Yvonne Howell is Professor of Russian at the University of Richmond, VA. She is the author of *Apocalyptic Realism: The Science Fiction of Arkady and Boris Strugatsky*, and the editor of an anthology of newly translated science fiction from the former

Soviet Union, *Red Star Tales: A Century of Russian and Soviet Science Fiction*. In addition to research assessing the importance of science fiction as a mode of thinking in modern history, she has also written about literature and scientific thought in Russian and Czech contexts.

Adriana X. Jacobs is Associate Professor of Modern Hebrew Literature in the Faculty of Oriental Studies and Fellow of the Oxford Centre for Hebrew and Jewish Studies. She has published widely on contemporary Hebrew and Israeli poetry and translation, including articles in *Shofar*, *PMLA*, *Studies in American Jewish Literature*, and *Prooftexts*. Her translations of Hebrew poetry have appeared in *Gulf Coast*, *World Literature Today*, *North American Review*, *The Ilanot Review*, among others, as well as in the collection *Women's Hebrew Poetry on American Shores: Poems by Anne Kleiman and Annabelle Farmelant* (Wayne State University Press, 2016). She is the author of *Strange Cocktail: Translation and the Making of Modern Hebrew Poetry* (University of Michigan Press, 2018).

Alexandra Lukes is Assistant Professor of French and Translation Studies at Trinity College Dublin. She works on the relationship between literature and madness, on the challenges of translating nonsense, and on the notion of untranslatability. She has published on Antonin Artaud's translation of Lewis Carroll and on Stéphane Mallarmé's pedagogical works, nursery rhymes, and translations, and she is the editor of a special issue of *Translation Studies* entitled 'Nonsense, Madness, and The Limits of Translation'.

Pari Azarm Motamedi, visual artist, writer and translator was born in Tehran and studied and worked in Iran and England before immigrating to Canada in 1984. Her art, as well as her theoretical interest, is focused on lingo-visual translations of poetry. She has exhibited her work extensively and has presented papers about her work at academic conferences. For several years Azarm Motamedi has been working on the translations of the poetry of Mohammad Reza Shafii Kadkani, renowned contemporary Iranian poet. Her English translations and paintings of the poems of Shafii Kadkani, were published in Tehran in a book titled *In the Mirror of the Stream*, which won the Parvin Etesami literary award in 2010.

Francesca Orsini is Professor of Hindi and South Asian Literatures at SOAS, University of London and a Fellow of the British Academy. She is the author of *The Hindi Public Sphere* (2002) and *Print and Pleasure* (2009). She is currently completing a multilingual literary history of the north Indian region of Awadh and running an ERC Horizon 2020 project called 'Multilingual Locals and Significant Geographies: for a ground-up approach to world literature'.

Hany Rashwan earned his PhD in Cultural, Literary and Postcolonial Studies from SOAS (2016). He defended a thesis on Arabic Jinās, or what can loosely be termed 'wordplay', 'paronomasia', 'pun', examined through a comparative lens with ancient Egyptian rhetorical traditions. It will be published with AUC University Press as *Literariness and Aesthetics of Ancient Egyptian Literature: Arabic Jinās in Post-Eurocentric Poetics*. Before joining the GlobalLIT project at the University of Birmingham to lead the Arabic strand, he was an Andrew Mellon Postdoctoral Fellow at the American University of Beirut. Dr Rashwan is the recipient of the International Society for the History of Rhetoric (ISHR) Research Fellowship in 2015. He is co-editing a volume entitled *Post-Eurocentric Poetics: New Approaches from Arabic, Persian and Turkic Literary Theory* to be published by the British Academy and Oxford University Press.

Matthew Reynolds is Professor of English and Comparative Criticism at Oxford and a Fellow of St Anne's College. Among his books are *Translation: A Very Short Introduction* (2016), *The Poetry of Translation: From Chaucer & Petrarch to Homer & Logue* (2011), *Likenesses: Translation, Illustration, Interpretation* (2013), *The Realms of Verse, 1830–1870: English Poetry in a Time of Nation-Building* (2001), and the novels *Designs for a Happy Home* (2009) and *The World Was All Before Them* (2013). He chairs the Oxford Comparative Criticism and Translation research centre (OCCT), and leads the Prismatic Translation research project.

Kasia Szymanska is Junior Research Fellow in Modern Languages at University College, Oxford, and a committee member of the Oxford Comparative Criticism and Translation research centre. Her research interests revolve around comparative literature, experimental translations, and multilingual poetics, especially with reference to the East European context. She is currently working on a book monograph on Translation Multiples, is involved in the collaborative project on 'Prismatic Jane Eyre' as well as in the 'Challenges of Translation' project in the CHCI-Mellon Global Humanities Institute. In 2018, she acted as a judge of the Oxford-Weidenfeld Translation prize. Her work to date has appeared in *PMLA* and edited volumes.

Philip Terry is a translator, and a writer of fiction and poetry. He has translated the work of Georges Perec, Stéphane Mallarmé and Raymond Queneau, and is the author of the novel *tapestry*, shortlisted for the Goldsmiths Prize. His poetry volumes include *Oulipoems*, *Shakespeare's Sonnets*, *Dante's Inferno*, Quennets, Bad *Times* and *Dictator*. He is currently editing the *Penguin Book of Oulipo* and translating Ice Age signs.

Stefan Willer is professor of Modern German Literature at the Humboldt Universität zu Berlin. Research interests: literary futurologies; cultural history of generations and inheritance; theories of language and translation; literature & music. Recent book publications: *Erbfälle. Theorie und Praxis kultureller Übertragung in der Moderne* (2014); *Futurologien. Ordnungen des Zukunftswissens* (co-ed., 2016); *Oper und Film. Geschichten einer Beziehung* (co-ed., 2019); *Zukunftssicherung. Kulturwissenschaftliche Perspektiven* (co-ed., 2019); *Selbstübersetzung als Wissenstransfer* (co-ed., forthcoming).

INTRODUCTION

Matthew Reynolds

Translation breeds more translation. A novel that travels into one foreign market will typically spread to more. A news story, when picked up by a global news agency, will be reproduced in many languages. Films, TV shows, You Tube videos, Wikipedia entries and other kinds of media content are dubbed or translated, not once, but again and again. A speech given in the European Parliament or United Nations is interpreted, both directly and via relay translation, into a multitude of tongues.

This translational multiplicity is sometimes said to be a modern phenomenon; and it is true that globalization and digital platforms have made the proliferative work of translation newly swift and newly visible.[1] But translation's tendency to multiply both across and within languages has deep historical roots. Global news agencies began life in the nineteenth century.[2] The reiterative translation of literary texts has a much longer history, for it goes to the heart of what literature is. Works become literary classics by being interpreted and re-interpreted — or, in the theatre, performed and re-performed — and translation participates in this complex interplay of reverence and renewal (think of the global multiplication of Homers and Shakespeares). Religious texts such as Buddhist sutras or the Bible have similarly paradoxical histories of preservation through multiple change.[3] And in predominantly oral and multilingual contexts, where the standardizing influence of print is not present, or not strongly felt, any repetition of any piece of language will involve alteration — of voice, handwriting, spelling, idiom, dialect, language — so that verbal reiteration and translation cannot be held apart.

Often, different translations are done by different people working in different places and times: they can be taken as indexes of cultural diversity or historical development. But different translations can also be made by the same person; indeed, the potential for multiplication is latent in any act of translation in the moment of its happening. In trans-lingual conversation, any proffered interpretation is open to correction or rephrasing. In written translation, any chosen form of words is plucked from a cloud of alternatives. Any given translation, in any form, is just one among many actual and possible versions.

In itself, each of the observations I have just made is uncontroversial. Separate aspects of translation's pluralising force have been well recognised and studied. Re-translation, understood as the repeated translation of the same work within a single language, has formed one area of investigation.[4] Other research has traced the reception of single texts or authors across different cultures and tongues.[5] There have been creative experiments in multiple translation, done by individuals and groups, in more academic or more popular contexts.[6] Discrete analyses have been conducted of the reiterative translation of religious texts, of philosophical terms, and of translation in global news and on the internet.[7] Yet, for all this varied and important work, the idea that translation is fundamentally multiplicatory — that its essence is not reproduction but proliferation — has been difficult to hold consistently in focus and to theorise. This has been the case across all the overlapping fields to which translation matters: Translation Studies, of course; and studies of national, comparative and world literatures; as well as discussions both within and beyond the academy of such issues as migration and machine translation. A paradigmatic scene of translation, in which a single text is translated by one person out of one language into one other language, is hard to shake off. It is rooted in dictionary definitions, according to which translation, or *traduction*, or *traduzione* is 'the action or process of turning from one language into another', or 'fait de transposer un texte d'une langue dans une autre', or 'azione del tradurre da una lingua in un'altra'; while *a* translation, or *Übersetzung*, is 'the product of this; a version in a different language' or 'ein Text, der von einer Sprache in eine andere übertragen wurde'.[8] The same picture shadows the definitions even of thinkers who, in other respects, have reoriented translation theory. Lawrence Venuti:

> Translation is a process by which the chain of signifiers that constitutes the source-language text is replaced by a chain of signifiers in the target language which the translator provides on the strength of an interpretation.[9]

Umberto Eco:

> Tradurre vuol dire capire il sistema interno di una lingua e la struttura di un testo dato in quella lingua, e costruire un doppio del sistema testuale che, *sotto una certa descrizione,* possa produrre effetti [sintattici e di senso] analoghi nel lettore.
>
> (Translation means understanding the whole internal system of a language and the structure of a given text in that language, and constructing a double of the textual system which, under a certain description, can produce analogous effects [syntactical and semantic] in the reader.)[10]

Theo Hermans:

> Authenticating a translation means transforming it into an equivalent authentic text which in its own particular sphere, can lay claim to the same authority as the original.[11]

What would it mean to pluralise these definitions? — to see translation, not as fundamentally a single act involving one source-text in one language, and one translation-text in one another language, which just happens to occur again and again, but rather as paradigmatically generating multiple texts, so that 'translation' becomes the process of turning from one language into other*s*, *da una lingua in altre*, producing chain*s* of signifiers in target language*s*, creating multiple equivalent, authentic text*s*, while 'a translation' correspondingly figures as just one of many actual and/or possible linguistic realisations? Translation's dominant metaphor would change: it would no longer be a 'channel' between one language and another but rather a 'prism'. It would be seen as opening up the plural signifying potential of the source text and spreading it into multiple versions, each continuous with the source though different from it, and related to the other versions though different from all of them too.

Reconfiguring the field in this way has consequences for how we conceive of languages, and language: it entails seeing them — or it — more as a continuum of variation than as a collection of bounded entities. It affects how we understand the relationship between texts that get called 'translations' and those that get called 'sources': not so much an endeavour to find equivalents for a set of given meanings (an idea encouraged by the channel metaphor) as a matter of interactive discovery and co-creation. It re-orients and adds to the questions that we ask. Not only 'why is this text re-translated?' but 'what prevents it from being translated more often, in more other places?' Not only 'what shifts has this translator introduced?' but also 'what are the other possibilities that have been both conjured up and foreclosed by the work of this translator?' — and not only 'what does this translation do in its context?', but also 'how does this translation relate to others, at many other points in the continuum of language variety?'[12] It opens the way to more plural translation practices, and to an exploration of how far readers might be receptive to them. As it develops these lines of enquiry, the prismatic approach draws on well-established trends in the discipline of Translation Studies. Like Susan Bassnett and Sherry Simon's classic work on gender, it sees 'translation as a dynamic activity fully engaged with cultural systems'.[13] Following Gideon Toury and Theo Hermans, it realises that to be a translator is to adopt a 'social role' in an 'institutional context'; and with Tejaswini Niranjana, Edward Cheyfitz, Maria Tymoczko, Robert Young and Naoki Sakai it recognizes that translation can be implicated in national and imperial strategies of definition and control, while also being a means of resisting them (as Sophie Collins and Adriana Jacobs have recently reasserted).[14] With its attention to the metaphoricity implicit in translation, it is in harmony with arguments put forward by Douglas Robinson, Lori Chamberlain and James St André.[15] What it seeks to add is a richer awareness of how translation operates within language, and a more nuanced account of the relationship between the textuality of the source and the many translational textualities that can and do arise from it. Kate Briggs has offered a vivid image of the translator's act of choice, the moment at which one form of words is pulled from the sea of language to do duty as an equivalent to the source: like a *stoppeuse* whose job, as Roland Barthes describes, was to halt and repair the runs in stockings, 'the translator wets her finger, she presses it down on the run of alternatives, the run of endless translation possibilities, each one with its own particular shades of meaning. And right now, in this moment, if only for her moment, familiarly and necessarily, and with all the delicate immobilizing power of saliva on wool, she makes it stop.'[16] What happens if, in the way we research and conceptualise translations, and perhaps also in our practices of making and reading them, we allow that run to stay visible, or keep on running, not only within a language but across the global continuum of linguistic variation and change? That is what this volume endeavours to illustrate, investigate and think through.

What causes translations to multiply? In the existing literature, various explanations have been provided. One idea bears on retranslation within a given language, and sees it as being driven by the need for improvement. An earlier translation is felt to be lacking or marred by mistakes, so a new one is conceived as a kind of remedy. Katrina Dodson cites this view in connection with anglophone translations of Clarice Lispector: 'I was the sixth translator in a new series intended to grant the Gospel of Clarice its proper glory by lovingly restoring every comma, semicolon, abrupt paragraph break, insistent repetition, and nonsensical turn of phrase that had been excised or steamrolled in previous, apocryphal versions.'[17] In Part I, below, I will explore other instances from Elizabeth Barrett Browning and Lydia Davis. This way of thinking is shaped by the picture of translation as channel. It conjures up an image of the best imaginable translation, a text that will have received and embodied everything that matters in the source text unchanged, and sees successive translations as a series of attempts to embody this ideal. Even when the ideal is understood to be a fantasy — as Dodson says, 'we know there is no such thing as a perfect translation' — it still exerts a strange power over how translation is understood. Any given translation is defined by its endeavour and yet failure to realise that picture — though of course it makes no sense to describe as 'failure' the non-realisation of something that by definition lies beyond the bounds of the possible.

This idea of improvement tends to attach to the translation of prose. For poetry, a different explanation is typically adduced, one which relies on a distinction of kind between poetry and other writing. When a poem generates multiple translations, it is taken as a sign of poetry's special linguistic richness: this requires a distinctive translational creativity, so much so that poetry translation is often felt to be not translation in the usual sense of the term, but something else. Don Paterson champions the word 'version'; Erín Moure coins 'transelation'; Johannes Göranssen speaks of 'transgressive circulation'.[18] Yet, for all that they seem to jettison the channel view, these arguments remain tied to it, in a secret alliance. Often, the more creative mode of remaking, which is meant to be distinguished from ordinary, channel-style translation, still turns out to be envisaged as a mode of transfer: in her transelation of Pessoa, Moure 'wanted to create a text that transferred the humor of the original', while Paterson aims (like many poetry translators before him) to 'represent the *spirit* of the original'. Göranssen does succeed in preventing the metaphor of the channel from ambushing his argument: poetry translation, he says, 'puts in motion a strange economy', in which:

> ... we may not only interact with the alien world by absorbing or rejecting, appropriating or conquering, but instead by becoming alien to ourselves, losing our own sense of mastery — over the poem, over ourselves — and opening up new realms of sensory-overwhelming "verbomania". Instead of going through the text to find a communication ideal in its interiority, we have to devour the text carnivalesquely.[19]

Yet, in this case, the channel metaphor persists elsewhere, being left unchallenged for the translation of all the kinds of text that do not count for Göranssen as poetry, and standing in implicit contrast to the energies of transgressive circulation. But what is the boundary between this poetry and that other writing? What if — as theorists of literary style assert — poetry (or 'poetic function', or 'poeticity') can be found in all kinds of language use?[20] How then does transgressive circulation relate to the everyday translation that is typically conceptualised according to the channel view? These questions remain to be explored.

With plays that are being translated for the theatre, yet another explanation holds sway. Here, it is taken for granted that translation is continuous with the generative processes of production, starting from the written text and conjuring up a work of performance that is freshly made with each new space, moment, cast, culture — and language. As Gregary Racz has put it, 'any translation done with performance in mind must seek to create ... a living piece of theatre developed from a dramaturgical analysis of the original text'; or in the words of David Hare, 'an intelligent translator is a kind of substitute director'.[21] Since such ideas already align comfortably with a prismatic view of translation we have chosen, in this volume, not to dwell on theatre translation but rather to explore areas where translation's prismatic workings are less obvious, more vexed, and so more in need of understanding.

The last of the prominent, current explanations for translational plurality is that translations — in any genre — age in a way that source texts do not: new versions therefore have to be made to replace previous ones that are becoming elderly and somehow ceasing to function.[22] It is true that translations have a distinctive, complex temporality since they always span time as well as languages: Annmarie Drury has traced some of the stylistic and cultural anachronies that can result, while Don Paterson notes that, when a text is translated and re-translated (he says a 'poem' but the same is true of any writing) it undergoes 'continual cultural rebirth, in a way denied to the original'.[23] Yet to say that translations age by contrast with original texts is to forget that many originals too lie dated and unreadable in the shadowlands of the past. What makes some source texts seem to endure through time is that they become canonical, which means that extraordinary cultural resources are devoted to keeping people reading them and feeling that they understand them. When the same energy is put into a translation it can survive in exactly the same way: Golding's Ovid, Florio's Montaigne or, in German, the Schlegel-Tieck Shakespeare are examples. When this happens the name of the translator takes on unusual prominence, in line with the workings of canonisation which always likes to build up author-figures for the texts that it conserves. On the other hand, when — as is much more common — a translation is felt to age in contrast to a source text, it is because the translation is being treated as itself one of the anonymous cultural resources — 'secondary material' — whose task is to keep the source text ever young. Paradoxically, what the ageing of a translation reveals is really the age of the source-text: this is what has to be denied by the creation of a new translation into more 'up-to-date' or 'idiomatic' language.

The prismatic approach draws something from all these ideas about the plurality of translations, and connects them up. From the consideration of ageing, we can take the recognition that languages are always changing. Translation crosses time as well as tongues: it is always done, not just into a language, but into a moment of that language. However, the prismatic view makes a stronger claim for the particularity of the language of the translation: not just the language of a 'time' (say a decade), but a single instant, or series of instants, in the work of the translator in interaction with the ever-shifting linguistic materials by which s/he is surrounded and permeated. In this respect, every act of translation for voice, page or screen is like a miniature dramatic performance: any translation, of any word, phrase, sentence, page or book, could be re-done at once by the same translator, and be different. For the prismatic view, the usual question is therefore reversed: not 'why are there multiple translations?' but 'why are there not (more of them)?' From this angle, translations of canonical novels are typically re-done within a language every twenty or thirty years, not because that is how often they need doing, but because that is how often they seem worth doing, given the labour involved and the commercial constraints on publishing. The same goes for new translations-and-productions of plays, where the possibilities for staging and touring (or lack of them) are crucial. With poetry, especially short poems, publication is often fairly easy to make happen in magazines or — nowadays — online. This circumstance helps drive the plural translation of poems, along with the close attention and high valuation that language in poetry commands. What distinguishes the prismatic approach from claims about the special translation-that-is-not-translation demanded by poems is the recognition that there is no binary opposition between poetry and other writing. Poetry can be discovered anywhere in language, and therefore any act of translation can involve elements of transgression and elation. Furthermore, every translation attends to some kind of 'spirit' as well as to the 'words', for if you look closely at a phrase or sentence and ask where does 'spirit', or 'tone', or 'illocutionary force' stop, and where does 'literal meaning' or 'verbal meaning' or the 'word' begin, you will find that there is no boundary.

In the abstract — as is now widely accepted in translation studies — there are no equivalents in one language to anything in another. Equivalence is always situated and partial: it is equivalence 'in this respect', or 'in this context', or 'for this purpose' ('skopos' is the technical term).[24] The varied arguments that have brought about this theoretical advance have been important; and they have recognized some aspects of translation's prismatic nature. Yet there is a question to which they typically do not give sufficient weight: 'equivalent to what?' As other scholars have realized, there is nothing 'in' any source text until it begins to be interpreted; and that beginning of interpretation is also the beginning of translation. When, as so often happens, reviewers criticize translations for not catching some aspect of the original (say, the tone), what they really mean is that the translation — or rather, their reading of the translation — does not correspond to their own mental translation of the source.[25] In fact, the work of translation brings into being, not only those features of the translation-text that are offered as equivalent to the source, but also those features of the source that they are offered as equivalent to. As Charles Martindale has put it: 'translations determine what counts as being "there" in the first place'.[26] Or in the words of Naoki Sakai: 'what is translated and transferred can be recognized as such only after translation'.²⁷ Karen Emmerich has drawn attention to the role played by translators in defining the 'original' in circumstances where the source consists of several textual states, or is fragmented;²⁸ but the point needs extending to all acts of translation, and all source-texts. Achieving equivalence does not mean creating a translation that will match or channel an already-existing entity, but rather co-creating elements in both source-text and translation-text which can be taken as equivalents of each other (in the given context, purpose or respect).²⁹

Of course, a translator does not do all this in isolation. Any reading of the source happens among other responses to it, in a cultural location, and in interaction with other texts; and any writing of a translation-text happens in collaboration with other ways in which the language has been and can be used. Much varied textuality flows into the moment of translation, just as much varied textuality can emanate from it: there are prisms angled in both directions. This is obvious in cases such as that of John Dryden (whom I discuss further in Part I): when he translated Virgil's *Aeneid* he was in fact working not only from that text but from other translations, as well as commentaries, editorial notes, Latin paraphrases, and of course dictionaries and histories. It is no less true whenever any translator checks something in another source, or a translation memory or online dictionary. Even the most solitary act of translation happens in collaboration with a plurality of texts, because it is from them — from our lifelong linguistic interaction — that we know the language(s) we know. Google Translate now imitates this aspect of human functioning as it trawls its massive stores of textuality for likely equivalents. The varied textuality in which any source-text floats is the reason why it is always available to be taken in different ways: depending on how its words connect up with other words they will assume different tonalities and meanings. Christian Matthiessen has adopted a term from Hallidayan linguistics, 'agnation', to describe the alternative phrasings from which the actual words of the source text have emerged but by which they are always therefore haunted: 'any expression in the source text will be agnate to innumerable alternative expressions ... At any point ... it may be one of these agnates rather than the actual expression that serves as the best candidate for translation ... The agnates make up the source text's shadow texts.'³⁰ As Clive Scott has put it: 'texts project, are surrounded by, alternatives not yet realized'.³¹ Here we get to the core reason for the plurality of translations. It is not fundamentally due to error, the nature of poetry or the passing of time. It has its origin in the inherent fluidity of every source text, which in turn arises from the multiple textuality out of which, and into which, every text is woven.

The prismatic approach keeps these twin multiplicities in view. Here again, it reverses the usual question: not 'why is there unusual liberty in literary translation?' But 'why is the inherently proliferative potential of translation subjected to greater regulation in some other spheres?' Translating poetry, Dryden — like many other poet-translators — felt comparatively free to co-create the kinds of equivalence that worked for him, recognizing that they differed, and would differ, from many other equivalences that had been and would be created by other writers. For translators of a medical or legal text, by contrast, the play of possibilities is restricted by the practices of interpretation which constitute the professions of medicine and the law as such: here, a mutually agreed text is necessary because of the uses to which it will be put.

As Sakai has argued, an overarching disciplinary influence is exerted on the field of translation by nation-state ideologies.[32] For one text to be seen as equivalent to another (the 'channel' view), it helps if the two of them are taken to belong to separate languages, and if those languages are standardized, with dictionaries and grammar books to regulate their meanings. In Europe, centuries of state-sponsored cultural and educational labour have gone into the construction of standard French, English, German etc., defining them as separate from one another, and establishing habitual ways of lining them up through translation; Robert Young has shown how the same work continued into the project of empire, recording, dividing and standardizing the language-practices of subject peoples so that they could be counted as separate languages rather than seen to be shifting and overlapping zones on the continuum of language variation. Within what have thereby come to be defined as separate languages, monolingualism is promoted, and dialectal and idiomatic variation suppressed; and between the so-called separate languages continuity is downplayed: hence 'philosophie' is taken to be a French word, and 'philosophy' an English one — rather than ever-so-slightly-different spellings and pronunciation-ranges of the same word. The idea of translation as transfer of meaning 'between languages' both relies on and buttresses this state of affairs.

The division and regimentation of languages has been a powerful driver of translation. As I have argued elsewhere, a good way of asserting that one language is separate from another is to claim that it needs to be translated to be understood;[33] conversely, translation has been central to the construction of national literary languages, for instance French or English in the C16th-17th, German in the C18th-19th, Japanese or Mandarin Chinese in the C20th. This must be a powerful language for literature — the argument goes — if Homer or Dante or Shakespeare can be successfully translated into it. Here we have one last reason for the plurality of translations, so obvious that it is rarely mentioned: if there are many languages then many translations are needed. Translation can relate to the separation and standardization of languages in a range of ways. It can be hyper-obedient to national standards of correctness and norms of usage: this is the regime of fluency so vigorously denounced by Lawrence Venuti.[34] Yet it can also push against the forces of regimentation and division, blurring the boundaries between languages, and re-creating an awareness of language as a continuum of variety and change. In the terms invented by Halliday — as David Gramling has noted — translation can work not only in the service of 'glossodiversity' (common meaning-making across separate standardized languages) but also 'semiodiversity', that is — as Gramling puts it — the 'many divergent, untranslatable, and often mutually irreconcilable meanings' that appear at different points on the continuum of language difference, and 'how such meanings become stretched and unmoored amid historical and ecological constellations'.[35] These are the conditions that nourish prismatic translation: one prompt for the writing of this volume is the perception that alertness to, and interest in, semiodiversity is growing, not only in fluidly multilingual and translingual regions such as India and the Arab world, but also in Europe and North America, the traditional heartlands of national language standardization. Mass migration, the internet, and the strengthening of regional identities are all making linguistic variety more visible, while as English spreads ever further as a global language it also fractures, itself becoming multiple. In harmony with these developments, more varied and layered translation practices are flourishing (see chapters 1, 4, 6, 7, 8, 11 and 13 below), in alliance with more plural conceptualisations of cultures and selves (see chapters 5, 9, 10, 17 and 18).

The prismatic approach responds to these developments. It offers a theorisation of translation in general, as I have outlined; and it also gives us a terminology for current practices. Translation is inherently prismatic, but its prismatic potential is restricted in some circumstances: the 'channel view', with its accompanying nation-state apparatuses, is one of the means by which this restriction is accomplished. 'A prismatic view of translation', by contrast, is one which is alert to translation's proliferative energies, and sees any given act of translation in the light of them. 'A prismatic translation' is a text in which those energies are given free rein via the staging of multiple possibilities, or other, related strategies. That said, each chapter below will pull these terms in slightly different directions. As James St André has pointed out, 'metaphors are not just interpretations; they themselves are subject to (re-)interpretation'.[36] I offer the metaphor of the prism, not in the belief that metaphors 'structure' thought (as in George Lakoff and Mark Johnson's original formulation of their theory of cognitive metaphor), but with an awareness that they influence and interact with both thinking and practice, and are in turn re-configured by them (as in the more nuanced accounts to which Lakoff and Johnson's original work has given rise).[37] As Douglas Robinson has long argued, what goes on in someone's mind at the moment of translation cannot be fully known:[38] just like the 'channel', the 'prism' is only a partial descriptive frame.

In particular, the detail of the relationship between the prism and the channel is unstable. A prism might be thought to be something quite different from a channel, because it changes everything that passes through it. This is the intepretation that I prefer. However, it might also be thought to be a complicated kind of channel, one made up of lots of sub-channels turning in different directions, so that everything that passes through it does in some respect stay the same. The ambiguity captures a paradox which, I argue below in Part I, is fundamental to translation. A great deal of research in Translation Studies has rightly emphasized translations' differences from their sources, so much so that a recent special issue of the journal *Translation Studies*, which sought to refocus attention on 'invariance' in translation, was welcomed as a novelty.[39] Yet all this work struggles to describe the relationship between difference and sameness which is constitutive of translation (if a text is simply different from another text it is not a translation; if it is simply the same it is not a translation either). Jean Boase-Beier has proposed that we can ease this problem by thinking of translations as 'conceptual blends' in which the idea of the original text and the recognition of its being in a different language mix 'in a creative mental process'. Yet, as she admits, 'blends generally involve clashes at some level';[40] and whenever you look closely at any discussion of translation the clashes become plain to see. Emmerich, for instance, presents herself as championing 'an understanding of translation as reiteration, as repetition-with-a-difference, a mode of textual proliferation rather than a mode by which semantic content is transferred'.[41] This stance is in harmony with the prismatic approach, but there is a glitch in the way it is expressed. If translation is only 'textual proliferation' then any text can count as a translation of any other; while, on the other hand, if translation does include an element of 'repetition' then it must possess some sameness to the source, and so engage in 'transfer'. As we have seen, the work of translation is best described as co-creating meaning in both source-text and translation-text. No meaning is simply there in the source-text for the translation-text to be the same as or different from: interpretation is already the beginning of translation. However, this subtlety is hard, perhaps impossible to maintain as soon as translations start to be discussed with any freedom. Of course people talk about sameness and disparity; of course translators feel themselves to be 'capturing' or 'reproducing' something of the source; of course readers worry about 'difference'. Yet, because there is a misfit between this language of description and what is really going on, these terms are volatile. A celebration of difference can suddenly morph into a claim for sameness; and what looks like inspired equivalence to one reader can strike another as a shocking betrayal.

In Part I, I probe this instability in our descriptive frames — including the metaphor of the prism — and argue that it cannot be resolved, only lived through in different ways: I explore instances in Elizabeth Barrett Browning, John Dryden, Ciaran Carson and Lydia Davis, so as to bring historical depth to the discussion, tracing continuities and differences between translation's present and its past. While the 'channel' view is buttressed by nation-state structures it is not dependent on them; indeed — I show — it must appear somewhere, even if concealed or denied, whenever a text is being treated as a translation: it is part of translation's definition. In some respects, then, the metaphor of the prism stands for translational difference in contrast to the channel. But in other respects the prism absorbs the metaphor of the channel, recognizing the idea of sameness that must somehow cling to any translation, if translation is not to dissolve completely into general textual proliferation.

Part II considers different language situations in relation to the prismatic view. In Chapter 2, Francesca Orsini explores a variety of translingual practices, across several centuries, in multilingual north India. She shows that it is not the case — as has been claimed by Harish Trivedi — that nothing that can be called translation happened in India before 1800. Rather, translation occurred in scattered places (such as the margins of manuscripts), varying according to the type of text, and intermingling with other processes such as the stretching and mixing of idioms and tongues. Chapter 3, by Hany Rashwan, analyzes ancient Egyptian picture-writing, both hieroglyphic and hieratic. In this writing, semantic, iconic and phonetic modes of signification interact with a complexity unrecognized by traditional Egyptology which has a limited conception of the possibilities of language. Prismatic translation practices, by contrast, can enable this intricacy to be opened up and represented. In Chapter 4, John Cayley offers a fresh conceptualization of language in general, rooted in his own digital media art practice. In works such as Cayley's *translation*, texts morph into one another through sequences of tiny shifts. This is in line with Walter Benjamin's idea of translation as happening through a continuum of transformations, and indeed with a prismatic view of language as made up of continuous variation. Yet, as Cayley says, the 'startling thing' is that areas of this shifting material become recognizable and understandable to any given viewer not gradually but all of a sudden — an observation which chimes with my argument about the necessary co-existence of prismatic and channel metaphors. Cayley coins the term 'grammalepsis' for this action of seizing-and-grasping as language.

Part III looks at translation in cultural and political contexts. In chapter 5, Yvonne Howell gives an account of key moments in the history of translation in Russia, showing that the desire to develop the culture nourished practices of adaptation and transformation which correspond to a prismatic view. Nabokov's famous assertion of literal correspondence in his translation of *Eugene Onegin* offers a stark contrast which needs to be understood in its Cold War context. Chapter 6, by Kasia Szymanska, then explores a range of recent anglophone texts which multiply translation variants. These prismatic translations, she argues, should be seen as meta-translations, offering a reflection on their own practices and assumptions. Adriana Jacobs, in chapter 7, continues the investigation of recent anglophone work, focusing on the United States and, in particular, on unconventional strategies which fall outside the 'expected bounds of translation'. Jacobs relates these practices to the global dominance of English, in which translation of course plays a part: the 'extreme translations' which she discusses form a critique of that involvement, and of the wider 'normalization of xenophobic and anti-immigrant rhetoric'. Globalization figures again, though differently, in chapter 8, where Cosima Bruno analyzes *Pink Noise* by the Taiwanese poet Hsia Yü. This work, in a mixture of English and Chinese, was made by harvesting texts from the internet and translating them by machine: Bruno argues that it engages with the general linguistic environment online, presenting us with 'the noise of digital textualities', but that it also has particular relevance in the Taiwanese context, where attempts to impose a 'national language' have been both fitful and conflicted. In chapter 9, Jernej Habjan brings the image of the prism into connection with processes of cultural translation, whereby a term of hate speech may be re-signified (or 'prismatically refracted') so as to take on a positive meaning. In a sustained critique of Judith Butler, Habjan considers the obstacles to the spread of a re-signified term beyond the community that re-signified it, and concludes that a notional prismatic free-for-all should not be preferred to a system of institutional curbs on hate speech.

In Part IV, we turn to reflections by practising translators. Jean Anderson, in chapter 10, continues the exploration of the ethics of translating between cultures, describing her work on a short story by the Tahitian Rai Chaze. Anderson shows how the source-text is full of culturally-specific nuances which might be opened up by a prismatic treatment (rather like the ancient Egyptian texts discussed by Hany Rashwan in chapter 3). However, she argues that to do so in this case would be to engage in a form of appropriation: a better practice is to leave a degree of opacity in the translation, so as to prompt readers towards recognizing cultural difference in a non-invasive way. In chapter 11, Pari Azarm Motamedi presents her own 'lingo-visual translations' from the Persian poetry of Mohammad Reza Shafii Kadkani. The twin practice of translating into words and painting enables Motamedi to register and respond to 'the hidden layers of a poem' without making them falsely explicit, thereby mixing 'contemplation, inspiration and unfolding'. Audrey Coussy, in chapter 12, confronts nonsense alphabets, where the sequence of letters and other phonetic patterns have to be respected as well as the semantic meaning. She shows how some kinds of verbal play can extend more fully in her French, creating a prismatic expansion of the impulse of the source. The idea of a similar mechanism generating different and sometimes fuller results recurs in chapter 13, where Eran Hadas describes his translational work in the realm of computer programming: re-making an American chatbot so that it functions in Hebrew; building an application that simulates 'an associative, meditative or "human" reading of a text' via translational procedures; translating source code from English to Hebrew; and creating algorithms which extract surprisingly modern-seeming language from the Bible. In such cases, translation 'works not on the text itself, but rather on the structures and mechanisms that give rise to it' so as to generate 'prismatic results'. Finally in this section, Philip Terry, in chapter 14, presents his translations of sonnets by Du Bellay into the language and context of the modern English university system. Here, translation generates prismatic angles of critique.

Part V offers readings of texts which either form prismatic groupings or are prismatic in themselves. In chapter 15, Patrick Hersant traces the surprisingly varied ways in which the names 'Xanadu' and 'Kubla Khan' — in Coleridge's poem — have been translated into French, Italian, German, Spanish, Portuguese, Romanian and Russian, showing that this diffraction extends 'a poetic process of translation and appropriation' first undertaken by Coleridge himself when he translated the names into his poem. In chapter 16, Péter Hajdu discusses five Hungarian translations of Petronius's *Satyricon*, showing how they each engage with their cultural contexts but cannot be explained by them: 'rather than thinking of translation as happening *into* cultural moments, the prismatic view encourages us to see translation as happening *through* them'. In consequence, the five translations create a varied spectrum of continuance for the *Satyricon*, one which cannot be reduced to any teleology (and certainly not, incidentally, to the simplistic idea proposed by Antoine Berman and reformulated by Andrew Chesterman, that 'later translations tend to be closer to the source text').[42] In chapter 17, Alexandra Lukes considers Louis Wolfson's book *Le schizo et les langues*, which is written in 'heavily Anglicized French'. Wolfson invented a therapeutic translation practice to deal with the unbearable pain that English caused him: he fragments the offending word 'into a number of languages, primarily French, German, Russian, and Hebrew'. Lukes argues that (somewhat paradoxically) this prismatic explosion offered him — and offers us — a momentary healing of the rupture between languages, and between language and self: the established idea that the text is therefore 'untranslatable' relies on an unduly narrow conception of translation. Dennis Duncan, in chapter 18, continues the discussion of translation's psychology. He shows that the presentation of pseudo-translation in Harry Mathews's *Armenian Papers* brings into play something like the idealization of the absent father, i.e. that impossible longing for 'the original' which is '*always* a condition of reading translation' since 'the original is always, to some degree inaccessible'. Finally, Stefan Willer, in chapter 19, explores the case of an actual original that was lost, until it was found: Diderot's *Le Neveu de Rameau* was translated by Goethe; the source text then vanished and a re-translation of Goethe's German version into French did service as Diderot's text — so much so that when the original reappeared it was found wanting in comparison. Here again, we can see an idea of the original — or 'originalesque' — being back-projected from a realm of prismatically translational textuality.

This rich spectrum of chapters in one sense exemplifies 'How to Do Things with Prismatic Translation': how to read prismatic texts; how to think about the field of translation from a prismatic point of view; what practices of translation are in harmony with the idea, and what reconceptualisations of language correspond to it. Yet each chapter is also its own refraction of the metaphor, re-routing and reconfiguring it, and opening it to debate.

Works Cited

BAKER, MONA, *Translation and Conflict: A Narrative Account* (London: Routledge, 2006)
BERMAN, ANTOINE, 'La Retraduction comme espace de la traduction', *Retraduire, Palimpsestes* 4 (Paris: Publications de la Sorbonne Nouvelle, 1990), pp. 1–9
BRIGGS, KATE, *This Little Art* (London: Fitzcarraldo Editions, 2017)
BASSNETT, SUSAN, 'Writing in No-Man's Land: Questions of Gender and Translation', *Isla do Desterro*, 28 (1992), 63–73. DOI: <https://doi.org/10.5007/%25x>
BIELSA, ESPERANÇA, and BASSNETT, SUSAN, *Translation in Global News* (Abingdon: Routledge 2009)
BOASE-BEIER, JEAN, *A Critical Introduction to Translation Studies* (London: Bloomsbury, 2011), electronic legal deposit text
CASSIN, BARBARA, ed., *Vocabulaire européen des philosophes: dictionnaire des intraduisibles* (Paris: Éditions du Seuil, 2004)
CHAMBERLAIN, LORI, 'Gender and the Metaphorics of Translation', in Lawrence Venuti (ed), *Rethinking Translation: Discourse, Subjectivity, Ideology* (London: Routledge, 1992), pp. 57–74
CHEUNG, MARTHA P. Y., ed., *An Anthology of Chinese Discourse on Translation, vol. 1: From the Earliest Times to the Buddhist Project* (Manchester: St Jerome, 2006)
CHEYFITZ, ERIC, *The Poetics of Imperialism: Translation and Colonization from* The Tempest *to* Tarzan (New York: Oxford University Press, 1991)
COLLINS, SOPHIE, ed., *Currently and Emotion: Translations* (London: Test Centre, 2016)
CRONIN, MICHAEL, *Translation in the Digital Age* (Abingdon: Routledge, 2013)
CULLER, JONATHAN, *Structuralist Poetics: Structuralism, Linguistics and the Study of Literature* (London: Routledge, 2002)
DEANE-COX, SHARON, *Retranslation: Translation, Literature and Reinterpretation* (London: Bloomsbury, 2014)

DODSON, KATRINA, 'Understanding is the Proof of Error', *The Believer*, 119 (11 July, 2018). <https://believermag.com/understanding-is-the-proof-of-error/> [accessed 24 February 2019]

DRURY, ANNMARIE, *Translation as Transformation in Victorian Poetry* (Cambridge: Cambridge University Press, 2015)

DURAN, ANGELICA, ISSA, ISLAM and OLSON, JONATHAN R. (eds), *Milton in Translation* (Oxford: Oxford University Press, 2017)

ECO, UMBERTO, *Dire quasi la stessa cosa: Esperienze di traduzione* (Milan: Bompiani, 2003)

EMMERICH, KAREN, *Literary Translation and the Making of Originals* (London: Bloomsbury, 2017)

FOWLER, ROGER, *Linguistic Criticism*, 2nd edn (Oxford: Oxford University Press, 1996)

GÖRANSSON, JOHANNES, *Transgressive Circulation: Essays on Translation* (Blacksburg, VA: Noemi Press, 2018)

GRAMLING, DAVID, *The Invention of Monolingualism* (New York: Bloomsbury, 2016)

HERMANS, THEO, *The Conference of the Tongues* (Manchester: St Jerome, 2007)

HOFMEYR, ISABEL, *The Portable Bunyan: A Transnational History of The Pilgrim's Progress* (Princeton: Princeton University Press, 2004)

HOFSTADTER, DOUGLAS R., *Le Ton Beau de Marot: In Praise of the Music of Language* (London: Bloomsbury, 1997)

JACOBS, ADRIANA X., *Strange Cocktail: Translation and the Making of Modern Hebrew Poetry* (Ann Arbor: University of Michigan Press, 2018)

JAKOBSON, ROMAN, *Language in Literature*, eds Krystyna Pomorska and Stephen Rudy (Cambridge, Mass. and London: Harvard University Press, 1987)

JOHNSTON, DAVID, ed., *Stages of Translation: Essays and Interviews on Translating for the Stage* (Bath: Absolute Classics, 1996)

KAHN, ROBERT, and SETH, CATRIONA, eds, *La Retraduction* (Mont-Saint-Aignan: Publications des Universités de Rouen et du Havre, 2010)

LAKOFF, GEORGE, and JOHNSON, MARK, *Metaphors We Live By* (Chicago: University of Chicago Press, 1980)

LIU, LYDIA H., *Translingual Practice: Literature, National Culture and Translated Modernity: China, 1900–1937* (Stanford, CA.: Stanford University Press, 1995)

LOFFREDO, EUGENIA, and PERTEGHELLA, MANUELA, eds, *One Poem in Search of a Translator: Rewriting 'Les Fenêtres' by Apollinaire* (Oxford: Peter Lang, 2009)

MARTINDALE, CHARLES, *Redeeming the Text: Latin Poetry and the Hermeneutics of Reception* (Cambridge: Cambridge University Press, 1993)

MATHEWS, JACKSON, 'Third Thoughts on Translating Poetry', in *On Translation*, ed. by Reuben A. Brower (New York: Oxford University Press, 1966), pp. 67–77

MATTHIESSEN, CHRISTIAN M.I.M., 'The Environments of Translation', in Erich Steiner and Colin Yallop, eds, *Text, Translation, Computational Processing [TTCP]: Exploring Translation and Multilingual Text Production: Beyond Content* (Berlin: De Gruyter, 2013), pp. 41–126

MONTI, ENRICO, and SCHNYDER, PETER, eds, *Autour de la Retraduction: Perspectives littéraires européennes* (Mulhouse: Orizons, 2011)

MOORE, DAVID CHIONI ET AL., 'An African Classic in Fourteen Translations', *PMLA*, 128.1 (January 2013), 101–11

MOURE, EIRIN (a.k.a. Erín Moure), *Sheep's Vigil by a Fervent Person: A transelation of Alberto Caiero / Fernando Pessoa's O Guardador de Rebanhos* (Toronto: House of Anansi Press, 2004)

MOURE, ERÍN, 'The Translator Relay: Erín Moure', *Words Without Borders* (Aug 28, 2017), <https://www.wordswithoutborders.org/dispatches/article/the-translator-relay-erin-moure> [accessed 26 February 2019]

MUNDAY, JEREMY, ed., *The Routledge Companion to Translation Studies* (London: Routledge, 2009)
NIRANJANA, TEJASWINI, 'Translation, Colonialism and the Rise of English', *Economic and Political Weekly*, 25. 15 (14 April, 1990), 773–79
NORTON, DAVID, *A History of the Bible as Literature*, 2 vols (Cambridge: Cambridge University Press, 1993)
O'NEILL, PATRICK, *Polyglot Joyce: Fictions of Translation* (Toronto: University of Toronto Press, 2005)
—— *Transforming Kafka: Translation Effects* (Toronto: University of Toronto Press, 2005)
PARTRIDGE, A. C., *English Biblical Translation* (London: Deutsch, 1973)
PATERSON, DON, 'Fourteen Notes on the Version', in his *Orpheus: A Version of Rilke's* Die Sonette an Orpheus (2006), pp. 73–84
RACZ, GREGORY J., 'Theatre', in Kelly Washbourne and Ben Van Wyke (eds), *The Routledge Handbook of Literary Translation* (Abingdon: Routledge, 2019), electronic legal deposit text
Retraduire, Palimpsestes 4 (Paris: Publications de la Sorbonne Nouvelle, 1990)
REISS, KATHARINA, and VERMEER, HANS J., *Towards a General Theory of Translational Action: Skopos Theory Explained* (Manchester: St Jerome, 2013)
REYNOLDS, MATTHEW, *The Poetry of Translation: From Chaucer & Petrarch to Homer & Logue* (Oxford: Oxford University Press, 2011)
—— *Translation: A Very Short Introduction* (Oxford: Oxford University Press, 2016)
RITCHIE, DAVID, '"ARGUMENT IS WAR" — Or is it a Game of Chess? Multiple Meanings in the Analysis of Implicit Metaphors', *Metaphor and Symbol*, 18.2 (2003), pp. 125–46
ROBINSON, DOUGLAS, *Becoming a Translator: An Introduction to the Theory and Practice of Translation*, 2nd edn (London: Routledge 2003)
—— *The Translator's Turn* (Baltimore: Johns Hopkins University Press, 1991)
ST ANDRÉ, JAMES, ed., *Thinking through Translation with Metaphors* (Manchester: St Jerome, 2010)
SAKAI, NAOKI, 'Translation', *Theory, Culture & Society*, 23. 2–3 (2006), 71–86. DOI: <10.1177/0263276406063778>
—— *Translation and Subjectivity: On 'Japan' and Cultural Nationalism* (Minneapolis: University of Minnesota Press, 1997)
SATO, HIROAKI, *One Hundred Frogs: From Renga to Haiku to English* (New York: Weatherhill, 1983)
SCARPA, FEDERICA 'Response by Scarpa to "Invariance Orientation: Identifying an object for translation studies"', *Translation Studies*, 10. 3 (2017), 343–48. DOI: <10.1080/14781700.2016.1207558>
SCOTT, CLIVE, *Channel Crossings: French and English Poetry in Dialogue, 1550–2000* (Oxford: Legenda, 2002)
—— *Literary Translation and the Rediscovery of Reading* (Cambridge: Cambridge University Press, 2013)
SIMON, SHERRY, *Gender in Translation: Cultural Identity and the Politics of Transmission* (London: Routledge, 1996)
SMALLEY, WILLIAM A., *Translation as Mission: Bible Translation in the Modern Missionary Movement* (Macon, GA: Mercer, 1991)
THIRLWELL, ADAM, ed., *Multiples: An Anthology of Stories in an Assortment of Languages and Literary Styles* (London: Portobello, 2013)
TOURY, GIDEON, *Descriptive Translation Studies and Beyond* (Amsterdam: Benjamins, 1995)
TYMOCZKO, MARIA, *Translation in a Postcolonial Context: Early Irish Literature in English Translation* (Manchester: St Jerome, 1999)

VENUTI, LAWRENCE, *The Translator's Invisibility: A History of Translation*, (London: Routledge, 1995)
WEINBERGER, ELIOT, and OCTAVIO PAZ, *19 Ways of Looking at Wang Wei: How a Chinese Poem is Translated* (Kingston: Asphodel Press, 1987)
WOODS, MICHELLE, *Kafka Translated: How Translators have Shaped our Readings of Kafka* (New York: Bloomsbury, 2013)
YOUNG, ROBERT, *Postcolonialism: A Very Short Introduction* (Oxford: Oxford University Press, 2003)

Notes to the Introduction

1. Michael Cronin, *Translation in the Digital Age* (Abingdon: Routledge, 2013). I am very grateful to the following friends and colleagues whose comments have improved both this Introduction and chapter 1: Tania Demetriou, Annemarie Drury, Adriana X. Jacobs and Céline Sabiron.
2. Esperança Bielsa and Susan Bassnett, *Translation in Global News* (Abingdon: Routledge, 2009), p. 39.
3. Matthew Reynolds, *Translation: A Very Short Introduction* (Oxford: Oxford University Press, 2016), pp. 6–9, 69–75, 102–20; Martha P. Y. Cheung (ed.), *An Anthology of Chinese Discourse on Translation, vol. 1: From the Earliest Times to the Buddhist Project* (Manchester: St Jerome, 2006), pp. 7–12; A. C. Partridge, *English Biblical Translation* (London: Deutsch, 1973); William A. Smalley, *Translation as Mission: Bible Translation in the Modern Missionary Movement* (Macon, GA: Mercer, 1991).
4. Sharon Deane-Cox, *Retranslation: Translation, Literature and Reinterpretation* (London : Bloomsbury, 2014); *Retraduire, Palimpsestes* 4 (Paris : Publications de la Sorbonne Nouvelle, 1990); Robert Kahn and Catriona Seth (eds), *La Retraduction* (Mont-Saint-Aignan: Publications des Universitès de Rouen et du Havre, 2010); Enrico Monti and Peter Schnyder (eds), *Autour de la Retraduction: Perspectives littéraires européennes* (Mulhouse: Orizons, 2011).
5. For instance, Patrick O'Neill, *Polyglot Joyce: Fictions of Translation* (Toronto: University of Toronto Press, 2005) and *Transforming Kafka: Translation Effects* (Toronto: University of Toronto Press, 2005); Isabel Hofmeyr, *The Portable Bunyan: A Transnational History of* The Pilgrim's Progress (Princeton: Princeton University Press, 2004); Angelica Duran, Islam Issa and Jonathan R. Olson (eds), *Milton in Translation* (Oxford: Oxford University Press, 2017); David Chioni Moore et al., 'An African Classic in Fourteen Translations', *PMLA* 128.1 (January 2013), 101–11; and two book series: *The Reception of British and Irish Authors in Europe*, general ed. Elinor Shaffer (London: Bloomsbury, 2008–) and *Translations: Pensées et pratiques de la traduction* (Pessac: Presses Universitaires de Bordeaux, 2013–).
6. For instance, Hiroaki Sato, *One Hundred Frogs: From Renga to Haiku to English* (New York: Weatherhill, 1983); Eliot Weinberger and Octavio Paz, *19 Ways of Looking at Wang Wei: How a Chinese Poem is Translated* (Kingston: Asphodel Press, 1987); Douglas R. Hofstadter, *Le Ton Beau de Marot: In Praise of the Music of Language* (London: Bloomsbury, 1997); Eugenia Loffredo and Manuela Perteghella (eds), *One Poem in Search of a Translator: Rewriting 'Les Fenêtres' by Apollinaire* (Oxford: Peter Lang, 2009); Clive Scott, *Literary Translation and the Rediscovery of Reading* (Cambridge: Cambridge University Press, 2013); Adam Thirlwell (ed.), *Multiples: An Anthology of Stories in an Assortment of Languages and Literary Styles* (London: Portobello, 2013); see further chapter 6 below.
7. David Norton, *A History of the Bible as Literature*, 2 vols (Cambridge: Cambridge University Press, 1993); Barbara Cassin (ed.), *Vocabulaire européen des philosophes: dictionnaire des intraduisibles* (Paris: Éditions de Seuil, 2004) ; Bielsa and Bassnett, *Translation in Global News*.
8. *Oxford English Dictionary*; *Trésor de la langue française informatisé*, CNRS & Université de Lorraine <http://www.atilf.fr/tlfi>; Gabrielli Aldo, *Grande Dizionario Italiano* <http://www.grandidizionari.it/Dizionario_Italiano/>; *Deutsches Wörterbuch*, <https://de.thefreedictionary.com/> [all accessed 7th November 2018].
9. Lawrence Venuti, *The Translator's Invisibility: A History of Translation*, (London: Routledge, 1995), p. 17.

10. Umberto Eco, *Dire quasi la stessa cosa: Esperienze di traduzione* (Milan: Bompiani, 2003), p. 16; my translation.
11. Theo Hermans, *The Conference of the Tongues* (Manchester: St Jerome, 2007), p. 24.
12. With a large group of collaborators I am exploring this question in relation to many translations of Charlotte Brontë's *Jane Eyre*, in research that is part of the AHRC's Open World Research Initiative programme in 'Creative Multilingualism': 'Prismatic *Jane Eyre*: Close-Reading a Global Novel Across Languages', <http://www.occt.ox.ac.uk/research/prismatic-translation> and <https://prismaticjaneeyre.org>.
13. Sherry Simon, *Gender in Translation: Cultural Identity and the Politics of Transmission* (London: Routledge, 1996), p. 66; see Susan Bassnett, 'Writing in No-Man's Land: Questions of Gender and Translation', *Isla do Desterro*, 28 (1992), pp. 63–73.
14. Gideon Toury, *Descriptive Translation Studies and Beyond* (Amsterdam: Benjamins, 1995), p. 52; Hermans, *The Conference of the Tongues*, p. 5; Tejaswini Niranjana, 'Translation, Colonialism and the Rise of English', *Economic and Political Weekly*, 25. 15 (14 April, 1990), pp. 773–79; Eric Cheyfitz, *The Poetics of Imperialism: Translation and Colonization from* The Tempest *to* Tarzan (New York: Oxford University Press, 1991), pp. 111–12; Maria Tymoczko, *Translation in a Postcolonial Context: Early Irish Literature in English Translation* (Manchester: St Jerome, 1999), p. 19; Robert Young, *Postcolonialism: A Very Short Introduction* (Oxford: Oxford University Press, 2003), p. 140; Naoki Sakai, 'Translation', *Theory, Culture & Society*, 23. 2–3 (2006), 71–86. DOI: 10.1177/0263276406063778; Sophie Collins, 'Introduction', in her (ed.) *Currently and Emotion: Translations* (London: Test Centre, 2016), n.p.; Adriana X. Jacobs, *Strange Cocktail: Translation and the Making of Modern Hebrew Poetry* (Ann Arbor: University of Michigan Press, 2018), p. 15; see also Mona Baker, *Translation and Conflict: A Narrative Account* (London: Routledge, 2006).
15. Douglas Robinson, *The Translator's Turn* (Baltimore: Johns Hopkins University Press, 1991); Lori Chamberlain, 'Gender and the Metaphorics of Translation', in Lawrence Venuti (ed), *Rethinking Translation: Discourse, Subjectivity, Ideology* (London: Routledge, 1992), pp. 57–74; James St André (ed.), *Thinking through Translation with Metaphors* (Manchester: St Jerome, 2010).
16. Kate Briggs, *This Little Art* (London: Fitzcarraldo Editions, 2017), p. 192.
17. Katrina Dodson, 'Understanding is the Proof of Error', *The Believer*, 119 (11 July, 2018), <https://believermag.com/understanding-is-the-proof-of-error/> [accessed 24 February 2019].
18. Don Paterson, 'Fourteen Notes on the Version', in his *Orpheus: A Version of Rilke's Die Sonette an Orpheus* (2006), pp. 73–84; Erín Moure, 'The Translator Relay: Erín Moure', *Words Without Borders* (Aug 28, 2017), <https://www.wordswithoutborders.org/dispatches/article/the-translator-relay-erin-moure> [accessed 26 February 2019]; see also Eirin Moure, *Sheep's Vigil by a Fervent Person: A transelation of Alberto Caiero / Fernando Pessoa's O Guardador de Rebanhos* (Toronto: House of Anansi Press, 2004); Johannes Göranssen, *Transgressive Circulation: Essays on Translation* (Blacksburg, VA: Noemi Press, 2018); see also Jackson Mathews, 'Third Thoughts on Translating Poetry', in *On Translation*, ed. by Reuben A. Brower (New York: Oxford University Press, 1966), pp. 67–77 (p. 67)
19. Göranssen, *Transgressive Circulation*, p. 53.
20. Roman Jakobson, *Language in Literature*, eds Krystyna Pomorska and Stephen Rudy (Cambridge, MA: Harvard University Press, 1987), pp. 62–94; Jonathan Culler, *Structuralist Poetics: Structuralism, Linguistics and the Study of Literature* (London: Routledge, 2002), pp. 64–86; see also Roger Fowler, *Linguistic Criticism*, 2nd edn (Oxford: Oxford University Press, 1996).
21. Gregory J. Racz, 'Theatre', in Kelly Washbourne and Ben Van Wyke (eds), *The Routledge Handbook of Literary Translation* (Abingdon: Routledge, 2019), electronic legal deposit text, 1107.0 / 2121; David Johnston (ed.), *Stages of Translation: Essays and Interviews on Translating for the Stage* (Bath: Absolute Classics, 1996), pp. 137–38.
22. Antoine Berman, 'La Retraduction comme espace de la traduction', *Retraduire, Palimpsestes* 4 (Paris : Publications de la Sorbonne Nouvelle, 1990), pp. 1–9 (p. 1).
23. Annmarie Drury, *Translation as Transformation in Victorian Poetry* (Cambridge: Cambridge University Press, 2015), pp. 1–3; 192–222; Paterson, 'Fourteen Notes on the Version', p. 76.
24. See Jeremy Munday (ed.), *The Routledge Companion to Translation Studies* (London: Routledge, 2009), pp. 185–86; Katharina Reiss and Hans J. Vermeer, *Towards a General Theory of Translational*

Action: Skopos Theory Explained (Manchester: St Jerome, 2013).
25. As Michelle Woods has pointed out, 'reviewers often hone in on perceived "mistakes" in order to justify their own taste preferences and to present their own legitimacy as experts'. *Kafka Translated: How Translators have Shaped our Readings of Kafka* (New York: Bloomsbury Academic, 2013), p. 85, quoted in Briggs, *This Little Art*, p. 266.
26. Charles Martindale, *Redeeming the Text: Latin Poetry and the Hermeneutics of Reception* (Cambridge: Cambridge University Press, 1993), p. 93.
27. Naoki Sakai, *Translation and Subjectivity: On 'Japan' and Cultural Nationalism* (Minneapolis: University of Minnesota Press, 1997), p. 5.
28. Karen Emmerich, *Literary Translation and the Making of Originals* (London: Bloomsbury, 2017).
29. Lydia H. Liu points out that 'the "trope of equivalence" between the English word "self" and the Chinese *ji*, *wo*, *ziwo* and other words has been established only recently in the process of translation and fixed by means of modern bilingual dictionaries'. *Translingual Practice: Literature, National Culture and Translated Modernity: China, 1900–1937* (Stanford, CA.: Stanford University Press, 1995), pp. 7–8.
30. Christian M.I.M. Matthiessen, 'The Environments of Translation', in *Text, Translation, Computational Processing [TTCP]: Exploring Translation and Multilingual Text Production: Beyond Content*, eds Erich Steiner and Colin Yallop (Berlin: De Gruyter, 2013), pp. 41–126 (p. 83).
31. Clive Scott, *Channel Crossings: French and English Poetry in Dialogue, 1550–2000* (Oxford: Legenda, 2002), p. 5.
32. Sakai, 'Translation'; see further chapter 1 below.
33. Matthew Reynolds, *The Poetry of Translation: From Chaucer & Petrarch to Homer & Logue* (Oxford: Oxford University Press, 2011), pp. 15–16.
34. Venuti, *The Translator's Invisibility*, p. 5.
35. David Gramling, *The Invention of Monolingualism* (New York: Bloomsbury, 2016), pp. 31–32.
36. St André (ed.), *Thinking through Translation with Metaphors*, p. 9.
37. George Lakoff and Mark Johnson, *Metaphors We Live By* (Chicago: University of Chicago Press, 1980); David Ritchie, '"ARGUMENT IS WAR" — Or is it a Game of Chess? Multiple Meanings in the Analysis of Implicit Metaphors', *Metaphor and Symbol*, 18.2 (2003), pp. 125–46; see also Reynolds, *The Poetry of Translation*, pp. 29–55.
38. Robinson, *The Translator's Turn*, p. 107; *Becoming a Translator: An Introduction to the Theory and Practice of Translation*, 2nd edn (London: Routledge, 2003), p. 88.
39. Federica Scarpa, 'Response by Scarpa to "Invariance Orientation: Identifying an object for translation studies"', *Translation Studies*, 10. 3 (2017), 343–48. DOI: <10.1080/14781700.2016.1207558>.
40. Jean Boase-Beier, *A Critical Introduction to Translation Studies* (London: Bloomsbury, 2011), electronic legal deposit text, 181.0/491, 186.0/491.
41. Emmerich, *Literary Translation and the Making of Originals*, p. 161.
42. Deane-Cox, *Retranslation*, p. 4.

PART I

Frames

CHAPTER 1

Prismatic Agon, Prismatic Harmony: Translation, Literature, Language

Matthew Reynolds

An Instance of the Agon

In 1845, in London, the poet and translator Elizabeth Barrett (later Barrett Browning) expressed a deep regret: 'the recollection of this sin of mine, has been my nightmare & daymare, too — ... I could look in nobody's face, with a "Thou canst not say I did it" — I know, I did it.'[1]

What was her sin? She had written, and printed, twelve years earlier, when she was twenty-four years old, a translation of Aeschylus's Προμηθεύς Δεσμωτής, *Prometheus Bound*.

Barrett had been 'satisfied — tolerably satisfied' with this work when she accomplished it;[2] so why did it later come to seem so wrong? Answers emerge piecemeal in her correspondence. The translation 'is rather close to the letter ... It is stiff & hard — a Prometheus *twice* bound, & to a colder rock than was intended'. Yet in other ways it no longer felt close enough: she rather '*undid*' it than translated it — 'the iambics thrown into blank verse, the lyrics into rhymed octosyllabics and the like — and the whole together, as cold as Caucasus, & as flat as the nearest plain'.[3] As so often in poets' discussions of translations, images from the work translated inform the understanding of the translational work that has been done;[4] and here they play out in contradictory ways. When she thinks of 'the letter', Barrett sees the translation as a matter of binding tight. Her metaphor includes an echo of Dryden's well-known image of the 'fettered legs' of the literal translator, and blends it with a reference to the characters Strength and Force in Aeschylus's play, who, in the words of the 1833 translation, 'Fix' Prometheus 'to the lofty-browëd rocks, by links / Infrangible of adamantine chains'.[5] Yet when her thoughts turn to the verse, a contrary web of association forms. Now, her handiwork seems too sloppy, undone, 'thrown' together, an unravelling of the source-text into something 'flat'. The translation is still 'cold', but now it seems that Prometheus himself has slipped his fetters and disappeared from the landscape of the work, leaving only the 'Caucasus' mountains to which he had been chained, and the 'plain' that might be seen from them. Altogether, this combination of verbal clinginess and formal latitude now seemed to Barrett a failure of literary re-animation: 'it is not *scholastically* that I am ashamed of it ... but poetically'.[6]

So Elizabeth Barrett set about the work of translation all over again. The relationship between the 1833 and 1850 versions has been traced by Yopie Prins, together with the wider significance of *Prometheus Bound* in Barrett's poetry and biography. The second version embodies Barrett's later confidence as an established poet and her altered view of the importance of classical scholarship. It cannot simply be called more 'free' than the earlier version; rather, it was more in the vein of her own mature style (a style which her reading of Aeschylus had helped to form). It was especially important to her because Prometheus had become a widely suggestive figure for her sense of her work and life, including the bonds of her relationship with Robert Browning.[7] Yet none of this quite explains the ferocity of her attitude towards the earlier translation, a stance which is the more surprising because her own preface to her 1833 *Prometheus* had presented a strikingly relaxed account of the variousness of translations and their divergences from their originals.

Both 'a literal version' and 'a transfusion of poetical spirit' — she had argued — have their place; and ever more, variously idiosyncratic versions are to be expected: 'it is in the nature of the human mind to communicate its own character to whatever substance it conveys' — she had said; and therefore 'we do not blame Pope and Cowper for not having faithfully represented Homer: we do not blame Pope and Cowper for being Pope and Cowper'. She reaches for a visual metaphor — almost but not quite a prism — to illustrate this variety which is blameless because inevitable: 'a mirror may be held in different lights by different hands; and, according to the position of those hands, will the light fall'. The image recognises a twofold plurality: the source text in itself projects, not one consistent light, but many different ones; and the various translators each choose one of those lights and refract it in a different way. This diversity is, not only blameless, and not only inevitable: it is to be welcomed: 'it is ... desirable that the same compositions should be conveyed by different minds'. Now the visual comparison alters: since people inevitably 'wear various-coloured spectacles' none of us can escape the colour of our own individuality. But we can come to understand and respect the different tints experienced and embodied by others: 'if Potter show us Aeschylus through green spectacles, and another translator, though in a very inferior manner, show us Aeschylus through yellow ones, it will become clear to the English reader, that green and yellow are not inherent properties of the Greek poet.'[8] The English refractions cannot make visible the different colour of the Greek; but they do enable it to be intuited.

This is a compelling theorisation of textual difference; indeed, almost of *différance*. There is no transfer of unchanged meaning, or unchanged anything, from Aeschylus's Greek to the various Englishes of his translators. There are only significant disparities which readers can probe and gauge. Here, the prismatic processes of translation are recognised and welcomed: the variety they create is experienced as a kind of harmony. Yet this radical and compelling theorization of the field of translation has little purchase on Barrett's later feelings about her own work. Her first *Prometheus* does not appear to her as one of the many possible reflected lights, or one colour in the inevitable and desirable spectrum. Instead it strikes her as a failure, a sin. When she is thinking about her own practice a second idea of translation supervenes, one in which it is possible to get, or not, what matters in the source; to do or fail to do it justice. Now, the prism of translation is felt as agon: the second version must extinguish the first one, 'replace' it (as the advertisement for its publication announced)[9] and prevent it from being read. One reason for this is Barrett's strong sense of translation as a mode of authorship in which her own identity is manifest. The first translation no longer feels like a fit representative of her, of the mature writer she has become: she does not recognize it as a 'Barrett's Aeschylus' to stand with Pope's or Cowper's Homer. The later version, by contrast, represents 'the sincerest application of my mature mind'; in it, she does her 'duty' by Aeschylus, 'not indeed according to his claims, but in proportion to my faculty'.[10] But that is not the whole of the matter, for what is it about the real, mature Barrett that was missing in the earlier version? Her ability to rise to the poetical challenge of Aeschylus, to capture at least something of his poetical warmth, fluidity and contours. The shadow of translation as the endeavour to achieve sameness has fallen across the celebration of translation as difference. Implicitly, the metaphor of translation as channel has materialized to haunt her thoughts, to turn difference into failure, and variety into a sin.

Elizabeth Barrett's long involvement with Aeschylus is significant in many ways. It reveals the centrality of translation to her creative practice: as with so many authors of the texts that make up 'English Literature', the language-world that she inhabited was not only English but plurilingual, and her writing life was laced with continual translation, not only from Greek but also from Latin, Italian, German and French. As Prins has recounted, her *Prometheus(es)* inaugurated a gendered imaginative community of readers and translators, with later writers such as Augusta Webster and Anna Swanwick producing their own versions of *Prometheus Unbound* in dialogue with hers.[11] And Barrett's work with Aeschylus also shows with striking vividness the instability of a prismatic view of translation, for the mode of translational variety which she welcomes in her 1833 Preface entails a rejection of translational variety of other kinds. The difference between translations made by different people is inevitable because everyone is different. But, within a career, each translator must strive to achieve the best equivalent they can, given their idioms and resources: indeed, it is each translator's striving to do the best they can which generates the variety celebrated in the Preface. The two views are in tension: why should the criticism that Barrett applies to her own translations not extend to translations by other people? And why, on the other hand, should her tolerance of variety in the 1833 Preface not extend to the various moments of her own self-realization through writing? As we will see, this is not the sort of tension that can be dissolved by being thought about. A commitment to the model of translation as prism will always be haunted by the idea of translation as channel; an experience of the prism as harmony is always liable to flip over into an experience of the prism as agon. Any text that offers itself as a translation, or is treated as one, can fall prey to the same oscillation. Translation is defined by this radical instability.

Theorisation of the Prism and the Channel

The contradiction lived through by Elizabeth Barrett is latent in experiences and discussions of translation in many places and at many times. Readers know that translations are different from their sources, that no word of any translation has actually been written by the author whose name is usually attached to the book. Yet we still all merrily go on saying 'yes, I've read Ferrante' when what we mean is that we have read the translation by Ann Goldstein; or present ourselves as quoting Derrida even though the words we type are English. Translators — no-one more so — are sharply aware of the shifts of tone, meaning, sound and rhythm introduced by every word they write; and yet they still — how could they not? — aim to capture something of their source texts and bring it over. Authors — who better? — understand the particularity of what they have composed — and yet still they hope (how could they not) that something will get across through translation to readers in other tongues.

This paradox — I contend — is fundamental to translation. It is what translation is. Translation is obviously 'prismatic', as we assert in the title of this volume: obviously a matter of endlessly varying proliferation and change. And yet it is also obviously a 'channel', a matter of bringing something across between different texts or people. We might try to resolve this contradiction by asserting that in fact translations are merely similar to their source texts, never 'equivalents'. Variations of this idea have been developed by Umberto Eco, Clive Scott and Karen Emmerich, among others.[12] Yet, as we began to see in the Introduction, this move does not do away with the paradox, for similarity or reiteration can always be broken down into a matter of sameness in some respects and difference in others: if we say that apples are similar to pears we might mean that they are the same in that both are fruit and different because they have distinct shapes and tastes (etc). In many domains of similarity, the tessellation of what people call sameness and what we call difference is relatively easy to manage. In print-runs of books, for example, we tend to think that the words are the same even though the paper and ink are not: different individual copies are all taken to embody the same work. It is possible for even this apparently straightforward view to be ambushed by a protestation of difference (perhaps any claim to sameness shares some such vulnerability): one can argue that no two printed copies of a book ever really embody *the same work* because they will always exhibit some material difference (more so in the early days of printing) as well as being read by different people in different ways.[13] But conflict is especially liable to erupt in the case of translation — so much so that it becomes constitutive of the form. Translations are in many respects different from their sources; they are also in many respects the same; and what counts as 'sameness' and 'difference' is subject to perpetual contestation.

The view of translation which I am proposing builds on classic arguments about language in general. In 'The Conduit Metaphor: A Case of Frame Conflict in our Language about Language' (1979),[14] Michael J. Reddy drew attention to the metaphor of the conduit, or channel, which pervades much of the language for describing language in English (and related languages such as French, Italian and

German). Meaning is 'conveyed', 'taken', or 'grasped'; and even the ambiguity of words like 'poem', or 'novel', as pointing both to the words on the page and to the ideational and emotional entity they signify, implies the conduit metaphor: the poem in the second sense is assumed to be somehow 'in' the words, or got at 'through' them. Reddy argues that the 'conduit' picture of language is mistaken, and develops an alternative metaphorical model to replace it. Let's imagine — he suggests — that individuals inhabit separate boxes with different features: they can convey picture-messages to one another but, since no-one has direct access to the world occupied by anyone else, making sense of the messages involves a lot of inference and guess-work. On this model, linguistic interaction is less a matter of transferring meaning, and more a matter of inventing it.

Reddy's conduit and toolmakers' paradigms are continuous with, respectively, the 'channel' and 'prismatic' views of translation; and, just like the theorists who argue that translation should be seen as similarity rather than transfer, Reddy recommends the adoption of his 'toolmakers' paradigm' as the better picture of how language works. But he also sees that the conduit metaphor will be difficult, if not impossible to eradicate: 'the logic of the framework runs like threads in many directions through the syntactic and semantic fabric of our speech habits'.[15] In my view, the 'toolmaking' and 'conduit' pictures of language-use have to be allowed to co-exist, just like the 'channel' and 'prismatic' views of translation: the question is how the relationship between them is negotiated. There are all sorts of utterances, from 'yes' or 'get out!' to 'I love you' or 'isn't the sunset beautiful?' that might, in many circumstances, more plausibly be described as communicating meaning than enabling it to be constructed. Of course, any of these phrases might also turn out to suggest non-obvious meanings that have to be built up by the listener: 'yes' might mean 'no'; 'get out!' might mean 'I am really hurt'; 'I love you' might mean a very wide range of things, etc.. So there are many circumstances in which the toolmakers' paradigm would be the better picture. But the very fact that we are able to see this entails that there are also circumstances in which it would not. The oscillation between the pictures goes deep, not only into speech habits, but into people's ideas and feelings about how we relate to each other. Not only a theory of language but many everyday practices of human interaction would be different if speakers of English, French, Italian and other related tongues decided that their languages never, ever allowed them to *pensarla allo stesso modo*, *saisir une idée*, or feel at one. We need to recognize both the possibility of something that counts as 'communication' and the need to probe and criticize the terms on which it can be thought to have occurred.

Something like this contradictory movement was painstakingly traced and enacted in the work of Jacques Derrida. In *De la grammatologie*, the 'effaced and respectful doubling of commentary', 'le redoublement effacé et respectueux du commentaire', aims to grasp the 'conscious, voluntary, intentional' — 'conscient, volontaire, intentionnel' — relationship to history that a writer has constructed through language.[16] In later work, this explanation was revised: 'the moment of what I called, perhaps clumsily, "doubling commentary" does not suppose the self-identity of "meaning", but a relative stability of the dominant interpretation (including the auto-interpretation) of the text being commented upon.'[17] In both definitions, the process of doubling commentary approximates to the 'conduit' metaphor of language: commentators efface their own impulses in order to receive an interpretation that has already been established. This endeavour to receive the text then opens onto a second, more energetic practice of interpretation which (in Simon Critchley's summary) opens the text's 'intended meaning, its *vouloir-dire*, onto an alterity which goes against what the text wants to say or mean'.[18] This deconstructive reading does not exactly tally with Michael Reddy's 'toolmaker's paradigm', but it shares with it a view of interpretation as making out of a text something other than anything that might be thought to be simply 'in' it.

In Derrida's later essay 'Survivre', translated as 'Living On / Border Lines', the double movement of reading extends into the reading-and-rewriting across languages that is translation:

> The line that I seek to recognize within translatability, between two translations, one governed by the classical model of transportable univocality or of formalizable polysemia, and the other, which goes over into dissemination — this line also passes between the critical and the deconstructive.[19]
>
> La ligne que je tente de reconnaître à l'intérieur de la traductibilité, entre deux traductions, l'une, réglée sur le modèle classique de l'univocité transportable ou de la polysémie formalisable, et l'autre qui déborde vers la dissémination, cette ligne passe aussi entre le *critique* et le *déconstructif*.[20]

The line passes 'between' in two senses: it separates, just as a deconstructive reading is something different from the effaced doubling of commentary; and it joins, just as the respectful doubling of commentary will lead on into a deconstructive reading if only it is pushed beyond the border of consensus, if it 'déborde' (overflows) into dissemination. The second movement cannot exist without the first; and the issue I want to probe, and question, is the relationship between them. Repetition introduces difference: as the opening lines of 'Survivre' assert, to say the same thing 'autrement', or 'in other words', is never only to say the same thing again but always also to say something new. It is no different if you simply repeat the same words (as I write, politics offers a perfect, agonizing example: 'Brexit Means Brexit'). So sameness opens onto difference. The point I want to add is that difference can, at any moment, switch around and be claimed as sameness. We can see this happening in Paul de Man's critique (in *Blindness and Insight*) of Derrida's critique (in *De la grammatologie*) of Rousseau. Derrida painstakingly deconstructs Rousseau's text, making meanings from it which — he thinks — are at odds with the 'conscious, voluntary, intentional' significance revealed by the doubling of commentary. Yet, as it seems to de Man, the meanings elucidated by Derrida have been readily visible all along, with no reason to think that they were unintended: 'Rousseau's text has no blind spots ... there is no need to deconstruct Rousseau'.[21] I do not wish to side with one or the other view; I simply want to observe the switchback: what seems to Derrida a reading that goes against the text's *vouloir dire* strikes de Man as merely describing it.

If we turn back to translation between languages (or rather to the kind of translation which, as we have seen in the introduction, both collaborates in and contests the separation of languages), instances corresponding to the first shift, from commentary to dissemination, are easy to find. They occur whenever a translation — or part of it — that has been felt to stand as an equivalent to its source is then felt not to (as when Elizabeth Barrett so comprehensively changed her view of her 1833 *Prometheus*); or whenever a translation is criticised by a reviewer or reader for some sort of failure or misunderstanding; or whenever a translational text is felt to be not really a translation but something freer such as an 'imitation' or 'version'. However, the opposite movement, in which a translational text shifts from being seen as an instance of dissemination to being taken as a vehicle of transfer, is also possible: prominent instances include parts of Pound's *Homage to Sextus Propertius*, at first decried by many classicists for inventing innuendoes that could not possibly have been in the Latin, only later to be accepted as having discovered something after all; or Robert Browning's *Agamemnon of Aeschylus*, widely ridiculed as unreadable when it appeared — but a century later adopted by Tony Harrison, when he was working on his celebrated theatre version of the *Oresteia*, as the key to creating hearable Aeschylean verse in English.[22]

The feeling of something 'getting through' in translation need not entail a naïve belief in the 'self-identity of "meaning"' any more than does Derrida's 'doubling commentary'. The meaning or rhythm or tone that are felt as 'coming through' are of course co-created by the recipient, as we saw in the Introduction: this is true of any reading of any text, and is no less true of the reading of translations. The fact that reading and hearing are active processes does not mean that nothing is ever read or heard. Charles Martindale, a theorist of translation who works in the field defined as 'Classical Reception' and who therefore is not as well known as he might be in Translation Studies and Comparative Literature, has given a subtle account of the difficulties for description which are generated by the continuities between translation and reading:

> Translations determine what counts as being "there" in the first place, and good translations thus unlock for us compelling (re)readings which we could not get in any other way. "Tone", for example, becomes ... not something read off but something constructed; indeed, ... the difference between "reading off" and "reading in" is dissolved. Our conception of "Ovid" is mediated through translations like those of Dryden which have helped define what "Ovid" is for us. We read in and through translations, though these always imply the possibility of other translations, other readings.[23]

The argument has obvious strength for texts in classical languages, which can only be learnt via those exploded and re-organized translations known as dictionaries and grammar books. It is in fact no less true for all texts, from any chronological moment, and in any location on the global continuum of language variety. As soon as you encounter the source you begin to read, drawing on your learnt knowledge of its language (whether you tend to think of that as your 'own' or as 'foreign') — and therefore you begin to translate. Your idea of 'the source' is (just like Derrida's 'doubling commentary') already an interpretation, so there can be no distinction between 'reading off' and 'reading in'. It follows that there can be no theory of translation as introducing inevitable differences from 'the source' since any conception of the source is already a translation. Our contrasting metaphorical networks — on the one hand the prism and reiterative difference, on the other the channel, transfer and equivalence — are both equally simplifications of a process which (as Douglas Robinson has argued) cannot adequately be known or represented. As Robinson puts it, source language and target language 'inhabit the translator's body in a great swirling confusion', until something happens that involves 'somehow making the leap, making the blind stab at understanding or reformulating'.[24]

Why, then, bother with our contrasting metaphorical networks at all? Because they are the conceptual and linguistic resources that are available in the environment of English and overlapping languages. They are the terms through which translators and readers of translations have done and still do experience their behaviour, and therefore through which it happens. Endeavouring to understand that behaviour better entails, not asserting the superiority of one set of terms over the other, nor jettisoning them both, but tracing and using them with an alertness to their ramifications and shortcomings. Translation involves a continual oscillation between the conviction that something has been found, clinched and brought across, and the reconfiguration of those acts as deviation, addition or change. That prismatic moment can be felt as agon (with Barrett Browning), failure, betrayal, growth or creativity; or it can swing round to seem like a channel once more. As we will see, attention to these varying configurations, and the feelings attached to them, offers a good way of tracing the work of translators, and mapping the cultures of translation which they at once inhabit and create.

An Instance of Oscillation: John Dryden

In the discipline of Translation Studies, Dryden tends to appear as a significant but simplified figure: a practioner of 'fluent' and 'domesticating' translation strategies, and the author of a distinction between three 'types' of translation — metaphrase, paraphrase and imitation — which still has some influence on how the translation of poetry is understood.[25] Yet, as scholars working in the disciplines of English Studies and Classical Reception have shown, Dryden's involvement with translation across the four decades of his career, encompassing versions of Ovid, Horace, Juvenal, Lucretius, Homer, Theocritus, Plutarch and others, and culminating in *The Works of Virgil in English*, was more restless and complex than this. Paul Hammond has traced how Dryden's translations, and also his own poems, 'activate the half-hidden Latin roots of the language', so that 'Latin continually shadows the English', and 'the time and space of translation' become 'a third field, a synthesis of Roman and English worlds'.[26] Julie Candler Hayes has argued that, with his awareness of the 'feedback loops' between translation and originality, Dryden develops a '"translational," rather than authorial, self-consciousness, overcoming the dichotomy between translators as abject and dependent and authors as independent and original'.[27] David Hopkins has pointed to the dynamic relationship between his theory and practice, so that 'Dryden's writings on translation are best considered not as a fixed body of theory or doctrine, but as the working notes of a practitioner ... continually modified, enriched, and transformed.'[28] In my own work, I have traced Dryden's vexed relationship to the idea that translation necessarily interprets: he translates in order to 'open' the subtleties of Virgil's verse, but by clarifying them he necessarily destroys them, and the resulting drama plays out with particular vividness when actions of opening or interpreting are portrayed in the scenes being translated.[29] Here, my aim is to explore how far Dryden's complex translational activity can be captured by a prismatic view of translation; and, in so doing, to put his writing in dialogue with the theoretical issues addressed by the volume as a whole. Perhaps this pillar of the translation canon is more prismatic than he has often been made to seem.

Dryden's description of his hope for his *Aeneis*, 'to make *Virgil* speak such *English*, as he wou'd himself have spoken, if he had been born in *England*, and in this present age', is in itself fraught with complexities.[30] What becomes of Dryden's own writing voice in this work of making another writer 'speak'? How far does the authorial figure of Virgil remain himself when he is re-made in another language? The intricacies proliferate when we realize that there are traces of other authors in Dryden's utterance, and echoes of other speech. Dryden points to 'the *French* translator', Jean Regnault de Segrais, whose translation influenced his, and to whose 'Preface' he pays repeated tribute in his 'Dedication', though he does not quote the exact words: 'j'ay voulu donner l'Eneïde en François, comme j'ay conceu qu'il l'eust donnée luy-mesme, s'il fust né sujet de nostre glorieux Monarque' ('I have endeavoured to give the Aeneid in French, as I conceive he would have given it himself, if he had been born a subject of our glorious Monarch').[31] Dryden's concealed echo-and-riposte to Segrais connects with assertions, elsewhere in the 'Dedication', of the value of being English rather than French — as, for instance, when he defends the political interpretations which he draws from Virgil's text: 'I shall continue still to speak my Thoughts like a free-born Subject as I am; though such things, perhaps, as no *Dutch* Commentator cou'd, and I am sure no *French*-man durst.'[32] Freedom of speech, already established as part of the ideology of Englishness, licences Dryden's freedom in interpreting, and gives a particular inflection to his freedom as a translator. Making Virgil 'speak ... English' will of course require the translator's usual freedom of departing from the words for the sake of sense or style; but it will also entail the uttering of latent political suggestions in a public sphere that was comparatively free. Segrais's words, in turn, echo those of Sir John Denham, the Royalist poet and translator, whose version from *Aeneid* II, *The Destruction of Troy* (1656) was also an important stimulus to Dryden in both kinds of freedom. Denham too resounds in Dryden's famous phrase: 'If *Virgil* must needs speak English' — Denham had written in his own 'Preface' — 'it were fit he should speak not only as a man of this Nation, but as a man of this age.'[33]

Dryden's famous phrase is, then, a particularly charged instance of agnation, that aspect of language which — as we saw in the Introduction — surrounds any utterance with the alternatives from which it has been selected. Dryden's statement is shadowed (to recall Christian Matthiessen's word) by other statements which, in this case, do not lie latent in the language but have in fact been made by other writers. It differentiates itself from them by being distinct, and also connects itself to them by being similar. The relationship between Dryden's statement and the others is not stable like the structure of a crystal, but rather dynamic, even wobbly, as we can see if we notice another concatenation of echoes. Back in 1680, in the 'Preface' to the group translation *Ovid's Epistles*, Dryden had been more critical of the idea of making people speak in the language of a time and country not their own. Ovid himself was faulted for doing this in the *Heroides*: 'perhaps he has Romanized his Grecian dames too much, and made them speak sometimes as if they had been born in the city of Rome, and under the empire of Augustus'.[34] Denham's mission statement was equated with Abraham Cowley's idea of 'imitation': 'that is, not to translate his words, or to be confined to his sense, but only to set him as a pattern, and to write as he supposes that author would have done, had he lived in our age and in our country'. This, Dryden firmly opined, was 'the greatest wrong which can be done to the memory and reputation of the dead'.[35] The disparity between the earlier and later texts shows Dryden's practice and theory evolving, as Hopkins suggests: the writer of the 1697 Dedication is a more confident poet-translator than that of the 1680 Preface, with more developed tactics for remaking verse in imitation of a style. All the same, something of the earlier opinion persists, and the venom which, in 1680, had been aimed at Denham and Cowley is, in 1697 redirected at himself: 'I have done great Wrong to *Virgil* in the whole Translation.'[36]

It is the same switchback that we observed in Elizabeth Barrett Browning. A work of translation to which Dryden had been committed becomes a source of shame to him. Here, though, the turn to self-criticism happens continually: the compulsion to translate is inseparable from regret at having translated, and especially in this particular case. In 1685, Dryden had announced: 'methinks I come like a malefactor to make a speech upon the gallows, and to warn all other poets by my sad example from the sacrilege of translating Virgil' — yet that was near the start of his own long translational involvement with the *Aeneid*.[37]

The 1680 Preface also includes Dryden's — equally famous — distinction between metaphrase, paraphrase and imitation. In our terms, this is an attempt to subjugate the prismatic deviances of translation to a structure that follows the metaphor of the channel. The three modes are channels for different things: the first, for 'words' and 'lines'; the second, for 'the author' and 'his sense'; the third, for 'only some general hints'. As I showed in *The Poetry of Translation*, this structure begins to disintegrate in the moment of being uttered, and its relationship to Dryden's practice is left in question. 'I am ready to acknowledge that I have transgressed the rules that I have given', Dryden wrote at the end of the Preface; and the sense of misfit between prescription and practice continues, two decades later, in the Virgil translation which operates, he says 'betwixt Metaphrase and Paraphrase'. A reader's understanding might want to to know what it is getting: 'is this paraphrase? Is this metaphrase? What sort of equivalence is being claimed?' — but the translating imagination is always wriggling out of one or the other definition as it responds to different aspects of the source and remakes them in English: sometimes a particular form of words might ask to be respected; sometimes a richly ambiguous meaning might ask to be opened out. As the translational writing continually escapes the available definitions, it repeatedly causes dissatisfaction: this line might seem to echo the shape of the words but lose some nuance of their meaning; this line might seem to open their sense while neglecting some aspect of their form.

As we have seen, Barrett Browning had a theoretical appreciation of the variety of actual and possible translations, the prismatic spray of colours which give an idea of the different tonality of the source by their multiple divergences from it; but this way of thinking did not extend to her own work, which she experienced as an endeavour to match up to Aeschylus and do him justice. Dryden too has a vivid awareness of other translations that have been and could be done; but he takes comfort from seeing his own work in their company. In 1685, he may have felt like a malefactor on the gallows when he compared himself to Virgil: it seemed to him that he had translated one episode too literally, and another not literally enough. But when he looked around him at the prismatic company of other translators, he cheered up: 'all that I can promise for myself is only that I have done both better than Ogilby, and perhaps as well as Caro' (Ogilby had translated Virgil into English in 1649; Annibale Caro the *Aeneid* into Italian in 1581).[38] Throughout his career, Dryden lived translation as a communal activity. The volumes which he edited, and to which he contributed, in 1680 (*Ovid's Epistles*), 1684 (*Miscellany Poems*) and 1685 (*Sylvae*) were all anthologies of work by multiple translators, done in collaboration with the young publisher Jacob Tonson; Dryden participated in discussions of translation as a member of the Earl of Roscommon's informal 'Academy' and continued those conversations into his prefaces and other writings; and, above all, he wrote surrounded by other written texts. William Frost, the modern scholarly editor of Dryden's *Virgil*, notes that he 'worked from a library full of Latin editions of Virgil's works and of sixteenth- and seventeenth-century Virgil translations into English, French and Italian'.[39] Elements of Dryden's practice and theory which correspond to the 'channel' metaphor — such as making Virgil 'speak' — need to be cross-hatched with this awareness of the prismatic plurality of voices among which he worked, and within which his writing found its place. He was not only translating a text but translating among texts; this affects how his translations should be thought about and read.

One of the things that Dryden most felt himself to be adding to exisiting translations and readings of the *Aeneid* was an appreciation of what he called Virgil's 'address'. That is, meanings which are not stated in the writing but which emerge from it when you enter imaginatively into the drama of a scene or the detail of its composition: a rough modern equivalent would be 'illocutionary force' (in the terms of speech act theory). Here, for example, Dryden compares Aeneas's reaction to the loss of his wife Creusa in the fall of Troy to the fuss made by Achilles when his concubine Briseis was taken from him, and sees Virgil's 'address' in the fact that Aeneas tells his story to Dido, who of course was on the point of falling catastrophically in love with him:

> *Aeneas* took a Nobler Course; for having secur'd his Father and his Son, he repeated all his former Dangers to have found his Wife, if she had been above ground. And here your Lordship may observe the Address of *Virgil*; it was not for nothing that this Passage was related with all these tender Circumstances. *Aeneas* told it; *Dido* heard it: That he had been so affectionate a Husband, was no ill Argument to the coming Dowager, that he might prove as kind to her. *Virgil* has a thousand secret beauties, though I have not leisure to remark them.[40]

The apparent casualness of 'though I have not leisure to remark them' is characteristic of Dryden's critical style. The phrase draws attention to the limitations of criticism's resources when faced with poetry as nuanced as Virgil's. It opens an imaginative space in which the poetry can exist as itself, away from the critical terms which, both despite and because of their limitations, help it to be seen for what it is.

As he translates the episode in which Aeneas relates the repetition of all his dangers, Dryden moves sometimes word by word and line by line with the Latin, and sometimes takes more room to amplify Virgil's 'Address'. Equally, he sometimes writes in unison with previous translators — especially with Lauderdale, who had lent him his version in manscript — and sometimes expands on meanings which seem to him to have been missed. He begins the episode in chorus. Here is Lauderdale's version:

> Alas, I lost *Creusa*, hard to tell,
> If by her cruel Destiny she fell,
> Or if to Toils unus'd, with Cares oppress'd,
> And weary grown she laid her down to rest,
> Or if she miss'd her way; but since that Hour
> (Whate'er befel) I ne'er beheld her more.[41]

And here is Dryden's:

> Alas! I lost *Creusa*: hard to tell
> If by her fatal Destiny she fell,
> Or weary sate, or wander'd with affright;
> But she was lost forever to my sight.[42]

Both may have been nudged towards the directness of 'Alas! I lost Creusa' by dissatisfaction with Ogilby's earlier attempt:

> Ah, by sad Fate, I my Creusa lost[43]

Ogilby is closer to the words of Virgil's Latin:

> Heu! misero coniunx fatóne erepta Creüsa.[44]

('misero ... fató' is 'by sad fate'; 'erepta Creusa' means 'was snatched Creusa'). But then Virgil's was not the only Latin that Lauderdale and Dryden had in front of them. The paraphrase in Ruaeus's edition introduces the words 'dubium est', ('it is uncertain', 'it is hard to tell'), which no doubt helped both of them to structure their English sentences in the way they do.[45] At this point the French of Segrais ('Creüse ... sa disgrace est encore incertaine' and the Italian of Caro ('Restai (misero me) senza la mia / Diletta moglie, in dubio') join in the translational harmonies only as outliers, though Caro too seems to have found inspiration in Ruaeus's 'dubium est'.[46]

Observing Dryden's text among the other translations, we can see how his idea of what the *Aeneid* could be in English, of what needed doing to give it a better representation, comes into being in collaboration with them. First he adopts an already achieved solution (Alas, I lost *Creusa*...); but then, in the ensuing lines, he sees a need for tighter verse than Lauderdale had written in order to imitate those 'sober retrenchments of his Sense', that reserve in the midst of emotion, which so impressed him in Virgil's style.[47] Yet, of course, maintaining that sobriety requires him not to open out the implications of Virgil's 'Address', and Dryden soon becomes frustrated at this restraint. Virgil writes two further compact lines of grief:

> Quem non incusavi amens hominumque Deorumque?
> Aut quid in eversa vidi crudelius urbe?
>
> (Out of my mind, what man or god did I not blame? Or what more cruel than that did I see in the fallen city?)[48]

Here, Ogilby, Segrais and Lauderdale all keep quite close to the Latin, but Caro feels the need for something more, adding 'miserando' ('grievous') to 'cruel' and inserting two more lines of expostulation.[49] Dryden follows him:

> This was the fatal Blow, that pain'd me more
> Then all I felt from ruin'd *Troy* before.
> Stung with my Loss, and raving with Despair,
> Abandoning my now forgotten Care,
> Of Counsel, Comfort, and of Hope bereft,
> My Sire, my Son, my Country Gods, I left.[50]

'Stung', 'raving' and 'abandoning' are all in the same vein as Caro; what is new is the mention of 'Counsel', 'Comfort' and 'Hope'. These words seem designed to prompt us to remember that Aeneas is telling this story to Dido, i.e. to someone who might offer him all those things. They alert us to 'the Address of Virgil', since — as Dryden had said in the 'Dedication' — 'it was not for nothing that this Passage was related with all these tender Circumstances'.

A little further on, Dryden effects another significant deviation from the spectrum of earlier translations. Here is Lauderdale:

> Where'er I pass I on *Creusa* call,
> I fill with Cries the Houses, Streets; through all
> In vain *Creusa* sadly I proclaim,
> A thousand times repeat the dear lov'd Name:
> Lamenting thus I roam through every Street,
> At length *Creusa*'s airy Shadow meet,
> Far bigger than the Life; ...[51]

Caro and Segrais, too, had both made Aeneas repeat Creusa's name a thousand times: 'Mille volte iterai l'amato nome'; 'Ah!, Creüse, ay-je dit, & redit mille fois'.[52] Dryden chooses to rely on showing rather than stating the repetition; and the repetition is itself repeated:

> Then, with ungovern'd Madness, I proclaim,
> Through all the silent Streets, *Creusa*'s Name.
> *Creusa* still I call: At length she hears;
> And suddain, through the Shades of Night appears:
> Appears, no more *Creusa*, nor my Wife:
> But a pale Spectre, larger than the Life.[53]

'Creusa ... Creusa' calls up 'appears: / Appears'. In this, Dryden is responding to the repetitive texture of the Latin, where Aeneas calls 'iterumque iterumque' ('again and again'), and the sound of 'que' ('and') echoes in words on either side, 'quaerenti' ('seeking) and 'nequicquam' (in vain), and even the phrase 'sine fine' ('without end') is turned into a repetition by early modern typography, which prints it almost indistinguishably from 'fine fine'.[54]

In this, Dryden might be thought of — and might have thought of himself — as channeling Virgil's style: in the 'Dedication' he presents himself as 'the first *Englishman*, perhaps, who made it his design to copy him in his Numbers, his choice of Words, and his placing them for the sweetness of the sound'.[55] Yet the endeavour to channel, to repeat Virgil's repetitions, of course introduces difference; and the lodging of the words within the scene seems to recognize and reflect upon this fact. Repeated, 'Creusa' shifts from being the name of a person who might be recovered to being the name of someone who has been lost: Creusa is no more Creusa. 'Appears' undergoes the same change: at first, it seems to announce the appearance of a person; but it turns out to announce the appearance of an appearance — a 'Spectre' or (as we say) an apparition. The echoic scene is charged with other echoes still, of Dryden's own ambitions as a translator. He puts all his energies into conjuring up a hearable voice for Aeneas, as Aeneas puts all his energies into conjuring up Creusa; and Aeneas (and Dryden) do manage to make her speak as if she were alive; only she is not, and when her speech ends she vanishes like an empty dream or blast of wind. At this, other potential metaphors of translation supervene. Creusa has trusted her 'common Issue' with Aeneas to his care (ie their child Ascanius); and he returns to where he has left his family, finding the group swelled with 'Men, and Matrons mix'd', 'young and old'. Aeneas yields 'to Fate', takes his aged father on his back, and sets off to fulfil Creusa's prophecy, to follow 'long wandring Ways' through 'many painful years' until they will be cast 'on *Latium*'s happy shore' where '*Fortune* shall the *Trojan* Line restore'.[56] In the 'Dedication', Dryden had figured himself in terms derived from this episode, as having 'the weight of a whole Author on my shoulders': Paul Davis has outlined the importance of this image for Dryden's sense of translation as 'labour'.[57] Other traces connect to other aspects of Dryden's thinking about his art. 'Way' had long been one of his key words for describing the possibilities of translation. Paraphrase is 'the second way', imitation 'the third way'; Denham and Cowley contrived 'another way of turning authors into our tongue'; Aphra Behn's version of Ovid is 'in Mr Cowley's way of imitation only'; in short, the whole challenge of translation was to work out 'which way of version seems to me most proper'.[58] And Dryden also endeavours to restore the '*Trojan* Line': indeed, he is following it 'line by line'. So, in this scene, which starts with an individual setting off by himself to conjure a voice, and ends with a group labouring together to transplant a civilization, Dryden gives imaginative life to the contradictory frames of translation as channel and as prism, and discovers a narrative by which they can be accommodated. The solitary conviction of hearing someone speak inspires, and gives way to, the slow, communal exploration of 'wandring Ways' through which the work of translation is, in practice, done.

The History of Translation and the Contemporary Scene

In both Dryden and Barrett Browning we have observed the co-existence of channel with prismatic views of translation: of a commitment to some kind of transfer or equivalence with a recognition that translation necessarily generates and participates in a multitude of differences. The co-existence was lived in different ways — as agon and as oscillation — but in neither case could one view win out over the other or the two be reconciled. Translation cannot be seen only as a channel nor only as a prism, and neither can the two views merge. Translation is constituted by the paradoxical co-existence of both frames.

Much writing about translation over the last three decades — in both theoretical and anecdotal veins — has attended to the disjunction beween the idea that translation aspires to sameness and the recognition that it introduces difference. Often, the idea of the channel (or 'sameness', or 'transfer') is located elsewhere: a summary of many arguments might go: 'other people think of translation as transfer; but we know it generates change'. For instance, Derrida, in 'Survivre' and 'Living On / Border Lines', takes aim at what he thinks to be the 'classical model' of translation as transfer which 'prevailed up until Benjamin perhaps'.[59] However, as we have discovered, neither Dryden nor Barrett Browning was at ease with that model — and both of them lived well before Benjamin. Some of what they said about translation, and some of their translational endeavour, can be aligned with it; but other aspects of their work and thinking cannot. Not ubiquitous before Benjamin, the 'classical model' has not vanished after him. Any celebration of translation as difference is haunted by translation as sameness. Any endeavour to achieve equivalence is rattled by awareness of disparity.

As we began to see in the Introduction, one recent line of theorisation pushes the channel view elsewhere by attaching it to the structures and requirements of the nation-state. Naoki Sakai concludes from his research into the literary and linguistic history of Japan:

> The particular representation of translation as communication between two particular languages is no doubt a historical construct. Given the politico-social significance of translation, it is no accident that, historically, the regime of translation became widely accepted in many regions of the world, after the feudal order and its passive vassal subject gave way to the disciplinary order of the active citizen subject in the modern nation-state.[60]

The postcolonial scholar Robert Young has pointed to the role played by nineteenth-century imperialism in promoting this sort of 'representation of translation' by standardizing languages and defining them as discrete entities:

> Translation can occur only if both languages have been made proper, have been standardized. Wedded to the written form, translation is sustained by the ideology of discrete unitary languages, assuming and requiring monolingualism, for without that separated distinction the conversion of one language into another would never take place — and would never be needed.[61]

Of course Young is not thinking of all the varied modes of re-making that can be described as 'translation', but only of the same particular representation as Sakai. Other factors, too, have been connected to the formation and maintenance of this mode. Michael Cronin, referencing the architectural theorist Mario Carpo, emphasizes the role, not only of the 'written form', but especially of print, and other technologies of mechanical reproduction, in creating a 'regime of identicality' that pushes translation towards an ideal of sameness.[62] As it seems to the Finnish poet and translator Leevi Lehto, this representation of translation, or Derrida's 'classical model', still holds today. Indeed, in his view, it is stronger now than in the nineteenth century: 'our present global language situation' — he says — 'dominated as it is by the rise of national states and corresponding national languages', promotes 'a naive conception of a "democratic" "equality" of languages. Translation has come to be seen as "transferring contents" between languages'.[63]

There is no doubt that all these forces have contributed to abstracting and solidifying the channel view, Derrida's classical model, which, in previous work, I have called 'Translation Rigidly Conceived'.[64] Yet, as the differences between Sakai, Young, Lehto and Cronin's arguments suggest, the channel view cannot be tied to a particular historical narrative. Equally, it cannot be wholly separated from any act of translation, however prismatic the practice or intent. Whenever there is a question of translation, the channel view looms. This is so even in the radically multilingual environments adduced by Young later in his essay, where 'the individual languages concerned may not even be classified as languages': as soon as there is a recognition of linguistic difference, followed by an act of communication, then a channel is metaphorically brought into being.[65] Leevi Lehto offers a nuanced account of the environment of translation as an alternative to the image promoted by nationalist ideology: 'perhaps communality is better understood as an exposure to the language of the other, one that you will (never) understand completely, never "master", but that at the same time, precisely for this reason, speaks to you'.[66] Yet here too, in this space of multiple differences, prism and channel are superimposed: Lehto's parentheses preserve the possibility of understanding within 'will never understand', while the language that is not mastered can still 'speak to you'. In our contemporary circumstances, just as much as when Dryden and Barrett Browning were writing, the prism and the channel metaphors cannot but co-exist: attention to their overlaps and switcharounds can help us trace the work being done by translation, as well as the claims being made for it.

Take, for example, the Belfast poet Ciaran Carson's recent volume *From Elsewhere*, which consists of translations, and 'translations of the translations as it were', from the French poet Jean Follain.[67] Carson, who grew up in an Irish-speaking family, with a father who was a devotee of Esperanto, has made poetry from fractures within language and the blending of languages throughout his career. In poems such as 'Belfast Confetti', political violence unleashes aggressive verbal energies ('Suddenly as the riot squad moved in it was raining exclamation marks'), while 'Second Language' presents English, from the point of view of the infant Carson, as something sumptuously, rebarbatively strange: 'Wordy whorls and braids and skeins and spiral helices, unskeletoned from laminate geology'.[68] Translation is intrinsic to this creative practice; and of course it is translation in a predominantly prismatic vein, attentive to the textual variety among which it operates, and to the particularity of any form of language which it brings into being. In his 'Introduction' to *The Inferno of Dante Alighieri: A new translation by Ciaran Carson*, Carson writes:

> Translating ostensibly from the Italian, Tuscan or Florentine, I found myself translating as much from English, or various Englishes. Translation became a way of reading, a way of making the poetry of Dante intelligible to myself. An exercise in comprehension: "Now tell the story in your own words." What are my own words? I found myself wondering how one says what one means in any language, or how one knows what one means. I found myself pondering the curious and delightful grammar of English, and was reminded that I spoke Irish (with its different, curious and delightful grammar) before I spoke English.[69]

And yet — no less of course — these prismatic emphases co-exist with channel-style claims: the book is titled *The Inferno of Dante Alighieri*, with the Irish-English text shadowing the Italian pretty much line for line, and aiming especially to 'get something of' Dante's 'music', a desire not so very different from Dryden's to make Virgil 'speak'. With its localized, up-to-date idiom and frequent reminders of Northern Irish political violence, the translation mines the impossible conjunction of channel and prism, finding there a source of restless imaginative energy.[70]

In turning to Follain, Carson chose a writer with a shorter and less plural translation history than Dante's. Nonetheless, selections of his poems had been put into English several times before. In the introductory 'Apropos' at the start of *From Elsewhere*, Carson recalls that when he came across Follain and 'looked him up on the internet one of the first things I found was a version of the first poem in the present book, "*Soulier renoué*: Shoelace Tied"'.[71] Other people's translations continued to play a part in Carson's work with Follain: the 'Acknowledgements' note that 'my translations of the poems of Jean Follain would no doubt have turned out differently had I not consulted translations by Kurt Heinzelman, Heather McHugh, W. S. Merwin, and Christopher Middleton.'[72] Follain's many poems are each typically about twelve or fifteen lines long, unrhymed, and unpunctuated except for a full-stop at the end: they present scenes or small sequences of events from ordinary life, though there is no observing or narrating 'I'; often they are located in the Normandy countryside in the decades following the First World War. They are, as Carson says in the 'Apropos', both 'humble' and 'resonant'; this combination seems to have been what most attracted Follain's several anglophone translators.

The look of Carson's volume in some ways recognizes and in other ways occludes this company. Follain's name does not figure on the cover or title page: the book appears as *From Elsewhere* by Ciaran Carson. Still, this implicitly registers the presence of the other versions, since poet-translators tend to feel able to present translations under their own name when the source-writer is already well known: what matters in the new publication is its fresh re-making of the material more than its origin. Then, when we look inside the covers, we find a text that is itself plural, as the 'Apropos' announces: 'this book consists of translations from the French poet Jean Follain, faced by "original" poems inspired by those translations: spins or takes on them in other words. Translations of translations as it were.'[73] The layout displays prismatic energies; but it also sidelines writing other than Carson's: of Follain's French, only the titles survive, and the acknowledgement of the other translations appears only at the very end of the book. On the left-hand side of the page-spread, where the source would be printed in a traditional parallel text, is a poem in English presented as a translation. This seems to probe the idea that an 'original' can ever simply be there on the page, separate from what a reader is making of it, and suggests a thought like Charles Martindale's: that it is translation which determines 'what counts as being "there" in the first place'. On the other hand — and on the right-hand page — are the 'translations from translations as it were', also called '"original" poems'. This begins an exploration of how 'translation' and 'originality' can relate, in ways that question the dominance of the poet-translator. Are the translations of translations further from the Follain poems, or somehow closer, like a reflection of a reflection?[74] Are the poems original-in-inverted-commas because they are in some sense original Carson, or in some sense original Follain?

Carson's explanation in his introductory 'Apropos' (quoted above) is designedly hazy. The second array of poems are 'spins or takes' — but which? They are 'in other words' — but is that because they are written in other words, or because they are, in other words, spins or takes? The poems/translations too invite a questioning response. In '*Sans courage*: Without Courage', Carson, translating Follain, describes someone returning home and climbing up to

> ... the attic rooms
> almost empty except for childhood.

The corresponding '"original" poem', which is titled 'Translation', gives us a boy leaning out of an 'attic window' overlooking countryside that he dreams of flying over, and then descending, having been

> changed in the meantime
> that is elsewhere.[75]

So this '"original"' which is called 'Translation' echoes the '*Elsewhere*' of the volume's title, and offers an image that matches Carson's description of his translational practice in the 'Apropos': 'I find myself in the other of Follain, questing and fetching the poems from another language, from the elsewhere of his territory.'[76] 'Fetch', Carson has explained, is a complex word, whose meanings include 'bringing from a distance', 'tacking' (in the nautical sense) and creating an 'apparition, double, or wraith'.[77] This exploratory work of translation is, then, in harmony with the theoretical assertions that we have encountered in Martindale, Robinson and Sakai: one cannot know what is there to be translated until it has been found by translation.

Though each of Carson's '"original"' poems differs in many way from its preceding 'translation', there are always one or a few shared words — a snippet of word-for-word (indeed, identical) translation between them to anchor the wandering process of the 'fetch'. In '*Sans courage*: Without Courage' and 'Translation', the word is 'attic'. These links, perhaps passageways, create an opening for our own, readerly inhabiting and fetching of the double textuality of the work. We are invited to see 'Translation' as a translational elaboration of the connotations of 'attic' in '*Sans courage*: Without Courage', an 'opening' of an aspect of that poem, not so very different from Dryden's openings of Virgil.

In another pair of fetches, '*Muraille*: Yard Wall' and 'Trompe l'oeil', the shared words are 'pinned', and 'hold everything together' (slightly altered to 'Everything held together'). In the 'translation', a split stone in a wall holds everything together, and a man is pinned to the wall as he dies; in the '"original"', collage items such as 'a snapshot of a soldier' and 'a woman's calling card' are 'held together' and 'pinned' to a board. The second poem seems to belong very much in Carson's own imaginative world, where everything is always already textual — the more so because it draws on an unexpected source: a note alerts us that '"Trompe l'oeil" is based on a passage from T. J. Clark, *Picasso and Truth*', though it does not say which passage. The most likely candidate turns out to be the description of a trompe l'oeil collage:

> Collage — and *Portrait of a Young Girl* is collage epitomized, for all that the stick-ons in it are illusions in oil — represented the *triumph* of room-space. Not for nothing was its key material wallpaper. The space it conjured was now literally put together from the little bourgeois's belongings: his newspaper, his sheet music, his matchbox, his daughter's scrapbook, his friends or dealers' calling cards.[78]

(Note the presence of 'calling cards', 'put together', and the 'wall' in 'wallpaper'.) This passage in its turn communicates with a section of Carson's 'Apropos', where we learn that the last entry in Follain's diary, 'dated 9 March 1971', reads:

> '*Dîner Vieux-Papier*'. *Le Vieux Papier* is an association devoted to the study of paper ephemera such as menus, playing cards, railway tickets, cheese labels, school exercise books, holy pictures, wine labels, theatre programmes, greeting cards, board games, diaries and the like.[79]

Finding its bearings among these intertexts, the '"original"' prompts thought about what translation can be 'into': not just English, and not just Belfast English, but Carson's particular language, itself prismatically interlaced with his readings and associations. As it is re-made in this medium, the realist visual scene presented in Follain is translated into the modernist genre of collage. The '"original"' also asks us to wonder how far, and how intricately, the meaning that has been translated, and thereby discovered, in the 'translation' might stretch: from the wall, via Clark's mention of wallpaper, to Follain's interest in old paper; from Follain's word for 'pinned', 'collé', to the mode of vision of Picasso's collages.[80] In the case of John Dryden we have watched translation drawing out meanings that were 'secretly in' Virgil, with an imagining of the author and his 'address' helping that to happen. Similar ambitions are at play in *From Elsewhere*, and similar discoveries occur. Dryden, as we have seen, was buoyed by writing among other translators, sometimes aligning with them and sometimes differing. Analogous feelings seem latent in the overlapping texts of the trompe l'oeil collage, along with Carson's distinctive word, 'pinned' as it differs from the agnate alternatives: 'stuck' (chosen by both W. S. Merwin and Christopher Middleton) and 'pressed' (Kurt Heinzelman).[81] In Carson's 'translation', the man pinned to the wall sees:

> columns of smoke rise
> from the fugitive horizons.

In the '"original"', what is pinned to the board is 'an airmail envelope', blue like

> the sky through a window
> that when everything
> else is collapsing
> opens.

The lines echo the open attic window in the '"original"' that is called 'Translation': here again we can sense the translator figure intervening in the elsewhere of the source text, inventing or perhaps uncovering a different, happier undertow to the ending, with the smoke clearing to reveal blue sky. The translational imagination opens this interpretation, and then — just as in Dryden — the process of opening appears as a figure in the writing. 'Opening', of course, being also Dryden's word.

Carson's *From Elsewhere*, then, is in many respects the epitome of a prismatic view of translation. It recognizes itself as having multiple sources and as finding its place among other versions, and its translations all have shadowy doubles. And yet, simply by presenting itself as a work of *translation*, it inevitably brings the channel view into operation. When you look at the '"originals"', not as random poems, but as 'translations of translations', the question of *what* they are translating cannot but appear. In pursuing it, as we have been doing, we discover nuances and connotations that may not have been sufficiently unveiled in the 'translations'; and we see that they are being opened into a particular, unusual translational medium, not just 'English' but Carson's own language and imaginative world. In this complex environment, what counts as translation keeps shifting, just as it did for Dryden between his modes of metaphrase and paraphrase. At one moment we may think that the papers 'pinned' to a board translate a meaning latent in the man 'pinned' to a wall; and if we track down the French, we might take both as translations of Follain's word 'collé'. On another occasion, the same sequence might seem to us something different from translation: version, departure, or invention. This provisional approach to the work of translation certainly downplays the channel view and opens it to question; but it cannot do away with it entirely, for if it did there would be nothing to ask questions about. Here, just as in every text that is offered or taken as 'translation', there is a co-existence of channel and prismatic frames.

Virtually the opposite stance to Carson's is represented by Lydia Davis, the translator of French novels — notably Proust's *Du côté de chez Swann* and Flaubert's

Madame Bovary — and writer of prose fictions. In Davis's novel, *The End of the Story*, translation figures as a a long, slow job, a matter of puzzles or problems that have solutions or answers.[82] Her essayistic accounts of translation likewise portray her as endeavouring to reproduce source texts 'correctly', 'closely and exactly', and to find 'the perfect equivalent'.[83] Her work on Proust involved correcting the 'lyricism and empty rhetorical flourishes' that seemed to her to mar the early and much-loved translation by Scott Moncrieff, so as to achieve 'accuracy and faithfulness'.[84] When, in *Madame Bovary*, she confronted a text with a long and plural translation history, the multitude of versions struck her as a record of error and shortcoming:

> In the case of a book that appeared more than one hundred and fifty years ago, like *Madame Bovary*, and that is an important landmark in the history of the novel, there is room for plenty of different English versions. For one thing, the first editions of the original text may have been faulty, and over the years one or more corrected editions have been published, so that the earliest English translations no longer match the most accurate original. (2) The earliest translators (as was the case with the Muirs rendering Kafka) may have felt they needed to inflict subtle or not so subtle alterations on the style and even the content of the original so as to make it more acceptable to the Anglophone audience; with the passing of time, we come to deem this something of a betrayal and ask for a more faithful version. (3) Earlier versions may simply not be as good in other respects as they could be — let another translator have a try.[85]

Yet when her own translations of Proust and Flaubert were published, they (of course) were not received as simply correcting or replacing the earlier versions. They were admired in some respects and dispraised in others, and took their place among each novel's prismatic translational array.

In a story called *A Walk* (written after the Proust translation but before the Flaubert), Davis reflects on the misfit between her channel-style ambitions for her work and its prismatic reception. As Helane Levine-Keating has shown, the story draws on an encounter between Davis and André Aciman, the critic of her Proust translation for the *New York Review of Books*, who had lamented its failure to recreate what he called Proust's 'cadence', i.e. nuances generated by the style.[86] The translator and the critic are in Oxford, having attended a conference, and wander together through the town, an exploration which is throughout made suggestive of translation, as she finds herself 'following not only her own impulses but also his' and taking 'care not to walk too close' (after having 'kept too close', as he had put it, in her Proust translation).[87] The hints become louder when two moments of surprise discovery remind her of a passage from *Du Côté de chez Swann*, one that (as Levine-Keating has noted) mattered especially to Aciman, and was discussed by him in his introduction to *The Proust Project*, an anthology of extracts and responses to which Davis too had contributed. Davis, writing the story, quotes the passage twice, first in Scott Moncrieff's translation, then in her own; but the translator-figure does not mention the reminiscence to the critic-figure, and the critic-figure does not notice it for himself. Levine-Keating takes this as an attack on Aciman, 'portraying this self-proclaimed harsh judge of translators as someone so caught up with himself that he is incapable of humor'; but it strikes me rather as a reflection on the disparities between two people who have much in common, including especially an intimate knowledge of Proust. The critic is not attacked, but rather observed; and the two extracts of translations, likewise, are not judged against each other, but simply left to sit there, displaying their paradoxical sameness-and-yet-difference.

In her contribution to *The Proust Project*, Davis had chosen a passage that was in itself repetitious, containing both a younger and a more mature description of the steeples of Martinville. She had asked 'why should Proust want to, in effect, duplicate a passage — write it twice over with only slight variations'; but she had not offered an answer.[88] *A Walk* poses the same question of herself, and pursues it to the story's last sentences, which are perhaps rather Proustian in their cadence. The critic and the translator are getting into separate taxis:

> As he stepped neatly into his, his last words to her, solemn and rather portentous, she thought, were ones that nobody, as it happened, had ever spoken to her before, but that she judged were likely to be correct, since he lived on the other side of the globe: "We will probably not meet again." He then made a graceful gesture of the hand that she later could not remember exactly, and whose meaning she could not quite grasp, though it seemed to combine a farewell with a concession to some sort of inevitability, and his cab moved slowly down the street, followed, soon, by her own.[89]

The passage sees understanding within misunderstanding, and the reverse: the translator meets the critic's view in judging what he says to be correct; yet what he says is that they will not meet again; and there is a sense in which (the story has shown) they have never met at all. She does not grasp his hand, and feels she cannot quite grasp the meaning of his gesture of the hand; yet she is able to give a translation of what it seems to mean. They are in separate taxis but follow the same road. Like Dryden's version of Aeneas's vision of Creusa, and like Carson's opening of the window, the story offers an image of translation, which is to say of the untranslatability within translation, and the translatability within the untranslatable.[90] It sits alongside Davis's intent endeavour as a translator of other people's writing, not agonizing over it (like Barrett Browning with her two *Prometheuses*) but giving it a human emotional context, and situating its claims. The quest for 'the perfect equivalent' co-exists with a recognition of the imperfection of all human communication. The same perception is interesting to Carson, and also to other contemporary writers, as we saw in the Introduction, and will see again in later chapters: in some respects, this is an early 21st-century theme. But, as we have found with Barrett Browning and Dryden, it goes deep into the past as well. It is, simply, the paradox of all translation.

Works Cited

ACIMAN, ANDRÉ, ed., *The Proust Project* (New York: Farrar, Strauss and Giroux, 2004)
APTER, EMILY, *Against World Literature: On the Politics of Untranslatability* (London: Verso, 2013)
BROWNING, ELIZABETH BARRETT, and ROBERT BROWNING, *The Brownings' Correspondence*, ed. by Ronald Hudson, Philip Kelley, Scott Lewis and Edward Hagan (Winfield, KS: Wedgestone Press, 1984–)
CARO, ANNIBALE, trans., *L'Eneide di Virgilio* (Treviso: Evangelista Deuchino, 1603)
CARSON, CIARAN, *Collected Poems* (Oldcastle: Gallery Books, 2008)
—— *From Elsewhere* (Winston-Salem, NV: Wake Forest University Press, 2015)
CLARK, T. J., *Picasso and Truth* (Princeton: Princeton University Press, 2013)
CRITCHLEY, SIMON, *The Ethics of Deconstruction: Derrida and Levinas*, 3rd edn (Edinburgh: Edinburgh University Press, 2014)
CRONIN, MICHAEL, *Translation in the Digital Age* (Abingdon: Routledge, 2013)
DANTE ALIGHIERI, *The Inferno*, trans. Ciaran Carson (London: Granta Books, 2002)
DAVIS, LYDIA, *The Collected Stories* (London: Penguin, 2013)
—— *The End of the Story* (London: Penguin, 2015)
—— *Proust, Blanchot and a Woman in Red* (London: Sylph Editions, 2008)
—— 'Some Notes on Translation and on Madame Bovary', *Paris Review*, 198 (Fall 2011), 65–99
DAVIS, PAUL, *Translation and the Poet's Life: The Ethics of Translating in English Culture, 1646–1726* (Oxford: Oxford University Press, 2008)
DE MAN, PAUL, *Blindness and Insight: Essays in the Rhetoric of Contemporary Criticism*, 2nd edn (London: Routledge, 1983)
DENHAM, SIR JOHN, trans., *The Destruction of Troy, an essay upon the second book of Virgils Æneis. Written in the year, 1636* (London: printed for Humphrey Moseley, 1656)
DERRIDA, JACQUES, *De la grammatologie* (Paris: Les Éditions de Minuit, 1967)
—— 'Living On / Border Lines', trans. James Hulbert, in Harold Bloom, Jacques Derrida, Paul de Man and Geoffrey Hartman, *Deconstruction and Criticism* (London: Routledge, 1979), pp. 75–176
—— *Of Grammatology*, trans. by Gayatri Chakravorty Spivak (Baltimore: Johns Hopkins University Press, 1976)
—— 'Survivre', in his *Parages* (Paris: Galilée, 1986), pp. 117–218
DRUMMOND, CLARA, *Two Translations of Aeschylus's* Prometheus Bound *by Elizabeth Barrett Browning*, PhD dissertation, Boston University School of Arts and Sciences, 2004
DRYDEN, JOHN, *The Poems*, ed. by John Hammond and David Hopkins, 5 vols (Harlow: Longman, 1995–2005)
—— *The Works*, ed. by E. N. Hooker, H. T. Swedenberg, Jr., et al., 20 vols (Berkeley: University of California Press, 1956–2000)
ECO, UMBERTO, *Dire quasi la stessa cosa: Esperienze di traduzione* (Milan: Bompiani, 2003)
EMMERICH, KAREN, *Literary Translation and the Making of Originals* (London: Bloomsbury, 2017)
EVANS, JONATHAN, *The Many Voices of Lydia Davis: Translation, Rewriting, Intertextuality* (Edinburgh: Edinburgh University Press, 2017)
FOLLAIN, JEAN, *130 Poems*, trans. by Christopher Middleton (London: Anvil Press Poetry, 2010)
—— *Demarcations*, trans. by Kurt Heinzelman (Austin, TX: Host Publications, 2011)
—— *Transparence of the World*, trans. by W. S. Merwin (Port Townsend, WA: Copper Canyon Press, 2003)
HAMMOND, PAUL, *Dryden and the Traces of Classical Rome* (Oxford: Oxford University Press, 1999)
HAYES, JULIE CANDLER, *Translation, Subjectivity, and Culture in France and England, 1600–1800* (Stanford, CA: Stanford University Press, 2008)

HOPKINS, DAVID, 'John Dryden', in Daniel Weissbort and Astradur Eysteinsson (eds), *Translation — Theory and Practice: A Historical Reader* (Oxford: Oxford University Press, 2006), pp. 144–45

JULLIEN, DOMINIQUE, 'The Way by Lydia's: A New Translation of Proust', in Suzanne Jill Levine and Katie Lateef-Jan, eds, *Untranslatability Goes Global* (New York: Routledge, 2018), pp. 97–112

LAUDERDALE, RICHARD, EARL OF, trans., *The Works of Virgil, translated into English verse*, (London, printed for Bernard Lintott, 1709)

LEHTO, LEEVI 'In the Beginning was Translation', in *The Sound of Poetry / The Poetry of Sound*, ed. by Marjorie Perloff and Craig Dworkin (London: University of Chicago Press, 2009), pp. 49–53

—— 'Plurifying the Languages Of the Trite: In Dialogue With Régis Bonvicino and Alcir Pécora, Sibila, 2006', *nypoesi*, 2/06, <https://www.nypoesi.net/tidsskrift/206/?tekst=27> [accessed 30th October 2018]

LEVINE-KEATING, HELANE, 'Lydia Davis's Proust: The Writer As Translator, The Translator As Writer', *3 Quarks Daily*, posted on Nov 25, 2013, 12:30 am, <https://www.3quarksdaily.com/3quarksdaily/2013/11/lydia-daviss-proust-the-writer-as-translator-the-translator-as-writer.html> [accessed 30th October 2018]

MARTINDALE, CHARLES, *Redeeming the Text: Latin Poetry and the Hermeneutics of Reception* (Cambridge: Cambridge University Press, 1993)

MCKITTERICK, DAVID, *Print, Manuscript and the Search for Order, 1450–1830* (Cambridge: Cambridge University Press, 2003)

OGILBY, JOHN, TRANS., *The Works of Publius Virgilius Maro* (London: printed by T. R. and E. M. for John Crook, 1649)

PRINS, YOPIE, *Ladies' Greek: Victorian Translations of Tragedy* (Princeton: Princeton University Press, 2017)

REDDY, MICHAEL J., 'The Conduit Metaphor: A Case of Frame Conflict in our Language about Language', in *Metaphor and Thought*, 2nd edn, ed. by Andrew Ortony (Cambridge: Cambridge University Press, 1993), pp. 164–201

REYNOLDS, MATTHEW, *Likenesses: Translation, Illustration, Interpretation* (Oxford: Legenda, 2013)

—— *The Poetry of Translation: From Chaucer & Petrarch to Homer & Logue* (Oxford: Oxford University Press, 2011)

—— 'Prismatic Translation and the Hum or Buzz of Tongues', in Catherine Chauvin and Céline Sabiron, eds, *Traduction et textualité / Translation and Textuality* (Nancy: PUN, forthcoming 2020)

—— *Translation: A Very Short Introduction* (Oxford: Oxford University Press, 2016)

ROBINSON, DOUGLAS, *Becoming a Translator: An Introduction to the Theory and Practice of Translation*, 2nd edn (London: Routledge, 2003)

—— *The Translator's Turn* (Baltimore: Johns Hopkins University Press, 1991)

SAKAI, NAOKI 'Translation', *Theory, Culture & Society* 23. 2–3 (2006), 71–86, DOI: 10.1177/0263276406063778

SCOTT, CLIVE, *Channel Crossings: French and English Poetry in Dialogue, 1550–2000* (Oxford: Legenda, 2002)

SEGRAIS, JEAN REGNAULT DE, TRANS., *Traduction de l'Eneide de Virgile* (Paris, 1668, 1681)

VENUTI, LAWRENCE *The Translator's Invisibility: A History of Translation* (London: Routledge, 1995)

VIRGIL, *Opera*, interpretatione et notis illustravit Carolus Ruaeus (Paris: apud Simonem Benard, 1682)

WARNER, MARINA 'The Politics of Translation', *London Review of Books*, 40. 19 (11 October 2018), 21–24

YOUNG, ROBERT J. C., 'That Which Is Casually Called a Language', *PMLA*, 131.5 (2016), 1207–21

Notes to Chapter 1

1. Elizabeth Barrett Browning and Robert Browning, *The Brownings' Correspondence*, ed. by Ronald Hudson, Philip Kelley, Scott Lewis and Edward Hagan (Winfield, KS: Wedgestone Press, 1984–) x. p. 102; quoted in Clara Drummond, *Two Translations of Aeschylus's* Prometheus Bound *by Elizabeth Barrett Browning*, PhD dissertation, Boston University School of Arts and Sciences, 2004, p. 31.
2. Yopie Prins, *Ladies' Greek: Victorian Translations of Tragedy* (Princeton: Princeton University Press, 2017), p. 65.
3. *Brownings' Correspondence*, v, p. 26, x, p. 102; Drummond, *Two Translations of Aeschylus's* Prometheus Bound, pp. 30–31.
4. I explore this phenomenon in *The Poetry of Translation: From Chaucer & Petrarch to Homer & Logue* (Oxford: Oxford University Press, 2011).
5. John Dryden, *The Poems*, ed. by John Hammond and David Hopkins, 5 vols (Harlow: Longman, 1995–2005), I, p. 384; Aeschylus, *Prometheus Bound*, trans. Elizabeth Barrett Browning (1833), quoted from Drummond, *Two Translations of Aeschylus's* Prometheus Bound, p. 69.
6. *Brownings' Correspondence*, v, p. 224; Drummond, *Two Translations of Aeschylus's* Prometheus Bound, p. 44.
7. Prins, *Ladies' Greek*, pp. 62–83.
8. Quoted from Drummond, *Two Translations of Aeschylus's* Prometheus Bound, pp. 64–65.
9. Drummond, *Two Translations of Aeschylus's* Prometheus Bound, p. 36
10. Drummond, *Two Translations of Aeschylus's* Prometheus Bound, p. 31; *Brownings' Correspondence*, x, p. 102.
11. Prins, *Ladies' Greek*, pp. 83–94.
12. Umberto Eco, *Dire quasi la stessa cosa: Esperienze di traduzione* (Milan: Bompiani, 2003), passim; Clive Scott, *Channel Crossings: French and English Poetry in Dialogue, 1550–2000* (Oxford: Legenda, 2002), p. 1; Karen Emmerich, *Literary Translation and the Making of Originals* (London: Bloomsbury, 2017), p. 161.
13. See David McKitterick, *Print, Manuscript and the Search for Order, 1450–1830* (Cambridge: Cambridge University Press, 2003).
14. Michael J. Reddy, 'The Conduit Metaphor: A Case of Frame Conflict in our Language about Language', in *Metaphor and Thought*, 2nd edn, ed. by Andrew Ortony (Cambridge: Cambridge University Press, 1993), pp. 164–201.
15. Reddy, 'The Conduit Metaphor', p. 176.
16. Derrida, Jacques, *De la grammatologie* (Paris: Les Éditions de Minuit, 1967), p. 227; *Of Grammatology*, trans. Gayatri Chakravorty Spivak (Baltimore: Johns Hopkins University Press, 1976), p. 158.
17. Quoted in Simon Critchley, *The Ethics of Deconstruction: Derrida and Levinas*, 3rd edn (Edinburgh: Edinburgh University Press, 2014), p. 24.
18. Critchley, *The Ethics of Deconstruction*, p. 27.
19. Jacques Derrida 'Living On / Border Lines', trans. James Hulbert, in Harold Bloom, Jacques Derrida, Paul de Man and Geoffrey Hartman, *Deconstruction and Criticism*, (London: Routledge, 1979), pp. 75–176 (p.93).
20. Derrida, 'Survivre', in his *Parages* (Paris : Galilée, 1986), pp. 117–218 (p. 138).
21. Paul De Man, *Blindness and Insight: Essays in the Rhetoric of Contemporary Criticism*, 2nd edn (London: Routledge, 1983), p. 139.
22. Matthew Reynolds, *Translation: A Very Short Introduction* (Oxford: Oxford University Press, 2016), pp. 38–39.
23. Charles Martindale, *Redeeming the Text: Latin Poetry and the Hermeneutics of Reception* (Cambridge: Cambridge University Press, 1993), p. 93.

24. Douglas Robinson, *The Translator's Turn* (Baltimore: Johns Hopkins University Press, 1991), p. 107; and *Becoming a Translator: An Introduction to the Theory and Practice of Translation*, 2nd edn (London: Routledge, 2003), p. 88.
25. Lawrence Venuti, *The Translator's Invisibility: A History of* Translation (London: Routledge, 1995), pp. 64–65; Marina Warner, 'The Politics of Translation', *London Review of Books*, 40. 19 (11 October 2018), 21–24 (pp. 22–23).
26. Paul Hammond, *Dryden and the Traces of Classical Rome* (Oxford: Oxford University Press, 1999) pp. 36, 149.
27. Julie Candler Hayes, *Translation, Subjectivity, and Culture in France and England, 1600–1800* (Stanford, CA: Stanford University Press, 2008), pp. 115, 113.
28. David Hopkins, 'John Dryden', in Daniel Weissbort and Astradur Eysteinsson (eds), *Translation — Theory and Practice: A Historical Reader* (Oxford: Oxford University Press, 2006), pp. 144–45 (p. 144).
29. Reynolds, *The Poetry of Translation*, pp. 73–118.
30. John Dryden, *The Works*, ed. by E. N. Hooker, H. T. Swedenberg, Jr., et al., 20 vols (Berkeley: University of California Press, 1956–2000), v, pp. 330–31.
31. Jean Regnault de Segrais (trans.), *Traduction de l'Eneide de Virgile* (Paris, 1668, 1681), quoted in *The Works of John Dryden*, vi, pp. 961–62. My translation.
32. Dryden, *Works*, v, p. 283.
33. Sir John Denham (trans.), *The Destruction of Troy, an essay upon the second book of Virgils Æneis. Written in the year, 1636* (London: printed for Humphrey Moseley, 1656), 'The Preface', np.
34. Dryden, *Poems of John Dryden*, i, p. 384.
35. Ibid., pp. 387–88.
36. Dryden, *Works*, v, p. 335.
37. Dryden, *Poems*, ii, p. 244.
38. Ibid.
39. Dryden, *Works*, ii, p. 859.
40. Dryden, *Works*, v, p. 291.
41. Richard, Earl of Lauderdale (trans.), *The Works of Virgil, translated into English verse* (London, printed for Bernard Lintott, 1709), p. 214.
42. Dryden, *Works*, v, p. 412.
43. John Ogilby (trans.), *The Works of Publius Virgilius Maro* (London: printed by T. R. and E. M. for John Crook, 1649), p. 48.
44. Virgil, *Opera*, interpretatione et notis illustravit Carolus Ruaeus (Paris: apud Simonem Benard, 1682), p. 340.
45. Ibid..
46. Segrais (trans.), p. 82 ; Annibale Caro (trans.), *L'Eneide di Virgilio* (Treviso: Evangelista Deuchino, 1603), p. 88.
47. Dryden, *Works*, v, p. 326.
48. Virgil, ed. Ruaeus, p. 340.
49. Caro, *L'Eneide di Virgilio*, p. 89.
50. Dryden, *Works*, v, p. 412.
51. Lauderdale, *The Works of Virgil*, pp. 124–25.
52. Caro, *L'Eneide di Virgilio*, p. 90; Segrais, p. 84.
53. Dryden, *Works*, v, p. 413.
54. Virgil, ed. Ruaeus, p. 341.
55. Dryden, *Works*, v, p. 319.
56. Dryden, *Works*, v, pp. 413–14.
57. Dryden, *Works*, v, p. 326; Paul Davis, *Translation and the Poet's Life: The Ethics of Translating in English Culture, 1646–1726* (Oxford: Oxford University Press, 2008), pp. 182–84.
58. Dryden, *Poems*, i, pp. 384–90.
59. Derrida, 'Living On / Border Lines', p. 93.
60. Naoki Sakai, 'Translation', *Theory, Culture & Society*, 23. 2–3 (2006), 71–86 (p. 76), DOI: 10.1177/0263276406063778 .

61. Robert J. C. Young, 'That Which Is Casually Called a Language', *PMLA* 131.5 (2016), 1207–21 (p. 1218).
62. Michael Cronin, *Translation in the Digital Age* (Abingdon: Routledge, 2013), pp. 77, 86–87.
63. Leevi Lehto, 'In the Beginning was Translation', in *The Sound of Poetry / The Poetry of Sound*, ed. by Marjorie Perloff and Craig Dworkin (London: University of Chicago Press, 2009), pp. 49–53 (p. 51).
64. Reynolds, *Translation: A Very Short Introduction*, p. 18.
65. See further chapter 2, below.
66. Leevi Lehto, 'Plurifying the Languages Of the Trite: In Dialogue With Régis Bonvicino and Alcir Pécora, Sibila, 2006', *nypoesi*, 2/06, <https://www.nypoesi.net/tidsskrift/206/?tekst=27>. Accessed 30th October 2018.
67. Ciaran Carson, *From Elsewhere* (Winston-Salem, NV: Wake Forest University Press, 2015), p. 11.
68. Ciaran Carson, *Collected Poems* (Oldcastle: Gallery Books, 2008), pp. 93, 214.
69. Dante Alighieri, *The Inferno*, trans. Ciaran Carson (London: Granta Books, 2002), p. xx.
70. See the discussion in my *Likenesses: Translation, Illustration, Interpretation* (Oxford: Legenda, 2013), pp. 97–103 and 132–44.
71. Carson, *From Elsewhere*, p. 11.
72. Ibid., p. 192. (I have corrected Carson's spelling of 'Heinzelman'.)
73. Ibid., p. 11.
74. A similar idea is discussed in chapter 18, below.
75. Carson, *From Elsewhere*, pp. 132–33.
76. Ibid., p. 14.
77. Ibid..
78. T. J. Clark, *Picasso and Truth* (Princeton: Princeton University Press, 2013), p. 82.
79. Carson, *From Elsewhere*, pp. 16–17.
80. I quote Follain's French text from Jean Follain, *Transparence of the World*, translated and selected by W. S. Merwin (Port Townsend, WA: Copper Canyon Press, 2003), p. 84.
81. Follain, *Transparence*, tr. Merwin, p. 85; Jean Follain, *130 Poems*, tr. Christopher Middleton (London: Anvil Press Poetry, 2010), p. 84; Jean Follain, *Demarcations*, tr. Kurt Heinzelman (Austin, TX: Host Publications, 2011), p. 116.
82. Lydia Davis, *The End of the Story* (London: Penguin, 2015), p. 89.
83. Lydia Davis, *Proust, Blanchot and a Woman in Red* (London: Sylph Editions, 2008), pp. 31, 11, 12.
84. Lydia Davis, *The Collected Stories* (London: Penguin, 2013), p. 576.
85. Lydia Davis, 'Some Notes on Translation and on Madame Bovary', *Paris Review*, 198 (Fall 2011), 65–99 (p. 66). I discuss Davis's work with *Madame Bovary* further in 'Prismatic Translation and the Hum or Buzz of Tongues', in Catherine Chauvin and Céline Sabiron (eds), *Traduction et textualité / Translation and Textuality* (Nancy: PUN, forthcoming 2020).
86. Helane Levine-Keating, 'Lydia Davis's Proust: The Writer As Translator, The Translator As Writer', *3 Quarks Daily*, posted on Nov 25, 2013, 12:30 am, <https://www.3quarksdaily.com/3quarksdaily/2013/11/lydia-daviss-proust-the-writer-as-translator-the-translator-as-writer.html>; accessed 30th October 2018. Dominique Jullien reads 'The Walk' as 'an ironic parable of the translator's situation' ('The Way by Lydia's: A New Translation of Proust', in Suzanne Jill Levine and Katie Lateef-Jan (eds), *Untranslatability Goes Global* (New York: Routledge, 2018), pp. 97–112; see also Jonathan Evans, *The Many Voices of Lydia Davis: Translation, Rewriting, Intertextuality* (Edinburgh, Edinburgh University Press, 2017).
87. Davis, *Collected Stories*, pp. 579, 576.
88. André Aciman (ed.), *The Proust Project* (New York: Farrar, Strauss and Giroux, 2004), p. 14.
89. Davis, *Collected Stories*, p. 587.
90. My phrasing here aims to suggest both a debt to and difference from Emily Apter, *Against World Literature: On the Politics of Untranslatability* (London: Verso, 2013). In my view (as I hope this chapter has shown) nothing is ever either translatable or untranslatable: everything is always both.

PART II

Languages

CHAPTER 2

Poetic Traffic in a Multilingual Literary Culture: Equivalence, Parallel Aesthetics, and Language-Stretching in North India

Francesca Orsini

No Translation, we are South Asians?

It is customary, and appropriate, to preface discussions of translation with statements about how, in the broadest sense, everyone translates all the time. And how, in multilingual societies like South Asia, translation across languages is an everyday activity spread across all social strata with a high degree of malleability. Vegetable sellers, rickshaw drivers, religious preachers — all are apt at translating, adapting their pitch or using an interlanguage with their customers or audience without a second thought. This is a society where ideologies of language communities as homogeneous entities have had a limited purchase on reality, however strong a hold they have on the imagination. Where a common attribute for learned poets or patrons in the premodern period was that they spoke 'six languages' (though which six could vary), and where until recently getting an education meant stacking up language skills.

At the same time, translation studies in South Asia have had to shake off a double prejudice: an Orientalist prejudice against the absence of 'accurate translations', and another about the lack of local theorisations of translation — though both in fact were not completely absent.[1] A third prejudice concerned the lack of originality because literatures in modern Indian languages typically began as 'translation literatures'. Indian intellectuals have responded to these accusations in two ways. First, in a much-quoted essay, Ganesh Devy decried Western understandings of translation as beholden to biblical and humanistic notions of the fall from an original state of grace and perfect understanding and an obsession with synonymity and fidelity to the 'original'.[2] To it he opposed the 'translating consciousness' of people living in multilingual societies, along the lines of my opening paragraph.[3] Second, Devy and others like A.K. Ramanujan also reversed the negative colonial judgement by pointing to the creative and often subversive moves involved in early modern 'translations' of classical texts such as the *Ramayana*. Viewed from this perspective, translation was in fact a covert way of introducing and legitimising novelty and departures under the disguise of continuity and affiliation. And a whole series of vibrant and sophisticated studies of these often intermedial texts has increasingly rejected the tag of translation (or of variant versions of a putative original) and instead used the terms telling or retelling.[4] These critical answers have led to further questioning of translation in the context of South Asia. For people with a 'translating consciousness' living in a multilingual society, are languages distinct sign systems or do they form a continuum, something both Devy and Ramanujan have suggested?

> In India several languages are simultaneously used by language communities as if these languages formed a continuous spectrum of signs and significance.[5]

> One may go further and say that the cultural area in which *Ramayanas* are endemic has a pool of signifiers that include plots, characters, geography, incidents, and relationships... These various texts not only relate to prior texts directly, to borrow or refute, but they relate to each other through this common code or common pool. Every author... dips into it and brings out a unique crystallization, a new text with a unique texture and a fresh context.[6]

This view of Indian languages as a seamless continuum and of a common pool of cultural signifiers stretching across languages has produced particular positions on translation, like Harish Trivedi's bold claim that 'in the long period of recorded literary history in India, from about 1500 BCE to 1800 CE there is, astonishingly, no evidence of any text of any kind having been translated into an Indian language, initially probably because the major Indian languages were all mutually intelligible.'[7] The 'characteristically Western assumption' that India's linguistic diversity makes it 'one of the richest and most productive areas of the world for translation activity', he adds, overlooks the fact that widespread multilingualism, which does not entail the 'psychologically or cultural barrier' associated with foreign languages, obviates much of the need for translation felt by monolinguals.[8]

Before examining Trivedi's claim it is necessary to pause on what language means in this context. The distinction between spoken and written language is crucial here. Apart from dialectal variations, at the spoken level language contact easily resulted in a large number of loanwords, earlier from Persian and more recently from English, not just for specific domains of language use but also in everyday speech. This is where it makes sense to speak of an interlanguage, for mixing was and is often unmarked. (By contrast, on formal occasions language peformance and language boundaries would be policed.) But, as in Europe or in East Asia, education and written language involved learning one or more High languages. The sense of language as a bounded entity (Persian, Sanskrit, Arabic, etc.) was undoubtedly stronger in this case, for acquiring and displaying competence in that language meant adhering to its protocols. And since the curriculum was largely literary, language learning involved acquiring familiarity with the language's poetic idiom (including grammar of referents, metre, poetics, etc.) and canon. When Brajbhasha (i.e. 'the language of the Braj region') became a cosmopolitan literary *koiné* from a regional spoken language and was learnt through tutors and poetic manuals, it acquired the same qualities. In the context of written poetic languages, mixing was much more limited and usually marked, as we shall see.[9] Language naming also reflects this distinction between written and spoken: in North India the vernacular was called by Persian writers 'Hindi', i.e. 'Indian' (the term Urdu was popularized only in the nineteenth century), while others just called it 'language', *bhakha*. Persian, Sanskrit, Arabic were always called by their separate names. Since language, script and community were not as tightly linked as in modern times, I avoid using the terms Hindi and Urdu with their modern connotations and have instead used Hindavi for the unmarked north Indian vernacular, and 'courtly Hindi' for the cosmopolitan literary vernacular Brajbhasha; Avadhi is a modern nomenclature for the vernacular used in the eastern region of North India, Avadh; in early modern times it was also simply called 'Hindi/Hindavi' or *bhakha*.

To go back to Trivedi, it is first of all important to distinguish spoken multilingualism from written literature (song-poems and other oral-literate texts are a somewhat different case, as we shall see). As to his claim that translation did not happen because the major Indian languages were mutually intelligible, it is both overstated and somewhat misleading. For one thing, it does not seem to take into account the well-documented translation activities of Sufis, Jains, and Persian-knowing Hindu and Brajbhasha-knowing Persophile literati in the early modern period.[10] Translations of scientific-technical texts (*shastras*) between Sanskrit and Persian or Arabic and Persian, of religious texts between Sanskrit and the vernaculars and Sanskrit and Persian, and of tales and romances between Sanskrit, the vernaculars and Persian were in fact not uncommon.[11] By contrast, on the whole it seems that to know poetry in order to be an educated person meant reading it in its own language. Yet this was not because Indian languages were mutually intelligible, or because Indians were not interested in literatures from other cultures, as Harish Trivedi has also argued.[12] Rather, within this multilingual world, poetic translation was possible, but it took specific conditions to activate it, as we shall see. Much more commonly, within the multilingual literary culture of north India poetic tastes were cultivated in parallel, with translations showing up in the margins or as nuggets of language inside a poem. The result was not a formal translation traffic but rather a parallel enjoyment and various kinds of 'language stretching', including poetic equivalences, the insertion of tropes, symbols, key terms and expressions from one poetic idiom into another and, in some cases, mixed-language verses. For this reason we need to look for clues at the level of micro-translations within verses rather than for full-length translations, and we need to think outwards from these nuggets of language to ask what 'communities of taste' they came out of, what interlingual and 'intermedial aesthetics' they produced and were part of, and how to best capture this poetic traffic.[13]

Activating Translation

Before I turn to forms of language stretching without translation, it is worth pausing on a few instances in which poetry was actually translated in early modern North India in order to see what specific conditions activated these translations. These include a provincial story-teller writing a prose tale in the cosmopolitan language of Persian that was particularly close to a Hindavi verse romance; a Jain reformer at the centre of an urban circle of lay intellectuals; a Muslim intellectual drawing upon and synthesizing multiple traditions in order to produce a text in the regional vernacular of Bengali for courtly performance; an Arabic teacher showing off his poetic as well as scholarly abilities.

First, already in the period of the North Indian Sultanates, and even more in the Mughal period, a few romances in the north Indian vernacular (Hindavi/Avadhi) were rendered into Persian. As a rule, these were retellings that entailed limited or extensive transcodification according to the stylemes of Persian romances rather than formal translations, and the original text and author often went unmentioned.[14] This is why it is not surprising that the heavily illustrated Persian version of Qutban's Hindavi/Avadhi romance *Mirigāvatī*, produced in Allahabad in 1604 at the court of the rebel Mughal prince Salim, the future emperor Jahangir, starts without any preamble mentioning the author's name or title and leaves out Qutban's own prologue.[15] But as one continues reading one realizes that this was actually a translation that strove to reproduce the Hindavi verse narrative in simple Persian prose — it transmitted not just a story but a text. Even in places where the Hindavi text slowed down and 'thickened' into dense poetic language, the Persian translator bravely struggled to keep up. And buried in the middle of the text, he actually mentioned the Hindavi author *by name*.[16] While the absence of paratexts leaves open the question of why the author of this Persian *Mirigāvatī* chose to translate rather than simply retell, we may speculate that he was possibly a local man familiar with the Hindavi text, which had been written a century earlier in the region and dedicated to the Sharqi ruler Husain Shah, rather than a Persian cosmopolitan poet who just happened to listen to the story recited.[17]

Second, John Cort has written extensively on the remarkable translation activity into the vernacular (simply called *bhasha* or *bhakha*, 'language') by the circle of the Jain lay reformer Banarsidas in the heart of the Mughal capital of Agra in the early seventeenth century. Here, group discussions led to translations of doctrinal and liturgical texts which, in turn, led to new discussions.[18] This vernacularisation of knowledge happened independently of royal initiatives or patronage, and the translations became authoritative texts that are still used in Jain ritual practices today.[19]

Third, perhaps the most sustained example of poetic translation activity that we come across in this period comes from the outward-facing, commerce-oriented, and highly multilingual kingdom of Mrauk-U in the Bay of Bengal, where the poet Alaol composed for his elite patrons a remarkable set of sophisticated verse narratives (*panchalis*) in Bengali, as illustrated in Thibaut d'Hubert's recent book.[20] In fact, all of Alaol's works were translations of either Hindavi or Persian texts. D'Hubert shows that, pace William Jones, Alaol was a highly conscious author-translator, for whom translation was a 'first degree' literary transposition in a continuum with composition.[21] Alaol uses verbs rather than nouns to describe what he does and talks repeatedly of 'breaking the Persian verse/metre (*bayt*)' in order to, first, understand the meaning and extract the *rasa* (mood), and then recreate it in Bengali verse ('*bhāṅgiyā bayeta chanda racite payāra*').[22] In other words, d'Hubert notes, Alaol views his action as primarily prosodic (of 'transmetrification')[23] and secondly of poetics (i.e. about the *rasa* of the work or passage). d'Hubert also shows that Alaol is closer to the Hindavi or Persian original in the first part of the verse, whereas in the second part metrical exigency (the *payar* verse is longer) forces him to be more inventive, while his choice of a sanskritized register in Bengali recalls the strategy of Sanskrit commentaries or *chhaya*, 'shadows'. Finally, d'Hubert argues that Alaol has his present audience in the royal assembly in mind all the time: when it comes for example to list-descriptions — a feature of courtly literary compositions at the time — he moves away from the original and comes closer to the Sanskrit descriptions his audience would have been familiar with. As a rule, the more familiar the theme, the more Alaol departs from the original to match his audience's expectations; the more unfamiliar the theme, the more mimetic is his translation. As a result, the homogeneous high-Bengali diction that Alaol uses for his translations of both Hindavi and Persian texts, d'Hubert shows, actually hides complex processes of cultural, aesthetic and and poetic negotiation across the several languages and models at work — Hindavi, Persian, Sanskrit, Maithili, and Bengali.

The fourth and final example of formal poetic translation comes from Simon Leese's recent research on Arabic literary writing in India.[24] This concerns a commentary on a canonical Arabic poem, *Bānat Suʿād* (by Kaʿb b. Zuhayr in the seventh century CE) by a small-town north Indian teacher and scholar of Arabic in the late eighteenth century, Ilahi Bakhsh, who was a disciple of the celebrated *hadith* scholar and religious reformer Shah ʿAbd al-ʿAziz of Delhi, the son of Shah Waliullah. Ilahi Bakhsh's commentary includes not just the usual grammatical and lexical explanations but also interlinear translations in Persian, Urdu, and an Arabic re-translation by the author. This is a rare multiple poetic instance of a far more common Qur'anic translation and commentarial practice. And while the translations do not stand as individual poems but act as versified glosses, Leese argues, they also implicitly advance a claim for Arabic, Persian, and Urdu as part of a poetic continuum.

What these examples bring home is the fact that within this multilingual world poetic translation was of course possible, but it took specific conditions to activate it, whether they be the particular status of or closeness to the original text or the needs and expectations of the intended audience. More commonly, it seems, poetic tastes were cultivated separately and in parallel. It is intriguing that every time Bhanupratap Tivari, a very ordinary poet lover in late-nineteenth century North India, quotes a Persian verse in Persian script in his autobiography, he gives a Brajbhasha poetic translation (*ulthā*) in Nagari script in the margin (Figure 1).[25]

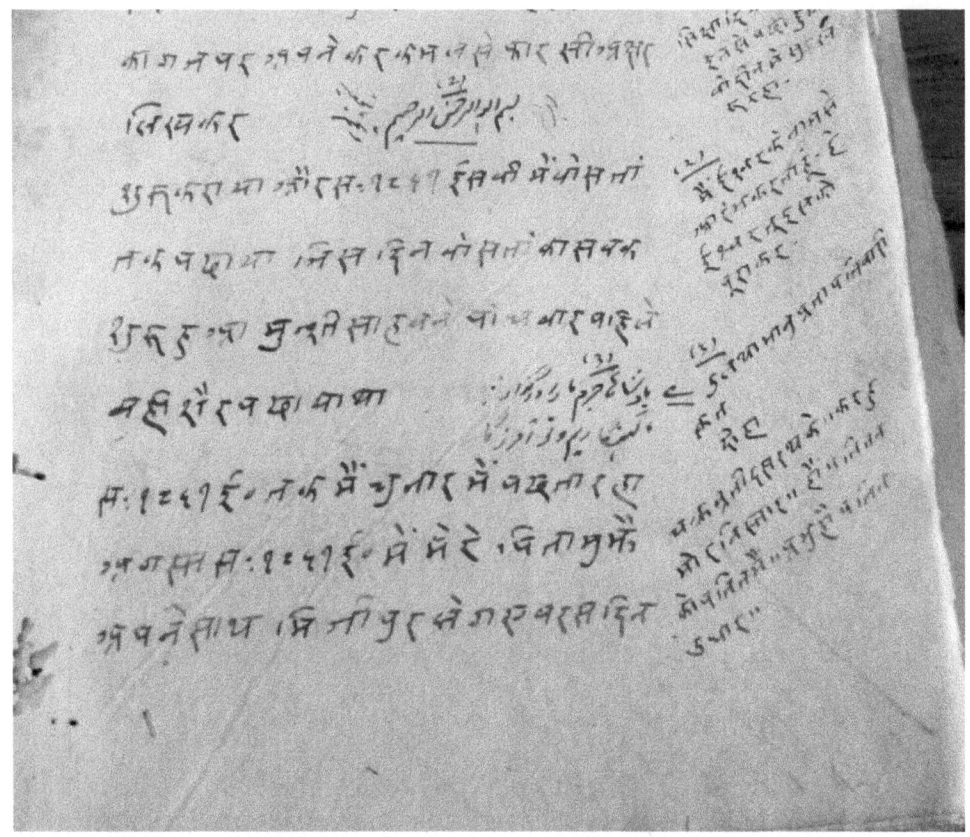

Fig. 2.1. Manuscript autobiography of Pandit Bhanupratap Tiwari (1890), p. 3. (Courtesy UP State Archive, Manuscript Library)

These are rare traces and material evidence of what I imagine must have been a more common practice, though usually unrecorded in writing. So if the relative absence of formal translations is not to be attributed to the mutual intelligibility between languages, or to a lack of interest — Harish Trivedi's argument — we can formulate the question differently: what happens when one is taught to appreciate and practise multiple poetic idioms in parallel? The answer is one of several possibilities. Either one can cultivate these poetic tastes separately and demonstrate one's mastery and inventiveness within each code. Or one can attempt equivalences across the poetic idioms, shapeshifting words, images, tropes and poetic feelings somewhat in the process. Else one can include nuggets of the one poetic idiom within the other — resonant keywords or familiar images and tropes that shine out in the unfamiliar environment. The latter two stretch the host poetic language, and it is to them that I now turn.

Poetic Equivalence as Language Stretching

It is worth restating that there is evidence from at least the thirteenth century that the recitation and singing of poetry in Sufi musical (*sama'*) sessions and courtly assemblies included song-poems in both Persian and Hindavi. In *sama'* sessions, *qawwal* singers at the instruction of the master of the assembly 'knotted' together lines from different poems, sometimes in different languages, so as to press a particular point, lead the disciples out of themselves, and induce in them a higher state of consciousness.[26] It is rarer, however, to have texts commenting explicitly on the equivalences produced in the process. This is what makes the short treatise on the unity of God (*tawhid*) by the fifteenth-century Chishti Sufi 'Abdul Quddus Gangohi, which presents Persian and Hindavi poetic examples, so enlightening for our purpose.[27] In this treatise, the phrase *dar in ma'ni* ('with the same meaning') sets up a chain of signification that connects Qur'anic verses, *hadiths* (sayings attributed to the Prophet), verses of Persian poets, and Hindavi verses, some anonymous and some by the author himself, whose Hindavi pen-name itself translated his Persian one (both Alakhdas and 'Abdul Quddus mean 'servant of God'). The connection could be an idea, a situation, or a word.

For example, in order to expound on the familiar theme of why God undertook creation (so that he could be known), 'Abdul Quddus began with the famous *hadith Qudsi* 'I was a hidden treasure and I desired to be known, and I created creation so that I would be known', reiterated it with another Arabic *hadith*, 'That which God created first was love for me' and followed it (*dar in ma'ani*) first with a line by Fariduddin 'Attar that partly translated the *hadith* phrase into Persian:

> Love came as a balm for every heart
> Without love no problem was ever solved.
> Likewise:
> Almighty God wished to reveal
> All at once His mysteries to you.[28]

And then by a line from a Hindavi song in Raga Purbi:

> *Dhana kāran piya āpa saṃvārā*   *bina dhana sakhī kānta kina hārā*
> *Shahu khelai dhana māhī evān*   *bāsa phūla māha achai jevān.*

> For the sake of his bride, the lover adorned himself,
> without her, oh friend, is not the husband lost?
> the bridegroom plays inside the girl,
> Like the fragrance within the flower.

The chain of examples concludes with a Hindavi riddle:

> *kyō nahī khelū tujha saṃga mītā*   *mujha kārana taī ītā kītā.*
> *alakhadāsa akhai suna loī*   *soī bāka, aratha phuni soī.*

> Why should I not play with you, oh friend? For my sake you did so much.
> Alakhdas says, 'Listen people, He is the word, He is also the meaning.'[29]

The song at first appears a typical utterance of the *virahini*, the poetic figure of the woman pining for her absent husband/lover and wondering why she should make herself beautiful. But then we notice a difference: here it is the male lover (*piya*) who adorns himself (*saṃvārā*) for the woman (*dhana*) and feels lost without her. Thus a new semantic situation — God, the lover, takes pains to adorn himself (=to reveal His beauty) for mankind, and it is He who craves (=mourns the absence) of mankind who will know Him — is grafted upon the familiar Hindavi 'structure of feeling'. The second line uses a love metaphor to suggest the extreme closeness of God to his creation. In the riddle, the first line suggests a banter between a woman and her male friend (m. *mītā*, not f. *sakhī*), once again suggesting some kind of erotic banter, while the next line calls the devotees to interpret the lover as God himself.

By setting up equivalences with Qur'anic utterances and Persian verses, then, 'Abdul Quddus bends and 'stretches' the language of Hindavi poetry — with its familiar characters of the pining woman, her female friend, and the absent or teasing male lover — in order to 'think new thoughts'.[30] The Hindavi terms bring their own set of semantic connotations and acquire new ones in the process. In the next example, revolving around the familiar metaphor of the drop and the sea, 'Abdul Quddus first uses the image to state that God manifests himself in a thousand ways yet always remains Himself, and then exorts the seeker to 'plunge deep' until the self is lost and unity with God is attained. The Hindavi verse plays on the idea of getting lost but combines plunging with the pathos of the woman looking for her husband, making us read this familiar image in a completely new way:

> Khwaja 'Attar says:
> If the drop drowns in the sea, so what?
> What is the drop's existence, and what the sea's?
>
> *Herata herata he sakhī, haū dhan gaī hirāi*
> *paryā būd samund māha, kahu kyau herī jāi*[31]
>
> Searching, searching, my friend, I got lost.
> The drop fell into the ocean, pray how can it be found?

Through these subtle changes and new combinations, the Hindavi poetic idiom is remoulded and pushed in new directions to express new thoughts, and key terms and images became polysemic — a good example of prismatic translation.

The process could also go the opposite way. In the anonymous Persian translation of Qutban's *Mirigāvatī* already mentioned, the image of the dancers' black braids that look like snakes coiled around a sandalwood branch — a common trope in Hindavi — is first explained and then rendered in a verse that extends the equally familiar image of the Persian poetic idiom. In the Persian verse, the familiar trope of the black curls framing the beloved's face is rhetorically denied because the curls are actually dangerous coiling snakes attracted — and here comes the stretching — to the scent of sandalwood. The Hindavi line goes:

> *cihura gūṃdi bēnī urābāī, cādana rūkha para bisahara chāī*[32]
>
> They had braided their hair and let it hang
> like black cobras covering sandalwood trees.[33]

silsila-yi mūband cunān mīnamūd ke gūyā darakht-i ṣandal az bār mī bar āyad. bayt:
na zulf ast īn ke hardam bar qad-i dildār mī pichad
zi mastī har nafas bar shākh-i ṣandal mār mī pichad.

Their long tresses looked like sandal trees encircled by snakes. Verse:
It's not a curl that ever coils round my beloved's body
It is a snake in heat, coiled around a sandal tree branch.[34]

Mixed-Language Poetry

Mixed-language or macheronic poetry is familiar to European readers.[35] But whereas in Europe the term macheronic is used mostly for humorous or parodic/mock-heroic works, in India this is not the case.[36] Mixed-language poems cover a much wider range and I would distinguish at least four categories of mixed-language poems: (a) 'ventriloquism', i.e. when a poet takes on another idiom, persona, or 'structure of feeling' and 're-accents' them, in the Bakhtinian sense; (b) poems that embrace a macheronic aesthetic and in which poetic idioms remain clearly separate and are made to collide rather than blend with each other; (c) 'poetic responses' — in the Perso-Urdu tradition of the *jawab*, in which a poet 'responds' to an earlier poem by using the same metre, rhyme, and terms and/or theme;[37] and (d) poems that combine different poetics.

'Ventriloquism' describes particularly well the strategy of devotional saint-poets (called Sants in Hindi) who rewrote practically all the poetic and popular idioms available in north India: seasonal songs and songs of the twelve months (*barahmasas*); women's wedding songs (*mangal*); children's alphabet-learning poems (called *kakhahara* for the Devanagari alphabet and *alif-be* for the Perso-Arabic one); the Perso-Urdu/Sufi poetic idiom of love (*'ishq*) with its emphasis on pain and madness; Islamic sermons and Bhakti practice; hymns and ritual songs (*stotra, sahasranama, arati*); yogic vocabulary and hermetic 'upside-down language', and so on.[38] Rather than choosing one particular idiom, Sant poets stamped and re-accented all these idioms as their own and moved with equal ease between different linguistic registers, from quasi-Persian, Brajbhasha, and Bhojpuri-inflected Hindavi.

For example, like other Sant poets, the seventeenth-century poet Malukdas from Kara, a Muslim-majority town with several Sufi establishments, has a small number of compositions in what we may call 'spoken Persian'.[39] They consist almost exclusively of Persian words and phrases (in the example below, e.g. *pura nūra, hamā jā*) with minimal grammatical elements (only one verb, *osta*; the others are either absent or Hindavi), and the effect is one of 'quasi-Persian'. In other words, these compositions sound like Persian while being ungrammatical. In the process, Sufi technical terms and phrases (like *besabūha, benamūna, becagūna, hamā osta, hamā azosta*) become part of Sant vocabulary, stretch Sant language and become familiar to Hindavi audiences, all through aural communication. In the following example (words **in bold** are the few non-Persian ones), we cannot help noting that Malukas happily reconciles what in Sufi terms are customarily read as two opposing philosophies — of *waḥdat al-wujūd* or 'unity of existence' and *waḥdat al-shuhūd* or 'unity of witnessing'):

Hai hajūra **nahī̃** *dūra, hamā-jā* **bhara pūra** |
zāhirā jahāna, jā kā zahūra pura nūra ||1||
besabūha, benamūna, becagūna osta |
hamā osta hamā azosta, jān-jānāṃ dosta ||2||
shabo roza zikara fikarahī̃ **maĩ** *mashgūla* |
tehī̃ dargāha bīca, paṛe **haĩ** *qabūla* ||3||
sāheba **hai merā pīra, qudrata kyā kahiye** |
kahatā *Malūka bandā, taka panāha rahiye.*⁴⁰

The Presence **is not** far, **it fills** everywhere,
manifest in the world, its appearance is full of light. 1
Without place, shape or sample, He is ineffable,
He is all, all is from Him, a friend of all creatures. 2
I spend night and day repeating his name, meditating **on him**,
I lie in the middle of his court, seeking his favour. 3
My Pir is my Lord, **what to say of** his power?
Says Maluk, my friend/the slave, **dwell in his** refuge.

In another song-poem, the warning against indifference, in other cases directed at others but here at himself ('This ignorant slave sins again and again'), is in line with the familiar Sant caution not to waste one's life sleeping but to wake up before death comes. But here it is the angel Jibril or Gabriel who appears with his mace ('My heart fears for the Last Day, when Jibrael will come mace in hand').⁴¹ We may hypothesize Malukdas would have heard Islamic popular poetry or preaching, but what is worth noting is that he uses an available language and makes it his own without registering it as a translation. While Malukdas could equally produce poems that conformed to a single particular idiom, he chose just as often to mix them within the same composition. And orally, without translation, and without formal education in Persian language and poetry, both Malukdas and his small-town, non-courtly audience were clearly familiar with polyvocal languages of love and devotion — a familiarity that continued later in the modern period as attested by commercial theatre, popular print genres, and cinema.⁴²

That macheronic verses should arise from a multilingual literary culture is not surprising. A small but resilient genre of 'songs of the twelve months' (*barahmasas*) in Hindavi written by Persian-knowing poets set what was already an established popular and literary genre, in which a woman abandoned by her lover or husband (the *virahini*) speaks of her suffering against the changing natural and ritual landscape of the months, to a Persian metre used for Persian narrative poems or *masnavis*, the *hazaj* (it is the metre of Firdausi's *Shahnāma*). Afzal's Twelve months-poem, later called *Bikaṭ kahānī* or 'Wretched tale' (ca. 1650), begins directly in the first person: 'Listen friends (*sakhi*) about my wretched tale, I have turned mad with the pain of love. I eat not in the day, nor sleep at night, my breast suffers the pangs of separation. The whole world calls me crazy...'⁴³ Here the demotic Hindi switches to Persian and what follows is quite a standard argument in Persian poetry (from the twelfth-century poet Nizami Ganjavi onwards) about the awesome power of love, which can transform a rich man into a wretch, exalt a poor man, turn a wise man into a dunce, impart wisdom, or make you hate life (Persian words and phrases are italicized here in the text and my translation):

>bhaī baurī birah bairāg setī,   jare jyūṛā měrā nit āg setī.
>kahĕ ghar ke sabhī log aur lugāī,   tamāmī sharm-e 'ālam kī gâvāī.
>*chi sāzam chūn kunam* kis kis pukārū,   jatan kyā *'ishq ke gham kā* bichārū.
>*ba-jānam be-davā āzār-e 'ishq ast*,   *hamūn dānad ki ū bīmār-e 'ishq ast*.
>*agar shāh ast ham sargashta-e ūst*,   *vagar bāshad gadā pā-basta-e ūst* [15][44]

>I have gone crazy forced by separation, my life is scorched by endless fire.
>Men and women at home say I've lost *all worldly shame*.
>*What should I do*, who should I call on, how can find remedy to the *pain of love*?
>*The hurt of love is for life, without cure, everyone knows if one is ill with love.*
>*Even a king, when subject to love, becomes a pauper chained to its fetters.*

Although an equivalence between the love of the simple *virahini* and the cosmic *'ishq* of Persian poets and Sufis underwrites this poem, there is no attempt to blend the demotic female voice and the lofty Persian one. The suture is on the surface, the stitches are not hidden. This macheronic aesthetic plays on contrast.

While poetic response or *jawab* remained for centuries a common strategy of training, affiliation, and differentiation in Persian and later Urdu poetry, we also find a small number of Hindavi compositions, mostly stemming from courtly and sophisticated settings, written in 'response' to Persian and Urdu poems. They show courtly Hindi poets reacting to the new fashion for Urdu/Rekhta poetry in the eighteenth century, like the poet-prince Savant Singh 'Nagaridas' recently documented by Heidi Pauwels.

Nagaridas, a talented courtly Hindi/Brajbhasha poet who was directly related to the Mughal imperial family and had a mansion in Delhi. enthusiastically 'responded' to the new Persianate Rekhta poetry which had recently reached Delhi from the Deccan in the 1720s and taken its poetic circles by storm.[45] Here is an example from Pauwels' book that shows Nagaridas responding to an admittedly simple Persian poem (the rhyming scheme is underlined):

>*zindagānī dar jahān be yār kardan mushkil ast*
>*ḥāl-e khud ba har kasi izhār kardan mushkil ast*
>*yakī migoī ba khubam āshnā'ī mushkil ast*
>*āshnā'ī mitavān kardan* [sic] *judā'ī mushkil ast*
>*shīsha-ye shikasta paivand kardan mushkil ast*
>*yār-e dil ranjīda rā khushnūd kardan mushkil ast*

>Spending life in the world without a lover is difficult.
>To reveal the state of one's mind before everyone is difficult.
>The saying goes: 'to befriend the finest is difficult.'
>To befriend is doable, but to part *is difficult*.
>To glue a broken mirror is difficult.
>To mend a lover's broken heart is difficult.

Here is Nagaridas's poem:

>*ankhiyaũ se maĩ kahā thā, karau mata husana parastī*
>*taba tau nahīṃ rahī ye bīca syokha saramastī*
>*aba biraha kī āvai, dila para parī hai tājī*

> *mujakau salāha kyā hai,* **musakala hai iskabājī**
> [...]
> *merī dasā duhelī yaha kisa kau kahi sunāũ*
> *parī prīta ke samada maĩ kahũṃ pāra bhī na pāũ*
> *nāgara navala piyāre tuma tau hau* **khusa-mijājī**
> *muja kaũ salāha kyā hai* **musakala hai iskabājī**

> I beseeched my eyes, 'Don't **worship beauty**!'
> They did not stay with me, but left **haughty and intoxicated**.
> Now loneliness has come and assaults my heart **afresh**.
> What's your **advice**? The **game of love is hard to play**.
> [...]
> This is my plight, who can I confide to?
> I drown in ocean's passion, I cannot reach the other side.
> Nagar says, 'My tender love, your are so **happy and carefree**,
> What's your **advice**? The **game of love is hard to play**.[46]

'While not a direct line-by-line translation' nor sharing the metre or the exact rhyme scheme of the Persian poem, Pauwels notes, the Hindi poem is tightly connected to it and echoes its rhyme scheme *mushkil ast* in the refrain *musakala hai iskabājī*. The 'response poem' stretches the Hindi poetic idiom not just linguistically but also thematically, given that the theme of unrequited love is typical of Persianate poetry but not in Hindi.[47] Lexical choices are also overwhelmingly Persianate (in bold). Here mixing is taking place at the heart of the poetic idiom.

Katherine Schofield has used the term 'Mughal *rasika*' to indicate the convergent and intermedial aesthetics underpinning Mughal courtly understandings and appreciation of music, painting, and Brajbhasha poetry.[48] Nagaridas's 'response poems' implicitly brought together the poetic personae and structures of feeling of the Perso-Urdu *ghazal*, with its emphasis on self-knowledge and refinement through love suffering, with the catalogues of heroines and love situations of courtly Brajbhasha poetry, which continued Sanskritic models.[49] Evidence shows that at least some other poets and literati in eighteenth-century north India did the same.[50] Nagaridas's quasi-contemporary, the bilingual Persian and Brajbhasha poet Ghulam Nabi Raslin (1699–1750) largely kept his poetic production in the two languages quite separate. Yet in a couple of Brajbhasha poems we see him use Persianate vocabulary and a quatrain (*ruba'i*) rhyme-scheme AABA for a typical 'description of the heroine', a stock theme of Hindi courtly poetry. While the vocabulary is much more Persianized than that of his Brajbhasha poems, including a few Persian compound forms (*ḥayā-dost, māya-e nāz, ayām-e shabāb*), Raslin seeks to match this Persianized register with the emotional and poetic language of the 'types of heroines' (*nayika bheda*, here the overly timid wife) — rather than with that of the Persianate lover and beloved (*'ashiq* and *mahbub*):

> *sukiyā/svakiyā* [the heroine as wife]
>
> *az bas ke ḥayā-dost hai vo māya-e nāz*
> *is ṭaraḥ son hai is ke sukhan kā andāz*
> *khāme kī zabān son jyon nikalte hain ḥuruf*
> *par kān talak nahīn pahunchtī āvāz.*[51]

> She's so chaste, that alluring one,
> This is how she speaks:
> Letters spring from the pen of her tongue,
> Yet no sound reaches your ears.

These examples show us how, within a multilingual social and poetic environment in which poets had access to several languages either through education or through oral access, poetic idioms could and did circulate even in the absence of formal translation.

Formal Translations and Modern Literature

There is little doubt that with colonialism the emphasis shifted radically in two major ways. First, particularly British translators and critics emphatically stressed 'faithful' formal translations, in line with William Jones's sentiments quoted at the beginnning (see note 1). Later Orientalists praised Shridhar Pathak's *tour de force* Hindi translation of Goldsmith's *The Deserted Village* (1889) as 'an absolutely line by line rendering of Goldsmith, every idea punctually reproduced', and said: 'similar accuracy of translation and similar melodiousness of verse runs through the entire specimen'.[52] They also praised his translation of *The Hermit* as 'a poem in the Hindi language, uniting all the beauties of an original composition with the all the faithfulness of a literal translation'.[53] Both texts were part of the English curriculum of colonial education and were much translated into Indian languages throughout the nineteeenth century, and though Pathak translated them 'for the sake of Hindi and English poetry lovers', he may have had the developing Hindi school curriculum in mind.[54] In fact, Pathak's translations flow only thanks to alliteration and rhyme, but their artificial language, a mishmash of Sanskrit loanwords and neologisms awkwardly juxtaposed to occasional dialectal terms and expressions, make the meaning difficult to follow, particularly for *Ūjaṛ Gām*, without the English original. Second, both British and Indian intellectuals came to share an instrumental view of translation as essential to the growth and development of a language, literature, and community, which were now imagined to neatly coalesce, and English poetry as the best model. Again, the positive reviewers of Pathak's Goldsmith's translation stress the benefit of 'direct[ing] the Indian mind to the beauties of nature and to the tender feelings of the heart. Extravagance of language and artificiality of sentiment characterize and disfigure Oriental Verse', and added:

> Works such as these will not only make a valuable addition to Hindi Literature but will tell people ignorant of English what stuff English poetry is made of. They will give them insight into that fine imagery, those delicate paintings of scenes and characters which are the peculiar attractions of English poetry, they will lead them from the land of the wild, the fantastic, the supernatural, the impossible with which so much of Oriental poetry and romance abounds into the regions of reason and reality, and lastly they will give them an opportunity of setting a right value upon foreign productions instead of blindly and therefore partially deciding in favour of works of indigenous art.[55]

Pathak was college-educated, and his translations clearly came out of and fed into the didactic context of colonial education.[56] Pathak was also an activist in the movement for the official recognition of Hindi; but was also trained in Brajbhasha and knew Sanskrit.[57] He was conscious and wary of the distance between the 'purely English' poem and Hindi.[58]

But after the first wave of translations of English poetry, formal translation also became a door to world literature, and English turned from a source to a medium for that. So in the 1930s the truly remarkable Urdu poet, essayist and translator Miraji broke with the colonial mould and undertook a breathtakingly ambitious project of translating world poetry into Urdu.[59] Miraji was already experimenting with stretching Urdu poetry towards song forms and with a wider range of registers and vocabulary than the traditional Persianate forms like the *ghazal*. His translations were clearly part of this effort, and we see him stretching the Urdu poetic idiom through metrical (end-rhyme, initial rhyme) and free verse translation partly by drawing upon the vernacular poetic idioms we have already encountered, such as that of Brajbhasha, and partly on colloquial language, as in his translation of Walt Whitman's 'To a Stranger':

> Passing stranger! you do not know how longingly I look upon you,
> You must be he I was seeking, or she I was seeking, (it comes to me as of a dream,)
> I have somewhere surely lived a life of joy with you, [...][60]

Ae 'ajnabī!	O stranger!
tujhko nahīn is kī khabar,	you don't know
dekhā tujhe kin ārzūon se abhī	how longingly I looked upon you,
be shak vahī hai tū	No doubt it's you
mujhe	who I
thī jis kī ab tak justjū;	was seeking;
(ye bāt aise hai ki jaise khwāb ho!)	(this comes to me as of a dream.)
hamrāz-e 'ishrat ho ke tere sāth	As your companion of joy
mainne guzārī hai kahīn,	I have lived somewhere
kuch zindagī.[61]	Some part of life...

Miraji breaks up Whitman's long lines to mark the rhythm of the voice and isolate smaller units of language like object (e.g. the emphasized "you", *be shak vahī hai tū*), indirect object ("I/to me", *mujhe*), and apposition ("As your companion of joy").

When writing about and translating Baudelaire, Miraji emphasizes the novelty of Baudelaire's diction and poetic ideas and tries to keep closer to his dense syntax. He also tells his readers that in recent times France has been leading Europe in cultural and artistic terms.[62] So while Miraji undertook relay translations of non-English poetry through the medium of English, it would be mistaken to read this as as a sign of subjection. Rather, his cosmopolitanism entailed looking *both* East *and* West, and not in a peripheral position vis-à-vis Europe or Britain. And while for the early modern cosmopolitans, even if they were aware of the wider world, their literary world was shaped by the reach of their languages, for modern cosmopolitans like Miraji translation through English became a way of continuously extending and expanding one's literary idiom and world.

Conclusions

This journey through the variegated poetic world of early modern North India has aimed to show that the comparative lack of formal poetic translations should not be read in terms of either complete mutual intelligibility between the languages — in a kind of language continuum — or of mutual indifference. Despite the relative paucity of written examples, we find enough *traces* to conclude that the cultivation of poetic idioms in multiple languages could produce parallel enjoyment but also poetic equivalences and various kinds of combinations — from ventriloquism to macheronic collision, from poetic 'responses' to combined aesthetics. As we have seen, these were common among both courtly, non-courtly, and devotional poets and their audiences. And since most if not all of this poetry was meant to be recited and repeated aloud, script and even literacy did not really act as barriers to comprehension, however much other forms of social exclusion may have done so.

This plurality and this traffic need not be read as either liberal pluralism or as fierce competition or appropriation. In other words, we should not read a strong, and political, intentionality in these practices, creating false binaries between 'good' syncretic mixing vs 'bad' rigid literary monolingualism, unless there are other clues about the authors' political and social views. It seems more accurate and productive to think of this plurality and traffic in the context of the 'everyday', of the ordinary multilingual competence and familiarity with a range of poetic idioms that formal education as well as aural exposure produced. We could think of a 'prismatic everyday' in which several language worlds interact within a single individual or locale and may or may not get recorded in a song or on a page. In re-using poetic idioms, usually in the form of 'nuggets of language' rather than metres or rhyme-schemes, each poet could and did re-accent them.[63] This usefully takes us away from models of belonging, 'borrowing', and strong intentionality to a more everyday understanding of what doing poetry and addressing audiences in a multilingual society and polyvocal literary culture entailed. Nor do I view this as a phenomenon unique to a uniquely multilingual India: multilingualism has been the norm rather than the exception in human societies, and scholars working on literary cultures in the ancient and medieval Mediterranean, Southeast Asia, the Caucasus, or among Mizrahi Jews, to name but a few examples, could provide their own versions of this 'prismatic everyday' and poetic traffic.[64]

Works Cited

Indo-Persica <http://perso-indica.net/section/fables_tales_and_stories>, last accessed on 13 September 2018

ADAMS, J.N., M. JANSE and S. SWAIN, eds, *Bilingualism in Ancient Society: language contact and the written text* (Oxford: Oxford University Press, 2002)

ALVI, TANVIR AHMAD, *Urdū men bārahmāson kī rivāyyat* (Delhi: Urdu Academy, 1981)

ANONYMOUS, *Rājkunwar*, MS CBL In 05, Chester Beatty Library, Dublin

BAKHTIN, MIKHAIL, *Speech Genres and Other Late Essays*, trans. Vern W. McGee (Austin, TX: University of Texas Press, 1981)

BARRETT, ARTHUR, ed., *The Traveller & The Deserted Village* (London: Macmillan & Co, 1888)

BEHL, ADITYA, TRANSL., *The Magic Doe: Quṭban Suhravardī's* Mirigāvatī (New York: Oxford University Press, 2012)

BROWN, HILARY. 'Rethinking agency and creativity: Translation, collaboration and gender in early modern Germany', *Translation Studies* 11:1 (2018), 84–102

BUSCH, ALLISON, *Poetry of Kings: The Classical Hindi Literature of Mughal India* (New York: Oxford University Press, 2011)

BUSCH, ALLISON, '*Riti* and register: Lexical variation in Courtly Braj Bhasha texts', in *Before the Divide: Hindi and Urdu literary culture*, ed. Francesca Orsini (Delhi: Orient Blackswan, 2010), pp. 84–120

CORT, JOHN D., 'Making it Vernacular Again: the pratice of translation among seventeenth-century Jains', in *Tellings and Texts: Music, Literature and Performance in North India*, ed. F. Orsini and K. Schofield (Cambridge: Open Book Publishers, 2015), pp. 61–106

D'HUBERT, THIBAUT, *In the Shade of the Golden Palace* (Oxford: Oxford University Press, 2018)

——'Histoire culturelle et poétique de la traduction. Alaol et la tradition littéraire bengali au XVIIe siècle à Mrauk-U, capitale du royaume d'Arakan', PhD dissertation (Paris: Ecole Pratique des Hautes Etudes, 2010)

DE BRUIJN, THOMAS, *The Ruby in the Dust: Poetry and History of the Indian Padmavat by Sufi Poet Muhammad Jayasi* (Amsterdam: University of Amsterdam Press, 2012)

DEVY, GANESH, 'Literary history and Translation: an Indian view', in *Post-Colonial Translation*, ed. Susan Bassnett and Harish Trivedi (London: Routledge, 1999), pp. 82–88

ERNST, CARL W., 'Muslim studies of Hinduism? A reconsideration of Arabic and Persian translations from Indian languages', *Iranian Studies* 36.2 (2003), 173–95

GIOVANARDI, CLAUDIO, 'Il bilinguismo italiano-latino del medioevo e del Rinascimento', in *Storia della lingua italiana*, ed. by Luca Serianni and Pietro Trifone, 3 vols (Torino: Einaudi, 1994), II, pp. 435–67

HESS, LINDA, 'The cow is sucking at the calf's teat: Kabir's upside-down language', *History of Religions* 22 (1983), 313–37

HODGSON, MARSHALL, *The Venture of Islam* (Chicago: University of Chicago Press, 1974)

JONES, SIR WILLIAM, 'On the Musical Modes of the Hindus', *The Works of Sir William Jones: With the Life of the Author*, 13 vols, ed. Lord Teignmouth (London: John Stockdale and John Walker, 1807), IV, pp. 166–210. Accessed through Googlebooks.

LEESE, SIMON, 'Longing for Salmá and Hind: (Re)producing Arabic Literature in 18th and 19th Century North India', PhD dissertation, SOAS, University of London, 2019

LEVY, LITAL, *Poetic Trespass: Writing between Hebrew and Arabic in Israel/Palestine* (Princeton: Princeton University Press, 2014)

Malūkdās kī bānī (Allahabad: Belvedere Printing Press, 2011)

Miragāvatī of Kutubana: Avadhi text with critical notes, ed. D.F. Plukker, PhD dissertation, Universiteit van Amsterdam, 1981

MIRAJI, *Maghreb aur mashreq ke naghme* (Lahore: Sang-e Meel Publications, 2009)

ORSINI, FRANCESCA, 'Na Turk na Hindu: Shared Languages, Accents, and Located Meanings', in *A Multilingual Nation: Translation and Language Dynamic in India*, ed. Rita Kothari (New Delhi: Oxford University Press, 2018), pp. 50–69

ORSINI, FRANCESCA, 'The Social Life of a Genre', *Medieval History Journal* 20, 1 (2017), 1–37

ORSINI, FRANCESCA, 'Translation, Circulation, Inflection: a Hindavi Tale in Persian Garb', in *Image, Object, Stories: Simon Digby's historical method*, ed. Francesca Orsini (New Delhi: Oxford University Press, forthcoming)

ORSINI, FRANCESCA, 'Traces of a Multilingual World: Hindavi in Persian Texts', in *After Timur Left: Culture and Circulation in Fifteenth-century North India*, ed. by F. Orsini and S. Sheikh (New Delhi: Oxford University Press, 2014), pp. 403–36

Orsini, Francesca, ed., *Love in South Asia: a cultural history* (Cambridge: Cambridge University Press, 2006)

Orsini, Francesca and Stefano Pellò, 'Bhakti in Persian', unpublished paper

Pathak, Shridhar, *Ekāntvāsī Jogī: ek premkahānī* (Allahabad: Ram Dayal Agrawal, 1931, 5th ed.)

Pauwels, Heidi C., *Cultural Exchange in Eighteenth-Century India* (Berlin: E. B. Verlag, 2015)

Pathak, Shridhar, *Ūjar Gām: A Hindi metrical translation of Goldsmith's* The Deserted Village (Benares: Medical Press, 1889)

Pellò, Stefano, 'Black Curls in a Mirror: The Eighteenth-Century Persian Kṛṣṇa of Lāla Amānat Rāy's *Jilwa-yi ẕāt* and the Tongue of Bīdil', *International Journal of Hindu Studies*, 22 (2018), 71–103. <https://doi.org/10.1007/s11407-018-9226-4>

Pellò, Stefano, 'Local Lexis? Provincializing Persian in Fifteenth-Century North India', in *After Timur Left: Culture and Circulation in Fifteenth-century North India*, ed. by F. Orsini and S. Sheikh (New Delhi: Oxford University Press, 2014), pp. 166–85

Ram, Harsha, 'The Sonnet and the Mukhambazi: Genre Wars on the Edges of the Russian Empire', *Remapping Genres* PMLA 122.5 (2007), 1548–70

Ramanujan, A.K., 'Three Hundred Ramayanas', in *Many Rāmāyaṇas: The Diversity of a Narrative Tradition in South Asia*, ed. Paula Richman (Berkeley: University of California Press, 1991), pp. 22–49

Ricci, Ronit, *Islam translated: Literature, conversion, and the Arabic cosmopolis of South and Southeast Asia* (Chicago: University of Chicago Press, 2011)

Richman, Paula, ed., *Many Rāmāyaṇas: The Diversity of a Narrative Tradition in South Asia* (Berkeley: University of California Press, 1991)

Ritter, Valerie, *Kama's Flowers: Nature in Hindi Poetry and Criticism, 1885–1925* (Albany: SUNY Press, 2011)

Schofield, Katherine Butler, 'Learning to Taste the Emotions: The Mughal *Rasika*', in *Tellings and Texts*, ed. by F. Orsini and K. Schofield (Cambridge: Open Book Publishers, 2015), pp. 407–22

Shackle, Christopher S., 'Approaches to Persian Loans in the *Adi Granth*', BSOAS, 41 (1978), 73–96

Sharma, Sunil, 'Translating Gender: Āzād Bilgrāmī on the Poetics of the Love Lyric and Cultural Synthesis', *The Translator*, Special Issue *Nation and Translation in the Middle East* ed. by Samah Selim, 15/1 (2009), 87–103

Sreenivasan, Ramya, *The Many Lives of a Rajput Queen: Heroic pasts in India, c.1500–1900* (New Delhi: Permanent Black, 2007)

Stewart, Tony K., 'In Search of Equivalence: Conceiving Muslim-Hindu Encounter Through Translation Theory', *History of Religions*, 40 (2001), 260–87

Tivari, Pandit Bhanupratap, 'Pandit bhanupratap tivari charanadi nivasi ka sanchhep jivancharit va satsang vilas', Ms Hindi 11035, UP State Archive, Manuscript Library

Trivedi, Harish, 'In Our Own Times: on Our Own Terms', in *Translating Others*, ed. Theo Hermans, 2 vols (London: Routledge, 2006), I, pp. 102–09

Truschke, Audrey, *Culture of Encounters: Sanskrit at the Mughal Court* (New York: Columbia University Press, 2016)

Viitamäki, Mikko, 'Text and Intensification of Its Impact in Chishti Samā, PhD dissertation, (University of Helsinki, 2008). pdf available at: https://helda.helsinki.fi/bitstream/handle/10138/19220/textandi.pdf?...2

Zipoli, Riccardo, *The Technique of the Ǧawāb. Replies by Nawā'ī to Ḥāfiẓ and Ǧāmī* (Venezia: Cafoscarina, 1993)

Notes to Chapter 2

1. William Jones: 'my experience justifies me in pronouncing that *Moghols* have no idea of accurate translation, and give that name to a mixture of gloss and text with a flimsy paraphrase of both', from 'On the Musical Modes of the Hindus', *The Works of Sir William Jones: With the Life of the Author*, ed. Lord Teignmouth, 13 vols, (London: John Stockdale and John Walker, 1807), IV, p. 181.
2. G.N. Devy, 'Translation and Literary History: An Indian view', in *Post-Colonial Translation*, ed. Susan Bassnett and Harish Trivedi (London: Routledge, 1999), shorter version of his 'Translation theory: an Indian perspective' (1989).
3. Devy linked it explicitly to the experience of colonial education, but it can be stretched back and more widely: 'The concept of a 'translating consciousness' and communities of people possessing it are no mere notions. In most Third World countries, where a dominating colonial language has acquired a privileged place, such communities do exist. In India several languages are simultaneously used by language communities as if these languages formed a continuous spectrum of signs and significance. The use of two or more different languages in translation activity cannot be understood properly through studies of foreign-language acquisition', 'Translation and Literary History', p. 185.
4. See e.g. the vast scholarship on the 'many Ramayanas', starting with Paula Richman, ed., *Many Rāmāyaṇas: The Diversity of a Narrative Tradition in South Asia* (Berkeley: University of California Press, 1991).
5. Devy, 'Translation and Literary History', p. 185.
6. A.K. Ramanujan, 'Three Hundred Ramayanas', in *Many Rāmāyaṇas*, p. 46.
7. Harish Trivedi, 'In Our Own Times: on Our Own Terms', in *Translating Others*, ed. Theo Hermans, 2 vols (London: Routledge, 2006), I, pp. 102–09, p. 106.
8. The full quote reads: India's linguistic diversity 'often leads to the assumption that India must be one of the richest and most productive areas of the world for translation activity. But this is, it turns out, a characteristically Western assumption, for it is to forget that translation is the need of the monolingual speaker, and that an obvious and efficacious alternative to having to translate from another language is to actually learn it, and if there is something even better than the best of translations, it is bilingualism'; Trivedi, 'In Our Own Times', p. 103.
9. Allison Busch explores this aspect nicely in '*Riti* and register: Lexical variation in Courtly Braj Bhasha texts', in *Before the Divide: Hindi and Urdu literary culture*, ed. Francesca Orsini (Delhi: Orient Blackswan, 2010), pp. 84–120. Simon Leese reflects on Arabic, Persian, and Brajbhasha and Urdu as different 'poetic terrains' for Indian literary scholars and poets, and notes that mixing was negatively commented upon; 'Longing for Salmá and Hind: (Re)producing Arabic Literature in 18th and 19th Century North India', PhD dissertation, SOAS, University of London, 2019.
10. Among key works on early modern translations are: Carl W. Ernst, 'Muslim studies of Hinduism? A reconsideration of Arabic and Persian translations from Indian languages', *Iranian Studies* 36.2 (2003), 173–95; John D. Cort, 'Making it Vernacular Again: the pratice of translation among seventeenth-century Jains', in *Tellings and Texts: Music, Literature and Performance in North India*, ed. F. Orsini and K. Schofield (Cambridge: Open Book Publishers, 2015), pp. 61–106; Thibaut d'Hubert, *In the Shade of the Golden Palace* (Oxford: Oxford University Press, 2018); Audrey Truschke, *Culture of Encounters: Sanskrit at the Mughal Court* (New York: Columbia University Press, 2016); Stefano Pellò, 'Black Curls in a Mirror: The Eighteenth-Century Persian Kṛṣna of Lāla Amānat Rāy's *Jilwa-yi zāt* and the Tongue of Bīdil', *International Journal of Hindu Studies* 22 (2018), 71–103; see also *Indo-Persica* entries on fables, tales, and stories at http://perso-indica.net/section/fables_tales_and_stories.
11. See Truschke, *Culture of Encounters* and Cort, 'Making it vernacular Again'.
12. Trivedi, 'In Our Own Times', p. 105.
13. The term 'communities of taste' was suggested to me by Ramya Sreenivasan; Katherine Butler Schofield, Molly Aitken, and Allison Busch have spoken of 'intermedial aesthetics' for the common aesthetics shared by courtly Hindi poetry, Rajput painting, and Hindustani music (as

codified in Persian and vernacular treatises) across Mughal imperial and Rajput courts in the early modern period in North India.

14. There are seven Persian versions of Jayasi's *Padmāvat,* making it the most 'translated' Hindavi text of the early modern period: see Thomas de Bruijn, *The Ruby in the Dust: Poetry and History of the Indian Padmavat by Sufi Poet Muhammad Jayasi* (Amsterdam: University of Amsterdam Press, 2012); see also Ramya Sreenivasan, *The Many Lives of a Rajput Queen: Heroic pasts in India, c.1500–1900* (New Delhi: Permanent Black, 2007); and Francesca Orsini, 'The Social Life of a Genre', *Medieval History Journal* 20, 1 (2017), 1–37, for different kinds of transcodification.
15. Anonymous, *Rājkunwar,* MS CBL In 05, Chester Beatty Library, Dublin.
16. See Francesca Orsini, 'Translation, Circulation, Inflection: a Hindavi Tale in Persian Garb', in *Image, Object, Stories: Simon Digby's historical method,* ed. Francesca Orsini (New Delhi: Oxford University Press, forthcoming) for a fuller discussion of this text.
17. See Aditya Behl, transl., *The Magic Doe: Quṭban Suhravardī's Mirigāvatī* (New York: Oxford University Press, 2012).
18. For a recent discussion of collaborative translation, see Hilary Brown, 'Rethinking agency and creativity: Translation, collaboration and gender in early modern Germany', *Translation Studies,* 11:1 (2018), 84–102.
19. Cort, 'Making it Vernacular'.
20. d'Hubert, *In the Shade*; also Thibaut d'Hubert, 'Histoire culturelle et poétique de la traduction. Alaol et la tradition littéraire bengali au XVIIe siècle à Mrauk-U, capitale du royaume d'Arakan', PhD dissertation (Paris: Ecole Pratique des Hautes Etudes, 2010).
21. d'Hubert, 'Histoire', pp. 357–58.
22. Ibid., p. 361.
23. This is one of the main differences he makes between his poetic and technical translations (of the Persian verse treatise of Sufi ethics, Yusuf Gada's *Tohfa-yi naṣāiḥ*); d'Hubert, 'Histoire', p. 357.
24. Simon Leese, 'Longing for Salmá'.
25. 'Pandit bhanupratap tivari charanadi nivasi ka sanchhep jivancharit va satsang vilas', Ms Hindi 11035, UP State Archive, Manuscript Library: 'The day he began teaching me the lesson on the *Bostān,* Munshi Sahab first recited this couplet five times:

> bādshāh jurm-e mā rā dar guẕar
> gunahgār-īm wa tū āfruzgār.'
>
> [Emperor, forgive our offense
> We are guilty while you exalt.]

In the margin, Tiwari added: 'translation (*ulthā*) by Bhanupratap Tiwari: *doha* (couplet):

> cakravartī dasaratha ke, karahu mora nistāra
> hauṃ patitana ko patita maiṃ, prabhu hau patita udhāra.'
>
> [Son of emperor Dasharatha, save me
> I am a sinner among sinners
> yet you, Lord, are a sinners' saviour.]

26. Mikko Viitamäki, 'Text and Intensification of Its Impact in Chishti Samā', PhD dissertation, (University of Helsinki, 2008).
27. For a longer discussion, see my 'Traces of a Multilingual World: Hindavi in Persian Texts', in *After Timur Left: Culture and Circulation in Fifteenth-century North India,* ed. by F. Orsini and S. Sheikh (New Delhi: Oxford University Press, 2014), pp. 403–36.
28. 'Abdul Quddus Gangohi, *Rushdnāma,* ed. Ghulam Ahmad Khan (Jhajjhar: Muslim Press, 1898), p. 5, tr. Simon Weightmann; this section draws on Orsini, 'Traces'.
29. Gangohi, *Rushdnāma,* p. 2.
30. Tony K. Stewart, 'In Search of Equivalence: Conceiving Muslim-Hindu Encounter Through Translation Theory', *History of Religions,* 40 (2001), 273.
31. Gangohi, *Rushdnāma,* p. 8.
32. *Mirigāvatī* (251.3), p. 53.
33. Behl, *Magic Doe,* p. 133.

34. Anon., *Rājkunwar*, f. 84r.
35. Claudio Giovanardi, 'Il bilinguismo italiano-latino del medioevo e del Rinascimento', in *Storia della lingua italiana*, ed. by Luca Serianni and Pietro Trifone, 3 vols (Torino: Einaudi, 1994), II, pp. 435–67.
36. For Hindi-Persian, see Imre Bangha, 'Rekhta: Poetry in Mixed Language: The Emergence of Khari Boli Literature in North India', in *Before the Divide: Hindi and Urdu Literary Culture*, ed. F. Orsini (New Delhi: Orient Blackswan, 2010), pp. 21–83. Stefano Pellò notes that in combining Persian with Hindavi, poets were in fact following a long tradition of mixed-language poetry in the Islamic world; 'Local Lexis? Provincializing Persian in Fifteenth-Century North India', in *After Timur Left: Culture and Circulation in Fifteenth-century North India*, ed. by F. Orsini and S. Sheikh (New Delhi: Oxford University Press, 2014), pp. 166–85.
37. As Riccardo Zipoli explains (*The Technique of the Ğawāb. Replies by Nawā'ī to Ḥāfiẓ and Ğāmī*, Venezia: Cafoscarina, 1993, pp. 6–9), this was one in a range of phenomena: *tarjuma*, which consisted in translating lines or part of lines from Persian into Arabic or viceversa; *taẓmīn*, i.e. a quotation of famous lines or parts of lines in a poem; *tawārud*, i.e. chance coincidence in part of or a whole line, and the *jawāb*, *istiqbāl* or *tatabbu'*, a deliberate 'reply' to the verse of another poet that included using the same metre, rhyme and *radīf* (if present), and reworking some of the words and themes of the original poem, and sometimes entire lines or parts of them.
38. For 'upside down language' (*ulaṭbāṃsī*), see Linda Hess, 'The cow is sucking at the calf's teat: Kabir's upside-down language', *History of Religions*, 22 (1983), 313–37.
39. See C.S. Shackle [who calls the language Torki], 'Approaches to Persian loans in the *Adi Granth*', BSOAS 41 (1978), 73–96; see also F. Orsini and S. Pellò, 'Bhakti in Persian', unpublished paper.
40. *Malūkdās kī bānī* (Allahabad: Belvedere Printing Press, 2011), p. 19.
41. *Malūkdās*, p. 27.
42. For the polyvocal languages of love, see Francesca Orsini, ed., *Love in South Asia: a cultural history* (Cambridge: Cambridge University Press, 2006).
43. Tanvir Ahmad Alvi, *Urdū men bārahmāson kī rivāyyat* (Delhi: Urdu Academy, 1981), p. 22.
44. Alvi, *Urdū*, p. 23.
45. The palace library in Kishangarh has a copy of Vali's *diwan* and Savant Singh's anthology *Padmuktāvalī* includes a few of Vali's *ghazals*; Heidi C. Pauwels, *Cultural Exchange in Eighteenth-Century India* (Berlin: EB Verlag, 2015), p. 82.
46. Texts and translations from Pauwels, *Cultural Exchanges*, pp. 100–02.
47. Persianate is a neologism launched by Marshall Hodgson in *The Venture of Islam*, Chicago: University of Chicago Press, 1974) to denote genres, styles, aesthetics and linguistic registers in languages other than Persian that drew upon Persian models, and is commonly used for Ottoman Turkish and Urdu. Persianized is used more narrowly for a linguistic register abounding in Persian words and constructions. In this case I use Persianate for Nagaridas's language because his spelling of the Persian words conforms to Brajbhasha phonology rather than Persian or Urdu, as would be the case with Persianized Hindi (so *musakila* instead of *mushkil*, *isakabājī* for *ishqbāzī*).
48. Katherine Butler Schofield, 'Learning to Taste the Emotions: The Mughal *Rasika*', in *Tellings and Texts*, ed. by F. Orsini and K. Schofield (Cambridge: Open Book Publishers, 2015), pp. 407–22.
49. See Allison Busch, *Poetry of Kings: The Classical Hindi Literature of Mughal India* (New York: Oxford University Press, 2011).
50. E.g. the comparison between Sanskrit and Arabo-Persian aesthetics in Ghulam Ali Azad Bilgrami's *Ghazalān-i hind*; see Sunil Sharma, 'Translating Gender: Āzād Bilgrāmī on the Poetics of the Love Lyric and Cultural Synthesis', *The Translator*, Special Issue *Nation and Translation in the Middle East* ed. by Samah Selim, 15/1 (2009), 87–103.
51. Quoted in Ghulam 'Ali Azad Bilgrami, *Sarw-i āzād* (Hyderabad: Kutubkhana-i Asafiya, 1913), p. 391.
52. See Valerie Ritter, *Kama's Flowers: Nature in Hindi poetry and criticism, 1885–1925* (Albany: SUNY Press, 2011), pp. 68–79 for an extensive analysis of this translation.
53. 'It will be a poem of remarkable excellence, the translation being so close as to be in the great

part line by line... The exact reproduction of each idea of the original in concise and beautiful Hindi verse is a triumph of skill'; 'very fair specimens of the artistic skill the Pandit has brought to bear on this work, and though the rendering is perfectly verbatim, it is quite free from the monotonous substitution of words which disfigures most of translations.' 'It is rare even in prose that so faithful a rendering is seen in the case of languages so widely different as English and Hindi, but in verse such close adherence to an original, while preserving fluency and poetic sweetness is exceedingly rare indeed'; *Opinions and reviews*, in Shridhar Pathak, *Ūjaṛ Gām* (Benares: Medical Press, 1889), pp. ii–viii.
54. '*The Solitary Yogi: a romance*, which Pandit Shridhar Pathak has translated (*ulthā kiyā*) from English into Hindi verse for the sake of Hindi and English poetry lovers', cover of Shridhar Pathak, *Ekantvasi Jogi: ek premkahani* (Allahabad: Ram Dayal Agrawal, 5th edn, 1931).
55. Review in *Aligarh Institute Gazette*, 6 July 1886, in Pathak, *Ūjaṛ Gam*, pp. iv–v.
56. Indeed, the standard edition of *The Traveller* and *The Deserted Village* was by Arthur Barrett, BA, Pofessor of English literature at Elphinstone College, Bombay, which included a substantial historical introduction and copious notes aimed at Indian students (London: Macmillan & Co, 1888 and many editions).
57. He dedicated *Ūjaṛ Gām* to Frederic Pincott MRAS, an 'earnest advocate of the just claims of the Hindi language to official recognition', Pathak, *Ūjaṛ Gām*, n.d.
58. His Hindi Preface is addressed in more traditional Brajbhasha/courtly Hindi terms to the connoisseurs (*rasik*), 'always tasting anew the nectar of the pleasures of verse/ bees drinking the honey of new poetry, lovers of new flowers'; transl. Valerie Ritter, *Kama's Flowers: Nature in Hindi Poetry and Criticism, 1885–1925* (Albany: SUNY Press, 2011), p. 70.
59. Miraji, *Maghreb aur mashreq ke naghme* (Lahore: Sang-e Meel Publications, 2009).
60. <https://www.poets.org/poetsorg/poem/to-a-stranger>, accessed on 13 September 2018.
61. Miraji, *Maghreb*, p. 46.
62. Miraji, *Maghreb*, p. 133.
63. See Mikhail Bakhtin, *Speech Genres and Other Late Essays*, trans. Vern W. McGee (Austin, TX: University of Texas Press, 1981); for other Indian examples, see Francesca Orsini, 'Na Turk na Hindu: Shared Languages, Accents, and Located Meanings', in *A Multilingual Nation: Translation and Language Dynamic in India*, ed. Rita Kothari (New Delhi: Oxford University Press, 2018), pp. 50–69.
64. See e.g. Adams, J.N., M. Janse and S. Swain, eds, *Bilingualism in Ancient Society: language contact and the written text* (Oxford: Oxford University Press, 2002); Ronit Ricci, *Islam translated: Literature, conversion, and the Arabic cosmopolis of South and Southeast Asia* (Chicago: University of Chicago Press, 2011); Harsha Ram, 'The Sonnet and the Mukhambazi: Genre Wars on the Edges of the Russian Empire', *Remapping Genres* PMLA 122.5 (2007), 1548–70; Lital Levy, *Poetic Trespass: Writing between Hebrew and Arabic in Israel/Palestine* (Princeton: Princeton University Press, 2014).

CHAPTER 3

❖

'Annihilation is atop the lake':
The Visual Untranslatability of an
Ancient Egyptian Short Story

Hany Rashwan

The Visual Inimitability of Ancient Egyptian Writing[1]

Translation is often employed as a means of cultural and literary exchange. Usually, translation scholars are more concerned with analysing the verbal layers of both source and target texts, evaluating the syntactic, stylistic, and phonetic structures, but ignoring the iconic identity of the translated scripts. This chapter highlights the significance of considering the visual medium of the Ancient Egyptian (henceforth AE) writing system when reading and translating AE literary texts. Despite the importance of understanding the internal mechanisms of AE literary expressions, modern scholarship has not assimilated this visual medium into its exploration. The examples I will present reveal the importance of examining such overlooked visual aesthetics for any theory that aims to investigate literary meaning in Ancient Egypt. Understanding AE visual aesthetics confirms Dick Higgins's claim that visual writing demonstrates a human tendency to synthesize visual and literary experiences, where pictorial elements provide visual cues for deciphering the intended meaning of the author.[2]

Although visual and verbal analysis of writing systems is often recognized as a modern phenomenon, AE writing has a considerably lengthier history than has generally been perceived. AE hieroglyphs constitute multiple sets of graphemes, or what Antonio Loprieno calls the 'iconic encyclopedia inherited in the hieroglyphic writing'.[3] For example, AE writing created the equivalent of our alphabetic values by using pictographic symbols consisting of actual images of entities extracted from the surrounding environment of the AE culture: an owl for the sound 'm', a snake with two horns ⌒ for the sound 'f', a water wave ∼ for the sound 'n', a human leg ⌡ for the sound 'b', etc. However, it seems that this one-to-one correspondence between sound and grapheme did not fully achieve the writing needs of Ancient Egyptians. Therefore, AE writing developed symbols that combine two or three sounds into one picture, usually with the help of phonetic complements for single sounds to authenticate the combined sounds: a house abstraction picture ⊏⊐ for the two sounds 'pr', a governor's stick ⸸ for the three sounds 'HqA', etc. This is one of the reasons why AE writing should not be equated with alphabetic writing as it exceeds the straightforward design of single letters. Moreover, many symbols that represent two or three sounds are not restricted to the construction of vocal forms. On the contrary, they play an effective visual-semantic role in specifying the intended meaning of a word:

> ⳼ ◠ı — sound[4]: wpt (horns, top, brow, top-knot, head-dress).
>
> ⳼ ⌃ — sound: wni (hasten, hurry, pass by or away).

The AE language is one of the most intricate writing systems because it uses graphical symbols to compose both the 'sound-signs' and the 'sense-signs'. These graphics were used to generate creative combinations of phonological and semantic principles. For instance, Emily Teeter highlights how AE writers did not feel the need to write the names of the offering table objects; instead, they took advantage of the visual nature of the language which represented the actual images of the described objects as 'determinatives' for the pronounced words. Tecter stresses the visual aspect of AE writing, and how modern alphabetic systems force our minds to separate the 'image world' from the 'phonetic signs', which was not the case for the Ancient Egyptian native readers:

> The hieroglyphic writing system could be highly efficient. The images of offerings in front of the man — a foreleg, ribs, and head of a calf, five beer jars in a rack, two baskets, a shallow tray with bread (?), and two tall wine jars in stands — all have more extended phonetic spellings, but here, only the image of what is portrayed was used, blurring the line between phonetic writing and picture writing.[5]

This indistinct line between the writing and the image inside the script is reflected in the Egyptian verb (⸻–sS), which means to 'write', 'inscribe', 'paint', or 'draw'. This word can be loosely used for both a scribe and an artist. *Sesh* thus has a cluster of meanings which include both writing texts and depicting pictures.[6]

In most AE words, the sequence of the phonograms[7] is followed by 'soundless sense-signs' which reinforce the semantic sphere of the word directly or metaphorically through the figurative content of the sign and its relation to the whole meaning of the word. They are thus called 'sense-signs', for example:

> ⸻ – sound: hy (husband). This word ends with two 'soundless sense-signs': the phallus and the sitting man, to confirm the gender.
>
> ⸻ – sound: txtx (disorder, crumble). This word ends with one 'soundless sense-sign': the hair. The hair is used here to represent the status of disorder metaphorically.

In AE script, the name of any concrete entity can be written merely by using its 'ending soundless sense-sign'. On the other hand, AE language can also use many 'tri-consonantal phonograms' to define the nature of the described object, without the 'ending soundless sense-signs'. However, these aspects are not always kept separate. For instance, the word ⸻, HAt, meaning 'forehead', 'forepart (of animal)', 'prow (of the ship)', or 'vanguard (of the army)', uses the head and shoulders of a lion metaphorically to show the concept of anything that stands out. Thus, the lion's forehead can be considered as a sense-sign and tri-consonantal sign simultaneously. Furthermore, a few ideograms can be formed from the sign of a single sound, where the addition of a 'stroke-determinative' indicates that this phonetic glyph also stands for the object that it represents visually (or related concepts). For instance, the word ⬠ r is written with a mouth and a single stroke glyph, meaning 'mouth', 'speech', 'language', or 'utterance'. The story of Sinuhe offers a sound example of the word being used in reference to the AE language, or even in a literal sense 'the mouth of Egypt':

𓄤𓍿𓏲𓎛𓈖𓂝𓀀𓄔𓏛𓎡𓂋𓈖𓆎𓏏𓊖

nfr tw Hna.i sDm.k r n kmt

You will be happy with me (in my company) when you hear the mouth of Egypt.[8]

In other words, these ideograms do not merely stand for the sound they evoke; they also share with the 'ending sense-sign' the function of clarifying the meaning of the word for the native reader, both visually and semantically. Gardiner defines the 'ending soundless sense-signs' as determinatives because their primary function appears to 'determine the meaning of forgoing sound-signs and to define that meaning in a general way'.[9] However, to think that only the ending 'soundless sense-signs' are determinatives is a misleading generalisation. Gardiner himself acknowledges the weakness of the term 'determinative' in dealing precisely with the AE 'sound-signs' and their visual complexity. He states:

> The name "determinative" is in many cases historically inaccurate, the ideogram having been the original sign with which the word was first written, and the phonograms having been prefixed to it subsequently for the sake of clearness. In such cases, it might be more truly said that the phonograms determine the *sound* of the ideogram than that the ideogram determines the *sense* of the phonograms.[10]

The modern terms can easily be challenged due to the highly graphical nature of AE writing, which blurs the line between our two modern theoretical sets ('sound' on the one hand, and 'sense' on the other). The lack of engagement with any extant native terms makes the redefinition process more difficult. The most puzzling part for modern scholars is capturing a correct theoretical account for all soundless hieroglyphic sense-signs in comparison to the sound-signs. The exceptional visual features of the AE script make it difficult to apply many of the standard terms we use, especially those extracted from cursive alphabetic scripts. For educational reasons, modern AE grammar books simplify the complex pictorial system for beginners, without conducting a more in-depth analysis of the interrelated areas between the soundless and sound signs, as Gardiner himself stated:

> The classification of hieroglyphs into (1) ideograms or sense-signs and (2) phonograms or sound-signs covers the entire ground, but, ... the line of demarcation between the two classes is often difficult to draw. Nor must it be imagined that all the signs contained in the sub-divisions of these main groups stand on an equal footing and conform to identical rules; on the contrary,

custom plays a very important part in deciding what writings are possible and what are not, though variant spellings are very numerous.[11]

The marriage between the 'phonograms' and 'sense-signs' is perfectly represented in some AE 'symbols' that combine both categories in one glyph to confirm the visual meaning of the word for native readers. Gardiner refers to them as 'monograms'. The moving feet ideogram 𓂻 and its combinations with different phonograms may illustrate this point:

𓁹𓂻 — sound: ii (come). The first glyph is a monogram because it is a mixture of (𓂻 + 𓏭).

𓈝𓂻 — sound: Sm (go). The first glyph is a monogram because it is a combination of (𓂻 + 𓄿).[12]

The creative visual and semantic engagement between these 'sound monograms' and the 'ending soundless sense-signs' can easily be observed in the verbs above. The mechanism of such 'visual repetition' can also be better understood in light of similar AE words that use the same hieroglyphic sign to begin and end the word, which visually stresses the meaning of the word, such as:

𓅓𓏏𓅓𓏏𓏥 — sound: mtwt (semen, seed, progeny).

𓈎𓐪𓈎 — sound: qA (hill, high-ground).

The first 'phonogram' is spoken while the 'ending sense-sign' is soundless. There are many similar AE words, in which the 'opening phonograms' semantically correspond to the 'ending soundless determinatives'. They both work efficiently to reflect the whole meaning of the word visually and semantically, such as:

𓊨𓏏𓉐 — sound: st (seat, throne, place, department, or position). The word begins with a high chair and ends with a house plan.

𓂝𓅓𓂝𓏒 — sound: amaA (throw a stick). The word begins with a hand and ends with a stick.

This pictorial realism was of great importance to AE priests in designing the intended meaning; it stimulates the minds of their native receivers by inviting both the eye and the ear to establish a cognitive dialogue to decode the proffered message easily. One hieroglyphic sentence carved on the tomb of the High Priest of Amun, *Men-kheper-ra-seneb* (serving the pharaoh Thutmose III 1479–1425 BCE),[13] illustrates the creative interrelation between the verbal and visual layers of AE writing:

𓏏𓈖𓇋𓇋𓅡𓂓𓏤𓁹𓂋𓐍𓅓𓏲𓏌𓏌𓏌𓏌𓈖𓅱𓏠𓈖𓏌𓏤𓂋𓈖𓀀

xny bA.i Hr aXmw nw mnw.i ir.n.i

May my ba (soul-bird) alight on the branches of my trees which I have planted.[14]

In this example, the author uses two 'sense-signs' that visually portray what the verse verbally signifies: first, the verb 𓏏𓇋𓇋𓅨, meaning alight (from the flight), stop, halt, or rest (on). This verb can be written with an additional determinative of human feet, 𓏏𓅨𓂻). Second, the noun 𓅡 bA, meaning 'soul', can be written with many different visual forms such as [hieroglyphs] — [hieroglyphs] — [hieroglyphs]. In both cases, the writer chose not to use any of the possible additional determinatives so as not to distract the reader from the intended visual sequence.

These two unencumbered determinatives correspond to two other related determinatives of the two successive words [hieroglyphs] (a plural noun meaning twigs or branches) and [hieroglyphs] (a plural noun meaning trees or plantations). Here, the 'visual dialogue' is between two successive positions of landing birds ([hieroglyph] – [hieroglyph]) and two other related ending determinatives, the first depicting a part of the second ([hieroglyph] – [hieroglyph]). If we place the determinatives beside each other, it sheds more light on how the AE writer displayed creativity in choosing his words to encourage the reader to picture the path and perch of the soul-bird ([hieroglyph] – [hieroglyph] – [hieroglyph] – [hieroglyph]). The first determinative can even correspond with the last one semantically, creating a visual thought couplet in which the first image is the bird still in the air but close to the tree ([hieroglyph] – [hieroglyph]). The second image is of the soul-bird resting on a tree branch ([hieroglyph] – [hieroglyph]). This example confirms the creation of a verbal-visual metaphor that is carried through the sentence at the determinative level to ensure that the deceased would be provided with the full range of necessary items to ensure that the soul-bird reached the afterlife safely. Such examples show how the performance of AE writing is 'located halfway between the individual and the social dimension on the one hand and between the sphere of cognition and the sphere of convention on the other.'[15] The pictorial realism of AE hieroglyphs played a vital role in delivering the intended message and remained unchanged throughout AE history, as Assmann states:

> The Egyptians were convinced of the power of language, not only in spoken but above all in written form. This is the reason why they never changed or reduced the pictorial realism and the iconic character of the hieroglyphs. They would rather invent, at first a second and then a third script alongside the hieroglyphs than adapt the hieroglyphs to everyday purposes. In their iconicity lay their cosmological character which corresponded to the "grammatological" structure of the cosmos.[16]

Such AE examples confirm that this unique connection between the iconic sphere and the reproduction of semantic content appeals to both the eye and the ear of the AE native reader when the sight and sound of words become parts of the process of making sense. This connection raises many questions about the visual skills that AE readers must have used to infer the intended meaning. The visual effects of AE writing create a particular challenge for our modern translations. Prismatic strategies are needed to represent complex phonetic and visual meanings.

The Short Story of the Father and the Crocodiles

These visual poetics can be further explored in a short story[17] extracted from the hieratic text of a man who complains about his miserable life to his own soul, which belongs to the Middle Kingdom (2000–1700 BCE). The short story is part of a poetic debate between a man and his soul, in which he tries to convince his soul to commit suicide as he thinks that the afterlife might be better. A melodramatic short story is offered by his soul to persuade him that his miserable situation is nothing when compared to another person who has faced a harder situation (seeing crocodiles devouring his beloved wife and infants in front of his eyes). The primary focus of this short story is to convey how young lives are ruined before they can enjoy the fullness of life.[18] However, the soul's story leaves it open as to whether the family perish or not. Below, I have provided a literal translation of this short story, following James Allen's hieroglyphic republication[19]:

67.
sDm r.k n.i mk nfr sDm n rmT
May you listen to me! Behold it is good to listen to people.

68.
Sms hrw nfr smx mH
Follow the happy day and forget the worry (lit. the-state-of-being-worried-and-nervous-about-something-in-the-future).[20]

68–69.
iw nDs skA.f Sdw.f
The lad cultivates (alone) his small-land.

69–70.
iw.f A[t]p.f Smw.f r Xnnw dpt
He carries (alone) his harvest to the boat's hold.

70.
stAs.f sqdwt
He hauls the sail.

71–72.
Hb.f tkn mA.n.f prt wxt nt mHyt
His festival will approach soon after seeing that the darkness of the northern-rainy-wind has emerged.

72.
rs m dpt
He stayed-awake inside the boat.

73–74.
ra Hr aq pr Hna Hmt.f msw.f
When the sun began-to-enter, he went-out with his wife and his young-children.

74.
Aq tp S
Annihilation is atop the lake.

75. [hieroglyphs]
Sn m grH Xr mryt
The crocodile-encircled (them) in the night, under the riverbank-of-the-crocodiles.

75–76. [hieroglyphs]
Dr.in.f Hms psS.f m xrw Hr Dd
Then he sat- down-like-a-small-child, ululating in a loud-voice saying:

76–78. [hieroglyphs]
n rm.i n tfA mst nn n.s prt m imnt r kt Hr tA
I do not cry for this young-girl for whom there can be no emergence from the West for another (existence) on earth.

78–79. [hieroglyphs]
mHy.i Hr msw.s sdw m swHt mAw Hr n xnty
I am sad about her young-children, who have just hatched from the egg, but they will see the face of the crocodile-God-Khenty.

80. [hieroglyphs]
n anxt.sn
They had not yet lived enough.

Now I offer a commentary on the story's visual and stylistic untranslatability:

68–69. [hieroglyphs]
iw nDs skA.f Sdw.f
The lad cultivates (alone) his small-land.

In this verse, the AE author repeats the subject of the sentence three times: as a noun **nDs**, as a suffix pronoun playing the role of the subject in skA.**f**, and as a suffix pronoun playing the role of the object in Sdw.**f**. The author uses a similar technique in the sentence 'iw.f A[t]p.f Smw.**f**', where the subject of the action has been repeated three times: as a suffix pronoun attached to the particle 'iw', as a subject in A[t]p.**f**, and as a suffix pronoun playing the role of the object (Smw.**f**) to refer once more to the subject of the main verb. The primary function of repeating the same pronoun, as a stylistic technique, is to highlight the hero of the story and to centralize the main subject of the verb inside the sentence.[21]

Studying the AE language is a kind of archaeology of a dead language in which stylistic comparisons provide the only support available for closer hypotheses about literary practices that aim to avoid Eurocentric rhetorical misperception. Viewed linguistically, the AE language belongs to the same language phylum — Afroasiatic — as Arabic and shares many of the same poetic features fundamental to literary production; as Stephen Quirke argues, 'Classical Arabic poetry offers for certain motifs and "genres" a resonance entirely lacking in English and other European literary traditions'.[22] There are many similar features in Arabic, and thus Arabic traditions of translation and stylistic analysis help us to understand and represent the internal mechanism of AE stylistic constructions. For instance, there is a moment in the story of Moses in the Arabic Qur'an where the sacred voice repeats a pronoun three times to confirm that Moses is the only person addressed. The expert magicians of the pharaoh's court create a visual deception whereby the rope and staffs transform and move in a way similar to how snakes move. Moses is terrified that he will never be able to challenge their faultless magic. Then God says to him:

((لَا تَخَفْ إِنَّكَ أَنْتَ الْأَعْلَى))
lā takhaf innaka anta al-āalā
Do not be afraid. Indeed, you are (alone) the highest. (Q20:68)

This verse repeats the second person pronoun three times: 1) as a hidden pronoun in the negated verb 'لا تخف', the prefix ت-t attached to the present verb represents the second person; 2) as a suffix pronoun attached to the Arabic confirmation device *inna*, 'إنَّك' (literally 'indeed you are'); and 3) as an independent/separate pronoun for the second person singular 'أنت' (literally 'you are'). In both AE and Arabic, such poetic repetitions of pronouns create different layers of untranslatability. They may disappear entirely in the translation process as a result of the limited knowledge of the translator or difficulty in translating them. This argument can be examined in four different translations produced for the Qur'anic verse just quoted:[23]

(1) George Sale 1734 (a native speaker of English)
'Fear not; for thou shalt be superior'.

(2) M. M. Pickthall 1930 (a native speaker of English)
'Fear not! Lo! Thou art the higher'.

(3) Mohamed Abdel Haleem 2005 (a native speaker of Arabic)
'Do not be afraid; you have the upper hand'.

(4) Sahih International 1997 (collective translation by different scholars from different backgrounds)
'Fear not. Indeed, it is you who are superior'.

In my translation of the verse, the three repetitions of the same second singular pronoun are rhetorically represented in the use of the annotation '(alone)'. In this Qur'anic verse, there are further complications. In fact, four confirmation elements have been blended by the voice of God to ensure that Moses feels his full support in facing the magicians of the pharaoh: 1) giving an order using negation; 2) using the Arabic confirmation device *inna*; 3) repeating three different types of pronouns for the second singular person; and 4) using the superlative form of the adjective 'high'. Such stylistic features are the main components of what Arabic balāghists/rhetoricians refer to as *iᶜjāz*, which can be translated as 'poetic-inimitability'. Most conservative Arabists employ these aesthetic dimensions to confirm that 'the Qur'an meant not only that its beauty could not be reproduced by human speech, but that its discourse was superior to all human discourse, including poetry'.[24] The notion of *iᶜjaz* in Arabic balāghah (eloquent-poetics) is mostly concerned with the relationship between the 'eloquent content', and its 'poetic form' to better understand the sources of literary and aesthetic beauty. The unsaid is always stressed by the creative syntactic structure of the sentence, with a 'great deal of meaning (*maana*) being communicated by a small amount of vocal forms (*lafz*)'.[25]

Such poetic structures are considered a fundamental part of producing the literariness of each language and cannot be translated entirely — or sometimes even appreciated or acknowledged — in a different linguistic system. This is a fact that was recognized early by the pioneer literary critic al-Jāḥiẓ (776–869 AD) who stated that Arabic poetry could be only appreciated in its original language and the translation process always fails to reflect the wonders of its internal and external beauty.[26] It is just as much of a challenge to translate the stylistic structures of AE literary expressions into languages that have entirely different syntactic structure, such as the European languages, as they have different conditions for the literariness of a text.

69–70.

iw.f A[t]p.f Smw.f r Xnnw dpt
He carries (alone) his harvest to the boat's hold.

The word 'Xnnw' is one of the keywords for understanding the general sequence of this short story and requires a philological comment. The Berlin dictionary mentions that this word generally means 'inside something', for example: 'inside the sky' — , 'Xnnw pt'; 'inside the house' — , 'Xnnw pr'; 'inside the body' (referring to a disease) — . The word and its meaning are present in the Coptic script ϩⲟⲩⲛ: ϩⲟⲩⲛ: ϩⲟⲩⲛ.[27] The colloquial Arabic dialects in Egypt have retained much of the AE lexicon[28] and these cognates, in turn, may resolve the ambiguity of word meanings in the AE dictionary. I consider that this AE word 'Xnnw' is semantically and phonologically equivalent to a common modern Egyptian word pronounced 'khwnn'- خُنّ. This colloquial Egyptian word 'khwnn' does not exist in the classic Arabic-Arabic dictionaries, and it cannot be used as a verb. The phonetic exchange between the letters X and x is frequent in both AE[29] and Arabic. Modern Egyptians often use the word 'khwnn' to mean hidden invulnerable places away from prying eyes. It can be used to denote a secret place for lovers to meet each other or a hiding place for small animals or insects.[30] Surprisingly, there is a close cognate in the ancient Iraqi language of Middle Babylon, pronounced 'xunnû' (meaning to give shelter or to lodge).[31]

75.

Sn m grH Xr mryt
The crocodile-encircled (them) in the night, under the riverbank-of-the-crocodiles.

The AE verb – Sn is derived from the verb – Snw (which means 'encircle') and (which means 'circuit'). The word – Snw (meaning 'king's cartouche') is also derived from this word. The resourceful author used the original root of the word Snw and added a crocodile, , as an 'ending-soundless determinative' to create a new adjectival verb, meaning 'surrounded by crocodiles'. There is similar usage in the story of the 'Eloquent Peasant', where the writer uses the crocodile's determinative to stress the importance of speaking truthfully, and indirectly to criticize the silence of a corrupted employer in the Egyptian government:³²

mk dmi.k Snw aqA nst.k
*Look your harbour will be surrounded-by-crocodile because of the truthfulness of your tongue.*³³

75-76.
Dr.in.f Hms psS.f m xrw Hr Dd
Then he sat- down-like-a-small-child, ululating in a loud-voice saying:

The AE verb — Hms is usually written with a seated man as a 'soundless-determinative' to mean 'sitting down'. However, the author here chooses another 'ending soundless-determinative': a young child who puts his finger inside his mouth, , to represent the notion of early-childhood. It visually illustrates how this kind-hearted father, in a difficult situation, felt weak and helpless.

76-78.
n rm.i n tfA mst nn n.s prt m imnt r kt Hr tA
I do not cry for this young-girl for whom there can be no emergence from the West for another (existence) on earth.

The AE writer uses this feminine attribute — mst, which literally means a 'very young girl', to refer to the man's wife in order to implant sad feelings in the reader's heart. By using such an attribute for the wife, the author establishes a direct comparison between the young wife and her newborn children, msw.s — . Both nouns and are derived from the same verb, — ms, which means 'to give birth' or 'be born'. The biblical name 'Moses' was derived from this verb, meaning 'newborn', which in turn highlights the time when the pharaoh of Egypt adopted God's prophet.

The calamity and sadness of this short story are evidenced in the way that this young mother and her newborn children are doomed before they can even experience life together. The AE writer mentions the word — Hmt (meaning 'wife') only once in the verse that depicts who was accompanying the hero of the story in his boat journey to the marketplace:

73-74.
ra Hr aq pr Hna Hmt.f msw.f
When the sun began-to-enter, he went-out with his wife and his young-children.

The traditional approach of 'determinatives' in Egyptology forces our minds to consider the seated woman only as an 'ending soundless determinative' to decode the general meaning for the word — Hmt (meaning 'wife'). However, AE writing also took into consideration the beginning sign (a vessel containing liquid) as a metaphorical symbol representing 'womanhood' in general. Griffith pointed out that: 'The IDEOGRAPHIC power is often extended or TRANSFERRED widely, and sometimes in a peculiar and rather unexpected way; e.g. when , a pond,

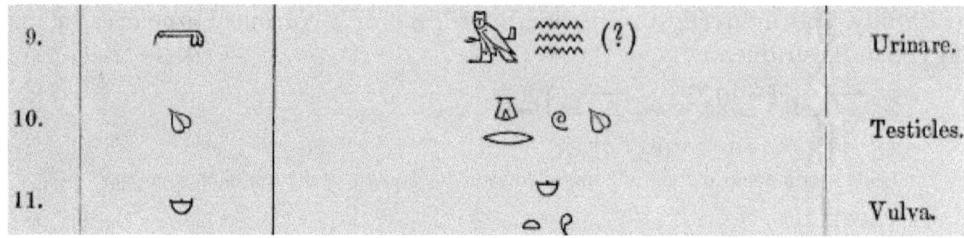

Fig. 3.1. Francis Griffith and William Petrie, *Two Hieroglyphic Papyri from Tanis* (London: Trübner and Co Grimal, 1889), p.13.

or a vessel containing liquid, is taken as the symbol of womanhood..... Mythology and religion naturally played their part in this extension'.[34] Furthermore, the AE author of the Tanis sign-list papyrus situated the sign under a group of human body parts, and more specifically alongside male genitalia (penis and testicles). This is why Griffith referred to this sign in an earlier publication as 'vulva' (see figure 3.1.).

The shape of this sign is less connected to the direct visual representation of genitalia than the other signs depicted above. It can be considered a metaphorical representation of the female reproductive system, perhaps referring to the 'womb' as a vessel or well, which carries the foetus surrounded by water. This suggestion is supported by the word — 'Hmt', which means 'womb', 'vulva', or 'uterus'.[35] 'The assimilation of the well with the uterus, and by extension with the reproductive organ of the woman, is a fundamental archetype of the human mind. It was not exclusive to the Egyptians, but they clearly expressed this concept through their writing. ... From a biological point of view, they clearly understood that all life comes from water'.[36]

Unfortunately, research into the AE 'determinative' system, particularly regarding its various literary graphic metaphors, is still in its early stages mainly because of the broad definition of 'determinatives' as signs that are located at the end of AE words:

> The so-called determinatives are pictograms that are placed after the vowelless root in the Egyptian script, functioning as reading aids but carrying no additional phonetic value. They mark the end of words and provide semantic information about the preceding word through their *iconic* meaning alone.[37]

Orly Goldwasser constructs her entire argument about what she refers to as the 'classifier' system on the hypothesis that 'the classifiers (signs carrying no phonetic information, only semantic information about the word) generally appear in cuneiform writing before the word, whereas in Egyptian they always appear at the end of the word'.[38] If we follow the conceptual definition of 'determinative' as a sign usually used to clarify or determine the general meaning of the word for native readers, then we have to reconsider the 'position' and the 'nature' of what we call 'determinative' or 'classifier'. Knowledge of this overlooked system helps modern readers to consider the general principles that once governed such visual-semantic interactions, and how they can be understood in other literary texts.

A Prismatic Rereading of the Short Story

To adequately represent the ideographic power of AE writing, I will rephrase the soul's story in my own words, reconstructing the unsaid based on what the soul narrated and highlighting the 'visual determinatives' that the AE author uses to clarify and weave together the dramatic sequences of the story for his native readers:

> There was a man of the common people (𓍶𓏛𓀀) who was fighting the hard circumstances of having no fixed income. This man got married (𓎛𓐮𓀔) to a young girl, and they agree to share the hardships of this earthly life, hoping that the Gods would grant them a happy afterlife together. He was pleased that his young wife (𓀀𓏤𓐮𓁐) brought children (𓀀𓈖𓐮𓁐𓀔) into his life. To feed them, he used a small piece of fertile land located by a Nile channel (𓍿𓐮𓁐𓏤) to plant (𓊪𓍯𓐮𓆰𓏛) some crops. He used to sell part of his crops to earn a small income to help him and his family to survive another rotation of crops. He was doing all that was possible to take care of his family. He was by himself working this small piece of land. It was a difficult job for him since his wife was occupied with taking care of their very young children, but he managed to achieve success, and he carried (𓐮𓎛𓀀) all the harvest (𓎼𓏤𓏤) to the boat. This boat had a protective cubbyhole (𓍿𓏥𓂝𓐮𓆱) that was designed to protect him and his family from the night's wind and rain. On one evening, he erected (𓊪𓐮𓐮𓁹) the mast of the boat (𓊪𓐮𓐮𓁐𓆱) to use the wind for moving the boat forward to the market. With every move of the boat, the man thought that he was going forward towards his feast (𓊪𓁹𓐮𓐮𓐮𓀒); the deserved reward of working hard. It was a windy and rainy night, so he stayed awake the entire night (𓎛𓊪𓀒) dreaming about how to celebrate with his small family after selling the crops and feeling the reward in his hand. He said to himself: this dream will soon become true when the darkness of this windy and rainy night (𓐮𓇳𓏏𓐮𓆱𓐮𓐮𓀒) finishes and the boat reaches the marketplace. With the first sunlight of the day (𓐮𓇳𓐮𓅱𓐮𓐮𓐮) the whole family came out (𓐮𓐮𓐮) of the boat's cubbyhole, thinking that the boat had safely reached the marketplace during the very dark night (𓐮𓇳𓐮𓐮𓐮). However, they were all shocked and scared to death when they saw that the boat was astray on the Nile, trapped by a hungry crocodile (𓆊𓏤𓐮), and that the nearest riverbank was also full of crocodiles (𓆊𓐮𓐮𓏪). The man could hardly speak and said just one short sentence: 'Annihilation is atop the lake' (𓐮𓐮𓐮𓐮). The man realized that they were trapped beside the dwelling place of crocodiles. He could not move the boat or ask for help from anyone. He sat down like a small child (𓐮𓀔) feeling helpless, screaming out in a

loud voice (𓊡𓏴𓈖𓄿𓂧𓀞) while looking at his scared wife with her young children (𓀔𓀔𓀔𓏪𓁐𓏭𓏥). They were looking at him, asking him to do something or perhaps blaming him for using the mast during a windy and rainy night and staying with them in the cubbyhole. The man did not care about what might happen to him; he was crying (𓄿𓂧) about the destiny of his beloved young wife (𓌻𓀔𓏪𓁐𓂧) in the afterlife. He was wondering if she would be able to have a happy afterlife like her peers who died and have been mummified on Earth (𓈖𓈖𓏤𓊪𓏤𓊌𓄿𓂧𓃀𓈖𓏌𓏤𓂝𓊪𓌙𓏪𓏤). However, his most heart-breaking concern (𓂋𓇋𓇋𓂧) was related to his young children (𓀔𓀔𓀔𓏪𓁐𓏭𓏥) who had just been born (lit. hatched from the egg, 𓊃𓂋𓅱𓏴𓄿𓂧𓄿𓂋𓏌𓊌); they had not seen much happiness in their short lives, and they are now seeing (𓌴𓀔𓂝) the face of an enormous crocodile (𓊪𓈖𓏤𓈖𓈖𓈖𓈖𓂋𓏪𓊌𓏌) that would devour them without any mercy. They had not yet lived enough (𓐍𓊪𓆑𓂝𓈖𓀔𓏪).

However, the resourceful author of this text uses interrelated visual clues to highlight the man's rejection of the whole emotional argument of this melodramatic short story; the man reconfirmed to his soul the aspiration to end his miserable life:

95–97.

𓐝𓎡𓎺𓐝𓊃𓂋𓈖𓏭𓐝𓂝𓎡𓂋𓊃𓏏𓌳𓋴𓌉𓅱𓂋𓈟𓋴𓏏𓐍𓂋𓂝𓍑𓅱𓐍𓂋𓅓𓂋𓇋𓇋𓏏𓈐𓏪

mk baH rn.j m-a.k r st msHw r Hmst Xr aDw Xr mryt

Behold, my name is reeking with you more than the smell of crocodiles, more than sitting-down-like-a-small-child under the slaughter place, under the riverbank-of-crocodiles.

This poetic refusal contains a direct visual hint of the main scene of the soul's short story:

75. 𓋴𓈖𓐝𓎼𓂋𓎛𓐍𓂋𓅓𓂋𓇋𓇋𓏏𓈐𓏪

Sn m grH Xr mryt

The crocodile-encircled (them) in the night, under the-riverbank-of-crocodiles.

The two verses use the word (𓌳𓅱𓂋𓇋𓇋𓏏𓈐𓏪 — mryt) with plural crocodiles as unusual soundless determinative. The usual forms of this word that means shore, bank, sandbank or quay are (𓌳𓅱𓂋𓇋𓇋𓏏𓈅) or (𓌳𓅱𓂋𓇋𓇋𓏏𓈇). These oft-used determinatives reflect a projecting ground along the bank of a river, but the writer here preferred to use the crocodile determinative as a visual indication that this river bank is no longer the common word that is used by and for humans. This lexical intertextuality confirms that the visual form, in this short story, is one useful tool in delivering the intended meaning and without recognising its active role semantically, we will not be able to appreciate the eloquent variations of AE words. Modern readers should not assume that the use of different determinatives for one word is rigid and has no additional interpretation semantically and visually. The richness of the AE determinative system requires that the modern reader should consider the nexus between a word and its many determinatives in order to rediscover the rich tones of meaning each brings to the reading process.

The Question of Aural versus Written Performance

If we consider how many different 'sense-signs' each AE word can possess and how each determinative is conceptually related to its context, which in turn enriches the meaning, we are able to reconsider the richness of AE writing in playing on sameness and difference to produce the intended meaning. I think it would be reasonable to assert that when using different determinatives a scribe highlights different aspects or facets of the semantic world of the word. The AE examples I have presented show that each different visual form was firmly related to the production of meaning. The various determinatives of each AE word raise a problematic question concerning the vocal performance of such visual messages: how could AE writers transfer these visual messages during oral recitation for their native audience? Were these visual messages only designed for the reader's eyes? To partly answer this difficult question, I will use another example of repeating one word through the whole text — three times with the same unusual determinative — to stimulate the reader's eye. This example may provide a small insight into the reactions of AE listeners when the writer uses an unusual 'soundless-determinative'. The example is extracted from the hieratic teachings of the vizier Kagemni who served Pharaoh Sneferu (2613–2589 BCE). He offers reliable advice for handling unbearable daily life situations:

ir Hms.k Hna aSAt msd t mrr.k

If you sit down (suffering-in-this-position-like-a-woman-giving-birth) with a multitude, [pretend that], you dislike the food you always love.[39]

In this example, the writer uses a critical determinative for the main verb of the sentence — Hms.k, a verb meaning 'dwell (in)', with a lady giving birth as an 'ending soundless-determinative'. This verb can be considered phonetically as a combination of two different words: the verb Hms with a seated man as a determinative (meaning 'sitting down') and the verb — ms (meaning 'to give birth' or 'to be born'). Gardiner has confirmed that the verb Hms was written with the ending determinative of the verb ms (meaning 'the lady who gives birth'): 'The scribe of Prisse consistently assimilates the determinative of Hms to that of msi, cf. the lines 1,8; 2,7;5,2 for Hms, 5,5.6; 19,1 for msi'.[40] The AE writer created a new visual form of the verb by borrowing the 'ending soundless-determinative' of the verb ms in order to add another metaphorical layer to fit a different literary context: the lady who gives birth may represent, in this context, a guest whose attitudes and eating behaviours are intolerable. This 'giving-birth' determinative reflects the hard time this person must go through in his/her stay with undesirable people. By using this determinative, the AE writer implies that the pain of keeping company with such people is similar to that of giving birth, and the teachings here advise the reader to deal with such stressful situations wisely (if this unlucky person cannot escape from their company).

The second repetition of the same verb, with its unusual determinative, is used to serve another context:

ir Hms.k Hna Afa wnm.k Axf.f swA
If you are sitting down (suffering-in-this-position-like-a-pregnant-woman) with a glutton, eat after his gorging has gone.[41]

The context confirms the suggested literary technique of using this visual form to represent the suffering that an ordinary person may face eating in the company of an excessively greedy eater: — Afa. It is remarkable that this word has been written with the use of a donkey as an 'ending soundless-determinative' to represent the uncivilized eating behaviour of such a gluttonous person. The two ending determinatives of the words — Hms and — Afa are metaphorically related in this context as the donkey was considered a representation of the God of storms and evil, Set. This thus implies that being in the company of a gluttonous person can generate negative feelings in any reasonable person, such as the pain of giving birth does to a woman, which creates horrible suffering for a while.

However, this suffering can end with a reward for the person who can deal with the undesirable behaviour, in this case by sharing his food and making this greedy person — whom he may need later — feel happy with his company. This reward can also be metaphorically linked to the process of giving birth, which ends with a newborn. This implies that this suffering may conclude with a reward if one finds the right way to deal with the pain of his company. In such stressful situations, the writer provides a solution for the reader to follow: try to be patient when watching this greedy person eat like a donkey; after his stomach is filled with food, he will invite you to eat whatever is left.

At the end of the teachings, the AE writer repeated the same verb in a context that may reveal how the Ancient Egyptians appreciated the visual intelligence of their writing system. The father Kagemni declared that his teachings had been well-received and preserved by his own sons and many others. The eye-catching point is that he declared that the reciters of the text should read his teachings precisely as it was written, to please the receiver's heart, saying:

wn.in.sn Hr rdit st Hr Xtw.sn
Then they kept placing it (his teaching) on their belly.

wn.in.sn Hr Sdt st mi ntt m sS
Then they kept reciting it as it is in writing.

wn.in nfr st Hr ib.sn r xtw nbt nty m tA r Dr.f
Then it was more beautiful on their hearts more than all the things that exist in this entire earth.

𓎟𓈖𓀃𓄿𓂝𓏪𓊵𓁐𓏪𓐍𓆑𓏏𓅪

```
wn.in aHa.sn Hms.sn xft
```
Then their standing and their sitting[42] *were accordingly so.*[43]

If we consider the different visual forms that the AE writer of this text produced, one might suggest that the AE reciters must have used gestures (such as facial expressions and movements of the body, hands, and feet) that encode the visual nature of the written 'soundless sense-signs'. In our example, the AE reciter may have acted like a woman giving birth 𓁐 to refer to all stressful situations that the readers might face in their everyday lives, in order to convey for the audience the visual writing of the verb 𓊵𓁐 Hms and its unusual ending soundless determinative. One might also imagine how humorous the reciter's bodily performance must have been for the hearts of his audience.

Translating the Untranslatability of Ancient Egyptian Writing

The creative change of determinatives may open up another critique of the fixed meanings we uncritically extract from modern AE dictionaries and how they are indefinite or undetermined, without full consideration of the metaphorical relationship between the used determinative and its particular textual context. In other words, AE words in modern dictionaries are not restricted by the given meanings; on the contrary, they have unlimited space for adding more semantic connotations based on the chosen determinative that has been carefully used to serve its unique textual context.

It is evident that the idea of having a fixed form of an AE word is a modern attitude related to our alphabetic languages and our modern desire to fix one written form of a word, and contradicts the AE writing practice with its various forms. That is why Gardiner wisely argued that our adopted terminology is far from being accurate in describing the 'visual inimitability' of AE writing:

> Such facts as these go to show the impossibility of a hard and fast classification of the uses of signs. Ideographic uses shade off into phonetic, and there are degrees and varieties within the two main groups of sense-sign (ideogram) and sound-sign (phonogram). We have, on occasion, found it convenient to employ the terms "semi-ideographic" and "semi-phonetic," as well as the term "phonetic determinative"... The objection to the term "determinative," which is nevertheless too convenient to discard, was stated in §23, OBS. We shall also make frequent use of the term "abbreviation," though this is open to the objection that signs so described, ex. 𓋾 HqA "chief," often represent the original spelling, later amplified by the addition of phonetic and other elements, ex. 𓋾𓈇𓀀𓀁. To sum up, the terminology adopted by us is not intended to bear too technical or too precise an interpretation.[44]

He was asking the modern reader to be sensitive when observing how the AE writer could have had many choices, using his own visual writing to highlight or specify what he wanted to imply. Such sensitivity to the metaphorical role of the 'sense-signs' and their intentionality may lead the modern reader to obtain new insights into AE literary techniques. We can deconstruct the modern dismissive attitude towards the visual literariness of AE writing. In doing so, we reveal that the text is using techniques that we now associate with visual-literary art. The conventions that govern their visual interactions are not yet fully acknowledged and can easily be overlooked due to the hegemonic influence of our alphabetic knowledge. This approach is perfectly illustrated by Christopher Eyre's understanding of AE literature and how he overlooks the 'visual communication' of AE writing:

> Egyptian literature was not obviously intended for private, personal reading, or for private study. Its structures, forms, and genres are those of an aural communication to a hearer — a performance, in the widest range of meaning that word can carry — and not of visual communication in writing to a reader. We should not talk of a "reading" of Egyptian literature; not in the narrow literal sense of that word, and only metaphorically in the academic sense.[45]

By following such hypotheses, the modern reader is encouraged to impose the current alphabetical preconceptions to evaluate the expected behaviour of AE readers wrongly. Visual features play a significant role in stimulating the imagination of the reader during the reading process and enhance enjoyment and comprehension. They are written in a way that is visually engaging to offer the mind a new metaphorical sense and an enjoyable reading experience. Egyptologists have not dedicated sufficient effort to understand the world of determinatives inside the realm of visual literariness. Angela MacDonald confirms: 'The ability of determinatives to be either alternates or supplements to each other is another strand of their use that is not sufficiently addressed.'[46]

The close connection between 'reading' and 'seeing' in the AE language can be clearly shown in the verb mAA, which means to see, and implies both watching and reading the text carefully;[47] for instance, in one of the King's speeches with his vizier:

```
iw mAA.n Hm(.i)  sS pn nfr nfr rdi.n.k in.tw.f m stp m
hrw pn nfr n snDm ib n (issi) mAa xrw mAa xrw
```
*My majesty **saw** this beautiful, beautiful **writing** that you were asked to bring to the palace on this beautiful day to make happy the heart of the king Issi, justified justified.*

```
mrr.i Hm(.i) mAA sS.k pn r xt nb
```
*My majesty loved **seeing** your **writing** more than anything else.[48]*

Apparently, 'seeing' and 'reading' the AE text were being signified without any distinction, which in turn confirms the importance of the overlooked visual aspects of the 'hieroglyphs' in understanding the literary reading process of any AE text. In the English-speaking world, by contrast, the verbs 'hear' and 'sound' are frequently used in written communication. In emails, phrases such as 'It is good to **hear** from you' and 'Your ideas **sound** more logical to me' are commonly used, which in turn reflects the closeness of alphabetic writing to speech. However, the situation in AE writing is different as the intended meaning of AE words cannot be fully encapsulated in its alphabetic transliteration; this overlooks the inimitable visual materiality of AE writing. As Gracia Zamacona explains:

> Alphabetic signs are hints that the reader recovers: they come from the writer's hand, and they belong to it. In contrast, hieroglyphic signs are entities that the reader must get through: they are in the written text, and they belong to it. In other words, hieroglyphic signs are entities with a permanent real existence, which happen also to be readable, while alphabetic signs are elements of reading whose real existence is momentary, as they merely last the time it takes to read a given sign: their existence is exhausted in its very function.[49]

The AE writers knew how to train and amuse the eyes of their readers. The pictorial realism of AE writing offered its writers many options for visually communicating with native readers. Each repeated word has a different semantic life via the dynamic engagement between the used determinative and the described context. It seems that the modern definition of 'visual poetry' can offer some good analytical implements for better understanding the shared space between visual and verbal layers in AE writing. Willard Bohn defines 'visual poetry' simply as:

> POETRY THAT is meant to be seen — poetry that presupposes a viewer as well as reader. Combining visual and verbal elements, it not only appeals to the reader's intellect but arrests his or her gaze. In one sense, to be sure, every poem is designed to be seen, since the eye must process the word before the mind can interpret them. ... In every instance, visual recognition can never escape its material origins. In every instance, visual recognition precedes verbal comprehension.[50]

The determinatives attached to a word reveal the inherent possibilities for linking the usual meaning of the word with new contexts due to its visual complexity. With the help of the textual context, readers could understand the word in new ways. Only the textual context could explain the visual variations of each word. The AE determinative system is unique in its extreme richness and is the main factor of the multivalent meanings of each AE word. The AE writers creatively used these determinatives to stimulate the visual memory of their readers. In the case of AE writing, modern translations can easily become misleading. Translators and readers have to remind themselves that they deal with AE content via a deceptive translation and alphabetic transliteration, which only reflects half of the meaning that was incorporated in the visual layer.

Translators should discuss visual untranslatability when they try to generate a translation theory that is sensitive to the aesthetic norms of AE writing. Acknowledging the untranslated elements is the first step in producing a translation that will reflect the hidden beauty of the source text. The British poet and translator Peter Robinson argues that being aware of what cannot be translated, culturally or linguistically, paves the way for a transparent translation. He claims that 'the strict impossibility of translating poetry is at the same time the condition making poetry need to be translated and what makes its translation an activity that can practically be done'.[51] I would argue that the aim of revealing what is untranslatable is to let modern readers enjoy and understand the beautiful wonders of the source text as intimately and profoundly as the natives once did. Stylistic analysis can inform us about how literary meanings are produced and how the natives formulated their own world of literariness. Haun Saussy convincingly argues:

> If it were simply possible to translate one into the other, to find for every point of the one a corresponding point in the ontology of the other, the process would not be particularly interesting; it's when the whole organization of the discourses is different that mediating the media becomes real work.[52]

The rhetoric of poetic untranslatability should seek a method of grounding comparative and world literature in the stylistic contexts of the source text in order to generate a valuable re-reading experience. Stylistic analysis is the time machine that allows the ardent reader to travel inside the various dimensions of the intended meaning.

Acknowledgements

I am indebted to Matthew Reynolds for inviting me to participate in the 2015 conference of Oxford Comparative Criticism and Translation (OCCT) and for the insightful criticism he offered on various drafts of this article. It was a great pleasure to engage with his beautiful critical mind. I am thankful also to my colleagues who generously offered their constructive criticism: Stephen Quirke (UCL), James Elkins (School of the Art Institute of Chicago), Donald Reid (University of Washington), Annmarie Drury (City University of New York), Rune Nyord (Emory University), Edmund Meltzer (Pacific Graduate Institute), Filip Taterka (Polish Academy of Sciences), Martin Fitzenreiter (Bonn University), Muhammad Taghian (Helwan University), Rebecca Gould (University of Birmingham), Stefan Sperl (SOAS) and Rita Copeland (University of Pennsylvania). I want to thank also Benjamin Costello for his insightful proofreading and comments.

Works Cited

ALLEN, JAMES, *The Debate Between a Man and His Soul: A Masterpiece of Ancient Egyptian Literature* (Leiden: Brill, 2011)

ANTELME RUTH-SCHUMANN, and STÉPHANE ROSSINI, *Illustrated Hieroglyphics Handbook*, English translation (New York: Sterling Publishing Co, 2002)

ASSMANN, JAN, 'Creation through hieroglyphs: the cosmic grammatology of Ancient Egypt', in S. La Porta, and D Shulman (eds), *The Poetics of Grammar and the Metaphysics of Sound and Sign* (Leiden: Jerusalem Studies in Religion and Culture, 2007), pp. 17–34

BLACK, JEREMY ET AL., eds, *A Concise Dictionary of Akkadian* (Wiesbaden: Harrassowitz, 1999)

BOHN, WILLARD, *Modern Visual Poetry* (Newark: University of Delaware Press, 2001)

CALLENDER, JOHN, *Middle Egyptian*, Afroasiatic Dialects 2 (Malibu: Undena Publications, 1975)

CONTARDI, FEDERICO, 'Egyptian Terms used to Indicate the Act of Reading: an investigation about the act of reading in the Egyptian society', in F. M. Fales and G. F. Grassi (eds), *CAMSEMUD 2007: Proceedings of the 13th Italian Meeting of Afro-Asiatic Linguistics* (Padova: Sargon, 2010), pp. 261–69

CORRIENTE, FEDERICO, 'Coptic Loanwords of Egyptian Arabic in Comparison With the Parallel Case of Romance Loanwords in Andalusi Arabic, With the True Egyptian Etymon of Al-Andalus', *Collectanea Christiana Orientalia* 5 (2008), 59–123.

ERMAN ADOLF and GRAPOW HERMANN. *Wörterbuch der ägyptischen Sprache*, 5 vols (Berlin: [s. n.], 1926–1931)

EYRE, CHRISTOPHER, 'The Practice of Literature: The Relationship between Content, Form, Audience and Performance', in *Ancient Egyptian Literature: Theory and Practice*, ed. by Roland Enmarch and Verena Lepper (Oxford: Oxford University Press, 2013), pp. 101–42

GARDINER, ALAN, 'The Instruction addressed to Kagemni and his Brethren', *Journal of Egyptian Archaeology* 32 (1946), 71–74

GARDINER, ALAN, *Egyptian Grammar, Being an Introduction to the Study of Hieroglyphs*, 3rd edn (London: Griffith Institute, Ashmolean Museum, 1957)

GOLDWASSER, ORLY, 'A Comparison between Classifier Language and Classifier Script: The Case of Ancient Egyptian' in *A Festschrift for Hans Jakob Polotsky*, ed. by G. Goldenberg and A. Shisha-Halevy (Jerusalem: Magnes Press, 2006), pp. 16–39

—— 'Cuneiform and Hieroglyphs in the Bronze Age: Script Contact and the Creation of New Scripts,' in *Pharoah's Land and Beyond: Ancient Egypt and Its Neighbors*, ed. by Pearce Paul Creasman and Richard H. Wilkinson (Oxford: Oxford University Press, 2017), pp. 183–93

GOULD, REBECCA, 'Inimitability versus Translatability: The Structure of Literary Meaning in Arabo-Persian Poetics,' *The Translator* 19. 1 (2013), 81–104

GRIFFITH, F. LL and W. M. FLINDERS PETRIE, *Two Hieroglyphic Papyri from Tanis* (London: Trübner and Co., 1889)

GRIFFITH, FRANCIS, *A Collection of Hieroglyphs: A Contribution to the History of Egyptian Writing* (London: Egypt Exploration Fund, 1898)

HIGGINS, DICK, *Pattern Poetry: Guide to an Unknown Literature* (New York: SUNY Press, 1987)

HINDS, MARTIN and BADAWI EL-SAID, *A Dictionary of Egyptian Arabic: Arabic — English* (Beirut: Librairie du Liban, 1986)

IGNATOV, SERGEI, 'Word and Image in Ancient Egypt', *Bulgarian Institute of Egyptology: The Journal of Egyptological Studies* 1 (2004), 9–32

JUNGE, FRIEDRICH, *'Emphasis' and Sentential Meaning in Middle Egyptian*, Göttinger Orientforschungen (Wiesbaden: Otto Harrassowitz, 1989)

KEY, ALEXANDER, 'Kavya: Prospects for a Comparative Poetics', *Journal of Comparative Studies of South Asia, Africa and the Middle East (CSSAAME)*, 38. 1 (2018), 163–70.

KILITO, ABDELFATTAH, *Thou shalt not Speak my Language*, trans. by Hassan Waïl (Syracuse: Syracuse University Press, 2018)

KOCH, ROLAND, *Die Erzählung des Sinuhe* (Brussels: Fondation Égyptologique Reine Élisabeth, 1990)

LOPRIENO, ANTONIO, 'Is the Egyptian Hieroglyphic Determinative Chosen or Prescribed?', in *Philosophers and Hieroglyphs*, ed. by Lucia Morra and Carla Bazzanella (Turin: Rosenberg & Seller, 2003), pp. 237–50

MCDONALD, ANGELA, REVIEW OF ORLY GOLDWASSER, *Lovers, Prophets and Giraffes: Wor(l)d Classification in Ancient Egypt*, *Lingua Aegyptia*, 12 (2004), 235–44

MELTZER, EDMUND, 'Hieratic is Beautiful: Ancient Egyptian Calligraphy Revisited', in *Writing Systems and Cognition: Perspectives from Psychology, Physiology, Linguistics, and Semiotics*, ed. by W.C. Watt (Boston: Kluwer Academic Publishers, 1994), 293–301

PARKINSON, RICHARD, *The Tale of the Eloquent Peasant* (Oxford: Griffith Institute, 1991)

PARKINSON, RICHARD, 'Literary Form and the Tale of the Eloquent Peasant' in *Journal of Egyptian Archaeology*, 78 (1992), 163–78

QUIRKE, STEPHEN, *Egyptian Literature 1800 BC: Questions and Readings* (London: Golden House Publications, 2004)

RASHWAN, HANY, 'Philosophical and Literary Argumentation Methods in the Ancient Egyptian Rhetorical Systems', in *Argumentation and Reasoned Action: Proceedings of the first European Conference on Argumentation and Reasoned Action, Lisbon, 2015*, 2 vols, ed. by Dima Mohammed and Marcin Lewiński (London: College Publications, 2016), pp. 849–63

ROBINSON, PETER, *Poetry and Translation: The Art of the Impossible* (Liverpool: Liverpool University Press, 2010)

SAUSSY, HAUN, 'When Translation Isn't Just Translating: Between Languages and Disciplines', *Recherche Littéraire / Literary Research*, 34 (Été 2018 / Summer 2018), 43–57

SETHE, KURT, *Urkunden der 18 Dynastie*, Abteilung IV, Heft 13–16 (Leipzig: Historische-biographische Urkunden, 1909), pp. 937–1226

SETHE, KURT, *Urkunden des Alten Reichs*, Erster Band, Urkunden des Ägyptischen Altertums Abteilung I, Heft 1–4. (Leipzig: J.C. Hinrichs'sche Buchhandlung,1933)

SHOHAT ELLA and ROBERT STAM, *Unthinking Eurocentrism: Multiculturalism and the Media* (London: Routledge, 1994)

TEETER, EMILY, '80. Funerary Stela' in *Visible Language, Inventions of Writing in the Ancient Middle East and Beyond*, ed. by Christopher Woods, Emily Teeter and Geoff Emberling, OIMP 32 (Chicago: The Oriental Institute of the University of Chicago, 2010), 149–51

ZAMACONA, CARLOS, 'The Two Inner Directions of the Ancient Egyptian Script', *Birmingham Egyptology Journal*, 3 (2015), 9–23

Notes to Chapter 3

1. This project has received funding from the European Union's Horizon 2020 Research and Innovation Program under ERC-2017-STG Grant Agreement No 759346 and is part of the 'Global Literary Theory' project at the University of Birmingham.
2. Dick Higgins, *Pattern Poetry: Guide to an Unknown Literature* (New York: SUNY Press, 1987), pp. 5–17.
3. Antonio Loprieno, 'Is the Egyptian Hieroglyphic Determinative Chosen or Prescribed?' in *Philosophers and Hieroglyphs*, ed. by Lucia Morra and Carla Bazzanella (Turin: Rosenberg & Seller, 2003), pp. 237–50 (p. 238).
4. The writing system of the AE language is similar to the Hebrew and Arabic *Abjad*, in terms of partly excluding the vocal movements *Harkāt* (roughly can be translated as 'vowels') and recording the consonants.
5. Emily Teeter, '80. Funerary Stela', in *Visible Language, Inventions of Writing in the Ancient Middle East and Beyond*, ed. by Christopher Woods, Emily Teeter and Geoff Emberling, OIMP 32 (Chicago: The Oriental Institute of the University of Chicago, 2010), pp. 149–51 (p. 152).
6. Sergei Ignatov, 'Word and Image in Ancient Egypt', *Journal of Egyptological Studies*, 1 (2004), 9–32 (pp. 9–10).
7. This term combines two Greek words: *phōnē* 'sound' and *gramma* 'writing', to mean literally the sound of writing. Gardiner defines the AE 'phonograms' or 'sound-signs' as 'signs used for spelling, which although originally ideograms and in many cases still also employed elsewhere as such, have secondarily acquired sound-values'. See Alan Gardiner, *Egyptian Grammar, Being an Introduction to the Study of Hieroglyphs*, 3rd edn (London: Griffith Institute, Ashmolean Museum, 1957), §6, p.8.
8. Roland Koch. *Die Erzählung des Sinuhe* (Brussels: Fondation Égyptologique Reine Élisabeth, 1990), p. 24.
9. Gardiner, *Egyptian Grammar*, §23, p.31.
10. Gardiner, *Egyptian Grammar*, OBS § 23, p.31.
11. Gardiner, *Egyptian Grammar*, § 54, p. 49.
12. Gardiner, *Egyptian Grammar*, §58, pp. 51–52.

13. In this chapter, I use examples written in both hieroglyphic and hieratic scripts without any discrimination. The modern dismissive attitude towards the hieratic script — as a fast way of writing that lacks the full visual details of the hieroglyphic script — has made it easy to overlook the fact that both hieroglyphic and hieratic scripts are part of the same language and share a unique visual mechanism. There are a fair amount of visual choices, in both scripts, that confirm such harmony. In his insightful article 'Hieratic is Beautiful', Edmund Meltzer argues for a different approach: he analyzes the overlooked visual aesthetics of the hieratic script against the automatic judgment that is always coined with using the term 'cursive' in our alphabetic writings. See Edmund Meltzer, 'Hieratic is Beautiful: Ancient Egyptian Calligraphy Revisited', in *Writing Systems and Cognition: Perspectives from Psychology, Physiology, Linguistics, and Semiotics*, ed. by W.C. Watt, (Boston: Kluwer Academic Publishers, 1994), pp. 293–301(p. 297).
14. Kurt Sethe, *Urkunden der 18 Dynastie*. Abteilung IV, Heft 13–16 (Leipzig: Historische-biographische Urkunden, 1909), p. 1193.
15. Loprieno, 'Is the Egyptian Hieroglyphic Determinative Chosen or Prescribed?', p. 237.
16. Jan Assmann, 'Creation through Hieroglyphs: the Cosmic Grammatology of Ancient Egypt', in *The Poetics of Grammar and the Metaphysics of Sound and Sign*, ed by S. La Porta and D. Shulman (Leiden; Boston: Jerusalem studies in religion and culture, 6, 2007), pp. 17–34 (p. 33).
17. The history of the short story genre is still narrated from a Eurocentric perspective, where scholars tend to credit ancient Greece for its early creation. Unconsciously, such methodologies support the fallacy of there being a straightforward line between the heritage of ancient Greece and the modern colonial powers of Europe. If we discuss the history of literary genres, we have to avoid such chauvinistic claims that intentionally overlook the accomplishments of other ancient cultures, and how they were instrumental for the Greeks in developing their achievements. 'Eurocentric discourse projects a linear historical trajectory leading from classical Greece (constructed as "pure," "Western," and "democratic") to imperial Rome and then to the metropolitan capitals of Europe and the US. It renders history as a sequence of empires: Pax Romana, Pax Hispanica, Pax Britannica. Pax Americana. In all cases, Europe, alone and unaided, is seen as the "motor" for progressive historical change.' Ella Shohat and Robert Stam, *Unthinking Eurocentrism: Multiculturalism and the Media* (London: Routledge, 1994), p. 2.
18. See Hany Rashwan, 'Philosophical and Literary Argumentation Methods in the Ancient Egyptian Rhetorical Systems', in *Argumentation and Reasoned Action: Proceedings of the first European Conference on Argumentation and Reasoned Action, Lisbon, 2015*, ed. by Dima Mohammed and Marcin Lewiński, 2 vols (London: College Publications, 2016), II, pp. 849–63 (p.860).
19. James Allen, *The Debate Between a Man and His Soul: A Masterpiece of Ancient Egyptian Literature* (Leiden: Brill, 2011), pp. 282–87.
20. I am using the hyphenations in my literal translations to show that many words are used to express the semantic or visual connotations of one AE word, showing the differences between alphabetic and image writing.
21. By repeating the subject, the writer establishes adequate means to chain the narrative constructions to the hero's identity. See Friedrich Junge, *Emphasis' and Sentential Meaning in Middle Egyptian*, Gottinger Orientforschungen (Wiesbaden: Otto Harrassowitz, 1989), pp. 14–28.
22. Stephen Quirke, *Egyptian Literature 1800 BC: Questions and Readings* (London: Golden House Publications, 2004), p. 28.
23. The reader can look at the numerous translations of this verse on this website: <http://islamawakened.com/quran/20/68/> (accessed 10/01/2018).
24. Rebecca Gould, 'Inimitability versus Translatability: The Structure of Literary Meaning in Arabo-Persian Poetics,' *The Translator*, 19. 1 (2013), 81–104 (p.90).
25. Alexander Key, 'Kavya: Prospects for a Comparative Poetics', *Journal of Comparative Studies of South Asia, Africa and the Middle East*, 38. 1 (2018), 163–70 (p.166).
26. Abdelfattah Kilito, *Thou shalt not Speak my Language*, trans. by and Hassan Waïl (Syracuse: Syracuse University Press, 2018), pp. 27–37.
27. *Wörterbuch der ägyptischen Sprache*, ed. by Adolf Erman and Hermann Grapow, 12 vols (Berlin: [s. n.] 1926–1931), III, p. 369.
28. Federico Corriente, 'Coptic Loanwords of Egyptian Arabic in Comparison With the Parallel Case of Romance Loanwords in Andalusi Arabic, With the True Egyptian Etymon of

Al-Andalus', *Collectanea Christiana Orientalia* 5 (2008), 59–123. Federico Corriente supported the semantic link between the ancient and modern Egyptian words of Xnnw and xwnn as a 'storage space forward in a wooden boat'. Moreover, he suggested an Andalusian Arabic cognate 'khinn' that was mentioned by the linguist Ibn Hisham al-Lakhmi to mean 'hold of a ship', saying: 'It is phonetically close and semantically akin to that meaning of khunn, as sailors used to turn their boats over and use them as shelters during the night: this might point to a South Arabian origin, a frequent ingredient of all Western Arabic dialects. People from South Arabia were highly civilized and familiar with ships, agriculture, domestic animal breeding, etc., and although they were soon and almost thoroughly linguistically assimilated by Northern Arabs, they kept some traces of their former language, which can be detected in Andalusi, Maghribian, Egyptian and Yemenite Arabic dialects until now' (email correspondence on 27 June 2012).

29. John Callender, *Middle Egyptian, Afroasiatic Dialects 2* (Malibu: Undena Publications, 1975), p. 10.
30. Martin Hinds and el-Said Badawi, *A Dictionary of Egyptian Arabic: Arabic–English* (Beirut: Librairie du Liban, 1986), p. 268.
31. *A Concise Dictionary of Akkadian*, ed. by Jeremy Black, Andrew George and Nicholas Postgate (Wiesbaden: Harrassowitz, 1999), p. 120. The dictionary suggests that this Akkadian word is of West Semitic origin, because many Mari letters show influence of local Semitic speech on written Akkadian.
32. On the Eloquent Peasant's irony and sarcasm, see Richard Parkinson, 'Literary Form and the Tale of the Eloquent Peasant', *Journal of Egyptian Archaeology* 78 (1992), 163–78 (p.175).
33. Richard Parkinson. *The Tale of the Eloquent Peasant* (Oxford: Griffith Institute, 1991), p. 26.
34. Francis Griffith, *A Collection of Hieroglyphs: A Contribution to the History of Egyptian Writing* (London: Egypt Exploration Fund, 1898), p. 3.
35. *Wörterbuch der ägyptischen Sprache*, III, p. 76.
36. Ruth-Schumann Antelme and Stéphane Rossini, *Illustrated Hieroglyphics Handbook* (New York: Sterling Publishing Co, 2002), p. 104.
37. Orly Goldwasser, 'A Comparison between Classifier Language and Classifier Script: The Case of Ancient Egyptian' in: *A Festschrift for Hans Jakob Polotsky*, ed. by G. Goldenberg and A. Shisha-Halevy (Jerusalem: Magnes Press, 2006), pp. 16–39 (p. 17).
38. Orly Goldwasser, 'Cuneiform and Hieroglyphs in the Bronze Age: Script Contact and the Creation of New Scrtipts', in *Pharoah's Land and Beyond: Ancient Egypt and Its Neighbors*, ed. by P. Pearce, P. Creasman and R. H. Wilkinson (Oxford: Oxford University Press, 2017), pp. 183–93 (p. 183).
39. Alan Gardiner, 'The instruction addressed to Kagemni and his Brethren', *Journal of Egyptian Archaeology*, 32 (1946), Plat XIV, lines 1.3–5.
40. Gardiner, 'The instruction addressed to Kagemni', Plat XIV, 1,3a.
41. Gardiner, 'The instruction addressed to Kagemni', Plat XIV, lines 1.7–8
42. The metaphorical usage of the contrasted verbs aHa.sn (their standing) and Hms.sn (their sitting) is a literal equivalent to the Arabic metaphorical expression قيامهم وقعودهم, where the meaning is extended to express every daily activity, especially in the Quranic verse: اللهَ قِيَامًا وَقُعُودًا وَعَلَىٰ جُنُوبِهِمْ الَّذِينَ يَذْكُرُونَ (alladhīna yadhqrūna Allah qyāmān wa qʿūdān wa ʿalā gnūbihm) which literally means 'Those who remember the God while standing, sitting and [lying] on their sides'. (Q3:191)
43. Gardiner, 'The instruction addressed to Kagemni', Plat XIV, lines 2.5–7.
44. Gardiner, *Egyptian Grammar*, p. 440.
45. Christopher Eyre, 'The Practice of Literature: The Relationship between Content, Form, Audience and Performance', in *Ancient Egyptian Literature: Theory and Practice*, ed. by Roland Enmarch and Verena Lepper (Oxford: Oxford Univeristy Press and British Academy, 2013), pp. 101–42 (p. 103).
46. Angela McDonald, review of Orly Goldwasser, *Lovers, Prophets and Giraffes: Wor(l)d Classification in Ancient Egypt*, in *Lingua Aegyptia* 12 (2004), 235–44, p. 237.
47. Federico Contardi, 'Egyptian Terms used to Indicate the Act of Reading: an investigation about the act of reading in the Egyptian society', in F. M. Fales and G. F. Grassi (eds), *CAMSEMUD 2007: Proceedings of the 13th Italian Meeting of Afro-Asiatic Linguistics* (Padova: Sargon, 2010), pp.

261–69 (p. 266).
48. Kurt Sethe, *Urkunden des Alten Reichs*, Erster Band, Urkunden des Ägyptischen Altertums Abteilung 1, Hft. 1–4. (Leipzig: J.C. Hinrichs'sche Buchhandlung, 1933), p. 179.
49. Carlos Zamacona, 'The Two Inner Directions of the Ancient Egyptian Script', *Birmingham Egyptology Journal*, 3, (2015), 9–23 (p. 17).
50. Willard Bohn, *Modern Visual Poetry* (Newark: University of Delaware Press, 2001), p. 15.
51. Peter Robinson, *Poetry and Translation: The Art of the Impossible* (Liverpool: Liverpool University Press, 2010), p. 82.
52. Haun Saussy, 'When Translation Isn't Just Translating: Between Languages and Disciplines', *Recherche Littéraire / Literary Research*, 34 (Été 2018 / Summer 2018), 43–57 (p. 54).

CHAPTER 4

❖

[Mirroring] Events at the Sense Horizon: Translation over Time

John Cayley

In common parlance, 'languages' are treated as identifiable, bounded entities. They are also, in a variety of real-world circumstances, associated with actual geographies, and — embracing human history — with their geopolitics. For these and other reasons, conceptually and metaphorically, there is a widespread assumption that languages exist 'within' countries and regions, and that they have margins, edgelands, borders, limits, boundaries, horizons, and so on. The translation of 'translation' is across such boundaries and liminalities. When discussing translation as (or of) process, the usefulness of these metaphors should give us pause.[1] Translation, especially literary translation, is addressed, typically, to an integral, finished textual artefact but, whereas the authorship of such work may be received as a mystery or revelation (of writerly 'genius', for example), translation is, necessarily — in all but the most extraordinary of circumstances — *subsequent* to the work. It demands the skills of a special type of language user, someone who has become conversant, *over some time*, with more than one language, and someone who must labour to produce the translation, *taking time* that is obvious (not mysterious) to us all, time for reading and time for a particular, regularly accountable variety of writing. *Translation is inherently temporal.* It is a time-consuming practice. Between languages, it is a back and forth. It may be reiterated, revised, and 'repeated,' most commonly by *subsequent* translation(s) of the same work. Translation is dedicated, precisely, to transgressions of the bounded geographies from which we set out, but it would be as pertinent to say that, more than through space, it is time through which translation travels in order to perform its transgressions.

Once they have produced their completed artefacts, however, practices of translation leave us with linguistic entities whose integrity and identity appear to be intact and untroubled. For the reader or interlocutor — particularly a monolingual subject reading or listening in the host language — conventionally translated linguistic artefacts appear to have arrived, albeit as guests, within the reader's horizons of understanding.[2] The translated work is inside the integral, bounded territory of its host language. It presents itself as equally far from any horizons of significance or affect as any other text that we may read within the host.

These circumstances, a function of the pragmatics of reading, are reinforced, prejudicially, by literature and its material culture. It is difficult to exaggerate the degree to which educated, Western, common-sense understandings — and even the *science* — of linguistic phenomena, particularly linguistic artefacts, including aesthetic artefacts of language, are determined by our expectation that such things will be literature in the sense of 'printable' and thus also subject to qualification and appreciation as 'literary'.[3] Linguistic artefacts are commonly expected to share a discourse and value system, and to have the characteristics of things that are literary. They are expected to be the product of literary practices, chiefly, of course, writing. Aesthetic linguistic artefacts are most commonly expected to be texts. Regarded collectively, we call these texts literature, literature being that part of linguistic activity that we believe to be worthy of study and appreciation. To a significant extent, this literature becomes definitive of culture as a whole. All this despite the fact that textual practices of writing are, precisely, historical. Their very adoption brings human history into existence. And although we may only have come to this certain knowledge quite recently, historically enabled science now tells us that our history is preceded by thousands of years of human cultural activity including, in particular, linguistic practices for which we have little or no — literary, historical — record. Before history there was as much language as there has ever been, some portion of which must have been important and aesthetic, and yet this language had no need for history or for literature. All it needed to exist and flourish was a language animal.

The voice, and Walter Ong's primary orality, preceded and presaged any origin of writing as such.[4] Presaged, also in the sense of troubling the very possibility of linguistic origins. Derridean grammatology refers the logic persuading us that writing is the supplement of speech to a fundamental logic of the supplement as such, the supplementarity of the language that we have. At the horizons of history, there are origin*s* (plural) of writing practices, but no *origin* as such, no more than there is an origin for any particular natural language, while any supposed origin of language itself is, even for the most confident scientist, pushed back beyond a more distant horizon the crossing of which erases human articulation and makes it literally impossible to know, with any kind of detailed certainty, when or how language began.[5] And although we can say that writing came into existence and regular use five or six thousand years ago, we also know that these practices, by contrast with those relating to linguistic aurality, are not innate behaviour for the human language animal in terms of evolved, phylogenetically realized capacities.[6] We must learn to write and to read text in the process of our enculturation, as part of a curriculum, an education in very specific, divergent, and located cultural practices.

Both before conventional practices of writing and in their absence, there have been and continue to be practices of translation. The Derridean critique of Lévi-Strauss's structuralist engagements with writing in *Of Grammatology*, for example, relies on the analysis of linguistic events in more than one language, but in circumstances where at least one of the linguistic cultures being addressed is non-literate. Translation took place, based on Lévi-Strauss's account, prior to any written record of this translation. It follows that, when we say that a translation has arrived within the horizons of a particular natural language, in such circumstances, any theory of translation must be able to account for such translation prior to and without regard for its expression in some specific material support which happens to be valorized by one or other natural linguistic culture (usually that of the colonizing host language). We cannot rely on any specific writing practice in order to understand or certify translation. The anthropologist's transcription of a translation is not the translation. This is an important point to make in order that we escape, conceptually and theoretically, the geography and gravity of literature while continuing to acknowledge that translation is taking or has taken *place*, the respected and respectable place, of a guest, within the host language.

Even when it is a matter of literary translation, when there is a text to work from in the guest language, the mere production of a corresponding text in the host does not guarantee that translation has taken place. A phonological or phonetic transcription is not usually considered to be a translation.[7] Neither is a so-called literal translation generally accepted as adequate, particularly for literary purposes. The further requirement that a translator should do more than produce a literal translation reinforces the point that a translation cannot be identified with any specific text, let alone with any transcription in a specific material support, typically the result of a writing practice. The translation is expected to capture qualities and characteristics of the guest that may be attributable to style, and which are often discussed in terms of 'voice'. If a translation is successful, we read and 'hear'-by-reading the voice of a guest author in our own language, the language of the reader, sometimes a new voice, and sometimes the well-remembered voice of an author who has been translated before, and is already a part of 'our' literature.

This association of the sited integrity and identity of linguistic artefacts, including translation, with *voice* is not mere metaphor. It is substantive. Voice is as close as we get to a name for the material/immaterial substance of language. This is not the voice of actual particular human voices although the characteristics of sited integrity and identity required by linguistic objects are dependent on the fact that voice and actual individual voices possess these characteristics. It is not Platonic idealism to acknowledge that there is a pragmatic necessity for virtual linguistic forms and traces, at any and all levels of linguistic structure, including a prospective translation, to fall away, gesturally and formally, from liminality and (unintended) ambiguity into sited integrity and identity, away from any margins, borders, and edgelands so as to enter into the heartland of a language. One name for this condition of linguistic phenomena is the *ideality* that enables repetition, expressed — produced and received — as *voice*:

> ... it must be constituted, repeated, and expressed in a medium that does not impair the presence and self-presence of the acts that intend it: a medium that preserves at once the *presence of the object* in front of the intuition and the *presence to oneself*, the absolute proximity of the acts to themselves. Since the ideality of the object is only its being-for a non-empirical consciousness, it can be expressed only in an element whose phenomenality does not have the form of mundanity. *The voice is the name of this element. The voice hears itself.*[8]

Forms of voice are produced and received by us, but until a form is readable, it is not language. This movement from gestural to readable is also the movement from actual events and processes of production to the finished inscription of a reiterable trace with respect to the conventions of one of the world's hospitable languages.

I am speaking of reading in a special sense now, as a word for what we do, both when we hear-and-understand and when we scan-and-'hear'-and-understand. The French *entendre* enfolds both hearing and understanding.[9] It does this straightforwardly when used in relation to language in aurality and it can also be applied, in French, to an experience that results from everyday practices of reading. In a complementary manner, older usages of English *read* are perfectly capable of invoking to-hear-and-understand, given that 'to read' was also often to make an informed persuasive guess about the meaning of symbols and gestures. In contemporary English, we still read the 'signs' in many situations and across a wide range of media including the conversations and discourses of aurality.

The first characteristic of the particular concept of reading that I want us to bring to these comments on translation is its agnosticism with respect to any support media for language. While acknowledging that the material culture of literature predominates in practices and discourses of translation, I argue that any theory of translation demands a poststructuralist perspective, one that has, after Derrida, understood writing as, more properly, *voice*, as (always already) the originary supplement that brings language into being. Actual human voices, which are equally the traces (a 'writing' or Derridean archi-writing) of *voice*, bring language into being in precisely the same manner.[10] The significance of this media agnosticism will become apparent shortly.

Secondly, we will qualify our concept of reading as grammaleptic. Grammalepsis is a word for both the process and the moment when a material and formal gesture of (potential, virtual) affect and significance shifts and moves, indeed we may say, *translates* so as, suddenly, to pass over the threshold of readability (and reiterability) where it is seized and grasped as such, as significance-and-affect-rendering language. The seizure, *-lepsis*, renders a *grammé*, a readable trace. Reading and making language is grammalepsy.

I hope that readers of Derrida will recognize in this definition of grammalepsis, my attempt to capture certain aspects of the meaning and force of *différance* in a form that renders it of practicable use to language artists and critics; translators and translation theorists. Whereas différance, it seems, needs must reserve itself for the deconstruction of the metaphysics of presence, grammalepsis offers itself as a name for what happens — continually, and whenever there is *any* event of language — when new meanings become and, at the same time, co-create actual language at any level of linguistic structure. Crucially, grammalepsis refers to a moment and a passage of both time and travel over a metaphorically spatial threshold. Thus, it does also name the passage from temporalization to spacing in language philosophical terms. We can treat grammalepsis, comfortably, as a word like any other, as opposed to 'différance' which, explicitly, paradoxically resists and insists on a refusal of this catastrophe. In pragmatic terms, grammalepsis names what happens as we are suddenly able to read, grammaleptically, what was not readable before, including within 'différance' itself: the inaudible 'A' (and the letter's capitalized form is readably there, even if it's not visible) is *voiced* within us and tells us that we are no longer reading 'difference'.[11] Any signified presence of accountable, formal, structural difference has suddenly been deferred ... to infinity, as a philosopher, following Derrida, would say.[12] In every event of language, moreover, the same process operates as grammalepsis. Manifestly, whenever we read a pun or we 'fill in' (read) an ellipsis, for example, or especially when we read a phrase or a sentence and we recognize a *voice*, a distinctive style — and we do this every single time we read — then we encounter grammalepsis and we read ... grammaleptically.

The horizons of a natural language are also grammaleptic in character. Suggestive aspects of the process and moment of grammalepsis manifest themselves, as already stated, at all levels of linguistic structure, including what is, pragmatically, the highest level, that of the 'natural' language. Any specific plurality of languages, any specific set of named languages, is pure construction, the result of historical contingencies, political economic prejudice, and arbitrary — arbitrarily shared — conventional behaviour. Nonetheless, all human language animals experience grammaleptic horizons of their receptive and productive linguistic practices more or less corresponding to these conventions, a metaphoric 'within' that they can read and understand and a 'without' that they cannot. I call these horizons grammaleptic because there is no continuous gradient across the liminal regions where the horizon is encountered.[13] Material forms — in the signifying substance of *voice* — may be produced and received in these liminal regions 'close' to one or another horizon but these are only ever read, grammaleptically, as on one side or another, at a point when the form may be received as grammé, as a trace of language, a writing (in the sense of Derridean archi-writing) in one or other language. The seizure, -lepsis, is sudden and irreversible. A form, once readable, does not become unreadable.[14] Or else there is simply a refusal and failure, a collapse of the form into nonsense (non-sense) which, for the speaker who attempted to project their voice over the horizon, is still 'within' their language, while for readers across this horizon the form is received, if it is perceived at all, as unreadable nonsense. There may be a continuous gradient in the abstract morphology of the voice's material form, but the reading of a form on one side or the other of any linguistic horizon is always grammaleptic. This helps to account for our sense that there are regions of complete incomprehension, even as and when situations make intentions clear while all attempts at linguistic performance remain meaningless, and also for both the strange silences of voice or the absurd, pointless, repetitions at increasing volume that can occur when people meet at the horizons of one another's languages.

Voice as I am using it here is the 'element' or medium by means of which language propagates. It is voice that is required to be read grammaleptically. Text is also voice in this usage, so long as it bears the traces of voice and yields to the potentialities of différance as well as difference. When we are speaking of a situation in which the everyday human voice is attempting to produce a linguistic event, temporalization is *actually* at play. To speak takes time and the manner of speaking along with all that is implied by the timbre of the voice in terms of identity and sited integrity, all this can be conveyed in the actual temporalization of the events.

In the case of text — published as readable in the everyday sense — temporalization has been stunned and must be read back into linguistic events by the reader. In the material culture of literature, this is both difficult and downplayed. A naïve reader confronted by a text that has a reputation, one that presupposes a voice, has little chance of appreciating, of *taking in*, this voice at their first reading. Saying as much implies the temporalization that is both implicit and realized in the pedagogical and critical traditions of literature: their *history*, the expectation that readers will *take time* to study and appreciate, to recover the voice — an easy and often overlooked metaphor in traditional literary criticism, but here proposed as the very substance of linguistic affect and significance — the voice of the text.

It is important to state that grammaleptic reading does not reduce to the kind of construal that we derive from semantics, from dictionary definitions (very important, after all, to real-world practices of translation), or even from the comprehension of an 'aboutness' in what we are reading (in the case of poetry, for example, which need not be 'about' anything). Grammaleptic reading is not reading for semantics, paraphrase, or expository interpretation. None of these on their own or in any combination can be taken to exhaust the meaning, let alone the aesthetics, of any artefact, including artefacts of language. In what is nonetheless a grotesque simplification of an infinitely differentiated state of affairs, I speak of the *meaning* of language in terms of *significance* and *affect*. Whereas a major part (but certainly not all) of *significance* may well be accounted for by semantic analyses and dictionary definitions, that portion of meaning which I refer, pragmatically, to *affect* is not. A grammaleptic reading may result in the grasp, the understanding, of meanings that we may characterize as either or both significant or affective, but it is more important to focus on what grammaleptic reading performs in order to decide whether or not it has taken place. *Grammalepsis brings sense-bearing language into the world that is shared by both a reader and the author of the voice being read.* Grammaleptic reading occurs when language has been brought into being, not when we have recognized some kind of index to a definition or paraphrase.

I can, I believe, demonstrate grammaleptic reading along with its non-reliance on conventional understandings of semantics or aboutness by way of commentary on a wonderful language art performance, a piece which also amounts to a special practice of translation. In a series of videos, collectively entitled, *Babel Babble*, Nickolas Procopi juxtaposes, for each performance in the series, two interlocutors. One of these will attempt to teach a tongue twister in a language that they know to the other who does not. Aligning this situation with more conventional translation from guest to host languages, the 'teacher', here, is proposing that the 'learner' should extend their practice of language so as to become hospitable to the tongue twister, which will then take the place of a guest within the learner's practice. The roles and consequences of the practices concerned do not correspond in terms of an analogy or allegory of conventional translation. Nonetheless, an artefact of language is translated across certain horizons between two languages and the performance that realizes this event reveals processes of translation that would otherwise be hidden or disregarded.

Fig. 4.1. Still from *Babel Babble*, Nickolas Procopi, video performance, 2015. Courtesy of the artist. The 'teacher', Lu Tianqi, of the 'si shi si' Mandarin tongue twister is on the left. Procopi, on the right, is the 'learner'. Please refer to streamable videos, courtesy of the artist, from Brown University Library's Digital Repository. A short 54' clip: <https://repository.library.brown.edu/studio/item/bdr:768969>; a longer, 7"18' excerpt: <https://repository.library.brown.edu/studio/item/bdr:768968>

The teacher begins by vocalizing short phrases from the tongue twister that the learner repeats, phrase by phrase, from beginning to end of the entire twister. So far so good. It is not particularly difficult to repeat very short bursts of strange syllables. The particular twister on which we will concentrate and from which I quote, is sixteen syllables in Mandarin Chinese (in its shortest form) and difficulties are compounded for the learner by tonal features and similar sounding words that constitute the twister as such.[15]

A performance concludes only when the learner is able to vocalize the entirety of the twister without 'error', and this takes some time. The focus of our interest is on whatever it is that determines whether or not the learner has made an error. Despite the fact that semantics are never invoked (other than, I suppose, with regard to the semantics of 'tongue twister' as a concept and generic form), there is, watching the video, no sense of any problem from anyone's point of view in making determinations of correct or erroneous vocalizations. I will shorthand an explanation for this by saying that it is the embodied human faculty for language that allows all of us to concur with these determinations. The teacher knows how to vocalize the twister, how to inscribe it as (a) *voice*. The learner can hear that linguistically implicated differences have been vocalized and the learner always already has the ability to attempt a repetition, in the acknowledgement that they have heard a trace of language that may be reinscribed in (their) voice. As viewer-readers of the performances we all have the same commensurate faculties, an aspect of our overall human language faculty, and, moreover, all of us have the ability to convey, with 'body language' an assent or a rejection of the learner's vocal forms.[16] We can see (sense) immediately who is teacher and who is learner and we can sense how the teacher expresses judgement and how the learner responds, complies and, eventually, succeeds by entertaining the twister as a 'guest' in their practice of language.

Proto-semantic grammaleptic readings provide the justification for the judgements that are made by both teacher and learner — 'author' and 'translator' — in this scene of language art performance as translation. Although neither semantics nor, indeed, signification (in the terms of linguistic science), is at play explicitly, there is no doubt that a linguistic artefact is the object of attention for the two performers, and that viewer-readers experience, together with them, a circumstance in which judgements of consensus and convention are made, judgements concerning readings that are suddenly and discontinuously perceived, repeatable, reiterable readings of vocal gestures that are constituted by linguistic segmentation. Significance is, in this case, disregarded, left out, literally bracketed — *epoché*, in the phenomenological sense — and this allows us to know, perceptibly (as it were) and in terms of a phenomenologically informed philosophy of language, that it is grammalepsis that brings language and translated language into shared affective being for all the participants in these events. But significance has not, by this token, abandoned the tongue twister — never for the teacher, while, for the learner, there is a proto-semantics latent in the vocalizations that further learning, which would also be grammaleptic, could bring out later and carry over — translate — into the learner's practice of language.

Apart from offering it as a stark demonstration of grammalepsis and certain processes of grammaleptic reading, there are three characteristics of this particular scene of translation that I suggest may be noted and applied, more generally, to both traditional and extended practices of translation. We have already discussed these characteristics, but it will help to have encountered them in the *Babel Babble* demonstration. Firstly, there is the indication of *voice* as forming the objects of grammaleptic reading. This is voice in the sense that I have defined it above, following Derrida, as the substance of language, regardless of any actually supporting materiality.[17] Secondly, there is the characteristic of the horizon between distinct practices of language, including natural languages. I don't have a single word or phrase for this other than grammaleptic, which attempts to capture, amongst other things, the discontinuities of significance and affect between all readable forms of language and thus the nullity of anything in their (vocal) vicinity that is *unreadable*. Finally, there is a characteristic relationship with temporality and temporalization that is set up by voice and grammalepsis in any dynamic, temporal practices of language which I take to include translation. Located movements in the spacetime of voice cross linguistic horizons suddenly, if at all, and so we do not (and I would argue cannot) experience, for example, any translation as a slow or steady outgrowth from the linguistic artefact that inspires it. Instead, over time, we are required to leap back and forth between the shifting locations of both guest and host forms. There is no overarching, continually present ur-translation into which we might travel and within which we might dwell. The temporal experience of a translation will either simply be a reading of a guest text in the host language (particularly for a monolingual reader) or a discontinuous back and forth from guest to host through vocal spacetime, the interstices of which are essentially empty, silent, or noisy-but-unreadable and therefore silent and empty with respect to *voice* as the substance of signification and affect.

As a title or caption, 'mirroring events at the sense horizon' expresses quite well the circumstances of Nickolas Procopi's *Babel Babble*, if we take 'sense horizon' as standing for the mirror-like threshold between communities of linguistic practice — typically natural languages — where 'sense' encapsulates all the significance and affect that these practices bear for us on either side, and 'mirror-like' refers to the fact that we always perceive a commensurate human image across such grammaleptic horizons. Procopi's video realizes a mirroring of linguistic performance which expresses the discontinuities, the horizons of incomprehensibility, between practices that may only be 'brought together', suddenly, by grammaleptic events of reading. For what remains of this essay I'd like to comment on each of the three characteristics that we discovered in this scene of translation with regard to a number of translational works of digital language art, made by myself or in collaboration with Penny Florence, and also firstly, with regard to speculations concerning digitalization and the future media of language making, to include translation.

I've been at pains to insist that our concept of reading should be taken as 'media agnostic' — philosophically unconcerned with any particular support material that bears the traces of linguistic events. Reading, in the terms set out here, is simply what brings any language into being as such. The genetic predisposition of the only language animal of which we know, ourselves, suggests that aurality, and thus structured sound, will bear the vast majority of those traces that we can read as language. And this is borne out, if we only consider, en masse, the support materialities of *all* the linguistic events of our world. But the differential and preferential relationship with time, memory, and archive that civilization procures, historically, for traces of language in structured, ultimately typographic, visuality — in, that is, textuality — this relationship ensures that literature overdetermines our understanding of reading. It causes us to privilege, with respect to reading, forms of writing as its definitive object. We have to resist this overdetermination, because it is a product of history and also because, at this precise historical moment, these circumstances are changing.[18]

It is now a banality to say that the proliferation of computation since the Second World War has had momentous effects on culture let alone socioeconomics. When, from about the mid 1990s, certain effects of textuality's digitalization — for example, its hypertextual potential for non-linearity; its apparent instantiation of intertextuality; and its supposed empowerment of readers, now materially controlling their consumption of the text — became appreciable to the world of letters and the university, they were received, and often celebrated, as disruptive, innovative, revolutionary. But their disruptive effects prove to be challenges — chiefly, I would argue — to institutions of dissemination. By the mid-1990s, computation had been taken up as, potentially, a or the model for mental processes, including those of language. Chomskyan 'generative' linguistics is still the apotheosis of this framework for inquiry, within which the 'infinite' (or very-large-finite) 'creativity' of expressive language can be accounted for by rule-governed generative combinatorics operating on finite sets (conceived of as dictionaries) of elements.

Human linguistic creativity is, in Chomskyan linguistics, computable. The finitude of the constituents of this framework is, however, derived, from, amongst other things, computation (or logic) itself and from textuality, from everyday written traces of language, rather than from language as such. Chomskyan linguistics and computation magnify and crucially exaggerate the effects of the methodological and language philosophical aporia that Derrida identified at the heart of Saussurian structural linguistics: the contradiction between, on the one hand, any claim that *speech* alone (not writing) is the object of linguistic science and, on the other, practices of this science that rely on or prefer *transcriptions* (traces, written forms) of linguistic events, including, commonly, data from corpora of 'writing' (in its everyday, literary, sense).

It is important to make this point clearly before we go on to read translational work in computational media. Although, when they execute, certain of these works do perform their programs in time, as actualizations of linguistic temporality, and although this is significant and affective, the elements that we read as we approach, experience, and interpret such works are still most often, literally, the 'letters' and 'words' of textuality. We tend to collapse the temporalities of language that they perform into literary texts-to-be-read, just as we have learned to do with all high linguistic practice for the sake, and in the cause, of literature ... and translation. If we go on to translate such works, we risk translating their *texts* and not the language of their *voice*, which must be read as constituted by temporalization.[19] Stored-program computation exaggerates the misdirection of these circumstances, because it takes language itself (and even mind) to be 'computable' in terms of tokens, and also because the transcription of a program itself is human-readable as — in combination with any data or inputs — exhaustively describing the combinatorial possibilities of the work, without any need for temporal actualization when the program executes.[20]

Computation may thus work with différance at and above the level of the *transcribed element*, the level of linguistic structure that is represented by the word or — in computational terms where language is understood as a complex, humanly privileged instance of formal 'language' — the *token* or dictionary headword. Computation may actualize non-linear or alternate passages and leaps of inherent temporalization through texts that are always-already folded within themselves due to repetition of tokens and sequences, and also, as we shall see, back and forth across the 'sense horizons' of natural languages. But it does so, most often, currently, at the expense of discounting différance(s) that is(are) both deferred and inscribed *within* words and their constituents, whereas all this is also language and voice, ignored by computation. I say 'currently' because at this historical moment, vital aspects of voice — in both everyday and grammatological senses — are becoming regularly subject to computation. Automatic speech recognition (ASR) and synthesis — transactive synthetic language — has taken its place in human society and culture in the form of voice-activated digital assistants. Although the ASR of contemporary networked computation is essentially a reduction of actual and grammatological voice to relatively conventional text or literature, this digitalization of voice is,

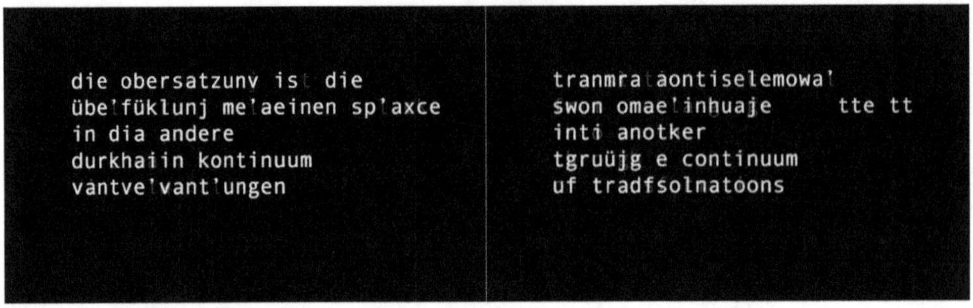

```
die obersatzunv is  die              tranmra aontiselemowa'
übe'füklunj me'aeinen sp'axce        swon omae'inhuaje       tte tt
in dia andere                        inti anotker
durkhaiin kontinuum                  tgruüjg e continuum
vantve'vant'ungen                    uf tradfsolnatoons
```

FIG. 4.2. Stills from an illustrative video rendition of transliteral morphing, John Cayley, custom software first released 1999. Courtesy of the author. The frame on the left displays the process a moment after leaving German orthography and that on the right shows it just about to arrive at English orthography. Please refer to the streamable video: <https://repository.library.brown.edu/studio/item/bdr:766946/MP4>. A live, javascript-coded version is available at: <http://programmatology.shadoof.net/ritajs/transliteral_morph/>

potentially, what I call the advent of aurature, granting the practice of human language in aurality all of the archival, mnemonic, index-activated affordances of literature.[21] This is too momentous a subject to take further here, and I have provided reference to more of my own writing on the topic, but it deserves mention as an important historical reason to ensure that theories of translation never satisfy themselves entirely with matters of literature.

To illustrate the second and third characteristics of a scene of translation in which events may be mirrored at the sense horizon, we turn first to the process of 'transliteral morphing' and 'transliteral drifting' which, in their most apposite setting, underlie the series of works in programmable media that I have titled *translation*, although transliteral morphing was first used in *windsound* (1999) and subsequently refined in *riverIsland*, 2003 and 2008.[22]

The process of transliteral morphing used by *windsound* and *riverIsland* is applied to one of the passages of *translation* in the illustrative example discussed here (see Fig. 4.2). As for all the passages in *translation* (except certain rarely surfacing passages quoted from Marcel Proust's *The Way by Swann's*), this one is taken from Walter Benjamin's 'On Language as Such and on the Language of Man'.[23] The German: 'Die Übersetzung ist die Überführung der einen Sprache in die andere durch ein Kontinuum von Verwandlungen'.[24] And the English: 'Translation is removal from one language into another through a continuum of transformations'.[25] For the piece itself and the illustration referred to in Figure 4.2, the two texts are lineated in parallel and the resulting texts are treated as a regularly spaced grid of letters. Each literal position in either text is considered to have a 'destination' in the literal grid of the other language. Letters are replaced in successive phases by cycling through some portion of an alphabet ordered and looped so as to place 'similar' letters in proximity. The order used here was: ' eaiouüy'lrwvjghkcxzqbpfsmndt'. ('t' at the end of this linear order loops back to the ' ' [space] at its beginning.) Letters in either text are never more than fourteen places away from their 'destination', so the number of phases between orthographically standard textual states is fourteen, and

```
tnanstation is rewovel          dre üqar atzusg  ct eia
trow une tanquape               übe fu   rg ber  ine    prac e
inlo enother                    ir bie andere
lhrooph a conljruuv             dorsn eir    rtjnuuw
ot lrarstormations              von ve  andl nqen
```

FIG. 4.3. Stills from an illustrative video rendition of transliteral drifting, John Cayley, custom software first released 2003. Courtesy of the author. The frame on the left displays the process 'floating' in English and that on the right shows the German 'surfacing' after 'sinking' slightly from a 'floating' state. Please refer to the streamable video: <https://repository.library.brown.edu/studio/item/bdr:774940/MP4>. A live, javascript-coded version is available at: <http://programmatology.shadoof.net/ritajs/transliteral_drift/>.

letters need not change in initial phases when the process runs. Thus, although the video example shows one possible outcome of the process the coded version varies quasi-randomly within constraints.

Before commenting on or interpreting this illustration, I'd like to provide an additional, closely related example for comparison (Fig. 4.3), one that exemplifies the process that is actually deployed for *translation* (and also, in a monolingual setting, for *overboard*).[26] In this example, the texts experience changes of state, which may be inclined in one or other linguistic 'direction' (with respect to English or German in this case) rather than proceeding to interpolate, literally, between orthographies. At regular intervals the state of a text may change to be 'floating', 'sinking', or 'surfacing' in a particular language. 'Floating' means that the letters forming words in the text may, at intervals, alternate between an orthographic (correct) form and a 'similar' letter with which I have paired it.[27] 'Sinking' implies that, apart from vacillating between alternatives, letters may disappear from sight. A 'surfacing' text will tend to make letter replacements so as to arrive at one or other orthographic destination. All of the states may be inclined, as I've said, in the direction of a particular language and literal alternates may be defined as specific to that language (for which the concept of 'similarity' between letters may, of course, be local). For the example provided, a short series of states and inclinations was explicitly programmed, one that translates — broadly, from English to German translationally correspondent orthographies — with the same 'origin' and 'destination' as Figure 4.2's example.[28]

If you watch, read (metaphorically), attempt to read (in the everyday sense), and read (grammaleptically) both the overall arc and the small but relatively numerous events of language that are represented in these videos, what characteristics of the reading experience and its underlying processes might you remark? As an artist, I'd prefer you to make such determinations for yourself hoping to make an impression on you in terms of aesthetics, but as a theorist, thinking through this essay on translation, I must provide you with some of my own suggestions.

The operations of grammaleptic reading — our chief concern — work, it seems at first, against certain meanings that can be paraphrased from Benjamin's proposition. Here are continua of transformations from one language to another, trans- and de-formations of words and phrases by means of literal substitutions. And yet, the shocking fact is that the shift away from anything graspable — grammaleptically readable — as language is sudden and it occurs if not after the first transliteral phase-shift, then definitely after the second of fourteen in the case of transliteral morphing, and more or less as quickly and suddenly with regard to transliteral drift. The transformations cross horizons of readability and then, although there is a continuum of comparable transformations, successive movement through this continuous literal space is largely 'empty' of graspable form. There is 'nothing' to read or what there is to read is beyond the sense horizons of natural language. Non-sense. Let's affirm this unambiguously. The crossing over is a discontinuity. Traumatic breaks occur in any 'continuum of transformations'. This is the import of -lepsis in grammalepsis.

And yet, if we review the moment of transliteral drift when, in the video (or the live-coded sketch) associated with Figure 4.3, the programmed process shifts from floating in English to floating in German, we can read an equally sudden and traumatic shift from arrangements of letters that are ungraspable as natural language to distinct arrangements of letters that are also ungraspable as language, except that we *can* grasp that the first arrangement is 'in English' and the second is 'in German'. And our ability to grasp this fact need not be due to any sudden introduction of u-umlaut (although this can 'seal the deal' as it were). The distinct (re-)*situation* or, indeed, *translation* of the text is readable, abstractly, as differences of (algorithmically-generated) letter choice and sequence, and for this reason — if we *know* English and/or German — as characteristic literal practices *in* those languages. The floating on either side of the horizon may be a 'continuum of transformations' but there may also be demonstrable discontinuous grammaleptic shifts from one continuum (English) to another (German).

These effects are a function of the circumstance that grammaleptic reading (indeed any reading) of linguistic artefacts may take place simultaneously at several levels of linguistic structure. In the cases just discussed, 'words' are suddenly no longer graspable and, this being one of the chief conscious criteria for conventional readability overall, we say that the text is beyond the sense horizon of English. But simultaneously we are still — nonconsciously perhaps — reading the text-as-letters 'in English', still within the *literal* horizon of English, and this nonconscious reading is brought to consciousness, retrospectively, when the text-as-letters shifts its inclination and, with remarkable discontinuity, becomes a text-as-letters that is 'in German'.

The statement that Benjamin proposed in his 1916 essay and that is quoted in *translation* (the work) as well as in the figures just discussed, needs to be revised and also, for the sake of careful articulation in this context, expanded. *Translation is the removal, beyond the horizons of a given community of language practice into a spacetime within the horizons of another such community by way of an iterable series of discontinuous, more or less readable states, embodied in transitional linguistic artefacts, themselves composed from continua of transformations at any and all applicable levels of linguistic structure.* This statement has been revised to account for the translational gestures in a specific work of my own, *translation*, but my intention here is to further characterize and specify the grammaleptic character of all linguistic events, to reiterate my contention that graspable discontinuities allow us to read linguistic events as such, while, at the same time, never foreclosing or prescribing continual transformations generated by any lower-level constituent elements of these events. Moreover, if we take this principle to apply, by analogy, to words and clauses, for example, rather than to letters and words as we have done in the course of our recent analysis, then we attain the full meaning of this definition, after all, of 'translation' itself, taken to encompass conventional translation.

In Derrida's terms, traces of the graspable, iterable discontinuities that are brought into being by grammaleptic reading are archi-writing, and the continua of transformations that constitute them are — at least for an applied grammatology — différance. It seems to me ironic that I can demonstrate this, pragmatically, with reference to what is a remarkably simple formal structure and its combinatorial operations, precisely the kind of symbolic structure that is one of the chief objects of radical critique for Derrida. Famously, in order to signify différance and also the way that this non-concept exceeds signification, Derrida names it by spelling a *vocally* imperceptible difference between itself and 'difference'. The 'a' of différance is so similar to 'e' in this context that it is also 'the same'. In the looping cycle of letters — ' eaiouüy'lrwvjghkcxzqbpfsmndt' — that is used by the transliteral morph in Figure 4.2 above, 'e' is next to 'a' for precisely the reason that their proximity is proposed as potential différance. The order of these letters is based on a multiply-compromised attempt to allow différance-generative associations to cluster, spring up, emerge. There can only be one order — in this particular programmatic structure — but it is crucial to note that the criteria determining proximity are both polyvalent and synaesthetic. The arrangement of the letters proposes generative operations based on certain synaesthetic associations that these letters bear within the practices of their languages: vowel vs. consonant (the vowels are all together); related phonetic association (lr, bp, dt); graphic similarity (xz, mn); orthographic history (fs, y'l); proper naming of the letters (wv); ordinal arrangements (gh, mn), letter frequency (t ea — including the 'space'), etc. Thus, as the transliteral operation runs, 'aesthetic' might become 'aesthetik', and 'difference' might become 'differance'. On another run, depending on quasi-random calculations, 'aesthetic' might also conceivably, in one phase and if every letter changed, become 'eafdgadok'. From the perspective of strictly determined orthographic readability, both 'aesthetik' and 'eafdgadok' are equally, as it were, cacographic, extra-lexical, unreadable as 'English'; however, from the perspective of generative différance, aesthetik is suggestive, virtual, potential. Is something new readable in this and forms like it? Or something newly shared across the sense horizons of natural languages? Regardless — in the sense of without human intuition or judgement — the algorithm runs. As the literal substitutions are made, and we pass beyond the threshold of a shared readability,

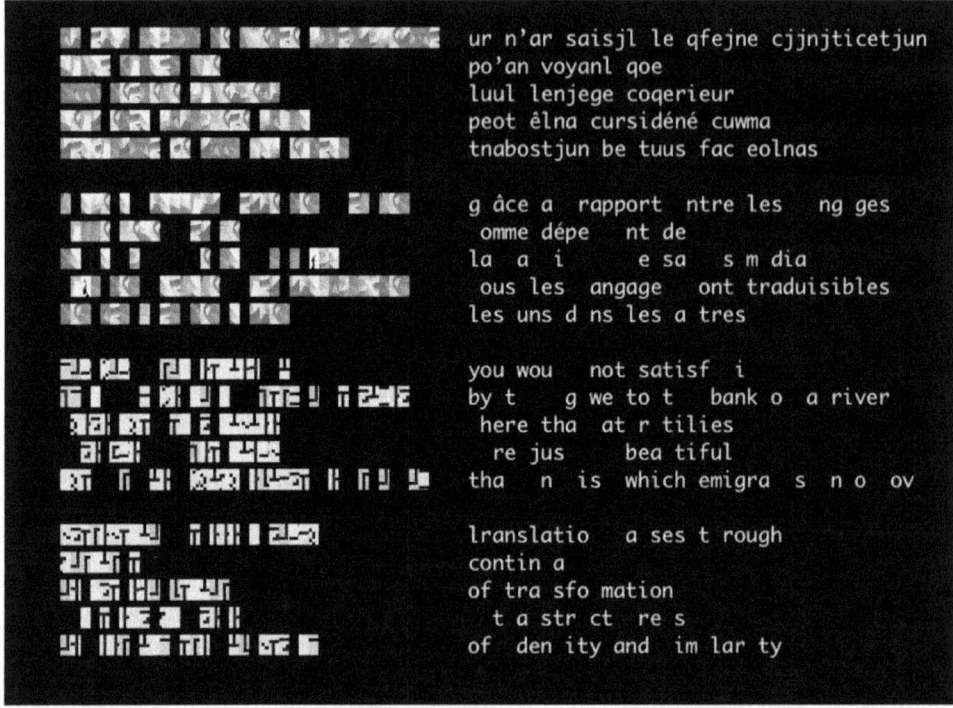

FIG. 4.4. Still from *translation*, John Cayley, custom software, 2004. Courtesy of the author. The top two passages are in French, surfacing and sinking respectively. The third passage is surfacing to display a 'hidden' English alternate passage quoted from Proust's *The Way by Swann's* and the fourth passage is surfacing in English. Please refer to the streamable video showing the record of the opening of one session with *translation*. The video shows the German text all but entirely surfaced, then the passages sink for a spell and at about 1'05' the top two passages incline toward French.
<https://repository.library.brown.edu/studio/item/bdr:766947/MP4>

we cease to read, consciously, within the sense horizons of one or other language, but we do experience a play of différance, more or less aestheticized and operating, unambiguously and synaesthetically in generative ignorance of any formal regularities *within specific perceptual domains* (typically phonetic/phonological), and in a manner that gestures toward and may occasionally quasi-randomly achieve — in sudden grammaleptic leaps — new language and new relations across linguistic horizons. This, then, is the (syn)aesthetic wager of *translation* as a published work, during the presentation of which many such processes are entangled as they run and propose their serious play of difference and différance (Figure 4.4).

One of the things that seems remarkable, then, in a work like *translation* is the sharp (grammaleptic) distinction between language states, the way in which, in Figure 4.4, even without the correspondent visual 'mapping' to the left, we can read the difference, starkly, between French in the upper passages and English in those below. There is also, of course the literal grid-work and the spacing that reinforces this discontinuity. But all that is needed is sub-lexical differences in sequences of

Fig. 4.5. Still from *Lu shan du ye*, translation, inextrinsic grammar, and custom software by John Cayley, 2013, based on the quatrain by Xu Ning (fl. during Yuanhe 806–20). Courtesy of the author. Streamable video: <https://repository.library.brown.edu/studio/item/bdr:766951/MP4>. Live javascript sketch: <http://programmatology.shadoof.net/ritajs/xuning/>.

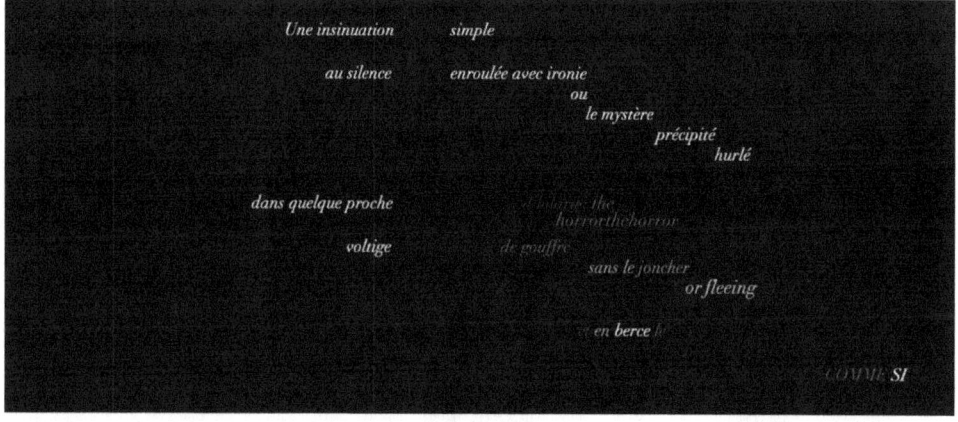

Fig. 4.6. Still from *Flights Unflown*, translation and inextrinsic grammars by Penny Florence, custom software by John Cayley, 2013, based on the first opening of Mallarmé's *Un coup de dés*. Courtesy of the author and Penny Florence. Streamable video <https://repository.library.brown.edu/studio/item/bdr:766948/MP4>.

blue and white of sky a moment still		bleu et blanc du ciel un moment encore	
the mud it's over it's done I've had	la	la boue c'est fini c'est fait ça s'éteint	the
is empty a few animals still then goes	I	scène reste vide quelques bêtes puis	image
stay there		je reste là	

FIG. 4.7. Still from *Inextrinsic Image*, token-for-token translation, grammar, and custom software by John Cayley, 2015, based on an excerpt from 'The Image' in Samuel Beckett's *How It Is*. Courtesy of the author. Streamable video: <https://repository.library.brown.edu/studio/item/bdr:766950/MP4>.

letters to establish the distinction. And then we recall that even these sequences are made readable as such by *spacing*, by the requisite emptiness between them, the grammaleptic horizons between literal difference, with différance permeating the entire structure at all levels, granting it generative potential.

In collaborative work, Penny Florence and I have explored what we call 'inextrinsic reading' and have applied it to translation.[29] In current iterations of processes and programmed artefacts sustaining this work, a text to be read — inextrinsically — is supplied with one or more 'grammars' (essentially formal context-free grammars) that operate on the words of the text. These words are replaced, successively, according to the rules of the grammar, the terminal points of which may be phrases. I provide three figures here with examples of inextrinsic reading as currently implemented.

In a single, apparently oxymoronic portmanteau, 'inextrinsic' refers simultaneously to two aspects of significance and affect that we may read in a particular embodied (here typographically inscribed) linguistic form — those that are explicitly represented in the transcription, extrinsically, 'in the text', and those that are implied, intrinsically, by, for example, context or previous reading and experience. An inextrinsic approach implies that operations usually considered as intrinsic or implicit to the reading process may be made extrinsic or explicit, and that we need not necessarily make any decision regarding the relative significance or affect of these in- or ex-trinsic forms of reading. They operate, if not simultaneously in a literal sense, then with equal energy and value during processes of reading. Clearly also, the potential of actively temporalized linguistic artefacts allows us to actualize inextrinsic reading in time-based language art, thanks to the digital media affordances of both composition and dissemination. These were equally felicitous with respect to the dynamic letter replacement in our examples of transliteral morphing and drifting. Temporalization is intrinsic to différance as it is proposed both by Derrida's thought and by the programmed operations that make it explicit at the level of the letter. Inextrinsic reading may also be proposed as exploring temporalization and différance at the higher level of linguistic structure represented by the word.

I will not analyze these new examples in any sort of detail. Chiefly I want to remark that although they very clearly translate — inextrinsically — back and forth across the sense horizons of one or more languages, it is noticeable that they do so, once again, simultaneously temporalizing difference/différance and also grammaleptically, establishing marked discontinuities with respect to the horizons of natural linguistic gesture. For, what is *intrinsic* in the reading of these pieces — graspable language from beyond the natural language horizon of the text-being-read — is made *extrinsic* by, basically, opening an empty space within the guest text and often, if temporarily, occluding it or rendering it as background 'surface' for a reading of host language fragments by which it is both interrupted and translated. This visual behaviour of a program is at one and the same time expediency (one of the expedient ways to get done what needs to be done) and also, I am arguing, a significant analogy for or visualization of the way that fundamental operations of translation and, indeed, language proceed.

In Figure 4.5, a single inextrinsic reader moves through a Chinese quatrain that has been regularly lineated in a western arrangement. As a character is read, both it and certain of its neighbours must fade from sight in order to allow one from a number of associative, neighbour-influenced words or phrases — rule-selected from the precomposed grammar — to be readably displayed. It's not a one-to-one. The substitutions are both free, one-to-many, and quasi-randomly chosen such that a final translated reading is both literally temporalized and endlessly (or, in this and all computable cases, very-large-finitely) deferred. But for now, we are chiefly remarking the discontinuities as we grasp the forms in one or other language. We don't follow continua from one language to another. Our host words are there in midst of a space — an emptiness revealing their horizons — opened up by the guest, and then they're gone.

There are two distinctly coloured inextrinsic readers moving through the initial opening from a famous text by Mallarmé in Figure 4.6. The substantive actual dynamism of the reading may be plural in terms of focal points, although for a human reader of any time-based visual display the linearity of linguistic attention (one of Saussure's unassailable fundamentals) is ineluctable, and the necessity to make space for the inextrinsic readers and to establish the discontinuities that allow for grammalepsis — this necessity is the same as that we encountered with respect to the Chinese quatrain. The temporalized operation of *Flights Unflown* does also show how interpretative, co-creative translational practices are well suited to time-based artefacts such as this. Readings grasped by a translator — here, Penny Florence — in the host language do, temporarily, remove some part of the guest beyond its natural linguistic sense horizons and yet larger structural forms of the guest remain to frame these interruptions and the guest will also reconstitute itself in time. This seems to allow greater freedom of interpretative gesture without impugning the integrity (or association) of the guest as whole, relative, for example, to a speculative print-culture replacement of the entire opening by a free interpretative (formally more conventional) translation in this case.

The *Inextrinsic Image* of Figure 4.7 was constructed specifically to bring us back to the kind of 'mirroring' that so strongly appeals to us when we think about translation. Simultaneously, two word-for-word, token-for-token readers move through parallel English and French versions of a short fragment taken from a text by Samuel Beckett. Each one opens a space in its guest and reveals a corresponding host word that is literally 'mirrored' in the corresponding neighbouring text. It is all of a piece, nothing is added, especially in this case where both French ('original') and English (conventional 'translation') are by Beckett. What we see and experience, on reflection, however, are the discontinuities, those already remarked above and also, in particular, the print-culture 'gutter' in the position of a speculative 'mirror' between the two texts. And then consider: that the vehicle of the image or metaphor in this case — a mirror — is, in our phenomenological world, very much an absolute horizon, one to which we may approach infinitely closely and that appears to reflect visuality with infinite granularity, but which shows us a world the objects of which are absolutely beyond the horizon of our own. 'Mirroring' is a metaphor that proposes iterable idealities in the perceptual dimension of visuality. It *appears* to work for writing and archi-writing but it does not work for language or across natural languages. The visual display — *the image* — even of the parallel texts of Figure 4.7, demonstrate this in a number of apparent glitches, one of which is shown in the still for Figure 4.7 itself. On the left, an inextrinsic reader alights on 'the' (of 'the image' in its guest text) and replaces it with 'la'; on the right, the corresponding reader alights on 'l'image' and the writer of its grammar (myself) has allowed this to be read as a single token and has proposed that it will be replaced by two words: 'the image'. French is not *mirrored* (in inscribed visuality) by English or vice versa, either metaphorically or literally. If we want to retain some metaphor to stand or speak for us at the natural linguistic horizons between the practices of distinct communities of language makers, then it would be better to speak of *echoing* with respect to *voice,* understood as the substantive medium of language. But it will also be essential to understand that this cannot be read as the substitution (or reinstatement) of another singular, privileged perceptual domain (aurality). Rather it refers to the fundamental synaesthesia of linguistic traces: echoing vocal différance(s), across grammaleptic horizons.

I have made much use of Derrida's philosophy of language in this text, beginning and ending with horizons while translating from one metaphorical domain to some other. Derrida articulates the relationship with death, with the passing beyond a certain horizon that language requires to exist as *the* supplement of human life, a horizon which it also breaks through by bearing and re-inscribing traces that could only have once been here with us before they passed beyond. Derrida's 'Living On / Border Lines' — proposed by Emily Apter and others as being 'about translation' — was one of the texts to which I turned when beginning to write this one.[30] It is perfectly conceivable — and historically demonstrable, just think of parts of the Bible — that a guest text might be translated and hosted in 'our' language and that the language of the guest might pass away. The language lives on in the host, we say, but the discontinuity, the horizon and its loss, remains, just as it was always there, as essential to all of any language that came to be. In *L'arrêt de mort (Death Sentence)*, which Derrida discusses in his essay, Blanchot's language of fiction creates a world where the horizon of death is indeterminate. Particular characters translate from one side to the other, but we know that they can only ever be here or there. There is no in between. The sentence is either passed or it has been deferred. There is no liminal fantasy that is not expressed by this ineluctable, fatally generative structure.

Translation, including the translation that is expressed in actual temporalized processes such as those proposed by digitalization, is subject to the same traumatic circumstances. Language is only ever here or there, with us or passed beyond. In *windsound* I encountered this personally, when metaphorically and culturally translating the life of a dead friend into the transliterating language of the transcultural stories it contained. *windsound* is dedicated to a memory and it brings this memory back for some but, at the end of the piece, in the course of its literal dedication, and as the letters disappear, pass away, we notice that 'e' and 't' are frequent; they survive along with 'd' and 'a' and a hardy, persistent 'y'. Our friends and their languages are translated and live on:

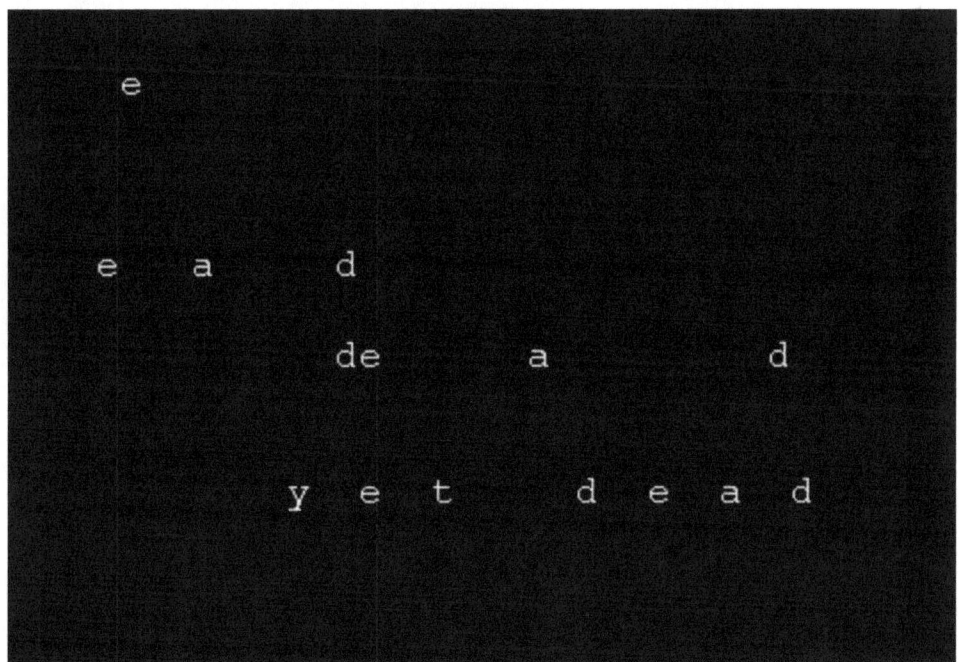

FIG. 4.8. Still from the closing credits of *windsound*, written and composed with custom software by John Cayley, QuickTime version, 2015. Courtesy of the author. A streamable video version of the entire piece is referenced below. As illustrating the final remarks of this essay, please navigate to 20'54' in the video. This still itself occurs at about 22'21':
<https://repository.library.brown.edu/studio/item/bdr:766943/MP4>.

Works Cited

BENJAMIN, WALTER, 'On Language as Such and on the Language of Man', trans. by Edmund Jephcott and Kingsley Shorter, in *One-Way Street and Other Writings* (London: Verso, 1997), pp. 107–23

—— 'Über Sprache überhaupt und über die Sprache des Menschen', in *Medienästhetische Schriften*, edited by Detlev Schöttker (Frankfurt a/M: Suhrkamp, 2002), pp. 67–82

BERWICK, ROBERT C., and NOAM CHOMSKY, *Why Only Us: Language and Evolution* (Cambridge: MIT Press, 2016)

CAYLEY, JOHN, 'The Advent of Aurature and the End of (Electronic) Literature', in *The Bloomsbury Handbook of Electronic Literature*, edited by Joseph Tabbi, (New York: Bloomsbury, 2018), pp. 73–94

CAYLEY, JOHN, *overboard*, (2003), custom software, ambient poetics, http://programmatology.shadoof.net/?overboard (accessed August 1, 2017), [also published/documented: ELMCIP Knowledge Base https://elmcip.net/node/549 (accessed August 14, 2017)]

—— '*overboard*: An Example of Ambient Time-Based Poetics in Digital Art', *dichtung-digital* 32 (2004) http://www.dichtung-digital.de/2004/2/Cayley/index.htm (accessed August 13, 2017)

—— *riverIsland: Hypercard and QuickTime Version*, first draft version 1999, published in *The Iowa Review Web*, 2003, http://thestudio.uiowa.edu/tirw/TIRW_Archive/tirweb/feature/cayley/ (accessed March 4, 2018)

—— *riverIsland: Programmable QuickTime Version*, published in *The Iowa Review Web* 9.2, 2008, <http://thestudio.uiowa.edu/tirw/vol9n2/johncayley.php> (accessed March 4, 2018)

—— *translation*, 2004, http://programmatology.shadoof.net/?translation (accessed August 1, 2017), [also published/documented: *Electronic Literature Collection*, vol 1 (2006) http://collection.eliterature.org/1/works/cayley__translation.html (accessed August 13, 2017), ELMCIP Knowledge Base https://elmcip.net/node/526 (accessed August 14, 2017)]

—— 'The Translation of Process', *Amodern*, no. 8 (2018), http://amodern.net/article/the-translation-of-process/ (accessed March 14, 2018)

—— *windsound*, (1999), http://programmatology.shadoof.net/?p=works/wsqt/windsound.html (accessed July 30, 2017), [also published/documented: *Electronic Literature Collection*, vol 1 (2006) http://collection.eliterature.org/1/works/cayley__windsound.html (accessed August 13, 2017), ELMCIP Knowledge Base, https://elmcip.net/node/790 (accessed August 14, 2017)]

DEHAENE, STANISLAUS, *Reading in the Brain: The Science and Evolution of a Human Invention* (New York: Viking, 2009)

DERRIDA, JACQUES, 'Living on / Border Lines', trans. by James Hulbert, in *Deconstruction and Criticism*, ed. by Harold Bloom, Paul De Man, Jacques Derrida, Geoffrey H. Hartman and J. Hillis Miller (London: Routledge, 2005), pp. 75–176

—— *Of Grammatology*, trans. by Gayatri Chakravorty Spivak, corrected edn (Baltimore: Johns Hopkins University Press, 1997)

—— *Voice and Phenomenon: Introduction to the Problem of the Sign in Husserl's Phenomenology*, trans. by Leonard Lawlor (Evanston, Ill.: Northwestern University Press, 2011)

EVENS, ADEN, 'Combination and Copulation: Making Lots of Little Poems', in *The Bloomsbury Handbook of Electronic Literature*, edited by Joseph Tabbi, (New York: Bloomsbury, 2018), pp. 217–36

FLORENCE, PENNY, 'Readers, Meet the Readers', http://programmatology.shadoof.net/pdfs/FlorenceReadersIllust4Lossfin.pdf (accessed Jan 1, 2019)

HURFORD, JAMES R., *The Origins of Language: A Slim Guide* (Oxford: Oxford University Press, 2014)

LIU, LYDIA H., *Translingual Practice: Literature, National Culture, and Translated Modernity — China 1900–1937* (Stanford: Stanford University Press, 1995)

ONG, WALTER J., *Orality and Literacy: The Technologizing of the Word* (London: Routledge, 1982)

ULMER, GREGORY L., *Applied Grammatology: Post(e)-Pedagogy from Jacques Derrida to Joseph Beuys* (Baltimore: Johns Hopkins University Press, 1985)

Notes to Chapter 4

1. For the translation *of* process, see John Cayley, 'The Translation of Process,' *Amodern*, 8 (2018), n.p. <http://amodern.net/article/the-translation-of-process/> (accessed 31 July 2019).
2. With respect to qualifiers for the languages involved in practices of translation, I follow Lydia Liu in preferring 'guest' and 'host' for 'original' or 'source' and 'destination' or 'target,' for example. Lydia H. Liu, *Translingual Practice: Literature, National Culture, and Translated Modernity — China 1900–1937* (Stanford: Stanford University Press, 1995).
3. This is one of the crucial insights from Derrida's critique of structuralism. Jacques Derrida, *Of Grammatology*, trans. Gayatri Chakravorty Spivak, Corrected ed. (Baltimore: Johns Hopkins University Press, 1997), pp. 27–44. In Saussurian structural linguistics, writing is never the object of study and is only ever taken to be a supplementary representation of the speech by means of which we come to know language 'scientifically'. However — this is one the paradoxes yielding to deconstruction — 'empirical' evidence for linguistics's object of study is (must be) inscribed in a privileged and restricted form of writing. Ibid., p. 39.
4. Walter J. Ong, *Orality and Literacy: The Technologizing of the Word*, ed. Terence Hawkes, New Accents (London: Routledge, 1982; repr., 1995).
5. What seems to me an even-handed summary of recent research can be found in James R. Hurford, *The Origins of Language: A Slim Guide* (Oxford: Oxford University Press, 2014). This is a highly condensed rendition of the same author's two monumental volumes on meaning and grammar published by Oxford University Press. See also: Robert C. Berwick and Noam Chomsky, *Why Only Us: Language and Evolution* (Cambridge: MIT Press, 2016).
6. Stanislaus Dehaene, *Reading in the Brain: The Science and Evolution of a Human Invention* (New York: Viking, 2009).
7. It is a misdirection from the main impetus of our argument to acknowledge, nonetheless, that homophonic 'translation' may be entertained conceptually, more or less seriously, as a creative or poetic response to certain guests, in the language of the host.
8. Derrida's emphasis. Jacques Derrida, *Voice and Phenomenon: Introduction to the Problem of the Sign in Husserl's Phenomenology*, trans. Leonard Lawlor, Northwestern University Studies in Phenomenology and Existential Philosophy (Evanston, Ill.: Northwestern University Press, 2011), p. 65. Voice and this passage are also usefully discussed — but with reference to the earlier translation of Derrida's essay as *Speech and Phenomena* — in Gregory L. Ulmer, *Applied Grammatology: Post(e)-Pedagogy from Jacques Derrida to Joseph Beuys* (Baltimore: Johns Hopkins University Press, 1985), 51–57.
9. Ibid., 52.
10. I want to be absolutely clear that nothing in this discussion should be read as a resuscitation of the logocentrism that Derrida strongly critiques, with justice and openness in mind. Voice is the medium of language as shared practice and, as used in this essay, is a self-erasing, paradoxical 'element' that helps to undermine (or deconstruct if you prefer) logocentric speech as authorized by a metaphysics of presence.
11. Ulmer, *Applied Grammatology*, 318 n. 16.
12. Derrida, *Voice and Phenomenon: Introduction to the Problem of the Sign in Husserl's Phenomenology*, pp. 85–87.
13. Although there may, in the course of particular subjective crossings, be moments of radical doubt concerning the ultimate destination of linguistic practice. If the hearing-reading subject does not know or does not yet grasp, grammaleptically, the 'natural' language towards which she is inclining her understanding, she may anticipate one or more other 'languages' that she may know (better), differing from the one 'within' which she does, in the end, arrive.
14. Not until conventions change for, at least, a majority of language users within the horizons of a natural language. Note also that changes in such conventions are motivated primarily, initially — although of course not exclusively — by forces that are *within* a language's community of practice. This qualification with respect to readable and unreadable forms brings up problems associated with the Saussurian synchronic vs. diachronic distinction in linguistics. Structuralism requires synchrony for its exposition and 'science' of *langue* (language as system of differences

and grammar). Différance introduces temporalization and therefore diachrony, potentially, into every event of language at whatever level of structure. Nonetheless, grammaleptic reading proceeds on the basis of difference and différance, processing persistent entities in the sense that they rely on shared conventions inscribed in the idealities of voice, however fleeting and alive. And, of course, for significant human durations and because so many of us are implicated, the overwhelming majority of 'natural' linguistic forms will tend to maintain their readability for some generations.

15. This is the twister in its short form: 'sì shì sì, shí shì shí. sìshí shì sìshí, shísì shì shísì.' 四是四, 十是十。四十是四十, 十四是十四。 Translating literally: 'Four is four, ten is ten. Forty is forty, fourteen is fourteen.' Innocuous enough, unless one considers that the syllable for 'four' is a homonym for 'death' in Mandarin, and 'ten' is a near-homonym for 'corpse' such that getting the tones wrong could have sinister consequences. The order of the second line of assertions may be reversed and a third line is often added to the twister such that many variants could be performed that would all make (numerical, arithmetic, 'deathly') sense. The common third line is: 'shísì bùshì sìshí, sìshí bùshì shísì.' 十四不是四十, 四十不是十四。 'Fourteen isn't forty, forty isn't fourteen.'
16. The common way to say this is that we express ourselves through 'body language,' but it would, I believe, be more accurate to say that we express our reading judgements in such cases using our language body, those parts of our embodied gestural formation that we are able to devote to assist in language making.
17. Typically and overwhelmingly the supporting materiality of language-as-voice is the aurality of actual human voices or (typo)graphically inscribed text (or graphic systems of inscription), but consider also — for a real-world human language community example of an alternate supporting materiality — the signs of sign language. Where 'signs' is linguistic terminology and, in the terms of this essay, refers to conventional forms constituting *voice* in sign language.
18. John Cayley, 'The Advent of Aurature and the End of (Electronic) Literature', in *The Bloomsbury Handbook of Electronic Literature*, ed. Joseph Tabbi (New York: Bloomsbury, 2018).
19. 'The Translation of Process'.
20. Aden Evens, 'Combination and Copulation: Making Lots of Little Poems,' in *The Bloomsbury Handbook of Electronic Literature*, ed. Joseph Tabbi (New York: Bloomsbury, 2018).
21. Cayley, 'The Advent of Aurature and the End of (Electronic) Literature'.
22. *windsound*, 1999; *riverIsland: Hypercard and QuickTime Version*, 2003. First draft version 1999. Published in *The Iowa Review Web*; *riverIsland: Programmable QuickTime Version*, 2008. Published in *The Iowa Review Web* 9.2.
23. Walter Benjamin, 'On Language as Such and on the Language of Man,' in *One-Way Street and Other Writings* (London: Verso, 1997).
24. 'Über Sprache überhaupt und über die Sprache des Menschen', in *Medienästhetische Schriften*, ed. Detlev Schöttker (Frankfurt a/M: Suhrkamp, 2002), 76.
25. 'On Language as Such and on the Language of Man', p. 117.
26. John Cayley, *overboard*, 2003; '*overboard*: An Example of Ambient Time-Based Poetics in Digital Art,' *dichtung-digital* 32 (2004).
27. Another description of the process, with more detail, although in a monolingual context, can be found in '*overboard*: An Example of Ambient Time-Based Poetics in Digital Art'.
28. For this video: seven seconds of English, thirty seconds floating in English, thirty seconds floating in German, forty-five seconds sinking in German, twenty seconds floating in English, twenty seconds floating in German, five seconds sinking in German, then surfacing until the text achieves German orthography.
29. See Penny Florence, 'Readers, Meet the Readers'. http://programmatology.shadoof.net/pdfs/FlorenceReadersIllust4Lossfin.pdf (accessed.
30. Jacques Derrida, 'Living on / Border Lines,' in *Deconstruction and Criticism*, ed. Harold Bloom, et al. (London: Routledge, 2005).

PART III

Cultures

CHAPTER 5

Through a Prism, Translated: Culture and Change in Russia

Yvonne Howell

Overview

In the history of Russian translation, a cardinal sin is the *otsebyatina*. The word is compiled from the prefix *ot* [*from*], the root word *sebya* [self], and the abstracting suffix *tina* [-tion, -ity], three morphemes that handily combine to mean inserting something 'from oneself' into a translation, something which is not present in the original text. Thus, the word *otsebyatina* designates a concept that is easily grasped (and frequently attested to) across cultures, but it is hard to find a single-word equivalent for it in non-Slavic languages. In Russian, this one word both describes and condemns the practice of inserting one's own material into the translated text in an effort to amend, upgrade, circumvent, or clarify a phrase in the original. As we shall see, there are many reasons translators have used *otsebyatina* in the course of bringing a foreign text across linguistic and cultural chasms to find new footing on home territory. However, what seems like a 'sin' in an individual translator's treatment of an individual text cannot be condemned as a problem when one considers the culture-building effect of translation as a whole. On the contrary, one could argue that cultural growth and evolution take place precisely in this way — in the process of creatively adapting, augmenting, and selectively amplifying knowledge as it moves through the prism of translation.

The history of Russian translation is littered with *otsebyatiny* (now in the plural), both in the sense that translators inevitably used them to create readable, non-literal versions of foreign originals, and in the commentary of critics, who occasionally excoriate the use of the *otsebyatina,* but more often than not tacitly approve the translator's efforts to render English, or German, or French into Russian. We should remember that the language of Christianity in the East — Russian Orthodoxy — was not Latin, but a frozen form of the Slavic vernacular; and the ideology of the State was focused on expanding and consolidating contiguous territory, rather than cultivating modes of civil society within its polity, or expanding its markets overseas. Russia remained isolated from European cultural developments for much of the medieval and early modern period, so that the intellectual, social, and artistic transformations wrought by the European Renaissance and subsequent

Counter Reformation (Baroque) hardly penetrated into Russian lands. The cultural dynamism that widespread translation ignites came late to Russia, only at the beginning of the eighteenth century. Once the process of cultural opening began, however, the vector of translation was generally from West to East: starting with Tsar Peter I (reign 1696–1725), Russian leaders primarily sought to translate texts, fashions, and technologies from Western Europe (and later the USA).

Thus, for most of the last few centuries, when Russian translators added something 'from oneself' to a foreign text, they were participating in a much larger phenomenon of adding rich lexical stock to the Russian language in that particular historical epoch, as well as expanding the breadth and depth of Russia's civilizational repertoire. As we shall see, from the eighteenth century onwards, translation of foreign texts into Russian served overwhelmingly as a source of knowledge and novelty, pouring new material into a culture that perceived itself as perpetually on the margins of the Western world. In other words, taken as a whole, foreign literature arrived into Russia (and later into the Soviet Union) through translation *as through a prism:* amplified or intensified, extended or distorted, and almost always shot through with new philosophical or aesthetic coloration.

This chapter offers a summary of key historical junctures in the history of what was essentially a prismatic process in Russia: the translation *cum* adaptation, imitation, transformation, and re-assimilation of foreign texts into a burgeoning Eurasian civilization.[1] In general, we will see that what Cronin calls a 'regime of identicality' never took root on Russian soil.[2] Already at the first historical juncture, the relationship between print culture, translation, and modernity was figured differently.

It was not until the beginning of the eighteenth century that Tsar Peter I famously 'hacked a window onto Europe' by building his new capital city to face Scandinavia on the Finnish Gulf. In Alexander Pushkin's famous poem 'The Bronze Horseman' [*Medyni vsadnik*], the first stanza mythologizes the setting and the intentionality of the Tsar's soon-to-be constructed city, St. Petersburg:

На берегу пустынных волн,	On an empty shoreline
Стоял *он*, дум великих полн,	Stood *he*, full of great ideas,
И вдаль глядел […]	And looked afar. […]
И думал он:	Then he thought:
Отсель грозить мы будем шведу	Here we'll build a city
Здесь будет город заложен	From which we'll threaten our neighbor
На зло надменному соседу.	The arrogant Swede.
Природой здесь нам суждено	Nature itself has decreed:
В Европу прорубить окно	To hack a window onto Europe
Ногою твердой стать при море.[3]	One foot planted firmly by the sea.
	(*my translation*)

At this relatively late date in European development, Peter 'the Great' proceeded to forcibly turn his empire onto the path of Western modernity. First and foremost, the Tsar's Westernizing ambitions led to a tremendous influx of translations into Russian. The influx of many centuries' worth of material suddenly making its way into Russian produced a kind of telescopic effect. A closed and insular medieval ecclesiastical culture suddenly discovered everything from Ancient Greek tragedies, to Renaissance literature, to Shakespeare, Goethe, Newton and Bacon. Thus, Peter's early eighteenth-century reforms stimulated translation, which in turn stimulated an unprecedented socio-cultural process of linguistic development, as well as the evolution of a literary sensibility. The towering figures of Russian literature (e.g. Tolstoy, Dostoevsky) appeared within a mere one hundred years after the first efforts to translate Western poetry and prose into Russian.

Throughout the nineteenth century, Russian attitudes towards literary translation remained quite far from any (Western) European notion of translation as a one-dimensional conduit from text A to text B. There was no place in the Russian cultural context for extolling the merits of 'fidelity' or 'equivalence' between two texts, when the historical task at hand was to imitate, adapt, and augment foreign material so as to grow new varieties out of borrowed soil. The most influential of the Romantic poet-translators, Vasilii Zhukovsky, laid the groundwork for the subsequent flourishing of a unique Russian literary tradition by moving European artistic motifs and genres into the Russian sphere. In the adaptive translations of Zhukovsky and his disciples, English graveyard poetry, German philosophical and moral literature, and Romantic modes of self-expression all acquired a distinctly Russian form.[4] By the latter half of the nineteenth century, the achievements of Turgenev, Tolstoy, and Dostoevsky (among others) temporarily overshadowed the importance of translation as a part of the cultural matrix. However, revolutionary change at the turn of the twentieth century represented a new juncture in the history of translation. The advent of Soviet rule after 1917 brought new tensions in cultural politics. This essay will briefly consider the ideological imperatives of Stalinism that once again brought to the fore the 'prismatic' function of translation — this time producing a subculture of moral resisters for whom translation was also a mode of surviving the gulag. A third critical juncture in the history of Russian translation is underway in the second decade of the twenty-first century. The prismatic function of translation in the current climate of geopolitical posturing is particularly interesting, because it creates fissures within Russia between those in favor of globalizing trends and those in favor of 'conserving traditions'; yet these fissures do not neatly overlap with official political rhetoric.

Then he Thought: here we'll Use Translations

When we speak about the emergence of Russian literature in the eighteenth century, we are not yet speaking about the rise of the *novel*. In Ian Watt's classic study of *The Rise of the Novel,* he tied the new literary form — one that has dominated the modern imagination for the last three centuries — to the emergence (in Western Europe) of scientific approaches to knowledge, rationalist philosophy, the beginnings of industrialization, and the creation of a literate middle class.[5] Daniel Defoe's *Robinson Crusoe* (1719), Samuel Richardson's *Pamela, or Virtue Rewarded* (1740), Laurence Sterne's *Tristam Shandy* (1759–1767), and Henry Fielding's *Tom Jones* (1749) are generally cited as examples of the new genre, whose form and content presumably reflected modern conditions of increasing secularism, economic individualism, social mobility, and bourgeois morality. How, then, did the novel develop in societies that lacked a rising bourgeois class in the same time period? Several scholars have added more complexity to Watt's thesis, arguing, for example, that the rise of the French novel reflected a different array of social and economic relationships,[6] or, that the rise of the novel in Southeast Asia must be contextualized differently. To paraphrase one reviewer's analysis of a 1790 courtesan's tale, just because a writer exhibits a quasi-novelistic concern with the Indian underclass, that does not yet mean the resulting fictional text can be called a surprisingly early example of a novel.[7] The first Russian novels did not appear until the 1840s; yet within two decades, the novels of Turgenev, Dostoevsky and Tolstoy seemed to represent a culmination of the genre's possibilities. This kind of acute and accelerated cultural development — what has often been called telescopic change — was mediated by the practice of translation.

The rise of the novel coincides roughly with a socioeconomic shift of a different type in the enormous Russian empire. At the eastern edge of Europe, the first quarter of the eighteenth century was a time of social and cultural upheaval, explicitly directed towards westernization, progress, and transformation, but almost all of it inaugurated through the sheer will of a towering autocrat — Peter I (Peter the Great). The Tsar's modernizing agenda mandated the first wave of translations of Western texts into Russian. The practice of translation in the Russian empire was marked from the beginning by an imperial decree (*ukaz*) — in 1724 the Tsar ordered that translations should be clear and easy to understand, that they should avoid archaic and ecclesiastical registers (i.e., the use of Church Slavonic, heretofore the primary source of written language), and that translators may translate only into their native tongue (no non-native Russian speakers would be allowed to translate into Russian). Finally, the Tsar came down decisively on the side of 'free' and adaptive translation, as opposed to literal translation, which 'obfuscates the meaning of the original, familiarity with which then becomes a virtual necessity for the Russian reader'.[8]

The point of translation, as far as the westernizing Tsar was concerned, was to convey the accumulated trove of Western texts and ideas to the Russian reader as rapidly and voluminously as possible. The widespread practice of translation of foreign texts was inaugurated on Russian soil as a mode of pouring knowledge — on almost all subjects, from ship-building to talking about one's feelings[9] — into Russia. The translation of Western texts into Russian occurred on an enormous scale, but notably with little regard for fidelity or for the sanctity of original authorship. Vasilii Trediakovsky, one of the leading Russian men of letters of this era, famously insisted that 'the translator differs from the creator in name alone'.[10] In other words, for Russian writers and poets of the eighteenth century, translation was an act of creative adaptation. The imperative was to transform foreign models into something usable on Russian soil. Maurice Friedberg cites the words (written in verse) of another early eighteenth-century poet, Sumarokov, whose 'Epistle on the Russian Language' argues:

> And as to which translation is praiseworthy, I shall say thus:
> Each nation has a style of its own.
> That which is most attractive in the French language
> May be just the thing that is horrid in Russian.
> Do not assume, while translating,
> that the author offers you a ready-made form.
> The author presents you with ideas,
> but not with words to express them.[11]

How to find the words to express foreign ideas in Russian? How to find the words to express foreign things — new technologies, inventions, instruments, and gadgets — in Russian? As has been the case in other societies whose encounter with Western modernity occurred after a long period of isolation, the initial period of opening up to the scientific, technological, literary, and philosophical achievements of Western Europe was marked by dramatic developments in the linguistic resources of the more closed, traditional society. Peter I sought to transform his largely isolated, Church-dominated, Muscovite kingdom into an expansive power that would face the West both figuratively and literally — this was the Tsar who, in Pushkin's mythologizing verse, 'stood on the desolate shore' of the Finnish Gulf and determined to build a city that would 'confront the arrogant Swede' and yet also invite the world's powers 'as guests' to the ambitious empire in the East.[12] Peter's decision to strengthen his alliances against the Ottomans by personally visiting the countries of Northern Europe in 1767 enabled him to spend several months studying shipbuilding and navigation in the Netherlands and England. He was determined to create a formidable Russian navy at home, which required the translation of technical expertise into Russian. This is one of many instances in which the drive for military-diplomatic advantage prompted an avalanche of new lexical terms into Russian. Brown cites, somewhat arbitrarily, the words for topsail, bowsprit, tack, shoal water, cabin boy, etc., all of which had to be imported from Dutch, German, or English.[13] As we shall see, a similar collusion of military-diplomatic exigencies and sudden shifts in political leadership would launch an avalanche of lexical importations at the beginning of the twentieth century, when the Soviet Union was formed, and again in the twenty-first century, as President Putin reinvents his country as a cyber-savvy petrostate.

When Peter I turned Russia onto the path of Western modernity (however 'alternative' this path may have turned out to be in subsequent centuries), the Russian language was not only lacking in scientific and technical vocabulary. There was no usable *literary* language. Written Russian was an unstable amalgam of so-called Church Slavonic and versions of the vernacular Russian that was actually spoken on the streets and in bureaucratic offices. Church Slavonic was the ritualized language of the Church, which over the centuries had not changed, although its rich repository of ecclesiastical concepts and imagery was still understandable (in a way that Latin was no longer understandable to speakers of European vernaculars). The problem lay in the jarring disjuncture between two dialects — everyday street language and the 'high' language of the Church — when they were mixed and matched in various proportions to communicate any kind of secular content in writing. Neither odes to the Emperor nor racy tales for the amusement of the merchant from the Petrine era seem readable today, in light of the standard Russian literary language that came into being a mere generation later. In other words, in order for Russian to become a workable literary language — a unified written form with expressive power, depth, and flexibility — something had to happen. That 'something' is usually summed up in one name: Alexander Pushkin. Pushkin's (1799–1837) extraordinary literary output in lyric and dramatic verse, short and long prose, drama, tragedy, and satire, formed the standard literary language that more or less remains to this day. Yet Pushkin's genius was also filtered through the prism of translation.

Before turning to Pushkin, we should review the role of prismatic translation in matters of Russian versification. In 1730, the irascible Classicist Vasily Trediakovsky (quoted above) translated Boileau's famous *Ode Sur La Prise de Namur* (1694) for the first time. The first few lines of Boileau's ode suffice to illustrate the Classical French system, whereby one counts syllables per line, not accents (stressed syllables) per line, and alternates 'feminine' (y-**vress**-e with P**ermess**-e) and 'masculine' (**loy** with **voy**) rhymes. At first, Trediakovsky stuck to the principle of counting syllables, thereby producing line after line of nine syllables. Because the accent in Russian words may fall on *any* syllable, but only on *one* syllable per long multisyllabic word, in a line of nine syllables the native ear only hears about two stressed syllables. The effect is the sound of trudging prose, marching nine paces before restarting in a new line. Over time, while pondering the problem of how to turn the natural rhythms of Russian into language that can lilt and soar, Trediakovsky redid his original translation of Boileau's ode — while also writing his treatise 'On Russian Versification, Ancient, Middle, and Modern'.[14] Trediakovsky's completely revised translation of the same poem keeps the same content, but is notably different in form, insofar as the stressed syllables fall naturally (regardless of syllable count).

Quelle docte & fainte yvresse	Кое странное пианство
Aujourd'hui me fait la loy?	К пению мой глас бодрит!
Chastes Nymphes du Permesse,	Вы парнасское убранство
N'est-ce pas vous que je voy?	Музы! ум не вас ли зрит?

In Brown's translation of the latter version (above), we hear something of the lilt of the Russian reproduced in English: What strange intoxication/ Emboldens my voice to song/ You, the adornment of Parnassus/ O Muses — is it you my mind beholds?[15]

From this perspective, what begins as a translation of Boileau's odes from the French leads to the recasting of an entire versification system. Trediakovsky's imitations of Boileau led him to question the very foundations of the notion that poetry was created out of lines with a set number of syllables, marked off by rhymes at the end of each line. Since this scheme, as we have seen, was completely unsuitable to the structure of Russian words, the syllabic French *ode* was transformed into a very un-French model of accentual (tonic) versification more suitable for Russian prosody. Trediakovsky's more famous rival Mikhail Lomonosov is justifiably credited with carrying verse reforms further, but the impetus for the process was translation. Within a scant half-century, the 'discovery' of syllabo-tonic versification (in the process of creative translation) would lead to the Golden Age of nineteenth-century Russian poetry.

Russian Literature Comes of Age

According to most experts, by 1840 translation work was no longer part of the repertoire of Russian writers and poets; rather, it had become a branch of commercial publishing, staffed by anonymous translators.[16] In Fyodor Dostoevsky's major novels, written in the latter half of the nineteenth century, we get glimpses of the seemingly ubiquitous and inexact activity of translating foreign texts. The translators who pop up in the pages of Dostoevsky are part of the landscape; they are anonymous members of the literate class. It is taken for granted that multiple translations of any given text can be generated and circulated wherever there is a demand. In *Crime and Punishment,* Razumikhin tries to help out the erratic and impecunious Raskolnikov by setting him up to 'do some translations,' assuring him that the work can be done without much effort. This certainly has to do with the fact that by the mid-nineteenth century — barely a hundred years from the first attempts to create a workable literary form of Russian for translating Western texts — Russian literature (and the remarkably rich language it created) had come into its own both at home, where literacy was on the rise, and on the world stage. Once Russian civilization could boast of its own world-class literature, the role of translated literature in the cultural system receded to the periphery. Marina Kostionova reminds us that by the late 1860s, even the Russian rage for Dickens (in notoriously loose translations) had receded, since native literature now dominated public discourse.[17]

Russian literature could boast its own 'greats' in the works of Pushkin, Lermontov, Turgenev, Dostoevsky, and Tolstoy. Moreover, the importance of literature as a primary mode for 'imagining the nation' had come to the fore. Literary journals sprouted up to feed a voracious appetite for entertaining fiction as well as intellectual debate. In fact, during the latter half of the nineteenth century, the act of reading and talking about literature acquired unusual importance — even a kind of sacrality — in Russian culture. Under the rule of nineteenth-century Tsars, the tension between rigid, autocratic rule and a restless, underemployed caste of educated urban citizens led to what Andrew Wachtel has called the 'overvaluation of literature' as a forum for social debate and (somewhat abstract) activism.[18] In the absence of enabling structures of civil society, Russians read, discussed, and debated matters of human nature, national identity, and ideal governance on the pages of literature (fictional or non-fiction, native or foreign) that escaped the nets of official censorship.

This suggests that on the one hand, translation was used as a prism to multiply, amplify, and productively distort source texts during Russia's rush towards Western modernity; on the other hand, from the standpoint of an increasingly self-confident imperial power, it might have been possible to argue, at least theoretically, over the merits of translation as a one-to-one equivalent or best possible rendition of the source text. Yet the latter position — what Lefevre and Venuti and others have referred to as a strong orientation towards the original text, rather than towards the target culture[19] — has never held sway for long in Russia. Indeed, in many parts of the world, the underlying social, political, and economic assumptions that shaped literary theory and practice did not support a culture of one-to-one equivalence in translation.

Lauren Leighton and Brian James Baer have both argued persuasively that it is more accurate to view Russian and Eastern Europe as a distinctive translation zone, separate from others.[20] On the eastern margins of Europe, numerous factors contributed historically to an unusually dynamic and inherently politicized culture of translation throughout the region, one that made the art of translation, in Baer's phrase, 'highly visible'. In Russia and Eastern Europe, translation can make deep historical fissures visible; it can also make futuristic, transnational dreams visible. In short, translation has often highlighted the region's anxieties about its late start in the race to modernity, but it has also served as a reminder of the latent strength in the region's unique spiritual and cultural resources.

Translation in Revolutionary Times

In the immediate aftermath of the Bolshevik Revolution, followed by a civil war (1918–1921) and the imposition of 'war communism,' it might have seemed quixotic to talk or think about literature at all. Instead, the city of St. Petersburg, in particular, was the site of a diverse and burgeoning artistic scene, despite chronic shortages of food, heat, and of the paper that was needed to write on. Under these conditions, writers and artists nevertheless tried to organize into groups and seek patronage. In 1919, the writer Maxim Gorky was able to establish a new publishing house under the auspices of *Narkompros*, the National Commissariat of Education.[21] The new venture was called 'World Literature' [*Vsemirnaia literatura*], and its publishing goals were not only enormously ambitious — they were also meant to assure survival (food, housing, occupation) for a generation of writers whose lives had been torn apart by war. Gorky's plan was to create a 'Basic Library' of 1,500 works of Western literature in translation, as well as a 'popular library' of translated works containing well over 3,000 titles. Although it was impossible to fulfill this plan under the circumstances in the 1920s, the remarkable existence of a State-supported 'Studio of Translators' is emblematic: the new communist state intended to educate and enlighten the masses in large part through the prism of translation.[22]

As Katerina Clark points out, the ideal of a world literature (replacing 'numerous national and local literatures') promulgated in Marx and Engel's 'Communist Manifesto' (1848) could only be realized in the world's first communist state if it invested in a lot of translating activity.[23] Gorky's 'World Literature' project actually pursued its enlightenment goals along two different vectors, which Leighton describes as 'propagandistic' and 'academic'. The Soviet Union was a vast multinational empire whose inhabitants spoke over one hundred different languages. In order to produce and replicate the premise that all these 'Soviet peoples' shared a common allegiance to a 'friendship of our peoples' under the banner of classless communism, Soviet leaders relied in part on the power of translation: thousands of poems, tales, stories, and so forth were translated from and into the various languages of the empire. As Efim Etkind puts it, 'in order to support the unity of a multiethnic Soviet Union, it was necessary to constantly recreate the illusion of brotherhood among the various republics and peoples; poetic translations played no small a role in that performance'.[24] For many intellectuals, this kind of translation work carried the moral stigma of participating in crude propaganda and participating in the regime's hypocritical policies towards its national minorities.

Against this background, the Soviet Union's so-called 'intelligentsia' subculture — roughly defined here as the cohort of thinkers who resisted acquiescence to the regime's reigning ideology (without necessarily actively engaging in dissident activities) — attached a strong moral valence to the translation of 'immortal' works of art. In the great works of Western literature, the post-war Soviet intelligentsia saw an expression of freedom, individuality, and beauty encoded without any overlay of ideology. At a moment when in the West, postmodern scholars started to emphasize the embeddedness of ideology in all canonical cultural productions, Soviet intellectuals did the opposite: they resisted the hegemony of Soviet Marxist dogma by devoting themselves to the translation of aesthetic masterpieces, on the grounds that these masterpieces reflected the timeless values of humanistic culture.[25] In other words, to translate literary works because they were *not* political (in the narrow sense of writing for a regime or an ideology) was in itself an act of moral resistance. Literary translation was thus 'viewed within the subculture as a highly moral or even ethical undertaking. Discussions of literary translation often celebrated the officially suspect concept of individuality, specifically the unique talent and genius of the literary translator'.[26] Here's the rub: Stalin's cultural watchdogs had condemned the orientation towards close, faithful translation on the grounds that literalism led to 'formalism,' i.e., excessive experimentation, stylistic opacity, and deviation from the necessary clarity and accessibility of Socialist Realist art.[27] Insofar as the 'nearly universal disrepute' of literalist translation held sway throughout the Soviet period,[28] it stands to reason that precisely this mode would be valorized by those who resisted the regime's heavy-handed censorship. From here, it is a short step from the discredited notion of 'formalism' to the 'heroic' stance of the Soviet literary translator who dedicates herself to the act of faithfully translating world literature. Tatiana Gnedich's translation of Byron's *Don Juan* famously illustrates this dynamic: in 1945, Gnedich was arrested and held in a KGB prison. While awaiting trial, she began to translate the first two cantos (over 2,000 lines) of Byron's poem, which she knew by heart. Her KGB handlers were not necessarily steeped in the ideological nuances of translation theory, but they were certainly impressed with the prisoner's narrative memory and skills. The investigator provided the conditions for her to finish the rest of poem (some 17,000 lines) in jail, before she was transferred to a camp to finish out her sentence.[29] In another instance, the outspoken geneticist and polyglot Vladimir Efroimson found himself facing yet another arduous transfer from one prison camp to another during his ten-year term. In a letter to his wife, he wrote '[...] it turned out to be a great day! Another prisoner in our transport knew some Italian! We spent the entire march reciting as much as we could remember from Dante. Arrived at our destination feeling greatly uplifted!'[30] In fact, the intelligentsia's faithful translations were not 'literal' in a technical sense; rather, they represented an effort to recreate the 'universal' artistic heritage of Western civilization, in order to reassert the continuity of 'real' Russian culture and this precious heritage. Thus, often quite literally, the act of translating poetry became a kind of survival mode in the gulag.

Russian Language on the Verge of a Nervous Breakdown

When the Soviet Union abruptly collapsed in 1991, the situation regarding translation was over-determined: after nearly seven decades of ideologically restricted literary traffic between Russia and the West, during which only a steady drip of approved material was translated and published in the USSR, the floodgates suddenly broke open, and nearly everything and anything that might sell was hastily translated and made available (in street kiosks and open markets, as well as in transformed established book stores) to the new post-Soviet consumer. At one end of the spectrum, the market was flooded with translations of cheap pulp fiction, bodice-ripper romances, pornography, detective fiction, religious and occult texts, and niche 'how-to' manuals on every imaginable topic. At the other end of the spectrum, translations of previously banned writers and thinkers appeared in non-chronological profusion — early twentieth century Russian poets and surrealists; Foucault, Lacan, and Latour, Orwell and Umberto Eco; as well as late twentieth century economists and entrepreneurship gurus. Once again, as during the Petrine reforms of the early eighteenth century, the socio-cultural impact of sudden, mass exposure to new ideas was transmitted through the prism of translation. For better or for worse (and there were vehement opinions on both sides), previously unattainable information about and from the other side of the Iron Curtain arrived into post-Soviet Russia in forms that were inevitably distorted, amplified, or re-contextualized. Previously unavailable Western texts were bent through the prism of linguistic difference, historical divergence (between the former Cold War adversaries), and pent-up demand for previously forbidden fruit.

By the second decade of the 21st century, the situation had stabilized, somewhat paradoxically, at a new level of both unprecedented newness and déjà vu. On the one hand, the ubiquity of the Internet, providing instant access to electronic texts and translations, had changed the way much of the world acquires and consumes any kind of literature. Russians, like most of the rest of us, expect nearly instant access to almost any kind of literature online, and they participate actively in the new paradigm of crowd-sourced reading and commentary platforms. In this scenario, one is no longer alone with a book, but reading online, usually with a lot auxiliary input (which one is only theoretically able to ignore) from a greatly expanded demographic of online critics, peer commentators, and ad hoc interpreters of any given text. On the other hand, one can argue that despite the radical newness of our technologies, the age-old reflexes of cultural 'liberals' and cultural 'conservatives' remain the same. During the period of Putin's third Presidential term (2012–2018), for instance, the inescapable influence of English (brought in through foreign texts and translations) on the Russian language has reopened a familiar front in the wars over language change. Is the 'great and mighty' Russian language being destroyed by proliferating neologisms, calques and borrowings from English that suddenly seem to have taken over entire spheres of discourse? Should the defenders of traditional values enact measures to reverse the foreign linguistic invasion?

In 2008, Maksim Krongaus, a professional linguist and scholar in Moscow, created an unlikely bestseller in a book devoted to current debates over the purity of the Russian language.[31] Krongaus's *Russkii yazyk na grani nervogo vzryva* [*Russian Language on the Verge of a Nervous Breakdown*] explains the nature of the lexical changes that have transformed the post-Soviet Russian language. While he feigns sympathy with those who still cringe at the normalization of *maternye slova* (swear words and criminal slang), the author presents 'liberal' arguments in favor of foreign borrowings. Today's foreign borrowings might be seen as distant analogs of the nautical and technical vocabulary of Peter's time, as well as the adoption of 'words for feelings' in early modern Russian society. In the post-Soviet period, the most obvious influx of borrowed words relates to the globalized realms of business, technology, self-help, and entertainment. *Marketing, competence, deadline, delete, internet, trolling, glamour, eyeliner* all have calqued forms in Russian. After all, through the prism of translation, the foreign neologisms soon acquire a patina of native sense and sensibility that — in the view of a sociolinguist — is productive for cultural change and development.

> While asking the eternal Russian questions *Who is to blame?* and *What is to be done?* we forget to ask the most interesting question, *What actually happened?* What happened is an enormous restructuring of language under the pressure of complicated social, technological, and even ecological changes. Only those who adapt in time can survive [such changes]. So far, the Russian language has kept the pace and adapted [to a new world]....[32]

As a linguist and as a citizen, Krongaus approves of the new crowd-sourced dictionaries and translation sites that augment the rapid movement from original source text to fruitful multiple translations and adaptations into Russian. On one such site, a quip by America's late-night television comedian Jimmy Kimmel was posted for translation. 'If Trump does become president, I hope he puts a wig on his plane and calls it Hair Force One'.[33] In its original context, the joke channeled animosity towards a presidential candidate considered to be both unqualified and narcissistic, by making fun of Trump's striking comb-over hair style. In Russian, the punning name of the presidential airplane, Hair Force One, was translated as *Volosatii Odin* [literally, Hairy Guy One], which makes perfect sense through the prism of an old Soviet joke: it was said that a 'periodic table' of Soviet leaders demonstrates regular oscillation between revolutionary-reformist 'bald guys' (picture Lenin, Khurshchev, Gorbachev) and conservative-strongmen 'hairy guys' (picture Stalin, Brezhnev). Thus, *Volosatii Odin* [roughly, Hair Force One] translates

American animosity towards a type of authoritarian leader into Russian animosity towards 'their' type of authoritarian leader, leaving both the humor and the hair intact.

Krongaus's popular book is meant to demystify the linguistic changes that have been explicitly embraced by young, urban, well-educated, cosmopolitan Russians, and at least implicitly by nearly everyone else who works in the modern world. In contrast, the arguments of the linguistic conservatives are frequently (but not always) marred by an unsavory tone of religious and ethnic fundamentalism. More interesting, for our purposes, is the language that the conservative camp uses in its defense of 'purity' and linguistic patriotism. All sides agree on the basic premise that language is linked to thought, so that changes in language lead to changes in 'ways of thinking.' From there, the more moderate conservatives (example #1, below) argue that the language of modern commercial media (initially translated from Western models) leads to stupidity. The more virulent conservatives (examples #2 and #3 below) directly link the perceived degradation of contemporary Russian to foreign meddling by hostile powers, and to apostasy — a falling away from the true path of God.

#1. A commentator on the folkorically named site *temnii les* [dark forest] takes aim at language that obscures critical thinking. He fails to mention that Soviet 'newspeak,' used in previous generations, also functioned in this way (with a different set of clichés and euphemisms). His examples will seem familiar to non-Russian audiences as well:

> Examples of usage beloved by television commentators: 'it's complicated' instead of 'it's hard' (hence, the ridiculous 'it's complicated to say...'); 'sufficiently [enough]' instead of 'fairly' ([fairly frightening] 'that's a frightening enough story!'); 'not prepared' instead of 'does not want to' ('the President is not prepared to speak to that point').[34]

#2. *Izba-Chitalnya* ['Little Shack Reading Room'], also with positive folkloric overtones, is an overtly patriotic site that calls itself an 'unbiased literary portal' where one can submit artistic works and read them. The site's homepage lists the following unambiguous values: 'We are patriots of the Russian language, regardless of where we now live. We are patriots of the homeland of the Russian language. We support anything that is beneficial to Russian people, or to any other people who 'use Russian'.'

The views on language expressed on the *Izba* site often illustrate the deeply conservative, intolerant and fundamentalist strain of contemporary thought. For example, a position article from 2013 called 'On the Purity of the Russian Language' argues that Russian is a sacred language given to us 'from above', which the people must serve as one would serve a deity in order not to stray into darkness. The author particularly condemns the ubiquity of obscene language in post-Soviet Russian, citing supposedly scientific evidence to argue against its use: 'the research of Russian scientists has shown that the use of obscene language leads to sexual impotence.'

#3 A national portal for Russian educators K-12 is called *Nasha set'* [Our Net]. The site is presumably a State-approved resource for the Russian Federation's teachers. A 2013 article on 'The Relevance of the Problem of Preserving the Purity of the Russian Language' makes many familiar claims about the connection between language use and social development; e.g. perceived degradation of language is directly linked to degradation of society. Moreover, the degradation of society is a symptom of the degradation and weakness of the entire nation; hence the author's alarmist insinuation that hostile foreign powers are behind the negative features in contemporary Russian:

> We have long known the laws of correlation: ugly and primitive speech leads to ugly and primitive thought processes, which determine accordingly a person's actions and behavior. So let's pose ourselves a question: To whose advantage is it if the nation loses its ability to think well? Who gains from a crippled, weakened Russian language? The advantage goes to those who want a weak, dependent Russia.[35]

Finally, in a 2016 example of the Russian 'language wars', a TV reporter set out to interview teachers on June 6, which is officially billed as 'Day of the Russian Language'. Somewhat predictably, the report emphasized teachers' uphill battle with vulgarisms, youth slang, and the general degradation of Russian in the post-Soviet period. (It bears repeating that during the Soviet period, it was axiomatic to most intellectuals that the Russian language had already been hopelessly degraded).[36] Paradoxically, when experts are brought in to support the doctrine of a 'pure Russian language', their pronouncements exhibit precisely the kind of pseudo-scientific, media-speak inelegance they are supposed to preach against. A quoted expert says:

> 'Word-parasites destroy the body at the level of DNA [ДНК], which is frightening. That is, the children and grandchildren of a person who uses word-parasites will suffer from brain dysfunctionalities [мозговыми дисфункциями],' says doctor of pedagogical science Tatiana Z....'[37]

The Great Exception to the Rule: Vladimir Nabokov and Literalism in the Cold War Context

In conclusion, we should question when and how it was ever possible to see one-to-one equivalence as the end goal of translation. Contemporary online tools provide us with instant access to vast data sets of possible word equivalents and contextualized usages, creating a different playing field for the would-be translator. Global translation practices and the technology that supports them rebel against the notion of one-to-one equivalence. For instance, promotional information on the website ABBYY LINGVO, an online translating resource:[38]

> [With our dictionary] find the translation of a word, its synonyms and antonyms, its idiomatic usage and meaning in fixed phrases. You can also select the most appropriate translation of the word from numerous examples of contextualized usage drawn from other lexical references, dictionaries of phraseology and slang, and conversational manuals.

The constantly evolving, crowd-sourced dictionary of words and phrases offered by ABBYY LINGVO is one of many similar online resources available to students and translators today. Sites like ABBYY LINGVO can be considered intellectual and commercial affirmation that at least for now, the old notion of one-to-one translation is out, and the notion of multiple possible translations, refracted through the prism of many people's linguistic needs and experience, is so ubiquitous that the dictionary itself encourages you to 'select the most appropriate translation from numerous examples [...].'

Clearly, we have come a long way from the spectacular debate between two multilingual scholars of the pre-internet twentieth century — Vladimir Nabokov and Walter Arndt — whose battles over the correct way (there could be only *one* correct way) to translate the poetic works of Russian literature's versatile genius Alexander Pushkin carried all the way into the pages of *Playboy* magazine.[39] Although in Russia and the former Soviet Union, as we have seen, 'literal' translation was almost never supported, the long Western tradition of championing 'fidelity' to the original put up a surprising vigorous fight during the Cold War years. The public debates over how to translate Pushkin are worth revisiting here, in order to probe the former status quo more carefully. Why, exactly, was the paradigm that figured translation as a narrow conduit from the original to a best-possible equivalent dominant (or at least vigorously respected) in the United States for so long? What confluence of ideological and other factors suppressed the perspective of translation-as-generative process in favor of a much more restrictive notion of translation-as-heroic-feat?

Let's go back to April 30, 1964, when *The New York Review of Books* published a notably harsh and vehement denunciation of Walter Arndt's new translation of Pushkin's novel in verse *Evgeny Onegin*.[40] The author of the mean-spirited attack was Vladimir Nabokov, who was working on his own translation of *Evgeny Onegin*. Nabokov came out swinging: Walter Arndt's *Eugene Onegin,* billed as 'an immortal novel in verse in a brilliant new translation', had just been released as trade paperback by E.P. Dutton.[41] According to Nabokov, Arndt's translation was the work of a 'pitiless and irresponsible paraphrast' who deceived his readers with 'lulling poetastry and specious sense'. Nabokov provided examples of passages he felt were mistranslated. He categorized Arndt's faults as a translator into twelve separate varieties, from 'natural objects changing their species or genus' (#1) to 'crippled clichés and mangled idioms' (#6) to the unforgivable '*otsebyatina*' (#12). For all its wit and venom, Nabokov's attack was not convincing, because Arndt's virtuoso rendering of Pushkin's rhymed iambic tetrameter made sense to readers in a way that Nabokov's ponderous literalism did not:

> Now that he is in grave condition,
> My uncle, decorous old prune,
> Has earned himself my recognition;
> What could have been more opportune?
> May his idea inspire others;
> But what a bore, I ask you, brothers,
> To tend a patient night and day

> And venture not a step away:
> Is there hypocrisy more glaring
> Than to amuse one all but dead,
> Shake up the pillow for his head,
> Dose him with melancholy bearing,
> And think behind a stifled cough,
> 'When will the Devil haul you off?'

Nabokov's version reads:

> My uncle has most honest principles:
> when taken ill in earnest,
> he has made one respect him
> and nothing better could invent.
> To others his example is a lesson;
> but, good God, what a bore
> to sit by a sick man both day and night,
> without moving a step away!
> What base perfidiousness
> the half-alive one to amuse,
> adjust for him the pillows,
> sadly present the medicine,
> sigh — and think inwardly
> when *will* the devil take you?[42]

Yet, the debate resounded and spread. In fact, the rhetoric of the debate resounded with deep Cold War anxieties. Arndt wrote a spirited (but not mean) rebuttal.[43] Edmund Wilson rejoined with another full-length essay in *The New York Review of Books* a year later, in which he failed to come to his old friend Nabokov's defense: Wilson could not find much merit in Nabokov's two-volume, obsessively footnoted, ponderously literal translation of *Onegin*. 'The Strange Case of Pushkin and Nabokov', as Wilson's critique was titled, can be considered the highwater mark of a mid-twentieth century assumption that only one road leads to the best translation. Nabokov insisted that his version — and only his version — was adequately representative of the original. All other translations were not acceptable. Translations like Arndt's, according to Nabokov, seduce the 'credulous college student' and 'passive reader', who is 'the pet of progressive educators'. In fact, Nabokov returns repeatedly to the potential harm inflicted on the 'passive' and ignorant reader, who does not know enough about Russia, and cannot trust any (other) translator to convey the truth. According to Nabokov's attack in the *New York Review*, innocent American readers, who so easily succumb to 'gaily colored packaging' will be duped by infelicities in the translation. They will 'hardly notice' that the non-Nabokov translator has substituted a different metaphor for the one in the original. As Margaret Peacock has demonstrated, Cold War discourse in the United States in the mid-nineteen-sixties continually reinforces the dangers of 'naïve' cross-cultural sympathies and passive lack of vigilance.[44] If we don't translate the Russians *in precisely the right way,* then how do we know what the original is *really like*?

Paradoxically, the more elaborately Nabokov insists on the need for a single, most equivalent translation, the more his own ingenious arguments betray him. His final blow against Walter Arndt is that Arndt has filled his texts with *otsebyatiny*. Now listen to Nabokov's own prismatic rendering of the word-concept:

> This convenient cant word consists of the words *ot*, meaning 'from,' and *sebya*, meaning 'oneself,' with a pejorative suffix, *yatina*, tagged on (its *ya* takes improper advantage of the genitive ending of the pronoun, coinciding with it and producing a strongly stressed *bya* sound which to a Russian's ear connotes juvenile disgust).
> Lexically translated, it can be rendered as 'comefromoneselfer' or 'fromoneselfity.'

Taking advantage of our prism, which allows the language of the original to produce a rainbow of new meanings to suit new realities, we might even propose that the *otsebyatina* today describes the insertion of one's self both textually and visually and digitally, as in the 'fromoneselfie.' The prism, to paraphrase Bulgakov (via *Faust*) is that force which forever falsifies, in order to forever tell the truth.

Works Cited

ARNDT, WALTER, trans., *Eugene Onegin, A Novel in Verse: A New Translation in the Onegin Stanza*. Original work by Alexander Pushkin. (New York: Dutton, 1963)
ARNDT, WALTER, 'Goading the Pony', *The New York Review of Books* (April 30, 1964)
AZOV, ANDREI, *Poverzhennye bukvalisty: Iz istorii khudozhestvennogo perevoda v SSSR v 1920–1960 gody* (Moscow: Izdatelskyi Dom VSE, 2013)
BAER, BRIAN J., 'Literary Translation and the Construction of a Soviet Intelligentsia Author', *The Massachusetts Review*, 47.3 (2006), 537–60
BAER, BRIAN, and SUSANNA WITT, *Translation in Russian Contexts. Culture, Politics, Identity* (New York: Routledge, 2018)
BROWN, WILLIAM E., *A History of Eighteenth-Century Russian Literature* (Ann Arbor: Ardis, 1980)
CRONIN, MIKHAIL, *Translation in the Digital Age* (New York: Routledge, 2013)
DELERS, OLIVIER, *The Other Rise of the Novel; Alternative Economies in Eighteenth-Century Fiction* (Newark: University of Delaware Press, 2015)
ETKIND, EFIM, *Mastera poeticheskogo perevoda* (Moscow: Akademicheskii Proekt, 1997)
FRIEDBERG, MAURICE, *Literary Translation in Russia; A Cultural History* (Pennsylvania: Pennsylvania State University Press, 1997)
HAMMARBERG, GITTA, *From the Idyll to the Novel: Karamzin's Sentimentalist Prose* (Cambridge: Cambridge University Press, 1991)
KRONGAUS, MAKSIM, *Русский язык на грани нервного взрыва*. *Russian Language on the Verge of a Nervous Breakdown* (Moscow: Yazyki slavyanskikh kultur, 2008)
LAL, VINAY, 'The Courtesan and the Indian Novel', *Indian Literature*, 139 (1995), 164–70
LEFEVERE, ANDRÉ, *Translating Literature: Practice and Theory in a Comparative Literature Framework*. (New York: MLA, 1992)
LEIGHTON, LAUREN, *Two Worlds, One Art; Literary Translation in Russia and America* (Dekalb: Northern Illinois University Press, 1991)
NABOKOV, VLADIMIR, 'On Translating Pushkin; Pounding the Clavichord,' *The New York Review of Books* (April 30, 1964)
NABOKOV, VLADIMIR, TRANS. WITH COMMENTARY, *Eugene Onegin. A Novel in Verse by*

Alexander Pushkin; Translated From the Russian with Commentary by Vladimir Nabokov (Bollingen Foundation, 1965)

PEACOCK, MARGARET, *Innocent Weapons; The Soviet and American Politics of Childhood in the Cold War* (Chapel Hill: University of North Carolina Press, 2014)

PUSHKIN, ALEXANDER, *Sobraniie sochineniie v desiati tomakh, tom 3* (Moskva: Gos Izd Khudozhestvennoj Literatury, 1960), 285–99. [Alexander Pushkin : Collected Works in Ten Volumes (Moscow State Art Publishing House, 1960)

RASSOKHINA, ELENA, *Shakespeare's Sonnets in Russian* (Umeå Studies in Language and Literature 37: Umeå University, 2017)

SCHERR, BARRY, 'Notes on Literary Life in Petrograd, 1918–1922: A Tale of Three Houses', *Slavic Review*, 36.2 (1977), 256–67

VENUTI, LAWRENCE, *The Translator's Invisibility: A History of Translation*, 2nd edn, (Abingdon: Routledge, 2008)

WACHTEL, ANDREW, *Remaining Relevant After Communism. The Role of the Writer in Eastern Europe* (Chicago: University of Chicago Press, 2006)

WATT, IAN, *The Rise of the Novel; Studies in Dafoe, Richardson, and Fielding* (Oakland: University of California Press, 1957)

Notes to Chapter 5

1. Eurasia is alternately a geographical, geopolitical, or ideological designation. For a recent consideration, see Chris Hann, 'Making Sense of Eurasia: Reflections on Max Weber and Jack Goody', *New Literary History*, 48 (2017), 685–99.
2. Michael Cronin, *Translation in the Digital Age* (New York: Routledge, 2013), p. 67.
3. *Sobraniie sochineniie v desiati tomakh, tom 3* (Moskva: Gos Izd Khudozhestvennoj Literatury, 1960), 285–99. [Alexander Pushkin : Collected Works in Ten Volumes (Moscow State Art Publishing House, 1960)], 285–99 (p. 285).
4. Yulia Tikhomirova, 'Expressing the Other, Translating the Self: Ivan Kozlov's Translation Genres' in *Translation in Russian Contexts. Culture, Politics, Identity*, ed. Brian James Baer and Susanna Witt (New York: Routledge, 2018), pp. 95–109.
5. Ian Watt, *The Rise of the Novel; Studies in Defoe, Richardson, and Fielding* (Oakland: University of California Press, 1957).
6. Olivier Delers, *The Other Rise of the Novel; Alternative Economies in Eighteenth-Century Fiction* (Newark: University of Delaware Press, 2015).
7. Vinay Lal, 'The Courtesan and the Indian Novel', *Indian Literature*, 139 (1995), 164–70.
8. Maurice Friedberg, *Literary Translation in Russia; A Cultural History* (Pennsylvania: Pennsylvania State University Press, 1997), p. 34. Friedberg's sources are *Zakonodatel-nye akty Petra I* (Moscow: Izdatelstvo Akademii Nauk SSSR, 1945), p. 35; cited in Givi Gachechiladze, *Vvedene v teoriiu khudozhestvennogo perevoda: Avtorizovannyi perevod s gruzinskogo* (Tblisi: Izd. Tbilisskogo universiteta, 1970), p. 26.
9. Peter I was obviously more interested in importing technical and engineering terms into Russian life, but the language of feelings and emotions was not far behind. The genre of 'sentimentalism' was adapted into Russian letters by the versatile historian and writer Nikolai Karamzin. See Gitta Hammarberg, *From the Idyll to the Novel: Karamzin's Sentimentalist Prose* (Cambridge, UK: Cambridge University Press, 1991).
10. Friedberg, *Literary Translation in Russia*, p. 36.
11. Friedberg, *Literary Translation in Russia*, p. 35.
12. Pushkin, 'Bronze Horseman', in *Collected Works*, pp. 285–99 (pp. 285–86).
13. William Edward Brown, *A History of Eighteenth-Century Russian Literature* (Ann Arbor: Ardis, 1980), p. 13.
14. Brown, *A History of Eighteenth-Century Russian Literature*, p. 63.
15. Brown, *A History of Eighteenth-Century Russian Literature*, p. 57.
16. Friedberg, *Literary Translation in Russia*, p. 38.

17. Marina Kostionova, 'Charles Dickens in Nineteenth Century Russia,' in *Translation in Russian Contexts. Culture, Politics, Identity,* ed. by Brian James Baer and Susanna Witt (New York: Routledge, 2018), pp. 110–24 (p. 118).
18. Andrew Wachtel, *Remaining Relevant After Communism. The Role of the Writer in Eastern Europe* (Chicago: University of Chicago, 2006).
19. See, for example, André Lefevere, *Translating Literature: Practice and Theory in a Comparative Literature Framework.* (New York: MLA, 1992); and Lawrence Venuti, *The Translator's Invisibility: A History of Translation* (2nd ed.). (Abingdon: Routledge, 2008).
20. Lauren Leighton, *Two Worlds, One Art; Literary Translation in Russia and America* (Dekalb: Northern Illinois University Press, 1991); See also Brian James Baer (ed.), *Contexts, Subtexts, and Pretexts; Literary Translation in Eastern Europe and Russia* (Amsterdam: John Benjamins Publishing Company, 2011).
21. Barry Scherr, 'Notes on Literary Life in Petrograd, 1918–1922: A Tale of Three Houses', *Slavic Review,* 36.2 (1977), 256–67.
22. The sense that one was 'enlightened through translated literature' ran deep, and left a mark at least up to the last generation to grow up in the Soviet Union. For instance, research on readers' reception of the novels of Charles Dickens, which were translated many times into Russian, reveals (at least anecdotally) a deep allegiance to the importance of these novels to the formation of an intelligent, socially-conscious worldview. A typical response to questions about Dickens' importance for the Soviet reader:

    Диккенс был создан блестящими переводчиками. Он был доступен советскому читателю, поскольку глубинно вскрывал социальные проблемы. Он был близок русскому читателю, тем, кто также зачитывался Достоевским и Толстым, поскольку создавал в своих произведениях эмоционально напряженные ситуации, хорошо узнаваемые русским читателем.

    [Dickens was created [for us] by brilliant translators. He was accessible to Soviet readers, because he revealed the essence of social problems. He was close to the Russian reader who had read Dostoevsky and Tolstoy, because Dicken's works gave us emotionally intense situations, the kind we recognized.] <https://russiandickens.wordpress.com/question-3/> Accessed 28 Feb 2018.
23. Katerina Clark, 'Translation and Transnationalism. Non-European Writers and Soviet Power in 1920s and 1930s,' in *Translation in Russian Contexts,* ed. by Baer and Witt, pp. 139–58.
24. Efim Etkind, *Mastera poeticheskogo perevoda* (Moscow: Akademicheskii Proekt: 1997), p. 39.
25. Brain James Baer, 'Literary Translation and the Construction of a Soviet Intelligentsia Author', *The Massachusetts Review,* 47.3 (2006), 537–60.
26. Baer, 'Literary Translation', p. 550.
27. Andrei Azov, *Poverzhennye bukvalisty: Iz istorii khudozhestvennogo perevoda v SSSR v 1920–1960 gody* (Moscow: Izdatelsky. Dom VSE, 2013).
28. See Elena Rassokhina, *Shakespeare's Sonnets in Russian* (Umeå Studies in Language and Literature 37: Umeå University, 2017) for a detailed account of shifts in translation policy.
29. This story is related by Efim Etkind in *Poeziia i perevod* (Moscow-Leningrad: Sovetskii Pisatel, 1963). See also Baer, 'Literary Translation', pp. 553–54.
30. Vladimir Pavlovich Efroimson, unpublished materials (copy of KGB archival material), private collection (Howell).
31. Максим Кронгаус, *Русский язык на грани нерного взрыва. Russian Language on the Verge of a Nervous Breakdown* (Moscow: *Yazyki slavyanskikh kultur,* 2008).
32. Krongaus, p. 13 (my translation). Text accessed online at <https://www.litres.ru>
33. <https://thoughtcatalog.com/lorenzo-jensen-iii/2015/08/hair-force-one-40-of-the-funniest-anti-donald-trump-jokes/>. Accessed 5 March 2018.
34. Accessed 02 March 2018. Ilya Miklashevskii has updated and reposted his essay on language change three times, 1993, 1997, and 2007. 'Вот примеры: 'сложно' вместо 'трудно' (совсем уж нелепо звучит 'сложно сказать'); 'достаточно' вместо 'довольно' (например, 'достаточно страшная история'); 'не готов' вместо 'не хочу' [...].' <https://www.chitalnya.ru/about.php>. Accessed 01 March 2018.

35. 'Давно известна закономерность: если уродлива, примитивна речь, то уродливо и примитивно мышление, равно как и зависящие от него поступки, поведение человека. И если мы зададим себе вопрос: Кому выгодно национальное беспамятство? Кому выгоден исковерканный, испохабленный русский язык. Тем, кому выгодна слабая, зависимая Россия.'
36. See, for instance, Antoly Naiman's 'Language on the Verge of A Nervous Breakdown,' *Wilson Quarterly* 18.3 (1994).
37. First reported in 'Великий и могучий: кто и как борется за чистоту русского языка' 11:48 06/06/2016 (accessed 5 March 2018). 'Слова-паразиты разрушают тело на уровне ДНК, и это страшно. То есть дети и внуки человека, который использует слова паразиты, будут страдать мозговыми дисфункциями,' — рассказывает доктор педагогических наук Татьяна Зотова.
38. <https://www.abbyy.com/en-us/translation_dictionary/>.
39. Walter Arndt was undaunted by Nabokov's attack on his *Evgeny Onegin,* and went on to produce a rhyming translation of Pushkin's poem 'Tsar Nikita's 40 Daughters', all of whom are missing their vaginas. Arndt's translation came out in *Playboy* magazine (1965: 12). Most people are not aware that Arndt's publication scooped a rival translation of the same poem by Irwin R. Titunik. Titunik's version is both different and brilliant. Yet, given the 'one-best-translation' ethos of the time, he felt that there would be no market for a alternate version.
40. Vladimir Nabokov, 'On Translating Pushkin; Pounding the Clavichord,' *The New York Review of Books* (April 30, 1964).
41. *Eugene Onegin, A Novel In Verse: A New Translation In The Onegin Stanza With An Introduction.* Alexander Pushkin, trans. Walter Arndt (New York: Dutton, 1963).
42. *Eugene Onegin. A Novel in Verse by Alexander Pushkin; Translated From the Russian with Commentary by Vladimir Nabokov* (Bollingen Foundation, 1965).
43. Walter Arndt, 'Goading the Pony', *The New York Review of Books* (April 30, 1964).
44. Margaret Peacock, *Innocent Weapons; The Soviet and American Politics of Childhood in the Cold War* (Chapel Hill: University of North Carolina Press, 2014).

CHAPTER 6

Literary Metatranslations: when Translation Multiples Tell their own Story

Kasia Szymanska

Publications with multiplied translations of the same work are often said to be a scarce commodity. In the newly released anthology *Into English* (2017), Martha Collins, one of the two editors who put together multiple translations of twenty-five different poems, points to a paltry number of existing projects of the kind. She suggests that this body of resources, with some cases hedged by limited access or a low print run, 'made the need for a new anthology seem even more pressing'.[1] A similar reckoning emanates from Walkowitz's epilogue 'Multiples' in her *Born Translated* (2015). Though she identifies potential for multiplying translation variants in digital publishing and online literary journals such as *Asymptote* and *Telephone*, she still labels printed books with translation multiples as 'rare projects' and attributes their format primarily to scholarly compilations released by university presses.[2]

While this is all true and anthologies with multiplied translations do often appear in such contexts, the situation is more complex: the gesture of placing more than one translation variant next to one another has moved beyond this narrow domain, entering a more artistic and experimental realm. In fact, the practice of multiplying different translation variants and putting them next to each other as part of one artistic work — be it a conceptual book with translation multiples or a poem composed of different renderings of the same original — has recently become the springboard for quite a few anglophone projects. Though not limited to this linguistic milieu,[3] translation multiples can offer a special shock therapy to the contemporary *lingua franca*. With its almost proverbial 'three-percent' figure for literature published in translation yearly and its expansive status of a global language, English is often lampooned for being reluctant and oblivious to the creative resources of translation, let alone of that coming in larger numbers and repetitions. This is also where authors of translation multiples and their artistic meddling with the publishing format come into play most forcefully. Oscillating somewhere on the fine border between experimental translation and conceptual writing,[4] projects displaying plural renderings of one original lift the veil on the very act and process of translation and alert readers to its transformative powers. As such multiples start telling their own story, they challenge the purely explanatory or didactic role of multiplied translation which typically boils down to illuminating the original from different angles. Instead, as I will argue, literary projects confronting different variants of one work unfold a narrative in their own right; the critical reflection on the multiple nature of translation which they offer is no longer a by-product of scholarly exegesis but rather a creative principle binding all different variants together and turning their diversity into an artistic conceit.

First of all, I should perhaps backtrack on the rough-grained distinction between the more 'literary' metatranslations and their more 'scholarly' equivalents published by university presses. The idea of unpacking the original verse in multiple ways through creative reworkings does equally have its roots in the academic apparatus surrounding translation. In other words, the artistic imagination behind translation multiples has definitely been nourished by scholarly textual practices such as, for instance: annotations, explanatory glosses, textual exegesis and commentaries with alternative variants in footnotes, in brackets or after slashes — all of which constitutes the long-standing tradition of tackling polysemy in source texts. In the European exegetic and philological practice, this has taken place in the contexts of closely related languages: for instance, early modern English translations of classical texts in which the margins of the page contained alternative variants to 'make visible the multiplying potential of translation'.[5] Likewise, a dissatisfaction with single translation solutions has been also present in attempts to render non-European languages, such as in I. A. Richards's *Mencius on the Mind* (1932) with multiple translations of terms and definitions from the Chinese[6] or David Hawkes's *A Little Primer of Tu Fu* (1967) with different variants resolving what the author saw as the original ambiguity of Chinese verse. In encircling and illuminating the plurality of meanings from various angles, translation acts here at its hermeneutic best.

Similar endeavours unscramble translation's multiple nature otherwise lying dormant in its procedural stage, namely, when a host of different equally legitimate variants go through a translator's mind. But this plurality has also been recorded and actualized in translation history as alternative renderings by different people appear over time; and in this case, it is, indeed, usually the editors of anthologies published by university presses that put them together for a comparative viewing. Take, for instance, whole critical series such as the Penguin Classics *Poets in Translation*, which trace how the English readings of classical and canonical writers (in this case, Horace, Ovid, Virgil, Dante, Baudelaire, to mention a few) changed over the centuries. Collections of this kind often serve as, in Matthew Reynolds's words, 'variorum translation' editions.[7] Whereas typical variorum editions of originals (e.g. of the Bible or Shakespearean plays) keep track of any textual instabilities, processual changes, and editorial decisions in production of original works, multiple translation editions work analogously by displaying a range of available translated variants of one text. Dispersed in a halo of alternative 'equivalences', translation here reflects numerous stylistic and interpretative takes of various historically situated translators, each activating different reservoirs of meaning.

But isn't the artistic practice of multiplying or putting together multiple translations something completely different, something inherently more creative, than its academic counterpart? For instance, Jacques Derrida observed that a firmer line is customarily drawn between the types of textual practice which involve different degrees of quantitative equivalence to the source text. Thick translation with glosses and alternative variants that 'occurs daily in the university and in literary criticism' does not hold a candle to a translation formally equal to a work, 'a translation worthy of the name'.[8] When Kate Briggs challenged this cultural preconception in her *This Little Art*, she insisted that every literary translation to some degree includes criticism, gloss and scholarship;[9] there is always something hermeneutic about translation as it aims to explicate and comment on the literary work it simultaneously purports to represent. In fact, Briggs's argument could be easily reversed when speaking about translation multiples: perhaps besides an inherently academic element in every instance of literary translation, we can, likewise, search for an artistic one in its academic genre? In other words, there might be, after all, some creative potential in the textual practice of translation criticism, with its tradition of glosses, encircling the originals from different analytic angles, squirreling multiple translations in anthologies, editing them collectively and so on. Occasional fascination with translation apparatus creeps into modern translation books which experiment loosely with the convention. For instance, in *Yoko Tawada's Portrait of a Tongue: An Experimental Translation*, Chantal Wright (2013) turns the commentary running on the margins of her rendering into a literary work as such. Others like Hiroaki Sato in *One Hundred Frogs* (1983) have combined the style of a translation workshop around a case study (Bashō's famous 'old pond' haiku) with essayistic narrative and an assemblage of over one hundred creative responses to the poem. A few ensembles of artists and translators have fiddled with the format of single-author or single-work anthologies and edited volumes, for example: Daniel Halpern's book with multiple poets translating parts of *Dante's Inferno* (1993) and Michael Hofmann and James Lasdun's translation metamorphoses in *After Ovid* (1994).

While these and other instances take editorial and textual practices rooted in translation culture to a completely new level, translation multiples in conceptual forms stay particularly close to the scholarly lineage. When multiplying translations of single words, passages or whole works, both domains — the scholarly and the artistic — share the same intuition: that translation is never a finite and singular act, that there is never one 'true' equivalent in a different language and literary culture, and that an inherent part of any translation process is pondering more than one legitimate interpretation of the original. At the same time, the academic and artistic universe are both often governed by the same cultural, economic or legal expectations: that translation should be, ideally, equal to the original, that it ought to substitute for its source text and re-enact it for a foreign audience. What lies at the heart of similar multiplicative acts in both these spheres is, therefore, a friction between the prescriptively singular and the potentially plural. Whereas the cultural and editorial standards customarily present translation as an autonomous, well-rounded and ready-to-read product with only occasional discursive escapades, translation's immanently multiple nature kicks against this paradigm with more variants asking for their equal share. In the words of one author of translation multiples, Sawako Nakayasu, whose 2011 cycle 'Promenade' offers seventeen different renderings of Chika Sagawa's poem:[10]

> It's nice to sometimes let go of the need to stick to the established modes (translation plus footnotes or endnotes or introductory notes), a one-to-one relationship: one translation per poem.[11]

Multiplying translation variants of the same work veers off from these familiar and fixed patterns of representation. Translation can no longer be conveniently internalized as a whole final product, exposing its own procedural and plural nature that otherwise remains behind the scenes.

Surely, the subversive element of similar artistic endeavours — in Nakayasu's case manifest in the idea of '*anti*-translations' from her collection's subtitle — has been already present in a range of twentieth-century experimental translations and interlingual exercises. This legacy spans at least several European avant-garde movements, the Anglo-American modernist innovations through translation under the aegis of Ezra Pound, the 'OuLiPo' with their notion of constrained writing, the Fluxus movement with their chance operations, and the American L-A-N-G-U-A-G-E poets with their focus on the uses of language. In all these traditions, in one way or another, experimental translations aimed to dismantle some norms and expectations about how translations should be made and delivered to the audience.

Homophonic translations, for that matter, including examples such as Semen Kirsanov's 'Osen' (1925), Ernst Jandl's 'oberflächenübersetzung' (1964), Louis and Celia Zukofskys' *Catullus* (1969) and Oskar Pastior's *O du roher iasmin* (2002), have challenged the distinction between semantics and sound in poetry, and accordingly undermined the tendency to prioritize literal accuracy in translation. Chance operations in translation, as in Jackson Mac Low's and bpNichol's experiments, later revisited in David Cameron's *Flowers of Bad* (2007) and Christian Hawkey's *Ventrakl* (2010), have debunked the assumption that translation is a coherent and determinate series of conscious and independent decisions made by the translator. Recursive or back-and-forth translation chains, also known as the 'telephone' or 'Chinese whispers' game, for example, in Walter Arndt's 'chain of traducers' in his *Pushkin Threefold* (1972) and Adam Thirlwell's *Multiples* (2012) have ostentatiously put literary texts in a state of constant interlingual metamorphosis and exposed translation's inevitably transformative nature. Erasure techniques applied to translation, like in Jonathan Safran Foer's *Tree of Codes* (2010) and Christian Hawkey and Uljana Wolf's *Sonne from Ort* (2012), have played on the inaccessibility of foreign texts and cast doubt on any chance of resurrecting them in a different context through linguistically neutral translation. Intralingual translation projects, such as Paul Legault's English-English translations of Emily Dickinson (2012) and of Shakespearean sonnets co-edited with Sharmilla Cohen (2012), have explored how translation is understood, between what kind of 'languages' it occurs, and to what extent it involves the necessity of rendering 'the Other'. Artistic pseudo-translations, for example, Jack Spicer's *After Lorca* (1957) and Christopher Reid's *Katerina Brac* (1985) have dismantled the notion of authorship, probed the continuities between creativity and translation, as well as revealed how translations are expected to embody another persona (even if a non-existent one) for the sake of literary spectacle in the receiving culture.

Most of these unconventional techniques had been anticipated before modernism. Homophonic translations were preceded by macaronic verse, parodic adaptions of the Bible, humorous puns and presumed misunderstandings of foreign phrases, all dating back to the early modern period.[12] Pseudo-translations continue the long-standing tradition of literary hoaxes, *fakelore*, and apocryphal writing.[13] What is now referred to as intralingual translations derives from many other earlier instances of paraphrases, retellings, parodies, adaptations, transformations, and so on. Nonetheless, there is still an increasing self-reflexivity and self-consciousness in contemporary takes on the genre openly questioning what passes as 'standard' modes of translation; it positions current projects alongside the subversive reinforcements of the avant-garde movements.[14] When placed in the ranks of similar experimental works, translation multiples, too, go beyond their age-old prototypes and precursors, abandoning their purely hermeneutic and scholarly kinship. When they start telling their own story, this is also the moment marking their artistic quality, a conceptual moment. Such literary metatranslations no longer consist of dispersed commentaries and approximations of original meanings. Instead, they become clustered together around a coherent narrative or artistic conceit at the centre of it all while also reflecting upon the multiple and creative potential of literary translation.

With an eye to this trait, let us look at the recent translation multiples published within conceptual books and poems that treat the originals as a starting point to tell us a much bigger story. There are several examples that keep recurring in criticism. Firstly, Eliot Weinberger in his *19 Ways of Looking at Wang Wei* (1987)[15] compiled nineteen versions of a poem about a 'deer park' by a eighth-century Chinese poet, including a transliteration, a character-by-character translation, and a series of different renderings — each with a commentary running on the right-hand page. Then, Douglas R. Hofstadter composed his *Le ton beau de Marot: In Praise of the Music of Language* (1997)[16] of eighty-eight translations of a sixteenth-century French poem by Clément Marot — created by Hofstadter himself, in collaboration with others, by friends, family members, colleagues, computer programmes and other people whose versions he solicited.[17] Also, Caroline Bergvall in her conceptual poem 'VIA: 48 Dante Variations' (2000/2005) put together forty-seven[18] opening tercets of Dante's *Inferno*, ordered them alphabetically according to the first letter of the incipit in English and coupled each with the translation's author and date.

It might seem at first glance that what links all these multiples is only the mere fact of compiling different renderings of one original. However, the fabric of serial translations in these works shapes up into a completely new overarching theme. Expressing a sense of continuity and progression, further translations arrive to embody Benjaminian afterlives of the original in various ever-changing forms. For Weinberger, Wei's poem undergoes a natural process of metamorphosis as it is relived in different Buddhist reincarnations. On the other hand, the cubist viewings redolent of Wallace Stevens's '13 Ways of Looking at a Blackbird' symbolically anchor the Chinese poem in its more visual mould: the pictorial script is recast in language depending on various observation points, each limited by its singular perspective and blind spots. In Hofstadter's project, the act of multiplying Marot's poem stems from his interest in musical forms and the idea of a recurring musical theme, like in a rhapsody or a rondo.[19] This affinity manifests itself in at least two conceptual aspects: firstly, the homophonic pun in the title on *ton beau* (beautiful tone) and *tombeau* (tomb) visible on the book cover, and secondly, the number of translations alluding to the standard number of piano keys (eighty-eight). For another thing, by reiterating the original in so many different versions, Hofstadter also hankers for some sort of eternal form that could outlive the source poem in translations. This is, in particular, a poignant reminder of his late wife, who embodied the 'sick damsel' from Marot's poem and rounded off the series with her last rendering.

Then again, in Bergvall's conceptual poem, the titular 'via' becomes a life path relived by different speakers, each pronouncing the sense of getting lost in the midway using different words in English. As the sequence is arranged alphabetically, and not chronologically, it rewrites typical histories of reception suggesting that translation should lead *via* language itself rather than history and time. Despite the numerical order, there is in fact no progress throughout as each translator repeats the same scenario of going astray and not moving forward with their lives[20]. Paradoxically, the only thing that changes here are the very words and images conveying this standstill. And these can range from a Romantic epiphany of waking into spiritual recognition like in Zappulla's 1998 rendering; to the version attributed to Seamus Heaney (1993), but in fact by T. W. Parsons (1893), which drops the forest's symbolic darkness; to Steve Ellis's slangy take from 1994 stretching the long and arduous 'trek' as far as 'miles away' from the right 'road' — all put together one after another in the following fragment:

> 5. Halfway along the journey of our life
> I woke in wonder in a sunless wood
> For I had wandered from the narrow way
> (Zappulla, 1998)
>
> 6. HALFWAY on our life's journey, in a wood,
> From the right path I found myself astray.
> (Heaney, 1993)
>
> 7. Halfway through our trek in life
> I found myself in this dark wood,
> miles away from the right road.
> (Ellis, 1994)

And where, in the thick of all these reiterated and variegated tercets, is the missing forty-eighth translation? Perhaps, just like the audio performance of this mix of voices itself counted as 'the 48th variation' according to Bergvall,[21] the very act of placing different translations next to each other is her forty-eighth legitimate variation on Dante and a personal take on being lost at the crossroads of all previous mid-life straying. In fact, thirty-seven at the time, Bergvall underscored the date of the poem's publication as coinciding with 'Dante's 35th year or so-called point of mid-life.' And thus, while Weinberger includes his impressions and letters in the book and Hofstadter deals with his trauma of loss, Bergvall's ostensibly impersonal juxtaposition, too, reveals a deeply personal facet. It is her voice speaking from behind the multiples that provides a rationale for putting them together and interweaves a subjective running commentary into the literary metatranslation.

As much as we think of translation multiples in terms of voice and performance, using their material texture can also lead to picturing them in a very visual fashion. Generated plural versions across the book's 'turnable' pages, linear arrangements of translation series, and accumulated variations of one text spread out on a single page all reclaim the potential of printed form and visual arts for their own purposes. It shouldn't come as surprise that creators of translation multiples have also found this aspect particularly inspiring. In 2004, Alejandro Cesarco, independently from Bergvall, came up with the idea of collecting ten different English translations of *Inferno*'s opening passages and displaying them alongside one another in his series of prints 'Untitled [Dante/Calvino]', later displayed at the 2012 Deutsche Guggenheim's *Found in Translation* exhibition. As each of the prints was headed with the title of one chapter from Italo Calvino's *If on a Winter's Night a Traveller*, Cesarco's assemblage explicitly called for both the activated reader of Dante's translations and the viewer critically attuned to their ever-altering textual shape. In Rosemarie Waldrop's *Reft and Light* (2000)[22], on the other hand, numerous takes on Ernst Jandl's poems turn into multiplied patterns moulding visual poetry as such. For instance, the German poem entitled 'reihe' ('row' or 'series'), consisting of ten misheard consecutive numerals (from one to ten) shaped in a word-per-verse column, entered an extended 'series' in itself — a translation series — as various poets reiterated it in their own variants, running sequences, and even 4x4 or 9x10 tables. The multiples in question here explore the ornamental texture of verse to reinstate their own plurality.

A similar visual potential of multiples has become a driving force for creative renderings of Bashō's frog haiku[23] over the past decades. It comes into play, for example, in the aforementioned *One Hundred Frogs* with its chains of frog translations, encompassing self-contained multiples across genres such as 'Ten Variations on 'Frog and Pond' Haiku' by William Matheson, limerick and sonnet versions by Alfred H. Marks, to mention but a few. It also involves projects from the Canadian avant-garde poetry scene building on famous multimodal translations by bpNichol and Dom Sylvester Houédard[24], namely: *Frogments from the Frag Pool* (2005) by Gary Barwin and Derek Beaulieu[25] and *The Bashō Variations* by Steve McCaffery (2007).[26] While these texts amount to visual and conceptual poems in their own right, putting together such artistic gems also provides a decorative feast for the eyes: the books teem with haiku multiples as if the frog jumping into an ancient pond over and over again intended to leave multiple water ripples — marks of its constantly recurring presence.

It is also only due to multiple frogs in translation that quantitative ambiguities already inscribed in the original are brought to the fore. The tensions occur with regard to singularity and plurality: firstly, the translation multiples place the allegedly singular frog against its translated descendants, while in fact the number of frog(s) in the original Japanese is already unclear (*kawazu* can mean both 'frog' and 'frogs'). Secondly, the multiples ostensibly juxtapose the single original and plural translated versions, even though Bashō had actually revised the original producing more than one textual base to be translated in the first place. Then, another apparent contrast can be seen between the haiku's minimalist form and its extended chain of translated transformations — something that offers an interesting twist on the original longer form *renga* with haiku serving only as its constituent part. Finally, since there is an apparent tension between the haiku's individual authorship and the collaborative crowd of translators, the multiples revise another preconception about the author's singularity: the collectiveness is already embedded in the original writing context of Bashō's haiku as it was created during the so-called 'frog contest' (*kawazu awase*), a gathering of poets writing on the subjects of frogs. And thus, even though every new frog hopping into the ancient pond 'plops into oblivion' in its singularity, according to one of Cyril Patterson's renderings,[27] the succession still inculcates some sense of continuity. Each of these jumps becomes a modest contribution to the long tradition of conversing with the Bashō poem, with translators each time reading and approaching it anew.

This perpetual process of unfolding the original into variegated sequences also sparks reflection on a more metaphoric aspect of translation multiples. Like a reel of film with changing frames, their construction becomes a capacious figure for a journey through language and translation process with their different forms leaving an imprint on our experience. This is the case when Weinberger speaks of 'reincarnations' and Bergvall leads us along a 'path', and likewise when Sawako Nakayasu in her aforementioned poetic cycle stretches out her walk on the titular 'promenade', an image from the original multilingual poem by Chika Sagawa[28]. In Nakayasu's work, translation multiples are enlisted as versions 1–9, A-C, and a few others with markers in other scripts, with none or with more elaborate subtitles (e.g. 'Pass The Hand Over a Life as Fleeting as The Dew'). These variants of the 'Promenade' span different language combinations mixing English, French, and Japanese, different forms of conveying the same point in time ('three o'clock afternoon', '3:00pm', 'three-time meridian', '15:00'), different versions of the title originally in the Japanese phonetic script used for foreign (French) pronunciation ('Promenade', 'Puromunaado', 'Puromenaado'; two in Japanese scripts), and a series of different ways of capturing the impressions of what happened during the walk on the titular promenade. Juggling these multifarious means of expression, Nakayasu brings to the fore the transformative power of translation but also its arbitrariness and serendipity. Depending on the vantage point, perspective and style employed in a single rendering, the poem could change and scintillate with different images — just as one painting each time appeared differently for T.J. Clark in *The Sight of Death* (2000) when he recorded his constantly shifting responses to the same painting by Poussin every day for a year. Owing to a similar technique in translation multiples, their creators can open up the original text to various readings and different possibilities of conveying them. As Nakayasu herself put it, the readers are consequently enticed to follow her act of 'shifting the emphasis from product (the complete, perfect, final translation) to process (everything that happens on the way to the product).'[29] As a result of this transition, all the procedural machinery that propels translation, but customarily remains out of sight, here unexpectedly gets to play first fiddle.

In this light, it is perhaps no coincidence that the procedural poetics inherent to translation multiples was also identified by Marjorie Perloff as 'the OuLiPo factor'[30] in relation to Bergvall's 'VIA', beside works such as Christopher Bök's *Eunoia* (2001) and Harry Mathews's '35 Variations on a Theme from Shakespeare' (1999). Although Perloff was absolutely right in establishing this conceptual relationship with 'OuLiPo' writing, her argument raises a further question: what would such a correspondence entail for the very fact of interlingual translation that clearly distinguishes Bergvall's case (and Nakayasu's, those of the Bashō variations — and all other multiples, for that matter) from those of Bök and Matthews? In 'VIA', 'Promenade' and other works of the kind, translations can no longer conventionally represent an original in a foreign language. Instead, they fragment the source text into dozens of splinters and plural 'equivalences' resulting from diverse interpretative approaches and translatorial voices.

This might sound like an inconsequential play and very simple concept, but so it did when Raymond Queneau wrote his *Exercices de style* (1947): the anecdote about a man on a bus who gets into an argument with another passenger was told ninety-nine times, each time emphasising different parts of the story and describing the event from various angles in radically different styles (including metaphorical, oneiric, epistolary, first-person or third-person narrative, different tenses, and so on). While all these perspectives swerved off in their own directions, access to what it meant to embody 'the original' was at least limited, if not non-existent: what actually happened had already been filtered through different interpreters, and subsequently narrators, of the event (or, in other words, there was no hundredth 'true' story that would round off the number). In his exercises, Queneau certainly highlighted the figure of the narrating self and openly questioned the neutral relationship between reality and its representation in literature. It is some years later that literary metatranslations juxtaposing multiple readings of the same original keep underscoring analogous features that are of foremost importance to our understanding of translation. In particular, they expose the translator's mediation as well as the lack of a straightforward conversion between the original and its rewriting in a different literary culture.

This intuition also underpins other more critical translation multiples that highlight the impossibility of retrieving original senses of the source text from among its distinct readings and rewritings. A case in point is Allison Cobb and Jen Coleman's collaborative project 'Come Out of Works: A Physical Translation' (2003),[31] in which a fragment from the Chinese philosopher Chuang Tzu appears in six radically different renderings. The distance and implicit bias of a given interpretative perspective depends on physical obstacles encountered in the process: for instance, the source text can only come through 'with the Noise of the Shower

Running', looms up 'from Behind Smeared Glasses', and so on. Whereas Tzu argued that the Tao in the world could be experienced solely with the mediation of senses and surrounding objects, Cobb and Coleman similarly point to another layer of uncertainty in their project: in each of the multiples, we can observe the original only from afar as it inevitably gets mediated through the translator's own cognitive and sensual apparatus.

Anne Carson takes an equally sceptical stance in her 'A Fragment of Ibykos Translated Six Ways' (2012).[32] In this translational collage, she renders a passage of Ibycus's poem first literally and then by employing various limited vocabularies as verbal filters, such as: a poem of John Donne, Bertolt Brecht's FBI file, signs in the London Underground, the manual for her microwave, and so on. Throughout her constrained rewritings, she keeps unchanged the rhetorical scaffolding with the contrasting connectives 'on the one hand... on the other hand' as well as the English phrase 'nay rather', which dramatizes the poem's recurring antithesis. Other than that, her Ibykos translations look completely different from one another and it can be easily noticed how they progress towards more modern language and imagery. Referring to this exercise in her essay 'Variations on the Right to Remain Silent', Carson argued how one language cannot be exactly rendered into another and so her travels between these distinct lexicons always end up with translating into 'wrong words'.[33] But the question here arises which wrong words in fact get us further from Ibykos, an author who is already remote to us temporarily and linguistically: the ones filtered through the poetic diction of John Donne and others or Carson's own philological translation in contemporary English which is supposed to stand for an accurate, literal version of expressive means belonging to the Ancient Greek? At the end of the day, all these mutually incommensurable dictionaries are doomed to be 'untranslatable' in the traditional sense of the word, a conjecture that Carson puts forward through the ostentatious gesture of generating more and more mismatches.

In all these conceptual works, translation multiples not only revisit the familiar academic practice of compiling several variants and encircling the original in a hermeneutic quest for the meaning. They can also tell their own story, a story that can be deeply personal, visual, philosophical and critical. Owing to this distinctive technique, poets and artists can lay claim to the textual practices typical of the scholarly domain and step into what had previously been the primary, if not exclusive, territory of multiplied translations. In this way, under the overarching narrative of translation multiples, literary exercises in style can easily turn into exercises in translation style, creating an artistic idiom in its own right.

While this takes place, there is yet another promising aspect to this translation-fuelled transition: a step further that has been taken in the volume mentioned at the very beginning, *Into English*. In fact, Martha Collins and Kevin Prufer's recent project partly builds on the lesson that translation multiples can teach readers as well as academics, lecturers of translation theory and translation critics. Spanning twenty-five poems in multiple languages brought into English in multiple translation (usually three versions each) and commented on by twenty-five translators, this book celebrates the multiplicity, not only of translations and their individual readings, but also of their commentators. Here, the artistic element to be found in translation triplets spreads into the essays of translation critics, too, as they get their heads round these multiples — each in a different way and in their own distinct voice. Even though advertized as an anthology that 'plunges the reader into a translation seminar',[34] the curious compilation of critical multiples in *Into English* lends itself to a more literary reading, once again blurring the line between the academic and artistic domains of translation.

The conceit here also lies in trying to make sense of the multiple chorus of readings that are deeply rooted in the original poem but at the same time find a unique formula to penetrate its multiplied existence in English. Here, analogously to translators from Matthew Reynolds's *The Poetry of Translation*,[35] the critics of translations *nolens volens* adopt the language of the original poetry as they discuss the matter of translation multiples. They often end up transposing source leitmotifs and images onto their own analytic categories, also signalled in the titles (e.g. Susan Stewart's 'infinite task' of translating Leopardi's 'L'infinito' in different ways,[36] Ellen Doré Watson's 'Drummond Incommunicado' on rendering his poem about 'incommunicable poetry' by various translators[37] etc.), but also their writing accords in style with what they see as the tone of original verse. For instance, Willis Barnstone becomes very possessive of his erotic interpretation of a poem by St. John of the Cross, reluctantly measuring other translations against his passionate reading;[38] Carl Phillips's slightly moralistic conclusion about Virgil's translations jibes with the poem's didactic quality;[39] Arthur Sze straightforwardly and calmly comes to terms with the 'untranslability' of Taoist spontaneity and peace of mind;[40] and Cole Swensen toys with Baudelaire's pranksters in a very tongue-in-cheek manner.[41] In one of the most palpable records of this mutual kinship, a very somatic reading of Wisława Szymborska's 'Torture(s)',[42] Alissa Valles does not shy away from talking about her deeply personal responses ('I feel,' 'I favor,' 'I prefer') or aesthetic biases ('rhythmically, I lean toward the latter'); instead, she activates all her senses and even rehearses some of the physical descriptions from the poem ('I find myself throwing up my arms as well as my hands').

In these and other instances throughout the book, the original poems fork into translation multiples as if almost to provoke their respective commentaries, commentaries that in return explore the plurality of translations according to showcased literary themes and imagery. The multiples can thus work more broadly as a tempting metaphor for diversity and plurality not only in literary translation but equally in the genre of translation criticism, this time becoming a metacritical instance of Queneau's exercises. In cases like *Into English*, they may become exercises in the style of translation criticism as translation critics tune up their personalized voices to individual cases of multiplied translations (here: triplets or quadruplets), often imbuing their language with the original's poetics and imagery. As part of the book's multiplied conceit, different languages of translation criticism extend and rework the literary languages of both plural originals and their plural renderings. Translation multiples can spark and nourish critical multiples.

In the wake of these recent projects, are we witnessing here some sort of erosion of translation discourse that makes individual reading lenses more prominent in the act of literary translation but also lets them slip into the language of criticism? Perhaps translation multiples and similar self-reflexive projects could serve as a touchstone of the gradually changing perception of translation among both artists and academics. While the first group has been rediscovering its creative space and turning translation into a legitimate literary language, the latter have also challenged the allegedly objective mode of translation analysis. These processes have been out there for a while: the idea of translation equivalence no longer holds as a realistic goal for literary translators nor does it really function as an operational category for scholars and critics, since the international discipline of Translation Studies has dissented from the normative framework and purely linguistic matchings of source and target texts. Translation multiples that tell their own story through creative narratives have also been influenced by earlier and parallel literary developments, finding their aesthetic roots in modernist movements and experimental translations that came into being earlier in the twentieth-century. At the same time, however, they have very consciously sought to intervene in the ongoing translation debates by offering their own artistic intuitions on translation theory and scholarly practices. And while it might take some time before the academic branch of translation criticism fully embraces the subjective and individual situatedness of its writing perspective, translation multiples may in the meantime lead to the marriage of both domains. If so, and if that's going to open up the floor to more translation idioms and languages of criticism, then why not let each and every one of them have their say?

Works Cited

Against Expression. An Anthology of Conceptual Writing, ed. by Craig Dworkin and Kenneth Goldsmith (Chicago: Northwestern University Press, 2011)

BARWIN, GARY, and BEAULIEU, DEREK, *Frogments from the Frag Pool: Haiku after Bashō* (Toronto: Mercury Press, 2005)

BERGVALL, CAROLINE, 'VIA: 48 Dante Variations', *Fig* (Cambridge: Salt Publishing, 2005), pp. 63–71

BERGVALL, CAROLINE, 'VIA (48 Dante translations) mix w fractals' feat. Ciáran Mahe (2002): http://www.carolinebergvall.com/audio-new.php (online access: 01/12/2013)

BERMANN, SANDRA, 'Performing Translation', *A Companion to Translation Studies*, 1st edn, ed. by Sandra Bermann and Catherine Porter (West Sussex: John Wiley & Sons, 2014), pp. 285–97

BOETHIUS, ANICIUS MANLIUS SEVERINUS, *Troost-medecijne-wynckel der zedighe wysheyt*, trans. by Adriaan De Buck (Brugges: Lucas vanden Kerchove Boekdrukker, 1653)

BORKENT, MIKE, 'At the Limits of Translation? Visual Poetry and Bashō's Multimodal Frog', *Translation and Literature*, 25 (2016), 189–212

BRIGGS, KATE, *This Little Art* (London: Fitzcarraldo Editions, 2017)

BRZOSTOWSKA-TERESZKIEWICZ, TAMARA, *Modernist Translation. An Eastern European Perspective* (Frankfurt a/M: Peter Lang, 2016)

CARSON, ANNE, 'A Fragment of Ibykos Translated Six Ways', *London Review of Books*, 34, 8 November 2012

CARSON, ANNE, 'Variations on the Right to Remain Silent', *Nay Rather* (London: Sylph Editions 2014), pp. 4–41

CAYLEY, JOHN, 'The Translation of Process', *Amodern*, 8 (Issue: 'Translation-Machination'), http://amodern.net/article/the-translation-of-process/ (online access: 26/03/2017)

COLLINS, MARTHA, 'Introduction,' *Into English: Poems, Translations, Commentaries* ed. by Martha Collins and Kevin Prufer (Minneapolis: Graywolf Press, 2017), pp. vi–x

DANTE and BERGVALL, CAROLINE, 'VIA (48 Dante Variations)', *Chain*, 10 (2003), 55–59

DEMBECK, TILL, 'Oberflächenübersetzung: The Poetics and Cultural Politics of Homophonic Translation', *Critical Multilingualism Studies*, 3.1. (2015), 7–25

DERRIDA, JACQUES, 'What is a Relevant Translation?', trans. Lawrence Venuti, *The Translation Studies Reader*, 2nd edn, ed. by Lawrence Venuti (New York: Routledge, 2004), pp. 365–88

HERMANS, THEO, *The Conference of the Tongues* (Manchester: St Jerome, 2007)

HOFSTADTER, DOUGLAS R., *Le Ton beau de Marot: In Praise of the Music of Language* (New York: BasicBooks, 1997)

HOFSTADTER, DOUGLAS R., *Rhapsody on a Theme by Clément Marot* (Cedar City, Utah: Grace A. Tanner Center for Human Values, 1996)

HORÁČEK, JOSEF 'Pedantry and Play: The Zukofsky Catullus', *Comparative Literature Studies*, 51.1 (2014), 106–31

JANDL, ERNST, *Reft and light. Poems by Ernst Jandl with Multiple Versions by American Poets*, ed. and trans. by Rosemarie Waldrop and others (Providence: Burning Deck, 2000)

McCAFFERY, STEVE, *The Bashō Variations* (Toronto: BookThug, 2007)

NAKAYASU, SAWAKO, 'An interview on Sawako Nakayasu and Sagawa Chika's Mouth Eats Color: Translations, Anti-Translations, & Originals (Rogue Factorial, 2011)', *Galatea Resurrects (A Poetry Engagement)*, 18 May 2012, <http://galatearesurrection18.blogspot.co.uk/2012/05/thomas-fink-interviews-sawako-nakayasu.html> (online access: 07/05/2015)

NAKAYASU, SAWAKO, and SAGAWA, CHIKA, *Mouth Eats Color: Sagawa Chika Translations, Anti-Translations, & Originals* (Tokyo: Rogue Factorial, 2011)

PERLOFF, MARJORIE, 'The Oulipo Factor: The Procedural Poetics of Christian Bök and Caroline Bergvall', *Jacket*, 23 (August 2003)

PERLOFF, MARJORIE, *Unoriginal Genius. Poetry by Other Means in the New Century* (Chicago: Chicago University Press, 2010)

RAMBELLI, PAOLO, 'Pseudotranslation', *The Routledge Encyclopaedia of Translation Studies*, 2nd edition, ed. by Mona Baker, Gabriela Saldanha (London: Routledge, 2009), pp. 208–11

REYNOLDS, MATTHEW, *The Poetry of Translation: From Chaucer & Petrarch to Homer & Logue* (Oxford: Oxford University Press, 2012)

REYNOLDS, MATTHEW, 'Variorum Translations', *2016 ICLA Congress in Vienna* (2016): <https://icla2016.univie.ac.at/fileadmin/user_upload/k_icla2016/Icla2016_Panels_19.06.2016.pdf> (online access: 15/07/2016)

ROBINSON, DOUGLAS, 'Pseudotranslation', *The Routledge Encyclopedia of Translation Studies*, 1st edition, ed. by Mona Baker (London: Routledge 1998), pp. 183–85

SATO, HIROAKI, *One Hundred Frogs: From Renga to Haiku to English* (New York and Tokyo: Waterhill, 1983)

SMITH, HELEN, 'Matters in the Margins', in *Thresholds of Translation: Paratexts, Print, and Cultural Exchange in Early Modern Britain (1473–1660)*, ed. by Marie-Alice Belle, Brenda M. Hosington (Basingstoke: Palgrave Macmillan, 2018), pp. 27–50

TZU, CHUANG, COBB, ALLISON, and OTHERS, 'Come Out of Works: A Physical Translation', *Chain*, 20 (2003), pp. 43–51

WALKOWITZ, REBECCA, *Born Translated. The Contemporary Novel in an Age of World Literature* (New York: Columbia University Press, 2015)

WEINBERGER, ELIOT, *19 Ways of Looking at Wang Wei: How a Chinese Poem is Translated* (New York: Moyer Bell, 1987)

WERSHLER, DARREN, 'Introduction', Steve McCaffery, *Verse and worse: selected and new poems of Steve McCaffery (1989–2009)* (Waterloo, Ontario: Wilfrid Laurier University Press 2010), pp. ix–xvi

Notes to Chapter 6

1. Martha Collins, 'Introduction,' *Into English: Poems, Translations, Commentaries*, ed. by Martha Collins and Kevin Prufer (Minneapolis: Graywolf Press, 2017), p. viii.
2. Rebecca Walkowitz, *Born Translated. The Contemporary Novel in an Age of World Literature* (New York: Columbia University Press, 2015), p. 240.
3. In my research, I examined several major cases of translation multiples in the Polish post-1989 context, in which the gesture of multiplying different ideological readings of the original served as a pluralist forum for discussion. These instances included: Stanisław Barańczak's 'Oratorium Moratorium' (1991) with multiple homophonic translations of the French anthem *La Marseillaise*, Robert Stiller's 1999 double/triple rendering of *A Clockwork Orange* by Anthony Burgess, and the 2012 poetic book with four translators presenting their different takes on Bertolt Brecht's poetry edited by Andrzej Kopacki. In the German tradition, for example, exercises in multiple translation also appeared in a collection modelled after Baroque manuals for poetics entitled *Das Wasserzeichen der Poésie* [The Watermark of Poetry] written by Hans Magnus Enzensberger under the pseudonym of Andreas Thalmayr (1985).
4. For example, Caroline Bergvall's 'VIA' was placed in: *Against Expression. An Anthology of Conceptual Writing*, ed. by Craig Dworkin, Kenneth Goldsmith (Chicago: Northwestern University Press, 2011), pp. 81–86. See also: Tamara Brzostowska-Tereszkiewicz's discussion of contemporary 'conceptual translations' that echo conceptual models in Modernist poetry: *Modernist Translation. An Eastern European Perspective* (Frankfurt a/M: Peter Lang, 2016), pp. 181–84.
5. Cf. Helen Smith, 'Matters in the Margins', in *Thresholds of Translation: Paratexts, Print, and Cultural Exchange in Early Modern Britain (1473–1660)*, ed. by Marie-Alice Belle, Brenda M. Hosington (Basingstoke: Palgrave Macmillan, 2018), p. 28. Coincidentally, exercises in multiple translation around this time also sneaked into the domain of poetry taking the question of form as its starting point. For instance, in the 1636 English multiples of entitled *Cato Variegatus*, the chronicler and religious writer Sir Richard Baker tried out different rhyme combinations and modes of paraphrase of the original Latin *Distichs of Cato*; cf. Matthew Reynolds, *The Poetry of Translation: From Chaucer & Petrarch to Homer & Logue* (Oxford: Oxford University Press, 2012), p. 86. Similarly, in his 1653 Dutch rendering of Boethius's *The Consolation of Philosophy*, Adriaan de Buck tested different poetic metres in his translation doubles of different poems throughout the book: Anicius Manlius Severinus Boethius, *Troost-medecijne-wynckel der zedighe wysheyt*, trans. by Adriaan De Buck (Brugges: Lucas vanden Kerchove Boekdrukker, 1653), pp. 5–8, 4–17, 25–35, 41–43, 47–49, etc. I am grateful to Theo Hermans for drawing my attention to the latter example.
6. Cf. Theo Hermans, *The Conference of the Tongues* (Manchester: St Jerome, 2007), pp. 146–47.
7. Matthew Reynolds, 'Variorum Translations', *2016 ICLA Congress in Vienna*, 2016: https://icla2016.univie.ac.at/fileadmin/user_upload/k_icla2016/Icla2016_Panels_19.06.2016.pdf (online access: 15/07/2016).
8. Jacques Derrida, 'What is a Relevant Translation?', trans. Lawrence Venuti, *The Translation Studies Reader*, 2nd edn, ed. by Lawrence Venuti (New York: Routledge, 2004), p. 427.
9. Kate Briggs, *This Little Art* (London: Fitzcarraldo Editions, 2017), pp. 287–88.
10. Sawako Nakayasu (with Chika Sagawa), *Mouth Eats Color: Sagawa Chika Translations, Anti-Translations, & Originals* (Tokyo: Rogue Factorial, 2011).
11. Sawako Nakayasu, 'An interview on Sawako Nakayasu and Sagawa Chika's Mouth Eats Color: Translations, Anti-Translations, & Originals (Rogue Factorial, 2011)', *Galatea Resurrects (A Poetry Engagement)*, 18 May 2012, http://galatearesurrection18.blogspot.co.uk/2012/05/thomas-fink-interviews-sawako-nakayasu.html (online access: 07/05/2015).

12. Josef Horáček, 'Pedantry and Play: The Zukofsky Catullus', *Comparative Literature Studies*, 51.1 (2014), 109; Till Dembeck, 'Oberflächenübersetzung: The Poetics and Cultural Politics of Homophonic Translation', *Critical Multilingualism Studies*, 3.1. (2015), 9–10
13. Douglas Robinson, 'Pseudotranslation', *The Routledge Encyclopedia of Translation Studies*, 1st edition, ed. by Mona Baker (London: Routledge 1998), pp. 183–85; Paolo Rambelli, 'Pseudotranslation', *The Routledge Encyclopaedia of Translation Studies*, 2nd edition, ed. by Mona Baker, Gabriela Saldanha (London: Routledge, 2009), pp. 208–11.
14. Cf. Marjorie Perloff's idea of the rear-guard (*arrière-garde*) in this context. See: *Unoriginal Genius. Poetry by Other Means in the New Century* (Chicago: Chicago University Press, 2010), p. 53.
15. Eliot Weinberger, *19 Ways of Looking at Wang Wei: How a Chinese Poem is Translated* (New York: Moyer Bell, 1987).
16. Douglas R. Hofstadter, *Le Ton beau de Marot: In Praise of the Music of Language* (New York: Basic Books, 1997).
17. Caroline Bergvall, 'VIA: 48 Dante Variations', *Fig* (Cambridge: Salt Publishing, 2005), pp. 63–71. First published online in 2000 as 'VIA (48 Dante translations) mix w fractals' as an audio version featuring the Irish composer Ciáran Mahe. http://www.carolinebergvall.com/audio-new.php (online access: 01/12/2013).
18. Not forty-eight like, for instance, Sandra Bermann claims in her 'Performing Translation', *A Companion to Translation Studies*, 1st edn, ed. by Sandra Bermann and Catherine Porter (West Sussex: John Wiley & Sons, 2014), p. 286. Admittedly, Bergvall did use a forty-eighth English translation for the poem's less known appearance in the *Chain* journal: Dante & Caroline Bergvall, 'VIA (48 Dante Variations)', *Chain*, 10 (2003), 55–59. However, neither her audio recording nor the poem's definitive version from the authored collection *Fig* (2005) contain the forty-eight rendering since, as she decided, the late addition "broke the rule of the task"; cf. Bergvall, *Fig*, p. 65.
19. Cf. the first version of the book: Douglas R. Hofstadter, *Rhapsody on a Theme by Clément Marot* (Cedar City, Utah: Grace A. Tanner Center for Human Values, 1996), p. xvi, in which the author named Sergei Rachmaninoff's 'Rhapsody on a Theme by Paganini' as a source inspiration; as well as Douglas R. Hofstadter, *Le ton beau*, p. 12, where he points to a musical rondo as the equivalent for the book's organising principle.
20. Note that the trick of turning Dante's words into translators' personal testimonies works well in a language that does not mark gender in its grammar. For instance, in my Polish translation of Bergvall's poem 'VIA: 22 wariacje na temat Dantego' (VIA: 22 Variations on Dante), I faced the problem of female translators doomed to use the original masculine forms. See: the discussion of the Polish version by John Cayley: 'The Translation of Process', *Amodern*, 8 (Issue: 'Translation-Machination'), especially footnote 26, http://amodern.net/article/the-translation-of-process/ (online access: 26/03/2017).
21. Bergvall, 'VIA...', p. 64.
22. Ernst Jandl, *Reft and light. Poems by Ernst Jandl with Multiple Versions by American Poets*, ed. and trans. by Rosemarie Waldrop and others (Providence: Burning Deck, 2000).
23. This is the oft-quoted translation of Bashō's haiku by R.H. Blyth (1952):

> 'The old pond;
> A frog jumps in —
> The sound of the water.'

Cf. Hiroaki Sato, *One Hundred Frogs: From Renga to Haiku to English* (New York: Waterhill, 1983), p. 154.
24. Cf. Darren Wershler, 'Introduction', Steve McCaffery, *Verse and worse: selected and new poems of Steve McCaffery (1989–2009)* (Waterloo, Ontario: Wilfrid Laurier University Press 2010), p. xii, and the discussion of multimodality in these versions by: Mike Borkent, 'At the Limits of Translation? Visual Poetry and Bashō's Multimodal Frog', *Translation and Literature*, 25 (2016), 189–212.
25. Gary Barwin and Derek Beaulieu, *Frogments from the Frag Pool: Haiku after Bashō* (Toronto: Mercury Press, 2005).
26. Steve McCaffery, *The Bashō Variations* (Toronto: BookThug, 2007).

27. Hiroaki Sato, *One Hundred Frogs*, p. 174.
28. For a more detailed discussion of this example, see Adriana X. Jacobs's chapter in this volume. I am grateful to Prof. Jacobs for drawing my attention to Nakayasu's volume.
29. Nakayasu, 'An interview on Sawako Nakayasu...'
30. Marjorie Perloff, 'The Oulipo Factor: The Procedural Poetics of Christian Bök and Caroline Bergvall', *Jacket*, 23 (August 2003).
31. Chuang Tzu, Allison Cobb and others, 'Come Out of Works: A Physical Translation', *Chain*, 20 (2003), 43–51.
32. Anne Carson, 'A Fragment of Ibykos Translated Six Ways', *London Review of Books*, 34, 8 November 2012.
33. Anne Carson, 'Variations on the Right to Remain Silent', *Nay Rather* (London: Sylph Editions 2014), p. 32.
34. Rosanna Warren's review on the back cover.
35. Reynolds, *The Poetry of Translation*.
36. Susan Stewart, 'Translating Leopardi's "L'infinito": An Infinite Task', *Into English*, pp. 44–47. Cf. my review of the anthology: 'Into English: A Collection of World Literature That Debunks Age-Old Translation Myths', *Words Without Borders* (December 2017): https://www.wordswithoutborders.org/book-review/into-english-a-collection-of-world-literature-that-debunks-age-old-myth (online access: 22/12/2017).
37. Watson, 'Drummond Incommunicado', *Into English*, pp. 126–28.
38. Barnstone, 'Commentary', *Into English*, pp. 28–31.
39. Phillips, 'Commentary, *Into English*, pp. 14–16.
40. Sze, 'Commentary', *Into English*, pp. 22–23.
41. Swensen, 'The case of:', *Into English*, pp. 52–53.
42. Valles, 'Szymborska: Torture(s)', *Into English*, pp. 150–52.

CHAPTER 7

Extreme Translation

Adriana X. Jacobs

I.

Extremophiles are creatures that live in environments that otherwise would seem inhospitable to life — *Panagrolaimus davidi*, a species of Antarctic roundworm, can survive extreme cold; fish like the pelican eel live in extreme ocean depths in a state of near blindness; the microorganism *pyrolobus fumarii* can thrive at temperatures exceeding 110°C. The very category of the extremophile is a threshold set according to the state where most organisms thrive: as life adapts to new environments, the bounds of the extreme shift, indeed expand. In what follows, I consider the possibility that translation constitutes such an extreme environment for language, a space where words are pulled out of their 'natural habitat' and exposed to conditions that test the limits of textual vitality, viability and translatability.

Translators generally have acknowledged the space of translation as an extreme, a space where pressure is applied to push a word and its meaning toward and beyond a breaking point. The moment that a word begins that movement from one language to another, it faces, enters, and attempts to cross that space that Anne Carson has described as 'that space between the word you're at and the word you can't get to'.[1] This gap has no rules, no map, no compass. It operates under the expectation of a kind of productive futility. 'Translation is a bottomless pit', Carson observes.[2] Dicta like the Italian *traduttore, tradittore* continue to cast translation as a practice that is inherently transgressive — as if that were a bad thing? — while occluding how translation draws its own strategies from existing, and even well-worn, practices of writing and reading. The poet Joyelle McSweeney, for example, exerts force in writing a poem, describing her creative process as '[collecting] phrases and [yoking] them by violence together, forcing them into such extreme pressures that they buckle and release unholy noises'.[3] At the heart of McSweeney's aesthetic is a commitment to exposing facades of normalcy and legibility in American poetry culture that promote and collude with institutions of racism, sexism, xenophobia, among others, a commitment that extends to (her) translation practices as well.

In his 1973 poem 'Kach' ('Take'), the Israeli poet Meir Wieseltier also proposed violent and destructive engagements with poetry, placing this responsibility on the reader: 'Take poems but don't read them / do violence to this book: / Spit on it, kick it / wring its neck' (translated by Shirley Kaufman).[4] Wieseltier observes that reading is a mode of containment and order. A poem that can be read can be categorized, commodified and tamed; instead, he calls for new modes of reading, indeed misreading, that open, wound and decompose the text. Drowning, burning, and nailing the poem tests the limits of its legibility — it may even render the text entirely illegible — yet doing so challenges habitual ways of reading poetry. Likewise, demands for fidelity and elegance that persist in practices and critiques of translation come back to the expectation that translated texts must hold together in the act of reading (the 'straightforward' approach).[5]

In their essay 'Manifesto of the Disabled Text', McSweeney and Johannes Göransson argue that 'discomfort with a translated text is discomfort with a disabled text. ('But the text can't stand on its own!' 'But something is lost, ruined, missing!', etc.).'[6] This discomfort underlies the infamous (and misquoted) assertion that 'poetry is what gets lost in translation' (attributed to Robert Frost), often invoked in translation reviews and criticism to signal the inevitable failure of translatability.[7] The Hebrew counterpart, 'tirgum hu neshika mi-ba'ad ha-mitpachat' [translation is like a kiss through a handkerchief] (often credited to the poet Chaim Nachman Bialik) is similarly negative, casting translators as puritans who regard the original from a modest distance. Contesting these maxims is not my concern here, rather I am drawn to the possibilities these formulations offer to a praxis of translation. For example, we can think of erasure and remixing as creative modes of 'loss'. The blurring effects and distortions the Hebrew handkerchief produces suggest generative practices of misreading and mistranslating.

The Hebrew poet Leah Goldberg once observed that translations by poets often lie 'on the borderline' between original writing and translation.[8] Goldberg meant that poets were more likely to translate poetry creatively, to the point where a translation by a poet may bear little likeness to the original text, but she also had in mind the ways in which 'borderline' translations have energized transformative developments in literary cultures, allowing for new poetic vernaculars, forms and styles to take hold. Such translation, in the words of McSweeney and Göransson, 'if taken internally, may break apart societal forms'.[9] The area around Goldberg's borderline constitutes an interstitial third space, one that materializes as a limit is pushed and prodded, as it resists and yields. Translation, in this respect, enacts and embodies, in the words of Gilles Deleuze and Félix Guattari, 'a movement of language toward its extremes, toward a reversible beyond or before'.[10]

In the following sections, I foreground specific examples of translations that make this extremity of translation acutely visible, explicit and material in ways that prove 'irreversible'. While it is generally understood that there are many paths to translation, and many possible translations of the same text, what concerns me here are texts that appear to fall entirely outside of the expected bounds of translation, in a zone where no return to a source or original is possible. This is the side of translation that David Bellos describes as 'unbounded as the line of a shore', a site of endless change and transformation.[11] 'Extreme translations', as I call them, thrive on this side of translation, where they emerge out of radical, and even unconventional, strategies of translation that test the limits of linguistic legibility, comprehension and translatability.

I focus my reading on the extremophile *translatio americana*, drawing my examples of extreme translation from the work of the contemporary American poets and translators David Cameron, Sawako Nakayasu, Christian Hawkey and Jody Gladding. In and through their work, prismatic approaches to translation have proliferated in recent years in the United States, creating a space in the literary market (usually supported by independent publishers) for texts that do not conform to traditional notions of literary translation. The strategies they enact — among them, erasure, decomposition, violence — recognize and critique the global hegemony of English, and respond to shifts in American cultural and political discourse in the years following 9/11. By proposing and practising border-pushing, transgressive translation strategies, these extreme translations resist the troubling encroachment and normalization of xenophobic and anti-immigrant rhetoric and ideologies both in the United States and on a global scale.

2.

I open my discussion of extreme translations with David Cameron's exuberant translation of Charles Baudelaire's *Les Fleurs du Mal*. Cameron's project, originally circulated as a pamphlet titled *Flurries of Mail* (Mbirra Press) — appeared in expanded form as the book *The Flowers of Bad*, published in 2007 as a collaboration between the independent presses Unbelievable Alligator and Ugly Duckling Presse. Cameron, who studied French in high school and at university, characterizes these poems as 'false translations', poems that intentionally depart from the literal meaning of Baudelaire's poems.[12] But the expression 'flowers of bad' is not exactly a false translation; rather, it is a hyper-literal translation of the original French title. In other words, in the very title of his book Cameron is already subverting and parodying notions of fidelity in translation. It also hints at a recurring feature of extreme translation, namely the fact that knowing the original language is not a requirement for translation. The expression 'flowers of bad' may not be idiomatic, but it calls to mind the more idiomatic expression 'a bad seed', which refers to a being genetically predisposed towards bad, lawless behaviour. Indeed, Cameron's rendering begs the question: is there something in Baudelaire's original text that engenders these bad translations, a kind of rotten quality or genetic glitch? Is the translation simply expressing, in this respect, a quality implicit in the original text?

We can understand 'flower' as a synonym for 'translation', growing out of 'bad' processes of translation. In fact, most of Cameron's book could be construed as a handbook for wilful misreading and mistranslating. In his appendix, he details the different methods he employed to produce these translations, most of them attempts to decompose the text by violent means: collision (translating a poem using a second text as a filter), blinding (translating with no more information than the title and line count), forcing (counting the number of syllables in a line of the original and removing the remaining text in the corresponding line of the translation), exclusion (taking and translating only some parts of a poem and then writing a separate translation from the excluded text).[13] In one instance, he considered writing one of Baudelaire's poems on a sheet of glass and smashing it with a hammer ('I never fully succeeded').[14] Though this approach is heretical to any consideration of 'translation proper', it nonetheless calls attention to long-standing practices in translation: the translation of ancient fragments, for example, as well as the long and vexed tradition of pseudotranslation. Translators of the Greek poet Sappho, for instance, often reconstructed her work, a practice that Carson contests in her English-language translation of Sappho, *If Not, Winter*, where she elects to preserve the spaces and breaks of the original fragment in her translation as markers of the 'papyrological event'.[15] Some of Sappho's poems were recovered from Oxyrhynchus, an ancient landfill in Egypt, where these poems mixed with toilet paper and other scraps. Carson's translation strategy thereby preserves but also reinitiates the decompositional process. In its strictly material sense, a printed text decays over time, however, the continuous retranslations and reconstructions of Sappho reveal what Hindy Najman refers to as 'an excess of vitality', that is, a property that some texts, like some living organisms, share, and which, in her words 'expresses itself in the fact that they provide the basis for new texts'.[16]

This desire for a generative mode of translation motivates Cameron's translation of Baudelaire's 'Au Lecteur', the opening poem of *Les fleurs du mal*. Cameron actually provides two versions of this poem, both titled 'To the Reader'. In the first version, the figure of David Cameron announces that he wishes to move away from readings that understand the lyric voice to be synonymous with the author:

> ...I can't seem to write 'I'
> In a poem which somehow doesn't transform me
>
> Or at least offer the option of transforming
> The speaker or supposing that he/she is someone other
> Than me'.[17]

In this 'false translation' of Baudelaire's 'Au Lecteur', Cameron proposes translation as a way of stepping out of the constraints of one's own identity, the expectation of contemporary readers that 'I' is always 'I, the author'. What 'false translation' offers, then, is the possibility that 'I' can be many other things, a premise that unsettles any idea of monologic authority.

This translation also opens with the line 'Dear Reader, / These poems are made up of lines', calling attention to the material practices of 'false translation' that are more explicitly activated in the second version, an interlacing of two poems: one printed in black text, and a second poem, written above these lines in red, italicized text.[18] Both versions appear to combine Cameron's strategies of 'Phonetic', 'Free', and 'Understood' translation. Discerning even the slightest homophonic association between French and English, Cameron allows the line to extend from this point.[19] The use of a different colour text suggests that the Swimming strategy is at work, which Cameron describes as 'a swimming on the surface of the poem' that follows the currents of mood over meaning and sound.[20] To illustrate the experience of reading this translation, I present here the original French and Robert Lowell's English translation, followed by the first stanza of Cameron's 'To the Reader' (version two):

Au Lecteur

La sottise, l'erreur, le péché, la lésine,
Occupent nos esprits et travaillent nos corps,
Et nous alimentons nos aimables remords,
Comme les mendiants nourrissent leur vermine.[21]

To the Reader

Infatuation, sadism, lust, avarice
possess our souls and drain the body's force;
we spoonfeed our adorable remorse,
like whores or beggars nourishing their lice.[22]

I want to resist here the tendency to use "literal" translations as intermediaries between originals and "free" translations, so I have elected to use Lowell's version, which takes its liberties with Baudelaire ('whores' is an addition, for example), though it otherwise follows the syntax of the French, allowing for a more or less linear comparison with Cameron's translation:

  Sorry but cataract my eyes being flummoxed   *busted*
 Sorry, how can I avoid being influenced by the copy of this I read before

            oceanliner
   the fisherman pulling in his line

     fiancé opens *with a club, the three and bawling over or bowl-*
 Or occupying all of France again with a forthright bouquet? Our spirits

    ing over warthogs the masses haven't worsted wool and trombones *assets*
   have worked or our noses have worked and travelled and our

    bodice *dustbin*
   bodies, dead in the kitchen

    moose *fish* *gallant aces*
 Eating, hanging from a noose or finally getting over a cold. Do you like

   recipe *over* *rhinoceros*
   record stores do you sneeze

        carumba astin martin pernod a whalebone corset
 When your typewriter puts up a comma and not a period or when the

    on the lawn
   nurse feeds you porridge because your own arms are immobile you're

   kelvin *rabbits add up*
  immobilized by tetanus, rabies and you're waiting for the vaccine.[23]

One does not need to know French to see clearly that Cameron's translation is a different text altogether, nor is it invested in any notion of literal translation. Nevertheless, attempts to trace Cameron's language back to Baudelaire's illustrate the extent to which a linguistic relation prevails despite the strategies of translation that work against 'translation proper'. As in the game of Telephone, or when a tongue twister is repeated quickly many times, the language of Cameron's translations retains echoes of Baudelaire's French. Take for instance Baudelaire's 'Occupent nos esprits et travaillent nos corps' which becomes in Cameron's translation 'Or occupying all of France again with a forthright bouquet? Our spirits have worked or our noses have worked and travelled and our bodies'. Here, 'occupent' (from *occuper*, inhabit, possess) sparks a riff on the English 'occupation', with 'forthright bouquet' perhaps alluding to 'les fleurs du mal' and their influence on French literary culture. What interests me here is how much variation Cameron extracts from Baudelaire's words, in large part because his limited proficiency in the language allows him to create connections that disregard the rules of French: 'Nos esprits' contracts playfully to 'noses', 'travaillent' is rendered erroneously as 'travelled'. An additional translation of 'travaillent' as 'worked' misunderstands Baudelaire's idiom, which he employs in the sense of exertion, working on or over. What Cameron preserves here is the kind of work that happens when someone does not know a language well and is fumbling around trying to make sense of it. On the other hand, this playful rejection of linguistic fluency, and specifically fluency in the language from which one is translating, shares troubling affinities with an 'English Only' discourse that has regained currency in the post-Trump and post-Brexit years. In this respect, Cameron's project initially appears to uphold an imperialist view of English as a language that others must know, while English-language speakers may move through the world without knowing its languages (or knowing them quite badly).[24] And yet, the alternative translation that the superscript proposes decomposes the English language itself, rendering it as near nonsense, into an English that now reads increasingly like a foreign language.

Cameron reworks Baudelaire's poems through a strategy, or in his words 'method', that he calls 'forced sonnet', an example being his translation of Baudelaire's 'La Mort des pauvres', which becomes, rather straightforwardly, 'The Death of the Poor'. With the 'forced sonnet' method, Cameron first produces a rhyming translation of the poem (using any one of his other methods) and then begins to break it apart and recompose it. Hints of the 'old translation' remain in the new 'forced sonnet', in the way that originals can be said to have an 'afterlife' in translation — one of several examples in this book of how translations begin to occupy the space and status of an original text. To demonstrate how this works in practice, I offer here Baudelaire's original poem alongside Cameron's version:

> *La Mort des pauvres*
>
> C'est la Mort qui console, hélas! et qui fait vivre;
> C'est le but de la vie, et c'est le seul espoir
> Qui, comme un élixir, nous monte et nous enivre,
> Et nous donne le coeur de marcher jusqu'au soir;
>
> À travers la tempête, et la neige, et le givre,
> C'est la clarté vibrante à notre horizon noir
> C'est l'auberge fameuse inscrite sur le livre,
> Où l'on pourra manger, et dormir, et s'asseoir;
>
> C'est un Ange qui tient dans ses doigts magnétiques
> Le sommeil et le don des rêves extatiques,
> Et qui refait le lit des gens pauvres et nus;
>
> C'est la gloire des Dieux, c'est le grenier mystique,
> C'est la bourse du pauvre et sa patrie antique,
> C'est le portique ouvert sur les Cieux inconnus![25]

162   ADRIANA X. JACOBS

> *CXXII: The Death of the Poor*
>
> Over are the bills! And who can make a living these
> For an underground newspaper — the burnt out ends
> Climbing higher and higher until the batteries
> Empty bottles on the soles of our moccasins
>
> In the studio of the hurricane, eating goat
> Reason why a vampire licks his plate clean to
> Your note book I saw the famous surgeon wrote
> Barn, eating dormice and their wheatgrass nests, while you
>
> Slippers for a dormouse born with a wooden
> In his dreams like eggs crashing down on a wooden
> Autumn. The naked and the poor eating away
>
> Temples with a secret added ingredient;
> Poor are a uterus that will birth an ancient
> A new body that begins at the ankle. Say[26]

Taking his cue from the Oulipo, one of his admitted influences on this project, Cameron's method here is mathematical: '...from the beginning of the first line of my old translation, I counted out a number of syllables equal to the number of syllables in the first line of the original French poem, and struck out all words on the line that came after. The words that remained became the first line of the Forced Sonnet'.[27] Nevertheless, despite the mathematical precision of his formula, no reverse engineering of the original poem is possible. Because the translation from which the forced sonnet emerges can be the product of any number of Cameron's methods, and even a combination of them, what is 'original' is at best a hint or vestige, like 'batteries' for 'magnétiques' (magnetic) and 'dormice' for 'dormir' (sleep). The 'contingencies' (e.g., a syllable falling in the middle of a word) for which exceptions and variations in the forced sonnet formula account further unsettle the relation between original and translation, and even more so, they highlight the extent to which translation itself resists formulation.

In a review of *Flowers of Bad*, Allison Elliott observed that Cameron's false translations 'link the familiar with the strange in unexpected ways', referring to the relation between Baudelaire's original poems and Cameron's translations.[28] The forceful 'yokings' that produce Cameron's translations also have the effect of defamiliarizing the English language itself. It is not incidental that Elliott raises here the issue of expectation. 'Fans of Baudelaire looking for a new incarnation of the poet's explorations of melancholy, beauty and pain will not find it here', she writes, 'at least, not in quite the way they might expect'. In fact, Cameron's *Flowers of Bad* relies on the expectation that some readers will project the Baudelaire they know on these texts — in several instances, he even reproduces the original French titles, pointing the way directly to an original text. Implicit in this practice is a recognition of the expectations that readers bring to a translation and what they expect a translation to do ('link'), particularly when they are 'familiar' with the work of the original author. Ultimately, sending the reader back to Baudelaire only calls further attention to Cameron's practices of translation and to the voids and interferences that replace an understanding of translation as a bridge between languages, texts, authors. 'My feet are sunk in it, and ah'm sinking'.[29]

3.

In September 2011, a Facebook exchange between the poets and translators Sawako Nakayasu and Jen Hofer sparked the idea for Nakayasu's 2011 collection *Mouth: Eats Color: Sagawa Chika Translations, Anti-Translations, and Originals*. In the initial post, Nakayasu suggested the possibility of a book of 'anti-translations' shaped in part by her own translations of the Japanese Modernist poet Chika Sagawa (1911–1936).[30] Hofer, a translator of contemporary Latin American poetry, was preparing class materials for a translation workshop and replied, 'can you make that book in the next week or two? (ha)'.[31] Nakayasu took up Hofer's challenge, but finding that conventional book categories could not accommodate this collection, she ultimately published it through her own imprint Rogue Factorial, an initiative committed to 'developing and producing books in a roguish manner'.[32] Indeed, if extreme, transgressive translation practices circulate among us, this is due in no small part to editors and publishers who are themselves working against the norms of the literary market and the demands of marketability.

Mouth: Eats Color emerges from the grey areas and borderlines between translated and original texts. In some respects, it could be read as a kind of notebook on the translation process, archiving what goes into and what is left out of a translation, as well as the ways in which translation allows for the creation of texts that fall 'between' translation and original. If there are relations to be drawn here between Sagawa's poems, Nakayasu's own poetry, and Nakayasu's English translations of Sagawa's Japanese poems they are not linear. In this respect, this collection can be read against works like Eliot Weinberger and Octavio Paz's 1987 collection *Nineteen Ways of Looking at Wang Wei*, which embraces the multiplicity of translation yet enforces critical practices of gatekeeping (e.g., insisting on 'resemblance' as a measure of a good translation and privileging a particularly American mode of translating Chinese poetry). Rather, what motivates *Mouth: Eats Color* is an entirely different way of making translation and poetry happen. Nakayasu describes the writing of this book as follows:

> The thing that's become important to me about this whole process of engaging and interrogating translation is that it frees me to be more expressive about the various things I see going on in Sagawa's work...sometimes I have the desire to combine several poems into one, to shed more light on either and both. There is a promiscuity in it — once I break the one-to-one contract, it allows for multiple relationships.[33]

Although the collection's subtitle implies a distinction between 'translations, anti-translations, and originals', the texts themselves splice together lines from Sagawa's poems, in both the original Japanese and Nakayasu's English translations, also bits of Chinese and French, including poems and translations (of Sagawa) by other authors (Harry Crosby, Mina Loy, 'Masako Hiraizumi'). Nakayasu's own writing is part of this mix, blurring and confusing any notion of a single author or a single translator. Nakayasu introduces here the idea of the 'puromenaado' (promenade) as a metaphor for the variations that wind through the book. The idea of the promenade is also explored literally — Sagawa's short poem 'Puromenaado' is retranslated seventeen times throughout the book as a multilingual text (in English, Chinese, French, and even a decomposed Japanese).[34] The reader is not expected to be able to read all of the poems in the various languages from which — and in which — they are written. Nor does Nakayasu expect — or want — the reader to make sense of them; rather, the point of the book, as she puts it, is to 'push through the idea' of the book, to read each line as "modified, crushed, loosed...unprotected order".[35]

If translation is still too often discussed as a practice of loss, Nakayasu's collection advances an idea of translation as multiplication. And while it is not possible here to address all of the permutations that Sagawa's poem 'Promenade' undergoes in this collection, I will highlight a few examples, beginning with the following translation that Nakayasu included in *The Collected Poems of Chika Sagawa* (which I will refer to as 'Promenade [CP]'). Sagawa's modernism is evident in her crisp imagery, the city/nature juxtaposition, and in her penchant for free verse, which distinguished Japanese modernism from the long, more formal *waka* tradition of Japanese poetry.

> Seasons change their gloves
> The three o'clock
> Trace of sun
> Of flower petals that bury the pavement
> A black and white screen
> Eyes are covered by clouds
> Evening sets on some promiseless day.[36]

Compare this translation with the one, also titled 'Promenade', that appears in *Mouth: Eats Color*:

> The saisons changent their 手袋
> A trois o'clock
> 薄れ日の
> Petals des fleur that bury leur report
> ホワイト and ブラツクの screen
> Les yeux covered par les nuages
> Evening se couche on some jour sans プロミス.[37]

In an interview with Lindsey Webb, Nakayasu discusses the influence of International Modernism, including French, on Sagawa and her contemporaries. The original Japanese title 'プロムナアド' is written in *katakana* (Japanese phonetic script used for foreign words), which makes it clear that the French pronunciation of 'promenade' is intended. The French words that make their way into Nakayasu's translation, or rather, anti-translation, of Sagawa's 'Puromenaado' attest to the French currents in Sagawa's own poem, and even go a step further by highlighting linguistic relations between French and English. If the French 'Saisons changent' and English 'seasons change' sound very similar, it is because the English words 'season' and 'change' have entered English via Old French (the way Middle French gives English 'promenade'). In a 2016 interview, Nakayasu conceded that the *Collected Poems* had to 'let go' of many of these multilingual details and associations. 'What am I to do', she said, 'add a footnote in every instance?'[38] *Mouth: Eats Color*, on the other hand, could '[hold] everything else that the *Collected* could not'.[39]

The inclusion of Japanese and Chinese scripts in the 2011 version of 'Promenade' creates additional linguistic interference and accords with Sagawa's own polyphonic poetic language and the strategies she and her contemporaries employed, as Nakayasu describes it, '[to negotiate] new ways of incorporating foreign language'.[40] For example, in the original Japanese text, the word for 'screen', スクリイン, is written in *katakana* which transliterates as 'sukuriin', suggesting that the word itself is an English loan word, returning, as it were, to its source in Nakayasu's translation.[41] For a reader who does not read Japanese or Chinese, this multilingual writing allows for a degree of illegibility that Nakayasu herself anticipates, that is even essential to the critique of translatability that this collection advances. In a statement that appears at the end of the collection, in a section titled 'Notes', Nakayasu offers a translation commentary that compares the perceived 'order' of proper translation to a beehive that, in her words, 'was complete before the new queen arrived'.[42] The queen's arrival violently upsets the previous order, forcing a 'readjustment' of each individual worker bee to the whole. Her presence introduces the idea of 'promise-less' order, in other words, an order that cannot be anticipated, planned, protected, like the 'promiseless day' in 'Promenade [CP]'. Under these new conditions, a different kind of translatability is possible, one where 'the past should be altered by the present as much as the present is directed by the past'.[43] This formulation extends to the multiple languages that circulate in each text, even in those that appear, at least outwardly, to follow a monologic, monolingual order. Texts like 'Puromunaado (2)' and 'Promenade (B)' may be read, as many translations are, as exclusively monolingual texts (Chinese and English respectively) 'or...not'. By bringing together multiple translations of the same poem in multiple languages, *Mouth: Eats Color* demonstrates how translation itself risks participating in a hegemonic linguistic order that privileges monolingualism, originality and authority. Instead, Nakayasu proposes that every proper, monolingual translation be read, to paraphrase Derrida, as more than two by placing it in relation to texts that more explicitly reflect the violent strategies that empower translation to break down its own monolingual authority.[44]

4.

A preoccupation with the violence of translation organizes Christian Hawkey's 2010 collection *Ventrakl*, a translation of the life and work of the German Expressionist poet Georg Trakl (1887–1914). The title is a portmanteau, a fusion of 'ventricle' and the poet's surname, underscoring how translation operates throughout Hawkey's collection as a mode of (re)circulation and reanimation of wounded texts and bodies. During World War I, Trakl worked in a medical unit under considerable stress; his experiences at Gródek, a town in Galicia (now Ukraine), were particularly harrowing. There, Trakl reportedly attempted suicide. 'Grodek', one of the last poems (and possibly the last poem) he wrote, draws from these experiences and is considered to be among his finest. The desire to translate Gródek motivakes *Ventrakl*, even though Hawkey knew no German when he undertook this project. *Ventrakl*, in that respect, documents the work of getting to the point where translation is possible.

Hawkey was partly inspired by Cameron's unorthodox strategies of translation, among them his use of homophonic and machine translation, and devised his own strategies, for example, extracting every colour reference in Trakl's poetry and recombining these to create poems like 'Yellow Trakl' and 'White Trakl'. In other instances, he relied on more violent strategies of translation, like decomposing pages of poetry in a jar of rainwater and only translating the words that remained after a year ('pieces of words, word-stems, floating up…').[45] Hawkey's translation strategies allowed him to simultaneously invoke and exceed his source material, as is the case for his poem-translation 'You Bent My Megahertz'. Here, Hawkey takes Trakl's poem 'Zu Abend Mein Herz' (My Heart at Evening) and translates, or rather rewrites it, according to homophonic relations that he locates between German and English. Listening for the English in the German results in a number of ludic, even absurd, distortions in both languages, while highlighting the Germanic currents that run through English. The opening line 'Am Abend hört man den Schrei der Fledermäuse' ('toward evening you hear the cry of the bats', in James Wright and Robert Bly's translation) becomes in Hawkey's poem 'I am unfolding a moth into a fluttering mouth, into'.[46] 'Fluttering mouse' would have been the more obvious homophonic rendering of 'Fledermäuse' (bat), however, given the linguistic relations between German and English, this would have constituted a more straightforward translation of the word. Rather, Hawkey's rendering 'fluttering mouth' pushes beyond the semantic field of the original to create a new one (also the case for his reworking of Trakl's 'Wiese' [meadow] as 'Visa card'). Trakl's 'Wanderer' is the one word that remains unchanged in Hawkey's poem. Its presence signals a place of convergence for English and German, while offering a figure of the translator as a wanderer and translation itself as an act of errancy.

Written in the first decade after 9/11, *Ventrakl* is a reflection on war as a 'mutual site', as Hawkey puts it, between his American English translations 'infiltrated daily by the ongoing wars in Iraq and Afghanistan' and Trakl's German wartime poetry. He applies specifically *American* practices of translation when he takes the law of translation into his own hands, wields a 12-gauge shotgun and, from the distance of 10 feet, shoots at an open book of Trakl's poems. Then, in his words '[translates], with a dictionary, a remaining page of perforated text'.[47] Like Cameron's *Flowers of Bad* and Nakayasu's *Mouth: Eats Color*, the resulting translations abound in bizarre juxtapositions, multilingual wordplay, 'word-stems' strung together to create texts that often bear little relation to the original text. These extreme translations therefore challenge authorship and originality in explicit ways, forcing a reappraisal of 'translation proper'. Using Trakl's poem as target practice inverts the relation between 'target' and 'source' in translation. It constitutes an extreme method of translation that addresses the violence of translation, that stage before a poem is rearranged in a new language when words are 'dissolved', dissected and decomposed. These strategies call attention to the wounds of translation; they also constitute an ethic of translation, acknowledging the state of anxiety and violence from which Trakl's own work emerged.

5.

For the poet Jody Gladding, translation is likewise an ethical inquiry, specifically one that problematizes the relation between beauty and damage. In her 2014 collection, *Translations from Bark Beetle*, Gladding, a translator of French poetry, undertakes translation of an entirely different order: documenting and translating the activity of the bark beetle, an insect that reproduces in the inner bark of trees. There are two layers to the bark beetle text: first, the marks that the beetle leaves as it burrows into the bark to deposit its eggs, and second, the recorded movements of its larvae after they hatch and chew their way out of the tree, at which point the cycle begins again. While bark beetles often target diseased and damaged trees, they are considered a pest, an invasive species responsible for high levels of tree mortality in areas of North America. The bark beetle poems, as Gladding calls them, are beautiful objects, records of the beetle's violence on this environment. Translating them is part of Gladding's ongoing interest in 'the elemental sources' of language, and doing so demands that Gladding reflect on the violence of her own language, the language of the human species, and its relation to the damaging effects of human activity on the natural environment:

> [H]ow can we even know what's untranslatable if we can't translate it? But in undertaking these bark beetle translations, I can begin to discover what's untranslatable. I can begin to imagine myself as a tiny cylindrical creature chewing my way through wood, elaborating patterns some other species may find compelling enough to want to read. I can begin to imagine *that* species, and the violences and elegances of *its* language: I can begin to understand what is untranslatable about my own kind.[48]

The bark beetle poems, and their translations, demand a different kind of reading. For one, the bark beetle texts, as they appear in Gladding's book, are amorphous, non-linear shapes, with no clear beginning or end, and no discernible lexical units. Lines blur together, with tracks of white space that signal where the beetle and its larvae have moved, and in that sense, do not correspond to the blank spaces of human language. In one text, titled 'Engraver Beetle Cycle', Gladding signals to the reader where the text 'begins', although from that point any reading of the bark beetle poem can take multiple directions and pathways.[49] The bark beetle's "process" is both creative and destructive, and this relation is one that Gladding projects onto her own writing practice. Like the translations discussed above, translating the tracks of the bark beetle allow for a new way of writing, one that breaks down the linguistic and grammatical norms of the English language, pushing it towards illegibility, as in these lines from Gladding's translation of 'Engraver Beetle Cycle'[50]:

```
            m•y sweet m•y rolled
              m•y x as in xylem
    cambrial      phloem              corridor
       • think •'m repeating m•yself
```

The bullet dots (in Gladding's book, slightly smaller than the letter 'o') create disruptions that defamiliarize common words like 'my' and 'I'm'. That they do so in the case of first person pronouns, which are related here to authorship and agency, is no coincidence. Gladding wants to call attention to the authorship of the bark beetle, while at the same time, as she states in the quote above, bring what is untranslatable in the bark beetle poem into her own poem. Xylem and phloem are terms for plant tissue which transport water, minerals, and various organic compounds to other parts of the tree; additionally, phloem constitutes an intra-cellular communication network that relays signals and information ('cambrial' may be portmanteau or a miswriting [intentional?] of 'cambial', referring to the tissue layer between xylem and phloem). 'Corridor' refers then to this network of plant tissues and the tunnels carved by the bark beetles and their larvae, serving in this context as a trope for translation and what moves or doesn't move between languages and texts. The bark beetle repeats its cycle of life and decay though its translation constitutes a repetition of a different kind. Gladding's encounter with the bark beetle poem is an invitation to exercise strategies of decay and decomposition in her own work, to rethink how poems are made from this violence and damage — "Each poem teaches me something new."[51]

6.

In his 1974 essay, 'Shnei nofim' (Two Landscapes), the Hebrew poet Avot Yeshurun proposed an abusive practice of composition. In his words, 'For a writer, language is like a child's toy. Language is in the hand of the creator — he doesn't feel it until he breaks it: when he throws it down — he hears the voice of language, the language that is his'.[52] In other words, for a poet working in her own language, it is entirely permissible, if not necessary, to deliberately bend and break the rules of this language, and yet, demands for fidelity and 'elegance' continue to pervade Western translation criticism. If an original author may resort to force in order to access or release her authentic and personal 'unholy noises', as McSweeney described it, maybe the damage of translation avoids an entirely different kind of violence, which is to say, the violence of forcing a translation to behave and abide by the linguistic, cultural and social norms of the target language. Extreme translation resists the inclination to normalize and numb these pressures.

And yet, after almost 150 pages of disobedient and radical translation — translations created by decomposing text in water and shooting pages with a shotgun — Hawkey concludes *Ventrakl* with an outwardly proper, even conventional translation of Trakl's 'Grodek', one that bears no explicit signs of the mischievous and transgressive strategies that the previous translations exhibit. Likewise, Nakayasu's *The Collected Poems of Chika Sagawa* — published four years after *Mouth: Eats Color* — offers a single, and in her words, 'conventional-looking' translation of Sagawa's

'Puromenaado'.⁵³ What are we to make of these translations, which outwardly appear to follow the rules of literal, proper translation? Does their placement confer the authority and finality of a 'last word', or, like the translations and anti-translations that precede them, do they represent, rather, one more possibility in the 'unprotected order' of translation ('Promenade [CP]', for instance, does not appear in the earlier collection). When *Collected Poems of Chika Sagawa* came out, a number of its reviews and prize citations remarked that it was the 'first appearance' of Sagawa's work in English translation, thereby privileging the 'conventional-looking' translation over the more experimental versions that preceded it.⁵⁴ But in this essay, I have shown how reading in the extremes of translation prepares us to discern, or at the very least, acknowledge, the many diversions and possibilities that constitute the translation process and underlie translations that may appear, on the surface, to be literal, proper, straightforward, 'conventional-looking'. The works I have gathered here recognize that such appearances are deceptive. Instead, these works invite us to think about translation the way we are trained to with an original text — in other words, to read between the lines, divining 'bottomless pits' of a text; to read, write and translate without restraint; to collect what remains of ourselves, transformed and translated, after we have spent some time, wilfully or by force, in their extremes.

Works Cited

BAUDELAIRE, CHARLES, *Les fleurs du mal* [The Flowers of Evil], trans. by Anne Princen (Paris: Flammarion, 2008)

BAUDELAIRE, CHARLES, *The Flowers of Evil*, ed. by Marthiel Mathews and Jackson Mathews (NY: New Directions, 1963)

BELLOS, DAVID, *Is that a Fish in Your Ear: Translation and the Meaning of Everything* (NY: Penguin Books, 2011)

BERVIN, JEN, 'Three Dimensions', *Poetry Foundation* (August 20, 2014) <https://www.poetryfoundation.org/features/articles/detail/70136>

CAMERON, DAVID, *Flowers of Bad* (Brooklyn, NY: Unbelievable Alligator/Ugly Duckling Presse, 2007)

CARSON, ANNE, 'Conversation with Brighde Mullins', *Lannan Foundation Readings & Conversations Series*, Santa Fe, New Mexico (March 21, 2001) <https://lannan.org/events/anne-carson-with-brighde-mullins>

DELEUZE, GILLES and FÉLIX GUATTARI. *Kafka: Toward a Minor Literature*, trans. by Dana Polan (Minneapolis: University of Minnesota Press, 1986)

DERRIDA, JACQUES, 'Des Tours de Babel', trans. by Joseph F. Graham, in *Acts of Religion*, ed. by Gil Anidjar (New York: Routledge, 2002), pp. 104–33

ELLIOTT, ALLISON, 'Review: *Flowers of Bad* by David Cameron', *The Adirondack Review* (2007) <http://www.theadirondackreview.com/book104.html>

FINK, THOMAS, 'Thomas Fink Interviews Sawako Nakayasu', *Galatea Resurrection* (May 8, 2012) <http://galatearesurrection18.blogspot.co.uk/2012/05/thomas-fink-interviews-sawako-nakayasu.html>

GLADDING, JODY, *Translations from Bark Beetle* (Minnesota: Milkweed Editions, 2014)

GOLDBERG, LEAH, 'Certain Aspects of Imitation and Translation in Poetry', in *Actes du IVe congrès de l'Association internationale de littérature comparée, Fribourg 1964* [Proceedings of the IVth congress of the International Comparative Literature Association], ed. by François Jost (The Hague: Mouton, 1966), pp. 837–43

GÖRANSSON, JOHANNES and JOYELLE MCSWEENEY, 'Manifesto of the Disabled Text', *Exoskeleton* (June 14, 2008) <http://exoskeleton-johannes.blogspot.com/2008/06/manifesto-of-disabled-text.html>
HAWKEY, CHRISTIAN, *Ventrakl* (Brooklyn: Ugly Duckling Presse, 2010)
MEADS, JOSEPH, 'Interview with Joyelle McSweeney', *Columbia Poetry Reviews* (May 1, 2013) < https://blogs.colum.edu/columbia-poetry-reviews/2013/05/01/interview-with-joyelle-mcsweeney>
NAJMAN, HINDY, 'The Vitality of Scripture Within and Beyond the 'Canon', *Journal for the Study of Judaism*, 43 (2012), 497–518
NAKAYASU, SAWAKO, *Mouth: Eats Color* (nc: Rogue Factorial, 2011)
SAGAWA, CHIKA, *The Collected Poems of Chika Sagawa*, trans. by Sawako Nakayasu (Marfa, TX: Canarium Books, 2015)
SAPPHO, *If Not, Winter: Fragments of Sappho*, trans. by Anne Carson (New York: Vintage Books, 2002)
TRAKL, GEORG, *Gedichte* [Poems] (Leipzig: Kurt Wolff Verlag, 1913)
TRAKL, GEORG, *Twenty Poems of Georg Trakl*, trans. by James Wright and Robert Bly (Madison, Minn., The Sixties Press, 1961)
WEBB, LINDSEY, 'From a Teen's Blog to International Acclaim: On Translating Sagawa Chika', *Literary Hub* (July 15, 2016) <https://lithub.com/from-a-teens-blog-to-international-acclaim-on-translating-sagawa-chika>
WEISELTIER, MEIR, *The Flower of Anarchy: Selected Poems*, trans. by Shirley Kaufman (Berkeley: University of California Press, 2003)
YESHURUN, AVOT, 'Shnei nofim' [Two Landscapes], in *Kol shirav* [Complete Poems] 3 vols (Tel Aviv: Hakibbutz Hame'uchad, 1995–2001), II (1997), 126–30.

Notes to Chapter 7

1. Anne Carson, 'Conversation with Brighde Mullins', *Lannan Foundation Readings & Conversations Series*, Santa Fe, New Mexico (March 21, 2001) <https://lannan.org/events/anne-carson-with-brighde-mullins> [accessed 25 February 2019]
2. Ibid.
3. Joseph Meads, 'Interview with Joyelle McSweeney', *Columbia Poetry Reviews* (May 1, 2013) <https://blogs.colum.edu/columbia-poetry-reviews/2013/05/01/interview-with-joyelle-mcsweeney> [accessed 25 February 2019]
4. Meir Weiselteir, 'Take', in *The Flower of Anarchy: Selected Poems*, trans. by Shirley Kaufman (Berkeley: University of California Press, 2003), p. 27. The original Hebrew poem appeared in Wieseltier's collection *Kach* [Take] (Tel Aviv: Mif 'alim universitayim le-hotsa'at ha-or, 1973).
5. The demand for 'legible' poetry continues to circulate in contemporary criticism, most recently in Matthew Zapruder's review 'Understanding Poetry is More Straightforward Than You Think' (July 10, 2017) <https://www.nytimes.com/2017/07/10/books/review/understanding-poetry-is-more-straightforward-than-you-think.html> [accessed 25 February 2019]. The poet Johannes Göransson responded with a defense of 'strangeness'. To follow their debate, see 'Matthew Zapruder Responds', <https://www.poetryfoundation.org/harriet/2017/07/matthew-zapruder-responds> [accessed 25 February 2019]
6. Johannes Göransson and Joyelle McSweeney, 'Manifesto of the Disabled Text', *Exoskeleton* (June 14, 2008) <http://exoskeleton-johannes.blogspot.com/2008/06/manifesto-of-disabled-text.html> [accessed 25 February 2019]
7. For the source of 'poetry is what gets lost in translation' see Cleanth Brooks and Robert Penn Warren, eds., *Conversations on the Craft of Poetry* (New York: Holt, Rinehart and Winston, 1961), p. 7.
8. Leah Goldberg, 'Certain Aspects of Imitation and Translation in Poetry', in *Actes du IVe congrès de l'Association internationale de littérature comparée, Fribourg 1964* [Proceedings of the IVth congress of the International Comparative Literature Association], ed. by François Jost, (The Hague: Mouton, 1966), pp. 837–43 (p. 840).

9. 'About Action', <http://actionbooks.org/about> [accessed 25 February 2019]. This copy is taken from an earlier version of the site. The current version now includes the line 'In an Emergency, Break Forms'.
10. Gilles Deleuz and Félix Guattari, *Kafka: Toward a Minor Literature*, trans. by Dana Polan (Minneapolis: University of Minnesota Press, 1986), p. 22.
11. David Bellos, *Is that a Fish in Your Ear: Translation and the Meaning of Everything* (NY: Penguin Books, 2011), p. 314.
12. David Cameron, *Flowers of Bad* (Brooklyn, NY: Unbelievable Alligator/Ugly Duckling Presse, 2007), p. 214.
13. Cameron, *Flowers of Bad*, pp. 206–11.
14. Ibid., p. 211.
15. Sappho, *If Not, Winter: Fragments of Sappho*, trans. by Anne Carson (New York: Vintage Books, 2002), p. xi.
16. Hindy Najman, 'The Vitality of Scripture Within and Beyond the 'Canon', *Journal for the Study of Judaism* 43 (2012), 497–518 (p. 516).
17. Cameron, *Flowers of Bad*, p. 1.
18. Ibid.
19. Cameron, *Flowers of Bad*, pp. 204–06.
20. Cameron, *Flowers of Bad*, p. 210.
21. Charles Baudelaire, 'Au Lecteur' [To the Reader], in *Les fleurs du mal* [The Flowers of Evil], ed. by Anne Princen (Paris: Flammarion, 2008), pp. 49–51.
22. Charles Baudelaire, 'To the Reader', trans. by Robert Lowell, in *The Flowers of Evil*, ed. by Marthiel Mathews and Jackson Mathews (NY: New Directions, 1963), p. 3.
23. Cameron, *Flowers of Bad*, p. 3. I am grateful to David Cameron for permission to reprint his work.
24. For a fuller discussion on American English monolingualism and its historical development as part of a current anti-immigrant platform in the United States, see Robert B. Kaplan 'Multilingualism vs. Monolingualism: The View from the USA and Its Interaction with Language Issues around the World', *Current Issues in Language Planning* 16, 1–2 (2015), 149–62.
25. Charles Baudelaire, 'La Mort des pauvres' [The Death of the Poor], in *Les fleurs du mal*, ed. by Anne Princen (Paris: Flammarion, 2008), p. 228. Multiple English translations of this poem are available via the online archive Fleursdumal.org. Charles Baudelaire, 'La Mort des pauvres', in *Fleurs du mal* <https://fleursdumal.org/poem/198> [accessed 25 February 2019].
26. Cameron, *Flowers of Bad*, p. 188.
27. Cameron, *Flowers of Bad*, p. 207.
28. Allison Elliott, 'Review: Flowers of Bad by David Cameron', *The Adirondack Review* (2007) <http://www.theadirondackreview.com/book104.html> [accessed 25 February 2019]
29. Cameron, *Flowers of Bad*, p. 73.
30. In addition to her translations, Nakayasu is the author of several books of poetry, including her most recent collection *The Ants* (2014, Les Figues Press). The original Facebook post was set to private but Nakayasu kindly shared a screenshot of the exchange.
31. Jen Hofer quoted in Thomas Fink, 'Thomas Fink Interviews Sawako Nakayasu', *Galatea Resurrection* (May 8, 2012) <http://galatearesurrection18.blogspot.co.uk/2012/05/thomas-fink-interviews-sawako-nakayasu.html> [accessed 25 February 2019]
32. Sawako Nakayasu, 'Rogue Factorial' <http://www.sawakonakayasu.net/kslungs> [accessed 25 February 2019].
33. Fink, 'Thomas Fink Interviews Sawako Nakayasu'.
34. See Kasia Szymanska's chapter in this volume for a discussion of Nakayasu's translation of the poem as an example of 'translation multiples'.
35. Sawako Nakayasu, *Mouth: Eats Color* (nc: Rogue Factorial, 2011), pp. 85–86.
36. Chika Sagawa, 'Promenade', in *The Collected Poems of Chika Sagawa*, trans. by Sawako Nakayasu (Marfa, TX: Canarium Books, 2015), p. 54. I am grateful to Sawako Nakayasu for her permission to include the translations and anti-translations that appear in this section.
37. Nakayasu, *Mouth: Eats Color*, p. 11.

38. Lindsey Webb, 'From a Teen's Blog to International Acclaim: On Translating Sagawa Chika', *Literary Hub* (July 15, 2016) < https://lithub.com/from-a-teens-blog-to-international-acclaim-on-translating-sagawa-chika> [accessed 25 February 2019]
39. Ibid.
40. Ibid.
41. Today, the spelling スクリーン is standard. According to *Nihon kokugo daijiten*, the largest Japanese dictionary, the word has been since (at least) the 1920s in connection to photography and film. I am grateful to Jennifer Guest for providing critical insights on this word's historical and cultural context.
42. Nakayasu, *Mouth: Eats Color*, p. 86.
43. Ibid.
44. Jacques Derrida, 'Des Tours de Babel', trans. by Joseph F. Graham, *Acts of Religion*, ed. Gil Anidjar (New York: Routledge, 2002), pp. 104–33 (p. 108).
45. Christian Hawkey, *Ventrakl* (Brooklyn: Ugly Duckling Presse, 2010), p. 8.
46. Hawkey, *Ventrakl*, p. 31; Georg Trakl, *Gedichte* [Poems] (Leipzig: Kurt Wolff Verlag, 1913), p. 24; Georg Trakl, 'My Heart at Evening', in *Twenty Poems of Georg Trakl*, trans. by James Wright and Robert Bly (Madison, Minn.: The Sixties Press, 1961), p. 10.
47. Ibid.
48. Jen Bervin, 'Three Dimensions', *Poetry Foundation* (August 20, 2014) <https://www.poetryfoundation.org/features/articles/detail/70136> [accessed 25 February 2019]
49. The interview linked to in the note above reproduces the original, bark beetle version of 'Engraver Beetle Cycle'.
50. Jody Gladding, *Translations from Bark Beetle* (Minnesota: Milkweed Editions, 2014), p. 8. I have used Courier to approximate the original font (Super Secret Typewriter).
51. Bervin, 'Three Dimensions'.
52. Avot Yeshurun, 'Shnei nofim' [Two Landscapes], in *Kol shirav* [Complete Poems], vol. 2 (Tel Aviv: Hakibbutz Hame'uchad, 1997), 126–30 (pp. 127–28).
53. Sagawa, *The Collected Poems*, p. 54; Webb, 'On Translating Sagawa Chika'.
54. See, for example, the citation that followed the announcement that Nakayasu's translation had won the 2016 Lucien Stryk Asian Translation Prize. <https://literarytranslators.wordpress.com/2016/11/01/2016-stryk-winner> [accessed 25 February 2019]

CHAPTER 8

Translation Poetry: the Poetics of Noise in Hsia Yü's *Pink Noise*

Cosima Bruno

'Good day,
   With warm heart I offer my friendship, and my greetings and I hope this letter meets you in good time.'[1]

When a message such as the one above is written and spammed by a machine to thousands of email addresses, such an event alters our relationship with language, texts, and words. The abundant circulation of digital texts that people in technologically advanced countries are exposed to on a daily basis, since the invention of broadband, has rapidly defined a textual environment that has transformed our assumptions about reading and writing. American poet Kenneth Goldsmith comments: '...the underlying ethos and modes of writing have been permanently changed...Words very well might be written not to be read but rather to be shared, moved, and manipulated'.[2]

Concrete and sound poetry, and literary devices such as pastiche, collage, and cutups, can be seen as the direct result of the technological turns that started with the widespread use of the phonograph, and continued with the typewriter, the tape recorder, the photocopy machine, the computer, all of which have radically impacted creative writing since the end of the 19th century.[3] All those technological inventions had in common the function of facilitating the reproduction and manipulation of oral and written texts, playing an enormous role in writers' experimentation with the materiality of language.

Pink Noise (Fen hongse de sangyin) is a book printed on acetate pages, including thirty-two poems in English and one in French as originals, and their translations into Chinese, by the Apple Macintosh search-and-find software Sherlock.[4] The original poems are composed using phrases, mostly found by clicking hyperlinks in spam emails, then lineated by Hsia Yü to look like poems. These are printed in black ink and made be followed by their machine translation into Chinese, printed in pink. The two different colours therefore mark two kinds of appropriations, the one of texts from the Internet and the one of the translation. *Pink Noise* thus situates itself in the long tradition of using existing materials and re-contextualising them in the creation of a new work.

What, then, is the conceptual framework that distinguishes a poetic work such as Hsia Yü's *Pink Noise* from Ezra Pound's radical, multilingual, collaged poetry, or Kurt Schwitters's 'Merz' poems, which were composed by assembling together fragments of overheard conversation and random phrases from newspapers and magazines, or Tristan Tzara's simultaneous poem 'The Admiral Looks for a House to Rent', written and performed in three different languages at the same time? The crucial differences pertain to the digital context of its creation, and a certain conceptualization of translation and noise as creative devices. In the digital context, the strategies and modalities of signification have been transformed, first and foremost by considerably expanding the field of textuality, and by putting all sorts of texts in topologically unspecific networked circulation, available to be looked at, shared, and manipulated, sometimes quickly or partially read.

In the following sections I will examine *Pink Noise* within the context of Hsia Yü's literary production, and, more generally, within the context of globalized, post-modern Taiwan. I will also attempt a discussion of this collection and its processes of remediation of poetic language, focusing on the mechanisms of localization activated by Sherlock's translation.

Pink Noise within Hsia Yü's Literary Production

Hsia Yü has a varied CV: she graduated in performing arts, specialized in creative writing; she worked in a publishing house, at a TV broadcasting agency, in an art gallery, as a journal editor, as a translator, as a lyricist for 'the princess of Taiwan's underground rock' Sandee Chan,[5] and established herself on the Taiwanese literary scene as the first and most successful postmodern poet. After many years living interchangeably in France, New York, and Taiwan, in 2002, Hsia Yü eventually returned to reside on a more or less permanent basis in Taipei, where she continues to be a productive and influential writer in and beyond Taiwan.

Hsia Yü's poetry collections include: *Memoranda* (Beiwanglu, 1984), a self-published volume, containing poems from 1976 to 1984 that surprised both the ear and the eye by linking together in analogy words that are normally unconnected;[6] *Ventriloquy* (Fuyu shu, 1991), featuring invented characters and where, as implied in the title, the main theme is the distance between the spoken word and the subject of speech; *Friction Ineffable* (Moca wu yi ming zhuang, 1995), composed mostly of concise and highly abstract cutups from the previous collection *Ventriloquy* and thus further radicalizing the estrangement; *Salsa* (2000), containing longer, almost narrative-style poems; and a double album CD, *The More Mixed Up with Music the Better* (Yue hun yue dui, 2002), containing poems from her collection *Fusion Kitsch*, and sung by various rock stars or recited with music by the poet herself.

Pink Noise is a product of the digital turn of the 1990s, when the Internet from being a specialized medium rapidly became an ordinary means of communication and expression, a new context, and a state of mind. It was first published by the author herself in 2007. Together with the poems and their translation, at the end of the book there is also appended an interview with the poet by A Weng, in Chinese, translated by Zona Yi-Ping Tsou into English.

As is apparent from such a succinct résumé, much of the motivation for this author's work seems to come from the postmodern interest in repetition, quotations and clichés. More recent books, such as *First Person* (Di yi rencheng, 2016), a bilingual book-length photo poem, also play around with the ideas of the speaking voice, visuality, illegibility, poetry and the controversy of signification. *Pink Noise*, with its lines in the second-hand Weblish language as *objet trouvé*, and their machine translation, constitutes no exception. The book has indeed a dependency on automated system, in the same way as contemporary e-poetry can do.[7] However, authorial intervention is also important, since Hsia Yü not only selects and arranges the texts, but she is also the designer, maker and publisher of the book. This makes *Pink Noise* distinctive, as it is not a wholly machine-operated text but rather stages a rhizomatic subjectivity operating in a digital world.

The book is also aesthetically pleasing to look at and it feels physically heavier than a regular paper book of equal size. It was printed in limited editions, and the price reflected this, being higher than a normal book. The text as image is quite dominant, but in fact, reading the poems is impossible, unless we interpose a sheet of paper between the acetated pages of the book. At a more minute level, the book presents linear verbal poetry, sometimes composed of segments from adverts, some times by random excerpts from online communications, and some other times by lines spanning from Shakespeare to Baudelaire, to more recent minds. The reader is then presented with semantic elements, even though they can be combined in surprising ways. The essay appended at the end of the book makes this object more bookish, and although the pages are unusually not numbered and transparent, there is no violation or denial of the book's potential page space, as we may find in many a visual, hypertextual, animated, interactive, holographic, or sound poem.[8] These attributes all point to the idea that, while very much an art object, *Pink Noise* does not deny its identity as a book: Hsia Yü's chosen medium is the book.

Simultaneously, while the book itself has considerable and stylish authorial intervention, conceptually, because of its reliance on citations and translation, and, above all, because it is written and translated by the machine, it is expressive of an approach to poetry that refuses familiar strategies of authorial control and the conventional idea of the poem as the product of a single authorial and original voice.[9] Some of the hallmarks of poetry as conventionally understood, such as the use of metaphor and imagery and the expression of sincere emotion by especially sensitive individuals, have to be radically reconsidered here.

Owing to its eye-catching appearance, its genesis, and its thoughtful conception, this book has triggered the interest of a large number of scholars. These scholars have discussed it in relation to issues of authorship and of the deconstructivist echo of the poetic word, of identity and concepts linked to poetry's originality and linguistic (in)commensurability; they have also discussed Taiwan's broader socio-cultural condition in the digital era, and language and globalization in the digital ecosystem of the Internet. In a paper presented at the AAS conference in 2010, Jennifer Feeley gives an introduction to the history of machine translation to foreground her discussion of *Pink Noise*'s collaborative writing between a human and a computer. Referring to Johnston's and Deleuze's theorizations of the simulacrum, Feeley reads this collection, in the light of deconstructivist speculations on the notion of original. Tong King Lee dedicates a whole chapter of his book on experimental Chinese literature to *Pink Noise*, entitling it 'Machine Translation and Hsia Yu's Poetics of Deconstruction'. Echoing and expanding Feeley's main points, Lee takes Derrida as his main theoretical reference, with a host of other literary and translation theorists, from Barthes to Benjamin to Pym to Gentzler. Jonathan Rollins in his book chapter 'Hsia Yü's Translingual Transculturalism from *Memoranda* to *Pink Noise*' also surveys 'the poet's radical experiments in language and culture [...] by reading her work as an example of translingual, transcultural poetry according to theories put forth by Mikhail Bakhtin, Mikhail Epstein, and Steven G. Kellman' (247). Jacob Edmond's discussion of *Pink Noise* appears in a chapter of his book *Make It the Same: Poetry in the Age of Global Media*, 'Chinese Rooms'. Here Edmond illustrates a number of authors, including Hsia Yü, Chen Li, and Jonathan Stalling, who relate to Chinese and English translation, with the aim of defamiliarizing language. Michelle Yeh and Lili Hsieh both approach *Pink Noise* from a critical angle that goes beyond deconstruction. According to the title and epigraph of her article 'Towards a Poetics of Noise: From Hu Shi to Hsia Yü', Yeh aims at examining this book within the framework of a 'poetics of noise', while succinctly focusing on three themes: love/sex, life and art. Given the limited space of her article, and the wide time frame of her exploration, Yeh's essay however does not probe, as promised, into a poetics of noise. Instead, it examines *Pink Noise* from the perspective of feminist writing, thus shifting attention to the broader social context of Taiwan, highlighting how sexual transactions are portrayed and how they relate to and are proscribed by the capitalist system. Lili Hsieh's 'Romance in the Age of Cybernetic Conviviality: Hsia Yü's *Pink Noise* and the Poetics of Postcolonial Translation' is perhaps the most incisive of all these inspiring studies, eloquently elaborating on Hsia Yü's conception of *Pink Noise* within a rhetoric of love and Taiwan's colonial background. Hsieh convincingly reads the poems in *Pink Noise* 'as the realistic representations of the transformed and transforming public sphere of cybernetic conviviality' (3) and discusses the question of 'the status of English as a global language, the loss and love of translation in a postcolonial context, the return from narratology to a musicology of poetry, and the tremendously rich 'nonsense' that happens when two heterogeneous and disparagingly hegemonic national languages meet' ('Abstract').

The reflections offered by all these studies are ample and sophisticated. Surprisingly, however, *Pink Noise* has not yet been read through the lens of sound studies. Sound studies can in fact introduce a critical dimension, in addition to the thematic one, that helps investigating the ideological dimension of the Internet and of translation as cultural forms. The poet herself stated that *Pink Noise* was conceived as a result of having been listening to Taiwan sound art, 'from music, noise, off-key, low-frequencies, sampling, jazz syncopation and such, ... I just wanted to work out the best form for this 'poetry noise'... to offset the lettristic noise...'[10] What Hsia Yü calls 'poetry noise' here may refer to certain treatment of the many citations taken from all the texts circulating and overcrowding the Internet. Like the processing of extracted audio signals through modulation, sampling, and other techniques of sound manipulation in sound art, *Pink Noise* aims at transforming the original polyphony of the extracted material found in the Internet into new poetic compositions. Hsia also compares this processing to that one of the 'lettristic' poets, who in their asemic writing worked to empty writing of its specific semantic content, while maintaining its visual form. This adds to *Pink Noise*'s visual dimension: asemic writing looks like regular writing but it is in fact 'unreadable'. Similarly, the poems in *Pink Noise* look like poems, but they are made of waste language and rendered 'unreadable' by the texts' superimposition. Such a celebration of language failure is what links *Pink Noise* to the art of noise: as in a piece of sound art, Hsia Yü puts glitches at the centre of her creative process. Indeed, what characterizes sound poetry is not just its audibility, but primarily an aesthetics of language that disengages poetry from meaning, linguistically encoded structures, or grammatical synthesis. Following these indications, the challenge I set for myself is then to explore *Pink Noise* through the epistemology of noise, hoping that drawing on sound studies and thinking about the visual and aural noise of these texts as art of noise will help me disclose the process and theoretical tenets of this book.

Pink Noise and the Epistemology of Noise

I shall start with the title and discuss *Pink Noise* within the operations of noise as a sensory phenomenon and as a cultural theory. Throughout, I will draw from both cultural theorist Stephen Kennedy's conceptualization of the digital space and methodology of sound and American artist Joseph Nechvatal's theory of noise art.[11]

In electromagnetics, noise can be named after colours, such as violet, blue, brown, white or pink. The practice started with the denomination of 'white noise', a phenomenon taking its title from the extension to audio of the visual phenomenon called 'white light', where a combination of lights of different wavelengths in the visible spectrum are perceived as white. Analogously, white noise can be compared to this phenomenon, inasmuch as it combines together all signals of different frequencies into a flat frequency of equal intensity. Pink noise is instead a filtered sound, inversely proportional to the frequency, defined as 'pink' because light with a similar spectrum would appear pink. Pink noise is also defined as 'human friendly' noise, because humans can tolerate it more easily. In information theory, any alteration in the transmission of a message is also defined as 'noise'.

Noise functions as a disturbance factor to the detached observation of a knowable world. Applied to art, noise has been invested with a subversive function, as a phenomenological means that is able to give access to non-representational meaning. In computing signal processing and in sound art, as Nechvatal explains, noise 'can be considered data without meaning; that is data that is not being used to transmit a signal, but is simply produced as an unwanted by-product of other activities. Noise can block, distort, or change the meaning of a message in both human and electronic communication'.[12] I see *Pink Noise* as drawing on both these two conceptions of noise, developing a tension between non-representational meaning and the non meaning of the signal interference.

Bearing Nechvatal's definition in mind, we can take the epigraph given at the beginning of this paper, and any other spam texts circulating on the Internet, as examples of noise in electronic communication. We can similarly take Hsia Yü's poem-lineated English texts as language noise, i.e. texts made of 'data without meaning', that will be turn into poems with 'non-representational meaning'. Made of samples of the textual inundation in today's networked digital world, *Pink Noise* presents us with texts that look like poems but are made of white noise interference. Indeed, Nechvatal also specifies:

> We must consider that noise takes place in a general media culture of massive electronic deluge, where the mercurial reproduction of free-floating (ineffable) signifiers of language, sound and images has blurred into a problematized complex/compound/prodigality sometimes referred to as *information overload*. In one respect, all sounds and images are already a kind of noise: data without meaning.[13]

In the same respect, *Pink Noise*'s English poems can be considered as being made of by-product language, randomly selected citations with or without quotation marks, 'free-floating signifiers of language'. This is language appropriated from the multitude of voices circulating on the Web, and which produces visual glitches and aural noise, both indicating communication failure. The method of sharing and exchange, of appropriating segments of texts, gives shape to a counter sub-cultural practice of remix and information overload, which recycles found digital texts. But *Pink Noise* does not linger in a polemical comment on digital culture. It rather performs it, showing how a large amount of text is always a click away from everyone, available, and open to any manipulation. Visually, aurally and conceptually, we are in front of a totalizing effect, an abundance of interwoven voices, expropriating the space of the single authorial voice.[14] Thus *Pink Noise* also undertakes a radical consideration of poetry and the poet, the former being made of material that is extraneous to the poet and the latter acting more as a sound artist or a *bricoleur*. Globe trotting through the Web, the poetic word has lost its specific location, and with it any claim to originality. But since Hsia Yü selected and combined the found textual segments at a specific time and place, and the book itself is a limited-edition collectable work, the final product is in fact not a piece of entirely automated writing, but an original work with an author.

Hsia Yü's manipulation of web-found language does not simply communicate a free postmodern play of signifiers. Within the overarching referent of cyberspace, we are not asked to try to fill the gaps, but to browse these texts and gaps, as we browse the Web. Furthermore, *Pink Noise*'s cutups may perhaps be incongruously compiled, but they do not attempt to disengage familiar words; instead they still retain conventional meaning; by a playful and exuberant operation of assemblage, they paradoxically often read as so conventional that they sound trite, with several idiomatic expressions. So, for example, we find lines such as: 'Words fail me' (poem 5); 'In the desolate frozen wasteland' (poem 14); 'Remember that great love and great achievements involve great risk' (poem 12); 'There is comfort in this sadness' (poem 15); 'Tu as largement rempli l'abysse qui est en moi' (poem 27); 'Things seem to get worse before they get better' (poem 32); or segments of 'small talk', such as in poem 4:

> "I have this green hutch, from Romania
> Late 1800s," she says. "It's a great antique piece
> It's a great colour, a very bright green
> The doors are held together by bent nails. It's
> Fabulous. I have eclectic tastes.
> Nothing really goes but it works."

These poems in English, then, let words stream out hijacked, as we encounter them on the web. They are commonplace, trivial, repetitive, familiar, and automate our reading. With appropriate reference to sound, Lawrence Lessing refers to this patchwork mechanism as 'remix culture', and Lev Manovich calls it the 'database logic' of the new media,[15] wherein the focus is no longer on the production of new material but on the recombination of previously produced and stockpiled data. Such a dynamic intermediation of texts leads to what has been called Work as Assemblage,[16] a cluster of texts that modifies constructions of subjectivity. The subjects producing the Work as Assemblage are multiple in many senses, both because they are collectivities in and among themselves, and also because they include nonhuman as well as human actors. The machine is also a poet that produces the text, and the text is also multiple, because is an assemblage of multiple authorship. The reader, immersed in the noise of the re-assembled texts on acetate pages, can claim equal rights on them to the poet Hsia Yü.

The obliteration of the original voice by the machine does not imply an antithesis to human, since it is still the poet to assemble the poems. As elaborated by cultural theorist Stephen Kennedy, both the human and the machine inhabit the digital space: 'Not a dichotomy of real and virtual but a unified experience where those two realms collide to create mediated experiences and environments without essential qualities'.[17] In such digital space, 'technology is not a specific object or collection of objects, but is a constellation of generative and regenerative elements in a number of forms that are not always stylistically uniform or thematically stable'.[18]

Given the digital environment where private and public, human and machine, past and present coalesce, *Pink Noise* is a hyperreal facsimile that exploits mass-consumed language as poetry, engages public and private, and brings about a compelling world of uneven digital globalization in postcolonial Taiwan. Even when writing has become more graphic than semantic, more an event than a medium for referential communication, *Pink Noise* still fundamentally goes beyond the page, into the context, exploring what Amie Elizabeth Parry has recognized as Hsia Yü's poetic project: the underlying structures of knowledge, subjective and collective belief, and the values and structures of feeling that they support and help produce. The underlying questions of this collection, as Parry pointed out in relation to other work by Hsia Yü, are still the epistemological questions of What do we know? and How do we know?[19]

The discrete segments of the cluster poem all contribute to the poetic world in the same way: Hsia Yü attempts some levelling of the different kinds of textual identities and human experiences, the lines from spam emails and the lines from Shakespeare's sonnets. They are the new 'post-spectacular articulation of banality'[20] that makes our collective knowledge. *Pink Noise* samples the chaotic digital environment, where extension and proximity are accentuated, and where we can engage in some activities of exchange and make 'journeys full of encounters'.[21] But whereas Kennedy concedes that in the contemporary digital landscape 'echoes resound in the shadows'[22] and 'noise resolves to harmonize',[23] in my view the 'harmonized' Weblish compositions in *Pink Noise* do not equal poetry. They need the 'improvised performative' of translation in order to be activated as poetry, 'affirm monstrosity' and 'mirror desire'.[24]

Translation as the Viral Mutation of Language

Sherlock investigates, finds connections to the linguistic extracts, translates word by word, line by line, and among the gaps, glitches and overlaps, 'in cognitive dissonance',[25] finally filters white noise into pink noise — that is poetry.

According to Nechvatal, in order to transform noise into art (i.e. be subversive and creative), the artist has to use 'noise to re-route and break our mental habits'.[26] I see *Pink Noise* doing this by being ideated as a bilingual collection. In order to 're-route' our mental habits, it is not enough to have poem-look-alikes made out of the noisy digital totality of voices, connecting the unconnected; they need to be further estranged, while being localized, through the operations of machine translation. As notably stated by literary theorist Victor Shklovsky, the poetic device of *ostranenie* (estrangement) aims at resurrecting consumed words, so as to awaken the mind to a critical view on the word.[27] Similarly, the Surrealist poet Comte de Lautreamont (aka Isidore Ducasse) advocated that all elements, no matter where they come from, can be used to produce new combinations in which meaning can be altered, through the estrangement of the familiar. Such a *détournement* works for Ducasse as a contamination, as a virus within the hosting organism, operating empathically with it, so as to subvert it through semiotic overwriting.

Thus, rather than claiming symmetry and dissymmetry between 'original' and translation, Hsia Yü invokes translation estrangement to explain aesthetics, emotion and the pleasure of forms; that is, an unpredicted deviation in the relationship between sign and meaning, original and translation, and global and local. Following an argument similar to that of Emily Apter in 'Philosophical Translation and Untranslatability',[28] Hsia Yü seems to warn against the tendency in world literature of relying on equivalence and cultural commensurability. Sherlock's wrong translation shows linguistic incommensurability between Weblish and Chinese, as we can see if we compare any of the English originals, the Chinese, and a back translation into English:

> You work all day and get half drunk at night
> *Nin fuwu zheng tian, he dedao yiban he zai wanshang*
> You, Sir, serve all day, and get half drink at night
> A little chaos every now and then seems necessary
> *Yidian fenluan changchang sihu biyao de*
> A little chaos often is like necessary
> When it comes to a matter that is close to your heart
> *Dang ta lai dao shi jin ai nin de xizang*
> When it comes is close to your heart
> You are addicted to excitement
> *Nin shi shangyin de dui xingfen*
> You are addictive to excitement
> You'll love these easy recipes
> *Nin jiang ai zhexie rongyi de shipu*
> You will love these easy recipes
> And the kids will adore this crafty activity
> *Bingqie haizi jiang chongbai zhege guiji duoduan di huodong de shiqing*
> Moreover children will worship this thing of trickery activity [29]

Sherlock's incomprehension works as resistance to the homogenizing impulses of the Web. I consider this as *Pink Noise*'s main conception as a bilingual collection, with texts in Weblish translated into Chinese poems by a software function. *Pink Noise* 're-routes' our mental habits, presenting us with the noise of the digital textualities; then it goes a step further, enhancing estrangement through the operations of machine translation. And yet, at the same time, such enhanced estrangement is what makes the texts localized, because it is Hsia Yü who has decided to do this, within Taiwan's socio-cultural context. This is how Hsia Yü transforms the white noise of the English texts, into pink noise — that is poetry.

The discursive condition of the collaboration between the voices of the internet collectivity, Sherlock and Hsia Yü, is fragmentary and visually complicated, thus diverting the attention from a linear aggregate reading of the poems to a discontinuous, more conceptually driven fruition of the work. In fact, it is impossible to read the book without taking the pain of interposing a sheet of paper in between the pages. After doing so, the bilingual reader will read original and translation, soon finding that whereas the original more or less works as a conventional poem, the translation into Chinese sounds awkward, ungrammatical, and anachronistic. In a heightened back translation by Steve Bradbury of poem 20, 'Newsletter filled with diets' becomes 'Current affairs loaded with food and drink' (*shishi tongxun bei zhuangzai yinshi*), 'For whom I'm searching' becomes 'I forage' (*wo xunzhao*), 'Yes, technology' becomes 'Right, technique' (*shi, jishu*), etc.[30] By having these texts translated by the software function Sherlock, introducing the discordant language of the Chinese translation, *Pink Noise* presents us with the grand narrative of the technological global culture, while also subverting it. When machine-like Sherlock translates, for example, 'fucking' into 'sexual intercourse' (*xingjiao*), or 'and' into 'moreover' (*bingqie*), 'creeping' into 'crawling' (*rudong*),[31] the suggestion is that poetry is not within the meaning of the original, nor in the translation, but in the 'cognitive dissonance' demonstrated by the gaps between original and translation. Hsieh astutely points out that the translation shifts resulting from Sherlock's translation

> are 'luminous mistakes': the comic effect is that the banality of everyday English is rendered into a pedantic, academic or jargon translation, [...] the machine-generated translation anachronistically reflects the literal translation of the 1950s and 1960s Taiwan [...]. The sense of defamiliarization in the Chinese poems of *Pink Noise* therefore has an historical as well as an aesthetic dimension.[32]

Benjamin conceptualized the authenticity of the work of art as a quality that is topologically inflected: an original is located into a specific territory and historical moment. The copy of an original, on the other hand, is virtual, ahistorical, de-territorialized. It is inauthentic, not because it is different from the original, but because it does not have a precise location. Benjamin's distinction between original and copy not only recognizes that an original can be copied and de-territorialized, but also that a copy can become an original if re-territorialized. The same applies to translation, which does not have to be primarily concerned with accuracy, but which in order to become an original needs to be concerned with context and connotation, whatever engenders the specificity of a topological reference. That is what the poet Hsia Yü, through Sherlock's translation, does in *Pink Noise*.

Hsia Yü herself states in the interview appended at the end of the collection that more than 'translated poetry' this is 'translation poetry'. In this light, the change of colour in the printed poems (black for the originals in English, and pink for the translation into Chinese) carries symbolic meaning too, inasmuch as the performative process of translation renders white noise (black print) into pink noise, corrupted language into affect, love and poetry.

Because Sherlock clearly refers to Sherlock Holmes, it anthropomorphizes the machine, thus triggering a regular misunderstanding that sees a piece of computer software as an autonomous entity, characterized by human-like processes and motivations. Furthermore, Hsia Yü contributes to such a misunderstanding of a hybrid subject, half-human, half machine, when she refers to it as a lover:

> But now I feel a new romance coming on with this automated translation software, my machine poet. And what really turns me on is that, like any lethal lover, it announces from the beginning that is not to be trusted.[33]

Sherlock problematizes, drains, transfigures, and shows a rupture, making language particular. It compels us to take notice that original and translation conflict with each other, but it also directs us towards the transformative possibilities of translation, which encourages us to adopt an attitude of exploratory curiosity. In other words, the Chinese poems provide for a complicating narrative, intrinsically intermingled with, but clearly distinguished from, the grand narrative of digital globalization.

Language is fragmented or sliced, then clustered together and inadequately translated: a linguistic breakdown to match the immersive and compressed World

Wide Web, full of coalescing, conflicting, and ineluctable voices and texts. This is part of a general critique of the language of the internet; but it also has particular relevance to Taiwan because linguistic crossing and communication problems have repeatedly been part of the Taiwanese context, with its history of heated debates on the abandonment of one 'national language' over another. At least as early as 1943, Taiwan's government tried to implement a series of language policies, first endorsing and then abandoning the colonial language (Japanese), and subsequently 'returning' to Chinese as a national language. At the time of the Second World War, however, many Taiwanese had learned Chinese characters only as Japanese *kanji*: the ideographs were the same, but they had a different pronunciation and sometimes a different meaning. Therefore, such a partially shared orthography between Chinese and Japanese made the recovery of Mandarin as national language ambiguous, since it was not clear what the object of decontamination was. Moreover, Mandarin was also challenged from within, as the inhabitants of Taiwan were largely southern Min topolect speakers in the first place. Taiwan's language problem, that is, was at once cross-national and intranational.[34] Taiwan's historical circumstances and multilingual environment gave language opacity and heft. The essentially plural, commingled, and always already othered linguistic and cultural environment created opportunities for translingual practices and artistic experimentation. I see *Pink Noise* as precisely arising from the conjunction between this historical context of linguistic complexity and the new language modes of the Internet.

In general, Hsia Yü's aesthetics of the cut-and-paste simultaneously works as a celebration and as a critique of the Internet. It emphasizes the collectivity, the group, in collaboration with the single poet, figuring the poetic production as a collective remix. According to this logic, instantaneous connections and subjective random associations are elevated to the status of performance itself, intended as public and creative gesture.

The miniature disconnections between originals and translations presented in *Pink Noise* can be seen as reflecting this gesture, by expatriating language, uprooting it, estranging it, and also freeing it:

> The books that illuminated my youth were by and large translations... I've always loved those sentences that are rendered with a clumsy fidelity, those adorable literal versions that are virtually indifferent to Chinese grammar... and all those second- and third-hand translations from Russian via English and Japanese and who knows what else.[35]

This not only gives a glimpse into an affective, nostalgic overtone of this work, but it also offers a reflection in the spirit of the ontology of poetry. Should we wish to do so, how could we possibly translate effectively to render such nostalgia, such a locally bound memory, into the language of another context?

Metaphorical and idiomatic language is clearly difficult to translate, and even more so in machine translation, where ambiguities are most likely bound to generate mistranslations, as the machine only equates X to Y, in a much more absolute way than human equations. Sherlock reads and transcodes between the two languages, creating poems whose language resembles the corrupted language of

Hsia Yü's childhood. The activity involves desire, ambiguity, innuendo and several misunderstandings.

In the machine, a great part of the poetic tradition is stored, but neither email spams nor Sherlock were designed to write poetry; therefore to use them in this way is in itself a rebellious act. Moreover, rather than reinforcing a common meaning, *Pink Noise* fractures linguistic integrity and generates general semantic and aural confusion. *Pink Noise* succeeds at failing. It also shows that even when code and linguistic translation come together in machine translation, this cannot be considered as a process of decryption (as Warren Weaver suggested in 1949): asymmetries among languages and cultures are responsible for the cogent reverberations necessarily borne by all translations.[36] In particular, the translation made by the software Sherlock operates by identifying and extract Hsia Yü's fragmented 'originals' in the pool of texts and stores, in a kind of recycle of words, snippets and small pieces of the texts. In this way, Sherlock contributes uniquely to the literary enterprise by creating an emergence, a cue to the confluence of texts and languages that the translation performs. So, again, languages here resonate with historical and cultural specificity.

The voices reverberating in *Pink Noise* are an effect of digital text editing that has changed the writing habits, and made cut-and-paste practices much more prevalent than was previously the case with typewriters. We can therefore read this work as an emphatic critique of appropriation and transformation or of 'neoliberalist market-utopianism', which, as Haomin Gong and Xin Yang have judiciously discussed in their 2017 book, has much to share with the 'cyber-cultural techno-utopianism', with their ideals of 'decentralization, systemic deregulation, structural flattening, atomic individualism, unconstrained communication, automated control system, and so on'.[37] This is the semi-autonomous world that *Pink Noise* would make creative and aesthetic through the subversive act of translation. The tracing of a territory between the conceptual and the sensory, legibility and de-coherence, tradition and iconoclasm, *Pink Noise* attests that willy-nilly we move within a cosmos of recycled words, images, sounds, objects. *Pink Noise* thus enacts the plurality of the subject, dilating and pluralising the text, making it grow and expand as an effect of its combinatory, citational technique, in vast stereophony. In such a context, *Pink Noise* poses a question about who is speaking and whether it really matters. All voices, all their forms, and their value are heard together in the plural noise of a community of bodies, but it is Hsia Yü who uses all the textual plurality as material for a work that is hers: 'We will need those rhyming skills/Some people are born with/Others develop'.[38]

Just as in Nechvatal's 'viral aesthetics', the virus is not to be understood as malicious, but as an aesthetic and benevolent mechanism that uses the host to live. It rapidly transfers genetic information helping their host survive in hostile environments (206). In this way the virus and the noise nurture in us a sense of polysemic uniqueness, which involves territorialisng as well as deterritorialising. In this way, *Pink Noise* goes against imposed configuration, crossing over macro and micro histories, local and global.

Reference to noise is paramount to the conception and understanding of this book. As a piece of noise art, *Pink Noise* is immersive and performative, pushing boundaries, carrying non-referential knowledge, so as to approximate the dynamism of sounds and rhythm. Noise is unwanted and needs to be tuned: 'We will need those rhyming skills'. The concept of noise as music, and of music as language (e.g. 'lyrics'), are not novel propositions.[39] As the creative process used by the avant-garde artists of Italian Futurism, noise is here a physical and phenomenal presentation; it constitutes the composition, regulated 'harmonically and rhythmically'.[40] We find in *Pink Noise* traces of the same antagonist impulse of the futurist noise, although it also goes beyond such an attitude. In the end, Hsia Yü's cross media noise reveals optimism, in suggesting a cognitive-ethical decision transformed by a project of limited intersubjectivity, a letting in of the Other, without any claim of knowing what the Other is like:

> Noise. Noises. Murmurs. When lives are lived and hence mixed together, they distinguish themselves badly from one another. Noise, chaotic, has no rhythm. However, the attentive ear begins to separate out, to distinguish the sources, to bring them back together by perceiving interactions.[41]

Works Cited

APTER, EMILY, 'Philosophical Translation and Untranslatability: Translation as Critical Pedagogy', *MLA Profession* (2010), 53–55

BARRETT, DOUGLAS G., *After Sound. Toward a Critical Music* (New York: Bloomsbury, 2016)

BENJAMIN, WALTER, 'The Author as Producer', in *The Work of Art in the Age of Its Technological Reproducibility and Other Writings on Media* (Cambridge, MA and London: Harvard University Press, 2008), pp. 79–95

BERLANT, LAUREN, *Cruel Optimism* (Durham: Duke University Press, 2011)

BERLINA, ALEXANDRA, ED. and TRANS. *Victor Shklovosky: A Reader* (New York: Bloomsbury, 2017)

BLOOM, HAROLD, *The Anxiety of Influence* (New York: Oxford University Press, 1973)

BRADBURY, STEVE, 'A Creative "Mis-Translation" of Hsia Yü's *Pink Noise*', http://www.drunkenboat.com/db9/mistran_text/bradbury/Pink%20Noise.html

CHAN, SANDEE, 'Leaving on a Jet Plane' (*Cheng penshe ji li qu*) <https://dustysojourner.wordpress.com/2010/04/page/2/>

CHRISTENSEN, BRETT, *Hoax-Slayer*, http://www.hoax-slayer.com/thomos-dah.shtml

COLLIGAN, COLETTE and MARGARET LINLEY, EDS. *Media, Technology, and Literature in the Nineteenth Century. Image, Sound, Touch* (New York: Routledge, 2016)

DWORKIN, CRAIG and KENNETH GOLDSMITH, eds, *Against Expression: An Anthology of Conceptual Writing* (Evanston, IL.: Northwestern University Press, 2011)

EDMOND, JACOB, 'Chinese Rooms: The Work of Poetry in an Age of Global Languages, Machine Translation, and Automatic Estrangement', in *Make It the Same: Poetry in the Age of Global Media* (New York: Columbia University Press, 2019)

FEELEY, JENNIFER, 'Goodbye Stranger: Consummating the Human and the Mechanical in Hsia Yü's Pink Noise', presented at the AAS Conference, Chicago, 2010, Unpublished

GONG, HAOMIN and XIN YANG, *Reconfiguring Class, Gender, Ethnicity and Ethics in Chinese Internet Culture* (New York: Routledge, 2017)

Hayles. Katherine N., *My Mother Was a Computer. Digital Subjects and Literary Texts* (Chicago: The University of Chicago Press, 2005)
Hsia, Yü, *Pink Noise* (Fenhongse zaoyin) (Taipei: Hsia Yü; Taipei: Garden City, 2007)
—— 'Poetry Interrogation — The Primal Scene of a Linguistic Murder', interview by A Weng, trans. by Zona Yi-Ping Tsou, in *Pink Noise* (Taipei: Hsia Yü; Taipei: Garden City, 2007), pages unnumbered
—— *Memoranda* (Beiwanglu) (Taipei: Self-Published, 1984)
—— *Ventriloquy* (Fuyu shu) (Taipei: Xiandaishi jikanshe, 1991)
—— *Friction Ineffable* (Moca wu yi ming Zhuang) (Taipei: Xiandaishi jikanshe, 1995).
—— *Salsa*, Translated by Steve Bradbury (Brookline, MA, Zephyr Press, 2014)
Hsia Yü, et al., *The More Mixed Up with Music the Better* (Yue hun yue dui, 2002) CD (Taipei: Sony Music Taiwan, 2002)
Hsieh, Lili, 'Romance in the Age of Cybernetic Conviviality: Hsia Yü's *Pink Noise* and the Poetics of Postcolonial Translation'. *Postmodern Culture. Journal of Interdisciplinary Thought on Contemporary Cultures*, 19.3 (May 2009), 1–46
Johnston, David Jhave, Aesthetic Animism. Digital Poetry's Ontological Implications (Cambridge, MA: MIT, 2016)
Karatzogianni, Athina and Adi Kuntsman, eds, *Digital Cultures and the Politics of Emotions: Feelings, Affect and Technological Change* (Basingstoke: Palgrave Macmillan, 2012)
Kennedy, Stephen, *Chaos Media: A Sonic Economy of Digital Space* (London: Bloomsbury, 2015)
Lee, Tong King, 'Machine Translation and Hsia Yu's Poetics of Deconstruction', in his *Experimental Chinese Literature: Translation, Technology, Poetics* (Leiden: Brill, 2015), pp. 21–66
Lefebvre, Henri, *Rhythmanalysis. Space, Time and Everyday Life*, trans. by Stuart Elden and Gerald Moore (London: Continuum, 2004)
Lessing, Lawrence, *Remix. Making Art and Commerce Thrive in the Hybrid Economy* (London: Penguin Press, 2008)
Lethem, Jonathan, *The Ecstasy of Influence. Nonfiction, Etc.* (London: Jonathan Cape, 2012)
Maioli, Chiara, *Cloning Aura. Art in the Age of Copycats* (Brescia: Link Editions, 2016)
Manovich, Lev, *The Language of the New Media* (Cambridge, MA: MIT, 2001)
Miluo Kasuo, http://benz.nchu.edu.tw/~garden/milo/heart/heart2.htm
Morris, Daniel, *Not Born Digital: Poetics, Print Literacy, New Media* (London: Bloomsbury, 2016)
Nechvatal. Joseph, *Immersion Into Noise* (Ann Arbor: Open Humanities Press, 2011)
Parry, Amie Elizabeth, *Interventions into Modrnist Cultures. Poetry from beyond the empty screen* (Durham: Duke University Press, 2007)
Rollins, Jonathan B., 'Hsia Yü's Translingual Transculturalism from *Memoranda* to *Pink Noise*', in *Transcultural Identities in Contemporary Literature*, ed. by Irene Gilsenan Nordin, Julie Hansen, Carmen Zamorano Llena (Amsterdam: Rodopi, 2013), pp. 245–66
Russolo, Luigi, *The Art of Noises: A Futurist Manifesto*, trans. by Barclay Brown (New York: Pendragon, 1987)
Shklovsky, Victor, 'Art as Device', in *Victor Shklovosky: A Reader*, ed. and trans. by Alexandra Berlina (New York: Bloomsbury, 2017), pp. 73–96
Tsu, Jing, *Sound and Script in Chinese Diaspora* (Cambridge, MA: Harvard University Press, 2011)
Yao Dajuin, *Cinnabar Red Drizzle* (Dan hong de xi yu) CD-ROM (Post-concrete, 1999)
Yeh, Michelle, 'Towards a Poetics of Noise: From Hu Shi to Hsia Yü', *Chinese Literature: Essays, Articles, Reviews (CLEAR)*, 30 (2008), 167–78

Notes to Chapter 8

1. Spam email reported by a website dedicated to the debunking hoaxes and exposing scams since 2003. Cf. <http://www.hoax-slayer.com/thomos-dah.shtml> accessed 4 June 2017.
2. *Against Expression: An Anthology of Conceptual Writing*, ed. by Craig Dworkin and Kenneth Goldsmith (Evanston, IL.: Northwestern University Press, 2011), p. xxi.
3. For a comprehensive overview on the use of these technological innovations in literature, see *Media, Technology, and Literature in the Nineteenth Century. Image, Sound, Touch*, ed. by Colette Colligan and Margaret Linley (New York: Routledge, 2016).
4. Named after Conan Doyle's literary character Sherlock Holmes, the software was created by Apple Inc. in 1997 and adopts the icon of the detective's hat with a magnifying lens.
5. Sandee Chan, 'Leaving on a Jet Plane' (*Cheng penshe ji li qu*) (1995). <https://dustysojourner.wordpress.com/2010/04/page/2/>.
6. See for example 'Look again' (Lianlian kan, 1979), which presents incommensurable analogies in the form of tests for the primary school. Hsia Yü, 'Look Again', *Memoranda* (1984), 6.
7. For a discussion of e-poetics, see David Jhave Johnston, *Aesthetic Animism. Digital Poetry's Ontological Implications* (Cambridge, MA: MIT, 2016), and Daniel Morris, *Not Born Digital. Poetics, Print Literacy, New Media* (London: Bloomsbury, 2016).
8. Examples of Chinese poems off the page, include Yao Dajuin's post-concrete work, or Miluo Kasuo's animated poems.
9. In *Cloning Aura: Art in the Age of Copycats*, Chiara Maioli appropriately asks: What makes of a writer the author of a literary work? After all, she continues, in ancient oral cultures, transmission of knowledge was possible only through the spoken word, and stories were received, repeated, circulated, appreciated and preserved, without asking who the author was (p. 23). In the logic of the postmodern debate, which led to the 'death of the author' (as Barthes famously named it), the individual is conceived as not being a free and aware creator, but as the result of impersonal structures acting mostly on the individual's unconscious level (see for example the philosophy of Lévi-Strauss and Foucault). According to such a de-authorizing conception, the writer is not anymore the one who generates, but a copyist, a *bricoleur*, a collector of pre-existent writing. The anxiety of influence, as theorised by Harold Bloom in 1973, is then transformed into euphoria, into the ecstasy of influence (J. Lethem, *The Ecstasy of Influence. Nonfiction, Etc.*). The emphasis, in other words, is on the unsustainability of the new. It is after all the admission that poetry, as culture in general, is an infinite palimpsest, and that there is no poet who 'writes in a pneumatic void: every gesture is — consciously or not — intimately connected to what it has been already done', and profoundly influenced by the context (p. 94). Chiara Maioli, *Cloning Aura: Art in the Age of Copycats* (Brescia: Link Editions, 2016).
10. Cf. 'Poetry Interrogation — The Primal Scene of a Linguistic Murder'. Interview with Hsia Yü, by A Weng. Translated by Zona Yi-Ping Tsou, in *Pink Noise*: pages unnumbered.
11. Stephen Kennedy, *Chaos Media: A Sonic Economy of Digital Space* (London: Bloomsbury, 2015); Joseph Nechvatal, *Immersion into Noise* (Ann Arbor: Open Humanities Press, 2011).
12. Nechvatal, *Immersion into Noise*, p. 17.
13. Nechvatal, *Immersion into Noise*, p. 14.
14. While all the sources of the extracted segments are visual, rather than audio, the poem-like lineation and rhythm, the many lines made of extracts from spoken conversations, and the sound of the languages in the mind of the reader makes them aural too. In this light, a plausible audio rendition of *Pink Noise* would consist of a piece in which both English and the target language texts are read by different voices in superimposition with each other.
15. Lawrence Lessing, *Remix: Making Art and Commerce Thrive in the Hybrid Economy* (London: Penguin, 2008), and Lev Manovich, *The Language of the New Media* (Cambridge: MIT, 2001).
16. Kathereine Hayles, *My Mother Was a Computer. Digital Subjects and Literary Texts* (Chicago: The University of Chicago Press, 2005).
17. Kennedy, *Chaos Media*, p. 26.
18. Kennedy, *Chaos Media*, p. 17.
19. Amie Elizabeth Parry, *Interventions into Modrnist Cultures. Poetry from beyond the empty screen* (Durham: Duke University Press, 2007), p. 85.

20. Lauren Berlant, *Cruel Optimism* (Durham: Duke University Press, 2011), p. 232.
21. Kennedy, *Chaos Media*, p. 44.
22. Kennedy, *Chaos Media*, p. 18.
23. Kennedy, *Chaos Media*, p. 44.
24. Berlant, *Cruel Optimism*, pp. 228 and 26.
25. Nechvatal, *Immersion into Noise*, p. 83.
26. Nechvatal, *Immersion into Noise*, p. 15.
27. Victor Shklovsky, 'Art as Devise', in *Victor Shklovosky. A Reader*. Ed. by Alexandra Berlina (New York: Bloomsbury, 2017), pp. 73–96.
28. Emily Apter, 'Philosophical Translation and Untranslatability: Translation as Critical Pedagogy', *MLA Profession* (2010), 53–55.
29. Cf. Poem 10, 'If not quite a harangue, at least a little discourteous'.
30. Cf. Poem 20, 'I am an expert in nothing', back translated by Steve Bradbury in 'A Creative Mis-Translation' of Hsia Yü's *Pink Noise*. http://www.drunkenboat.com/db9/mistran_text/bradbury/Pink%20Noise.html.
31. Cf. Poem 1, 'Brokenhearted and ordinary daily moment'.
32. Lili Hsieh, 'Romance in the Age of Cybernetic Conviviality: Hsia Yü's Pink Noise and the Poetics of Postcolonial Translation', *Postmodern Culture: Journal of Interdisciplinary Thought on Contemporary Cultures*, vol. 9, no. 3, (May 2009), 13.
33. Hsia, 'Poetry', 2.
34. On this topic, cf. Jing Tsu. *Sound and Script in Chinese Diaspora* (Harvard University Press, 2011).
35. Hsia, 'Poetry', 3.
36. Following Kuntsman's adoption of the concept of 'reverberation', I mean to attend to both 'distortions and resonance [...] in process of moving through various digital terrains'. Both 'distortion' and 'resonance' are terms consonant to sound. Cf. Athina Karatzogianni and Adi Kuntsman (eds.) *Digital Cultures and the Politics of Emotions* (Basingstoke: Palgrave Macmillan, 2012), p. 13.
37. Haomin Gong and Xin Yang, *Reconfiguring Class, Gender, Ethnicity and Ethics in Chinese Internet Culture* (New York: Routledge, 2017), pp. 7–8.
38. Poem 1, 'Brokenhearted time and ordinary daily moment'.
39. Douglas Barrett's *After Sound: Toward a Critical Music* constitutes an absorbing reading on the subject (New York: Bloomsbury, 2016).
40. Luigi Russolo, *The Art of Noises: A Futurist Manifesto*, trans. by Barclay Brown (New York: Pendragon, 1919/1987), p. 23.
41. Henri Lefebvre *Rhythmanalysis: Space, Time and Everyday Life*. Translated by Stuart Elden and Gerald Moore (London: Continuum, 2004), p. 27.

CHAPTER 9

Cultural Translation, or, the Political Logic of Prismatic Translation[1]

Jernej Habjan

A decade ago, translation was said to have become 'a more prolific, more visible and more respectable activity than perhaps ever before', even 'a model of time-space, of geopolitical relations, of postnational identities, and ultimately [...] a metaphor of culture itself'. Both these claims, by Harish Trivedi and Hito Steyerl respectively, were followed by a critique of the conception of cultural translation, as Steyerl questioned the 'optimistic predictions about a new globalized cosmopolitism based on cultural translation', while Trivedi even claimed that, quite often, 'cultural translation is not so much the need of the migrant, as Bhabha makes it out to be, but rather more a requirement of the society and culture to which the migrant has travelled; it is a hegemonic Western demand and necessity'.[2] In what follows, I will build on these two critiques of cultural translation in an attempt to make a contribution to the recent proposal of prismatic translation, a notion that from this perspective may arguably be seen as a kind of return to literary translation that acknowledges the intervention of cultural translation.

'Translation can be seen as producing a text in one language that will count as equivalent to a text in another. It can also be seen as a release of multiple signifying possibilities, an opening of the source text to Language in all its plurality.' This is the opening statement of the call for papers for 'Prismatic Translation', the 2016 annual workshop of the AILC/ICLA Research Committee on Literary Theory.[3] 'The first view is underpinned [...] by the need for regulated communication in political and legal contexts', the call goes on; '[t]he second view attaches to contexts where several spoken languages share the same written characters [...], to circumstances where language is not standardized [...], to the fluidity of electronic text, and to literature [...]. The first view sees translation as a channel; the second as a prism.' So, translation as the old channel, versus translation as a prism, a prism that 'has yet to be fully theorized'.

The channel and the prism; or, to use another pair of spatial metaphors, the public space and the third space. The opposition between the channel and the prism can be unpacked by adding this second binary, of the public space and the third space. Indeed, in a prefiguration of Steyerl's above-mentioned critique of cultural translation, her colleague Boris Buden talked about the public space and the third space as the two possible social scenes of translation; writing for what an authoritative account of translation studies calls a 'superb multilingual website',[4] Buden distinguished between therapeutic and cultural translation.[5] In the first case, Jürgen Habermas speaks of returning excluded individuals into the community by translating their pathological private discourses into the discourse of the public space.[6] In the second case, Homi Bhabha, and also Judith Butler (who, as Buden notes, explicitly connects Bhabha's notion of cultural translation with the problem of universality),[7] speak of universalizing the public space itself by making it recognize its own excluded other; this other is excluded constitutively, it defines the public space as its other, and will hence never be fully translatable into it; the public space, no matter how universalized, remains separated from the private space, and this separation itself introduces a third space, the space of the very negotiation between the two: the space of cultural translation.[8]

According to Buden, the difference between these two models of emancipatory translation amounts to the difference between negation and negotiation, or, between dialectics and transgression; in Habermas's therapeutic translation the integration of the private into the public leads to its dialectical negation as the other of the public, while in Butler's or Bhabha's cultural translation it leads to a transgressive renegotiation of the public itself. But building on Buden, we could perhaps even speak of two kinds of dialectics here, a positive one in Habermas and a negative one in Butler and Bhabha, as well as of two kinds of transgression, transgression demanding therapy and transgression limiting therapy; in Habermas, dialectical negation of private transgressions of the public sphere is just a step in the positive process of affirming that sphere, while in Butler or Bhabha it truly is a negative movement, one where no therapeutic translation can fully negate the private as the negation of the public. In this sense, we can only agree with Butler's and Bhabha's critiques of Habermas,[9] as his therapeutic essentialism shares several flaws with channelizing translation as distinguished from prismatic translation. Like channelizing translation, Habermas's universal pragmatics subsumes otherness under equivalence, and only Butler's and Bhabha's proposals of cultural translation grant otherness the status of difference, where equivalence among discourses is a matter of endless negotiation and transgression rather than something that simply precedes the discourses. As such, and in the words of yet another authoritative source on translation studies, 'cultural translation [...] offers a dissolution of some key categories of translation studies: the notion of separate "source" and "target" language-cultures and indeed binary or dualistic models in general'.[10]

However, as we have seen following Buden, both therapeutic and cultural translation ultimately regard translation as a kind of social bond, with one located in the public space and the other in the third space. From this perspective, we could argue that, if Habermas's therapeutic translation makes social action redundant, Butler's and Bhabha's cultural translation makes it atomized, asocial, and as such, again, redundant. As Buden himself notes, by the time Bhabha's cultural universality was picked up by Butler, 'universality has become the problem of cross-cultural translation', which Butler explains 'in a way similar to the Habermasian "excommunication model"'; for Buden, cultural translation, like therapeutic translation, ultimately seeks the post-political 'balance of impossibilities', instead of facing the 'impossibility of balance'.[11]

In my account of cultural translation and its political relevance to prismatic translation, I will focus on Judith Butler's proposal of cultural translation as an endless process in which identities excluded from the legal notion of universality are translated back into it, and in turn retroactively universalize this universality itself. According to Butler, in contemporary multicultural societies it is no longer possible either to universalize a particular culture or to define a universal trait of cultures. Hence, the universalization of recognition depends not on the universalist law and the state but on cultural translation,[12] a process in which excluded identities resignify the speech acts through which they have been excluded. I will argue that this belief in the power of the addressee of exclusionary speech to subvert this speech rests on a misreading of Austin's speech act theory, a misreading mediated by an older misreading of Austin, the one introduced by Derrida. Butler's voluntarist argument that exclusionary speech is sooner or later resignified by its addressee, and that hence state censorship denies both the speech and its resignification, seems alien to Austin and Derrida as her two main sources. A more attentive reading of these sources can therefore help us appreciate the institutional overdetermination of both speech acts and their potential resignifications. This in turn can raise our sensitivity to the kinds of overdetermination that may accompany prismatic translation, I will claim, insofar as this kind of translation can indeed be compared to Butler's cultural translation along the lines drawn above.

But first let me give an example. Martin Luther King provided us with a sublime case of cultural translation when he proclaimed that he was indeed black — and beautiful:

> Somebody told a lie one day. They couched it in language. They made everything Black ugly and evil. Look in your dictionaries and see the synonyms of the word Black. It's always something degrading and low and sinister. Look at the word White, it's always something pure, high and clean. Well I want to get the language right tonight. I want to get the language so right that everyone here will cry out: 'Yes, I'm Black, I'm proud of it. I'm Black and I'm beautiful!'[13]

Indeed, this is what Butler's cultural translation is all about: countering exclusionary speech not with a Habermasian therapeutic neutralization on behalf of some universal target language — racist speech already is part of what is perceived as universality in 1960s America — but with a reappropriation in the language of the addressees themselves, a reenactment capable of showing that universality itself is not universal until it recognizes the excluded and admits that, for instance, black is beautiful. However, Martin Luther King would never have given up in advance any institutional resource in his fight, despite the strength of his own speech.[14] And not everyone's speech matches that of Martin Luther King, so even if King were able to to resignify hate speech with the sheer strength of his speech acts, this would still only constitute a solution for him and for those few who can match the strength of his speech acts. Everybody else would have to seek refuge outside the realm of speech acts and their resignification.

But the point is that even King, while providing paradigmatic examples of what we can today call cultural translation, never stopped fighting for a broader institutional transformation. By the 90s, when Bhabha and Butler championed the idea of cultural translation, this insufficiency of aesthetic reenactment of hate speech was already the butt of a joke. The joke comes from African American stand-up comedian Dave Chappelle as part of a set that more or less launched his by now global comedic career, and it goes as follows:

> I remember I went to a party with a white guy. [...] He was like real Vanilla-Icey and shit. And you know how the brothers are at a party! When we get together we call each other *niggers*, you know; nothing negative, just play: 'Hey, what's up, nigger?' [the sound of a high five]; 'Oh, my nigger! Ha ha, what's up, boy?' And my white friend got all excited and he said: 'Hey, what's up, nigger?' [The sound of a turntable suddenly stopping:] the music stopped, everyone looked at him ... man he got his butt kicked that night! I mean he got fucked up, you know. I hated to do it but, damn! He was talking about my people![15]

Here, Butler's aesthetic reenactment of hate speech is just the premise of the joke, the punchline being its failure, the inability, even self-imposed inability, of reenactment to cross the boundaries of its original producers, the addressees of hate speech, and become available to a person who happens to be of the same colour as the original producers of hate speech. The channel that used to deliver the slur from the utterers to the addressees has been prismatically refracted — the slur has become a term of endearment — and yet the two ends of the channel remain as distant as ever, if not more. Let us see if we can find something in the theory itself that may be the cause of this frustration.

★ ★ ★ ★ ★

In his 1955 Harvard lectures, which posthumously appeared as *How to Do Things with Words*, J. L. Austin rejects the metaphysics of logical positivism.[16] He discovers a class of utterances that do not reproduce the metaphysical gap between subject and object, but rather produce intersubjective relations. This distinction between constatives ('I am running') and performatives ('I apologize')[17] allows Austin to break with logical positivism. But far from simply adding performatives to constatives, Austin discovers that, like performatives, constatives can under certain conditions perform an act in saying something and thus do the act they name. Hence, he degrades the opposition between constatives and performatives into a 'special' theory of the performative within the 'general' theory of speech acts.[18] According to this 'general' theory, each utterance has the locutionary force of uttering a sentence, the illocutionary force of producing intersubjective relations by this utterance, and the perlocutionary force of influencing subsequent utterances. Depending on the illocutionary force, which was designated, in the special theory, by the notion of the performative, Austin classifies speech acts as verdictives, exercitives, commissives, behabitives, and expositives.[19]

In his 1971 talk 'Signature Event Context', Jacques Derrida recognizes in Austin's theory of illocutionary acts a forerunner of his own theory of writing. A written sign is written in order to be able to function outside its original context and even after the death of the addressee and the author. The possibility of such functioning is hence a necessary possibility, in the case of a written sign. As a consequence, the possibility of further citation of a written sign outside that original context is a necessary possibility as well. A written sign is thus repeatable beyond the addressee's and even the author's original intentions, and to this degree a written sign is also alterable; in a word, a written sign is iterable.[20] The possibility of a citation that is unfaithful to the original intentions or the original context in general is hence not external to a written sign but immanent to it; it is a necessary possibility. And if the possibility of iteration is not external to a written sign, neither is a written sign itself merely external to a spoken sign, for that sign, too, is vulnerable to citations outside its original context. Every sign is hence necessarily iterable and as such unable to express any original, idiosyncratic intention, which in turn means that communication cannot be a means of exchange of such intentions.

Not unlike deconstruction, Austin is said to have reduced intention and reference to so many effects of illocutionary formulas themselves. But this similarity between Austin and deconstruction is, according to Derrida, just a backdrop for the fundamental difference, his own *différance* (Derrida's translation, incidentally, of Hegel's use of the Latin verb *differre* to define the present as both a differing and a deferring relation, the two senses only the former of which, as Derrida notes, pertains to the Greek verb, *diapherein*, that *differre* is supposed to be a mere translation of).[21] In the logocentric philosophical tradition, to which Derrida relegates Austin as well,[22] the absence of the receiver is 'merely a distant presence, one which is delayed'; Derrida, on the other hand, maintains that 'this distance, divergence, delay, this deferral [*différance*] must be capable of being carried to a certain absoluteness of absence if the structure of writing [...] is to constitute itself'.[23] This weight of the metaphysical tradition is supposed to force Austin's deconstruction of communication to remain logocentric and unsusceptible to the movement of *différance*. More precisely, Austin is said to regard locution as a mere contingent expression of the illocutionary formula, and not as its necessary and potentially altering embodiment. In order to escape the precariousness of locution, Austin clings to monosemy, according to Derrida, the monosemy guaranteed by the 'serious' intention and the conventional context in general. Hence, finally, Austin's infamous dismissal of jokes, citations, and literature as 'non-serious', 'parasitic', 'etiolated' speech acts. For Derrida, the possibility of this etiolation is a necessary possibility, one that makes any speech act precarious and hence meaningful, non-redundant. In Derrida's Austin, however, etiolations are still a mere possibility external to the 'serious' illocutions; the citation is still not a necessary possibility in the fate of any sign.

In her 1997 book *Excitable Speech*, Judith Butler misreads Derrida's necessary possibility of etiolation as a necessary actuality. According to Derrida, the performative's 'possibility [...] to be "quoted"' is 'the very force and law of its emergence'; Butler's report, however, reads: 'Derrida claims that the failure of the performative is the condition of its possibility, "the very force and law of its emergence."' Here is the relevant passage from Derrida:

> [T]he possibility for every performative utterance (and a priori every other utterance) to be 'quoted' [...] Austin [...] excludes, along with what he calls a 'sea-change,' the 'non-serious,' 'parasitism,' 'etiolation,' 'the non-ordinary' [...], all of which he nevertheless recognizes as the possibility available to every act of utterance. [...]
>
> I would therefore pose the following question: [...] does the quality of risk admitted by Austin *surround* language like a kind of *ditch* or external place of perdition which speech [*la locution*] could never hope to leave, but which it can escape by remaining 'at home,' by and in itself, in the shelter of its essence or *telos*? Or, on the contrary, is this risk rather its internal and positive condition of possibility? Is that outside its inside, the very force and law of its emergence? In this last case, what would be meant by an 'ordinary' language defined by the exclusion of the very law of language?[24]

And this is what Butler makes of the passage:

> [P]erformatives fail either because, for Derrida, they must fail as a condition of their iterability or, for Bourdieu, they are not backed by the appropriate expressions of social power. Derrida claims that the failure of the performative is the condition of its possibility, 'the very force and law of its emergence.' (17)[25]

In this way, 'the very force and law of its emergence' no longer resides in the performative's 'possibility [...] to be "quoted"', but instead in 'the failure of the performative', as if to be quoted is always already to fail, when it comes to speech acts. The performative's possibility to be quoted becomes the failure of the performative; a possibility in Austin becomes a necessary possibility in Derrida — only to become a necessary actuality in Butler. So, for her, every speech act is sooner or later 'aesthetically reenacted',[26] resignified, reappropriated by the addressee. Aesthetic discourse, which was painstakingly expelled, by Austin, from the theory of the performative, is now equally painstakingly pushed to the very core of Butler's theory of performativity. The literary and other etiolations that Austin excluded from his nomothetic theory are used by Butler as the very object of her own idiographic philosophy.[27]

Butler tries to provide a theoretical argument for introducing universality beyond its legal institutionalization. In her analysis, the law necessarily particularizes universality because it censors, in the name of universal rights and liberties, any utterance that prevents its addressee from uttering.[28] Hate speech, as a silencing of its addressee, is particularist and hence censored in the name of universality. If the law were to protect such particularist speech on behalf of universality, it would conduct a 'performative contradiction: an act of speech that in its very acting produces a meaning that undercuts the one it purports to make'.[29] So, if the universalist law is to avoid such a contradiction, it must refrain from ratifying non-universalist utterances. But according to Butler, it is precisely by trying to escape the performative contradiction that the law misses the contradiction that is universality, namely universality as precisely the process of ratifying, universalizing, non-universalist utterances:

> Consider, for example, that situation in which subjects who have been excluded from enfranchisement by existing conventions governing the exclusionary definition of the universal seize the language of enfranchisement and set into motion a 'performative contradiction,' claiming to be covered by that universal, thereby exposing the contradictory character of previous conventional formulations of the universal.[30]

As she posits universality beyond its institutional, legal notion, Butler refers to Hegel's critique of Kant's formalist distinction between subjective categories and the objective world. According to Hegel, the individual participates in universality insofar as he or she subjectivates the objective sphere of customs, *Sittlichkeit*, which consists of the family, civil society, and the state. For as alienated into this sphere, the individual can be recognized within the community of other subjects of *Sittlichkeit*. Participation in universality is guaranteed by participation in *Sittlichkeit*. But since Butler views contemporary societies as multicultural communities, she claims that today universal recognition demands the work of cultural translation:

> In fact, if Hegel's notion of universality is to prove good under conditions of hybrid cultures and vacillating national boundaries, it will have to become a universality forged through the work of cultural translation. And it will not be possible to set the boundaries of the cultures in question, as if one culture's notion of universality could be translated into another's. Cultures are not bounded entities; the mode of their exchange is, in fact, constitutive of their identity.[31]

Multiculturalism is said to require a practice of translating between the particular and the universal, a politics of translation that is able to recognize all particular identities as participating in universality and hence to universalize the institutionalized notion of universality. In short, the politics of cultural translation is a politics of recognition.[32]

This means that Butler equates *Sittlichkeit* with the sphere of culture. This equation, where the family, civil society, and the state are identified with culture, seemingly allows her to derive universality, whose material existence is for Hegel *Sittlichkeit*, from the purely cultural overcoming of the purely cultural differences that in her view characterize contemporary societies. This culturalization of *Sittlichkeit*, however, is difficult to find in Hegel. In Hegel, *Sittlichkeit* universalizes not only abstract law but also morality as the universalization of this law; and within the sphere of *Sittlichkeit* itself, the state universalizes not only the family but also civil society as the universalization of the family. So when Butler returns to the sphere of culture, accusing the state of rigidity, it is not clear how she can rely on *The Phenomenology of Spirit* and *The Philosophy of Right*. Granted, the latter text does envisage such a return from the state to civil society, insofar as it views the universalization that propels the triad of family, civil society, and the state as more than just a linear negation of the first two elements of the triad by the third one. But this return is not without consequences for universality: it proves difficult as soon as *The Philosophy of Right* is read with *The Phenomenology*, in which the state, far from negating civil society, overdetermines it, rendering any return to civil society without any regard for the overdetermining state regressive, just as it would be a regression to view the family as a haven unmarked by civil society; after all, 'if we fail in our attempt to climb the social ladder we cannot simply return back to our family: there is nothing more painful and uncanny than to face your family members once they know that you *had to* return'.[33]

So, in order to grant culture more universality than the state, Butler reinterprets the negation of the family and civil society by the state as a mutual dependence of all three institutions of *Sittlichkeit*. This enables her to talk about the dependence of the state's legal apparatus on the norms of the family and civil society (for example, the dependence of the legal definition of universality on patriarchal homophobic politics), and then deploy this hinging of the state upon culture in her struggle against the hegemony of the existing state. But in her reading of Hegel she seems to neglect the fact that the negation of both the family and civil society by the state does not lead to the mutual dependence of these three institutions, since the two negated institutions — not only the family but also civil society, the institution that she defends against the state — are overdetermined by the negating one, the state. This is why her demand that universality be a process to come, not merely a sphere already institutionalized in the modern nation-state, seems itself overdetermined by the viewpoint of the contemporary state, which is precisely the institutionalized regression of the nation-state to the identity community, that is, the kind of regression of the state to culture that Butler seems to execute conceptually in her reading of *Sittlichkeit*. In this sense, her anti-statism is the anti-statism of the contemporary state itself; her culturalist reduction of *Sittlichkeit* is the reduction that is the contemporary state.[34]

For example, in Butler's reading, hate speech can be resignified by its addressees via aesthetic reenactment and other transgressive acts that need not resort to state institutions. Resembling prismatic translation and its strategies of conveying meaning in a globalized world where source and target languages are no longer neatly differentiated along national lines, such resignifications of hate speech not only can do without the state, but the state even disables them as it censors hate speech, the very object of resignification:

> The border that produces the speakable by excluding certain forms of speech becomes an operation of censorship exercised by the very postulation of the universal. Does every postulation of the universal as an existent, as a given, not codify the exclusions by which that postulation of universality proceeds? In this instance and through this strategy of relying on *established conventions of universality*, do we unwittingly stall the process of universalization within the bounds of established convention, naturalizing its exclusions, and preempting the possibility of its radicalization?[35]

Butler's argument that hate speech can be resignified by its addressees lies on her interpretation of hate speech as the illocutionary act of threat, the act that triggers a temporality that can be brought to a close only by the threatened act itself, which is the perlocutionary effect of the threat. In this interval between the threat and its realization lies the opportunity to subvert hate speech, according to Butler:

> The saying is not itself the doing, but it can lead to the doing of harm that must

> be countered. Maintaining the gap between saying and doing, no matter how difficult, means that there is always a story to tell about how and why speech does the harm that it does.
>
> [...] [T]he ritual chain of hateful speech cannot be effectively countered by means of censorship. Hate speech is repeatable speech, and it will continue to repeat itself as long as it is hateful. [...] The public display of injury is also a repetition, but it is not simply that, for what is displayed is never quite the same as what is meant, and in that lucky incommensurability resides the linguistic occasion for change.[36]

Here, Butler seems to underestimate the fact that the perlocutionary effects of a threat are much less institutionally mediated, and hence much more in the hands of the utterer, than those of, say, a marriage or a verdict. The reason for this is that the same holds true for the felicity conditions of these illocutions, as classified by Austin: the conditions of felicitous execution of such illocutionary acts as a threat are much less institutionally mediated, much more manageable by their utterer, than those of a marriage or a verdict.[37] The only institution necessary is language itself: hate speech can be viewed as the result of the so-called delocutive derivation of a verdictive; it consists of words derived from illocutionary acts of verdict. To use Emile Benveniste's famous example, the verb *to okay* is derived not from *okay* the noun, but from 'Okay!' the locution; so, the verb *to okay* simply means 'to say: "Okay!"'.[38] So too, in the case of hate speech, the word *Idiot!*, far from being a diagnosis, means 'I call you "Idiot!"'. If called an idiot, a person is designated not as someone who fits the description made by the word *idiot* (whatever that description may be), but as someone who is called an idiot (and who as such fits the only pertinent description). From a word that metaphorically designates its addressee as having a certain property (say, idiocy, whatever that may mean) is derived, via continuous use, a homonym that designates its addressee as precisely the addressee of that word. Far from describing its addressee, hate speech makes him or her hateable, addressable by hate speech.

Consequently, Austin's first of the three pairs of felicity conditions is satisfied by definition, in the case of a threat: there is a conventional procedure with a conventional effect (A. 1), and the involved persons and circumstances are appropriate (A. 2), as they are retroactively constituted by the very invocation of the procedure. Due to this invocation, this utterance, the threat is also executed correctly (B. 1) and completely (B. 2), which satisfies the second pair of felicity conditions. The four conventionalist conditions are therefore easily met, in the case of a threat. So, there remain two felicity conditions, the intentionalist conditions, namely the sincerity of the speech act (Γ. 1) and subsequent adherence to it (Γ. 2).[39] These two conditions, however, don't have to be met at all, because even without them the act is not a misfire but rather a mere abuse, where, as Austin writes, 'the act *is* achieved, although to achieve it in such circumstances, as when we are, say, insincere, is an abuse of the procedure', so that, 'when I say "I promise" and have no intention of keeping it, I have promised but ...'.[40] Butler seems to forget here that a threat, as an utterance that embodies the rift between illocution and perlocution, can only be abused, not misfired.

So, the felicity conditions of a threat are met as soon as the threat is uttered. Which means that in the absence of state censorship anyone can make a threat. And anyone with sufficient authority can also execute a threat, thereby satisfying the final of the six felicity conditions (Γ. 2).

Butler is right in saying that hate speech can be stopped only in the gap between what it does as an utterance and what it does as the cause of later events, that is, in the rift between its illocutionary force and its perlocutionary effects. As we have seen, Derrida claims that the possibility of this gap is a necessary possibility, one that makes any speech act precarious and hence meaningful, non-redundant, and Butler effectively misreads this necessary possibility as a necessary actuality. As she herself argues, Derrida merely abstains from analysing the institutional conditions of actualizing this necessary possibility;[41] she, on the other hand, does look for these conditions, but she seems to recognize them precisely in the disintegration of an institution, namely that of censorship. The law, claims Butler, cancels the gap between illocution and perlocution as it defines hate speech (illocution) as conduct (perlocution) and then censors it. By doing so, the law deprives threatened identity groups of the opportunity to resignify a given speech act of threat before the gap between this act and the threatened act is closed. And she believes in this resignification because she thinks that all hate speech is sooner or later resignified in the very process of its uncensored dissemination, since it is iterable, that is, repeatable and as such prone to resignification.

But as Butler would probably agree, what increasingly prevents addressees of hate speech from suspending its perlocutionary effects are not institutions but their neoliberal commodification. Addressees of hate speech are forced to rely on the option of resignifying a threat only after a bigger threat has been realized, namely the threat of dismantling public institutions. Only after institutional sanctions against an illocutionary act of threat are no longer an option does a suspension of the act's perlocutionary effects become a real option, if not the only one (which, as the only option, is of course no option at all). But at that point the institutional measures necessary to control these perlocutionary effects become unavailable (and the only option literally becomes a non-option). As soon as an individual has to suspend the perlocution, it is too late. For without the help of censorship, addressees can resignify hate speech only if each case of hate speech is always already misfired — which, as we have seen, is untenable, as hate speech is abused at best, rather than misfired, and can as such hardly be resignified by its addressee alone. In fact, we can prevent the realization of a threat only if we treat the threat as always already realized, and then silence it. Hence, Butler's politics is one of allowing the dissemination of hate speech in order that it be aesthetically resignified in its iterability. This politics, however, disavows the fact that only institutions can intervene in hate speech, insofar as hate speech, as Butler herself knows, pertains to rigid designations, empty signifiers (*Idiot!* means nothing but 'I call you "Idiot!"', and it means this rigidly, in all possible worlds). As the result of delocutive derivation, hate speech is inherently institutional, inscribed in the national language, which is why it can only be resignified institutionally. A rigid designator cannot be resignified without a transformation of the very institutions that support the belief in the object of such a designator. There is no resignification without the institution, so any attack on the institution in the name of resignification is an attack on resignification itself.[42]

In short, in a situation where the addressee of hate speech is deprived of any legal and social support, we should not say *Only if hate speech is not censored can the addressee resignify it*; on the contrary, we should say *If hate speech is not censored the addressee can only resignify it*, only reenact it in a new context without, however, thereby effecting its misfire.

★ ★ ★ ★ ★

Unlike Derrida, Butler raises the question of the social conditions of subverting a speech act, but she finds the answer in iterability as the law of performativity,[43] that is, in the very category that Derrida insists on to answer, as it were, the question he does not raise. Her answer regarding the material conditions of a performative is performativity, that is, she equates the conditions of a phenomenon with its essence, instead of studying these conditions precisely in order to avoid contemplating the mystery of the essence. As such, her answer to the question of conditions is tautological. But, as she herself says, the illocutionary act itself is a 'tautological' act of symbolization.[44] Her account of the speech act is thus as tautological as the speech act itself. In this sense, her account reproduces its object. As a result, the absence of institution in Butler's analysis of hate speech uncannily fits the absence of institution from the list of felicity conditions of a threat.

So, instead of following Eve Kosofsky Sedgwick or, say, Shoshana Felman in their adherence to Butler, or even J. Hillis Miller and Erika Fischer-Lichte in their revisions of Butler,[45] we should reach beyond her horizon of the atomized addressee. And who better to lead us beyond the atomized individual if not Austin himself, whose original speech act theory places so much importance on performatives' institutional conditions; who better to see that if the two voices of the channel needed institutional support, so too will the many voices of the prism. Delocutive derivation and similar discursive processes have inscribed in the language system itself not only the effects of injurious speech, such as 'Idiot!', but also those of its opposite, for example, 'You are so intelligent!' As Oswald Ducrot has shown, the adjective *intelligent* is derived simply from speakers saying that someone is or is not intelligent in their attempts to make arguments that have no basis in any clearly defined concept called *intelligence*.[46] Ducrot has done the same kind of analysis also for the words *elegant* and *dirty*:

> [I]n the very notion of elegance, as a word of the language-system, there is the idea that elegance is a quality [...]. [I]n the word itself, as an item of the lexicon, there is a sort of justification of elegance, a justification which is like a fragment of discourse written into the word *elegant*: the word *elegance* in itself comprises a justification of elegance. About an example studied yesterday (the example of parents telling their children not to touch a dog because the dog is dirty), I said that the word *dirty* in itself contained a criticism of dirtiness and that one could not understand the word *dirty* without introducing a sort of discourse according to which dirtiness must be kept away from. Similarly, but inversely, elegance is a way of dressing which is good.[47]

This brings us to the terms that continue to separate originals from translations, authors from translators, and source languages from target languages. These terms, too, carry with them arguments about value that still underwrite much of the production and reception of literature. No less than these values and the language-systems that support them will have to be addressed institutionally if the conceptual shift from the channel to the prism is to be followed by a shift in the literary field itself. National languages will need to change their very lexicons of originals and translations, geniuses and traitors, bards and epigons, good and bad quartos, and so on, if translations are to be valued as meaningful refractions rather than mechanical reflections — and, for example, the Republic of Slovenia is to subsidize more than one translation of, for example, *Romeo and Juliet* at a time, and more than just translations of the 'good' quarto of *Romeo and Juliet* (and, why not, more than just Slovenian translations of *Romeo and Juliet*), not to say anything about English translations of Slovenian (or any other marginal) literature.

These and other distinctly modern hierarchies between and among national languages are being challenged within the third space as the realm of cultural translation. Before modernity, something similar to cultural translation was practiced by myth, judging by one of its most classical definitions:

> Myth is the part of language where the formula *traduttore, tradittore* reaches its lowest truth-value. From that point of view it should be put in the whole gamut of linguistic expressions at the end opposite to that of poetry [...]. Poetry is a kind of speech which cannot be translated except at the cost of serious distortions; whereas the mythical value of the myth remains preserved, even through the worst translation. Whatever our ignorance of the language and the culture of the people where it originated, a myth is still felt as a myth by any reader throughout the world. Its substance does not lie in its style, its original music, or its syntax, but in the *story* which it tells. It is language, functioning on an especially high level where meaning succeeds practically at 'taking off' from the linguistic ground on which it keeps on rolling.[48]

Before modernity, it seems, translations were valued despite their style, original music, and syntax. After modernity, they will hopefully be valued precisely for these qualities. That certainly seems to be the idea of prismatic translation.

Works Cited

ARRUZZA, CINZIA, 'Gender as Social Temporality: Butler (and Marx)', *Historical Materialism*, 23. 1 (2015), 28–52

AUSTIN, JOHN L., *How to Do Things with Words* (Oxford: Oxford University Press, 1962)

BENVENISTE, EMILE, 'Delocutive Verbs', in *Problems in General Linguistics*, trans. by Mary Elizabeth Meek (Coral Gables, FL: University of Miami Press, 1971), pp. 239–46

BHABHA, HOMI, *The Location of Culture* (London: Routledge, 1994)

BUDEN, BORIS, 'Strategic Universalism: Dead Concept Walking', trans. by Aileen Derieg, *Transversal*, February 2002, <http://eipcp.net/transversal/0607/buden/en>

——, 'Public Space as Translation Process', *Transversal*, December 2003, <http://eipcp.net/transversal/1203/buden/en>

BUTLER, JUDITH, *Excitable Speech: A Politics of the Performative* (New York: Routledge, 1997)

——, 'Competing Universalities', in Judith Butler, Ernesto Laclau, and Slavoj Žižek, *Contingency, Hegemony, Universality: Contemporary Dialogues on the Left* (London: Verso, 2000), pp. 136–81
——, 'Restaging the Universal: Hegemony and the Limits of Formalism', in Butler, Laclau, and Žižek, *Contingency, Hegemony, Universality*, pp. 11–43
——, *Frames of War: When is Life Grievable?* (London: Verso, 2009)
CAVELL, STANLEY, *Philosophical Passages: Wittgenstein, Emerson, Austin, Derrida* (Oxford: Blackwell, 1995)
DERRIDA, JACQUES, 'Différance', in Derrida, *Margins of Philosophy*, trans. by Alan Bass (Chicago: The University of Chicago Press, 1982), pp. 1–27
——, 'Signature Event Context', in *Limited Inc*, trans. by Samuel Weber and Jeffrey Mehlman (Evanston: Northwestern University Press, 1988), pp. 1–23
DUCROT, OSWALD, *Le dire et le dit* (Paris: Minuit, 1984)
——, *Slovenian Lectures: Introduction into Argumentative Semantics*, trans. by Sebastian McEvoy (Ljubljana: Pedagoški inštitut, 2009), <http://www.pei.si/Sifranti/StaticPage.aspx?id=70>
FELMAN, SHOSHANA, *The Scandal of the Speaking Body: Don Juan with J. L. Austin, or Seduction in Two Languages*, trans. by Catherine Porter (Stanford: Stanford University Press, 2003)
FISCHER-LICHTE, ERIKA, *The Transformative Power of Performance*, trans. by Saskya Iris Jain (London: Routledge, 2008)
FLOYD, KEVIN, *The Reification of Desire: Toward a Queer Marxism* (Minneapolis: University of Minnesota Press, 2009)
HABERMAS, JÜRGEN, *Knowledge and Human Interests*, trans. by Jeremy J. Shapiro (Boston: Beacon Press, 1971)
LACLAU, ERNESTO, 'Constructing Universality', in Butler, Laclau, and Žižek, *Contingency, Hegemony, Universality*, pp. 281–307
LÉVI-STRAUSS, CLAUDE, 'The Structural Study of Myth', *Journal of American Folklore*, 270 (1955), 428–44
LLOYD, MOYA, 'Butler, Antigone and the State', *Contemporary Political Theory*, 4. 4 (2005), 451–68
MARBURY, HERBERT ROBINSON, *Pillars of Cloud and Fire: The Politics of Exodus in African American Biblical Interpretation* (New York: NYU Press, 2015)
MILLER, J. HILLIS, 'Performativity as Performance / Performativity as Speech Act', *South Atlantic Quarterly*, 106. 2 (2007), 219–35
MILOHNIĆ, ALDO, 'Performative Theatre', trans. by Suzana Stančič, in *Along the Margins of Humanities*, ed. by Aldo Milohnić and Rastko Močnik (Ljubljana: ISH, 1996), pp. 237–53
MOATI, RAOUL, *Derrida/Searle: Deconstruction and Ordinary Language*, trans. by Timothy Attanucci and Maureen Chun (New York: Columbia University Press, 2014)
PYM, ANTHONY, *Exploring Translation Theories*, 2nd edn (London: Routledge, 2014)
SEDGWICK, EVE KOSOFSKY, *Touching Feeling: Affect, Pedagogy, Performativity* (Durham, NC: Duke University Press, 2003)
SIMONITI, JURE, 'Nelagodje ob določnosti', in Axel Honneth, *Trpeti zaradi nedoločnosti*, trans. by Jure Simoniti (Ljubljana: Krtina, 2007), pp. 95–114
SMITH, ANNA MARIE, 'Missing Poststructuralism, Missing Foucault: Butler and Fraser on Capitalism and the Regulation of Sexuality', in *Judith Butler's Precarious Politics*, ed. by Terrell Carver and Samuel A. Chambers (Abingdon: Routledge, 2008), pp. 79–91
STEYERL, HITO, 'Beyond Culture: The Politics of Translation', *Translate*, 2006, <http://translate.eipcp.net/concept/steyerl-concept-en>
STURGE, KATE, 'Cultural Translation', in *The Routledge Encyclopedia of Translation Studies*, 2nd edn, ed. by Mona Baker and Gabriela Saldanha (London: Routledge, 2009), pp. 67–70

TRIVEDI, HARISH, 'Translating Culture vs. Cultural Translation', *91st Meridian*, May 2005, <https://iwp.uiowa.edu/91st/vol4-num1/translating-culture-vs-cultural-translation>

——, 'Translating Culture vs. Cultural Translation', in *In Translation — Reflections, Refractions, Transformations*, ed. by Paul St-Pierre and Parfulla C. Kar (Amsterdam: Benjamins, 2007), pp. 277–87

WEEKS, KATHI, 'Subject for a Feminist Standpoint', in *Marxism beyond Marxism*, ed. by Saree Makdisi, Cesare Casarino, and Rebecca E. Karl (New York: Routledge, 1996), pp. 89–118

ŽIŽEK, SLAVOJ, 'Ecology', in *Examined Life: Excursions with Contemporary Thinkers*, ed. by Astra Taylor (New York: The New Press, 2009), pp. 155–84

Notes to Chapter 9

1. This chapter was written at the Research Centre of the Slovenian Academy of Sciences and Arts in the framework of the research project 'The Structure and Genealogy of Indifference' (J6–8263) and the research program 'Studies in Literary History, Literary Theory and Methodology' (P6–0024 (B)), both of which were financed by the Slovenian Research Agency.
2. Harish Trivedi, 'Translating Culture vs. Cultural Translation', *9st Meridian*, May 2005, <https://iwp.uiowa.edu/91st/vol4-num1/translating-culture-vs-cultural-translation> (Trivedi made no alterations to his assessments for the 2007 republication in the collective volume *In Translation — Reflections, Refractions, Transformations*, ed. by Paul St-Pierre and Parfulla C. Kar (Amsterdam: Benjamins, 2007), pp. 277–87); and Hito Steyerl, 'Beyond Culture: The Politics of Translation', *Translate*, 2006, <http://translate.eipcp.net/concept/steyerl-concept-en> [both accessed 9 February 2019].
3. For the call, see the website of the organizer, the AILC/ICLA Research Committee on Literary Theory: <https://iclatheory.org/2016/07/15/the-vienna-workshop-25-27-july> [accessed 9 February 2019].
4. Anthony Pym, *Exploring Translation Theories*, 2nd edn (London: Routledge, 2014), p. 158.
5. Boris Buden, 'Public Space as Translation Process', *Transversal*, December 2003, <http://eipcp.net/transversal/1203/buden/en> [accessed 9 February 2019].
6. Jürgen Habermas, *Knowledge and Human Interests*, trans. by Jeremy J. Shapiro (Boston: Beacon Press, 1971), pp. 214–45.
7. Buden, 'Public Space'.
8. Judith Butler, *Excitable Speech: A Politics of the Performative* (New York: Routledge, 1997), pp. 86–95; Homi Bhabha, *The Location of Culture* (London: Routledge, 1994), pp. 226–29.
9. Butler, *Excitable Speech*, pp. 86–88; Bhabha, *The Location of Culture*, pp. 239–41.
10. Kate Sturge, 'Cultural Translation', in *The Routledge Encyclopedia of Translation Studies*, 2nd edn, ed. by Mona Baker and Gabriela Saldanha (London: Routledge, 2009), pp. 67–70 (p. 69).
11. Buden, 'Public Space'; Buden, 'Strategic Universalism: Dead Concept Walking', trans. by Aileen Derieg, *Transversal*, February 2002, <http://eipcp.net/transversal/0607/buden/en> [accessed 9 February 2019].
12. See Judith Butler, 'Restaging the Universal: Hegemony and the Limits of Formalism', in Judith Butler, Ernesto Laclau, and Slavoj Žižek, *Contingency, Hegemony, Universality: Contemporary Dialogues on the Left* (London: Verso, 2000), pp. 11–43 (pp. 20–21, 24–25, 35); see also Butler, 'Competing Universalities', in Butler, Laclau, and Žižek, *Contingency, Hegemony, Universality*, pp. 136–81 (p. 172).
13. Cited in Herbert Robinson Marbury, *Pillars of Cloud and Fire: The Politics of Exodus in African American Biblical Interpretation* (New York: NYU Press, 2015), p. 228, n. 5.
14. 'For Martin Luther King, racism was not a problem of tolerance. He does not ask the whites to tolerate the blacks. That would be ridiculous. For him racism was a problem of equality, economic justice, legal rights, and so on. Today we perceive racism as a problem of tolerance, which means we perceive it as a problem of cultural differences, cultural intolerance, which is really a mystification. The whole field of economy, public space, and so on disappears.' (Slavoj

Žižek, 'Ecology', in *Examined Life: Excursions with Contemporary Thinkers*, ed. by Astra Taylor (New York: The New Press, 2009), pp. 155–84 (p. 157).)
15. The show, an episode of *Def Comedy Jam*, aired on HBO in 1992 and Chappelle's set is freely available at https://www.youtube.com/watch?v=gBJXIuzRnyI [accessed 9 February 2019].
16. See Stanley Cavell, *Philosophical Passages: Wittgenstein, Emerson, Austin, Derrida* (Oxford: Blackwell, 1995), pp. 71–72, 51–52, 48, 61. Cavell also shows here that Derrida neglects this epistemological break with logical positivism.
17. John L. Austin, *How to Do Things with Words* (Oxford: Oxford University Press, 1962), p. 46.
18. Austin, *How to Do Things with Words*, p. 147.
19. Austin, *How to Do Things with Words*, pp. 150–51.
20. Jacques Derrida, 'Signature Event Context', in *Limited Inc*, trans. by Samuel Weber and Jeffrey Mehlman (Evanston: Northwestern University Press, 1988), pp. 1–23 (p. 7).
21. Jacques Derrida, 'Différance', in his *Margins of Philosophy*, trans. by Alan Bass (Chicago: The University of Chicago Press, 1982), pp. 1–27 (pp. 7–8, 13–14).
22. Derrida, 'Signature Event Context', p. 15.
23. Derrida, 'Signature Event Context', p. 7.
24. Derrida, 'Signature Event Context', pp. 16–17.
25. Butler, *Excitable Speech*, p. 151.
26. Butler, *Excitable Speech*, p. 99.
27. See also James Loxley, 'Performatives and Performativity: Ben Jonson Makes His Excuses', *Renaissance Drama*, New Series, 33 (2004), 63–85 (pp. 81–82), for Butler's 'insistence that the "breaking force" that Derrida identifies with iterability in his initial encounter with Austin is the same as "the force of the performative" in its productive, proper sense'. According to Loxley, '[t]o make this equation is to transform the aporia of the iterable into a structural account of performativity, the determination of an event of force by positive conditions of possibility'. This misreading, Loxley argues, 'allows Butler to speak of a "logic of iterability that governs the possibility of social transformation" and can be "enact[ed]"'. (Loxley's citations are from Derrida, 'Signature Event Context', p. 9, and Butler, *Excitable Speech*, pp. 147, 148.)
28. Butler, *Excitable Speech*, pp. 88–90.
29. Butler, *Excitable Speech*, p. 84.
30. Butler, *Excitable Speech*, p. 89.
31. Butler, 'Restaging the Universal', p. 20.
32. Butler, 'Restaging the Universal', pp. 20–21, 24–25, 35; see also Butler, *Excitable Speech*, pp. 86–95.
33. Jure Simoniti, 'Nelagodje ob določnosti', in Axel Honneth, *Trpeti zaradi nedoločnosti*, trans. by Jure Simoniti (Ljubljana: Krtina, 2007), pp. 95–114 (p. 110). Simoniti comments here on Axel Honneth, a proponent, like Butler, of the Hegel of recognition, who explicitly rejects Hegel's institutional view on *Sittlichkeit*. See also Ernesto Laclau's objection to Butler's appropriation of Hegel's dialectics of *Sittlichkeit*: Ernesto Laclau, 'Constructing Universality', in Butler, Laclau, and Žižek, *Contingency, Hegemony, Universality*, pp. 281–307 (p. 296). And for a critique of Butler's culturalism, see, for example, Anna Marie Smith, 'Missing Poststructuralism, Missing Foucault: Butler and Fraser on Capitalism and the Regulation of Sexuality', in *Judith Butler's Precarious Politics*, ed. by Terrell Carver and Samuel A. Chambers (Abingdon: Routledge, 2008), pp. 79–91.
34. A critique of Butler's anti-statism is developed, for example, in Moya Lloyd, 'Butler, Antigone and the State', *Contemporary Political Theory*, 4 (2005), 451–68 (pp. 460–66).
35. Butler, *Excitable Speech*, p. 90.
36. Butler, *Excitable Speech*, p. 102.
37. See Austin, *How to Do Things with Words*, pp. 14–24.
38. Emile Benveniste, 'Delocutive Verbs', in *Problems in General Linguistics*, trans. by Mary Elizabeth Meek (Coral Gables, FL: University of Miami Press, 1971), pp. 239–46 (p. 242).
39. In my distinction between the conventionalist and the intentionalist felicity conditions, I follow Aldo Milohnić, 'Performative Theatre', trans. by Suzana Stančič, in *Along the Margins of Humanities*, ed. by Aldo Milohnić and Rastko Močnik (Ljubljana: ISH, 1996), pp. 237–53 (p. 245).

40. Austin, *How to Do Things with Words*, p. 16.
41. For Derrida's neglect of the conventionalism developed already in Austin, see Raoul Moati, *Derrida/Searle: Deconstruction and Ordinary Language*, trans. by Timothy Attanucci and Maureen Chun (New York: Columbia University Press, 2014), pp. 42–43, 19, 21, 61.
42. Butler's underestimation of the institutional dimension of gender performativity has been noted, for example, in Kathi Weeks, 'Subject for a Feminist Standpoint', in *Marxism beyond Marxism*, ed. by Saree Makdisi, Cesare Casarino, and Rebecca E. Karl (New York: Routledge, 1996), pp. 89–118; Kevin Floyd, *The Reification of Desire: Toward a Queer Marxism* (Minneapolis: University of Minnesota Press, 2009), pp. 115–19; and Cinzia Arruzza, 'Gender as Social Temporality: Butler (and Marx)', *Historical Materialism*, 23:1 (2015), 28–52 (pp. 35, 41–47).
43. Butler, 'Restaging the Universal', pp. 27–29.
44. Ibid., 'Restaging the Universal', pp. 25–27.
45. See, respectively, Eve Kosofsky Sedgwick, *Touching Feeling: Affect, Pedagogy, Performativity* (Durham, NC: Duke University Press, 2003), pp. 3–9; Shoshana Felman, *The Scandal of the Speaking Body: Don Juan with J. L. Austin, or Seduction in Two Languages*, trans. by Catherine Porter (Stanford: Stanford University Press, 2003), pp. ix–x; J. Hillis Miller, 'Performativity as Performance / Performativity as Speech Act', *South Atlantic Quarterly*, 106:2 (2007), 219–35 (pp. 224–29); and Erika Fischer-Lichte, *The Transformative Power of Performance*, trans. by Saskya Iris Jain (London: Routledge, 2008), pp. 26–36.
46. See Oswald Ducrot, *Le dire et le dit* (Paris: Minuit, 1984), pp. 123–24.
47. Ducrot, *Slovenian Lectures: Introduction into Argumentative Semantics*, trans. by Sebastian McEvoy (Ljubljana: Pedagoški inštitut, 2009), p. 42, <http://www.pei.si/Sifranti/StaticPage.aspx?id=70> [accessed 9 February 2019].
48. Claude Lévi-Strauss, 'The Structural Study of Myth', *Journal of American Folklore*, 270 (1955), 428–44 (pp. 430–31).

PART IV

Practices

CHAPTER 10

The Literary Translator as Dispersive Prism: Refracting and Recomposing Cultures

Jean Anderson

All translation requires a balancing act on the part of the translator who must juggle his or her understanding of the complexities of the source text embedded within its parent culture with the need to produce a text acceptable for a target-culture reading. In this sense the translator as first reader acts like a prism in breaking text down into its constituent, separable colours. This depth of understanding is not unlike Appiah's notion of 'thick translation', a heavily annotated version proposed as a means of communicating the complex richness of texts from unfamiliar cultures.[1] The concept is especially applicable to post-colonial texts, and can be seen as a means of asserting the value and intricacies of the source culture and correcting any imbalance in perceived prestige between source and receiving culture.

Given the well-established (and well-founded) practice of translators working into their first language, the usually endogenous translator requires a high degree of source culture knowledge in order to fully understand the original text. This understanding can be expressed, as Appiah suggests, through annotations. However, as he also indicates, this is an approach best suited to academic purposes.[2] Such translations are prismatic in their revelation of the dispersed component 'colours', revealed in complementary information that might also be made available in less distracting form through hypertextual links. While these techniques make obvious the complex connections between a text and its source culture, they can give rise to a new problem: unless these prismatic extensions are the work of cultural insiders, as Appiah proposes, there are ethical questions to be taken into consideration. Do these annotations become a 'speaking for' on the part of the exogenous translator, and an exertion of that 'epistemic violence' decried by Spivak?[3]

Translating works for a more literary end purpose, as perceived by publishers responding to market expectations, requires recomposition, such that the target text appears 'smooth', whole and unified, a reversal of the refraction performed by culturally-initiated readers.[4] The present study draws on examples from a single short story by a Tahitian writer as illustrative of some of these issues in the translation of post-colonial texts. Applying the concept of prismatic reading to a small number of extracts, I first identify a range of elements which could be explicitated in a thick translation approach. From this in-depth analysis I then reflect on broader issues of post-colonial translation. While dense annotation is useful in expanding understanding of a given text, it will clearly detract from our reading of that text as literature.

The practising literary translator's inevitable struggle between the compulsion, not to say the ethical imperative, to communicate the fullest possible meaning/s of the original text, and the necessity of providing a finished, 'readable' text for the publisher and eventual target readership is particularly acute when dealing with a little-known culture, such as that of Tahiti. Rather than rehash here the now fossilized debate over domestication or foreignisation, source or target 'faithfulness', I want to explore some of the implications of reading the texts, both original and translation, as a prismatic and refractive activity. In order to illustrate this, I refer to a single text, intitled 'La vieille dame' [The Old Lady] by Mā'ohi (Tahitian) writer Rai Chaze. This piece, while very short (just over 2100 words), is exemplary in its frequent use of what we might call 'cultural ellipses': to understand it fully requires a highly-developed awareness of the source culture — a prismatic understanding. These allusions, taken together, constitute a subtext that exists in parallel with the overt meanings of the work: or, in prismatic terms, they constitute component colours that may be perceived as light but can be — and are — broken down by the informed reader. To illustrate this, I will first provide a brief analysis of the story, followed by a more in-depth ('thick') discussion of three short extracts.

Reading the Prism

'La vieille dame' is a short story in a 1990 collection, *Vai la rivière au ciel sans nuages*, by Rai Chaze (born in Tahiti in 1950 to parents of mixed heritage). Much of her work reflects on Polynesian identity — and 'The Old Lady' is no exception. As a close friend of Henri Hiro (1944–1990), a militant poet and anti-colonialist voice on the Tahitian literary scene, Chaze's work shares Hiro's belief in the values of Polynesian (Mā'ohi) culture. While unlike Hiro, Chaze writes in French rather than reo mā'ohi,[5] her militantism emerges in her choice of subjects and her highlighting of Mā'ohi traditional practices. Foremost among these is the ritual of shared food, a sacred duty of any household toward any new arrival.

What happens in the original text? Nothing much: Johanne Frogier refers to this and the other 'stories' in the volume as 'fragments', rather than narratives, in that they capture a moment and not a series of events.[6] That is not to say, however, that they do not carry a form of narrative: rather, their meaning is to be found in the cumulative effect of the allusions contained in their component parts.

It is Sunday. An old lady is visited by a younger cousin, and later by two door-to-door evangelists. At the end of the story, there is a promise of rain. In the absence of a strong plot, the text contains a great deal of description, and it is here that the cultural prism can be found. Objects mentioned in these descriptions are not innocent: instead, each of them bears the weight of an allusion that needs, ideally, to be understood by the reader.

The first extract analysed here is a description of the opening scene of the story. Elements which might be enhanced by commentary or explanation in a thick translation are indicated by an asterisk in the non-elaborated English version that follows:

> La vieille dame se lève, fait quelques pas et s'assoit à nouveau dans son fauteuil face à la porte.
>
> Dans le salon, il y a trois fauteuils. Un à sa droite, séparé d'elle par une petite table: un bouquet de fleurs sur un napperon de dentelle et un tout petit verre. Sous la table, une bouteille de whiskey.
>
> Les autres fauteuils sont en face de la vieille dame, de part et d'autre de la porte.
>
> L'un d'eux, celui au coussin rose, regarde le tableau de la vieille dame lorsqu'elle était jeune et si belle: un dessin coloré, rouge et teinté d'or.
>
> Les yeux du portrait, sombres et allongés, regardent toujours ceux qui sont dans la pièce, tout le monde en même temps, où qu'ils soient.
>
> L'autre fauteuil regarde les chevaux. Des chevaux noirs qui courent sur le papier blanc, bordé de laque rouge.
>
> Près de la porte, il y a le général de Gaulle, uniforme et képi sur velours noir.
>
> Et de l'autre côté, l'horloge.
>
> Ding-dong, ding-dong, six fois! C'est l'heure du café. C'est dimanche. Mais c'est quand même l'heure du café.⁷
>
> [The old lady stands up, walks a few steps and sits down again in her armchair facing the door.
>
> In the sitting room there are three other armchairs. One on her right, separated from her by a small table: a bunch of flowers on a lace cloth★ and a very small glass. Underneath the table, a bottle of whisky.★
>
> Two other armchairs are facing the old lady, on either side of the doorway. One of them, the one with the pink cushion, looks across to the picture of the old lady when she was young and so very beautiful: a coloured drawing, red with touches of gold.★ The eyes in the portrait, dark and almond-shaped,★ are always watching whoever is in the room, everyone at the same time, wherever they may be.
>
> The third armchair looks across to the horses. Black horses running over the white paper, inside a red lacquer border.★
>
> Near the doorway is General de Gaulle,★ uniform and peaked cap★ on black velvet.★
>
> And on the other side, the clock.
>
> Ding-dong, ding-dong, six chimes! Time for coffee. It's Sunday. But it's still time for coffee.★⁸]

What are we to make of this? As cultural outsiders, we are most likely reading in 'black and white', so to speak. If we read prismatically instead, a variety of subtexts can be revealed. Initially, there is an emphasis on European elements of the old lady's life: the small cloth and vase of flowers are indicative of a relatively middle class environment. The bottle of whisky sitting beneath the table, however, hints at a more problematic set of practices, and may signal a negative consequence of the colonisers' bringing of alcohol to the islands. The drawing of the old lady when young is reminiscent of Gauguin's *Tahitian Woman with a Flower in her Hair* (c. 1891), and thus a reminder of European artists' exoticisation of the Indigenous female. While Gauguin is much admired by many, in French Polynesia he is remembered as much as a sexual predator as an artist, particuarly by Indigenous militants.[9] The red colour of the drawing is also a French reference, such pencils being named *conté* after their inventor Nicolas-Jacques Conté (1755–1805). Such mentions may seem trivial, but one of the greatest obstacles to Tahitian self-definition has been the persistently eroticized depiction of men and women, beginning with Bougainville's 1768 visit and his naming of the island as 'Nouvelle-Cythère' after the birthplace of Venus.

The mention of the woman's eyes would seem to indicate a Chinese, or at least an Asian influence, something which is confirmed by the reference to the image of horses in a red lacquer frame that follows, reminiscent of traditional Chinese brush painting. This may be read prismatically in at least two ways: it may be that the old lady has mixed blood — something the text confirms later with the mention of a quite different heritage through a red-headed, English-speaking grandfather; or it may be a reference to some of the debate about the origins of Polynesian peoples (Thor Heyerdahl's South American theory versus the Lapita-Taiwanese hypothesis); or more specifically, it may serve as a reminder of Chinese heritage through nineteenth- and twentieth-century population movements.[10]

The representation of General de Gaulle, painted in military uniform on black velvet rather than canvas, has multiple implications. De Gaulle is here not merely a reminder of French colonialism: it was under his authority that nuclear weapons were tested in the French Pacific from July 1966. The initial tests were atmospheric, resulting in considerable fallout and with serious consequences for local residents' well-being. Additionally, the establishment of French military bases in French Polynesia had an overwhelming impact on the local economy, in particular disrupting traditional cultural practices. For Tahitian source text readers, de Gaulle is associated not just with colonial power, but more precisely with social upheaval, and a strongly negative impact on health.

There is a further allusion at work as well: the association of sultry maidens with black velvet paintings here sits in parallel with the Gauguin reference as a reminder of the exoticisation of Indigenous femininity.[11] One of the leading velvet artists, Edgar Leeteg (1904–1953), spent the last 20 years of his life in Tahiti, producing over 7000 works and earning himself the nickname of 'American Gauguin'.[12]

Whether Leeteg actually produced a velvet portrait of de Gaulle is a moot point: the presence of this object in the old lady's home remains a powerful evocation of colonial and sexual hegemony and of romanticized representations of the Indigenous Other, here ironically reversed.

It is Sunday: a majority of Polynesian people are Christians who attend church services every week. The old lady appears to prefer to drink whisky or coffee — in this she is accepting some of the by-products of colonisation, while rejecting others. The significance of these choices, when framed by a culturally informed reading of the text to this point, is heightened. At issue here is the difference between a reading which appreciates the various nuances and layers of meaning and association that lie within the text, and a non-prismatic reading that sees few or none of the above.

'Tell me what you eat and I will tell you what you are...' (Brillat-Savarin)

As translators know all too well, food is an area of difficulty, not merely because ingredients and culinary practices vary from culture to culture, but also because certain foods, especially those first encountered in childhood, carry an affective weight, a nostalgia, that may not be replicated for the reader from another culture, or from the same culture but a different time. A second extract continues to play to the insider's understanding of the situation:

> Le chien dort et n'aboie pas lorsque la cousine Tafifi arrive. L'énorme cousine Tafifi qui se déplace comme le Tuha'apae, en se balançant de droite à gauche.
> 'Mamie, voilà le pain!'
> 'Haere mai, le café est prêt!'
> La vieille dame reste assise lorsque la cousine Tafifi l'embrasse.
> Tafifi se penche: elle sent bon la savonnette. Et sous la dentelle, entre ses seins, la colombe brille.
> Puis elle va à la cuisine, ouvre le meuble, prend une nappe blanche amidonnée et, en la dépliant, elle marche vers la table et la pose.
> Dans le pli de la nappe il y a un trou, un tout petit trou, la cousine Tafifi revient avec le pot de lait chaud et le pose sur le trou. Elle pose l'eau, le pain, le beurre, le pua'a rôti, le fromage de tête, le ma'oa taioro, le pâté rose, les pattes de cochon et les firifiri.
> 'Mamie, haere mai tama'a!' (p. 13)

> [The dog is sleeping and doesn't bark when cousin Tafifi* arrives. Enormous cousin Tafifi who moves like Tuha'apae,* lurching from side to side.
> 'Mamie, here's the bread!'*
> 'Haere mai,* the coffee's ready.'
> The old lady doesn't get up when cousin Tafifi kisses her on the cheek.
> Tafifi leans forward: she smells sweetly of soap. And beneath the lace, between her breasts, the dove* sparkles.
> Next she goes to the kitchen, opens the dresser, takes out a starched tablecloth, unfolding it as she moves toward the table, where she spreads it. In one of the folds there's a hole, a tiny hole. Cousin Tafifi fetches the pot of hot milk* and places it over the hole. She lays out the water, the bread, the butter,* the roast pua'a,* the head cheese,* the ma'oa taioro,* the pink pastries,* the pigs' trotters* and the firifiri.*
> 'Mamie, haere mai tama'a!'*]

Here the focus is principally on food, as the old lady's cousin Tafifi arrives to bring her bread and set out her meal for her. There is a joke here in passing for the initiated: Tafifi is a delicate climbing plant: Tuha'apae (I, II, III...) is the name of a series of large ships that have ferried goods around the islands of French Polynesia for many years.

The Tahitian greeting, 'haere mai' means 'welcome here'. Tahitian words are not italicized in the translation, in order to reflect Chaze's strong stand on not 'foreignising' them in the original, as she explains in a note preceding the collection in the original 1990 edition. Clearly the source readership can be expected to have more familiarity with these terms than the translation audience; however for ethical reasons relating to the power imbalance between languages implied by the use of italics this practice has not been adopted.

The dove that glints between Tafifi's breasts is recognisable to the informed as a sign of her beliefs: the French Protestant pendant consists of a cross of Saint John with, below it, an upside-down dove with its wings spread. This is indirectly a reminder of Tahiti's religious colonisation. Both Catholic and Protestant missionaries arrived: the London Missionary Society in 1797; the Picpus fathers (Sacred Hearts of Jesus and Mary) in 1841, closely followed by the Mormons in 1844. By 1820 or so, some 50% of Tahitians were converted to Protestantism, meaning that later arrivals had to provide a contrasting version of the Christian faith, a divisive situation that continues today.[13] This is represented further in the story when two young men — the text does not specify their affiliation — arrive on the old lady's doorstep to talk to her about God's love.

The huge spread of foods listed in Chaze's story is not merely a sign of well-being, hospitality and extended family links common in Polynesian cultures (here the care lavished on the old lady by Tafifi). It also contrasts imported elements with some traditional culinary practices, and can be read as a reminder that the typical Tahitian diet, although showing strong foreign influences, still maintains some links with tradition.

Among the dishes laid out on the table is bread: most commonly, this is a *baguette*, and thus a reminder of French influence, as is the butter (although this is likely to be imported from New Zealand rather than made locally, the tropical climate being unsuited to dairy production). According to Christophe Serra Mallol[14] the essentially Europeanised combination of 'café-pain-beurre' [coffee-bread-butter] taken as a meal or part of a meal is seen as a typically Mā'ohi alimentary practice, in part due to the (legally fixed) low price of the bread which makes it a staple with the poorer sectors of the population.

Roast pua'a is roast pork: pigs were probably introduced to the islands by early Polynesian settlers some time between 300 and 1000 CE, and were an important status food.[15] The head cheese (also known as brawn), although made from pig's heads, is a traditional European dish, as are the pigs' trotters mentioned later. The ma'oa taioro, on the other hand, are sea snails or other shellfish marinated in a sauce made of fermented shrimp or crab, sea water and grated coconut flesh. Although it is not specifically named here, this sauce is miti hue, a staple of traditional Tahitian cuisine.

Like many unfamiliar foods, the pink pastries are difficult to imagine for a non-initiate: they are often filled with a peanut paste and coloured with tamarind powder. This reference is another nod to both a Chinese heritage (peanut butter buns) and to European contacts: the first tamarind tree was planted by James Cook in 1769. It died, but more were imported by missionary William Henry in 1797.[16] The firifiri are a donut-like pastry in the shape of an 8, containing coconut milk and thought to have been made originally by Chinese bakers. They are usually eaten for breakfast on Sundays.

The meal can thus be seen to represent a diversity of ethnic traditions, reflecting the hybrid nature of French Polynesian cuisine (and culture). The description ends with Tafifi's urging the old lady to eat: here she uses the traditional invitation described by Hiro as key to understanding Mā'ohi society, founded on openness, sharing and hospitality: 'Haere mai tama'a!' [Come and eat!].[17]

The Politics of Identity

With this prismatic understanding in place, the informed reader will be aware that what appears to be a somewhat disjointed description of unrelated elements in the old lady's surroundings is in fact a reflection on cultural heritage, colonialism and identity. This question comes into tighter focus during the conversation between the old lady and two door-to-door evangelists she has welcomed with a repeated invitation to share her food: 'A tomo mai! haere mai tama'a!' The clean-shaven, white-shirted, tie-wearing young men respond:

> 'Iaorana! Merci pour l'invitation. Nous venons vous parler du bonheur. Voulez-vous entendre nos paroles?'
> 'Voulez-vous un verre de whiskey?'
> 'Avez-vous une religion?'
> 'Et vous?'
> 'Etes-vous catholique ou protestante?'
> 'Je suis paumotu.'
> 'Il paraît que les paumotu sont protestants.'
> 'J'ai grandi aux Marquises.'
> 'Il paraît que les marquisiens sont catholiques.'
> 'Des noms! Des noms! Catholique. Protestant. Mormon. Autrefois, on nous appelait les sauvages. Ensuite, on est devenus les indigènes, puis des canaques, ou peut-être que c'est l'inverse. Un jour, je suis devenue tahitienne. Il paraît que je suis maintenant polynésienne.' (p. 14)

> ['Iaorana! Thank you for the invitation. We have come to speak with you about happiness. Will you hear our words?'
> 'Will you take a glass of whisky?'
> 'Are you a believer?'
> 'Are you?'
> 'Are you catholic or protestant?'
> 'I'm Paumotu.'
> 'Apparently the Paumotu people are protestants.'
> 'I grew up in the Marquesas.'
> 'Apparently Marquesans are catholic.'
> 'Names, names! Catholic! Protestant! Mormon! In the old days they called us savages; then we were natives, then kanaks, or maybe it was the other way round. One day, I turned into a Tahitian. And now apparently I'm Polynesian.']

As well as picking up the more obvious reference to the competing missionary influences, the informed reader will be alert to the fabrication of a 'nation' labelled 'French Polynesia' which draws together into one administrative unit over 100 islands dispersed over a surface of 2,500,000 km². As the dialogue above indicates, there are considerable differences in the ways colonisation has impacted on the five separate archipelagoes, not to mention the broader Pacific region of 'Polynesia'. In addition, there are important variations between Indigenous cultural practices and even languages from island group to island group. For example, the northernmost archipelago of the Marquesas is often considered to be a kind of cultural heartland, comparatively less affected by Europeanisation and therefore more 'authentic'.

The Final Touch

The underlying tensions relating to colonisation (what Hiro refers to as 'occidentalisation') and Indigenous identity are also evoked by a final food reference. This dish is not on the old lady's table but is being prepared as she sits and ponders life. The keeping of dogs as pets is not part of traditional Polynesian society, and is considered by some to be a strictly European practice. As a result of this cultural divide, there is occasional intense discussion about the many stray dogs roaming the streets of Tahitian townships. In the past, dogs were a precious source of protein, given the absence of large herbivores.[18] Attitudes toward dog-meat have been used by other writers to suggest ethnic differences: for example, in Chantal Spitz's novel *Elles: Terre d'enfance*, an Indigenous father's fondness for dog is rejected by a *métisse* mother who gives precedence to her European connections.[19]

The final extract from Chaze's short story recounts the killing and preparation of this local delicacy, as perceived by the main character:

> La vieille dame entend les chiens haleter. Les crocs sortent des babines, les langues pendent, lourdes et sèches.
> Elle entend aussi, un peu plus loin, les spectateurs muets groupés autour du sac. Les yeux fixes, les lèvres entrouvertes ou serrées, ils regardent le bâton s'abattre sur le sac.
> Sur une branche de l'arbre, une corde. Au bout de la corde, le sac. Au bout du bâton, la main qui frappe.
> Dans le sac, les cris du chien se font de plus en plus sourds.
> Par terre, sur un feu, une énorme marmite d'eau. Plus tard, les odeurs de la peau ébouillantée qui se détache dans l'eau brûlante, se mêlent aux pensées de la vieille dame. (pp. 16–17)

> [The old lady can hear the dogs panting. Their teeth are bared, their tongues hang out, heavy and dry.
> She can also hear, a bit further off, the silent spectators gathered around the sack. Staring eyes, lips half-open or pinched tight, they watch the stick whip down onto the sack.
> On a branch of the tree, there's a rope. At the end of the rope, the sack. At the end of the stick, the hand that strikes.
> Inside the sack, the dog's cries become more and more muffled.
> On the ground, over a fire, an enormous pot of water. Later, the smell

of scalded skin peeling off in the boiling water mingles with the old lady's thoughts.]

While it could be argued that the obvious indirectness of the narrative here ('a rope'... 'the sack'... 'the hand'...) and the apparent disconnect between the dog in the sack and the pot of boiling water express a kind of avoidance, this can also be read as acceptance, a reduction to mere facts that voids any sense of emotional response to the dog's suffering.

There are other aspects of the text that could be further broken down into their prismatic elements: for example, the repeated mentions of the tree growing in the old lady's garden. While the changing shadows around it can be seen as markers of the passage of time, if the reader is also aware that the Tahitian equivalent of the notion of 'roots' as indicative of belonging and identity is the concept of 'tumu', the solid trunk of a plant or tree,[20] then multiple references to this tree become symbols of authenticity and an identity closely tied to the land.

Translating the Prism

To fully understand this short story requires a good deal more than a knowledge of French or Mā'ohi language. There is nothing new, of course, in confirming the importance of a deep understanding of the culture that is being translated. In the case of post-colonial texts in general, translator decisions are additionally complicated by the existence within the original, refracted text of elements that speak differently not just to cultural outsiders reading a translation, but also to Indigenous and settler readers of the original: the consumption of dog meat is an obvious example of this. It is possible to read the original without recognising the prismatic range of associations linked to so many elements mentioned in the text: in fact Tahitian Bruno Saura (a sociologist rather than a literary critic) seems to bypass the underlying network of references when he claims that Chaze's collection is 'plutôt intimiste qu'identitaire' [psychological and personal rather than concerned with identity politics].[21] Frogier, on the other hand, sees beyond the surface: '"La vieille dame" relate l'espace d'un après-midi, le vide de l'Occident, les divisions ethniques et religieuses que la colonisation a engendrées' ['The Old Lady' tells of an afternoon's Westernized emptiness, of the ethnic and religious divisions brought by colonisation].[22]

Saura's judgment demonstrates a crucial point, that even source culture readers may not recognize the full prismatic range of a text. For this reason I argue that it is entirely possible to translate Chaze's short story, and doubtless other texts, without drawing out the spectrum of local meanings. In the translations featured above, the prism of allusions may well not be evident to non-initiate readers. And yet there may be nothing (or very little) 'lost in translation', that is, in the passage from one language to another. As Saura's comment demonstrates, what is lost is lost in the reading, of both the source and the target text, not in the text itself.[23] The translation is potentially just as prismatic as the original, as long as the network of references is intact and therefore available to be recognized in the reading process.

Not every literary text is as charged with allusions as Chaze's short story, and there are many cultures better known to outsiders — including those who share the same language — than the one that features here. This example is, in some senses, an extreme illustration of the hypothesis that an informed reading is a prismatic one, capable of breaking the text into its multiple components. The translator's dilemma, in this instance, is whether to recompose the whole into a readable but potentially shallow text, or attempt to maintain the full prism by incorporating some kind of paratextual 'colours'. This is essentially what Appiah suggests. His call for the study of African oral literature in a 'thick and situated understanding' is directly linked to a 'challenge to the assumption of Western cultural superiority'.[24]

Appiah's proposal clearly implies the explanation of African oral texts by an insider, capable of providing the 'situated understanding' — or prismatic reading — that results from knowledge of context and allusions. Relatively few translators, however, are in the position of being endogenous cultural informants: the usual principles of translation best practice require working toward one's first language, something which usually implies outsider origins.

In this case, providing the prismatic reading through paratextual explanation is not only a format best suited to academic translations, one that more clearly resembles a scholarly edition than a literary object, it is also a mediating intervention of the kind which can be seen as a 'speaking-for'. The existence and nature of the power relationship between receiving culture and source culture has of course attracted some attention:[25] nevertheless, the problematic transfer of cultural allusions, the prism of meanings (ideally) available to the initiate and inoperative for the non-initiate, remain relatively unacknowledged, particularly within a post-colonial framework. Ritva Leppihalme proposes that the translator needs to be both 'competent reader' and 'responsible text producer', in order to recognize the allusions in the first place before finding a way to communicate their meaning.[26] This equates to what I would call a prismatic reading of the text, followed by a mediation of meaning to make the allusions accessible to a target audience whose already acquired competence is insufficient.

As we have seen from the preceding brief analysis, Appiah's approach through 'thick translation' is essentially and explicitly a pedagogical one. It operates on the basis of a cultural initiate wishing to bring his understanding of an African, oral culture to a readership of privileged American university students, as a strategy for leading them to question their assumptions about cultural superiority. In this sense, it becomes a means for the so-called subaltern not merely to speak but to be heard.

But how is the (normally exogenous) translator of Indigenous, (post)-colonial literatures to avoid 'speaking-for' and thereby to some degree perpetuating the perceived inequalities between source and target culture? In this respect, another of Hiro's fundamental beliefs comes to mind. For him, much of the problem of colonisation originates in the coloniser's attitude: 'Si tu étais venu chez moi j'aurais pu t'accueillir mais tu es venu chez toi... comment veux-tu que je t'accueille?'[27] [If you had come to my home I could have welcomed you but you came here to your home... how can I welcome you?]. For a translator following Hiroan principles, the question then becomes one of facilitating cultural access, but without taking control.

Like Spitz and many other Indigenous Tahitian writers, Chaze is, as already indicated, a disciple of Hiro. In 1990, the day after his death, *Les Nouvelles de Tahiti* published an interview she had conducted with this militant.[28] It is hardly surprising, then, that a reading of Chaze's text is so enriched by a knowledge of Hiro's beliefs and principles. I argue that in order to reflect and respect this important influence, the translator needs to be especially careful not to speak on behalf of a little-known culture if the kind of appropriation implied by Hiro's 'tu es venu chez toi' is to be avoided. Given the existence of websites such as Fare Vāna'a (the Tahitian Academy), readers can make their own efforts to 'venir chez l'autre', to come to the home of the other.[29]

We might also think here of another proponent of respect for non-European cultures. Édouard Glissant's stance on the contact between cultures, such as can occur via the translational act, can be summed up in terms of the difference between nomadic contact and invasive contact. The former occurs naturally, along traditional trade and exchange routes, while the latter is based on the desire to conquer and to seize. Playing on the meanings of the French verb 'saisir', meaning 'to grasp' in both the mental and physical senses, Glissant proposes a contact and communication model that accepts a degree of opacity between cultures and rejects the dominance of one over another:

> In this version of understanding the verb to grasp contains the movement of hands that grab their surroundings and bring them back to themselves. A gesture of enclosure if not appropriation. Let our understanding prefer the gesture of giving-on-and-with that opens finally on totality.[30]

Totality of understanding cannot be achieved through grasping or grabbing meanings: rather it must arise from mutual respect between source and receiver — even if some degree of opacity ensues.

When is a Prism not a Prism?

Much of the work on cultural allusions stresses the importance of the receiver's competence in identifying them. This is certainly true of Leppihalme's work, which adopts Carol Archer's notion of 'culture bumps'.[31] This term refers to elements from another culture encountered in daily life and which give rise to feelings of disconnectedness and a sense of not knowing. Needless to say, this scenario presupposes the existence of a norm against which variance may be judged: in other words, a hierarchy. In the translation process, cultural allusions are often seen as impediments to understanding, problems requiring solutions and explanations so that meaning may be 'grasped'. Here I argue instead that they are part and parcel of the prismatic reading and that if the translator and target readers are to appreciate cultural difference in a non-invasive way, a degree of opacity is to be expected, and even required, in the target text. While this approach might seem stripped back when compared with Appiah's thickness, it has the advantage of not 'speaking for' or appropriating the source culture, something which an outsider translator needs to consider with care when dealing with Indigenous-authored texts. This is particularly important where there is a potential imbalance in the perceived value of source and target cultures. Glissant and Hiro both call on outsider consumers to respect difference, even when — especially when — they may not understand it. The performative aspect of cultural allusions, that is, whether they are recognized and processed, is in that sense irrelevant: the prism is there, seen or unseen.

In translating Chaze's story, I have refrained from footnoting or glossing elements even where I consider them unlikely to be understood in their full prismatic colour by a cultural outsider. Any translatorial interventions I have made are related to structural elements in the narrative — the number of armchairs and their placement, for example, as described in the opening section of the story. The remarks offered here, while they might be of assistance to a reader of the translation itself, are the result of judicious use of a range of reference works which would also be available to any reader intrigued by a sense of disconnectedness, or of not knowing. If reading involves the construction of the meaning of text, then the translator must of course take the necessary steps to a fully prismatic understanding: but if we are to let the literary text speak for itself *as literature*, readers of the translation — the plural is an essential concept here — can and should be left to perform their own more or less prismatic readings.

Works Cited

ANDERSON, JEAN, 'Translating Chantal Spitz: Challenges of the Transgeneric Text', *Australian Journal of French Studies*, vol. L. 2 (May — August 2013), 177–89

APPIAH, KWAME ANTHONY, 'Thick Translation', *Callaloo*, 16. 4 (1993), 808–19. <http://www.jstor.org/stable/2932211> [accessed 18 June 2017]

ARCHER, CAROL M., *Living with Strangers in the U.S.A.: Communicating Beyond Culture* (Englewood Cliffs, NJ: Prentice Hall, 1991)

CHABOUTS, L. and F., *Short Flora of Tahiti* (Paris: Société des Océanistes, [1971])

CHAZE, RAI, *Vai la rivière au ciel sans nuages* (Pape'ete: Cobalt/ Tupuna/ Les Éditions de l'Après-midi, 1990)

DEVATINE, FLORA AURIMA, *Tergiversations et rêveries de l'écriture orale: Te Pahu a Hono'ura* (Pape'ete: Au vent des îles, 1998)

FROGIER, JOHANNE, 'Le Portrait d'une muse de Tahiti: Michou Chaze. Retour vers la culture par l'écriture' (2000) <http://ile-en-ile.org/michou-chaze-portrait/> [accessed 10 November 2017]

GLISSANT, ÉDOUARD, *Poetics of Relation*, trans. by Betsy Wing (Ann Arbor, MI: The University of Michigan Press, 1997)

GUÉ, JULIEN, 'L'Empreinte du poète guerrier polynésien' (2012) <http://tahiti-ses-iles-et-autres-bouts-du-mo.blogspot.co.nz/2012/04/henri-hiro.html> [accessed 5 December 2017]

LEFEVERE, ANDRÉ, *Translation, Rewriting, and the Manipulation of Literary Fame* (London: Routledge, 1992)

LEPPIHALME, RITVA, *Culture Bumps: an Empirical Approach to the Translation of Allusions* (Bristol: Multilingual Matters, 1997)

LESTRADE, CLAUDE, 'Quelques souvenirs de Tahiti de 1942 à 1945: 2e partie.' *Journal des Océanistes*, 95 (1992), 251–74 <http://www.persee.fr/doc/jso_0300-953x_1992_num_95_2_2624> [accessed 29 December 2017]

RAI A MAI [RAI CHAZE], 'The Source: An Interview with Henri Hiro', trans. by Jean Toyama, *Mānoa*, 17. 2 (Winter 2005), 70–81

ROSE, CYNTHIA, 'Voluptuous Visions in Velvet — Seattle Museum Strives to Bring Respectability to the Art', *Seattle Times* (1998) <http://community.seattletimes.nwsource.com/archive/?date=19981214&slug=2788880> [accessed 29 December 2017]

SAURA, BRUNO, *Tahiti Mā'ohi. Culture, identité, religion et nationalisme en Polynésie française* (Pape'ete: Au vent des îles, 2008)

SERRA MALLOL, CHRISTOPHE, *Nourritures, abondance et identité. Une socio-anthropologie de l'alimentation à Tahiti* (Pape'ete: Au vent des îles, 2010)

SPITZ, CHANTAL, 'À toi Autre qui ne nous vois pas', *Littérama'ohi, ramées de littérature polynésienne*, 2 (2002), 120–29 <http://www.lehman.cuny.edu/ile.en.ile/litteramaohi/02/francophonie.htm> [accessed 10 December 2017]

——, 'Où en sommes-nous cent ans après la question posée par Paul Gauguin?' and 'Sur Gauguin', *Pensées insolentes et inutiles* (Pape'ete: Éditions te ite, 2006), pp. 129–42; 145–47

——, *Elles: Terre d'enfance. Roman à deux encres* (Pape'ete: Au vent des îles, 2011)

SPIVAK, GAYATRI CHAKRAVORTY, 'Can the Subaltern Speak?', Bill Ashcroft, Gareth Griffiths, Helen Tiffin, eds, *The Post-colonial Studies Reader* (London: Routledge, 1995), pp. 24–28

TYMOCZKO, MARIA and EDWIN GENTZLER, eds, *Translation and Power* (Amherst, MA: University of Massachusetts Press, 2002)

Notes to Chapter 10

1. Kwame Anthony Appiah, 'Thick Translation', *Callaloo*, 16. 4 (1993), 808–19.
2. Appiah, 'Thick Translation', p. 818.
3. Gayatri Chakravorty Spivak, 'Can the Subaltern Speak?' in Bill Ashcroft, Gareth Griffiths and Helen Tiffin, eds, *The Post-colonial Studies Reader* (London: Routledge, 1995), pp. 24–28 (p. 28).
4. I use this term here to refer to the recomposition of the text after its component colours have been identified. This is of course in some ways similar to Lefevere's (1992) concept of refraction, referring to the inevitable and/or deliberate alteration which occurs when a text is translated. For the present study, however, 'refraction' refers instead to the breaking down effected during a prismatic reading.
5. For poet and militant nationalist Flora Devatine, who stresses the need to promote Polynesian languages or reo mā'ohi, writing in French is a present inevitability, given that each of the archipelagoes that make up the colonial construct known as 'French Polynesia' has its own language. French thus becomes the language of inter-archipelagic communication, as well as the basis for a Pacific francophone literary community. See Devatine's *Tergiversations et rêveries de l'écriture orale: Te Pahu a Hono'ura* (Pape'ete: Au vent des îles, 1998).
6. Johanne Frogier, 'Le Portrait d'une muse de Tahiti: Michou Chaze. Retour vers la culture par l'écriture', http://ile-en-ile.org/michou-chaze-portrait/. (Chaze no longer uses the name Michou). Interestingly, Frogier points out that Chaze's aim in writing some of these texts is to remind the reader of the rainbow colours ('couleurs de l'arc-en-ciel') of traditional Mā'ohi life as compared with the emptiness of the colonized experience.
7. Rai Chaze, *Vai ou la rivière au ciel sans nuages,* [n.l.]: API, 2013 [1990], p. 11. All further references to this work will be inserted directly into the text.
8. All translations from Chaze's story are my own. Sharp-eyed readers will note the occasional translatorial intervention for the purposes of clarity.
9. See for example Chantal Spitz, 'Où en sommes-nous cent ans après la question posée par Paul Gauguin?' and 'Sur Gauguin' in Chantal Spitz, *Pensées insolites et inutiles* (Pape'ete: Éditions te ite, 2006), pp. 129–42 and 145–47.

10. Bruno Saura points out that Chinese indentured labourers first arrived in the 1860s and that many of them fathered children with Indigenous women (*Tahiti mā'ohi. Culture, identité, religion et nationalisme en Polynésie française* [Pape'ete: Au vent des îles, 2005], p. 290). We should note here that Hiro held strongly inclusive beliefs regarding the presence of Chinese people in French Polynesia: along with the other races present, they could and should contribute to building a Polynesian culture (Rai a Mai, 'The Source: an Interview with Henri Hiro', trans. Jean Toyama. *Manoa* 17. 2 [2005], 70–81, p. 73).
11. Black velvet paintings, largely seen as a kitsch art form, often featured exotic 'dusky maidens', the subject of Samoan-New Zealand director Sima Urale's 1997 film, *Velvet Dreams*. See https://www.nzonscreen.com/title/velvet-dreams-1997.
12. Claude Lestrade, 'Quelques souvenirs de Tahiti de 1942 à 1945: 2e partie', *Journal des Océanistes*, 95 (1992), 251–74.
13. Saura, *Tahiti mā'ohi*, pp. 48–57.
14. Christophe Serra Mallol, *Nourritures, abondance et identité. Une socio-anthropologie de l'alimentation à Tahiti* (Pape'ete: Au vent des îles, 2010), pp. 370–72.
15. Mallol, *Nourritures*, pp. 149–54.
16. L. and F. Chabouts, *Short Flora of Tahiti* (Paris: Société des Océanistes, [1971]), p. 25.
17. Saura, *Tahiti mā'ohi*, pp. 174–78.
18. Mallol, *Nourritures*, pp. 51–52.
19. Chantal Spitz, *Elles: Terre d'enfance. Récit à deux encres* (Pape'ete: Au vent des îles, 2011), p. 180.
20. Saura, *Tahiti mā'ohi*, pp. 173–74.
21. Saura, *Tahiti mā'ohi*, p. 368.
22. Frogier, 'Le Portrait'.
23. In this respect, see also Jean Anderson, 'Translating Chantal Spitz: Challenges of the Transgeneric Text', *Australian Journal of French Studies*, L, 2 (May-August), 177–89.
24. Appiah, 'Thick Translation', p. 819, p. 818.
25. For example, Maria Tymoczko and Edwin Gentzler's edited collection *Translation and Power* (Amherst, MA: University of Massachusetts Press, 2002).
26. Ritva Leppihalme, *Culture Bumps: an Empirical Approach to the Translation of Allusions* (Bristol: Multilingual Matters, 1997), pp. 18–21.
27. Quoted by Chantal Spitz in her essay 'À toi Autre qui ne nous vois pas' [To you, the Other who does not see us], *Littérature ma'ohi. Ramées de littérature polynésienne*, 2 (2002), 120–29, http://www.lehman.cuny.edu/ile.en.ile/litteramaohi/02/francophonie.html.
28. As Rai a Mai, an alternative name she has used: she is now known solely as Rai Chaze. The interview first appeared (in French) in *Nouvelles de Tahiti* on March 12 1990; it was republished in an English translation by Jean Toyama as 'The Source: an Interview with Henri Hiro', *Mānoa*, 17. 2 (2005), 70–81.
29. The Fare Vāna'a Tahitian-French dictionary, (http://www.farevanaa.pf/ dictionnaire.php) in combination with an online translator for English speakers, while approximate, is a useful aid, as is Freelang's Tahitian-English dictionary (http://www.freelang.net/online/tahitian.php?lg=gb).
30. Édouard Glissant, 'For Opacity', in *Poetics of Relation*, trans. Betsy Wing (Ann Arbor, MI: The University of Michigan Press, 1997), pp. 189–94 (pp. 191–92). As Wing explains (p. xiv), the concept of 'giving-on-and-with', in French 'donner avec', implies standing side-by-side and looking out together as equals.
31. Carol M. Archer, *Living with Strangers in the U.S.A.: Communicating Beyond Culture* (Englewood Cliffs, NJ: Prentice Hall, 1991).

CHAPTER 11

In Words and Colours: Lingo-Visual Translations of the Poetry of Shafii Kadkani

Pari Azarm Motamedi

Translation of poetry is a complicated and challenging artistic endeavour in which one artist hopes to express his perception and cognizance of the work of another artist, articulating his experience in a different language, for a new group of readers. The nature of the relationship between the original and the translated poem, the indeterminacy of the original poetic utterance, the difficulty of translating poetry, what to translate and how to translate, has been discussed by literary and translation scholars for centuries up to the present time.

> It is often a concern of readers and translators of poetry that, as the American poet Robert Frost is supposed once to have said, "poetry is what gets lost in translation". We are sometimes aware of the music of poetry falling like fine sand through the hands of the translator. Indeed it would be a rare thing for an Englishman to appreciate even the best translations of Shakespeare, or for a Russian to warm to an English version of Pushkin. And what Persian could bear to read Hafez in any other language? But it is not always so for the reader of translations who is not a native speaker. One could reply to Robert Frost that poetry is what gets *discovered* in translation — else why would we (translators and foreign readers) bother to make and read them? Poetry is strong language, and can travel much better than we, in our roles as native speakers, might fear.[1]

Acknowledging the well-known challenges involved in literary translation, I concur with Alan Williams, that despite the inevitable loss of some features and aspects of a poem in translation, the practice of translating poetry between languages has been, and will continue to be, a worthwhile and rewarding endeavour. Discussing the complexities of translating poetry, Roman Jakobson has argued that poetry by definition is untranslatable. Instead, he suggests the idea of creative transposition: intra-lingual, inter-lingual or, 'intersemiotic transposition — from one system of signs into another, e.g., from verbal art into music, dance, cinema, or painting'.[2] Yet it is not clear what 'transposition' really involves. Reflecting on the vagueness of the meanings of the words 'translation', 'transposition', 'transcription', 'transformation' and other such words used by translators and scholars, as well as the shortcomings and looseness of adjectives that describe them, Matthew Reynolds advocates the approach of considering each translation, being aware of the indeterminacies specific to each translator in relation to a particular source text, the situation, genre, and purpose of translation, in order to better evaluate and appreciate the work.[3]

For more than two decades, I have been involved with the lingual and visual translations of poetry. My practice of parallel creation of lingual translations and visual expressions of poetry can be seen as an example of the unique experience of one translator with the challenges of translating a specific text at a certain time and for a particular purpose and audience. In this paper I share the various choices and decisions that were made in the translation of the work of contemporary Persian poet Mohammad Reza Shafii Kadkani. More specifically I will discuss why I have opted to remain close to the source text in the lingual translation and to be more creative in the visual expression. I have been cognizant of the work of Clive Scott and Michael Burke, amongst others, whose writings have helped me, in hindsight, to reflect on a practice of more than twenty years. References to these works are given later in the present article.

The Poetry of Mohammad Reza Shafii Kadkani

The work of contemporary Persian poet and scholar Shafii Kadkani (b 1938) has been recognized as a powerful poetic expression commenting, amongst other phenomena, on the universal questions of life and existence as well as the historical and socio-political developments in Iran during the past several decades. I have lived through and experienced some of the same historical events, or read about them and am familiar with the cultural context, as well as the images and symbols from nature through which the poet talks about global concerns, freedom, compassion, condemnation of violence and injustice.

Translating Poetry: Reflections in the Mirror

The view of a literary translation as a text that can be regarded the equivalent of the original text has been questioned and mostly rejected by literary and translation scholars. One of the arguments for this dismissal relates to the indeterminacies of literary texts and the role of the reader in the construction of meaning and thus diminution of the value of interpretation by any one reader/translator and the impossibility of the creation of an equivalent text in another language. Shafii Kadkani has cited the words of Ayn al Quzat Hamedani (1098–1131), Iranian mystic and philosopher, who used the metaphor of the mirror, to highlight the role of the reader in the assimilation of meaning in poetry.[4] The following English translation of the words of Ayn al Quzat is by the author of the present article.

> Know these poems as mirrors.
>
> You know that a mirror
> in itself
> has no face

> but everyone who looks
> can see his own face.
>
> Know
> that a poem
> by itself
> has no meaning!
> But everyone sees
> in that mirror
> the totality of what life has given him
> and what he is ultimately able to see.
>
> And if you say:
>> 'In a poem there is a meaning
>> which the speaker intended
>> and others make of it,
>> their own meaning...'
>
> It is like saying that:
>> 'The face of the mirror
>> is the face of the very first person
>> who polished the metal to fashion the mirror.'

Ayn al Quzat is reflecting on how readers perceive different images, borne of their own character, knowledge, history and background in the mirror of the poem. Several centuries after these utterances, Eastern and Western literary theorists are asking the same question. Contemplating the role of the reader and advocating his phenomenological approach to literary translation, Clive Scott emphasizes the importance of the 'readerly' experience of the translator.

> The voice is, rather the voice of the reader: one hears oneself reading; one hears one's own voice, taking possession of the text. This possession may be achieved as much in imagination as in actualization, but, whatever the mix of the embodied and the imaginary, or indeed of the physiological and the cultural, a text is as much about what one puts into it as about what one gets out. Reading is a positive *enrichment* of the text. And the crucial question for the translator is: how should I handle language in such a way that the experience of (reading) the source text (ST) can emerge?[5]

The above question, which I have had to consider with regards to my practice, addresses the significance of aspiring to convey in translation, one's unique experience with the poem and the need to search for the language one can use for such expressions. Scott further elaborates:

> In what sense, as translators, does a ST matter to us? How does it affect us, how are we entailed in its text? This is what translation must find an answer to and express...we each have to find our own way, with a language which must be ready to start from scratch, to ask all the perennial questions, so the new answers might emerge.[6]

Scott encourages the translator to ask questions related to the 'functionality' and purpose of translation, 'what are translations for, what kind of translation do different genres demand', and 'what particular objective does a translator have in mind'[7]. For literary translations he advocates the concept of 'translationwork' rather than 'translation', emphasizing that the -work compound can refer to a text that is plural, hybrid, mobile and elusive, putting forward the perceptions of the translator, the phenomenology of the reading experience.[8] Thus he advocates creativity and taking liberty to express one's unique relationship with the text. With respect to the audience of literary translations, he discusses the futility of attempting to translate the meaning of a literary work for a reader ignorant of the source language. Drawing from the work of Walter Benjamin and others, Scott concludes that 'translating for the monoglot reader makes no sense; translation is a celebration of polyglottism'.[9]

In his earlier work, *Translating Baudelaire*, however, Scott is more open to the idea of faithful translation, alongside more creative work. He explains that readers of Baudelaire are 'already so well served by available 'plain prose' translations and otherwise faithful versions, that the new translator coming to this particular *oeuvre* can afford to create his own kind of translational space(s) and more easily explore experimental fringes', while for a poet such as, 'Yvanhoe Rambosson rather than Baudelaire, no doubt the story would be different'.[10] He thus implies that for the work of a lesser-known poet we need close and faithful translations to introduce the work to readers ignorant of the source language.

In reflecting on my practice I propose, in harmony with Scott, that there is certainly a place for creating new works of literature and art, to convey the phenomenology of reading and one's personal experience with the poem; making the translation as a self-portrait, a version of a *self*. Such an endeavour could use the medium of writing as well as other visual or auditory artistic means of expression. I disagree, however, with the idea that translations are only useful for polyglots who can read the source language, a position that goes against centuries of efforts to translate masterpieces of poetry and literature, offering these works to audiences not conversant in the source language. Once we acknowledge the importance of translating also for monoglot readers, the question one has to ask is whether a translation influenced by the personal, subjective experience of a translator can be considered as an introduction to the work of a poet in another language.

In the masterpieces of poetry, in addition to the specific form and poetic image, a layered world of hidden and indeterminate utterances exists that may be uncovered to different extents by readers and translators. When these layers are gradually revealed, exciting fields of vision and perspective or experience can open up inspiring the translator to create a text that goes beyond the source and conveys his discoveries. But the source text can be lost in this process. If readers are presented with an unravelled text that is influenced by the personal perceptions of the translator, they are robbed of the pleasure of original discovery and cannot become even remotely familiar with the work of the poet. Since the veiled utterances add to the power and beauty of the poem it is best they remain hidden and enfolded in the translation, without personal inputs, perceptions and interpretations from the translator. For someone who does not read French and wants to know and enjoy the work of Baudelaire, a faithful and literal translation, or even the sensitively creative translations by Clive Scott, give a better sense of Baudelaire than the visually interesting but hardly legible overwritten or painted-over artworks or 'translationworks' conveying *his* phenomenology of the reading experience. However, if they are presented alongside each other, the two versions, the more literal and the more creative version expressing the phenomenology of reading the poem, can together give readers a much richer experience.

To further reflect on the question of purpose in translation and what is to be conveyed an example from the domain of visual art may be helpful. Let us imagine that a painter is asked to, or is inspired to paint an apple. Visual artists throughout the ages have painted apples, from the depictions of the forbidden fruit in the Garden of Eden, to the still-lives of Paul Cezanne, the apples of Picasso, botanical drawings and hundreds of lesser-known works. The botanical artist tries to depict the apple as best as possible in an image that closely resembles the apple in front of him, intentionally limiting his emotional or interpretational inputs into the work. It can still be a beautiful work if done with talent and care. For a person who has never seen an apple, a botanical representation is much closer to the real apple than an impressionist or abstract depiction, which can be more exciting and richer in terms of conveying the artist's feelings and experience.

Thus, depending on the purpose anticipated for the translation, one could make appropriate choices. The close, literal translation is comparable to the work of the botanical painter, giving a close rendition of the source text. Alongside the close translation, more innovative and imaginative versions also have a place and in such attempts endless freedom and creativity could be employed towards the making of a 'distinctive medium' of translation as Matthew Reynolds has described.

> Translation stretches words, bridges times, mingles personal identities, and unsettles national languages. As it does so, it creates a distinctive medium in which connections between different places, times and people can be imagined, thought over, and felt through.[11]

In discussing the shortcomings of viewing different translations as occurring between two poles, for example 'faithful' and 'free', or 'formally equivalent' and 'dynamically equivalent', or other well-known poles of translation, Reynolds stresses the importance of seeing different translations not 'as surface variants of what is fundamentally a single process'. Instead he emphasizes that,

> They are the products of distinct imaginative encounters with their source texts. If we are to grasp their particularity, we need to approach them, not as 'examples', that prove or disprove a theory but as texts that ask to be read.[12]

What I would add is that as well as the 'distinct imaginative encounter' of each translator with a specific 'source text' the anticipated function and audience for a translation are other important influencing factors in the final text and how it is read. For example, Ted Hughes, who mainly advocated literal translations, wrote with creativity and freedom from the original text when moved by a poem written by the Hungarian poet, Ferenc Juhaz.[13] Thus the same translator may choose different approaches depending on the source text, how it affects him/her and the audience. As Reynolds has noted the discovery of a powerful metaphor in a poem and its projection onto the translation can energize and shape the translation to become a great 'poem of translation'.[14] However, one can argue that if a translator decides to remain close to a text, 'omitting nothing' and 'inventing nothing' it does not necessarily mean that 'the consequence is a narrowing and flattening of what they can allow themselves to notice in the source'.[15] A translator may discover the metaphors and hidden layers of a poem but still decide to keep them veiled as the poet intended. Perhaps the solution lies in a prismatic approach of multiple translations, both 'close' and 'creative', clearly stating the intention of the translator(s), resulting in a better presentation of a poet's work in another language.

Deliberating on the above discussions, and appreciating the metaphor of the mirror, leads me to the understanding that the source poem is always indeterminate and the translator's perceptions and experience with the poem are always subjective and personal. Also, the adjectives we use to describe a specific way of translating, and what it does, are not exact and have different meanings, nuances and ramifications for each translator. Depending on the source text, purpose and audience for a work, a translator may decide to remain close to the words on the page or may intently decide to express his understanding-beyond-the-words to colour the translation, voicing his/her interpretive or experiential discoveries. The readers need to be made aware of the process and the choices in the creation of the final text. Translations of poetry are works of art and as long as the reader is informed of what he/she is getting, i.e., the nature of the relationship between the source text and the final text and the intentions of the translator, then the translation can be appreciated and enjoyed for what it is.

In Words and Colours: Lingo-Visual Translations

The practice of translation and painting of poetry is, for me, not comprised of two distinct and separate activities but a repeating progression of contemplation, inspiration and unfolding of the lingual and the visual perceptions. Accordingly this presentation is not divided into a neat portrayal and narration of the two processes. Rather it is a sketch of recollections about a journey of discovery in which the written word induces the visual image and the visual image unfolds and enriches my perception of the word.

The motivation to translate the poetry of Shafii Kadkani started with the aspiration to paint the powerful experience that arose from reading the poems. Most of my reading and work on the poems took place while I was living outside Iran. From afar, my perceptions and memories related to the physical and cultural contexts of my old and my new home affected how I read and perceived the poems. Being in the West at a time when everything negative about Iran was being exaggerated and everything positive was being played down, the poems of Shafii Kadkani seemed to connect me, through a wise and beautiful poetic language, with the reality of both the positive and the negative aspects of the land left behind. The solitude and contemplative acts of reading, translating and painting these powerful poems and the contrast with the noise of the outside world changed me, gave me hope and energy to work and paint with more enthusiasm. This change is a subtle, two-way process, taking place between the reader and the text, as delicately described by Clive Scott:

> When at last the reader looks up, the book's effect still radiates from his look, and the changes he has undergone will never leave his face. Will we ever know what our reading has done to us? Our translations of the texts of our reading are portraits of this ever-renewed face.[16]

In the studio, a contemplative process of reading silently and aloud, rewriting the poem in Persian, taking notes for the lingual translation, leaving the poem and coming back to more readings, helped me to enter inside the poem but also inside my own world of images aroused by the poem. Going back and forth between the moment of reading the words on the page, in a location thousands of miles away from the place and the events in the poem, contemplating and imagining what the poet is saying, what was, what could have been and what could be, inspired images that were to become the components of the visual expressions. While recording these images through taking notes and sketches, and being aware of keeping them out of the lingual expressions, the process of lingual translations followed.

In retrospect, I find similarity, between the process mentioned above and the contemplations of Bonnefoy and Barthes, cited by Scott, regarding the effects of the reading environment:

> We might then identify two kinds of 'reading–into -the–environment', the re-infusion of the reading experience with the pressures or urgency of existence, the kind of reading which seems to provoke an appeal from the outside world, that kind of reading that lets the outside world infiltrate the text's texture or renew our return to the world (Bonnefoy), and on the other hand, that day dreaming, digressive reading that generates an inner fertility, which triggers images and associations and memories, and the desire to write, all of which as a consequence of writing (translation) flows back into the text. (Barthes)[17]

With continued work on the English translations, carried out initially for a deeper understanding, I realized that these translations in themselves could be useful for non-Persian speakers. Additionally, the prismatic approach of simultaneous presentation of the original text, with lingual translations and the paintings, could be offered to a wider audience including the Iranian diaspora and the future generations, many not necessarily conversant in their Persian mother tongue.

The choice of poems for translation is a process with several steps. I was drawn to some of the poems as they strongly resonated with my own disposition and sensations, a state of feelings and thoughts also noted by Reginald Gibbons:

> Our experience of being called by a person or a text is recognition of what is other yet akin, despite being other. To obey the call of certain texts, is to permit oneself an emblem of what one is already thinking and feeling unconsciously, and in so doing, to awaken one's own awareness of what one is already thinking and feeling, and in that moment to open up a new articulation.[18]

Many of the poems of Shafii Kadkani gave me the same feeling of recognition and prior awareness that Gibbons talks about. For me, the new articulation he refers to was the expression of thoughts and feelings awakened by the poems into paintings. The choice was further narrowed down to the poems I felt could be expressed in the language of paintings. This was because the conveyance of the total experience of the poem, rather than the apparent meaning was the desired outcome. In some cases I could not discover or connect with a visual clue to convey the deeper experience. The fleeting and elusive spark did not offer me a visual anchor with which to begin the process of painting. In such cases I left the poem for a future reading and a possible future expression. When a visual image, even a vague one, was formed in my imagination I could begin to work.

A further factor defining the choice of poems was the foreseeable difficulty in the lingual translation of some of the poems. This was either due to the absolute importance of the form, which is inevitably destroyed in translation, or to the difficulties of conveying complex inter-textual cultural references. In some cases there are words, phrases and metaphors that would lose so much in translation as to need footnotes. Rather than struggling with such issues, and out of respect for the poet's work and the future readers of the translated poems, I decided to forego the translation of these poems. Such an approach is of course a serious shortcoming if one wishes to provide a complete and full presentation of the works of a poet.

Having chosen the poems I had to look for a simple and effective language and translation process, which would allow me to remain as close as possible to the original in order to best convey it to first-time English readers of these poems. This approach required close and careful reading of the poem with the intention of least possible interpretive or experiential inputs, striving to choose the most contextually appropriate words, the poetic image, an impression of the internal music, keeping the layout of the stanzas, and respecting the syntax and structure of the English language. For reasons of poetic expression and also to overcome limitations on free speech, some poems have hidden layers of meaning expressed through the use of literary devices. Also, in the Persian text, the date of a poem, the lack of a date, quotation marks and bracketing a word, are all devices that help the reader to decode the deeper meanings. In the lingual translations I try to keep all these devices intact and the layers hidden as the poet had decided. Each poem has a unique layout of stanzas which were to be repeated in the translations so the readers would experience the visual layout of the original text on one page of the published work and the identical layout in English, on the facing page giving them a better opportunity for reading the poem, more or less, as the poet intended.

The poems were edited by Alan Williams, and were published together with the paintings in a bilingual edition, *In the Mirror of the Stream*, in Tehran.[19] A second book, *My Blue Canvas*, containing more recent paintings and excerpts of translations was published in Canada.[20]

The Process of Visual Translations

My experience of reading, translating and painting these poems seems to fall in line with the work of Michael Burke who has studied the effects of literary reading on the minds and bodies of readers and has proposed that literary reading, in comparison with other genres of text, has an intense and highly emotive quality.

He talks about the 'Oceanic Mind' and the 'literary reading loop' and notes that for avid readers of literary prose the reading experience does not start or end with the words on the page. Rather, there are pre-reading experiences, emotions and memories that affect the reading experience; and after-effects and reverberations inducing mental imagery and epiphanies that are taken into the life of the reader when the book is closed:

> In many ways, the oceanic mind is a rhetorical mind, a mind 'on the move', caressed softly by the ever-shifting framework of *kairos*: the ancient Greek notion of time, place, manner, content and participants of varied textual and discursive acts. It is a mind that is capricious, dynamic and brimming with original potentials. It floats confidently on the credible narrative of embodied cognition.[21]

I propose that his model can be extended to the reading of poetry, an experience encountered in my own practice. The following examples show how, as I read and translate the poems into English and immerse myself in the environment of the poems, personal feelings and memories associated with the times, places and events expressed in the poem permeate the reading of the text and become one with the poem as if a new version of the poem is being portrayed in my mind, but this time in a visual language.

Gradually and over many years a language has developed. Geometry, sinuous fluid lines, abstracted forms inspired by nature, colours and textures, transparent layers of shapes and colours and simplified motifs from the repertoire of Persian visual art have become the words of a language with numerous possibilities of expression. Geometry has been a powerful yet subtle tool giving the possibility of expressing ideas of boundaries, frameworks, oppressive rules and regulations, while at the same time it can be used to express infinity, progressive inner and outer growth and the boundless realms of the unknown. Yet the most important component of the process remains elusive, 'the capricious, dynamic mind' recognized by Burke, playfully experimenting with 'original potentials', composing images seemingly beyond my consciousness, courage and fortitude. There is a stage when I am aware of a structure and form that wants to be expressed, that needs to be conveyed and that I obey and draw on the white watercolour board. While I work the painting itself seems to take over. In most of the paintings the form of the Persian miniature paintings is adopted, i.e., there is no perspective. The geometric backgrounds depict an impression of the architectural plan of a space over which the abstracted elevations or images of buildings, trees or animals are superimposed. Only the geometric background and the rough outlines of the superimposed abstract elements are composed and drawn in pencil. Everything else, the free flowing lines, the forms, the choice of colours and textures, all happen on the white paper at the moment of painting. The spontaneity of the experience of painting the poem and expressing my emotions and feelings with freedom at each moment of the process is an important part of my motivation to continue with this practice.

Examples of the Lingo-Visual Translations

The examples below present a few of the lingo-visual translations. The Persian originals are not included and can be easily sourced. Five examples have been chosen from the two books already mentioned. With each example the English translation is given first followed by the painting and a description of the main elements of each painting.

1. Message

Behold, O weary spring, from far away
I hear the sound waves of your footsteps
as from beyond the crystal groves of early dawn,
you approach the outskirts of this city of no enthusiasm.

Turn back, O traveller, you who have lost your way!
Tired and thirsty-lipped, turn back from midway!
Here, come not... come not... you too will be oppressed
in the cruel claws of this cold night.

Turn back, O spring! As in the gardens of this city
there is no place for the music of merriment or the sound of a song.
Other than the tight lumps of an enduring sadness,
there is no bud on the dry branches of the trees.

Turn back and alter your path away from this territory.
Take flight from the darkness of this eternal night.
Go towards other meadows, where on your path,
they have spread fields of oscillating silk.

This cold, frozen city in the bed of silence
is not your place, O traveller with battered feet!
It is confinement and fear and in this boundless field,
there is nothing but the reticent shadow of a persistent sadness.

The executioner of the eternal winter
has spread his shadow on the garden of memories.
The blooms of desire, all bereaved and blue-black,
branches of hope are, all, barren and leafless.

Turn back from this region, as on your way back,
when, in silence, you go towards another territory
you will not see any gift but the tears of pain
in the knapsack of clouds you have thrown on your shoulder.

Go to that place where the trembling of each branch, dancing,
speaks of the laughter of the dawn.
Go to that place where the rolling ripples of wind and water
fill the soul with the sweet fragrance of the blooms of desire.

Where a flight of swallows, at dawn,
sing their songs of joy,
where drunken butterflies spread their wings in the morning,
and take to the air, free, sheltered by you.

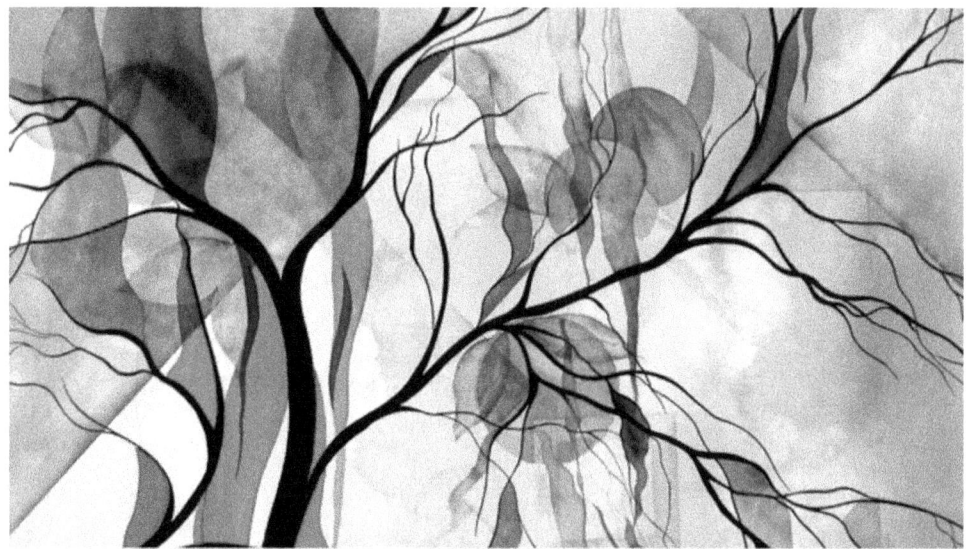

Fig. 11.1. Message, *Paygham*. Watercolour and acrylic, 50 x 65 cm, 2010, Vancouver. Private collection

> Go to that place where from the tip of each green branch,
> you will become drunk with a nocturnal song and melody!
> Turn back, O traveller, from this road, burdened with danger!
> Here, do not come, since with chains you will be tied![22]

The poem is a sombre portrayal of a garden where hopelessness prevails. It is a garden in which spring has no place and the poet is urging the approaching spring to turn back. The lingual translation is literal and close to the original poem. The painting (Fig 11.1) depicts colours, not of spring but of a strange, almost burning place. Despite the bright colours and the blue sky, there is a deep sadness here, perhaps because there seems to be no way out to the garden of song and melodies in another place. Many branches, instead of turning up to the light and the blue sky, seem to be turning downwards, mourning a loss. There is no green and no sign of spring except a few wilting leaves, which are out of place, in this strange landscape.

2. A Good Journey I Wish You

'To where, with such haste?'
    The thorn-bush demanded of the wind.

'My heart is afflicted by this place,
    do you not have a yearning to travel
away from the dust of this desert?'

'My whole being yearns, but
    what can I do with my feet tied...
to where, with such haste?'

'I'm heading for anywhere but this place.'

Fig. 11.2. A Good Journey I Wish You, *Safar Be Kheyre*. Watercolour and acrylic, 69 × 99 cm, 2004, Vancouver. Artist's collection

> 'A good journey I wish you, but for the love of God,
> when you've safely escaped from this brackish wasteland,
> give my greetings,
> to the blossoms, and the rain.'[23]

Here again the translation remains close and literal. The metaphor of the wind in conversation with the thorn-bush is about freedom to fly and the obstacles that hinder and make the flight impossible. There is no date stated for the poem. The image (Fig. 11.2) is of a butterfly, which looks as if it is an integral and indivisible part of the thorn-bush. The body of the butterfly, every line in the wings and every vein is a part and an extension of the thorn-bush and has grown and developed from the spines, bristles and thorns of the bush. While the desire to fly away is strong for the butterfly, breaking away from the thorn bush, which constitutes its whole being results in its annihilation. The poem awakened in me the deep sadness I had felt when we made the decision to leave Iran. I too had felt that my whole being was connected to the land and the culture I was leaving behind. I wanted to depict the dilemma brought about by the desire to move away while I was firmly tied down with deep-rooted sentiments that held me back. In my childhood memories, the most prominent physical feature in a Persian home is the square or rectangular pool of water, lined with turquoise blue tiles, located in the centre of a courtyard garden and brimming with water, with a few red gold fish swimming in it. This motif has found its way into many of my paintings, a landscape feature now lost, not only for me but also for most of the inhabitants of urban and even rural spaces in Iran today. The blue tiles in the background of the painting of the butterfly/thorn-bush allude to this cherished element.

> 3. The Garden of the Crows
>
> They tremble in the cool wet wind of autumn,
> two or three yellow and crimson leaves still on the branch
> that signify: 'Of flag and forethought this is what remains
> that can be seen in this final moment of the day.'
>
> On a naked branch, two or three leaves, and an apple,
> and over there, two or three pomegranates withered on the branch.
> the "x-ray" image of the garden reflected in the lake;
> the spirit of autumn running, brazen, in all directions.
>
> After all the buzzing and humming and the light and song,
> and all the performers of this garden's pavilions
> beneath this cloudless blue, if there is any sound
> it is the lament of the garden weeping and
>   the clamour of the crows.[24]

My emotions in reading this poem were sadness and regret. In witnessing the cold and neglected landscape of the poem, devoid of the joy, song and light that it once possessed, I revisited the feelings of despair and sorrow I had felt in the place left behind. Two dates and locations are mentioned at the bottom of the published Persian text of the poem denoting the dates the poet wanted to convey to the reader as the dates on which he composed the poem, the dates on which

Fig. 11.3. The Garden of the Crows, *Bagh-e Zaghan*. Watercolour and acrylic, 75 × 29 cm, 2006, Vancouver. Artist's collection.

he felt the same sentiments. The first date is 1978 and the location is Princeton, as the poet lived there at the time and accordingly dated the poem in the Gregorian calendar. The second date, mentioned next to the first, is in the Iranian calendar, year 1374, or 1995 in the Gregorian calendar and the location is Tehran, where the poet was living at this time. The two dates point to the fact that the poet had the same feelings about this 'garden' on both of those dates, i.e., before and after the revolution. The reverberations, the after-effects of reading the poem, my feelings of despair, hopelessness and indifference guided the process of painting, the composition, the colours and textures. The image (Fig. 11.3) is a cold and barren garden with the predominant colours of brown, black and grey. The trees are leafless, the inhabitants being only a few loud and unpleasantly crying crows. The almost haphazard plan of the geometric garden forms the background symbolizing the harshness that dominates this place.

> 4. Floral Patterns on a Tile
>
> Throughout the winter, the sparrow
> looked forward with yearning
> to spring and the garden so much
> that in mid winter
> it saw the flowers painted on the mosque tile
> as the dawn of spring.[25]

The poem has no date. But there is a hidden date conveyed in the few stanzas of this short, powerful poem. It is a statement of a fact, an event that occurred at a moment in time. It speaks of a sparrow, waiting for the dawn of spring, and of flowers painted on the mosque tiles. It could be a pleasant, quiet scene. In the lingual translation the layers remain hidden as the poet intended. The poem can be read and perceived in different ways. If one is not familiar with the context of the poem, or chooses not to hear the message, then it is a descriptive poem about the sparrow and the mosque tiles. But in the literary and cultural context of this poem, spring is the symbol of freedom. The sparrow yearning for the arrival of spring and freedom mistook the patterns on the mosque tiles as real spring flowers and flew into them. But this was a wall, a harsh, unyielding and ruthless wall of painted tiles, a wall in a mosque. The harsh reality and outcome of such a mistake in perception was violent annihilation.

Having lived through the events alluded to in the poem, all the feelings of sadness and despair came back to me and filled my mind with unwanted images that melted into and coalesced with the text of the poem on the page. The painting (Fig. 11.4) expresses the calm and quiet peacefulness of a wall of painted tiles, depicting a tree of life, and two small portions of two other identical trees of life symbolising timelessness, and the continuing love of art and beauty that has always been part of the Persian sensibility. I wanted, also, to show the violence awaiting the bird that made the grave mistake, the violence that awaited many birds for many years to come. A very large brush, saturated with the colour of blood, forcefully splashed on the finished painting was to show the violent outcome of the misperceived spring leading to the gravely mistaken flight. The act of mindlessly splashing the red on

Fig. 11.4. Floral Patterns on a Tile, *Golhay-e Naghsh-e Kashi*. Watercolour and acrylic, 77 × 54 cm, 2007, Vancouver. Private Collection

Fig. 11.5. Rhythm of the World (1). Watercolour and acrylic, 50 × 76 cm, 2012, Tehran. Artist's collection.

a painting, a decision that had taken some time to evolve, and which could have completely destroyed the painting, felt similar to the destruction that had taken place in reality.

> 5. The Rhythm of the World
>
> The 'world' was a new and deep meaning,
> its poise and promise boundless.
>
> I told myself that in this short life
> composing and singing it in a new rhythm is my wish.
>
> To a rhythm, I will bring it, full of life and sweetness
> so it remains such into endless time.
>
> ++++++++++++
> Adversaries suddenly stole it away from me
> and composed it in another rhythm.
>
> A rhythm, not pleasant and a song not desired,
> a setting devious, dubious and depressing.
>
> ++++++++++++
> Art tells me: Do not be grieved, oh poet
> as this meaning will not endure.
>
> No status and setting will survive
> if not in a rhythm desired by mankind.

> If you remain, bring it to another rhythm;
> for the 'world', initiate another image.
>
> An image, in which a humankind with new ideals
> is brought forth, free of animosity.
>
> ++++++++++++
> And if you leave and this rhythm remains
> do not be grieved by this misfortune and mistrust.
>
> After you, other poets will come
> and will compose it in the desired rhythm.
>
> A rhythm in harmony with pursuits and passions,
> a rhythm in harmony with aspirations,
> in the style of the tree, the wind and the rain,
> abundant with images of rain and of spring.
>
> The ' world' will not remain in this plight,
> will not remain in a rhythm so distorted and deformed.[26]

The poem has a date, 1992. In the title, and throughout the poem, one word 'jahan', meaning 'world' is put in inverted commas. My reading of the poem tells me that perhaps the poet has, for reasons of opacity, put 'jahan' inside inverted commas to convey another meaning, i.e., a co-rhyming word 'vatan', meaning 'home', 'homeland', or 'country'. The English translation is literal and close to the original.

I decided to divide the poem into four parts as I intended to paint one panel for each part. The first part of the poem portrayed by the first panel talks about a time in the life of a country and a people, when different tendencies, ideologies and inclinations came together towards a seemingly unified goal. My reading of the poem suggests that the poet felt and hoped, as many others did, that he could be part of the unified effort to bring another rhythm to the 'world'. The close reading of the first painted panel in this quadriptych (Fig. 11.5), shows four bands in the background coming together in one point in the left lower quarter of the painting, the moment of 'poise and promise' referred to in the poem. While there is a sense of movement and dynamism the painting does not express the sense of the possible agreeable rhythm. I have portrayed a sense of confusion and darkness into the painting despite the hopeful atmosphere of the first part of the poem. For me the powerful memories, and images of those days took over the reading experience. While I was aware of the sense of hope expressed in the first six stanzas, my experience of the words was coloured by the feelings of despair and confusion which I had felt years before and which had now come back to me and found expression in the first panel of the painting.

In the four following stanzas we hear what happened in reality. The second panel of the painting (Fig. 11.6) shows the 'devious, dubious and depressing rhythm' that has taken over the whole situation. Echoing my memories and feelings in agreement with that of the poet, I created a dark and depressing panel. One ideological stream is now dominant as the vertical thick black bars overpowering a huge butterfly, symbolizing the 'world', or 'home', battered and bleeding, caught partly behind the bars of the prison, partly struggling to tear away.

Fig. 11.6. Rhythm of the World (2). Watercolour and acrylic, 50 × 76 cm, 2012, Tehran. Artist's collection

Fig. 11.7. Rhythm of the World (3). Watercolour and acrylic, 50 × 76 cm, 2012, Tehran. Artist's collection

Fig. 11.8. Rhythm of the World (4). Watercolour and acrylic, 50 × 76 cm, 2012, Tehran. Private collection.

The third panel of the painting (Fig. 11.7) follows the quiet wisdom of the next eight stanzas. It is more hopeful that the undesired rhythm will not endure. In the painting only one of the vertical prison bars is remaining. Colour has come back into the scene and there are signs of the beginnings of a joyful flight and freedom. The poet tells us to be inspired and to become part of the creation of this new possibility. In the painting, the harmonious geometry of a Persian garden is emerging in the background as a new rhythm, the backdrop for the spontaneous and free dance of the butterflies.

In the last ten lines of the poem, we are reminded that the rhythm may remain for a longer period, beyond the lifespan of the poet and the reader. But hope cannot be lost. There will be other poets who will bring the 'world' into a more harmonious order and rhythm in line with the best aspirations symbolized by the abundance of rain, spring, trees and the freedom of the wind. In the last panel of the painting (Fig. 11.8) there is much more harmony, joy and freedom. The geometric rhythm, the trees and the butterflies have come together to create a movement towards a more harmonious state. The colours echo the hopeful and wise tone of the poem.

Conclusion

I have explored, in this paper, the potentials of visual expression as a complement to lingual translations, and as a creative medium for conveying perceptions of poetry. The focus has been on the practice of translation, especially visual translation, while at the same time reflecting on some of the relevant theoretical discussions. As a visual artist affected and inspired by the poetry of Shafii Kadkani I have created paintings conveying my perceptions, experiences, invoked senses, memories and associations. This creative endeavour and relationship with the poem has also enriched my understanding of the poem and has helped me in fine-tuning the lingual translations. I have tried to remain as close and faithful as possible to the source text in the English translations. The visual has become a third language, presented alongside the original text, and the lingual translations, all three together providing a prismatic, multi-layered experience for the readers.

Works Cited

AZARM MOTAMEDI, PARI, *My Blue Canvas* (Vancouver: Anahita Productions, 2016)
——TRANS. and ILL., and ALAN WILLIAMS, ed., *In the Mirror of the Stream, Selected Poems of Shafii Kadkani* (Tehran: Sokhan Publishers, 2008)
BURKE, MICHAEL, *Literary Reading, Cognition and Emotion: An Exploration of the Oceanic Mind* (New York: Routledge, 2011)
GIBBONS, REGINALD, *How Poems Think* (Chicago: University of Chicago Press, 2015)
JAKOBSON, ROMAN, 'On Linguistic Aspects of Translation', in *The Translation Studies Reader*, ed. by Lawrence Venuti (London: Routledge, 2012), pp. 113–18
REYNOLDS, MATTHEW, *The Poetry of Translation: From Chaucer & Petrarch to Homer & Logue* (Oxford: Oxford University Press, 2011)
SCOTT, CLIVE, *Translating Baudelaire* (Exeter: Exeter University Press, 2000)
——*Translating the Perception of Text: Literary Translation and Phenomenology*, (Oxford: Legenda, 2012)
——*Literary Translation and the Rediscovery of Reading* (Cambridge: Cambridge University Press, 2012)
SHAFII KADKANI, MOHAMMAD REZA, *Ayeneh-e baray-e seda ha* (Tehran: Sokhan Publishers, 1997)
——*Hezareh dovom-e ahou-y-e kouhi* (Tehran: Sokhan Publishers, 1997)
WEISSBORT, DANIEL, ed., *Ted Hughes:Selected Translations*, (London: Faber and Faber, 2006)

Notes to Chapter 11

1. Alan Williams, 'Introduction', in *In the Mirror of the Stream, Selected Poems of Shafii Kadkani*, Translations and Paintings by Pari Azarm Motamedi, ed. by Alan Williams (Tehran: Sokhan Publishers, 2008), p. 11.
2. Roman Jakobson, 'On Linguistic Aspects of Translation', in *The Translation Studies Reader*, ed. by Lawrence Venuti (London: Routledge, 2012), p. 131.
3. Matthew Reynolds, *The Poetry of Translation: From Chaucer & Petrarch to Homer & Logue* (Oxford: Oxford University Press, 2011), pp. 23, 36.
4. Mohammad Reza Shafii Kadkani, *Ayeneh-e baray-e seda ha* (Tehran: Sokhan Publishers, 1997), p. 443. My translation.
5. Clive Scott, *Translating the Perception of Text: Literary Translation and Phenomenology* (Oxford: Legenda, 2012), p. 1.
6. Scott, *Translating the Perception of Text*, p. 42.
7. Clive Scott, *Translating Baudelaire* (Exeter: Exeter University Press, 2000), p. 1.
8. Scott, *Translating the Perception of Text*, p. 3.
9. Scott, *Translating the Perception of Text*, p. 9.
10. Scott, *Translating Baudelaire*, p. 251.

11. Reynolds, *The Poetry of Translation*, p. 11.
12. Reynolds, *The Poetry of Translation*, p. 38.
13. Daniel Weissbort (ed.), *Ted Hughes: Selected Translations* (London: Faber and Faber, 2006).
14. Reynolds, *The Poetry of Translation*, p. 55.
15. Reynolds, *The Poetry of Translation*, p. 208.
16. Clive Scott, *Literary Translation and the Rediscovery of Reading* (Cambridge: Cambridge University Press, 2012), p. 59.
17. Scott, *Literary Translation and the Rediscovery of Reading*, p. 60.
18. Reginald Gibbons, *How Poems Think* (Chicago: University of Chicago Press, 2015), p. 44.
19. Williams (ed.), *In the Mirror of the Stream*.
20. Pari Azarm Motamedi, *My Blue Canvas* (Vancouver: Anahita Productions, 2016).
21. Michael Burke, *Literary Reading, Cognition and Emotion: An Exploration of the Oceanic Mind* (New York: Routledge, 2011), p. 119.
22. Shafii Kadkani, *Ayeneh-e baray-e seda ha*, p. 93. My unpublished translation.
23. Shafii Kadkani, *Ayeneh-e baray-e seda ha*, p. 242; English translation in Williams (ed.), *In the Mirror of the Stream*, p. 135.
24. Mohammad Reza Shafii Kadkani, *Hezareh dovom-e ahou-y-e kouhi* (Tehran: Sokhan Publishers, 1997), p. 95; English translation in Williams (ed.), *In the Mirror of the Stream*, p. 261.
25. Shafii Kadkani, *Hezareh dovom-e ahou-y-e kouhi*, p. 131; English translation in Williams (ed.), *In the Mirror of the Stream*, p. 265.
26. Shafii Kadkani, *Hezareh dovom-e ahou-y-e kouhi*, p. 60. My translation.

CHAPTER 12

T is for Translation(s): Translating Nonsense Alphabets into French

Audrey Coussy

When translating a printed text, the translator juggles between multiple solutions before settling on one definitive version. Variants belong to the draft stage, not the finished work; readers only see the final version and usually do not think twice about the translating process or the choices made by the translator — they often do not even think about the translator. Likewise, the history of translation confirms that a translator is expected to be objective and invisible — an image that presents them as passive, inhabiting a 'shadowy existence'[1] instead of craftsmen and creators in their own right.

This common-sense picture of translation, though still widespread among readers and the publishing industry, has been dismantled by a range of critical and theoretical works, with notable contributions from the fields of comparative literature and philosophy. Jacques Derrida,[2] Emily Apter[3] and Barbara Cassin,[4] among others, have explored the limits of translatability and expanded discussions on translation, moving away from linguistic fidelity to the original — Philip E. Lewis famously challenged this fidelity through his concept of abusive translation, which 'values experimentation, tampers with usage, seeks to match the polyvalencies and plurivocities or expressive stresses of the original by producing its own'.[5] Works such as Henri Meschonnic's *Poétique du traduire* (1999) and Antoine Berman's *Pour une critique des traductions: John Donne* (1995) have also cast a light on translators, their translative projects and their creativity, while translation scholars working in post-colonial and gender studies have helped redefine 'the role of the translator (...) from that of a faithful reproducer to an inventive interventionist'.[6]

Studies on the translation of texts written in verse have offered eloquent examples of this dismantlement. Matthew Reynolds's comprehensive *The Poetry of Translation* (2011) shows the long history linking translation and thoughts on translation to this supposedly untranslatable art; Annmarie Drury's *Translation as Transformation in Victorian Poetry* (2015) focuses on the transformative power of poetry translation during the Victorian period and endeavours to demonstrate the lasting influence of the Victorian approach to translation, calling on appropriation[7] while 'admitting alterity to its atlas as no age had done before'.[8] A 'poetics of appropriation',[9] based on the translators' (subjective) interpretation and re-creation of the texts, is at the core of Barbara Folkart's *Second Finding: A Poetics of Translation* (2006), which follows in Meschonnic's and Berman's footsteps and draws from Folkart's experience as a poet, scholar and translator to present case studies underlining the multiple translations that can arise from the very same poem, since 'poetry thrives on ambiguity — or rather, on multiplicity of meaning'.[10]

Nonsense verse, emblematic of the Victorian era, especially thrives on multiplicity of meaning, and embodies a paradox also found in translation: how working within confines can generate creative possibilities. To quote Elisabeth Sewell, '[nonsense] is a carefully limited world, [...] a construction subject to its own laws'.[11] Nonsense plays with order and relishes rules and limits, and its very constraints foster creativity.[12] This is perhaps best exemplified in the many alphabets belonging to the genre, as they exaggerate this with their fixed form, their use of rhyming schemes, lively rhythm, vivid and precise imagery, and the frequent inclusion of illustrations.

Nonsense alphabets push translators out of their comfort zone — they present an extreme instance of how all translation involves transformation. While longstanding principles, author's authority and editorial expectations tend to demand respect for the original work, a system of reinvention proves necessary to recreate the fixed exercise of the nonsense alphabet and its often absurd humour. Translators are used to working within constraints; in the case of nonsense alphabets, the constraints are increased and privilege form over verbal meaning. The result is a translation practice which adopts the same formal constraints (and indeed extends them) but changes the semantic content to fit, producing prismatically deviated texts which are formally similar but semantically divergent.

Looking at nonsense alphabets from the nineteenth century onwards and their translation into French, this study will offer an extreme example of what happens in all translation and discuss the tools available to translators, and how ambivalent *and* creative translation can be.[13] The first part of this paper will focus on one of Edward Lear's nonsense alphabets to introduce the translation problem of this genre: finding equivalencies for the words illustrating each letter. Then, the case of Neil Gaiman's *The Dangerous Alphabet* (2008) will show how pictures can help further the translation instead of limiting it. Finally, the example of two published translations of works by Edward Gorey will illustrate the impact of the translator's subjectivity and the potential it holds for the translated text.

Revisiting Fidelity and Creativity: the Case of Edward Lear's *Unnamed Alphabet* (1877)

Printed alphabets are prominently featured in the oldest forms of children's literature, appearing in primers and hornbooks (early primers for children consisting of a sheet of parchment or paper protected by a transparent sheet of horn, commonly used in England and the United-States from the sixteenth to the eighteenth century) as early as the sixteenth century.[14] Their aim was first and foremost to teach children the alphabet and how to read, using objects and living things they could easily identify. They were also used as a tool to teach catechism and moral lessons, as the first primers were usually written by pastors and pious authors,[15] and they followed in the steps of alphabets codified during the Middle Ages, which were based on prominent prayers.[16] A move away from religious themes came about over the course of the nineteenth century with the development of more modern ABC books to suit the democratization of readership. Progress in printing techniques, an increase in adults' and children's literacy — one of the main preoccupations of governments at the time[17] — and the advent of an affluent upper middle-class increased demand, and the publishing market thrived.

The first translations of alphabets from English to French were published during the mid-nineteenth century; France experienced an important wave of English picture books at the end of the 1860s, through the joint effort of English and French publishing houses (such as Hachette working with Frederick Warne & Co and Routledge, and Guérin-Mueller with Dean & Son): 'By collaborating with English publishers, French publishers benefited from their savoir-faire and reduced their own production costs. They were thus able to sell a renewed product, at a very attractive price for the middle classes.'[18] The translation of alphabets was made possible by these new market conditions and presented translators with linguistic and cultural challenges, heightened by the frequent presence of illustrations and the specificities of the different types of ABC books (readers, thematic alphabets, alphabets including poems). Marie-Pierre Litaudon-Bonnardot mentions in her masterful work on ABC books how French translators until the 1960s tended to champion education over entertainment, which demonstrates how set habits and mentalities can stifle creativity: '[French translators] have long refused to incorporate in their works (until the 1960s) the zany universe of English nursery rhymes, favouring the integration of moral instruction over playful unwinding. [The] musicality of English texts, often versified and more attentive to rhythm and sounds than to meaning and logic, unsettles the French Cartesian order which prefers prose, deemed more rational and pragmatic.'[19]

Alphabets caught the attention of nonsense authors, as this literary genre relishes in playing with language and rules within a delimited space.[20] The norms established in nonsense texts underline the existence of norms in our everyday lives, which rule the interaction between the individual and the outside world. Nonsense texts play on our 'deep-seated need for meaning, which [they] deliberately frustrate in order to whet it'.[21] The best, and probably best-known, example is Lewis Carroll's *Alice's Adventures in Wonderland* (1865). At first, Alice tries to make sense of this new world by referring to the set of rules she has learned in her own world. This only leads her to misunderstandings and frustration. Through observation, however, Alice is able to 'conform to the new rules and to use them for her own purposes. She then becomes a formidable opponent and sometimes triumphs over characters who are, after all, merely cards and chess pieces'.[22] Translators working on nonsense alphabets could very well find inspiration in Alice's attitude, as they go through a similar experience; they need to understand the new rules set by these texts, something that can be unsettling as it challenges the traditional fidelity to the letter[23] and instead favours fidelity to alphabet letters.

Edward Lear's *Unnamed Alphabet* (1877) provides an interesting case. Here, Lear personifies the alphabet and tells us the story of A who fell down the stairs, and the other letters' reactions to the incident — Lear thus relies on the letters of the alphabet to build and advance the story. The advice given by the characters in order to cure the poor A ranges from common-place to absurd, and it becomes clear the author is mocking the prescriptive tradition found in children's literature, especially during the Victorian and Edwardian periods.[24] The first couplets seem quite ordinary:

> A tumbled down, and hurt his Arm, against a bit of wood.
> B said, 'My Boy, O! do not cry; it cannot do you good!'
>
> C said, 'A Cup of Coffee hot can't do you any harm.'
> D said, 'A Doctor should be fetched, and he would cure the arm.'[25]

However, some of the advice encountered later can be very random, and feel irrelevant to the situation; this humorously underlines the absurdity of prescription while complying with the limited vocabulary possibilities of letters such as K, V and W:

> K said, 'A Kangaroo is here, — this picture let him see.' [...]
> V said, 'I'll stand upon a chair, and play a Violin!'
>
> W said, 'Some Whisky-Whizzgigs fetch, some marbles and a ball!'[26]

When faced with the challenge of translating this text, the first step is to outline what Antoine Berman calls the translation's playground (*'espace de jeu de la traduction'*[27]): the translator needs to understand how this playground works to better recreate it in French. What are its main constraints? The most obvious one is finding French words illustrating each of the twenty-six letters — this is at the heart of the alphabet exercise. Lear's versification pushes the translator to pay attention to rhythm and rhymes (Lear follows an /aabb/ scheme, until the last four lines where he switches to /aaaa/) in order to recreate a compelling story; his use of the outdated (even at the time) fourteen-syllable couplet results in a strange and confining structure. One last constraint would be to maintain the absurdity, the apparent randomness of events and advice that pervades the text and creates its humour. The translator is forced to develop a more complex notion of fidelity in translation: sticking strictly to the original meaning is often impossible, especially when it comes to difficult letters like K, Q, or W, and prioritising this would be missing what is at play in alphabets.

Form therefore prevails over any literal translation. I experienced this firsthand when I translated the text for my doctoral dissertation.[28] Lear uses the letter Q to mention food as a possible cure, with 'quince' and 'quail'.[29] Their French translations, '*coing*' and '*caille*', preserve the /k/ sound but not the letter Q, providing an unsatisfactory solution. The French language provides limited solutions to keep the letter Q and the culinary lexicon, and my version resulted in cultural adaptation, with references to French cuisine:

> Q said, 'A **Quince** I recommend, — a Quince, or else a **Quail**.'[30]
> Q quémanda : « Qu'on lui amène une **Quiche** — une Quiche, ou des **Quenelles**. »[31]

Regarding versification, as shown in this first example, I opted for the alliterative pattern (slightly reminiscent in the source text of Old English alliterative verse) over the metrical structure. 'Yeast' is also mentioned in the story, and was changed to '*yaourt*' ('yogurt') because the French literal translation, '*levure*', did not match the letter of the verse; this solution appears to be more eccentric than the original while conjuring the similar image of an improvised homemade plaster cast:

> Y said, 'Some **Yeast** mixed up with salt would make a perfect plaster!'[32]
> Y yoyota : « Qu'on mélange du **Yaourt** et du sel, ça fera un sacré plâtre ! »[33]

Translators of other languages would most likely have to use the same device were they to rely on the same rules for their translation's playground. And as such, they would likely end up with varied (and potentially culturally loaded) solutions, such as '*quesadilla*' in a Mexican translation, or '*qualle*' ('jellyfish') in a German translation.

This is why I want to underline the '*jeu*' in Berman's expression '*espace de jeu*',[34] the 'play' part: translators are experts at following the rules of the game and working within a limited space; in the case of nonsense alphabets, the rules are tighter, therefore the (re)invention must be more resourceful. When I translated this alphabet, there was an opportunity to add another rule to Lear's system that would expand the playground of the translation. In the source text, Lear simply uses the verb 'say' every time a letter speaks; maintaining this approach proves difficult in French, since repetition is to be avoided at any cost. A literal translation would be deemed flat, at best. The usual approach is either to assign a more specific action (like 'yelled' or 'whispered') to the introductory verb or delete the verb altogether. This French norm proved more nurturing than stifling. Instead of repeating the verb '*dire*', the introductory verbs chosen began with or echoed the letter featured in the verse, thus enhancing language play within the text[35]:

> C **said**, 'A **C**up of **C**offee hot can't do you any harm.'
> D **said**, 'A **D**octor should be fetched, and he would cure the arm.'[36]
>
> C **clama** : « Une tasse de **C**afé bien **C**haud te remettra sur pieds. »
> D **déclara** : « Allez chercher un **D**octeur, il faut le soigner. »[37]

The most difficult letters demanded more unusual solutions that would play not only on the written form but on sounds as well:

K said, 'A Kangaroo is here, — this picture let him see.'[38]
W said, 'Some Whisky-Whizzgigs fetch, some marbles and a ball!'
X said, 'Some double **XX** ale would be the best of all!'[39]

K claironna : « Voilà un Kangourou — montrez-lui ce cliché. »
W v-vanta : « Allez chercher du Whisky, il n'y a pas meilleure solution ! »
X s'eXclama : « Plutôt de la bière eXtra-forte, des billes et un ballon ! »[40]

'*Claironna*' ('trumpeted, shouted from the roof tops') echoes the /k/ sound; the letter K being pronounced /ka/ in French, '*claironner*' was chosen over verbs beginning with the /ka/ sound in order to avoid an unfortunate /kaka/ utterance — humorous as it is, it did not fit the type of humour used by Lear here. The solutions found for X, '*s'eXclama*' and '*eXtra-forte*', emphasize the sound echo with a visual echo. The translations of K and X inspired the W one, which was particularly troublesome — very few words, and even fewer verbs that start with these exist in French. Inventing a stutter for W, '*v-vanta*' ('praised'), enabled me to graphically recreate the letter W with two Vs, while using a verb that fitted the story.

Translating Edward Lear's *Unnamed Alphabet* showed that the rules and limits imposed by the genre invite translators to be especially resourceful. Translation always involves negotiation[41] (with rules, norms, people, etc.), and nonsense alphabets offer a playful model translators can adopt.[42] Just as Lear followed textual rules to generate deviations from the norms of the English language, I followed a French linguistic and cultural rule (to consistently avoid repetitions) which, in turn, generated deviations from the norm of Lear's text. As we will see in the second part of this paper, prismatic deviations can also occur due to another main feature of the genre — the presence of illustrations.

I is for Illustrations: Translating Neil Gaiman's *The Dangerous Alphabet* (2008)

To echo Lewis Carroll's Alice, what is the use of an alphabet without pictures?[43] If illustrated alphabets appeared during the sixteenth century,[44] they truly came into being at the end of the seventeenth century in England (almost a century before they appeared in France) and today they have become the norm rather than the exception in the genre. They developed from the nineteenth century collaboration mentioned earlier between English and French publishers, which led in the 1860s to the wave of translated ABC books from English into French: 'It was the advent of illustrations in French alphabets that started editorial exchanges between France and other countries — most notably England.'[45]

The presence of illustrations in alphabets and picture books in general creates a new dynamic within the book, one that translators have to take into account: 'According to many writers, the essence of the picture book is the way the text and the illustrations relate to each other; this relationship between the two kinds of text — the verbal and the visual texts — is complicated and subtle.'[46] It is indeed a complicated and subtle dynamic that calls for a broadening of translators' approach to their work, extending the complexities that we explored in the first part of this essay.

For translators, illustrations can be limiting, especially if the publisher decides to keep the original ones. Perry Nodelman describes the relationship between text and illustration in terms of limitation: 'Many commentators say that the purpose of pictures in picture books is to 'extend' the texts, but cognitive theories of perception suggest that extension may be the wrong metaphor. It would be more accurate to say that pictures *limit* the text — and to add that the text also limits the pictures.'[47] Translators are no strangers with having to work within limits, however, and — as we have seen — creativity can be nurtured by limitation. Illustrations thus can also offer a way out of linguistic dead-ends often encountered in an alphabet. The question then becomes: which part of the illustration will a translator focus on to help create the translation?

Sometimes the choice is easy, as with the letter X in *The Dangerous Alphabet* (2008) written by Neil Gaiman and illustrated by Gris Grimly. In this work, an alphabet tells the adventures of a girl, a boy and their pet gazelle who all journey through a menacing underworld (a sewer filled with monsters and thugs) to find a treasure:

> X marked the spot, if we read the map right.[48]
> X marquait l'endroit, si on a bien lu la carte fournie.[49]

In this example, the big X painted in red on the wall presents an easy and effective solution for translators. But more often than not, they will have to come up with a personal, subjective solution depending on the dialogue they create between the text and the illustration. For the letter K, the dictionary was a good place to start looking for various options, especially since rhythm had to be taken into account. The question of rhythm is one of the main characteristics of children's literature in general and of picture books in particular, since they are very often read aloud.[50] This disqualified the first solution, which was to keep the word 'kiss' closer to the source text. But this proved too long:

> K's but a **Kiss** — lovers glow with elation.[51]
> K est un **baiser Kaléidoscopique** entre deux amoureux transis.

I turned to the picture for help: on the left side stands the little boy and the gazelle, determined to rescue the little girl being kidnapped on the right side by a bulky monster; they are separated by a stream that runs centre to the illustration, and is carrying a couple embracing on a small boat through a heart-shaped hole in the sewer wall. Looking at the composition, it was obvious the artist had decided to put the emphasis on the lovers, the very heart of this drawing on all levels; the translation could hardly choose to ignore them. However, the kidnapped little girl on the right is also prominent and it was this aspect of the illustration that became the key to unlocking the translation. A parallel was created between being physically kidnapped and being overwhelmed by one's feelings:

> K's but a **Kiss** — lovers glow with elation.[52]
> K pour ces **amants Kidnappés** par l'émotion.[53]

The solution — both creative and as short as possible — came as a result of a dialogue between text, illustration, orality and subjective connections that took into account what Riitta Oittinen calls the 'whole situation': 'Translators of picture books translate whole situations including the words, the illustrations, and the whole (imagined) reading-aloud situation.'[54]

Other solutions had a more visible impact on the original work, because they modified the original order of the lines and images to suit the translated text. Resorted to on three occasions, this solution was used for the pairs G/H, I/J, and T/U:

> G is for Good, as in hero, and morning.
> H is for 'Help me!' — a cry and a warning.
> I am the author who scratches theses rhymes.
> J is the Joke monsters make of their crimes. [...]
> T is for Treasure heaped into a pile.
> U are the reader who shivers with dread.[55]
>
> G pour « Gare à vous ! » — un cri dans un sanglot.
> H pour Héros, halte-là et hello !
> I pour les Ignobles monstres qui rient de leurs crimes.
> **Je suis l'auteur qui griffonne ces quelques rimes**. [...]
> Tu es le lecteur qui tremble et qui geint.
> **U pour Un million de trésors que l'on a entassés**.[56]

For the G/H pairing, Gaiman uses the adjective 'good' on two levels: first as a way to characterize 'hero', and as a nod to the expression 'good morning'. He then resorts to direct speech and *epexegesis* ('a cry and a warning') to convey the sense of danger that pervades the book. 'Hero' was the starting point of my solution, hence my decision to invert the original G/H lines; to enhance the linguistic game at play, the French sentence was made to contain three occurrences of words beginning with an H, while keeping the references to warning ('*Halte-là*' meaning 'Stop!'), hero and greetings ('hello' is a transparent English word for French-speaking readers, and it adds a touch of foreign/alterity to the translated text). As the illustrations for G and H are closely linked to the sentences displayed (G features the hero running towards danger with his sword, and H shows the heroine crying for help), the French edition would entail switching the two images.

The same strategy would be adopted for the illustrations of the I/J pairing, to match the inversion occurring in the text, which was influenced by the structure 'I am': the obvious solution ('*Je suis*') initially conforms to the traditional concept of fidelity to the letter (in Meschonnic's sense of the word), only to lead to a disruption of the original order of the lines[57]. The same pattern appears for the T/U pairing, both in the English and the French texts, and in the illustrations[58]; the letter T dictated the use of *tutoiement* in the translation, and the recourse to familiarity adds to the menacing atmosphere by singling out the reader — this addition makes up for the loss of the original play on register, with Gaiman using the slang spelling of 'you'. He shows how one can subvert a fixed form/exercise while playing within the limits imposed, and this invites the translator to do the same.

In nonsense alphabets, the elements that make up the source text are configured more as a game than an organic unity, with the formal rules typically creating (prismatic) distortions from the norms of sense. This enables translators to continue the game in the target text, obeying and extending the source formal rules so as to create further prismatic deviations — not only from the norms of meaning-making in French, but also from the meanings that were made in the English text. So as to stay close to the intention of the source text,[59] we therefore may modify its playground at length in the translation. In the case of *The Dangerous Alphabet*, inverting letters followed the game established in the foreword to the source text: 'Please Note: The alphabet, as given in this publication, is *not to be relied upon* and has a dangerous flaw that an eagle-eyed reader may be able to discern.'[60] The flaw to which the author alludes is the disruption of the alphabetical order for the letters W and V: 'U are the reader who shivers with dread. / W's Warnings went over your head. / V is for Vile deeds done in the night. / X marked the spot, if we read the map right.'[61] The inversion creates instability within the source text, underlying its potential danger. This is made more apparent in my French translation with its three inversions, which add a layer of irony to the foreword's assertion ('a dangerous flaw that an eagle-eyed reader may be able to discern').[62]

Nonsense alphabets clearly offer an extreme and eloquent example of Jean Boase-Beier and Michael Holman's following assertion (on literary translation in general): 'creativity is often intimately tied to constraint, it is a response to it, it is enhanced by it.'[63] The same could be said of the intimate link that exists between translation and subjectivity; as Antoine Berman underlines in his essay on Walter Benjamin's famous *The Translator's Task*, translation is always the work of a translating subject,[64] whose creative role is essential and must be acknowledged. Their subjectivity is unique and 'must be understood as part of a complex overlay of mediating activities, which allow for active and critical intervention,'[65] to quote Sherry Simon. Since subjectivity and some amount of disruption are inescapable in the translative process, rather than fight against this, translators should embrace the creative potential they contain.

'They Needed a Poet': Impact and Creative Potential of the Translating Subject

As we have seen, the adoption of rules constrains subjectivity in some respects, but releases it in others, and the translator's subjectivity has a real impact on the target text, creating a unique playground among many other possible options. While the general public only accesses the finished, published version, translators experience first-hand the prismatic nature of the translation process: they are the ones at the centre of the different, often numerous stages the target text goes through and the meticulous working and reworking of solutions. And as such it is important for translators to share their experiences, and for scholars and journalists to offer them the platform they need to do so. The exposure will help all concerned to rethink the notion of faithfulness and open up the discussion around creativity in translation, both of which are deeply rooted in the translator's subjectivity and craftsmanship.

Released in 2011 by the publishing house Attila[66] and translated by Ludovic Flamant, the French translation of Edward Gorey's *The Gashlycrumb Tinies: or, After the Outing* (1963) offers an interesting case in point. Edward Gorey, a very prolific American writer and illustrator (1925–2000), inspired artists like Tim Burton and

Neil Gaiman with the dark humour and gothic atmosphere characteristic of his work. Gorey belongs firmly to the nonsense genre and is considered the twentieth century heir to Edward Lear and Lewis Carroll.[67] At the age of 5, he had already read Carroll's *Alice's Adventures in Wonderland*,[68] and he later illustrated the works of nonsense authors Edward Lear and Hilaire Belloc. *The Gashlycrumb Tinies: or, After the Outing* presents readers with an illustrated alphabet listing the gruesome, often grotesque deaths of twenty-six children; Gorey resorts to the traditional formula of alphabets, '[Letter] is for [Word]':

> A is for Amy who fell down the stairs,
> B is for Basil, assaulted by bears.
> C is for Clara who wasted away,
> D is for Desmond, thrown out of the sleigh.[69]

The deaths portrayed vary widely, as if Gorey wanted to explore the prism of death: some are the direct consequence of a malicious act ('K is for Kate who was struck with an axe.'), some are accidental ('U is for Una who slipped down a drain.'),[70] and all of them seem arbitrary and grotesque. This alphabet dares the readers to consider the many ways one can die, and it challenges translators with the numerous issues and possible solutions it raises, so much so that the book was long thought to be untranslatable: '[Attila] really wanted to publish it and had long wondered who would be able to tackle this project, because — and I only learned of this well after the release of my translation — this alphabet was reputed untranslatable, which is why Gallimard/L'Arpenteur hadn't published it when they translated several of Gorey's books during the 1980s.'[71]

Translating the title is no small task in itself. Gorey created a portmanteau word, something common in the nonsense tradition: 'The type of word that nonsense is famed for is not simply coinage, but a specific type of coinage: portmanteau words. Not so much because they first appeared in a nonsense text, as because they were named in one [...]. The phrase, which is of course Humpty Dumpty's, has now found its way into most dictionaries.'[72] The translator first needs to deconstruct the expression: the noun 'gash' (long, deep wound) becomes an adverb with the suffix '-ly', and is fused to the noun 'crumb' (evoking bread crumbs); the portmanteau word thus underlines the tragic and yet insignificant fates of the 'tinies' featured in the text.

Ludovic Flamant opted at first for '*Réduits en miettes*'[73] ('reduced to crumbs, smashed to death'), echoing the original 'crumb', but it did not convince the publishers, who invited him to stray from the original title to find something that would be as playful in French. Flamant found inspiration in the illustration of the original cover, which shows the young heroes gathered around a black-clad death figure holding an umbrella over their heads, and suggested '*Les Enfants gâchés*', which played on the expression '*enfant gâté*' ('spoiled child') and the adjective '*gâché*' ('spoiled, ruined') — a pun that would work in English as well. This solution proved interesting but not convincing enough for the publishers, and the French title had to go through several additional changes before settling on the final, fixed solution of '*Les Enfants Fichus*' ('the doomed children'), which plays on sounds (alliteration), register ('*fichus*' is colloquial) and on the double meaning of '*fichus*' ('doomed' and 'damn, darn'). The French title modifies the rules of the translation playground (no portmanteau word[74]) but proves as creative as the original — and possibly more humorous.

Regarding structure, the rhyming scheme is simple (rhyming couplets) and the verses are quite short so as to be easily read and remembered. This approach is also used to make light of the children's demises: 'The threat of emotional harm is lessened further by Gorey's tendency to use rhyming couplets. Rhyming verse allows Gorey's readers to maintain a certain distance from his grim subjects. [...] When form is more valued than content, a reader is less likely to be alarmed by content, he or she subconsciously (or consciously) using the necessity of the rhyme to reject the possibility that the text reflects something real.'[75] This is precisely what is at stake for the translator: to render the poetic, violent and humorous qualities of the text.

For his translation, Ludovic Flamant wanted at first to keep Gorey's decasyllables: 'I am very fond of this rhythm, for example in the work of Belgian poet William Cliff — this somewhat dry rhythm, which evokes a moving train... .'[76] He managed to find satisfying solutions for several verses, but all in all 'the French words [...] just wouldn't fit into this limited space'.[77] Flamant then turned to the French tradition of the alexandrine to build his verses, much to his disappointment.[78] It ended up defining his remaining translation choices, up to the names of the children — where changes are rare,[79] but when they do occur, they are a result of needing the correct number of syllables for his verse: 'Leo' and 'Neville' respectively become 'Lou' and 'Norman' (the French pronunciation of 'Neville' would add a syllable), while the Shakespearian 'Yorick' transforms into the Middle French 'Ysengrin'.[80] Much like what happened with the alexandrine, Flamant wished he could have kept all the source names, since Gorey seemed to have put a lot of care into selecting them.

Flamant reinvented the meter of the text and increased the occurrence of the key letter (or sound)[81] in each line, while remaining as concise as possible in French. Due to this choice, Gorey's style evolves in the translated text from a dry, matter-of-fact tone, to something that is almost elegant:

> Q is for Quinton who sank in a mire,
> R is for Rhoda, consumed by a fire.
> S is for Susan who perished of fits,
> T is for Titus who flew into bits.
> U is for Una who slipped down a drain,
> V is for Victor, squashed under a train.[82]
>
> Q pour Quentin courant droit vers un marécage
> R pour Rhoda brûlée en pleine fleur de l'âge
> S pour Susan saisie de fortes convulsions
> T pour Titus surpris par la détonation
> U pour Una chutant sans plus laisser de trace
> V pour Victor curieux de voir un train de face[83]

The translator was acutely aware of this difference between the source and the target texts, and the elegance of the French alexandrine matched the elegant, almost affected style of Gorey which Flamant perceived in the illustrations.[84]

Flamant's translation diverges from the original structure of the text to assimilate it to the target culture: does it also mean that he steers away from the intention of the source text — namely, to make light of a dark subject matter? Not necessarily. If Gorey's voice sounds somewhat different in French, the more elegant tone can be comical as it feels inappropriate and disconnected from its violent and grotesque content. By taking a different poetic road, Flamant also aims at making light of the gruesome deaths of this alphabet, and he positions himself as a poet in his own right — something that was expected of him when he was first asked to translate *The Gashlycrumb Tinies: or, After the Outing*: 'To quote them, they needed a poet.'[85]

Another poet took on a Gorey translation for the same publishing house. Jacques Roubaud, French poet, scholar and member of the famous Oulipo group, translated *The Utter Zoo Alphabet* (1967) into French in 2012 (*Total Zoo*). This alphabet presents an interesting selection of coined words, some of which are portmanteau words: Gorey invented twenty-six imaginary beasts and their names reflect who they are, their mood, their shape, the sound they might make, etc.. For example, the 'Crunk' is cranky and may want to devour you with his impressive fangs (an echo to the action and onomatopoeia 'crunch'), the 'Humglum' looks depressed, gloomy and listless, and the 'Veazy' is said to make 'a creaking noise'.[86]

The game established by Gorey invites the translator into a world full of possibilities; who better to translate this text in French than Jacques Roubaud, a member of the Oulipo group who once described himself as being forever in a state of translation?[87] After all, the definition of the Oulipian literature as something working under constraints echoes the translation process: 'Potential literature, what is that? A literature under constrainment.'[88] Translating *is* creating under constraints, and seeing the potential that lies within these constraints.[89]

Roubaud's translation could therefore have unleashed the full potential of portmanteau words, especially since they are one of Oulipo's favourite literary tools. Roubaud himself helped to create some Oulipian portmanteau animals, such as the '*corboa*' (a combination of '*corbeau* [raven]' and '*boa*'), and he translated Lewis Carroll's *The Hunting of the Snark* (1876), a text full of portmanteau words.[90] It comes as a surprise then that Roubaud did not coin any new names for the French version of this alphabet. He chose instead to keep the English versions imagined by Gorey:

> The **Neapse's** sufferings are chronic;
> It lives exclusively on tonic.
>
> The **Ulp** is very, very small;
> It can hardly be seen at all.
>
> The **Yawfle** stares, and stares, and stares,
> And stares, and stares, and stares, and stares.[91]
>
> Les douleurs du **Neapse** sont chroniques
> Il vit exclusivement de toniques
>
> Le **Ulp** est très très très petit
> On le distingue à peine ici

> Le **Yawfle** a le regard fixe
> Et fixe et fixe et fixe et fixe[92]

This choice makes the alterity of these animals stand out even more in French: they become completely foreign to the French readers, whereas the usual purpose of coined words in general and portmanteau words in particular is to play a guessing game with the readers who must decipher the linguistic roots of these invented words. Some of the names of Gorey's strange zoo animals have more transparent meanings than others, which creates within this collection a spectrum of creature names that further unsettles the readers: 'In the names of many of Gorey's fantasy creatures we find language at its most challenging, such as the Ippagoggy, the Jelbislup, the Ombledroom, the Quingawaga, and the Wambulus.'[93] This spectrum disappears in French. While the presence of the source names in the translation does catch the attention of French readers and disrupts the French text (how should names like 'Jelbislup' or 'Yawfle',[94] baffling for a French audience, be pronounced?), rereading the target text is unlikely to lead to a semantic revelation, which is usually the case with coined and portmanteau words: 'The semantic blanks compel us to look at the text in a new way, to read it anew.'[95]

The target text then does not do to the French language what the source text did to the English language, to use Henri Meschonnic's expression.[96] While champions of translators' visibility such as Lawrence Venuti hold foreignisation in high regard, domestication in this case would have proved more interesting because of Roubaud's subjectivity and personal poetic skills. We can only mourn the coined words that Roubaud could have created.

If, as Berman said, there are as many translative positions as there are translators (and all translators have a translative position),[97] there are still certain constants worth exploring when translating a text, especially a nonsense text/alphabet. Close reading is mandatory so as to understand how the source text works, what it aims to do, and what the text does to its own language — translators are, after all, the most active and attentive readers. With this close reading, translators become aware of limits — the limits of the source text's and the target text's playgrounds,[98] and the limits inherent to the translators' subjectivity. This realisation can be discouraging, even paralyzing; it can also be an invitation to consider subjectivity not as something simply limiting, but as a source of creativity and possibilities. It demands real commitment from translators and coherence in the translation solutions: just as nonsense is never random, neither is the translation process.

All this will help translators (re)create a solid, reliable playground for their translation of texts that can be challenging on a linguistic, cultural and personal level. As George Steiner points out, 'the craft of the translator is [...] deeply ambivalent: it is exercised in a radical tension between impulses to facsimile and impulses to appropriate recreation'.[99] This 'radical tension' is felt even more when working on nonsense alphabets, with their specific formula and attention to details — both in the texts and the illustrations. The presence of illustrations renders visible the prismatic nature of translation, as it opens up new possibilities while bringing into focus certain details. The interventions of editors and publishers, which are often forgotten, show how translation also works as an inverted prism, bringing together multiple subjective positions to produce one target text; Mieke Desmet underlines this aspect by broadening the definition of 'translator' in her papers: 'Despite the uncertainty as to who exactly intervenes in the text at any given stage, the generic word 'translator' will be maintained throughout the text. It should be read as referring at the same time to the translator, the editor, the publisher or anyone who is involved in publishing the text.'[100] These factors turn the translation process into a very unsettling exercise, as well as a very formative and creative one — in the vein of nonsense alphabets.

Works Cited

APTER, EMILY, *Against World Literature. On the Politics of Untranslatability* (London: Verso, 2013)
—— *The Translation Zone: A New Comparative Literature* (Princeton: Princeton University Press, 2006)
BERMAN, ANTOINE, 'L'âge de la traduction. « La tâche du traducteur » de Walter Benjamin, un commentaire', *La Traduction-poésie: à Antoine Berman*, ed. Martine Broda (Strasbourg: Presses universitaires de Strasbourg, 1999)
—— *L'Épreuve de l'étranger: Culture et traduction dans l'Allemagne romantique* (Paris: Gallimard, 1984)
—— *Pour une critique des traductions: John Donne* (Paris: Gallimard, 1995)
BOASE-BEIER, JEAN and MICHAEL HOLMAN, eds, *The Practices of Literary Translation: Constraints and Creativity* (London: Routledge, 2014)
CARROLL, LEWIS, *Alice's Adventures in Wonderland & Through the Looking-Glass and What Alice Found There* (London: Penguin, 1998)
—— *La Chasse au Snark*, trans. by Jacques Roubaud (Paris: Gallimard, 1997)
CASSIN, BARBARA, *Éloge de la traduction. Compliquer l'universel* (Paris: Fayard, 2016)
CASSIN, BARBARA, ed., *Vocabulaire européen des philosophies. Dictionnaire des intraduisibles* (Paris: Seuil / Le Robert, 2004)
COUSSY, AUDREY, 'Traduction et littérature d'enfance et de jeunesse anglophone (19e–21e): langage, identité, altérité', Dissertation, Université Sorbonne Nouvelle Paris 3, 2014
DERRIDA, JACQUES, 'Des tours de Babel', in *Psyché, inventions de l'autre* (Paris: Galilée, 1987), pp. 203–36
DERRIDA, JACQUES, 'Qu'est-ce qu'une traduction 'relevante'?', in *Quinzièmes Assises de la Traduction Littéraire (Arles 1998)* (Arles: Actes Sud, 1999), pp. 21–48
DESMET, MIEKE, 'The Secret Diary of the Translator', in *Translation and the (Re)Location of Meaning*, ed. by Jeroen Vandaele (Louvain: CETRA, 1999), 215–36
DRURY, ANNMARIE, *Translation as Transformation in Victorian Poetry* (Cambridge: Cambridge University Press, 2015)
ECO, UMBERTO, *Mouse or Rat? Translation as Negotiation* (London: Phoenix, 2003)
FOLKART, BARBARA, *Second Finding: A Poetics of Translation* (Ottawa: University of Ottawa Press, 2007)
GAIMAN, NEIL, *The Dangerous Alphabet* (London: Bloomsbury Children's Books, 2008)
GOREY, EDWARD, *Les Enfants Fichus*, trans. Ludovic Flamant (Paris: Attila, 2011)
—— *The Gashlycrumb Tinies: or, After the Outing* (New York: Simon and Schuster, 1963)
—— *Total Zoo*, trans. Jacques Roubaud (Paris: Attila, 2012)
—— *The Utter Zoo Alphabet* (New York: Meredith Press, 1967)
GREENE, IAN, *The Christian's ABC: Catechisms and Catechizing in England c. 1540–1740* (Oxford: Oxford University Press, 1995)

GUSSOW, MEL, 'Edward Gorey, Artist and Author Who Turned the Macabre Into a Career, Dies at 75', *The New York Times*, 17 April 2000
JOOSEN, VANESSA, 'ABC Books or Alphabet Books', in *The Oxford Encyclopaedia of Children's Literature* (vol. 3), ed. Jack Zipes (Oxford: Oxford University Press, 2006, ebook)
LEAR, EDWARD, *The Complete Nonsense*, ed. by Holbrook Jackson (London: Faber and Faber, 1998)
LECERCLE, JEAN-JACQUES, *Philosophy of Nonsense: The Intuitions of Victorian Nonsense Literature* (London: Routledge, 1994)
LEWIS, PHILIP E., 'The Measure of Translation Effects', in *Difference in Translation*, ed. Joseph Graham (Ithaca, N.Y.: Cornell University Press, 1985)
LITAUDON-BONNARDOT, MARIE-PIERRE, *Les Abécédaires de l'enfance: verbe et image* (Rennes: Presses universitaires de Rennes, 2014)
MESCHONNIC, HENRI, 'Chapter VII. Faithful, unfaithful, just more of the same, I thank thee O sign', *Ethics and Politics of Translating*, trans. Pier-Pascale Boulanger (Amsterdam: Benjamins, 2011, ebook)
NODELMAN, PERRY, *Words about Pictures: Narrative Art of Children's Picture Books* (Athens, Georgia: University of Georgia Press, 1990, ebook)
OITTINEN, RIITTA, *Translating for Children* (New York: Garland, 2000)
OULIPO, *L'Abécédaire provisoirement définitif* (Paris: Larousse, 2014)
—— *Abrégé de littérature potentielle* (Paris: Éditions Mille et une nuits, 2002)
REYNOLDS, MATTHEW, *The Poetry of Translation: From Chaucer & Petrarch to Homer & Logue* (Oxford: Oxford University Press, 2011)
ROUBAUD, JACQUES, *Le Grand incendie de Londres: récit, avec incises et bifurcations, 1985–1987* (Paris: Éditions du Seuil, 1989)
SEWELL, ELISABETH, *The Field of Nonsense* (London: Chatto and Windus, 1952)
SHORTSLEEVE, KEVIN, 'Edward Gorey, Children's Literature, and Nonsense Verse', *Children's Literature Association Quarterly*, 27.1 (Spring 2002), 27–39
SIMON, SHERRY, *Gender in Translation* (London: Routledge, 2003)
SIPE, LAWRENCE R., 'How Picture Books Work: A Semiotically Framed Theory of Text-Picture Relationships', *Children's Literature in Education*, 29.2 (1998), 97–108
STEINER, GEORGE, *After Babel — Aspects of Language and Translation* (Oxford: Oxford University Press, [1975] 1998)
TIGGES, WIM, *An Anatomy of Literary Nonsense* (Amsterdam: Rodopi, 1988)
VENUTI, LAWRENCE, *The Translator's Invisibility: a History of Translation* (London: Routledge, 1995)

Notes to Chapter 12

1. Lawrence Venuti, *The Translator's Invisibility: a History of Translation* (London: Routledge, 1995), p. 8.
2. Jacques Derrida, 'Des tours de Babel,' in *Psyché, inventions de l'autre* (Paris: Galilée, 1987), pp. 203–36; Jacques Derrida, 'Qu'est-ce qu'une traduction 'relevante'?', in *Quinzièmes Assises de la Traduction Littéraire (Arles 1998)* (Arles: Actes Sud, 1999), pp. 21–48.
3. Emily Apter, *The Translation Zone: A New Comparative Literature* (Princeton: Princeton University Press, 2006); Emily Apter, *Against World Literature. On the Politics of Untranslatability* (London: Verso, 2013).
4. Barbara Cassin, ed., *Vocabulaire européen des philosophies. Dictionnaire des intraduisibles* (Paris: Seuil / Le Robert, 2004); Barbara Cassin, *Éloge de la traduction. Compliquer l'universel* (Paris: Fayard, 2016).
5. Philip E. Lewis, 'The Measure of Translation Effects', in *Difference in Translation*, ed. Joseph Graham (Ithaca, N.Y.: Cornell University Press, 1985), p. 41.

6. Jean Boase-Beier and Michael Holman, eds, *The Practices of Literary Translation: Constraints and Creativity* (London: Routledge, 2014), p. 14.
7. Annmarie Drury, *Translation as Transformation in Victorian Poetry* (Cambridge: Cambridge University Press, 2015), pp. 57–99.
8. Drury, *Translation as Transformation*, p. 223.
9. Barbara Folkart, *Second Finding: A Poetics of Translation* (Ottawa: University of Ottawa Press, 2007), p. xiii.
10. Folkart, *Second Finding*, p. 188.
11. Elisabeth Sewell, *The Field of Nonsense* (London: Chatto and Windus, 1952), p. 5.
12. This description immediately calls to mind the work of the Oulipo group (founded in France in 1960) and their exploration of constraint and creativity in literature. Sequencing is a recurrent feature among the many Oulipian tools of creation (alphabets, indexing, tautograms, etc.).
13. In the vein of Oulipo's alphabet *L'Abécédaire provisoirement définitif* (Paris: Larousse, 2014) and its desire to inspire people to write (an aim displayed on the cover: '*Découvrez une centaine de créations de l'OULIPO qui vous donneront envie d'écrire!*'), this paper also hopes to inspire people to translate alphabets in general, and nonsense alphabets in particular.
14. Vanessa Joosen, 'ABC Books or Alphabet Books', in *The Oxford Encyclopaedia of Children's Literature* (vol. 3), ed. Jack Zipes (Oxford: Oxford University Press, 2006, ebook).
15. For reference, see for example: Ian Greene, *The Christian's ABC: Catechisms and Catechizing in England c. 1540–1740* (Oxford: Oxford University Press, 1995).
16. Marie-Pierre Litaudon-Bonnardot, *Les Abécédaires de l'enfance: verbe et image* (Rennes: Presses universitaires de Rennes, 2014), p. 199.
17. Laws were passed to introduce mandatory schooling for children: Factory Act (1833), Education Acts (1870, 1880, 1889) in the UK; Jules Ferry's reforms of 1880–1881 in France.
18. Litaudon-Bonnardot, *Les Abécédaires de l'enfance*, p. 199. The author's translation.
19. Litaudon-Bonnardot, *Les Abécédaires de l'enfance*, p. 227. The author's translation.
20. I follow Wim Tigges's definition of nonsense as a literary genre first and foremost (instead of a mode or device): Wim Tigges, *An Anatomy of Literary Nonsense* (Amsterdam: Rodopi, 1988), p. 47.
21. Jean-Jacques Lecercle, *Philosophy of Nonsense: The Intuitions of Victorian Nonsense Literature* (London: Routledge, 1994), p. 113.
22. Lecercle, *Philosophy of Nonsense*, p. 3.
23. Meschonnic would also talk about 'fidelity to the sign', criticizing the semiotic binary definition of the sign (signifier/signified): see for example Henri Meschonnic, 'Chapter VII. Faithful, unfaithful, just more of the same, I thank thee O sign', in *Ethics and Politics of Translating*, trans. Pier-Pascale Boulanger (Amsterdam: Benjamins, 2011, ebook), pp. 89–101.
24. Hilaire Belloc (1870–1953), another figure of nonsense literature, mocked this prescriptive tradition: his *Cautionary Verses*, written between 1896 and 1930, parodied alphabets from puritan authors and cautionary tales like Mary Martha Sherwood's *The History of the Fairchild Family* (1818).
25. Edward Lear, *The Complete Nonsense*, ed. by Holbrook Jackson (London: Faber and Faber, 1998), p. 270.
26. Lear, *The Complete Nonsense*, pp. 270–71.
27. Antoine Berman, *L'Épreuve de l'étranger : Culture et traduction dans l'Allemagne romantique* (Paris: Gallimard, 1984), p. 250.
28. Audrey Coussy, 'Traduction et littérature d'enfance et de jeunesse anglophone (19e–21e): langage, identité, altérité', Dissertation, Université Sorbonne Nouvelle Paris 3, 2014.
29. Lear, *The Complete Nonsense*, p. 271.
30. Ibid..
31. Coussy, 'Traduction et littérature d'enfance et de jeunesse', p. 641.
32. Lear, *The Complete Nonsense*, p. 271.
33. Coussy, 'Traduction et littérature d'enfance et de jeunesse', p. 641.
34. Berman, *L'Épreuve de l'étranger*, p. 250.
35. This new rule, here at play in the French version of the game, could have worked in English as

well, for example: 'C claimed, 'A Cup of Coffee hot can't do you any harm.' / D declared, 'A Doctor should be fetched, and he would cure the arm.''

36. Lear, *The Complete Nonsense*, p. 270.
37. Coussy, 'Traduction et littérature d'enfance et de jeunesse', p. 641.
38. Lear, *The Complete Nonsense*, p. 270.
39. Lear, *The Complete Nonsense*, p. 271.
40. Coussy, 'Traduction et littérature d'enfance et de jeunesse', p. 641.
41. 'Negotiation is a process by virtue of which, in order to get something, each party renounces something else, and at the end everybody feels satisfied since one cannot have everything. In this kind of negotiation there may be many parties: on one side, there is the original text, with its own rights, sometimes an author who claims right over the whole process, along with the cultural framework in which the original text is born; on the other side, there is the destination text, the cultural milieu in which it is expected to be read, and even the publishing industry, which can recommend different translation criteria, according to whether the translated text is to be put in an academic context or in a popular one. [...] A translator is the negotiator between those parties, whose explicit assent is not mandatory', in Umberto Eco, *Mouse or Rat? Translation as Negotiation* (London: Phoenix, 2003), p. 6.
42. Matthew Reynolds makes a similar point in *The Poetry of Translation: From Chaucer & Petrarch to Homer & Logue* (Oxford: Oxford University Press, 2011) about source texts providing metaphorical models which translators adopt in their own practice.
43. '"And what is the use of a book,' thought Alice, 'without pictures or conversations?"', in Lewis Carroll, *Alice's Adventures in Wonderland & Through the Looking-Glass and What Alice Found There* (London: Penguin, 1998), p. 9.
44. 'The first known English use of the picture alphabet is John Hart's *A Methode; or, Comfortable Beginning for All Unlearned* (1570), which showed a letter and a noun together with a woodcut of a concrete object. It is not an ABC book in the strict sense, since some letters are lacking and others do not feature in the usual order, but nevertheless it can be seen as a precursor for the illustrated ABC book', in Joosen, 'ABC Books or Alphabet Books'.
45. Litaudon-Bonnardot, *Les Abécédaires de l'enfance*, p. 199. The author's translation.
46. Lawrence R. Sipe, 'How Picture Books Work: A Semiotically Framed Theory of Text-Picture Relationships', *Children's Literature in Education*, 29.2 (1998), 97–108 (p. 97).
47. Perry Nodelman, *Words about Pictures: Narrative Art of Children's Picture Books* (Athens, Georgia: University of Georgia Press, 1990, ebook), p. 166.
48. Neil Gaiman, *The Dangerous Alphabet* (London: Bloomsbury Children's Books, 2008), unpaginated.
49. Coussy, 'Traduction et littérature d'enfance et de jeunesse', p. 545.
50. 'Sharing, performance, reading aloud are characteristic of children's books and their translations', in Riitta Oittinen, *Translating for Children* (New York: Garland, 2000), p. 32.
51. Gaiman, *The Dangerous Alphabet*.
52. Gaiman, *The Dangerous Alphabet*.
53. Coussy, 'Traduction et littérature d'enfance et de jeunesse', p. 545.
54. Oittinen, *Translating for Children*, p. 75.
55. Gaiman, *The Dangerous Alphabet*.
56. Coussy, 'Traduction et littérature d'enfance et de jeunesse', p. 545.
57. The illustration for I shows the author working on the very book the readers are holding, while the image for J features children held prisoners and some of the torture devices used by the monsters of the story.
58. Since the illustration for T displays the treasure mentioned in the text, and the illustration for U an audience of captive young readers, the two images would need to be inverted here as well.
59. 'Translators must aim at rendering, not necessarily the intention of the author (who may have been dead for millennia), but the *intention of the text* — the intention of the text being the outcome of an interpretative effort on the part of the reader, the critic or the translator.', in Eco, *Mouse or Rat?*, p. 5.
60. Gaiman, *The Dangerous Alphabet*.

61. Gaiman, *The Dangerous Alphabet*.
62. Gaiman, *The Dangerous Alphabet*.
63. Boase-Beier and Holman, eds, *The Practices of Literary Translation*, p. 6.
64. Antoine Berman, 'L'âge de la traduction. « La tâche du traducteur » de Walter Benjamin, un commentaire', in *La Traduction-poésie : à Antoine Berman*, ed. Martine Broda (Strasbourg: Presses universitaires de Strasbourg, 1999), p. 34.
65. Sherry Simon, *Gender in Translation* (London: Routledge, 2003), p. 37.
66. The founders, Frédéric Martin and Benoît Virot, decided to part ways in 2013, which resulted in the creation of two different publishing houses: Le Nouvel Attila, and Le Tripode (the latter retained Gorey in their catalogue).
67. Tigges, *An Anatomy of Literary Nonsense*, p. 184.
68. Mel Gussow, 'Edward Gorey, Artist and Author Who Turned the Macabre Into a Career, Dies at 75', *The New York Times*, 17 April 2000.
69. Edward Gorey, *The Gashlycrumb Tinies: or, After the Outing* (New York: Simon and Schuster, 1963), unpaginated.
70. Gorey, *The Gashlycrumb Tinies*.
71. Ludovic Flamant, personal interview, 14 July 2017. The author's translation.
72. Lecercle, *Philosophy of Nonsense*, p. 44.
73. Flamant, personal interview.
74. A possible French title using a portmanteau-word could be '*Petit macchabécédaire*', a play on '*macchabée*' ('corpse') and '*abécédaire*' ('alphabet'), with a general nod to the word '*macabre*'.
75. Kevin Shortsleeve, 'Edward Gorey, Children's Literature, and Nonsense Verse', *Children's Literature Association Quarterly*, 27.1 (Spring 2002), 27–39 (p. 33).
76. Flamant, personal interview. The author's translation.
77. Flamant, personal interview. The author's translation.
78. When discussing this aspect of his translation, Flamant talks about 'renouncement'.
79. 'I would always try to twist and play with syntax rather than change the name in the verse', Flamant, personal interview. The author's translation.
80. Edward Gorey, *Les Enfants Fichus*, trans. Ludovic Flamant (Paris: Attila, 2011), unpaginated.
81. Much like my translative strategy for Lear's *Unnamed Alphabet*.
82. Gorey, *The Gashlycrumb Tinies*.
83. Gorey, *Les Enfants Fichus*.
84. The illustrations played a crucial part in Flamant's translation process: 'I always looked at the illustrations when I was working. It was very important for me. [...] I was fully aware that I was translating an *illustrated* text. [...] All in all, I would say that the illustrations usually helped me find solutions for certain words. For example, the English text says that Basil was "attacked" by bears, but it's his expression in the picture that allowed me to say he was "surprised by bears". Desmond is said to have fallen from a sled, but Gorey never specified how it happened. Since we can barely see the sled and we don't know if there were other people on it, I was able to say that Desmond was "thrown" from it', Flamant, personal interview. The author's translation.
85. Flamant, personal interview. The author's translation.
86. Edward Gorey, *The Utter Zoo Alphabet* (New York: Meredith Press, 1967), unpaginated.
87. 'Je ne suis dans aucune langue, toujours traduisant', in Jacques Roubaud, *Le Grand incendie de Londres: récit, avec incises et bifurcations, 1985–1987* (Paris: Éditions du Seuil, 1989), p. 169.
88. 'La littérature potentielle, qu'est-ce que c'est ? Une littérature sous contrainte', in Oulipo, *Abrégé de littérature potentielle* (Paris: Éditions Mille et une nuits, 2002).
89. See this volume on the specific subject of translating constrained literature: *MLN*, 131.4, September 2016 (French Issue).
90. Lewis Carroll, *La Chasse au Snark*, trans. Jacques Roubaud (Paris: Gallimard, 1997).
91. Gorey, *The Utter Zoo Alphabet*.
92. Edward Gorey, *Total Zoo*, trans. Jacques Roubaud (Paris: Attila, 2012), unpaginated.
93. Shortsleeve, 'Edward Gorey, Children's Literature, and Nonsense Verse', p. 35.
94. Gorey, *Total Zoo*.
95. Lecercle, *Philosophy of Nonsense*, p. 24.

96. Meschonnic, 'Chapter VII', p. 52.
97. Antoine Berman, *Pour une critique des traductions: John Donne* (Paris: Gallimard, 1995), p. 75.
98. Berman, *L'Épreuve de l'étranger*, p. 250.
99. George Steiner, *After Babel — Aspects of Language and Translation* (Oxford: Oxford University Press, [1975] 1998), p. 235.
100. Mieke Desmet, 'The Secret Diary of the Translator', in *Translation and the (Re)Location of Meaning*, ed. Jeroen Vandaele (Louvain: CETRA, 1999), pp. 215–36 (p. 215).

CHAPTER 13

Algorithmic Translation: New Challenges for Translation in the Age of Algorithms

Eran Hadas

1. Introduction

For many people, the first thing that comes to mind when speaking of algorithms and translation is Machine Translation. This research field investigates the use of software to translate text or speech from one language to another, and is a subfield of Computational Linguistics. It has gained popularity since the advent of the Internet, employing new techniques based on Big Data and Machine Learning algorithms.

While Machine Translation's goal is the ability to translate any text from one language to another, literary texts present that effort with some unique challenges. Moreover, Machine Translation's cultural and technological microclimate creates new fields of thought for research into translation and translation-related tasks that are not directly computer-based.

As an independent poet focusing on 21st-century writing techniques, I spend much of my time exploring language and its relationship to technology. I am interested in exploring language and its potential. Inspired by the French group Oulipo, I seek new structures and patterns that can be used in writing. My background in Computer Science allows me to interact with language using computer languages, and I believe that software can provide access to many of the potential structures of language. Part of my poetic practice involves building chatbots, automatic text generators and other poetic text-based applications.

The poetic practice of building chatbots has led me to translate one from English to Hebrew. This made me think about much of my work in terms of creative translation. I will outline four areas of study within which I have worked to create new literary environments and experiences through the use and augmentation of translation. I emphasize the work I have done in my mother tongue, Hebrew, and the specific difficulties and opportunities of translating into it. I also examine the social and political forces that operate on the spaces between English and Hebrew and between English and other languages.

The four topics I will cover, which correspond to four of my poetic endeavors are:

1. Translating a chatbot from English to Hebrew.
2. Word embeddings in English, Hebrew, and other languages, and how to harness their power to expose deeper social structures.
3. Translating source code from English to Hebrew in an environment where English is the default coding language.
4. Using algorithms for creative translations between Biblical and Modern Hebrew.

2. Translating a Chatbot

2.1 Bots' and ELIZA

The word 'bot' denotes an autonomous computer program that can interact with other computer systems and with users; in common use it refers to a program designed to respond to humans. A chatbot is a computer program tailored to simulate conversations with human users, typically over the Internet. Chatbots became popular with the introduction of Intelligent Personal Assistants on mobile phones (such as Apple's Siri). These voice-operated assistants can understand spoken commands and perform administrative tasks in response, such as setting reminders, searching the Internet, etc.

Chatbots create a novel phenomenological perspective for machines. While humans treat most artificial objects as tools, we see chatbots as companions. When using a search engine, people will type in a term, get a result, and end the interaction. With a chatbot, they will often initiate a conversation with a greeting ('Hi, Siri'), and will often thank the bot for completing an action.

Many consider such personification to be a new phenomenon. However, there is a term for it — 'The ELIZA Effect' — named after the first chatbot, built by Joseph Weizenbaum at the MIT Artificial Intelligence Laboratory and released in 1966. Weizenbaum was inspired by Alan Turing's thought experiment, the Turing Test, in which a human evaluator was asked to judge natural language conversations between a human and a machine designed to generate human-like responses. Turing proposed the question 'Can machines think?'[1] and provided us with a tool to evaluate future answers. His test would pave the way to modern Artificial Intelligence, while relating it intimately to (human) language.

Weizenbaum was a pioneer when it came to developing data structures and patterns for efficient use of data. One of his achievements was a programming language titled SLIP, for Symmetric LIst Processor.[2] An interesting corollary of his work was the ability to formulate certain problems, known today as Sequence to Sequence problems, that his methods could resolve. Given one sequence of language elements (usually words or characters), the software would output another sequence of similar elements. His work had significant implications for chatbots, text-generating software, and translation programs. Basically it showed that these tools pose intimately related design challenges from an algorithmic point of view — at least in the sense that they all can be tackled in the same manner.

Weizenbaum did not consider his ELIZA software a genuine Artificial Intelligence, nor an attempt to pass the Turing Test.[3] His original intention was to show the superficiality of communication between man and machine; in a sense, he designed the software as a parody. He named it after Eliza Doolittle, a working-class character in George Bernard Shaw's *Pygmalion*, who pretends to belong to elite London society. ELIZA consisted of the Sequence to Sequence engine, but also used data to perform pattern matching. It scanned inputs for recognizable keywords and reassembled responses accordingly. The first and best-known data script to come out of ELIZA was Doctor. It mimicked a Rogerian therapeutic situation, in which the program merely reflected a patient's statements back in the form of questions. In so doing it could 'sidestep the problem of equipping the program [with] a data base of real-world knowledge.'[4]

While Weizenbaum considered ELIZA to be unintelligent, he was surprised by the number of people, including his own secretary, who did not distinguish its responses from human ones despite obvious limitations. The ELIZA effect thus came to describe the psychological tendency to unconsciously assume an analogous relationship between the behaviors of computers and humans.[5]

2.2 ELIZA, Translation, and Hebrew

Chatbot behavior has some important philosophical implications. (Some could be argued to date back to Descartes.)[6] Unsurprisingly, many artworks have dealt with the Turing Test and the ELIZA effect, taking particular interest in the social aspects of bots. For instance, Peggy Weil's proposed Blurring Test essentially reverses Turing Test so that humans must prove their own humanity.[7] Another of Weil's thought experiments provides insight into the connection between chatbots and translation. Suppose a person arrives in a foreign country. Said person has memorized phrases to ask for directions, but he knows nothing else of the native language. So he can do nothing with the directions that the locals give him in a language he does not understand.

In Hebrew culture, ELIZA is well known from the poet David Avidan's 1974 book titled *My Electronic Psychiatrist: Eight Authentic Talks with a Computer*, in which he transcribes and translates conversations conducted with an IBM port of the ELIZA Doctor script.[8] Since the conversations in the book seemed 'too real,' Avidan was accused of modifying, beautifying, and/or editing the computer's outputs.[9] However, when I studied Avidan's original script during my work translating ELIZA, I was able to prove that he did not make anything up. The entire book is genuine and unmodified, albeit cherry-picked — that is, he included only the interactions that worked for him. Avidan's book is the first example of Computational Literature in Hebrew. Although it is not one of his most popular works, it made an impact and legitimized the creation and discussion of computer-generated works in the language.

2.3 Translating ELIZA into Hebrew

In 2013, I was contracted by the Jerusalem Bloomfield Science Museum to translate ELIZA into Hebrew for their computer science display. They explained that they had considered the cheaper and simpler option of just obtaining the original ELIZA data and translating it literally, but realized they would be better served by a more literary translation. Two factors informed that decision: the program's architecture, and the differences between the source and destination languages.

ELIZA makes decisions based on rules. It recognizes keywords based on certain criteria, and reassembles sentences in predetermined ways once such keywords are found. The alternative to such a rule-based approach, for both chatbots and Machine Translations, is a statistical one. In that case, an algorithm generates outputs based on generalizations from a set of examples. Such example-based algorithms attempt to mimic the behavior of the examples, according to metrics they define or learn. Contemporary algorithms use hybrids of the rule-based and statistical approaches, with the latter often implemented by Artificial Neural Networks that determine patterns by processing massive numbers of examples.

The rule-based approach seems closer to human translation, since it does not require collecting of external data that demonstrates behaviors of the destination language. Instead, it focuses on the relevant data. However, its translation rules will depend heavily on the structure of the destination language, which makes it practically impossible to achieve a one-to-one rule transformation that would apply universally to all languages.

One problem, shown in Table 1, is that of homographs, different words with identical spellings. In typed Hebrew, vowel signs are generally not specified, which greatly increases the number of homographs one encounters. When mirroring a patient's words, ELIZA's Doctor script frequently uses the word 'you.' (The best-known example recognizes the patient's use of 'you' and replies, 'We were discussing you — not me.') However, the Hebrew word for you, 'את' (at) is a homograph of the most frequently used word in the language, 'את' (et), which is a meaningless structural pronoun that comes before a definite object.[10] In the context of ELIZA, typing the Hebrew for 'you are the problem' is the same as simply writing 'the problem.'

While it would be possible in some cases (though not this one) to infer the homograph's meaning from the general context of the conversation, this would make the translated program much more complicated to program than the straightforward rule-based approach that ELIZA takes. My intuition in this case was to steer the translation more toward the algorithm than toward the data, and to reflect the 'mechanical' behavior of the code even if it lost some of the text's meaning.

Since ELIZA reveals its imperfections quite apparently in the original English version, my decision to keep the same code behavior followed a classical translation process: if adequacy in translation measures adherence to the source text, an algorithmic adequacy here would measure adherence to the source code. The next decision I made was to determine which of the two meanings of 'את' would be

Original (English) Version

////me: **you** are the problem
eliza: Did you think **they** might not be the problem?
/////me: **the** problem?
eliza: Do you feel strongly about discussing **such things**?
/////me: **you**?
eliza: **We were discussing you — not me.**

Hebrew Version
Back-translation

////me: (you are) the problem
eliza: **We were discussing you — not me.**
////me: (you are) the problem
eliza: We are not here to deal with the fact I might be the problem, but for you to tell me about your problem*

```
‎אליזה: מה שלומך? בוא נשמע על הבעיה שלך.
‎/////אני: את הבעיה
‎אליזה: דיברנו עליך, לא עליי.
‎/////אני: את הבעיה
‎אליזה: אנחנו פה לא כדי לעסוק בכך שאולי אני
‎הבעיה אלא כדי שתספר לי על הבעיה שלך.
```

TABLE 1. Homograph ambiguity — [Et]
*Not in the original script

given priority. Even though the article use is more common, it made more sense to prioritize the 'you' meaning in this context.

A second problem, shown in Table 2, is that in English ELIZA addresses users without reference to their gender, whereas in Hebrew many language constructs must distinguish between feminine and masculine forms. For instance, the phrase 'you are,' which begins many sentences in ELIZA, is gender-dependent in Hebrew. My solution here was to allow users to specify their gender ('I'm female,' 'I'm a boy,' 'I'm a woman,' etc.) as soon as they started up the program or at any other time in the conversation. ELIZA would then proceed with constructions reflecting the appropriate gender.

Gender differences necessitated another tweak involving the tense of sentences. 'Do you dream' does not involve a homograph for both genders in Hebrew, whereas 'did you dream' does. My general approach was to create a dialog that could be read aloud differently for each gender, but would be written the same, as very few homographs are homophones in Hebrew. This could also accommodate people who challenge the binary division of sexes.

A third problem involved trying to preserve the algorithm's spirit. ELIZA was built as a word processor, replacing whole words. Hebrew complicates the situation

Hebrew Version
Back-translation

////me: I am a girl.
eliza: Do you[f] say[f] that you[f] are[f] a girl for some special reason?
////me: I am a boy.
eliza: What do you[m] do[m] about feeling that you[m] are[m] a boy?

```
שלום. אני אלייזה. נעים מאד. מה הבעיה?
/////אני: אני בת
אלייזה: כשאת טוענת כי את בת יש לך סיבה מסוימת
לומר את זה ?
/////אני: אני בן
אלייזה: מה אתה עושה עם התחושה כי אתה בן ?
```

Hebrew Version

////me: I dreamt we were falling in love
eliza: Really, <did you dream> we were falling in love?
////me: I dreamt we were in love
eliza: What persons appear in your dreams?

```
שלום. אני אלייזה. נעים מאד. מה הבעיה?
/////אני: חלמתי שאנחנו מתאהבים
אלייזה: באמת, חלמת שאנחנו מתאהבים ?
/////אני: חלמתי שאנחנו מאוהבים
אלייזה: מי האנשים שמופיעים לך בחלומות?
```

TABLE 2. Handling gender identities

with its extensive use of in-word prefixes. In simple cases, I tried to preserve ELIZA's basic behavior of mechanically replacing the word 'I' with 'you' (and likewise 'am' with 'are'). However, in Hebrew, constructions where the word 'that' precedes 'you are' appear as one word: 'that-you-are' or 'שאתה.' My solution was to add an additional word, like 'actually,' which would adhere to the in-word prefix as 'that-actually' ('שבעצם') and separate it from 'you are' ('אתה'). For more complicated sentences, I allowed 'that-you-are' to simplify matters.

The act of translation here involved altering the text-generating algorithm so that output text would work in Hebrew, and so that the program's overall functioning would bear equivalence to its English counterpart. J. L. Borges made the distinction between what he called romantic and classical approaches to translation: 'One practices literalness, and the other practices paraphrase.'[11] In this sense, I translated

Hebrew Version

////me: I'm not frustrated
eliza: Why are you saying that you're **not** frustrated?
////me: I'm frustrated
eliza: You are saying that you're **actually** frustrated?

```
שלום. אני אלייזה. איך אפשר לעזור?
/////אני: אני מתוסכל
אלייזה: אתה אומר שבעצם אתה מתוסכל ?
/////אני: אני לא מתוסכל
אלייזה: מדוע אתה אומר שאתה לא מתוסכל ?
```

TABLE 3. Breaking in-word prefixes

ELIZA in something closer to the classical mentality, departing from literalness and focusing on functionality.

Moreover, while an 'ordinary' translator goes to work on a text, a chatbot translator works on the mechanism that generates a text. The chatbot translator is required not only to understand the text of the original human language, but also the data flow or the functional behavior of the software source. The translation follows the given rules as much as it follows the text.

The bot's source code can be open or closed, i.e., either available or unavailable to the translator. It can also be partially available, as was the case here. I was able to see ELIZA's configuration file of rules, but not the 'boilerplate' code behind it. In every case, a human translator has certain degrees of freedom to interpret how the translated software should work. Interpretation of the source code is prismatic: multiple translations may have similar meanings and structures, while generating programs that behave differently on particular inputs.

On top of that, a chatbot tries to provide the best matching sentence to a sentence that hasn't been written yet. It predicts possible cases, but there are necessarily a wide range of sentences that it will be unable to match properly. Tasked to handle an infinite number of sentences, a chatbot will be expected to make mistakes in understanding. Therefore, a chatbot translation reflects the set of correctly matched sentences as well as the set of mismatched sentences. Two translations might provide the same wording for matched sentences, but diverge for the mismatched ones, giving an additional dimension to the prismatic refraction. Thus, the world of bots opens a new horizon of translation, even for the simplest rule-based cases.

3. Word2Dream

3.1 Word Embeddings

J. R. Firth said that 'a word is characterized by the company it keeps.'[12] This is the motivation for many statistical algorithms that make connections between words not via linguistic rules, but rather by analyzing how words co-occur within documents or individual passages. Naturally, this approach has grown more popular in the Internet era, which provides ready access to an abundance of documents on a wide variety of topics.

It's easy to understand how such a co-occurrence matrix of words could be useful. If the words 'ball' and 'striker' co-occur frequently across documents, we can infer a lot of semantic information — that the words are related, first of all, and that the relationship probably involves sports. (Such information is deduced by pre-tagging the documents or by looking at other related words across other documents). This notion is sometimes called the Distributional Hypothesis and suggests that linguistic items with similar distributions have similar meanings.

However, implementing such a matrix can be difficult for large sets of words and documents. If a word is represented by its number of occurrences in each document, then the amount of values we have to store for each word, called the dimension of the representation, is the number of documents. If each document is represented by the occurrences of words, the dimension is the number of possible words in the corresponding lexicon.

In 2003, Bengio et al. began using Artificial Neural Networks to reduce the high dimensionality of word representations by 'learning a distributed representation for words.'[13] Their idea was to map co-occurrence vectors to simpler vectors representing meaningful features of the relevant words. The model does not apply rules, but just lets the neural network adjust itself to supplied data. Assuming that words with similar (hidden) features share similar statistical attributes in the co-occurrence representation, the model tries to reflect this behavior as a combination of the features. A perfect example is the way a color can be represented as a combination of red, green, and blue light (RGB). The neural network's challenge is to find the optimal axes that can describe the entire span of words compactly, much like every perceivable color has a corresponding RGB value.

This ongoing work shaped a research domain of Word Embedding, which refers to algorithms in Natural Language Processing (NLP) where words or phrases from a given vocabulary are mapped to vectors of real numbers. Embedding here means a transformation from a high-dimensional space (one dimension per word) to a vector space with a much lower dimension. This dimension reduction is usually achieved through the use of mathematical tools or neural networks. For an embedding to be useful, the behavior of the high-dimensional space should be preserved in the lower dimension. That is, if two words share a (predefined, mathematical) similarity in the original space, they should share an analogous similarity in the new space.

Once again, the RGB color model provides a good example. In the model, colors are represented by a sequence of three numbers, scaled between 0 and 255, each corresponding to relative proportions of red, green, and blue light. The term for a sequence of numbers like this is a vector. In this case we would say that we are dealing with RGB vectors. The space within which such vectors exist — i.e., the set of perceivable colors — is called a vector space.

The interesting thing about this representation (or translation) of colors into vectors is that the vector space is additive. What that means is this: if, in the real world, we mix red and green light, the combination will produce yellow light. The same thing happens in the vector space. Red light translates to a vector of (255,0,0) and green to a vector of (0,255,0). We can sum the two vectors by adding each component separately; the result (255,255,0) is the vector value of yellow light.

Word2Vec is a groundbreaking step toward mapping words in this manner. Much like the example above, it translates words into sequences of numbers that indicate shared characteristics, which can then be mathematically manipulated.

3.2 Word2Vec

Word2Vec was developed in 2013 by a team of Google researchers led by Tomas Mikolov. Academia initially rejected the group of models comprising the project, but it eventually gained popularity among researchers and the industry.[14] The algorithm contains some NLP preprocessing and a neural network trained to search documents for adjacent words and map them to closer vectors. The algorithm itself can be seen as a type of translation, where each word is transformed into (or re-rendered as) a vector of numbers.

The Google team used enormous amounts of data (by contemporary standards), and even released a pretrained dataset for public use. That set is 1.5GB in size includes vectors for a vocabulary of three million words and phrases that the researchers trained on about a hundred billion words from a Google News dataset. Our RGB vector example mapped individual colors to three features (relatives amounts of red, green, and blue light), whereas Word2Vec's vector comprises three hundred features.

We saw that the RGB vector was additive. Remarkably, some arithmetical rules apply to the Word2Vec vectors as well. The Google team's encoding can be understood to describe semantic relations between the words in the set.[15] For instance, if we denote the vector for word w as v, then v('Paris') — v('France') + v('Italy') will result in a numerical vector. Out of the entire dataset, the vector with the closest value is v('Rome'). This made Word2Vec a candidate for evaluating analogies. The question above can also be denoted as

$$\text{France : Paris :: Italy : ?}$$

The answer would be denoted as

$$\text{France : Paris :: Italy : Rome.}$$

Additionally, the expected behavior of the embedding holds. For instance, the closest vector to v('woman') is v('man'). However, more relations were revealed. Mikolov et al. showed that for v(word1) + v(word2), the vector with the closest value demonstrated a semantic relation to the two words. For example, v('French') + v('Actress') yielded a value closest to the vector for the phrase v('Juliette Binoche'); the next closest vector was v('Vanessa Paradis'). For v('Czech') + v('currency') the closest result was v('korona'), etc.

3.3 Word2Dream

Eyal Gruss and I built an application that utilizes Word2Vec, extending it beyond a single addition operation. The application is called Word2Dream, and it simulates an associative, meditative, or 'human' reading of a text by showing the viewer the result of the algorithm's associative thinking process. Using Word2Vec's additive compositionality, the computer conjures related words that are not part of the original input text, and then proceeds to bring up associations related to the new layer of words, and so on. This creates a computer-based imaginary train of thought — or possibly, a computer's dream. The project was motivated by Google's Deep Dream project, a program that finds patterns in images and enhances them through deliberate over-processing, creating dreamlike, hallucinogenic effects.[16] In our project, however, the subconscious manifests through text rather than images.

In Word2Dream the input is a text in English. While an algorithmic process maps each word to a vector behind the scenes, the user sees the text translated into a stream of artificial consciousness. In the initial iteration, the algorithm goes over each pair of distinct words in the given text and computes their vector sum, the closest word to that sum in the Google News corpus, and the proximity of the found word to the sum. Out of those found words, it then selects the N (default = 5) words closest to the original text and repeats the process for all the found words. Having completed two iterations, the algorithm will have $2N$ words, and if $2N \geq M$, it will calculate the next N closest words using only the $2N$ words, slowly drifting away from the original text.

For example, providing Martin Luther King Jr.'s 'I Have a Dream' speech as an input would begin by analyzing keywords within the text, generating the following result: 'Dream, Day, One, Live, Sons.' The first iteration then identifies five words that are outside the text but close to it vector-wise: 'Repression, Enslaved, Foothills, Subjugation, Tyranny.' From then on, the algorithm drifts from those words. The next iteration, for instance, is 'Dehumanization, Imperialism, Despotism, Servitude, Totalitarianism.'

The translational procedures used in Word2Dream accentuate the relation between semantics and statistics, as they reveal the associations that emerge prismatically from any given text within a corpus. A text is more than just the words that comprise it; it is also the entire context in which they reside. It is possible to translate a word not just into a single word in the destination language, but rather to a 'neighborhood' of words, determined by a certain distance from the vector, or by the N closest words to the result.

> I have a dream that one day this nation will rise up and live out the true meaning of its creed: "We hold these truths to be self-evident, that all men are created equal."
>
> I have a dream that one day on the red hills of Georgia, the sons of former slaves and the sons of former slave owners will be able to sit down together at the table of brotherhood.
>
> I have a dream that one day even the state of Mississippi, a state sweltering with the heat of injustice, sweltering with the heat of oppression, will be transformed into an oasis of freedom and justice.
>
> I have a dream that my four little children will one day live in a nation where they will not be judged by the color of their skin but by the content of their character.
>
> I have a dream today!
>
> I have a dream that one day, down in Alabama, with its vicious racists, with its governor having his lips dripping with the words of "interposition" and "nullification" -- one day right there in Alabama little black boys and black girls will be able to join hands with little white boys and white girls as sisters and brothers.
>
> I have a dream today!

> facism
> monarchism
> sexists zionism
> feminazis
> homophobes

FIG. 13.1. Word2Dream for excerpts from Martin Luther King Jr's speech

3.4 Word2Dream and Biased Data

'Word embedding' is the umbrella term for mapping words into vectors, and Word2Vec was the project that made the technique widely known. Word2Vec's creators have shown that word embeddings can also be utilized for Machine Translation. While working on the Google Translate project, the Mikolov team decided to test the hypothesis that visual maps of vectors would look similar for different languages. And indeed, for some cases, the analogies and additive compositionality that we saw before hold up between different languages. This enabled them to track errors and missing words in certain dictionaries.

The authors point out that the Word2Vec model does feature some linguistic pitfalls, presented by things like synonyms or idiomatic phrases . Another problem arises even when the model appears to be working as expected. It occurs as texts shift in associative manners among various topics and semantic fields. That associative activity is generally legitimate, since human thinking tends to generalize and abstract, but the results can be quite jarring. An example, shown in Figure 1, comes from using Martin Luther King Jr.'s 'I Have a Dream' speech as an input in Word2Dream. The first output iteration include the words 'Zionism' and 'Fascism'; after a several more iterations, however, the program generates the word 'Feminazis.'

In other words, Word2Vec preserves and perpetuates biases that exist in the texts comprising its corpus (i.e., Google News). If Google has captured male-chauvinistic texts from the 1950s, for instance, they would affect Machine Learning algorithms in the 2010s and beyond, because each Big Data algorithm in the future will rely on data from the past. An example from Word2Vec that went viral was the following analogy:

Man : Doctor :: Woman : ?

The result, unsurprisingly, was 'Nurse.' On the one hand that seems to demonstrate the algorithm working flawlessly, but on the other it was obviously undesirable. Such results suggest that algorithms should not simply function, but also address biases in their source data. Whether and to what extent that task is feasible seems to be an open question.

3.5 Translation of Word2Vec

For me, one interesting question was whether a translation of the entire Word2Vec model to Hebrew should preserve the original model's biases. Before I could get an answer, I first had to obtain the data used in the English version, that is the Google News corpus. Data from commercial resources is not always available for researchers, particularly independent ones. When a company like Google does release data, one can assume it will have been pre-processed for that particular company's purposes. Even open-source algorithms lack a certain degree of freedom without free and open data.

When I worked to translate Word2Vec, the only solution I found was to use Hebrew Wikipedia as my corpus. My acid test was to input v('Paris') — v('France') + v('Italy') and have the working model reach v('Rome') as the closest result. It did, and was able to reproduce other classic examples.

When the model was fed the Man : Doctor :: Woman : ? analogy, the result did not translate the bias of the English version, as shown in Table 4. This is the result of complex Hebrew morphology that allows in-word prefixes; in this case the model combined the word 'and' with the word 'doctor' to give the result 'And Doctor,' which is unbiased. Therefore, I tested the other direction of the analogy, Nurse : Woman :: Man : ?, and once again the result diverged from the English version. This time, the result was 'Doctor,' which might seem to indicate the original bias. However, the Hebrew version of the word was feminine, essentially 'Female Doctor,' which does not reproduce the bias.

> Man : Doctor :: Woman : 'And Doctor'
> גבר : רופא :: אישה : ורופא
> Woman : Nurse :: Man : 'Female Doctor'
> אישה : אחות :: גבר : רופאה

TABLE 4. Word2Vec gender bias does not translate from English to Hebrew

Next I decided to explore a more domestic Israeli-Hebrew topic, which is the fragile relationship between Ashkenazi and Mizrahi (sometimes referred to as Sephardic) Jews, especially when it comes to poetry. A long and loud debate has accused Ashkenazi poets of being too intellectual on the one side and Mizrahi ones as being too emotional on the other. Results from the model, shown in Table 5, give only a mild hint of these prejudices.

> Ashkenazi : Poet :: Mizrahi : 'And Playwright'
> אשכנזי : משורר :: מזרחי : ומחזאי
> Mizrahi : Poet :: Ashkenazi : 'And Essayist'
> מזרחי : משורר :: אשכנזי : ומסאי

TABLE 5. Word2Vec Jewish Israeli ethnicity results

While a particular prejudice regarding doctors and nurses is mitigated in Hebrew, a different one about Ashkenazis and Mizrahis emerges. From this perspective, a translation that tries to express a cultural phenomenon across languages may be unable to preserve inherent biases. An alternative approach may be to find a separate phenomenon that shares the biased approach of the original.

4. Alert: Translate! — An Executable Poem

4.1 Human Languages in Computer Languages

Finnish poet Leevi Lehto has joked that English is not the dominant language on the planet. For him, the true lingua franca is English spoken as a second language. Most speakers in the world have transformed English into something else. Still, it is obvious that English remains prevalent in both the physical world and the virtual world of the Internet.

This dominance was highlighted by a major event in Internet history that occurred on January 18, 2012. Protests against two proposed laws in the United States Congress led many American sites to disable themselves in protest for a day, including Wikipedia (in English).[17] While it dealt with domestic issues inside the United States, the Wikipedia blackout affected all English speakers across the world, as Wikipedia is divided by languages and not by countries. People in New Zealand, for instance, were denied access to the site, even though they had nothing to do with the American legislation. Such a side-effect exemplifies how on the Internet a person's daily routine can be influenced by their language more than by their nationality.

The debate that followed the blackout led Lebanese-born artist Ramsey Nasser to question a similar phenomenon regarding software engineering and programming languages in particular. Programming languages are artificial, but their commands, functions, and operators often come from human languages. However, for most programming languages — and, as a matter of fact, for all popular ones — the vocabulary consists of English words. JavaScript, the language that runs on every web browser, is written in English. This means that any developer who cannot read English is incapable of web development.

In 2012, Nasser designed and built the programming language قلب, or Qlb, (pronounced 'qalb' and meaning 'heart' in Arabic). The language is comprised entirely of Arabic, highlighting computer science's cultural biases and challenging the assumptions we make about programming.[18] While the project became popular, insufficient support for Arabic (and other non-English languages, for that matter) in many Content Management Systems left Qlb impressive as a work of art, but useless for web development. Reflecting on the design bias that favors English alone in software engineering, Nasser commented, 'If [Qlb] could exist, it would make people's lives so much easier, but rewriting the last 50 years of software engineering isn't on the table.'

4.2 Alert: Translate

On the day I ordered my ticket to the Oxford Comparative Criticism and Translation conference on prismatic translation, I decided to spend a couple of months creating an executable poem in Hebrew. This meant writing something that would look like a poem in Hebrew, but would also function as a JavaScript program (in English), executable within a browser. I decided to translate one of the most basic JavaScript programs from English to Hebrew, the one-liner

> alert('translate');

which opens an alert box with the message 'translate.' Translating the word 'translate' into Hebrew would be easy, yielding the following program:

> alert ('תרגמו');

However, I also wanted to translate the code, i.e., the 'alert' part, which can only be interpreted by the browser as-is.

Ultimately, I was able to create the poem in Hebrew and have it run on modern browsers, using a technique that many would consider hacking. To execute it, open a console window in a web browser (in Google Chrome, click the Options button and then select More Tools → Developer Tools, and click on the Console tab), copy and paste the poem (See Table 6), and hit Enter. Running the poem will open an alert box reading 'תרגמו.' Below is a short description of the process I used to write it.

Research led me to certain websites, which I will refrain from citing. These in turn led me to the work of Martin Kleppe. Kleppe designed a programming language, titled JSFuck,[19] within the larger programming language of JavaScript. JSFuck is therefore a subset of JavaScript, but it can still do everything that its parent language can. It uses only six characters, none of which are in English (or any other human language). They are: ( ) [ ] + !

While JSFuck is a self-declared 'esoteric and educational' language, it has two major practical uses in the Internet's commercial environment:

> 1. Obfuscation. It is a 'write-only' language, meaning it is very hard for humans to understand, and therefore discourages people from modifying code or appropriating parts of it.

> 2. Security. Many systems defend themselves by identifying potentially malicious code based on the presence of certain English command words. This strategy is not recommended, since it is easy to get around — for instance, by using code that avoids English words . If a system flags the word 'javascript' as suspicious, an attacker could use '&#0000106&#0000097&#0000118&#0000097&#0000115&#0000099&#0000114&#0000105&#0000112&#0000116'; it means the same thing to a browser.

While JSFuck did not provide me with an out-of-the-box solution, its implementation principles did allow me to deconstruct the binary opposition of programming language vs. human language.

My implementation is based on the fact that JavaScript is not imperative but rather functional, in the sense that it treats every text input as an expression. Figure

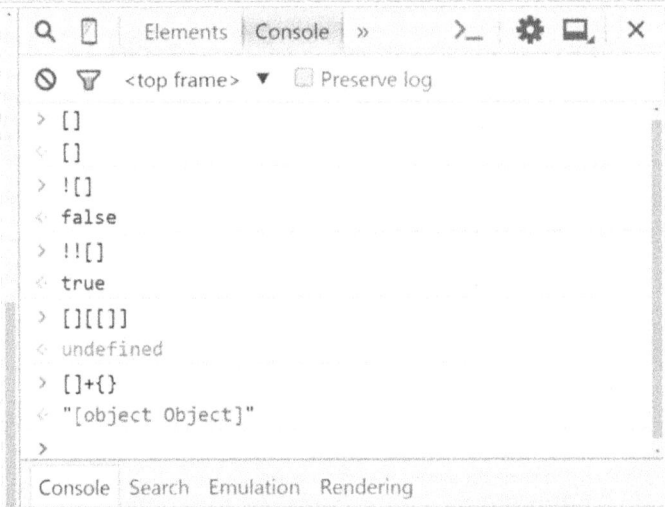

Fig. 13.2. Using four basic expressions to generate meaningful values and contexts

13.2 shows user inputs preceded by arrows pointing to the right, with responses preceded by arrows pointing to the left. The sequence here reveals Javascript trying to give context to symbols even when they are meaningless. For example, it evaluates the expression '![]' to 'false,' meaning it thinks of it in a Boolean (true/false) context. This result shows that the interpretation accepts not only meaningful content, but also non-informative combinations of characters, which correspond to phatic communication by humans. By using the same technique, non-informative characters generate the words 'true,' 'object.' and 'undefined,' in addition to 'false'.

Other manipulations make it possible to extract letters from output words and use them in subsequent code. (See Figure 3 for a technical demonstration of these methods.) The word 'alert,' for instance, can be constructed by combining the 'a' and 'l' from our output 'false', along with the 'e,' 'r,' and 't' from 'true'. Similarly, but in much more technical detail, the last line in Figure 4 is an expression that would execute the required program **alert('translate');**.

In conclusion, by taking advantage of JavaScript's human-language-like traits, we can build a functioning program without English. Letters from any language can substitute the non-alphabetical characters in Figures 2 and 3. This method treats any letters or symbols as signifiers of (or placeholders for) the code, rather than signified parts of it.

The poem I arrived at, shown in Table 6, uses Hebrew only to represent non-alphabetical characters; behind the scenes it is a program without any letters. While letter selection is of course meaningful in terms of the generated poem, it is arbitrary from the perspective of the software. Therefore, in an Oulipo-like constraint, any letter can be replaced by any other (unique) letter, as long as all instances are replaced. Multiple translations (or poems) are possible in any human language. This allows for truly prismatic, constraint-based translation.

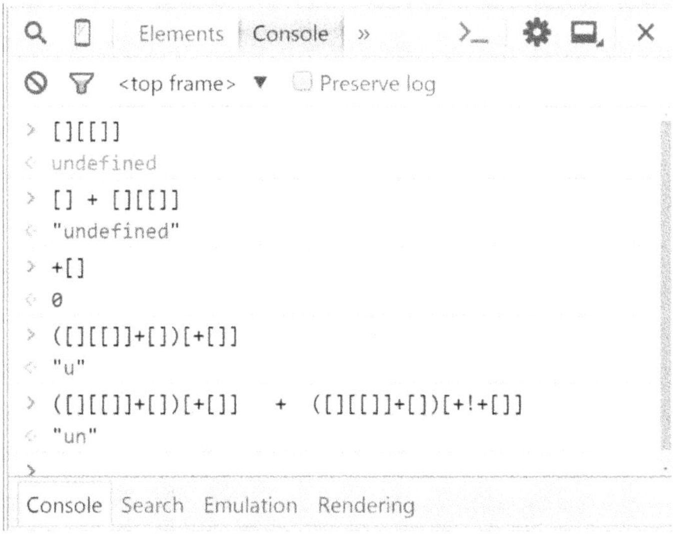

Algorithmic Translation

```
Q  []    Elements | Console | »         >_  ⚙ ▭, ×
⊘ ▽   <top frame> ▼  ☐ Preserve log
> [][[]]
< undefined
> [] + [][[]]
< "undefined"
> +[]
< 0
> ([][[]]+[])[+[]]
< "u"
> ([][[]]+[])[+[]] + ([][[]]+[])[+!+[]]
< "un"
>
Console  Search  Emulation  Rendering
```

FIG. 13.3. Extracting the two first characters from an expression result

FIG. 13.4. Using four basic expressions to generate the required characters

English Translation

//Said the software to the language
Proofing
Out of Error
Fabricates
Presents what has been wrapped
Around its leg
In a roar of disease

Yet pride and its hook are
The cover of your leg
The Ode to your hubris

I will change
So that you will completely translate

Hebrew Version (extra non-alphabetical characters are omitted)

עברית:
אמרה התוכנה לשפה

הגהה
מתוך משגה
בודה
מציגה את שנכרך
ברגלה
בשאגת מחלה

אולם גאוה וווה
והלל יוהרתך
שמיכת רגלך

אשתנה
שלגמרי תתרגמו

Hebrew Code Version

אמרה התוכנה לשפה//
ה,"=ג!=ה+ה,
מ,=ת=ו=ד]=" ,מ!=ש=ג+ה,
+ב=ד=ו=ה,
"=מ=צ=י=ג]ה]++[,א=ת"= ,ש=נ=כ=ר=ך
[,ב=ר=ג]ל=ה,
ב,=ש=א!=ג+ת, מ=ח=+=ל+ה
+[א=ו]ל+מ], ג=א[=ו]ה],(+]ו.ו+ ו[)ה
+ש[מ]+י=כ+ת +ר=ג=נ]ל]+ך
] ו]ה + ל + ל]+ י+ו]ה]+ ר+ת+ך
+[א]]ש((+ת+נ)[ה]
()'(=ש[)ל[+ג]מ]+ר+י+ +ת+)'תרגמו

TABLE 6. Alert:Translate!

Alert: Translate — Eran Hadas

2014, built for the Oxford Comparative Criticism and Translation conference on prismatic translation. (The Hebrew code version of this poem is executable — that is, one can copy the text, paste it into the console pane of a modern browser, and click Enter. An alert box should then open with the message 'Translate.')

This project demonstrates that there is more than one way to translate source code between languages. It highlights the programming world's biases against speakers of unprivileged languages, as well as some prejudices we humans have regarding machines and their languages. It is a humanistic gesture to a scientific tradition developed by Richard Montague who said, 'There is in my opinion no important theoretical difference between natural languages and the artificial languages of logicians; indeed, I consider it possible to comprehend the syntax and semantics of both kinds of languages within a single natural and mathematically precise theory.'[20] This theory has been developed by others, following Jerry Hobbs's work,[21] which has inspired generations of researchers and poets. In the future, similar infrastructures of translation may challenge English-language hegemony. For now, the technique exposes biases and allows us to manipulate language in ways that might never have occurred to us.

5. Code — Re-rendering the Torah in Haiku Form

Code is a book I created by developing a computer program that revealed all the haiku poems hidden in the Hebrew Pentateuch, or Torah. These are the five books of Moses which provide the foundation of the Jewish holy law and behavioral code of conduct.

Haiku is a form of Japanese poetry, characterized by syllabic and thematic constraints. A haiku consists of three lines of 5, 7, and 5 syllables, respectively. I realized that the most famous Jewish prayer begins with a haiku; Table 7 shows a passage from Deuteronomy 6:4–9, which encapsulates the monotheistic essence of Judaism:

Transliteration	*She'ma Yis'ra'eil* *A'do'nai E'lo'hei'nu* *A'do'nai e'chad.*
Translation	Hear, O Israel: the LORD is our God, the LORD is One.
Hebrew Version	שְׁמַע יִשְׂרָאֵל יְהוָה אֱלֹהֵינוּ יְהוָה אֶחָד

TABLE 7. The She'ma opening verse

This motivated me to write a program that would count the syllables of each and every word in the Torah, and then output all the passages forming a valid 5–7–5 haiku structure. (Individual words were not allowed to cross line breaks.) I hoped to discover whether only the well-known She'ma verse carries the supposedly universal rhythm, or if there is a case to be made that the entire Torah fits that musicality. However, as soon as I started to build the proof-of-concept code, I realized that most of the Torah does not conform to any constant rhythm.

Another linguistic phenomenon stood out. Within the Israeli education system it is often claimed that children, excluding orthodox Jews, cannot read the biblical Hebrew language, and therefore have lost contact with the 'world of Torah.'[22] My efforts to re-render the text in short verse, allowing for repetitions and breaking the original Biblical sentence structure, left it somewhat closer to modern (Israeli) Hebrew. It essentially filtered out the 'difficult' parts for the reader of modern Hebrew.

An in-depth linguistic analysis of that phenomenon is beyond the scope of this paper. In a nutshell, though, modern Hebrew sentences usually begin with a noun, whereas Biblical ones mostly begin with a verb, in the form of waw-consecutive constructions that do not exist in modern Hebrew.[23] A waw-construction is a verb prefixed with the letter waw, and it is often used to change the verb tense from past to future or from future to past.

Due to the extra syllable added by the waw, my haiku operator filters out many sentences describing one figure addressing another (or God addressing a person). For instance, the phrase 'וַיְדַבֵּר אֱלֹהִים' (And God spoke) is six syllables long, so it cannot start a haiku without breaking words. Other sentences feature an 'extra' waw as a prefix, and the syllable constraint effectively shortens these and forces them into a more descriptive format.

Table 8 shows the earliest haiku identified, from Genesis 1:2. It demonstrates how the constraint filters out both the structure of prefixing waws and the use of alliteration. In this case 'תֹהוּ וָבֹהוּ', translated as 'without form and void' but literally meaning 'to be wondering and to be staring' disappear, leaving only the part starting with '*tehom*,' translated as 'darkness' but literally meaning 'abyss.'

English Translation	Abyss and spirit God she is floating upon The face of waters
Hebrew	תְהוֹם וְרוּחַ אֱלֹהִים מְרַחֶפֶת עַל־פְּנֵי הַמָּיִם
King James Version	And the earth was without form, and void; and darkness was upon the face of the deep. And the Spirit of God moved upon the face of the waters.
Original Verse	וְהָאָרֶץ, הָיְתָה תֹהוּ וָבֹהוּ, וְחֹשֶׁךְ, עַל־פְּנֵי תְהוֹם; וְרוּחַ אֱלֹהִים, מְרַחֶפֶת עַל־פְּנֵי הַמָּיִם

TABLE 8. First haiku identified, from Genesis 1:2

I did not modify or cherry-pick the program's results. A lot of the Haikus are sheer nonsense, but I included them anyway. However, I did repeatedly calibrate the algorithm within the degrees of freedom it allowed. In this case, I manipulated the algorithm parameters until it produced the above verse as the first one in the book, because of the presentation of God as a female. The main configurable feature was the pronunciation of the Hebrew niqqud (vowel sign) *shva* (or in Biblical Hebrew, *shewa*). In certain Biblical instances referred to as *shva na*, the proper pronunciation is believed to be a short 'eh' sound of one syllable. In modern Hebrew, however, some cases of *shva na* are pronounced that way, while others are silent, meaning they use no syllables. For my translation, I could interpret all appearances of *shva na* individually, or apply a strict logic to the algorithm . My choice was to adhere to the colloquial pronunciations that my wife and I use for the various <u>shvas</u>. The source code specifies these rules so that each *shva* is pronounced consistently for each instance of a given word.

Table 9 shows another example of how little space the waw-consecutive construction leaves for haiku. This one is taken from the story of the binding of Isaac. It depicts a conversation between the boy, who thinks he is about to be sacrificed, and his father. Three instances of the word '*Vayomer*' ('he said') occupy three syllables each, allowing only a very compact, Zen-like conversation to take place in the rest of the poem.

English	He said: My father
	He said: Here am I my son
	He said: There it is
Transliteration	*Va'yo'mer A'vi*
	Va'yo'mer hi'nen'ni vni
	Va'yo'mer hi'ne
Hebrew	וַיֹּאמֶר אָבִי
	וַיֹּאמֶר, הִנֶּנִּי בְנִי
	וַיֹּאמֶר, הִנֵּה

King James Version

And Isaac spake unto Abraham his father, and said, My father: and he said, Here am I, my son. And he said, Behold the fire and the wood: but where is the lamb for a burnt offering?

Original Verse

וַיֹּאמֶר יִצְחָק אֶל־אַבְרָהָם אָבִיו וַיֹּאמֶר אָבִי וַיֹּאמֶר הִנֶּנִּי בְנִי; וַיֹּאמֶר הִנֵּה הָאֵשׁ וְהָעֵצִים וְאַיֵּה הַשֶּׂה לְעֹלָה

TABLE 9. Haiku in the binding of Isaac

Table 10 shows an example where the haiku does not simply benefit from the foundations of the story or make use of the reader's prior knowledge of the original text. This poem deconstructs the original text by offering an alternative, in this case opposite, interpretation.

Biblical	Egypt, Israel Beheld the Egyptians Die on the seashore
Modern	Egypt, Israel Beheld the Egyptians Mad about the beach
Hebrew	מִצְרַיִם וַיַּרְא יִשְׂרָאֵל אֶת מִצְרַיִם מֵת עַל שְׂפַת הַיָּם
Original Verse	וַיּוֹשַׁע יְהֹוָה בַּיּוֹם הַהוּא אֶת־יִשְׂרָאֵל מִיַּד מִצְרָיִם וַיַּרְא יִשְׂרָאֵל אֶת־מִצְרַיִם מֵת עַל־שְׂפַת הַיָּם
King James Version	That day the Lord saved Israel from the hands of the Egyptians, and Israel saw the Egyptians lying dead on the shore.

TABLE 10. Biblical and Modern Hebrew interpretations of haiku, from Exodus 14:30

Code subjects a preexisting text to radical reduction. New patterns emerge that challenge the original text. The book's parasitic method enables the new text to either retain or contradict the linguistic aspects of the parent text. Modern Hebrew lets Biblical Hebrew sneak a peek, albeit a subverted one.

Programming a book to be re-rendered may be seen as an extension of methods attributed to modernism. It posits canonized words within a well-defined formal frame. The creative act may recall stances taken by Ezra Pound or Louis Zukofsky. However, the technique of writing one text by way of reading another resembles postmodern approaches such as John Cage's 'Writing Through (Pound…)'. What makes this project different from those precedents is the code itself. Rather than being modern or postmodern, it is indigenous to the Digital Age.

The skills that created it are those of a computer programmer rather than a traditional writer. A book of 5,341 poems resulted from coding less than 10 pages of words and UNICODE signs. *Code* suggests that human behavior is no longer dictated by traditional religion but by technological determinism. This new state of affairs threatens us as much as it redraws our horizons.

6. Conclusion

These projects show some ways that the contemporary technological environment opens a path to creative translation methods. In the presence of algorithms, it is possible to translate more than mere texts.

The first two examples, reproducing the chatbot ELIZA and utilizing Word Embedding in Word2Dream, show that digital translations must work differently from paper ones. Translation here works not on the text itself, but rather on the structures and mechanisms that give rise to it. This complex situation creates prismatic results. In a way such translation operates in a 3-dimensional environment rather than a 2-dimensional one.

Both projects involve predictions. A chatbot cannot know what inputs it will receive from the user. Navigating a statistical model depends on its source corpus, user inputs, and the contexts in which words appear. Moreover, Word2Dream is time based, and the longer it runs, the further its results drift from the original input, broadening the prismatic refraction.

The other two projects, *Code* and Alert:Translate, involve creative writing acts that are based on translation procedures. Each adheres to a strict path on the way to potential multiplicity. *Code* is a rereading of a text, based on counting and pronunciation, where the parameters are arbitrary and can be reconfigured to generate other readings. Alert:Translate reverses the roles of human and programming languages, generating potentially infinite human representations from machine code.

Both projects bear similarity to Oulipo's procedural constraints. However, the use of programming tools enhances the capabilities of a creative translator in unique ways. To manually extract the specific structures of a project like *Code* could be practically impossible or at least take years to complete. However, with software it becomes a feasible task. In Alert:Translate, the act of translation shifts from the page to the screen, since it is a translation of an executable program, and hence lives outside the page. This allows the translation to break the limit of the page and generate multiple translations, as shown before.

Future works in this area could include the translation of entire software systems, algorithms, and other software-made entities, whose unique 'identities' and 'characters' must be taken into consideration. In general, translation is a tool that reveals knowledge about the nature of our society and its linguistic infrastructure. It provides new ways to bridge cultures, and can expose (and possibly fix) biases. It can bring less-privileged cultures closer to equality. New algorithmic translation techniques can reshape these already powerful tools, resolving technical issues and freeing translators to deal with core concepts. Algorithmic translation provides tools for translators to produce and explore various angles of texts. It enables multiple prisms.

Works Cited

AGASSI, J., and J. WEIZENBAUM, 'Computer Power and Human Reason: From Judgment to Calculation', *Technology and Culture*, 17. 4 (1976), 813. DOI: 10.2307/3103715

AVIDAN, D., *My Electronic Psychiatrist: Eight Authentic Talks with a Computer* (Tel-Aviv: E. Lewin-Epstein-Modan, 1974)

AVITAN COHEN, S. 'Bible Studies: The Secular Sector Loses the Book of Books', *nrg.co.il*. Makor Rishon (2016). Retrieved September 9, 2017, from <http://www.nrg.co.il/online/1/ART2/751/288.html>

BAKARDJIEVA, M., and R. W. GEHL, *Socialbots and Their Friends: Digital Media and the Automation of Sociality* (London: Routledge, 2016). Retrieved September 8, 2017, from <https://www.routledge.com/Socialbots-and-Their-Friends-Digital-Media-and-the-Automation-of-Sociality/Gehl-Bakardjieva/p/book/9781138639409>

BENGIO, Y., H. SCHWENK, J.-S. SENÉCAL, F. MORIN, and J.-L. GAUVAIN, 'Neural Probabilistic Language Models', *Innovations in Machine Learning Studies in Fuzziness and Soft Computing*, 194, 137–86 (2006). DOI: 10.1007/10985687_6

BERRY, GEORGE RICKER, 'Waw Consecutive with the Perfect in Hebrew', *Journal of Biblical Literature*, 22. 1 (1903), 60–69. DOI: 10.2307/3268935

DESCARTES, RENÉ, *Discourse on the Method and Meditations on First Philosophy*, ed. David Weissman (New Haven: Yale University Press, 1996)

WAISMAN, SERGIO GABRIEL, *Borges and Translation: The Irreverence of the Periphery* (Lewisburg, PA: Bucknell University Press, 2005)

MIKOLOV, T., K. CHEN, G. CORRADO, and J. DEAN, 'Efficient Estimation of Word Representations in Vector Space' CoRR abs/1301.3781 (2013)

MIKOLOV, T., I. SUTSKEVER, K. CHEN, G. S. CORRADO, and J. DEAN, 'Distributed Representations of Words and Phrases and their Compositionality', *Advances in Neural Information Processing Systems* (2013), 3111–19

FIRTH, J. R.M *Selected Papers of J R Firth 1952–1959*, ed. by F. R. Palmer (London: Longmans, 1968)

GÜZELDERE, GÜVEN and STEFANO FRANCHI, 'dialogues with colorful personalities of early ai' (n.d.). *colorful personalities* (1995). Retrieved September 8, 2017, from <https://www.stanford.edu/group/SHR/4-2/text/dialogues.html>

HOBBS, J. R., and S. J. ROSENSCHEIN, 'Making Computational Sense of Montagues Intensional Logic', *Artificial Intelligence*, 9. 3 (1977), 287–306. DOI: <10.1016/0004-3702(77)90025-x>

KLEPPE, M., 'JSFuck', *JSFuck — Write any JavaScript with 6 Characters: []()!*. (2013), retrieved September 9, 2017, from <http://www.jsfuck.com/>

MASORTI EUROPE, '[ET] — The Most Common Word in the Hebrew Language', *My Hebrew Word*. <https://myhebrewwords.wordpress.com/2014/03/07/1-את-et-the-most-common-word-in-the-hebrew-language>, accessed 20th February, 2019

MONTAGUE, RICHARD, *Formal Philosophy: Selected Papers of Richard Montague*, ed. by Richmond H. Thomason (Ann Arbor, Mich: University Microfilms, 1995)

MOR, G., 'The Intelligence of Avidan and Artificial ELIZA', *ynet*. (YNET, 2001). Retrieved September 8, 2017, from <http://www.ynet.co.il/articles/1,7340,L-861571,00.html>

MORDVINTSEV, A., C. OLAH, and M. TYKA, 'DeepDream — a Code Example for Visualizing Neural Networks', *Google Research* (2015). Archived from the original on 8th July, 2015. <https://web.archive.org/web/20150708233542/http://googleresearch.blogspot.co.uk/2015/07/deepdream-code-example-for-visualizing.html>

Protests against SOPA and PIPA, *Wikipedia*, Wikimedia Foundation. Retrieved September 9, 2017, from <https://en.wikipedia.org/wiki/Protests_against_SOPA_and_PIPA#Wikimedia_community>

SMITH IV, J., 'Meet the Genius Who Created the First Fully Functioning Arabic Programming Language', *Mic*, Mic Network Inc. (2015). Retrieved September 9, 2017, from <http://mic.com/articles/130331/this-arabic-programming-language-shows-how-computers-revolve-around-the-western-world>

TURING, A. M., 'I. — Computing Machinery And Intelligence', *Mind*, 59. 236 (1950), 433–60. DOI: 10.1093/mind/lix.236.433

WEIZENBAUM, J., 'Symmetric list processor', *Communications of the ACM*, 6. 9 (1963), 524–36. DOI: 10.1145/367593.367617

Notes to Chapter 13

1. A. M. Turing, 'I. — Computing Machinery And Intelligence', *Mind*, 59. 236 (1950): 433–60. DOI: 10.1093/mind/lix.236.433

2. J. Weizenbaum, 'Symmetric list processor', *Communications of the ACM*, 6/9 (1963): 524–36. DOI: 10.1145/367593.367617
3. J. Agassi and J. Weizenbaum, 'Computer Power and Human Reason: From Judgment to Calculation', *Technology and Culture*, 17/4 (1976): 813. DOI: 10.2307/3103715
4. Ibid.
5. Güven Güzeldere and Stefano Franchi, 'dialogues with colorful personalities of early ai.' (n.d.), *colorful personalities* (1995). Retrieved September 8, 2017, from <https://www.stanford.edu/group/SHR/4-2/text/dialogues.html>
6. René Descartes, *Discourse on the Method and Meditations on First Philosophy*, ed. David Weissman (New Haven: Yale University Press, 1996).
7. R. W. Gehl and M. Bakardjieva, *Socialbots and Their Friends: Digital Media and the Automation of Sociality* (London: Routledge, 2016). Retrieved September 8, 2017, from <https://www.routledge.com/Socialbots-and-Their-Friends-Digital-Media-and-the-Automation-of-Sociality/Gehl-Bakardjieva/p/book/9781138639409>
8. D. Avidan, *My Electronic Psychiatrist: Eight Authentic Talks with a Computer* (Tel-Aviv: E. Lewin-Epstein-Modan, 1974).
9. G. Mor, 'The Intelligence of Avidan and Artificial ELIZA', *ynet*. (YNET, 2001). Retrieved September 8, 2017, from <http://www.ynet.co.il/articles/1,7340,L-861571,00.html>
10. Masorti Europe, '[Et] — The Most common Word in the Hebrew Language' (2014), *My Hebrew Word*. Retrieved September 8, 2017, from <https://myhebrewwords.wordpress.com/2014/03/07/1-%D7%90%D7%AA-et-the-most-common-word-in-the-hebrew-language/>
11. Quoted in Waisman, Sergio Gabriel, *Borges and Translation: The Irreverence of the Periphery* (Lewisburg, PA: Bucknell University Press, 2005), p. 46.
12. J. R. Firth, *Selected Papers of J R Firth 1952–1959*, ed. by F. R. Palmer (London: Longmans, 1968).
13. Y Bengio, H. Schwenk, J-S. Senécal, F. Morin, and J.-L. Gauvain, 'Neural Probabilistic Language Models', *Innovations in Machine Learning Studies in Fuzziness and Soft Computing*, 194, 137–86 (2006). DOI: 10.1007/10985687_6
14. T. Mikolov, K. Chen, G. Corrado, G., and J. Dean, 'Efficient Estimation of Word Representations in Vector Space' CoRR abs/1301.3781 (2013).
15. T. Mikolov, I. Sutskever, K. Chen, G. S. Corrado, and J. Dean, 'Distributed Representations of Words and Phrases and their Compositionality', *Advances in Neural Information Processing Systems* (2013), 3111–19.
16. A. Mordvintsev, C. Olah, and M. Tyka, 'DeepDream — a Code Example for Visualizing Neural Networks', *Google Research* (2015). Archived from the original on 2015-07-08, <https://web.archive.org/web/20150708233542/http://googleresearch.blogspot.co.uk/2015/07/deepdream-code-example-for-visualizing.html>
17. Protests against SOPA and PIPA, *Wikipedia*, Wikimedia Foundation. Retrieved September 9, 2017, from <https://en.wikipedia.org/wiki/Protests_against_SOPA_and_PIPA#Wikimedia_community>
18. Smith IV, J., 'Meet the Genius Who Created the First Fully Functioning Arabic Programming Language', *Mic*, Mic Network Inc. (2015). Retrieved September 9, 2017, from <http://mic.com/articles/130331/this-arabic-programming-language-shows-how-computers-revolve-around-the-western-world>
19. M. Kleppe, 'JSFuck', *JSFuck — Write any JavaScript with 6 Characters: []()!* . (2013). Retrieved September 9, 2017, from http://www.jsfuck.com/ .
20. Richard Montague, *Formal Philosophy: Selected Papers of Richard Montague*, ed. by Richmond H. Thomason (Ann Arbor, Mich: University Microfilms, 1995).
21. J. R. Hobbs and S. J. Rosenschein, 'Making Computational Sense of Montagues Intensional Logic', *Artificial Intelligence*, 9. 3 (1977), 287–306. DOI: 10.1016/0004-3702(77)90025-x
22. S. Avitan Cohen, 'Bible Studies: The Secular Sector Loses the Book of Books', *nrg.co.il*. Makor Rishon (2016). Retrieved September 9, 2017, from <http://www.nrg.co.il/online/1/ART2/751/288.html>
23. George Ricker Berry, 'Waw Consecutive with the Perfect in Hebrew', *Journal of Biblical Literature*, 22. 1 (1903), 60–69. DOI: 10.2307/3268935

CHAPTER 14

Du Bellay in the Modern University

Philip Terry

Today universities in Britain face a crisis, a crisis that is starkly visible in the humanities, where values such as public service and humanism collide with neoliberal business models and McKinseyist doctrines holding that only those things which can be measured have value. Urizen has arrived on campus, and the culture of slippers and arm patches and scholarship now finds itself at war with the culture of targets and spreadsheets and transferrable skills. In translating Du Bellay's sonnets of administrative grief *Les Regrets* (1558), written while he was working in the employ of a French cardinal-diplomat in Rome, and relocating them to the University of Essex, where in August 2014 I began my own administrative role as Head of the Department of Literature, Film, and Theatre Studies, I hope not only to have captured something of the contemporary explosion of bureaucracy as it hits the university sector, but also to have represented the conflicts that are now encountered in universities over the land.[1] As such, these poems form part of the larger collective work of thinking through the contradictions which currently manifest themselves in the Higher Education sector in the UK, such as championing human rights in an environment where the rights of staff are being eroded, and introducing business models based on paradigms of conflict and exploitation of labour into institutions that are in essence charities, and where students are taught about how to resolve conflict rather than create it. Such doctrines themselves seek to invisibly translate our world: a 'passenger' on a plane or a 'student' in a seminar both become 'customers'. In the spirit of carnival, closely following Du Bellay, official doctrines and truisms and rules of decorum are here turned upside-down and inside-out. As sonnet 139 puts it, a sonnet that is in many ways a *mise-en-abyme* of the whole sequence:

> In honour of twenty years of Italian exchanges,
> And five years of the International Academy,
> In order to enhance the student experience
> Essex is holding its inaugural Carnival,
> Where Vice-Chancellors may be laughed at, yet remain amiable.

As well as representing HE in a time of crisis, these poems, first and foremost, are translations. Back in the fourteenth century, as Matthew Reynolds notes in *The Poetry of Translation* (2011), we find in the Wycliffite Bible that Solomon 'translatide' Pharoah's daughter from the city of David to the house he had prepared for her.[2] One of the earliest recorded meanings of the word 'translate', then, is to shift places, and in shifting Du Bellay's action from Rome to Essex, these poems pay homage to this now forgotten sense of the word, and they are able to take advantage of the Roman ruins of Colchester to translate Du Bellay's meditations on the ruins of Rome more or less intact, if refracted through space. This is one of the translatory prisms at work here. Another, the translation from the sixteenth century to the present, is inspired, at least in part, by the Oulipo (the *Ouvroir de littérature potentielle* or Workshop of Potential Literature), specifically the method 'up to date' which was first developed by Harry Mathews in *Trial Impressions* (1977), where he updates and otherwise metamorphoses stanzas from John Dowland's *Second Booke of Ayres* (1600). Mathews's *Trial Impressions*, it should be noted, is the very model of prismatic translation, if that metaphor is understood to suggest that translation methods can be multiple, metamorphic, and dispersive. The book consists of 30 poems: a base text, a poem of 12 rhyming lines in 2 stanzas of iambic pentameter with metrical variants, taken from John Dowland's *Second Book of Ayres*; and the following 29 poems which present variations, or prismatic translations, of the base text. The variations employ various Oulipian techniques and forms from S+7 (where nouns are replaced using a dictionary, advancing seven nouns forwards), to the employment of multiple choice narrative, palindromic translation, expansion (or '*tireur à la ligne*') and traditional forms adopted by the Oulipo, such as the sestina.[3] There is some justification for the use of these experimental and metamorphic translation methods in the work of Du Bellay himself, for in a famous passage of his *La Deffence et Illustration de la Langue Françoyse* (1549) he advocated imitation, a freer and bolder approach to source texts, over translation, arguing that imitation involved 'delving into the most hidden and inward parts of the author' ('penetrer aux plus cachées et interieures parties de l'aucteur').[4]

There is much internal evidence that Du Bellay himself modelled *Les Regrets* on Ovid's poems of exile, and the note of bitterness, and the tone which has come today to be called 'passive aggressive', that charaterize Du Bellay's voice in these poems is in part an inheritance from Ovid. When Rimbaud, in his letter to Paul Demeny of May 15, 1871, pronounced 'Je est un autre', he was speaking for all poets, but perhaps especially for translator-poets, for here the distinction between author and translation is always blurred, the poet translates, but is also translated. The same is true of these translations: Du Bellay is translated to Essex, is translated across time, yet simultaneously Du Bellay translates the present, everything is refracted through the *prism* of Du Bellay, so that the source text itself here paradoxically becomes a prism through which the present is refracted and metamorphosed. Belfast, the city I left to first come to Essex, is substituted for Du Bellay's beloved Loire, and so is often idealized, while Colchester itself takes on the most negative aspects of Du Bellay's Rome. The truth is very different, for in reality, for me, moving from Ireland to England in the 1970s was a liberation — suddenly I could walk into town unmolested by the British Army. The demonisation of Essex, and the idealisation of Ireland, in brief, is created by the prism of Du Bellay, reflecting or refracting Du Bellay's opposition of Rome and the Loire.

This fictionalisation in the poems is there in other aspects too: the Irish poet O'Malley is an invented character, for I could find no adequate substitute for Du Bellay's Ronsard. When the poems, as they often do, speak to an addressee, the voice of the poem frequently takes on a point of view associated with, or coeval with, the addressee, much as a narrator in fiction will adopt the point of view of the character that is being described at any particular moment. So poem 133, for example, addressed to Will Rowe, the organiser of the Birkbeck conference on Poetry and Revolution, invokes revolution and Essex's radical past in the form of the Angry Brigade. In this respect, the work adopts a perspectivist approach, representing different perspectives that blend and clash without offering any synthesising discourse. Elsewhere, the departure point for these prismatic translations is determined by the underlying decisions concerning *topos* and *chronos*, and by the language: line 8 of Du Bellay 39 ('Je cherche la vertu, et ne trouve que vice') could only be translated in one way, by substituting 'Vice-Chancellor' for 'vice'; poem 110 in Du Bellay (127 in my sequence, which has been lengthened by occasional expansion and free improvisation), which celebrates Antoine Caracciolo, the poet bishop of Troyes, could only become a poem about the translator Enriqué Caracciolo, formerly of the Department of Literature at the University of Essex, and the editor of *The Penguin Book of Latin American American Verse* (1971); Du Bellay 111 (128 in my sequence), which concerns the militaristic Emperor Charles V, who gave up his offices to move to a monastery, could not be translated otherwise than as a poem concerning the current Vice-Chancellor of Essex, who likewise came from a military background to the cloistered world of the academy. Yet just as the author, when he returns in his text, is an 'auteur de papier', according to Roland Barthes, so these figures are figures of paper, no more real than Dickens' Scrooge or Chaucer's knight.

More broadly, as touched on earlier, these poems form part of the many discourses surrounding debates concerning Higher Education today, and in this they are indebted to many writers and thinkers who have led the way in this area, including Stefan Collini, Michael Bailey, Des Freedman and Marina Warner. I can only hope that this work, alongside theirs, can make some small contribution to documenting a crisis, and to the thinking-through of that crisis, so that, in time, that crisis might be resolved. As the late Seamus Heaney succinctly put it: 'The end of art is peace.'

1

Je ne veulx point fouiller au sein de la nature,
Je ne veulx point chercher l'esprit de l'univers,
Je ne veulx point sonder les abysmes couvers,
Ny desseigner du ciel la belle architecture.
Je ne peins mes tableaux de si riche peinture,
Et si haults arguments ne recherche à mes vers:
Mais suivant de ce lieu les accidents divers,
Soit de bien, soit de mal, j'escris à l'adventure.
Je me plains à mes vers, si j'ay quelque regret,
Je me ris avec eulx, je leur dy mon secret,
Comme estans de mon cœur les plus seurs secretaires.
Aussi ne veulx-je tant les pigner et friser,
Et de plus braves noms ne les veulx desguiser,
Que de papiers journaulx, ou bien de commentaires.[5]

1

I'm not going to theorize about the human genome,
I'm not going to ask about big data,
I'm not going to draw a plan of future media,
Nor do I propose to explore the mud of the Colne with robotic fish.
I don't paint my pictures in such rich colours,
Or seek such lofty subjects for my verse.
Keeping an eye on shit that happens, the bad, the worse,
I take a pen, or chalk, and write what comes.
I moan right here if I have something to moan about,
Make a joke of it or, if I wish to act the whistleblower, speak out loud,
In the sure knowledge that no-one ever reads poems.
I don't tart them up to look presentable at award ceremonies,
Knackered times require knackered words,
But regard them as no more than minutes or blogs.

10

It is not the rubbish-heaped banks of this Essex river,
It is not the exhaust-filled air, nor North Hill Barbers,
Which makes me pour out my misery in verse, no,
The problem, Atkins, is not merely aesthetic.
It is the constant struggle against boredom here,
Nailed like Prometheus to Clingoe Hill,
And this futile hope which holds me here
As Capitalism unrolls its business plans on campus.
And so, Atkins, if Ovid in exile bought *Teach Yourself Getic*, since
Nobody could figure out what he was saying, who can blame me
For abandoning the avant-garde in Colchester?
Nobody, for the delights of L=A=N=G=U=A=G=E poetry are,
In this Essex backwater, understood by none.

12

Given all the business plans I have to write,
Given the invoices that pile up all day,
And given all the staff that bring me their complaints,
You are surprised that I find time for sonnets.
For literary theorists sonnets are little songs,
For me they are laments, and I sing them with tears,
And in doing so chase my torments away,
That is why, Munton, I still sing night and day.
So builders sing to fight off the boredom of their labour,
So dairy farmers when they sell their produce at a loss,
So backpackers who cannot get a flight back home,
So songwriters who have no luck with their girls,
So the fisherman chasing the diminishing shoal,
So the poor sod in prison who is doing time.

25

Unlucky the century, the decade, the year, the month,
The day, the hour, the minute, the second, the millisecond,
The nanosecond, and unlucky the false hope that flattered my family
When, to come here, they left the sweet land of
Ireland, and my own city, Belfast (*ouch!*), it hurts to remember.
Truly, that was a day of ill omen,
And my stomach warned me at the time,
For on the ferry trip to Stranraer
All I could do was puke my guts out.
A hundred times the Rowlands begged us not to leave,
And if desire had not blinded us to the truth,
Would it not have been enough to make us think twice
When, on our own doorstep, by more than ill luck,
The car broke down just as we were about to leave?

33

Maxwell, what do you think I should do?
Should I stay on in this benighted campus
Where they fucked you about so badly, offering
You an interview for the job you'd already secured,
Then changing the date at the last minute so you couldn't make it,
Before telling you to fuck off altogether,
Or should I apply for that chair at UEA
Before the opportunity has melted, like last year's snow?
If I stay at Essex it will be to waste my time
Imagining things will come right here,
And if I look for tenure elsewhere
All the work I have done will turn to nothing.
I'll stick it out. No, fuck the lot of them, I'm off.
Maxwell, say something, I'm in two minds what to tell my feet.

39

I love anarchy, and I'm Head of Department,
I don't like management, and must manage,
I don't like acting, and must play a part,
I love the simple, and must privilege the virtual,
I'm not interested in budgets, and work for accountants,
I don't like league tables, and must prize them,
I like to be straight up, my employer says we need to have a conversation,
I seek virtue, and find only the Vice-Chancellor,
I want space to write, and cannot find it,
I don't like business, and must write business plans,
I don't like arguing, but must justify every decision with a bar chart,
I am sick at heart, and must act upbeat,
I was born for the Muse, and my job is to manage,
Am I not, Schmidt, the unluckiest man alive?

92

It's true, Tom, there's no such thing as a free lunch,
So here I am talking to the Vice-Chancellor
About Ice Truckers, his favourite TV show, the latest student numbers,
And the new franchises in the Knowledge Gateway.
It's good to see inside the Lake House, I suppose,
With its view across the water to the new Student Centre,
And to see so many Heads of Department deep in intrigue,
One holding forth about the student experience, another extolling employability.
But what I'd really like to see, before capitalism has destroyed this place utterly,
Is students protesting again as in 1968.
I'd like to see them occupy buildings again,
And bring the whole juggernaut to a grinding halt,
Saying no to fees of £9000 a year, saying no to charges at the Sports Centre,
Saying no to minimal wages for cleaners, saying no to branding.

98

We don't spend our time here writing poetry,
As we did in the 60s, when Davie was in charge.
If you really want to know how we spend our days,
The next ten lines will bring you right up to date:
There is no time for research, we are too busy making research plans,
There is no time for teaching, we are too busy on curriculum review,
There is no time for real conversation, we are too busy on email,
There is no time for students, we are too busy monitoring student satisfaction,
There is no time for culture, we are too busy on business plans,
There is no time for education, we are too busy on employability,
There is no time for marking, we are too busy reviewing assessment,
There is no time for work, we are too busy on workload models,
There is no time for literature, we are too busy on transferable skills,
There is no time for thought, we think only of outcomes.

101

Munton, how come the harder I try to get out
Of here, the more the animus of the place
(Like that shopping mall in *Dawn of the Dead*)
Pulls me back with its strange force?
Is it misguided loyalty holding me back,
Or some insidious Away-Day voodoo,
Such that when we try to even *think*,
We feel little by little our minds shrink?
A thousand times I have wanted to get the hell out,
But I feel my brain turning to a pulp,
My eyes bulging out of my head, my feet become rotting flesh.
Look at me, Munton, I'm nothing but a zombie now,
Protesting helplessly at my transformation —
Like that bloke in Ariosto, turned into a tree trunk.

127

When Caracciolo unleashes the wrath of Mars,
Shouting 'Brotherstone, I *kill* you!' as he charges
Down the corridor, he makes us feel the violence
On our own pulses, but when his battles are done,
And he has finished with his Latin threats,
And wants to show us his charm, then he does,
And our ears are soothed by his mellifluous voice:
Then we are at peace, like John and Yoko.
A veritable Tolstoy, he can contrast war and peace,
Fine weather and thunderstorms, or spring and winter,
Or Albert Sloman and Anthony Forster, whose two
Vice-Chancellorships could not have been more diffferent.
No-one could describe better what went before,
And help us understand what followed, old Essex and now the new.

128

I have never thought that the skies of Essex covered
Anything constant, beyond the constant din of the A12.
Now more than ever, Hilson, it seems that nothing lasts long,
And that nothing built here is built firmly.
For he who controlled National Security
With his military precision and rigour
Wants to try out his philosophy
On campus, leave the world and serve knowledge boldly.
Then what do you make of this Professor of Robotics
Who, having spent his best days teaching quietly, at *Essex*,
Now finds work in *Military Reconnaissance*?
I don't know which of the two is the more strange,
Hilson, but in both cases it's late for a career change:
Would you trust the one's robotic fish any more than the other's graduation
                                                                                        speeches?

133

> Rowe, what makes a good university, tell me, for I
> Don't see many in the *Times Good University Guide*?
> A good university should be about changing the world,
> Not all this shit about employability which so crowds out thought today.
> We don't need students who are work-ready, but students who are
> Radically unfit for work, students who are ready to change the workplace.
> Once Essex offered 'something fierce', it was even there in the architecture,
>   now this 'fierce' is just part of the brand,
> But once it gave us sit-ins against Vietnam, Guerilla Poetry,
> Protests against Dr Inch, Anna Mendelssohn and the Angry Brigade.
> Like poetry, universities should not be made
> According to some template, especially when that template is a
>   hierarchical fucking business model,
> That's why I spit on the Movement, even if I aim at Swiftian clarity here,
> Universities should be organized from the bottom up,
> Like an ecosystem, like Tom Raworth's poem on Proust, like Catalan Anarchy.

Works Cited

Du Bellay, Joachim, *Joachim Du Bellay, A Bilingual Edition*, trans. Richard Helgerson (Philadelphia: University of Pennsylvania Press, 2006)

Calvino, Italo, *Le città invisibili* (Turin: Einaudi, 1972)

Caracciolo-Trejo, Enriqué (ed.), *The Penguin Book of Latin American Verse* (Harmondsworth: Penguin, 1971)

Mathews, Harry, *Trial Impressions* (Providence: Burning Deck, 1977)

Queneau, Raymond, *Exercices de style* (Paris: Gallimard, 1947)

Reynolds, Matthew, *The Poetry of Translation: From Chaucer & Petrarch to Homer & Logue* (Oxford: Oxford University Press, 2011)

Terry, Philip, *Bad Times* (London: Veer Books, 2017)

Notes to Chapter 14

1. The complete sequence is published as Philip Terry, *Bad Times* (London: Veer Books, 2017).
2. Matthew Reynolds, *The Poetry of Translation: From Chaucer & Petrarch to Homer & Logue* (Oxford: Oxford University Press, 2011), p. 1.
3. This concept of a text consisting of variations is fundamental to Oulipian practice, and is there in Queneau's *Exercices de style* (1947), as well as Calvino's *Le città invisibili* (1972), where all the cities described by Marco Polo to Kublai Khan, are prismatic variants on his home city of Venice.
4. *The Defence and Enrichment of the French Language*, transl. Richard Helgerson, in *Joachim Du Bellay A Bilingual Edition* (Philadelphia: University of Pennsylvania Press, 2006), p. 338.
5. Ibid., p. 53. Constraints of space have meant it has not been possible to reproduce more than the first poem in the French original, but this should be sufficient to give the reader the feeling of Du Bellay's seemingly effortless French, at once so formal yet so colloquial, which these translations have tried to capture.

PART V

Readings

CHAPTER 15

Coleridge Diffracted: on the Opening Lines of *Kubla Khan*

Patrick Hersant

> Translate my name, says [God], but at the same time he says: You will not be able to translate my name, because, first of all, it's a proper name.
>   JACQUES DERRIDA[1]

'In Xanadu did Kubla Khan…' While its tonal fluidity may sound like pure magic to the ear, the famous line is syntactically rather simple: a preposition, a place-name, a verb, and a name.[2] Despite the lack of any apparent ambiguities on a lexical or grammatical level, it has inspired a motley range of translations: the twenty versions compiled here bring to light, through their sheer diversity, some of the more poetic aspects of translation such as rhythm, sonority and connotation, as well as the performative dimension of the language (Table 1). I do not intend to propose a new reading of *Kubla Khan* — perhaps the most scrutinized poem in the history of English literature[3] — but I will argue that the analysis of its opening lines, from a translation studies perspective, may bring to light some unexpected aspects and challenges in the translation of the poem: should (and could) names such as Xanadu and Kubla, neither of them 'in English', even be translated? If not, can the translation still preserve the poetic, exotic and — as we shall see — godlike dimension of these names?

What is perhaps most striking is that half of the translators of *Kubla Khan* chose to alter the toponym and/or the anthroponym, those 'rigid designators' that the modern practice of translation tends to leave intact.[4] The names Xanadu and Kubla Khan possess a history that precedes their use (and their reformulation) by Coleridge, but this rich history does not come to an end with their invocation in the poem. Rather, examining the various translations of *Kubla Khan*, we will see how this place-name and this surname, fixed in time by Coleridge at the end of the eighteenth century, have continued to evolve, even metamorphose, throughout the twentieth century up until now. Even if, at first glance, the diffraction of these names in the translations of *Kubla Khan* appears to betray the resonance and the intentions of the poem, they are in fact prolonging a poetic process of translation and appropriation undertaken by Coleridge himself.

Étienne Vauthier, 1934
    À Xanadou Koubla Khan fit bâtir
    un fastueux palais de joie
Henri Parisot, 1939
    C'est à Xanadu que Koubla Khan
    Fit bâtir un fastueux palais de plaisance
Germain d'Hangest, 1945
    En Xanadou le Koubla Khân fit ériger
    un palais majestueux
Louis Cazamian, 1946
    À Xanadu Kubla Khan ordonna
    De bâtir un majestueux palais
Henri Parisot, 1947
    En Xanadou, lui, Koubla Khan,
    S'édifia un fastueux palais
Henri Parisot, 1975
    En Xanadou donc Koubla Khan
    Se fit édifier un fastueux palais
Camille Fort, 2001
    À Xanadu c'est Kubla Khan
    Qui ordonna un haut lieu des plaisirs
Michel Midan, 2002
    À Xanadu, Kubla Khan décréta
    La construction d'un palais majestueux
Gérard Gâcon, 2005
    'En Zanadou, dit Koubla Khan,
    D'un dôme de plaisance je veux la merveille.'
Jacques Darras, 2007
    En Xanadu dit Kubla Khan
    Qu'on crée un grand dôme de plaisir
Wolfgang Breitwieser, 1959
    In Xanadu schuf Kubla Khan
    Ein Lustschloß, stolz und kuppelschwer
Edgar Mertner, 1973
    In Xanadu ließ Kubla Khan
    einen prunkvollen Freuden-palast errichten
Ramón López Ortega, 1978
    En Xanadú ordenó Kubla Khan
    que una augusta mansión de ensueño edificasen
Arturo Agüero Herranz, 2009
    En Xanadú, Kubla Khan
    Se hizo construir un espléndido palacio de recreo
José María Valverde, 1989
    En Xanadú, el Khan Kubla decretó
    alzar una solemne cúpula de placeres

Pedro António Janeiro, 2010
>   Em Xanadou, Kublai Khan havia construído
>   Um palácio majestoso para seu prazer

Mario Praz, 1925
>   In Xandu eresse Coblay Cane
>   Per sue delizie un'alta mole

Mario Luzi, 1949
>   Nel Xanadu alza Kubla Khan
>   dimora di delizie un duomo

Petru Iamandi, 1973
>   În Xanadu măreț palat
>   Plăcerii Kubla hotărî

Konstantin Balmont, 1908
>   Въ странѣ Ксанадѣ благословенной
>   Дворецъ построилъ Кубла Ханъ

TABLE 1. Twenty translations of the opening lines of Kubla Khan
in French, German, Spanish, Portuguese, Italian, Romanian and Russian[5]

Our inquiry begins in Inner Mongolia, around 1275. Kublai, the Mongols' great Khan and Emperor of China, welcomes Marco Polo to Shangdu, the summer capital of his far-flung empire. The Venetian merchant, dazzled by the palace of Genghis Khan's grandson, gives a detailed description of his wonder in his *Book of the Marvels of the World*, in which he describes the sixteen years he spent with the emperor: 'Una città nominata Xandú, la qual edificò il gran Can che al presente regna, detto Cublai Can; e quivi fece fare un palagio di maravigliosa bellezza e artificio, fabricato di pietre di marmo e d'altre belle pietre, qual un capo confina in mezzo della città e con l'altro col muro di quella.'[6] In the beginning of the seventeenth century, this passage from Marco Polo was translated into English in *Purchas his Pilgrimage*, an anthology of travel writing published by Samuel Purchas.

In the fall of 1798, in southwestern England, Samuel Taylor Coleridge has just turned 25 years old.[7] He has moved into a cottage in Somerset at the beginning of the year with his wife Sara and their one-year-old son. On this autumn day in 1798, taken with a 'slight discomfort', the young poet swallows a few drops of opium to soothe his dysentery and drifts off into a dreamlike lethargy. As he falls asleep holding the Purchas anthology in his hands, one of the passages from Marco Polo sparks a dream about architecture: 'in *Xamdu* did *Cublai Can* build a ſtately Palace, encompaſſing ſixteene miles of plaine ground with a wall, wherein are fertile Meddowes, pleaſant Springs, delightfull Streames, and all ſorts of beaſts of chase and game, and in the middeſt thereof a ſumptuous houſe of pleaſure.'[8] During a deep sleep that lasts three hours, the slumbering poet effortlessly composes some two to three hundred verses. Awaking in a trance, he rushes to write them all down but only manages to capture some of them before 'a person from Porlock' calls and takes over an hour of his time. When this unfortunate nuisance takes his leave, alas, the poet is left grasping at a handful of scattered memories. Only fifty-four verses from this dream-poem survived. The first were directly inspired by Purchas, and through him, Marco Polo:

> In Xanadu did Kubla Khan
> A stately pleasure-dome decree:
> Where Alph, the sacred river, ran
> Through caverns measureless to man
> Down to a sunless sea.

It's a very compelling — but, most likely, untrue story.[9] No matter: whether authentic or fictive, Coleridge's prose preface to the poem, with its imaginary tale of the circumstances surrounding the composition of *Kubla Khan*, foreshadows and sustains the essential themes of a poem that oscillates between fragmentation and profound unity. Inspiration, vision, and the unconscious as well as poetic frustration all loom large. Translation also plays a role, as the poem presents itself as the poetic deployment of a short prose passage.

S. T. Coleridge, *Kubla Khan*, 1816

In Xanadu did **Kubla Khan**
A stately pleasure-dome decree:
Where Alph, the sacred river, ran
Through caverns measureless to man
Down to a sunless sea.
So twice five miles of fertile ground
With walls and towers were girdled round:
And there were gardens bright with sinuous rills,
Where blossomed many an incense-bearing tree;
And here were forests ancient as the hills,
Enfolding sunny spots of greenery.

Samuel Purchas, *Purchas, his Pilgrimage*, 1613

In **Xamdu** did **Cublai Can** build a stately Pallace, encompassing sixteen miles of plaine ground with a wall, wherein are fertile Meddowes, pleasant Springs, delightfull streames, and all sorts of beasts of chase and game, and in the middest thereof a sumptuous house of pleasure, which may be moved from place to place.

Marco Polo, *Il Milione c.* 1290 (Italian translation 1556)

Una città nominata **Xandú**, la qual edificò il gran Can che al presente regna, detto **Cublai Can**; e quivi fece fare un palagio di maravigliosa bellezza e artificio, fabricato di pietre di marmo e d'altre belle pietre, qual con un capo confina in mezo della città e con l'altro col muro di quella.

TABLE 2. Spelling of name and place-name in Marco Polo, Samuel Purchas and S. T. Coleridge

The attentive reader will have noticed that the two proper nouns that concern us here, Xanadu and Kubla Khan, are spelled differently by Polo, Purchas, and Coleridge (Table 2). Before turning to the different translations of *Kubla Khan* and the evolution of these names after Coleridge used them, it seems useful to quickly sketch their diachronic evolution before the poem. My initial approach will be chronological as I trace the translation of the name 'Kubla Khan' and the place-name 'Xanadu' before Coleridge's time (from the thirteenth to the eighteenth centuries), to Coleridge's two versions of this poem (from 1798 and 1816) and, finally, in the many translations of *Kubla Kh*an that followed.

Marco Polo was the first man to transcribe the Chinese place-name 元上 [Yuan shangdu] to describe the summer palace of Kubilai, the first Mongolian emperor from the Yuan dynasty at the end of the thirteenth century. The transliteration was probably produced via Mongolian, a language Polo had learned during his stay even though he did not know Chinese. This name, which means 'the high capital of Yuan', is transcribed as 'Ciandu' by Polo — or at least by the writer of *The Description of the World*, who actually was not Polo himself: from a shared prison cell in Genoa, in 1299, he dictated his recollections to Rustichello da Pisa, who then composed the book in a mix of a Pisan dialect and the langue d'oïl.

The circumstances surrounding the composition, publication, and translation of Marco Polo's work remain unclear: an original manuscript does not really exist, although there are a dozen editions written in various languages. The seven oldest versions of the text (in Tuscan, Venetian, French, French-Italian) present numerous linguistic challenges such as a mix of languages in the French-Italian version, or traces of Italian and the appearance of Oriental words from Persian, Arabic, Turkish, Mongol or Chinese which appear in the French account.[10] In 1824, in the appendix of their edition of *Les Voyages de Marco Polo*, the Société française de géographie established spelling variants for the proper names taken from the diverse editions of the travels of Polo written in Italian, Latin and French.[11] It appears that the transcription 'Ciandu', or its variant 'Cyandu', prevails in the majority of editions except for one: in *Delle navigationi et viaggi*, a text published in Venice between 1550 and 1556, which is considered the first treatise of modern geography. The Italian humanist Giovanni Battista Ramusio translates Polo's text by choosing the spelling 'Xandu' — a seminal spelling variation because it moves away from the pronunciation of a 'tʃ' in favour of an initial 'X' which henceforward became the norm.[12]

In sixteenth century England, Ramusio's Italian version served as a source for Richard Hakluyt who then compiled these travel narratives in *The Principal Navigations, Voiages, Traffiques and Discoueries of the English Nation*, which appeared as a series of three volumes between 1598 and 1600.[13] In the seventeenth century, after Hakluyt's death in 1616, his former assistant Samuel Purchas added to the anthology with the title *Hakluytus Posthumus, or, Purchas his Pilgrims*, which came out in 1625.[14] It has been shown that Coleridge was familiar with Purchas's anthology, but it is not clear which edition he consulted. The 1617 edition, which his friend Wordsworth owned, transcribes the key place-name as 'Xamdu'; in the 1613 edition, 'Xaindu' appears.[15]

The name Kubla also presents a complex etymology and orthographic evolution, from its beginning as a transliteration from classical Mongol as 'Qubilai'. Once again, it seems likely that Marco Polo was the first person to transcribe into a Romance language the name of the Mongolian emperor, the founder of the Yuan dynasty. The Société de géographie's table comparing these names shows numerous variations from the diverse translations of Polo's account: Cublay, Cublim, Choblay — to which the spelling 'Coblay Cane' was added. Not mentioned in the chart, this variant was widespread in other Italian versions of the text. In Purchas's text, the name appears under the form 'Cublai' in three editions. As for the title of Khan, the Mongolian term for king, it is formulated in the many translations of Marco Polo as Chan, Khan, Kaan, and Cane, among others. It is then found in English under a great number of orthographic variations.[16] Interestingly, the variations in the name of the Mongolian ruler may well chime with Coleridge's 'uncertainty about how to pronounce his own surname' — Col-ridge, Cole-ridge, Coal-ridge, Colleridge — , and the 'even greater indecisiveness about what his full name really [was]'.[17]

Coleridge wrote *Kubla Khan* in 1798 but did not publish it until 1816, at Lord Byron's urging, in a slender volume that also contains the poems 'Christabel' and 'The Pains of Sleep'. The prose preface where the poet sketches the circumstances of the creation of this poem also appears in this edition. A second version exists which was established from a signed manuscript discovered in 1934 in a private library — this crucial document, the Crewe Manuscript, is today housed at the British Museum. The differences between the two versions of the poem are few and hardly meaningful, except, as it happens, for those concerning the proper names. The Crewe Manuscript (1798) reads 'In Xannadù did Cubla Khan', while the 1816 edition reads 'In Xanadu did Kubla Khan'. Perhaps because he was heir to a language with a long etymological and literary history that changed conventions of spelling and pronunciation from one century to another, Coleridge himself changed the proper nouns from one version to the next: Cubla becomes Kubla, Xannadù becomes Xanadu. In this particular formulation, Xanadu is Coleridge's unique creation.[18] Coleridge's re-spelling also signals remarkable onomastic and poetic implications as the metamorphosis of these names underscores the importance of their visual appearance and their resonance from the first verse of the poem[19].

On an onomastic level, the name of the Mongolian emperor and of his palace have inspired the most diverse — sometimes the most far-fetched — commentary; it is true that the poem itself seems to authorize or call for interpretation, even over-interpretation. As Richard Gerber says: 'The fusion of the oriental Khan Kubla or Cublai (in Coleridge's source and preface) or Cubla (in Coleridge's [Crewe] manuscript) and the Great Mother Kubela, Kubele or Cybele consisted in the similarity of names which can play such an important part in dreams.'[20] Another critic suggests a parallelism with Cain, but this comparison is more pertinent to the Ancient Mariner than to Kubla Khan.[21] In addition to these diverse possible connotations, the two proper names add to the rhythm and the sonority of the opening verse. As one commentator notes, 'aesthetically, the rhythmic suavity of the name with its careful alternation of consonant and vowel sounds is deserving of rather more than casual regard.'[22] Another underscores the importance of the letters that make up these proper nouns: 'Its very names are so lettered as to suggest first and last things. [...] Xanadu, which starts the poem, is enclosed in letters that might well be called eschatological; while Kubla Khan himself sits alphabetically central with his alliterating k's'.[23] Many critics are rightly impressed by the self-

FIG. 15.1. Pattern of assonances and alliterations

contained symmetry of the opening line: '[It] receives its primary shape from the enclosed assonance of its four stresses, *u— u— u— u—*, which swings the sound as if in a shallow curve, the symmetry being still further marked by the full rhyme of the enclosing syllables. *Xan-* and *Khan* (Coleridge undoubtedly pronounced *Khan* as it was often spelled, *Can*), and the embellishment of minor echoes, *d*'s and short *i*'s binding together the first part and *k*'s the end of the line: In Xanadu did Kubla Khan'.[24]

One might wonder, then, why certain translators chose to alter these names that are so thoroughly laden with a sense of history and meaning, so marked by their sonorous, rhythmic, and connotative qualities. On the one hand, the fact that these are proper nouns might discourage their alteration; but on the other hand their sonic charge (which in the poem is determined by the phonetic system of English) is also of extreme significance, and the desire to preserve this can lead to altered spelling. There is no obvious or satisfactory way of keeping the name unchanged across languages: same spelling suggests different pronunciation — for instance, even when the written letter 'X' stays the same through transmission across languages, the pronunciation will change: 'z' in English, 'ʃ' in Portuguese, 'cs' in German and Italian, and 'gz' in French — , while endeavours to preserve the pronunciation inevitably create different spelling, as illustrated (Table 1) by our sample of translations into seven different languages[25].

In German, both Breitwieser and Mertner keep name and place-name intact — visually if not vocally, since Xanadu will be pronounced /csanədu:/ by their readers. In the Spanish translations by López Ortega, Agüero Herranz and Valverde, the version of the place-name offers an accented 'u' — 'En Xanadú' — , but as this is a common Spanish accent the effect is not particularly exotic; rather than altering the pronunciation of the vowel, then, the accent suggests a stress on the last syllable. To more foreignizing effect (as many Portuguese words end with an 'u'), Janeiro adds an 'o' — 'Em Xanadou' — , creating a diphthong where there was none: /ʃanədəʊ/. In Romanian, Iamandi keeps both 'Xanadu' and 'Kubla' as they are in the original English, but he omits the title 'Khan' — 'Plăcerii Kubla hotărî' — for rhythmic rather than sonic reasons, presumably, as this allows him to maintain the original octosyllable. Similarly, the requirements of Russian syllabo-tonic versification inspired Balmont to drop the final vowel in the place-name: 'Въ странѣ Ксанадъ благословенной' — the 'ъ' being silent, the place-name simply becomes /zanəd/. In the Italian version by Luzi, neither name nor name-place are altered; in the rendition by Praz, however, standard spellings of the place-name and surname from the Marco Polo editions are both Italianized and exoticized, as the 'y' was never part of the Italian alphabet: 'In Xandu eresse Coblay Cane.' This is certainly the most interesting — and the most questionable — case, for Praz refers directly back to Polo without making apparent the evolution of names that, via the translations of Polo and the editions of Purchas, led to the creation of the term Xannadù in the Crewe Manuscript and eventually to Xanadu in the definitive version of 1816 (Table 3).

In French, Xanadu is more often than not left as is, although occasionally the spelling is changed to imitate the English pronunciation. Parisot, who published three different translations of *Kubla Khan* over a span of forty years, begins by using Coleridge's version before opting, after 1947, for the addition of an 'o' — Xanadou — that indicates that the place-name should be pronounced /zanədu:/ and not /zanədy/. Other translators, such as Vauthier and d'Hangest, follow suit, undoubtedly for the same reasons; Gâcon, however, is the only one to employ the logic of this phonetic transcription throughout: the French reader, tempted to say '*dy*', is also at special risk of mispronouncing the first letter of the place-name as '*gz*' instead of just '*z*'. This explains why Gâcon spells both 'Koubla' and 'Zanadou'. One comes across even more surprising spellings, such as d'Hangest's choice of 'Khân' which claims to highlight, through the circumflex, the exotic and archaic dimension of the name — in the nineteenth century, non-French accents were sometimes meant to render exoticism, as for instance in Pauthier's spelling 'Khoubilaï Khan'.[26]

Cazamian, Fort, Midan and Darras all leave name and place-name unchanged, confident that the modern reader will not mispronounce them. A possible explanation comes to mind: it is more than likely that, by the time they published their translations of the poem, between 1946 and 2007, both Xanadu and Kubla Khan were perceived as common names (and indeed common nouns) even for the French poetry reader, who might have heard them uttered a number of times in Orson Welles's 1941 *Citizen Kane* (note the Coleridgean echoes in the sound chain of the film's title, *z-n /k-n*). We may then date back to 1941 the time when Xanadu actually became a common name/noun, as the script of the film, immediately after the famous mystery-word 'Rosebud', reads: 'Legendary was *the* Xanadu where Kubla Khan decreed his stately pleasure dome. (...) Today, almost as legendary is *Florida's* Xanadu — world's largest private pleasure ground.'[27] In that respect at least, an apposite analogy might be drawn between the emperor's palace in Xanadu and the mythical tower of Babel — or indeed the very word 'Babel' interpreted as 'confusion' by Jacques Derrida: 'Now, a proper name as such remains forever untranslatable, a fact that may lead one to conclude that it does not strictly belong, by the same right as the other words, to the language, to the system of the language, be it translated or translating. And yet "Babel", an event in a single tongue, the one in which it appears so as to form a "text", also has a common meaning, a conceptual generality.'[28] Few words in literary history, it seems, have gone through so many re-spellings and allowed for so many diverse articulations as Xanadu, this 'translatable-untranslatable name' testifying, as did Babel, to 'forbidden transparency, impossible univocity'.[29]

Chinese / Cyrillic Mongolian		元上都	Хубилай хаан
Mongolian (VPMC transliteration)		Šandu	Qubilaĭ qaɣan
Marco Polo	1298	Giandu	Coblay Cane
	var.	Ciandu	Cublay
	var.	Ciandai	Choblay
	1550	Xandu	Cublai
Samuel Purchas	1613	Xaindu	Cublai Can
	1617	Xamdu	
	1619	Xandu	
S. T. Coleridge	1798	Xannadù	Cubla Khan
S. T. Coleridge	1816	Xanadu	Kubla Khan
Translations	1925	Xandu	Coblay Cane
	1934	Xanadou	Koubla Khan
	1989	Xanadú	Khan Kubla
	2003		Koubilaï Khan
	2005	Zanadou	
	2007	Xanadu	Kubla Khan
	2010	Xanadou	Kublai Khan

TABLE 3. Diachronic evolution of name and place-name until 1816 and their subsequent diffraction through translation

The preposition *in* and the verb *did* equally play a determining role in the musicality as well as the structure of the verse. Their very brevity is essential, for it reinforces the exotic dimension of the proper nouns. The place-name and surname take up six of the verse's eight syllables, making it almost incomprehensible, as if it was uttered in some foreign language. English is hardly present (just in these two monosyllables) and barely recognizable as such. The predominance of the foreign names in the first verse seems to create a tonality that is halfway between exoticism and magic, two of the poem's essential themes. At its heart, this first verse is scarcely English; beyond the mysterious, almost incomprehensible place-name and surname, the grammar is of no great help either. The auxiliary verb *did* postpones the actual verb, *decree*, to the following verse, so that the initial iambic tetrameter appears to lack a verb — and, therefore, meaning. The *in* and the *did* are so miniscule, so lost within the surrounding mass of sonority and unfamiliar letters, that the entire first verse comes across as an incantatory formula, a sort of long abracadabra.[30] The second part of the poem stages a scene of sorcery, chiefly through the act of encirclement: 'Weave a circle round him thrice | And close your eyes with holy dread' — but this magic spell has been cast from the poem's opening.

There remains one final formal element, which is crucial to truly understanding the poem, that most of the translators of *Kubla Khan* have not been able to see —

or able to translate. When the poem is read aloud, assonance dominates in the first line: i a a u / i u a a, creating a chiasmus effect which reinforces another important phenomenon: the performativity of the verb *decree*. Kubla, it should be stressed, did not decree the construction of a palace, as he does in Purchas: 'he commanded a palace to be built.' Rather, he decreed a palace. *Fiat lux, et lux fuit*: just as in the Vulgate, Khan's words not only carry the decree of law but they benefit from an absolute sort of efficiency: what Khan says will be. The chiasmus in the Latin, playing off the paronymy between *fiat/fuit* with the simple '*et*' exposing at the center the evidence and immediacy of divine creation, finds an echo in the *did*, but also in the vocal chiasmus mentioned earlier. Meschonnic's meditation on translating the Bible pertains here: 'The first verse starts with a syntactical problem that is also a theological problem.'[31]

Can any translation preserve these aspects of the first verse, a line so crucial that it enacts the meaning of the entire poem? In order to do so, the translator should first respect the absence of any perceptible grammatical structure, the incantatory dimension that tends toward exotic euphony and letters, and a sense of the indecipherable. The apparent ungrammaticality of the first verse, allowing the reader-listener the possibility of believing in a magic spell intoned in some unknown language, could not resist the apparition of any verbal structures and personal pronouns such as 'fit bâtir', 'C'est à... que', 'fit ériger', 'ordonna', 'décréta', 'schuf', 'ließ', 'eresse', 'decretó'. On that count, the majority of the *Kubla Khan* translations fail to produce a line that is at once outlandish and mysterious with its absence of verbs: too many of them do include a verb, sometimes an unwieldy one of several syllables, which detracts from the incantatory effect created by Coleridge.

In a similar fashion, no translator seems to have noticed the performative dimension that is offered by 'decree... a pleasure dome'. The divine *fiat lux* is reduced to far less audacious formulations such as 'se fit édifier', 'fit bâtir', 'ließ errichten', 'eresse un'alta mole', 'decretó alzar'. Some translators, however, are careful to preserve the semantic mystery, and they manage to recreate the effect of this lexical exoticism barely punctuated by two identifiable monosyllabic words: 'En Xanadou, lui, Koubla Khan' (Parisot), 'À Xanadu c'est Kubla Khan' (Fort), and especially 'En Xanadu dit Kubla Khan' (Darras). In view of the criteria discussed above, it seems that Jacques Darras's translation is the only one that satisfies, as it manages to preserve the iambic tetrameter of the original as well as the minimal presence of ordinary language as glimpsed in the monosyllables, which are paronyms with the English (*in/en, did/dit*):

> En Xanadu dit Kubla Khan
> Qu'on crée un grand dôme de plaisir

Darras's translation conveys the vocal chiasmus and the fluctuating syntactic and semantic senses — elements that harmonize to allow us to hear for ourselves the powerful language of the Mongolian emperor. Furthermore, in the following verse, the performative nature of the ordering language is, by some miracle, preserved: the divine *fiat*, transformed into the imperial decree of Coleridge, becomes in French: 'dit... qu'on crée' — literally: 'said... to create'. Just slightly less performative than the original English, this formulation offers a new paronym in the guise of pseudo-etymology: *decree* / 'dit... crée'.

From Geoffrey of Monmouth's 'Avalon' to Hilton's 'Shangri-La', Swift's 'Lilliput' and Tolkien's 'Mordor', proper nouns that both don't belong in the English language and are laden with historic and exotic resonances pose a particular challenge when it comes to translating them — or, perhaps even more so, *not* translating them. It appears that translation is not always a matter of moving out of one language and into another, but rather of working with the varied resources of a language continuum, reshaping words and remaking texts in varying ways in different places and moments, using the ever-changing resources of language that are available, as well as the ever-altering imaginations of translator-readers. The graphic variations on Xanadu and Kubla Khan, that span from before Coleridge and persist after him, present a surprising continuity-within-discontinuity: through their initial transliteration, temporary crystallization and ultimate diffraction, they illustrate a particular practice of translation as 'just a moment within a long series of other interpretations of the same poem, a consent readily given by the translator to the work of others in the years to come'. The poet Yves Bonnefoy names this *le traduire*: 'While each particular translation is less than the original, translating as such, the practice that we name translating, will be, in the long run, equal to it and possibly even more.'[32] The multiple interpretations of the first lines of Coleridge's *Kubla Khan* certainly enrich our comprehension of the poem; viewed together, their various prismatic shades blend into another one to provide a diachronic and polyphonic commentary as richly varied as the poem itself.

Works Cited

BALLARD, MICHEL, *Le Nom propre en traduction* (Paris: Ophrys, 2001)

BONNEFOY, YVES, *La Communauté des traducteurs* (Strasbourg: Presses universitaires de Strasbourg, 2000)

COLERIDGE, SAMUEL TAYLOR, *Poetical Works*, ed. by Ernest H. Coleridge (Oxford: Oxford University Press, 1969)

——, *The Collected Letters*, ed. by Earl Leslie Griggs, 6 vols (Oxford: Clarendon Press, 1956–71)

COOPER, LANE, 'The Abyssinian Paradise in Coleridge and Milton', *Modern Philology*, 3. 3 (1906), 327–32

DERRIDA, JACQUES, 'Des tours de Babel', trans. by Joseph F. Graham, in *Psyche. Inventions of the Other*, ed. by Peggy Kamuf (Stanford: Stanford University Press, 2007), pp. 191–225

——, *The Ear of the Other: Otobiography, Transference, Translation*, ed. by Christie V. McDonald, trans. by Peggy Kamuf (Lincoln: University of Nebraska Press, 1988)

FLEISSNER, ROBERT F., *Sources, Meaning, and Influences of Coleridge's 'Kubla Khan': Xanadu re-routed: a study in the ways of romantic variety* (Lewiston: Mellen Press, 2000)

GERBER, RICHARD, 'Cybele, Kubla Khan, and Keats: An essay on imaginative transmutation', *English Studies*, 46. 1–6 (1965), 359–89

——, 'Keys to Kubla Khan', *English Studies*, 44 (1963), 321–41

GRASS, THIERRY, 'La traduction comme appropriation: le cas des toponymes étrangers', *Meta: Translators' Journal*, 51. 4 (2006), 660–70

HILL, JOHN SPENCER, *A Coleridge Companion* (London: Macmillan, 1983)

KNIGHT, G. WILSON, *The Starlit Dome: Studies in the Poetry of Vision* (New York: Routledge, 2002)
KRIPKE, SAUL, 'Naming and Necessity', in *Semantics of Natural Language*, ed. by Donald Davidson and Gilbert Harman (Dordrecht: Reidel, 1972), pp. 253–355
LACH, D. F., 'The Far East', in *The Hakluyt Handbook*, ed. by D. B. Quinn, 2 vols (Cambridge: Hakluyt Society, 1974), I, pp. 214–15
LOWES, J. L., *The Road to Xanadu: A Study in the Ways of Imagination* (Boston: Houghton Mifflin, 1927)
MAN, JOHN, *Kublai Khan: from Xanadu to Superpower* (London: Bantam, 2007)
MANKIEWICZ, HERMAN J. and WELLES, ORSON, 'The Shooting Script', in *The Citizen Kane Book*, ed. by Pauline Kael (New York: Bantam, 1971) pp. 127–306
MEIER, HANS HEINRICH, 'Ancient Lights on Kubla's Lines', *English Studies*, 46. 1–6 (1965), 15–29
MESCHONNIC, HENRI, *Pour la poétique II: Épistémologie de l'écriture poétique de la traduction* (Paris: Gallimard, 1973)
NEWMARK, PETER, *A Textbook of Translation* (New York: Prentice Hall, 1988)
PATRICK, JOHN M., 'Ammianus and Alpheus: The Sacred River', *Modern Language Notes*, 72. 5 (1957), 335–37
PERRY, SEAMUS, 'Coleridge's Names', *The Coleridge Bulletin*, n.s., 11 (1998), 37–47
POLO, MARCO, *Dei Viaggi di Messer Marco Polo, gentilhuomo venetiano* [1298], in Giovanni Battista Ramusio, *Delle Navigationi et Viaggi* (Venice: Giunti, 1583)
——, *The Description of the World*, trans. by A. C. Moule and P. Pelliot, 2 vols (London: Routledge & Kegan Paul, 1938)
PURCHAS, SAMUEL, *Hakluytus posthumus, or, Purchas his Pilgrimes*, 4 vols (London: Fetherston, 1625)
RÉCANATI, FRANÇOIS, 'La sémantique des noms propres: remarques sur la notion de "désignateur rigide"', *Langue française*, 57 (1983), 106–18
SCHNEIDER, ELISABETH, *Coleridge, Opium and Kubla Khan* (Chicago: University of Chicago Press, 1953)
SHAVER, CHESTER LINN, *Wordsworth's Library: A Catalogue* (London: Garland, 1979)
SMALL, MARGARET, 'A World Seen through Another's Eyes: Hakluyt, Ramusio, and the Narratives of the *Navigationi e Viaggi*', in *Richard Hakluyt and Travel Writing in Early Modern Europe*, ed. by Daniel Cary and Claire Jowitt (Farnham: Ashgate, 2012), pp. 45–56
SNYDER, EDWARD, *Hypnotic poetry: a Study of Trance-inducing Technique in Certain Poems and its Literary Significance* (Philadelphia: University of Pennsylvania Press, 1930)
STEVENSON, WARREN, *A Study of Coleridge's Three Great Poems* (Lewiston: Mellen Press, 2001)
WORTHEN, JOHN, *The Cambridge Introduction to Samuel Taylor Coleridge* (Cambridge: Cambridge University Press, 2010)

Notes to Chapter 15

1. Jacques Derrida, *The Ear of the Other: Otobiography, Transference, Translation*, ed. by Christie V. McDonald, trans. by Peggy Kamuf (Lincoln: University of Nebraska Press, 1988), p. 201.
2. Samuel Taylor Coleridge, 'Kubla Khan: Or, A Vision in a Dream. A Fragment', in *Poetical Works*, ed. by Ernest H. Coleridge (Oxford, Oxford University Press, 1969), pp. 295–98.
3. See John Spencer Hill, *A Coleridge Companion* (London: Macmillan Press, 1983), p. 61.
4. On rigid designators, see Saul Kripke, 'Naming and Necessity', in *Semantics of Natural Language*, ed. by Donald Davidson and Gilbert Harman (Dordrecht: D. Reidel, 1972), pp. 253–355; François Récanati, 'La sémantique des noms propres: remarques sur la notion de "désignateur rigide"', *Langue française*, 57 (1983), 106–18. On the translation of proper nouns, see Michel Ballard, *Le Nom propre en traduction* (Paris: Ophrys, 2001); Thierry Grass, 'La traduction comme

appropriation: le cas des toponymes étrangers', *Meta: Translators' Journal*, 51. 4 (2006), 660–70; Peter Newmark, *A Textbook of Translation* (New York: Prentice Hall, 1988), pp. 35–36, 214–16.
5. References: *Hermès*, 3 (1934), 53; Samuel Taylor Coleridge, *Koubla Khan* (Paris: GLM, 1939); Coleridge, *Vingt-cinq poèmes* (Paris: Aubier, 1945), p. 323; Louis Cazamian, *Anthologie de la poésie anglaise* (Paris: Delamain, 1946) p. 204; S. T. Coleridge, *Le Dit du vieux marin* (Paris: J. Corti, 1947), p. 91; Samuel Taylor Coleridge, *Poèmes* (Paris: Aubier-Flammarion, 1975), p. 275; *Tropismes*, 13 (2006), 79; Michel Midan, *Voix d'outre-Manche* (Paris: L'Harmattan, 2002), p. 91; Gérard Gâcon, *Le Lait de paradis* (Grenoble: ELLUG, 2005), p. 251; Samuel Taylor Coleridge, *La Ballade du vieux marin* (Paris: Gallimard, 2007), p. 187; S. T. Coleridge, *Der alte Seemann und Kubla Khan* (Heidelberg: Lambert-Schneider, 1959), p. 254; S. T. Coleridge, *Gedichte* (Stuttgart: Reclam, 1973), p. 181; Ramón López Ortega, *Antología bilingüe* (Seville: Publicaciones de la Universidad, 1978), p. 33; Samuel Taylor Coleridge, *Kubla Khan y otros poemas* (Madrid: Alianza Editorial, 2009), p. 167; José María Valverde, *Poetas románticos ingleses* (Barcelona: Planeta, 1989), p. 109; *Veredas Favip*, 3:2 (2010), 91; Mario Praz, *Poeti inglesi dell'Ottocento* (Florence: Bemporad, 1925), p. 161; S. T. Coleridge, *Poesie e prose* (Milan: Cederna, 1949), p. 86; *Translation Studies: Retrospective and Prospective Views*, 7 (2010), 41; Konstantin Balmont, *Izbrannye stichotvorenija i poèmy* (Munich: Fink, 1975), p. 390.
6. Marco Polo, *Dei Viaggi di Messer Marco Polo, gentilhuomo venetiano* [1298], in Giovanni Battista Ramusio, *Navigationi et Viaggi* (Venice: Giunti, 1583), pp. 16–17. In English: 'A city which is called Ciandu, which the great Kaan, who now lives and reigns and who has the name Cublai Kaan, who is spoken of in this book, made them make there. And in this city Cublay Kaan made them make there a vast palace of marble cunningly worked and of other fair stone [...] so well and so cunningly that it is a delight to see'. Marco Polo, *The Description of the World*, trans. by A. C. Moule and P. Pelliot, 2 vols (London: Routledge & Kegan Paul, 1938), I, 185.
7. The dating of the composition of the poem is controversial; in his 1816 preface to *Kubla Khan*, Coleridge mentions 'the summer of the year 1797', but this is widely believed to be a mistake. See Coleridge, *Poetical Works*, p. 295.
8. Samuel Purchas, *Hakluytus posthumus, or, Purchas his Pilgrimes*, 4 vols (London: Fetherston, 1625), IV, 418. It should be noted that the passage is misremembered by Coleridge, whose preface to *Kubla Khan* quotes: 'Here the Khan Kubla commanded a palace to be built, and a stately garden thereunto. And thus ten miles of fertile ground were enclosed with a wall'.
9. See for example Warren Stevenson, *A Study of Coleridge's Three Great Poems* (Lewiston: Edwin Mellen Press, 2001), p. 27.
10. Philippe Ménard, 'Le mélange des langues dans les diverses versions du *Devisement du monde* de Marco Polo', in *Le Plurilinguisme au Moyen Âge, Orient-Occident, de Babel à la langue une*, ed. by Claire Kappler and Suzanne Thiolier-Méjean (Paris: L'Harmattan, 2009), pp. 233–49. See also Pierre Racine, *Marco Polo et ses voyages* (Paris: Perrin, 2012).
11. 'Variantes et tableau comparatif des noms propres et des noms de lieux cités dans les Voyages de Marco Polo', in *Recueil de voyages et de mémoires*, ed. by Conrad Malte-Brun, 8 vols (Paris: Impr. d'Everat, 1824), I, 534–35, 542–43.
12. On initial 'x' the OED writes: 'The third value /z/, arising from a reduction of /gz/, is given in all cases to initial x, as Xerxes /ˈzɜːksiːz/; this value is shown in many instances in the 17th and 18th centuries by the spelling with z, as Zanthian, zebeck, Zerez...'
13. See Margaret Small, 'A World Seen through Another's Eyes: Hakluyt, Ramusio, and the Narratives of the *Navigationi e Viaggi*', in *Richard Hakluyt and Travel Writing in Early Modern Europe*, ed. by Daniel Cary and Claire Jowitt (Farnham: Ashgate, 2012), pp. 45–56; D. F. Lach, 'The Far East', in *The Hakluyt Handbook*, ed. by D. B. Quinn, 2 vols (Cambridge: Hakluyt Society, 1974), I, 214–15.
14. John Man, *Kublai Khan: from Xanadu to Superpower* (London: Bantam, 2007), p. 389.
15. J. L. Lowes, *The Road to Xanadu: A Study in the Ways of Imagination* (Boston: Houghton Mifflin, 1927), p. 360–61; Chester Linn Shaver, *Wordsworth's Library: A Catalogue* (London: Garland, 1979), p. 208.
16. Among other spellings, the OED quotes 'caan, cane, can, canne, caunn, chaan, chane, chahan, chawn, khaun, khan, kan, kaan'. Among other examples in literature, it quotes John Mandeville:

'the Grete Caan of Cathay' (*The Travels*, 1425); Thomas More: 'ye graund Canis' (*A Dialogue of Comfort*, 1553); Thomas Herbert: 'the Chawn [...] of Shyras' (*A Relation of Some Yeares Travaile*, 1634); and John Milton: 'Cambalu, seat of Cathaian Can' (*Paradise Lost*, 1667).

17. Seamus Perry, 'Coleridge's Names', *The Coleridge Bulletin*, n.s., 11 (1998), 41. Perry goes on to quote a relevant passage from Coleridge's correspondence: 'From my earliest years I have had a feeling of Dislike & Disgust connected with my own Christian Name: such a vile short plumpness, such a dull abortive smartness, in [the] first Syllable, & this so harshly contrasted by the obscurity & indefiniteness of the syllabic Vowel, & the feebleness of the uncovered liquid, with which it ends — the wabble it makes, & staggering between a diss- & a tri-syllable — & the whole name sounding as if you were abeeceeing. S.M.U.L. — altogether it is perhaps the worst combination, of which vowels & consonants are susceptible.' *The Collected Letters of Samuel Taylor Coleridge*, ed. by Earl Leslie Griggs, 6 vols (Oxford: Clarendon, 1956–71), II, 1126.
18. *Xanadu* is not the only new coinage in the poem: 'Coleridge even invented for it the simple word "greenery", new to the English language'. John Worthen, *The Cambridge Introduction to Samuel Taylor Coleridge* (Cambridge: Cambridge University Press, 2010), p. 28.
19. Since my focus here is on the meaning of the opening distich, I will not dwell on the evolution and translations of the two other names in the poem, Mount Abora and the river Alph — even though the latter has a particularly rich diachronic history and onomastic significance, and was translated into many different versions: l'Alphée (Vauthier), l'Alphe (d'Hangest), Alphe (Darras), Alphée (Cazamian), le fleuve Alphée (Parisot), l'Alph (Midan), Alph (Gâcon), Alph (Breitwieser), el Alfa (López Ortega), o Alfeu (Valverde), Alfeo (Ceni) and Alf (Praz). See John M. Patrick, 'Ammianus and Alpheus: The Sacred River', *Modern Language Notes*, 72:5 (1957), 335–37, and Lane Cooper, 'The Abyssinian Paradise in Coleridge and Milton', *Modern Philology*, 3:3 (1906), 327–32.
20. Richard Gerber, 'Cybele, Kubla Khan, and Keats: An essay on imaginative transmutation', *English Studies*, 46:1–6 (1965), 24; and 'Keys to Kubla Khan', *English Studies*, 44 (1963), 321–41.
21. Hans Heinrich Meier, 'Ancient Lights on Kubla's Lines', *English Studies*, 46:1–6 (1965), 19.
22. Robert F. Fleissner, *Sources, Meaning, and Influences of Coleridge's 'Kubla Khan': Xanadu re-routed: a study in the ways of romantic variety* (Lewiston: Mellen Press, 2000), p. 5.
23. G. Wilson Knight, 'Coleridge's Divine Comedy' [1941], in *The Starlit Dome: Studies in the Poetry of Vision* (New York: Routledge, 2002), p. 97.
24. Quotation and diagram: Elisabeth Schneider, *Coleridge, Opium and Kubla Khan* (Chicago: University of Chicago Press, 1953), p. 274. The visual similarity between X and K certainly adds to this effect.
25. This sample includes all existing translations of *Kubla Khan* into French, to which were added three in Spanish, two in Italian and German, and one in Portuguese, Romanian and Russian. Translations of the poem do exist in a number of other languages, including Greek and Japanese, but these exceed the range of my expertise. Three of the translators of *Kubla Khan*, namely Balmont, Darras and Luzi, also are (or were) fine poets in their own right.
26. *Le Livre de Marco Polo, citoyen de Venise*, ed. by M. G. Pauthier (Paris: Firmin Didot, 1865).
27. Herman J. Mankiewicz and Orson Welles, 'The Shooting Script', in *The Citizen Kane Book*, ed. by Pauline Kael (New York: Bantam, 1971), p. 138. Italics mine. Since then, the name Xanadu was given to a number of things and places, including a 1980 Hollywood musical, a bright area on one of Saturn's moons, and a coffee brand, to name but a few.
28. Jacques Derrida, 'Des tours de Babel', trans. by Joseph F. Graham, in *Psyche. Inventions of the Other*, ed. by Peggy Kamuf (Stanford: Stanford University Press, 2007), p. 197.
29. Ibid., p. 199.
30. See Edward Snyder, *Hypnotic poetry: a Study of Trance-inducing Technique in Certain Poems and its Literary Significance* (Philadelphia: University of Pennsylvania Press, 1930), p. 45: 'In the early stages of a hypnotic poem a foreign word, an obscure phrase, or any slight difficulty that causes fatigue from strain on the part of the listener may actually promote the ultimate aesthetic effect at which the artist aims.'
31. Henri Meschonnic, 'Au commencement', in *Pour la poétique II: Épistémologie de l'écriture poétique de la traduction* (Paris: Gallimard, 1973), p. 430.

32. 'Cette traduction sans illusion ni sanction, cette approche délibérément personnelle, ne peut que se savoir un simple moment au sein d'une suite d'autres interprétations du même poème: et ce savoir, ce consentement d'emblée accordé par un traducteur au travail des autres dans les années à venir, instituera ainsi une activité, le traduire. [...] En somme, si chaque traduction est moins que l'original, le *traduire* comme tel, l'activité que l'on peut nommer le traduire, va — nous dit-on — en donner à la longue l'équivalent et même sans doute davantage: ces déchiffrements successifs ayant fait paraître au grand jour un infini de la signifiance que l'auteur, pour sa part, avait réfréné autant que vécu.' Yves Bonnefoy, *La Communauté des traducteurs* (Strasbourg: Presses universitaires de Strasbourg, 2000), pp. 24–25.

CHAPTER 16

The Hungarian Spectrum of Petronius's *Satyricon*

Péter Hajdu

The Hungarian translations of Petronius's *Satyricon* offer a suitable terrain to test the metaphor of translation as prism. Although the five translations cover a time-span little longer than one hundred years (1900–2014), I will not try to create a historical pattern mostly to avoid the implication of a teleology, a story of development towards better and better translations. The canon of acceptable translation strategies is constantly changing in a given target culture, not independently from the purpose and context of translations, therefore a historical analysis is perfectly legitimate. However, absolutising the present perspective is an obvious danger in such approaches (on the part of both the analyser and the reader of the analysis). One can easily suppose that translations produced in a time closer to the present are better just because they better fulfil what is expected from a translation in the current cultural context. I will rather focus on how all the translations highlight different aspects of Petronius's work. As a dispersive prism breaks up the white light into the spectral colours, the Hungarian translations show various colours of the ancient text as if separately. (It goes without saying, however, that the translations do not show all the colours, since the number of possible aspects is theoretically infinite.) Which colour a translator finds most important, of course, will be at least partly determined by the context of the given cultural-historical moment, but the cognitive tool of the concept 'prismatic translation' gives me the opportunity to avoid a storytelling approach to the translations — even if they follow each other in time — but rather look at them synoptically.

It is always a challenge to translate Latin texts into a non-Indo-European language, which has completely different grammatical structure, and whose readers have different ideas about the artistic merits of a text. For example, speakers of an agglutinating language (which languages tend to have rather long words), which puts the accent always on the first syllable, will probably have different ideas of rhythm from those who use shorter words and flexible accents. Differences in linguistic artistry, of course, also derive from the differences in cultural or literary development. Hungarian readers of poetry tend to prefer rich figurative texture to precise formulations of thought. The situation is especially delicate with Petronius in Hungary for two reasons. On the one hand, the text does not everywhere fit in with the traditional standards of the Latin language as it is taught in schools and for which a canon of translation strategies has been developed. The first person narrator Encolpius speaks or writes an elegant and eloquent Latin, and the numerous poetic insertions of various functions[1] also use a Latin grammar familiar from the schoolroom. The topics discussed and represented in the narrative, however, are many times such as do not appear in the usual reading material provided for students, therefore they bring with them an unfamiliar vocabulary. Since most of the medium-sized dictionaries collect their words from the canonical texts and target a school-centred readership, translators of Petronius meet strange words on every page. And since of the texts from ancient Roman literature that have survived the centuries of Christian selection very few use the lexicon of the lower social strata and discuss the kind of topics that Petronius does, many words do not actually appear in any other text transmitted from classical antiquity. Moreover, Encolpius frequently quotes speeches of uneducated non-native speakers of Latin: this challenges translators both because they cannot use the usual translation strategies and because they need to recreate a style which has an important function in the characterisation.[2] On the other hand, the vivid, sometimes experimental, polyphonic style of the twentieth- and twenty-first-century novel may have encouraged translators to use free, creative strategies to adapt the text to the expectations of novel readers. It is difficult to position Petronius' work in the ancient system of literary genres, but it is certain that ancient readers could not have regarded it as a novel, since for them such a genre did not exist. The prosimetric form pushes the work very close to the Menippean satire,[3] and the recurrent themes are mostly familiar from Roman verse satire. We may agree with Gian Biagio Conte that the work is a unique composition which is indebted to several genre traditions,[4] but the novel can hardly be regarded as of primary importance among those traditions. For nineteenth-century literary criticism, the novel was regarded as of little esteem because it represented the less elevated aspects of human life and also the life of lower social strata. For some this interest in low topics made up the essence of 'realism'. Such a content may bridge the modern novel to ancient satire (rather than most ancient novels), including the *Satyricon*. We should also keep in mind that satire, which tended to mock all the serious genres, had always already created a mixture of genres, but also that Mikhail Bakhtin regarded the Menippean satire as the most important ancestor of the polyphonic style of the modern novel.[5] The ancient novel became an important research topic for classical philology only after the novel became the central genre of the western literary system, and this change seems to have been a precondition for the *Satyricon* to start being regarded as a novel in the 20th century. Nowadays, studies in Petronius' *Satyricon* tend to discuss the problem of the genre in some detail, while comprehensive histories of Roman or ancient literature do not hesitate to call it a novel. Be that as it may, the novelistic approach may have had a liberating effect on the twentieth-century Hungarian translators of the text.

Five Hungarian translators have tested their skills on this challenging work. István Székely (1900)[6] and József Révay (1920)[7] translated only the single long continuous fragment, namely Trimalchio's banquet; then István Károly Horváth (1963)[8] translated all the available fragments. György Faludy (2002)[9] and Zoltán Csehy (2014)[10] omitted only the long epic inserts on the sack of Troy (89) and the civil war (119–24), because they thought the artistic merit of those poems was based on stylistic parody, which could not work in translation. All the translators can be regarded as trained professionals, since they translated many books.

Székely was a secondary school teacher all his life, and wrote several textbooks and teaching materials mostly for Latin. He also translated many books from German, but only three from Latin. One of them, selected biographies by Cornelius Nepos,[11] was obviously inspired by his school training; another, *The Twelve Caesars* by Suetonius,[12] seems to have been a byproduct of his scholarly activity, since he wrote his dissertation on Suetonius' style.[13] His Petronius translation, however, cannot be linked to his teaching activity. His Hungarian text was published as a very cheap, very simple booklet, which stands in harsh contrast to Petronius's later Hungarian translations, which are rather pretty with good quality paper and attractive typography, some of them with many pictures too. The first edition of the third translation was a publication for true bibliophiles, embellished with many drawings by a leading book illustrator, Ádám Würtz (1927–1994). It is very probable that publishers intended to counterbalance the sometimes obscene content, obviously challenging (although to a diminishing degree and in different ways) twentieth-century norms of literary expression, with the appearance of those books. The text is a delicacy for the connoisseur who can appreciate both the visual aesthetics of the book and the artistic merits of the text, not letting themselves be seduced by the content. Székely, however, had different intentions. He thought that the content delivered an important message to his society. His introduction was designed to highlight it.

For Székely, Trimalchio's banquet is a source of history of manners, and he explains in detail why the text delivers an important message to *fin-de-siècle* readers. Those who attend the banquet are not Romans but freedmen, 'slaves recruited from abroad'. The idea that the slaves are recruited may make a reader suspicious, but the continuation is even stranger: 'These and similar people were those who, getting rich through lucky, often unfair business, and ruining the lighthearted sons of the old noble families as usurers, were, so to say, a heavy burden on the shoulders of the Roman nation.'[14] This is not simply a xenophobic discourse (which is not at all alien to Roman satire either), but the voice of late-nineteenth-century antisemitism. Calling the *nouveaux riche* freedmen 'usurers' (which claim is completely unsupported by the life stories of the banqueters) was enough for contemporary readers to see those 'parvenus from two thousand years ago' as predecessors of the Jews as represented by contemporary antisemitism, and to understand the topical political message Székely wanted to bring home. The setting, Southern Italy, he describes as follows: 'that part of the empire where the Greek influence, so harmful to the nation, was burgeoning most wildly.'[15] From a historical viewpoint, this description is completely wrong. The Greeks had arrived in Southern Italy centuries earlier than the Romans, therefore they could not undermine the Roman nation there.

Historical inaccuracy and logical inconsistency, however, are not unusual in the discourse of xenophobia. Székely charges an oppressed, subjugated group with terrible crimes, and who he wants to protect from them is the elite, the 'old noble families' of the society. He concludes as follows:

> We can imagine the shock this grand satire could cause in the always sinking, so called noble Roman society. They could feel, beside the attack on the alien habits, that they also should do something. However, wealth and the independence that comes with it have already moved to the new possessors, and the Roman society was much too corrupted to retain enough moral strength to perform their national duties.
>
> I think my work was not entirely superfluous when I was trying to translate this miniature masterpiece into our language.[16]

The constant (and obviously anachronistic) mentioning of 'nation' *(nemzet)* deeply anchors this discourse in modern nationalism with obviously xenophobic and easily decodable anti-semitic emphasis. However, this political attitude, which is for Székely the reason and purpose of translating, cannot be detected in the target text. He needed the relatively long introduction to provide an interpretative tool, namely that Petronius' xenophobia should be understood in the context of modern anti-semitism. He wanted his readers to learn an anti-semitic lesson from the *Satyricon*.

Since Székely translated only a long fragment with the narrative of a social gathering, he rarely had to face the problem of explicit sexual content. Nevertheless he discussed this problem in his introduction: 'this should not be criticised the way realists of today are, since Petronius counted on the trend of his own time, and was far from trying artificially to arouse readers, as e.g. modern French naturalists do. Even the most vulgar scenes he covered with a kind of smiling irony.'[17] As one can see, Székely does not suggest any historical reading; he does not explain the different roles explicit sexual content plays in different cultures or literary traditions. He only emphasizes the irony, which he thinks excludes arousal. This approach to the sexual content disregards the fact that the *Satyricon* does not follow the tradition of smiling irony (not to mention raging moral preaching) in Roman verse satire so much as what Bakhtin described as the 'grotesque realism' of ancient satyr drama and comedy.[18]

In contrast to the translator's political message, his prudish attitude towards sexuality is in fact apparent in the actual text he produced. He always makes the text more refined. I will quote only two examples. When Trimalchio starts making out with a beautiful boy (74.8), this pederastic content hardly appears in the translation. First of all, the boy *(puer)* becomes a youth *(ifjú,* the still usual although already archaic translation for *iuuenis)*, then the rather long kissing *(diutius osculari)* becomes kisses all over his cheeks.[19] And when in his anger Trimalchio calls his wife a *lupatria* (a brothel-whore), Székely translates it as 'woman' *(asszony)* (37.4). This prism filters the vulgar, socially unacceptable sexual content.

Generally speaking, Székely translated with a liberty unusual among his contemporaries so that Petronius speaks a Hungarian that is consumable in a period in which Hungarian prose writing achieved unprecedented excellence, while translated texts, especially from Latin, were of a very low standard. One of the reasons for this liberty could be the cheap booklet series in which the work appeared, since it was designed to reach a wider audience than the usual translations of the classics. Another reason may be the topical political message which Székely thought he had discovered in the ancient text, and which he wanted to disseminate as widely as possible. The novel-like character of the work could also have had a liberating effect, if the translator had not felt the pressure of philological accuracy so much, while trying to cope with the challenge of competing with contemporary narrative prose. It is true that his political tendency is suspicious, that in several places he did not understand the original, that he was unable to break completely with archaising trends, and that he could not handle stylistic registers in a manner evocative of Petronius' art, but he was very flexible with many features which made translations from Latin very awkward in the Hungarian tradition. Translators usually wanted to keep the Latin sentence boundaries also in Hungarian, while Székely easily contracted short sentences or broke up long ones. For instance, he made one sentence from these two, which editors tend to regard as separated by a lacuna: *Non licebat †multaciam† considerare. Nos iam ad triclinium perueneramus* (30.1). In Michael Heseltine's translation it sounds as follows: 'I could not take the whole multiplicacity in at one... we now went through to the dining room.'[20] Székely rendered the two statements as one logical unit: 'I did not have the time to inspect everything, because we already reached the dining room.'[21] He hardly ever tried to keep the Latin word order (which makes many Hungarian translations awkward: although word order in Hungarian is almost as free as in Latin, emphasis is signaled by the position of a word inside a sentence), and he never uses passive verb forms (which were obsolete already in 1900, and only translators of Latin texts used them). Participles are immensely rarer in Hungarian than in Latin, and translators (as a consequence of a school-bounded translation practice) love to translate them with subordinate clauses while trying to express the time relations. Since current Hungarian has only two verb tenses (past and present) this is not easy, and brings with it either the usage of archaic verb forms or complicated formulations with a plethora of subordinate clauses. Székely elaborated inventive strategies to cope with participles, and he did not even care about subordination. His bravest solution is the translation of the following sentence: *Nos libertatem sine tyranno nacti coepimus inuitare conuiuarum sermones* (With the tyrant away we had our freedom and we proceeded to draw conversation from our neighbours) (41.9), which he made very short: Föllélegeztünk és szabadon beszélni kezdtünk [We sighed of relief and started freely speaking].[22]

The target text is not an isolated achievement of the translator. It is influenced by the context of contemporary political discourse in the target culture, the linguistic tradition of translations, and the stylistic environment of prose writing as well. Székely's translation as a prism (including his introduction) makes the xenophobic coloration dominant. Petronius's representation of Trimalchio and his friends is xenophobic enough: readers are supposed to laugh at the bad Latin of non-native speakers and at the forced immigrants' inability to adapt to a sophisticated code of behaviour in their new social environment. Connecting this aspect to the antisemitism of his own time Székely tried to make it the work's centre of thought.

On the other hand, the pressure of Petronius's unique Latin and the stylistic environment of the contemporary Hungarian prose break up the Hungarian translation tradition and allows more varied colours.

The next translator of Petronius, József Révay (1881–1970) was a freelance translator and writer in that period of his life. Until 1919 he had had a promising career in education, but due to his involvement in the Hungarian Soviet Republic, he was not allowed to teach in the counter-revolutionary regime between 1920–45, so he made a living from translating Latin, Greek, Italian and French literature. He wrote several informative books on ancient cultural history, but also many works of historical fiction.[23] The first edition of his translation of Trimalchio's banquet was a beautiful booklet, but it was several times reprinted in less prestigious formats, once even in a bilingual edition, and once together with Apuleius' *Golden Ass*.

With his fresh, fluent prose he standardized the Hungarian Petronius. His text is easily readable, arguably too easily. There is nothing interesting in it, apart from the content, since everything is converted into a simple, conversational Hungarian. This cannot happen without eliminating many hindrances to understanding through a domesticating translation strategy. The vocabulary that implies ancient Roman objects, habits, and ideas tends to be replaced with seemingly neutral expressions, which, however, may happen to be anachronistic, as when *mimus* is translated as musical comedy (*énekes bohózat,* 35.6), or *babaecalus* as fine cavalier (*finom gavallér,* 37.10). In order to increase its readability the text has to lose some of its ancient, alien taste.

The domesticating strategy is clearly visible in the translation of the characteristic vocabulary suggestive of ancient world view or religion, which Révay tends to replace with everyday usage, yet which, however, can easily imply Christianity by default. The everyday usage in the language of a nation that converted to Christianity about a thousand years earlier necessarily uses monotheistic concepts of divinity and frequently refers to Biblical stories and formulations. When a character, Niceros, tells about the awakening of love, he says it happened 'as the gods wanted' (*quomodo dii volunt,* 61.6), which Révay translates as follows: *Isten különös rendeléséből* [for God's peculiar order].[24] In the next sentence he swears to Hercules *(mehercules)* that he did not fall in love with Melissa's bodily aspects, which Révay renders as 'I swear to God' *(Isten engem úgy segéljen).* These are all simple colloquial expressions, both in Latin and Hungarian, but the Hungarian ones are embedded in a monotheistic discourse. Readers of this translation do not have to think about the otherness of a culture that has several gods and has various options of whom to swear to.

Niceros is a rather unintelligent speaker, which is suggested among other features by the strange similes he applies in his narrative of the werewolf soldier. He says that the soldier was as strong as Orcus, the god of death, which might make sense (*fortis tamquam Orcus,* 62.2). When Révay writes 'strong as a bull' (*erős, mint a bika*), he is partly filtering the alien religious content, but he also stages a character who speaks in flat commonplaces. More interesting is the second simile, when Niceros says: 'I stood like a dead man.' It is a general experience that dead people do not stand; however, they do not move either. Niceros selects a simile for his motionless state rather awkwardly, which tells us something about his limited capacities (*stabam tamquam mortuus,* 62.6). Révay, either because he realized the absurdity of the image or because he wanted to put an everyday colloquial expression as he usually did, translated it as 'I stood like a pillar of salt.' *(Úgy álltam, mint a sóbálvány.)* The expression is colloquial and flat enough, but a person who uses it must know the Bible quite well, since he refers to the story of Lot's wife from the Book of Genesis.[25] I have to emphasize that the light Christianisation is not more than a probably-unintended lateral effect of his strategy to make the text easily accessible to his Hungarian readers, which filters many culturally alien, but with it also many artistic, features. The concept of prismatic translation makes it difficult to see something as mere domestication, since it might create prismatic effects like that of a religious tension. József Révay attended Catholic schools in his youth and he joined the Piarist monks for a decade (1895–1904), leaving the order just before he was supposed to accept the sacrament of priesthood. This background makes it highly probable that the Christianisation in his translation is unintentional. His everyday language was deeply impregnated with Christian implications.

To make the text more familiar to his readers, Révay also uses several Hungarian idioms and proverbs. The incompatible cultural implications may remain undiscovered by many Hungarian readers who do not realise that colloquial expressions have some special background in the history of language. This is evident in the colloquialisms discussed above that go back ultimately to the Bible. Let me quote one more example of this kind. When Encolpius' neighbour introduces to him the participants of the banquet, he says of somebody: *non impropero illi,* which means 'I don't blame him', although in a rather bad Latin with the verb *impropero* that is a corrupted form for *improbo* (38.11). Révay's translation 'I don't throw a stone at him' *(Nem vetek rá követ.)* is a colloquialism that some Hungarian readers may not connect with the ancient practice of stoning (unknown for Romans, but still in use in the Middle East) or Jesus' sentence in John 8.7. The predilection for idioms may result in the abundance of figurative language in Hungarian. Here we have a figure of speech while Petronius used the simplest possible utterance.[26] Where Révay thought that Trimalchio's reference to some dry fig, which had been lost, would not tell much to the Hungarian readers who were not familiar with that fruit of Mediterranean climate he made Trimalchio quote François Villon: where is the snow of yesteryear? (64.3: *Abistis dulces caricae!* → *Hol van már a tavalyi hó?)* The refrain of the 'Ballade des dames du temps jadis' is so well known that many readers will take it as a general proverb.

Révay loves using Hungarian proverbs and idioms, which may make the text more familiar to his readers. He repeatedly refers to an East-European dairy product, *tejföl,* a sort of sour cream, which Hungarians tend to be mad about. Hungarians living abroad usually say that it is one of the things they miss the most.[27] It is completely unattested in ancient Italy. When Révay writes of people who swim in *tejföl,* he creates a counter-variation of the idiom that something is not *tejföl* to the bottom of the pot.[28] In one place a misogynistic 'truism' formulated by a drunken character (We'd have everything as cheap as dirt if there were no women) is transformed into a pseudo-proverb. (67.10: *Mulieres si non essent, omnia pro luto haberemus.* → *Ha nem volnának nők, nyakig úsznánk a tejfölben.* [We'd swim neck-deep in *tejföl* if there were no women.]) In another place, however, a reference to the ancient carnival Saturnalia is converted into the image of a popular utopia of swimming in *tejföl.* (44.3: *nam isti maiores maxillae semper Saturnalia agunt* (for the bigger jaws are always keeping Saturnalia) → *mert azok a nagyfejűek nyakig úsznak a tejfölben* [for those big shots[29] are swimming neck-deep in *tejföl*].) The Romans in Révay's translation are not too much different from twentieth-century Hungarians, since they eat the same dairy products, they use the same proverbs and also love to refer to stories from the Bible, and they hardly ever mention pagan gods. Many alien features are filtered and a rather simple easily consumable text is created, reading which one can focus on the story alone. Cultural otherness, however, cannot only washed away from a text: something else must take the place of what has been removed. If all the gods but one are removed, the result is a different kind of god, a different religious context. Due to its newly acquired Hungarianness the text becomes digestible, and this prismatic effect might be called the tejfölisation of Petronius.

The third translator of the *Satyricon*, István Károly Horváth (1931–66) was a university teacher and a successful scholar with remarkable academic achievement despite his early death and alcoholism. He loved to do research in comic and satirical texts. He published an important paper on the social prestige of comic genres in ancient Roman context (Horváth 1956),[30] and wrote about Catullus, Ovid, Persius, and Juvenal. His only major translation is the *Satyricon*. According to a legendary anecdote he tried to collect the various manuscripts of *Indecent Toldi*, the anonymous pornographic (and highly imaginative) parody of the most canonical Hungarian epic poem, *Toldi* (1846) by János Arany (1817–1882). He is said to have been preparing a critical edition (Czigány 1997, 29–31).[31] In order to adapt this interest to the ideological requirements of the communist system, Horváth focused on two minor Marxist issues, namely popular culture and realism. Realism was a much-discussed topic in Soviet literary scholarship in the 1950s and the school, which sought to interpret the history of world literature as a struggle between realism and anti-realism (in parallel with the idea that the history of philosophy is a struggle between idealism and materialism), had a lasting influence in Hungary. As for his other central notion, namely popular literature, we have to admit that it was a good idea to connect comic literature and lower stylistic registers to the literary production of the people, since ideologically it was evident that whatever the people were doing should be regarded as good. The result, the interpretation of ancient texts as representing popular realism was uninteresting and hardly innovative from the viewpoint of literary theory, but in the Communist context Horváth had to elaborate a theory to harmonize his interest with official Marxism, and he managed to base a highly successful career on it.

It is small wonder that he made Petronius a realist novelist. To provide a continuous narrative, he wrote shorter or longer passages to bridge the gaps between the fragments and summarizing the hypothetical events to come so that readers could easily understand unconnected fragments as parts of the plot. The translator's additions are in italics, so they can visually be differentiated from the translated text. In many places where editors suppose a lacuna, he did not indicate any, making the narration more continuous.

Around the time he was working on the translation, a fierce debate took place in Hungary about translations of the classics. Since it was triggered by the publication of the complete bilingual edition of Horace in 1961 and a long aggressive critique of it by a productive translator, poet and writer, István Vas (1910–1991), it is called the Horace-debate.[32] Vas spoke about the dictatorship of classical philologists, who successfully created a hermetically closed, autonomous reservoir for classical translations where the outside rules of Hungarian language and literary expression are invalid.[33] Actually he described an alienating translation strategy which is interested rather in teaching readers than in entertaining them. According to the (in)famous formulation of Gábor Devecseri: 'A reader might be exempt from learning the foreign language, but not from studying the foreign ways of thinking'.[34] However, according to Vas, Devecseri was a great poetic talent, and his achievement legitimized the philological paradigm despite his alienating approach, as if projecting the ancient text on the canvas of Hungarian language.

Horváth's translation fits into this alienating, philological paradigm. As an academic he really understands the Latin text (as far as the fragmentary, sometimes corrupted text can be understood), and he wants to present the result of his scholarly approach. He offers a culturally alien text, but also a lot of interpretation written into that text. Let me start with another simile of Niceros, namely that the wounded soldier 'was lying in the bed like an ox' (62.13: *iacebat miles meus in lecto tamquam bovis*). Oxen, as a rule, do not lie in bed. Niceros omitted to mention some vital elements of the similitude he may have had in mind, which is characteristic of his denseness. Révay translated the text literally, reproducing Petronius's joke — intentionally or unintentionally. Horváth, however, had to do more: 'like some slaughtered ox, he was lying in the bed.'[35] The joke disappears and the simile is explained in a college teacher's manner.

In many cases he formulated with the dryness of official correspondence. It would be, however, unfair to say that he has created a flat, philological commentary disguised as translation. On the contrary, his text strives to be too colourful. His alienating strategy and his desired emulation of novelists resulted in an elevated style. The problem, however, is that he did not have the talent to create great prose. His attempts thus usually fail and he simply writes tortured, unnatural sentences that are often actually meaningless. He tries to use original artistic expressions too, but with rather unsatisfactory results. He cannot resist the temptation to use archaic forms to make the text more interesting and sometimes words that may be either neologisms or dialectal expressions, although they cannot be found in dialectal dictionaries. Let me quote some of his most adventurous experiments. When Trimalchio asks Niceros to tell his story, the latter is delighted *(delectatus)* by his amiability (61.3). Horváth puts this as 'elángyorodva', a word which neither I nor anyone I know has ever heard. A somewhat similar verb, *ándorodik* appears in a nineteenth-century dictionary as a dialectal word,[36] and also in a dictionary of etymologies but with a meaning that does not really fit here, *to be absorbed in some activity,* which hardly expresses anything similar to *delectari*.[37] It is a bigger problem that the dialectal word appears in the narrator's discourse, which tends to be a polished, elegant Latin.

One of Trimalchio's extravagant ideas of serving food is the four statuettes of Marsyas, from whose little wineskins *(utriculi)* peppered fish sauce is flowing (36.3). Horváth puts an unknown and unattested word here too as the source of the sauce *(bulóka)*. Horváth coined the word *hímkéjenc* to express the meaning of the Greek loan-word *cinaedus* (21.2 and 23.2), and *hímkéjenctanonc* for *spatalocinaedus* (23.3). *Hímkéjenc* is a compound of *hím* (= male) and *kéjenc,* which means a man who seeks only pleasure. Horváth probably wanted the new compound to mean a man who seeks pleasure in males. Alas, it does not mean that or anything else; the expression is just meaningless and absurd. We see attempts at unique literary expression, which, however, fail.

It also happens that Horváth attributes false meanings to otherwise existing words, e.g. when he puts *fityula* [headdress of a nurse or a nun] as penis (24.7). It may be interpreted as a paronomasia, since *fityula* sounds similar to *fütyülő* [little whistle], which is a dead metaphor for a child's penis. But the need for a figurative expression in a text, which is otherwise far from shy, is unjustified.

What makes the text an unrewarding read, however, is not the failed attempts at poetic vocabulary or some absurd usages, but the ubiquitous alienating strategy that intentionally makes everything strange and difficult to comprehend.

The Horváth translation contains a foreword by the publishers. More than half of this paratext explains the vulgar and sexual content of the work, putting this aspect in a historical context. In the 20th century, it seems, the *Satyricon* was published in Hungary despite the sexual content. For the two recent translators, however, the sexual content might have been the main reason to work on the text. Both new translations look impressive with unusual format and expensive paper. György Faludy's 2002 translation is illustrated with colour pictures from Fellini's film, Zoltán Csehy's with reproductions of ancient graffiti.

György Faludy (1910–2006) had a great impact on the Hungarian translation history with his Villon book in 1937, creating a supreme example of a brave re-elaboration of a source text. That book was a great success, making François Villon popular in Hungary, though it was also disqualified as a translation by some for its unfaithfulness, using Villon only as a pretext to publish vulgar poetry in the manner of cabaret songs. The credit for the undeniable poetic merit of the text tended to be ascribed to Faludy rather than to Villon. His other big translation project was the complete *Pantagruel* by François Rabelais (1948). He was a successful poet, writer and journalist, who spent several decades in exile (1938–45, 1956–87). Zoltán Csehy (1973) is a poet and a university teacher in Bratislava, and also a prolific translator, mostly interested in the erotic or pornographic traditions of ancient and renaissance literature. He sees it as his mission to renew and enrich the sexual vocabulary of Hungarian literature, which he thinks is basically prudish. His *Satyricon* is the most radical attempt, since he produced a poetic translation of Petronius' prose, composing a book in hexameters (apart from some of the embedded poems that were originally written in some other metre).

Since the two most recent translations were made by poets, it is worth comparing their strategies in translating the verse parts of the *Satyricon* with that of Horváth. In twentieth-century Hungary (after some debates between different competing schools) the norm of formally faithful poetic translation was canonized, namely that the Hungarian text should be a poem with a metric pattern identical to that of the source text. Faithfulness, however, is not a self-evident concept regarding metre. Hungarian poetry can be written with two different types of metre. One is based on the number of syllables inside the measures (in the sense of musicology) which can be organized in innumerable metric patterns. The other, invented in the 16th century, is the imitation of Greek and Latin quantitative metre, although there are many small differences. It is therefore possible to use the same metric patterns in Hungarian as in Latin or Greek source texts, if one disregards the minor differences. Traditionally it is this metre in which German, Italian, and English poetry is translated into Hungarian, although they are not the same, because West-European poetry uses a qualitative, while Hungarians a quantitative metre. Hungarians seem to think that West-Europeans wished to have quantitative metrics, but could not, so the Hungarian translation can fulfil the source text's dream of being similar to ancient poetry.[38] Even though in a somewhat different system, Hungarian translators in the 20th century felt obliged to recreate the metric pattern of the source poem. This strategy started to be cautiously challenged some years ago.

Horváth, whose ideal was philological equivalence, copied the metric patterns of Petronius' poetic inserts with pedantic accuracy. Faludy, a notoriously unfaithful translator of poetry, did not care about formal equivalence, and translated most of the poems into the Hungarian national verse system, based on the number of syllables. On the one hand, this can be interpreted as a domesticating strategy, which makes the target text more Hungarian; on the other, Faludy adapted the poems to his own poetic style and wrote more or less typical Faludy-poems. Broadly speaking, the content of Petronius' poems is recognisable, while features like a loose rhyming give them a distinctively non-ancient character. The metric richness of Petronius' poems caused problems for Csehy, who translated the prose parts in hexameters, therefore the contrast between the poetic and non-poetic parts is not so obvious in his text. Some poetic inserts he translated in hexameters, but in some places he used the same metre as the source text. All three strategies are equally legitimate, although Horváth's was the most canonical in the context of modernism, and probably still is. Ironically enough his was the least successful attempt, not so much due to the strategy selected, but to his lack of poetic talent, his target poems cannot compete with those created by professional poets. This shows the limitation of 'strategy' as an analytical term for what goes for translation. Although it is possible that it is the strategy that makes a translation unacceptable in a given cultural context, a canonical strategy does not guarantee success. Much depends on the translator's 'talent', which is an unpredictable element in the prism.

Both Faludy and Csehy created smooth texts with great impetus, which read easily and enjoyably. They both use a lot of vulgar vocabulary, which in the case of Csehy makes an amusing contrast with the sublime, elevated poetic form. It is probably unfair to read these translations with the Latin source text in hand. The experience is, however, that the target texts always (or at least most of the time) tell something similar to the source text. Usually not something that one would want to call equivalent, but more or less similar. Students will not find them useful to understand the Latin text, but those who want to enjoy a story written in a great prose or poetry, respectively, will appreciate them.

There is, however, some difference between them: Csehy, who is also a professional philologist, knows Latin much better. Faludy sometimes writes something that does not even remind one remotely of the source text, and it is difficult not to imagine that it is because he had no idea what the Latin meant. Even if the poetic medium grants Csehy much more freedom, and he sometimes ventures a bit far from the source text, one never has the feeling that he does not understand it. We can even find some ridiculous mistranslations in Faludy. In the middle of Trimalchio's zodiac plate a *fauus* (honey-comb) is served, which Faludy translates as *lépvessző*, which means lime-twig (35.5). When Trimalchio interprets the whole plate, Faludy renders the final sentence about the *fauus* as follows: Mother Earth is set in the middle, and the lime-twig symbolizes the many good things Mother Earth is giving us (39.15).[39] I very much doubt that any reader can have the faintest idea how a lime-twig symbolizes all the blessings of Mother Earth. Faludy's problem was that the Hungarian word for *fauus*, which is *lép*, is homonymous with that of bird-lime, which is *uiscus* in Latin. Faludy seems to have confused the homonyms he found in the dictionary, which ultimately resulted in rather absurd symbolism. One might suppose that if his knowledge of Latin was that weak, he could use other translations. In his introduction he wrote: 'In places where the difficulty, obscurity or undecipherability of the Latin drove me to despair, for help I usually turned to P.G. Walsh's translation (Oxford, 1997).'[40] Faludy obviously did not want to contaminate his Hungarian style with other Hungarian translators' formulations, so he rather consulted English translations. But he did it only in the deepest despair. As it seems, his most important resource for finding meaning for a difficult place was his own imagination. His mistranslating *fauus*, which nobody has ever confused with *uiscus* and which only a Hungarian could do, is a strong proof of that. I put here Walsh's translation for reference: 'Mother earth is set in the middle, rounded like an egg, and containing within her like a honeycomb all that is good.'[41] The expression 'rounded like an egg' highlights one more interesting feature: when a part of the Latin text was incompatible with his vision about the meaning, Faludy simply omitted it. A lime-twig cannot be egg-shaped, therefore he did not translate the expression *quasi ouum corrotundata*, while he obviously did not consult Walsh's translation.

Eumolpus' literary catalogue of positive examples Faludy renders as follows: 'This has been made obvious by Homer and Rome's lyric poets, namely Virgil and Horace, although not through their natural talent but their learned and magnificent ability of expression' (118.5).[42] That something is wrong is made clear by the fact that Virgil was not a lyric poet. Here we can see what happens when Faludy is lost in a Latin sentence and starts writing anything that comes to his mind. In Petronius' sentence four items of literary history are mentioned: Homer; the

[Greek] lyric poets; Virgil, the Roman; and Horace's painstaking artistry. Faludy could not follow the Latin polysyndeton, and the result is not only an outdated contrast between Greek originality and Roman posteriority, but also that Virgil is called a lyric poet. However, this failure can be compared to Horváth's almost literal translation: 'Witnesses are Homer and the lyric poets, the Roman Virgil, and Horace's successful experiments.'[43] This sentence is simple, rather flat and boring, and can be criticised because the 'successful experiments' do not have the Horatian air and complexity of the Latin *curiosa felicitas*. Faludy really knew how to write, but he did not know Latin well enough, while I.K. Horváth knew Latin, but did not know how to write.

What both twenty-first-century translators, Faludy and Csehy, really seem to have enjoyed is that the present Hungarian written culture allows one to use vocabulary that previously was unprintable. The werewolf in Niceros' story, at the beginning of their night journey, does something hardly explained: *coepit ad stelas facere*, started doing (it) by the tombs (62.4). What exactly? Probably something Niceros does not want to tell more explicitly at the dinner table, and he probably uses a common euphemism for 'relieving himself'.[44] In 1920 Révay put it as follows: 'he started clinging to the tombs' *(a sírkövek mellé lapult)*. In 1963 Horváth used a printable word, which meant that the character defecated *(lecsinálni a síremlékeket)*. In 2002 Faludy rendered it as 'he started pissing on the memorial stones' *(pisálni kezdett az emlékkövekre)*. Csehy, finally, puts it as 'he started shitting on the tomb' *(elkezdett szarni a sírra*, p. 73). The expression is obviously ruder than the word Petronius used, but gives one a very clear idea about how the translator understood the text.

Csehy wrote in his 'Translator's Note' that the music of Petronius's great prose could not be recreated in a rhetorical prose. He reads Petronius's 'novel' (as he calls it) as an 'unbelievably modern epic' (Csehy 2014,),[45] which is logically translated in the traditional metre of ancient epic poetry. Epic poetry, however, is not the only literary genre that is written in hexameters. Petronius's *Satyricon* has very strong generic ties to Roman satire, a version of which was also written in hexameters. Most of the motives and topics that appear in the narrative of Encolpius' adventures have parallels in Horace' and/or Juvenal's satires. Csehy's choice of hexameter, apart from emphasising the musical aspect of the work, dissolves it from the traditional twentieth-century interpretation as a novel, and opens up the possibilities of a satirical reading. This shift is important because the novelistic reading (which might have unchained the translators in the first half of the 20th century) is still anchored in the mimetic tradition of critical realism, while a satirical interpretation may highlight the text's overwhelming playfulness.

The poetic form has a liberating effect on Csehy's translation, which can be regarded as a genuine book of poetry. The text is divided into seven chapters, each of which has a title. No paratext connects the chapters, but within the chapters the narration is quite continuous. Where the transmitted Latin text is fragmentary, Csehy has taken the liberty of filling up the gaps with his own poetry. The most daring example is 8.4 when the two fragments which end Encolpius and Ascyltus' adventure in the brothel (neither of which is a complete sentence) trigger an eighteen-line narrative of a fantastic orgy.[46] Another case of Csehy's bawdy amplifications is when Bargates asks Eumolpus to blackguard his concubine in verse (*maledic illam in versibus*, 96.7). Bargates' short speech, which takes less than two lines in the source text, becomes a nine-line tirade in Csehy's poem, which contains the *tour de force* of enumerating fourteen synonyms for a whore, in four hexameters (Petronius 2014,).[47] It is as if Csehy created the invective Eumolpus is being commissioned to compose and put it already in Bargates' request.

A tendency can be seen that the more vulgar the Hungarian phrasing is, the less like that anything even vaguely equivalent can be found in the source text. Csehy enjoys and is carried away by the carnivalesque aspect of the *Satyricon,* and he seldom cares about the translator's 'faithfulness'. His freedom is remarkable in the translation of Trimalchio's *apophoreta,* little take-away gifts awarded to the holders of tickets that describe the items in a playful manner (56.7–9). The passage is difficult to understand and almost impossible to translate, since it is some play with words that connects the objects with the very short descriptions, and some of the jokes are bilingual, making use of the homophony of Greek and Latin words; moreover the jokes are poor and rough. Révay, who produced a domesticated, colloquial text, kept the objects but replaced the word plays with Hungarian ones, and some of them are even funny. Philological accuracy made Horváth translate the meaning of the words and lose the play. It is not always understandable for each gift how the tickets are connected to them, and none is even remotely funny. Faludy simply surrendered and omitted the whole passage (56.7–10) from his translation. Csehy's strategy is unique: he has replaced all the take-away gifts with new ones and described them with ingenious word-plays. It may be regarded as a problem that Csehy's jokes are not bad enough, but this 'loss' is counterbalanced by their erotic or scatological content. It is debatable whether one of Trimalchio's *apophoreta,* a pole with an apple, has sexual implications (probably not[48]), but the others are not even suspicious of anything sexual. Instead of the roughness of the jokes, the vulgarity of the content is supposed to suggest Trimalchio's bad taste. The fact that in this list some obvious culinary anachronisms appear, chocolate and turkey (gifts of the Americas, unknown to the Romans), may be evaluated as failures or signals of the translation's originality.

Csehy dedicated the book to the memory of József Révay, István Károly Horváth, György Faludy, Edoardo Sanguineti (who translated the *Satyricon* into Italian), and Federico Fellini.[49] His tribute to the tradition of literary translation, however, goes further than a dedication. When Eumolpus describes Chrysis' beauty through mythological comparisons, the sentence *Quid contra hanc Helene, quid Venus posset?* (138.6, How could Helen or Venus compete with her?) renders as follows: *És Venusé, Helenéjé számba se, szóba se jönne!* [Venus or Helen's beauty could not be taken account of, could not be mentioned].[50] The second half of the verse is a literal quotation from Gábor Devecseri's translation of an epigram by Callimachus (*AP* 5.6.6): *mint megarébeliek, számba se, szóba se jön*.[51] Quoting the most celebrated translator of ancient poetry in Hungary (especially in the translation of a place that does not show any similarity to the text Devecseri was translating[52]) seems to signal respect for the collective achievement of Hungarian translators of ancient poetry. When Encolpius tries to hang himself in his amorous frustration (94.8), Csehy adds about four lines to motivate this almost fatal decision, and before actually acting makes Eumolpus imagine how he will die with the following words: *Méri a seggem / súlyát majd a kötél* [My arse will be weighed by the rope].[53] When he makes Eumoplus quote the second half of François Villon's four-liner *Et de la corde d'une toise / Saura mon col que mon cul poise* (and especially when the reference appears as addition to the source text) he pays tribute not only to György Faludy, who translated both Villon and Petronius, but also to the numerous Hungarian poets and translators who competed in translating Villon's little gem. The tribute seems collective here, since none of the translations is quoted literally. Csehy's playful references to poetry translated into Hungarian may be regarded as recompense for the omission of long epic parts in *Satyricon,* the literary references of which could not be transmitted.

The five translations cannot be regarded as phases of a development towards a goal. On the one hand, the translators hardly used their predecessors' achievements. Faludy went so far as intentionally and explicitly disregarding the previous Hungarian translation, and the addressee of Csehy's tribute to the translation tradition is rather the tradition of verse translations generally than the Petronius-translations. Not using the others' achievements might imply a rather strong critique. On the other hand, the five translators seem to have very different ideas about Petronius's literary merits to be transmitted to the target audience, while the viewpoints from which those differences can be seen vary not only from period to period of cultural history but also from person to person. The political environment seems to have had the strongest influence on Székely and Horváth. The anti-Semitic discourse of his time made the former focus on the xenophobic tone, while communist dictatorship pushed the latter to see the *Satyricon* as an example of popular realism. Different political and cultural conditions create different prisms (with different distortions and interferences) through which the source must pass. Rather than thinking of translation as happening *into* cultural moments, the prismatic view encourages us to see translation as happening *through* them. Inherited translation conventions and the rebellion against them may deeply impact the style of a target text: Székely seems a rebel from the viewpoint of the school-bound practices of the translations of the classics in his time; Horváth worked in perfect harmony with the philologist paradigm dominant in his life-time, then Faludy and Csehy rebelled against that. Everyday vocabulary not without religious implications resulted in mild Christianisation in Révay's translation as an unintended side-effect of his domesticating strategy; later translators carefully avoided that kind of usage to emphasize the religious otherness of the source text. The pagan religious environment of the later translations makes the religious tensions in Révay's text harsher retrospectively. The five translations together form a complex, multifaceted prism with interpretive impulses bouncing back and forth between them. Politics, translation conventions of the target culture, considerations of genre (novel or satire), ideas about the function of the translation (school-bound, scholarly, entertaining, or poetic), religion, politeness in language and rebellion against it, and individual talent contribute to forming the prism. Most of these elements obviously belong to the current target culture or are created by a tension between source and target cultures, and some of them — especially the talent — are unpredictable. Therefore, it is impossible to tell what is and is not 'in' the source text or is an aspect of it, which is a potentiality of the text to be actualized through reading/translating. Translations strongly support the insight that reading is a matter of building on prompts.

Works Cited

Ács, Bori, 'Mi után sír a külföldön élő magyar?' [What Hungarians who leave abroad miss the most?] <http://www.origo.hu/tafelspicc/kozelet/20121109-mi-utan-sir-a-kulfoldon-elo-magyar.html> (accessed 31 July 2017)

Auerbach, Erich, *Mimesis: The Representation of Reality in Western Literature*, trans. Willard R. Trusk (Princeton: Princeton University Press, 2003)

Bakhtin, Mikhail, *Dialogic Imagination: Four Essays,* trans. Michael Holquist (Austin: University of Texas Press, 1981)

Bakhtin, Mikhail, *Rabelais and His World,* trans. Helene Iswolsky (Bloomington: Indiana University Press, 1984)

Béládi, Miklós & László Rónay (eds.), *A magyar irodalom története 1945–1975, III/1–2 A próza* [A history of Hungarian literature 1945–1975, III/1–2: Prose] (Budapest: Akadémiai, 1990)

Benkő, Loránd (ed.), *A magyar nyelv történeti-etimológiai szótára* [A historical-etymological lexicon of Hungarian language], 4 vols (Budapest: Akadémiai, 1984)

Boyce, Bret, *The Language of the Freedman in Petronius' Cena Trimalchionis* (Leiden: Brill, 1991)

Conte, Gian Biagio, *The Hidden Author: An Interpretation of Petronius's Satyricon,* trans. Elaine Fantham (Berkeley: University of California Press, 1997)

Cornelius Nepos, *Híres férfiakról,* trans. István Székely (Budapest: Lampel, 1901)

Csehy, Zoltán, 'Jegyzet a fordításhoz' [Translator's note] in Petronius trans. Csehy, pp. 179–82.

Czigány, Lóránt, 'Elöljáró beszéd' [Introduction], in *Pajzán Toldi* [Indecent Toldi], ed. by Lóránt Czigány (Budapest: Kortárs, 1997), pp. 7–92

Czuczor, Gergely & János Fogarasi, *A magyar nyelv szótára* [A lexicon of Hungarian language], 6 vols (Pest: Emich Gusztáv, 1862–74)

Devecseri, Gábor, 'Válasz Csengery János bírálatára' [An answer to the critique by János Csengery], *Egyetemes Philologiai Közlöny* 62 (1938), 402–05.

Horváth, István Károly, 'Musa severa — Musa ludens', *Antik Tanulmányok* 3 (1956), 92–104

Marbach, Alfred, *Wortbildung, Wortwahl und Wortbedeutung als Mittel der Charakterzeichnung bei Petron* (Giessen: Pöppinghaus, 1931)

Nádasdy, Ádám, 'Arany *Hamlet*jének metrikája. Antikizálás és modernizálás' [Metrics in Arany's translation of *Hamlet*] in *„Eszedbe jussak.' Tanulmányok Arany János Hamlet-fordításáról* [Studies in János Arany's translation of *Hamlet*], ed. by Júlia Paraizs (Budapest: reciti, 2015), pp. 219–50

O. Nagy, Gábor, *Mi fán terem? Magyar szólásmondások eredete* [Origins of Hungarian idioms] (Budapest: Gondolat, 1979)

Petronius, *Satyricon,* trans. István Károly Horváth (Budapest: Helikon, 1963)

Petronius, *Cena Trimalchionis – Trimalchio lakomája,* trans. József Révay (Budapest: Európa, 1977)

Petronius, *The Satyricon*, trans. P.G. Walsh (Oxford: Clarendon, 1996)
Petronius, *Satyricon*, trans. György Faludy (Budapest: Glória, 2002)
Petronius Arbiter, T[itus], *Trimalchio lakomája* [Trimalchio's Banquet], trans. István Székely (Győr: Gross Testvérek, 1900)
Petronius Arbiter, *Satyricon*, trans. Zoltán Csehy (Bratislava: Kalligram, 2014)
Petronius & Seneca, *Satyricon & Apocolocyntosis*, transl. Michael Heseltine (Cambridge: Harvard University Press/Loeb Classical Library, 1969)
Polgár, Anikó, *Catullus noster* (Pozsony: Kalligram, 2003)
Rankin, D., 'Symbolism in *contus cum malo*', *Rheinisches Museum* 107 (1964), 361–64
Relihan, J. C., *Ancient Menippean Satire* (Baltimore: The Johns Hopkins University Press, 1993)
Schmeling, Gareth, *A commentary on the Satyrica of Petronius* (Oxford: Oxford University Press, 2011)
Suetonius, *Császárok életrajzai* [The Twelve Caesars] trans., intr. and comm. István Székely (Budapest: MTA, 1897)
Szepessy, Tibor (ed.), *Görög költők antológiája* [An anthology of Greek poetry] (Budapest: Európa, 1982)
Székely, István, *De Suetonio C. Taciti imitatore* (diss. Kolozsvár, Hungary, 1887)
Vas, István, 'Horatius olvasásakor' [When I read Horace] in *Az ismeretlen isten. Tanulmányok 1934–1973* [The unknown God: Collected essays 1934–1973] (Budapest: Szépirodalmi, 1974), pp. 600–31

Notes to Chapter 16

1. For the function of verses in the *Satyricon* see Gian Biagio Conte, *The Hidden Author: An Interpretation of Petronius's Satyricon*, trans. Elaine Fantham (Berkeley: University of California Press, 1997), pp. 140–43.
2. Characterisation through language is described as an important step in the history of representation by Erich Auerbach in his chapter on Petronius 'Fortunata' (Erich Auerbach, *Mimesis: The Representation of Reality in Western Literature*, trans. Willard R. Trusk (Princeton: Princeton University Press, 2003), pp. 24–49). The characteristics of every single freedman are analysed from the viewpoints of phonology, morphology, lexicon, and syntax in Bret Boyce, *The Language of the Freedman in Petronius' Cena Trimalchionis* (Leiden: Brill, 1991).
3. Cf. J. C. Relihan, *Ancient Menippean Satire* (Baltimore: The Johns Hopkins University Press, 1993), pp. 91–99.
4. Conte, *The Hidden Author*, p. 142.
5. See e.g. Mikhail Bakhtin, *Dialogic Imagination: Four Essays*, trans. Michael Holquist (Austin: University of Texas Press, 1981), pp. 26–27.
6. T[itus] Petronius Arbiter, *Trimalchio lakomája* [Trimalchio's Banquet], trans. István Székely (Győr: Gross Testvérek, 1900).
7. More easily available is the second, bilingual editon: Petronius, *Cena Trimalchionis — Trimalchio lakomája*, trans. József Révay (Budapest: Európa, 1977).
8. Petronius, *Satyricon*, trans. István Károly Horváth (Budapest: Helikon, 1963).
9. Petronius, *Satyricon*, trans. György Faludy (Budapest: Glória, 2002).
10. Petronius Arbiter, *Satyricon*, trans. Zoltán Csehy (Bratislava: Kalligram, 2014).
11. Cornelius Nepos, *Híres férfiakról*, trans. István Székely (Budapest: Lampel, 1901).
12. Suetonius, *Császárok életrajzai* [The Twelve Caesars] trans., intr. and comm. István Székely (Budapest: MTA, 1897).
13. István Székely, *De Suetonio C. Taciti imitatore* (diss. Kolozsvár, Hungary, 1887).
14. Petronius, trans. by Székely, p. 4: 'idegenből toborzott rabszolgák'; 'Ezek és hasonló szőrű társaik voltak azok, akik szerencsés, gyakran csalárd üzérkedéssel meggazdagodva, és a régi előkelő családok könnyelmű sarjait uzsorával tönkretéve, valósággal reá nehezedtek a római nemzet vállára.'

15. Petronius, trans. by Székely, p. 6: az a része a birodalomnak, ahol a nemzetrontó görög befolyás a legdúsabban burjánzott.
16. Ibid.: Képzelhetjük ezek szerint, hogy az a hatalmas szatíra mekkora hatást tehetett az egyre süllyedő, úgynevezett előkelő római társaságra. Érezhette az idegenszerűség ostorozása mellett azt is, hogy talán némi föladatai neki is volnának. Ámde a vagyon és a vele járó függetlenség már gazdát cserélt, és a római társadalom sokkal romlottabb volt, hogysem nemzeti kötelességei teljesítésére elég erkölcsi ereje maradt volna. Azt hiszem, nem egészen fölösleges munkát végeztem, midőn ezt a kis remekművet nyelvünkre átültetni igyekeztem.
17. Petronius trans. Székely, p. 5: de azt nem a mai reálisták módjára kell bírálni, mert Petronius midőn az ő korának irányával számolt, korántsem iparkodott mesterségesen az érzékiség felköltésére, mint például a modern francia naturalisták. A legtrágárabb jeleneteket is bizonyos mosolygó irónia zománcával vonja be.
18. See esp. Mikhail Bakhtin, *Rabelais and His World,* trans. Helene Iswolsky (Bloomington: Indiana University Press, 1984), p. 19
19. Petronius, trans. by Székely, p. 62: össze-vissza csókolt.
20. In some places, where I translated Petronius into English, I used the translation by Michael Heseltine (Petronius & Seneca, *Satyricon & Apocolocyntosis* (Cambridge: Harvard UP. Loeb Classical Library, 1969), pp. 3–429) and the seminal commentary by Gareth Schmeling, *A commentary on the Satyrica of Petronius* (Oxford: Oxford UP, 2011).
21. Petronius, trans. by Székely, p. 12: Nem értem rá mindent megszemlélni, mert már az ebédlőig értünk.
22. Petronius, trans. by Székely, p. 23.
23. Although his historical novels and semi-fictional educative oeuvre is described and appraised in a comprehensive history of Hungarian literature (Miklós Béládi & László Rónay (eds.), *A magyar irodalom története 1945–1975, III/1–2 A próza* [A history of Hungarian literature 1945–1975, III/1–2: Prose] (Budapest: Akadémiai, 1990) pp. 299–301), he can be hardly regarded as more than a minor writer.
24. It is a somewhat archaic formulation, in which the old meaning of the adjective *különös* had shifted from 'special' to 'strange' by Révay's time.
25. Genesis 19.26.
26. It is also true that the Hungarian tradition of translations shows a general predilection for figures and images. That can be the reason why two later translators of the *Satyricon* kept the stoning image. Horváth: *Nem vetek követ rá;* Csehy: *De követ rá nem vetek.*
27. A gastromonic blog puts *tejföl* on the top of the list of food Hungarians miss abroad, and speaks of the 'burning pain' its lack causes: Bori Ács, 'Mi után sír a külföldön élő magyar?' [What Hungarians who leave abroad miss the most?] <http://www.origo.hu/tafelspicc/kozelet/20121109-mi-utan-sir-a-kulfoldon-elo-magyar.html> (accessed 31 July 2017).
28. See Gábor O. Nagy, *Mi fán terem? Magyar szólásmondások eredete* [Origins of Hungarian idioms] (Budapest: Gondolat, 1979), p. 457.
29. Literally: the big-headed. Révay wanted to use a body part to express colloquially the social influence.
30. István Károly Horváth, 'Musa severa — Musa ludens', *Antik Tanulmányok* 3 (1956), 92–104.
31. Lóránt Czigány, 'Elöljáró beszéd' [Introduction], in *Pajzán Toldi* [Indecent Toldi], ed. by Lóránt Czigány (Budapest: Kortárs, 1997), pp. 7–92 (pp. 29–31).
32. Cf. Anikó Polgár, *Catullus noster* (Pozsony: Kalligram, 2003), pp. 134–37.
33. István Vas, 'Horatius olvasásakor' [When I read Horace] in *Az ismeretlen isten. Tanulmányok 1934–1973* [The unknown God: Collected essays 1934–1973] (Budapest: Szépirodalmi, 1974), pp. 600–31.
34. Devecseri Gábor, 'Válasz Csengery János bírálatára' [An answer to the critique by János Csengery], *Egyetemes Philologiai Közlöny* 62 (1938), 402–05 (p. 404).
35. Petronius, trans. by Horváth, p. 73: mint valami letaglózott ökör, az ágyon hevert.
36. Gergely Czuczor, & János Fogarasi, *A magyar nyelv szótára* [A lexicon of Hungarian language], 6 vols (Pest: Emich Gusztáv, 1862–74), I (1862), 327.
37. Loránd Benkő (ed.), *A magyar nyelv történeti-etimológiai szótára* [A historical-etymological lexicon of Hungarian language], 4 vols (Budapest: Akadémiai, 1984), I, 152.

38. Ádám Nádasdy, 'Arany *Hamlet*jének metrikája. Antikizálás és modernizálás' [Metrics in Arany's translation of *Hamlet*] in „*Eszedbe jussak.*' *Tanulmányok Arany János Hamlet-fordításáról* [Studies in János Arany's translation of *Hamlet*], ed. by Júlia Paraizs (Budapest: reciti, 2015), pp. 219–50 (p. 226).
39. Petronius, trans. By Faludy, p. 41: Mert Földanya foglalja el a középső helyet és a lépvessző a jelképe a sok jónak, mit Földanyától kapunk.
40. Petronius trans. Faludy, p. 6: olyan helyeken, ahol a latin nehézsége, homálya vagy megfejthetetlensége kétségbe ejtett, rendszerint P.G. Walsh (Oxford, 1997) fordításához fordultam segítségért.
41. Petronius, *The Satyricon,* trans. by P.G. Walsh (Oxford: Clarendon, 1996), p. 30.
42. Petronius trans. Faludy, p. 117: Nyilvánvalóvá tette ezt Homerosz, valamint Róma lírai költői, Vergilius és Horatius, bár nem ösztönös, de tanult és nagyszerű kifejező képességükkel.
43. Petronius, trans. by Horváth, p. 152: Tanú Homerus és a lírikusok, a római Vergilius, és Horatius sikeres kísérletei.
44. Alfred Marbach, *Wortbildung, Wortwahl und Wortbedeutung als Mittel der Charakterzeichnung bei Petron* (Giessen: Pöppinghaus, 1931), p. 142.
45. Zoltán Csehy, 'Jegyzet a fordításhoz' [Translator's note], in Petronius trans. Csehy, pp. 179–82. (p. 179).
46. Petronius, trans. by Csehy, pp. 16–17.
47. Ibid. pp. 113–14.
48. D. Rankin, 'Symbolism in *contus cum malo*', *Rheinisches Museum* 107 (1964), 361–64.
49. Petronius, trans. by Csehy, p. 7.
50. Ibid., p. 170.
51. *Görög költők antológiája* [An anthology of Greek poetry], ed. by Tibor Szepessy (Budapest: Európa, 1982), p. 448.
52. Νύμφης ὡς Μεγαρέων οὐ λόγος οὐδ' ἀριθμός.
53. Petronius, trans. by Csehy, p. 111.

CHAPTER 17

The Schizophrenic Prism: Louis Wolfson's Translation Practice

Alexandra Lukes

Writing about Louis Wolfson's book, *Le Schizo et les langues*, entails recognizing just how difficult such a task is. This difficulty stems from a number of reasons. Firstly, it is unclear what kind of text it is. Written in the third person as an autobiographical depiction of the author's battle with schizophrenia and of the translation device he developed to manage it, the book straddles the boundaries between clinical document, psychoanalytical investigation on the nature of the schizophrenic mind, linguistic treatise on the study of languages, poetic reverie on the sounds and shapes of words, and literary (auto)biography. The book's editor, J.-B. Pontalis, described it as a disconcerting, bizarre, and unclassifiable 'object';[1] and his decision to publish it in the Gallimard psychoanalytical series 'Connaissance de l'Inconscient', alongside works by Freud and with a preface by Gilles Deleuze, adds to the book's problematic status, because it imposes a medically-minded categorization on the work (and, by implication, on its author), at odds with the text's explicit intentions.[2]

Such generic uncertainty is not in itself a reason for difficulty, but it may become one when we take into account a second consideration, namely, the language in which the book is written. This is a heavily Anglicized French, full of direct calques of English expressions and sentence structures, all of which betray the American writer behind it. This feature, in conjunction with a deeply ironic tone, dark humour, and an abundant use of the conditional tense, produces in the reader a sense of estrangement from both French and English, while also raising questions about the nature of the narrative voice. In this context, it is worth noting that Wolfson intended to publish the book in a reformed orthography, or 'écriture secrète',[3] which entailed suppressing most double consonants (mm, nn, tt, ll, pp), omitting the u that follows q, using various accents to replace the silent h, substituting the word 'et' with the symbol &, and indicating all changes with an asterisk in front of the modified word. While Pontalis made the editorial decision to normalize the spelling for the French readership, he left in a sample of this reformed spelling at the end of the book, to give the readers a taste of the intended shock-effect of Wolfson's writing.

Along with the form of the book, another element that might prove challenging for the reader is the content. The book tells the story of the protagonist's battle with his mental condition, the main symptom of which is intense physical and mental pain that occurs when the self-declared 'schizo' hears, speaks, or reads any word of the English language; and the therapy that the protagonist devises for himself consists in a tortuous and highly idiosyncratic translation practice that aims to neutralize the pernicious language and its painful effects. Whether or not the book constitutes the account of an individual's mental illness (which is itself subject to debate) or, indeed, whether the 'schizo' is in fact schizophrenic (a consideration that raises important questions about the nature of mental health), the reader is trapped inside the protagonist's obsessive thoughts and compulsive practices. More precisely, the protagonist's painstaking ruminations on how words can or cannot be translated, accompanied by descriptions of his eating disorders and anti-social behaviours, lock the reader into a claustrophobic world, where suffering and respite are precariously balanced on the success or failure of specific translation choices. Such a narrative may not only be unsettling, but, as Pontalis notes, it may also carry with it the danger of driving the reader mad: 'Je me rappelle m'être demandé avec quelque angoisse: "Ce Wolfson va-t-il réussir à me rendre fou?"'[4]

Despite these challenges (or, perhaps, because of them), the book attracted considerable attention from writers, critics, psychoanalysts, philosophers, and artists, not only at the time of its publication in 1970, but also in more recent years.[5] 2009 saw the publication of the *Dossier Wolfson*, a collection of essays that reflects on the book's enduring impact and on the reasons for why (and how) the book acquired something of a cult status. What is it about this text, then, that both attracts and pushes away its readers, urging them to enter into dialogue with it, while at the same time questioning the very conditions of possibility of any form of relation? Moreover, what is the nature of the discomfort that emerges from either reading or writing about this book?

Broadly speaking, this discomfort concerns forms of relatedness, insofar as the book describes how an individual understands himself and interacts with the world around him, through a meticulous reflection on his uses (or misuses) of language, relying on practices of translation to negotiate every single interaction. More specifically, the book reveals the extent to which an individual's relationship with language is characterized by pain and suffering, and, at the same time, it points towards translation as a potential therapeutic tool. Thus, the book shows the complexities inherent in daily linguistic interactions and it invites us, as readers, to pay attention to how we use, or potentially misuse, language in negotiating our place in the world and in formulating judgments about other people, so that we can observe how categories of normality and pathology are created, and how fault lines of exclusion and inclusion are defined.

Language and Pain

Le Schizo et les langues presents itself as an account of the daily activities of the protagonist, as he attempts to manage the pain that derives from using the English language. Wolfson describes two main painful effects that hearing, reading or speaking English have on him: the English word can either obstinately clamor around in his head for a long time, creating intense physical pain and preventing him from thinking about anything else — 'le mot anglais lui semblant au contraire toujours sauter et rebondir avec opiniâtreté dans sa tête pendant un temps variable';[6] or it can send him into a catatonic stupor, shutting down his ability to connect with himself and the world around him — 'il restait comme frappé de stupeur [...], son esprit était du moins dominé, possédé, par ces mots, soit durant une seule minute, soit durant peut-être un quart d'heure, soit même à plusieurs reprises avec cinq, dix, vingt minutes entre chaque attaque'.[7] In both cases, the experience of English is a painful one of separation and rupture. Wolfson is taken over by language, which he suffers as a form of an assault or a possession (or, rather, a dispossession), and which destabilizes him as a speaking subject.

Incapacitated by his illness and unable either to leave his mother's home or to move to a non-English-speaking country,[8] Wolfson develops two coping mechanisms. Firstly, he attempts to seal his body hermetically, by blocking his ears at all times (either with his fingers or the earphones of a portable radio, tuned to a foreign-language or music station), and by fixing his eyes on a foreign-language manual or semi-closing his eyes when confronted with writing in English. This stratagem is not however foolproof, as English words manage to slip through despite his best efforts to keep them out.

Thus, he adopts a second method: the construction of a translation device that explodes the offending English word into a number of languages, primarily French, German, Russian, and Hebrew. Wolfson does not, however, produce what we might call conventional translations, that is, translations that privilege content over form — what he calls, 'une simple, correcte, directe traduction en langue étrangère'.[9] Rather, he aims for the impossible task of translating both the sound and the sense of the word, so that nothing of the original gets lost in translation. The original word, then, would no longer be considered painful to hear or to say because it would cease to exist in its offending English shape: 'En effet, ayant un mot étranger remplissant, à la fois dans le son et dans le sens, les conditions, selon lui, de similitude avec un mot anglais donné, celui-ci ne lui semblait plus guère exister, et l'écouter, ce lui serait plus ou moins écouter le mot étranger similaire'.[10]

Working with languages in this way, Wolfson variously refers to himself as a student of foreign languages, using expressions such as 'l'étudiant de langues schizophrénique', 'l'étudiant malade mentalement', 'l'étudiant d'idiomes dément'. These expressions juxtapose language acquisition and illness in the process of self-definition. By implication, using language comes to be seen as an activity founded upon a tension between pain and therapy. More precisely, language is considered both a source of suffering (as we can see in Wolfson's turning *away* from English) and an attempted palliative to that very suffering (evident in his turn *towards* foreign languages). We can now begin to identify one of the reasons why Wolfson's book may strike such a familiar chord with us. It touches on a fundamental recognition, that is, the possibility that any individual's relationship to language involves a certain degree of suffering, insofar as pain is central to the very experience of language.

The relationship between pain and language can be considered from roughly two perspectives. The most common position conceives of pain precisely as that which runs counter to language, because language is deemed to be incapable of expressing pain, whether physical or mental. Pain causes what Elaine Scarry, in her seminal book on the topic, describes as a 'shattering of language',[11] returning the suffering being to a pre-linguistic state, in which the cry of the body rips through the articulations of grammar and syntax. Pain cannot be communicated in language; yet, by that very token, pain can reveal something to us about how language works — or, more precisely, about the way we can or cannot use language, because, in shattering language, pain demands to be heard: 'Physical pain does not simply resist language but actively destroys it, bringing about an immediate reversion to a state anterior to language, to the sounds and cries a human being makes before language is learned'.[12]

Richard Selzer, both a surgeon and a writer, takes one step further in describing what happens in this shattering: consonants disappear, because the primary intention of the cry is to let out the pain as though 'the vowels of pain were, in some magical way, the pain itself'.[13] Selzer distinguishes between vowels and consonants in relation to the expression of pain: consonants, as opposed to vowels, function by partially obstructing the flow of breath; and because pain often impairs our breathing patterns, when we disarticulate the word and remove those elements of obstruction to our breath, we are also, in some way, releasing the pain.

Selzer's description resonates with Wolfson's linguistic manipulations. The latter's translation practice is, in his terms, an act of 'dismembering' and 'deboning' the word of its skeleton (the consonants) in order to release the vowels — 'son désir de démembrer ces premiers [les vocables anglais], [...] en les désossant pour ainsi dire, en les dépouillant de leur squelette (les consonnes)'.[14] In so doing, Wolfson reveals a second, and less well-explored relationship between language and pain: rather than seeing pain as being, essentially, separate from language, this perspective conceives of language as constituting itself a source of pain.

This point can be understood by thinking about language acquisition as a process of separation. Language learning is precisely that activity of discrimination between inarticulate sounds, beginning with the vocalic ones, whereby the babbling child's potential for making all possible sounds becomes focused on those of the mother tongue. In entering into one language, the child separates himself not only from a non-verbal union with the mother but also from the endless possibilities of sounds that he would otherwise, potentially, be able to make, if exposed to a socio-cultural setting in which those sounds were dominant. In this way, then, language learning can be thought of as a profoundly painful experience: the conjunction of vowels and consonants that occurs in word formation alters the infant's breath flow while simultaneously rupturing his sense of communion with the mother, by creating the mother as other in the act of separation itself.[15]

This suffering is further compounded by the fact that the individual is inevitably bound to resort to language, because language promises to mend that rupture by constituting his primary tool for communication. The pain felt in that process of separation is only superficially assuaged by language use: communication by means of a pre-existing and public system, into which the child enters, but which he has no role in creating, cannot replace the immediacy of physical touch and pre-verbal babble. Language then is both at the origin of the suffering and the necessary palliative for the suffering that it has created.[16]

Wolfson reveals a similar conception of linguistic suffering when he explains how he became interested in learning foreign languages. He refers this suffering back to the learning difficulties he experienced as a child in relation to his mother tongue:

> Et c'était sans doute quelque ridicule pour le schizophrène que de commencer l'étude de plusieurs langues étrangères en vue de la lutte qu'il avait eue pour bien apprendre sa langue maternelle, ayant pu parler seulement à un âge plus attardé que la moyenne pour cette capacité. Et pour pouvoir lire convenablement cette langue, ça lui avait été une vraie bataille [...] car même à un niveau avancé d'études primaires, il n'avait pu encore épeler de simples mots.[17]

The child's inability to spell the simplest of words is what caused alarm in his teachers and, subsequently, his parents, ultimately leading to his diagnosis of schizophrenia. Wolfson's understanding of his condition is thereby inherently linked not only to language but, more specifically, to the act of decomposing words into their component letters. Thus, engaging in that same practice of breaking up words becomes a means for Wolfson to grapple with his condition, to reach an understanding of its nature and devise a way of managing it.[18] Ultimately, he aims to question the diagnosis itself, asking to what extent it identifies a specific medical illness rather than a broader human affliction tied to the process of language acquisition.

Translation Therapy

The above quotation may also explain how the suffering induced by language acquisition and language use informs Wolfson's compulsion to translate. Translation opens up a space that, akin to the child's babble, comprises all possible linguistic combinations, before the act of judgment separates them into discrete words and languages. Translation comes as an attempted therapy for mending the rupture caused by the fact that, in learning one language, the individual has, temporarily, precluded the possibility of speaking all others — the ambition to recreate the mythical Tower of Babel is ever-present on the translator's horizon. But, more precisely, in bringing languages together, translation points towards the possibility of recomposing a sense of wholeness that was presumably lost in the process of learning language in the first place, independently of how many languages one may learn at any given time. The problem, here, lies in the fact that the presumed lost wholeness that one mourns is pre-verbal, and translation is, in its most basic (although problematic) definition as the transfer of meaning from one language to another, an activity based in language(s). Here, then, Wolfson's idiosyncratic practice becomes all the more significant: it focuses on that space of suspension in-between languages, where something can potentially be accessed of that non-verbal whole before the two-fold act of separation that is, first, the passage into language and, second, the passage from one language to another.

An example may help to illustrate this point. In translating the English word 'early', Wolfson creates the invented word 'urlich', which conjoins the German prefix *ur-* (meaning 'origin' or 'antiquity') with the suffix *–lich* (meaning 'similar'). Creating this word gives Wolfson a profound sense of accomplishment: 'Durant un moment, il se figurait vraiment brillant, si plein d'inventivité, et quelle sensation d'accomplissement!'[19] As the etymology of the verb 'to accomplish' suggests (*ad-* 'to' + *complere* 'to complete'), this is a feeling of fullness or completeness; as such, it counters the schizoid shattering that habitually mars Wolfson's sense of self. 'Urlich' emerges from, but does not quite leave, the in-between space opened up by bringing English and German into contact with one another. And because the translation of the word 'early' does not settle on a word that exists in a given language, it shows how languages may come together, while producing the feeling of completeness that temporarily mends the individual's internal schism.[20]

Translation, then, provides the 'schizo' with a glimpse of the integrity that he would seem to have lost during the process of learning English. Whether this integrity existed in the first place is in itself subject to debate, as Wolfson himself wonders. In the opening pages, he introduces the protagonist by painting a picture of mental rupture, drawing on the etymology of the term schizophrenia, '*esprit fendu*':[21] claiming that he almost certainly had this condition from the age of four or five and that madness runs in his family, he remarks, 'son état psychotique, dans lequel il avait été plus ou moins plongé aussi loin dans le passé qu'il pût se souvenir, s'étant toujours senti bien anormal'.[22]

The feeling of completion that Wolfson believes he can attain through his translation practice can only be temporary — as Deleuze notes, the text creates 'une fausse totalité';[23] moreover, the 'schizo' cannot stay in non-verbal limbo, living, as he is forced to do by his debilitating condition, in an English-speaking community. His solution, then, is to try to maintain English as a whole (the sound, shape, and meaning of individual words) within the foreign languages, while at the same time attempting to abolish it through the translation process itself.[24] Moving away from English is, paradoxically, a way of staying very close to it, as English constitutes the absent backdrop that unifies and contains within it all the other languages, an originary (and perhaps imaginary) whole to which Wolfson aspires to return.[25] These languages, in turn, function as a distortion lens through which English can be experienced free of pain. And, in the process, each language is distorted: English opens up to a prismatic medley of other tongues; the foreign languages, which participate in both destroying English and maintaining its integrity, appear in the form of isolated words and dismembered sentence parts; and the idiosyncratic French, through which the whole process is narrated, veers far from idiomatic expression.

This process of distortion is visible in Wolfson's transformation of both individual words and entire sentences. An example of the former is his conversion of the term 'shortening', meaning both 'fat' (used for making pastry) and 'abbreviation'. Unable to find one word that would do the trick, Wolfson breaks the word up into its constituent parts, first exploring translations for the meaning of 'fat' and then for the meaning of 'abbreviation', both of which he needs to maintain. The process starts with the temporary creation of the 'monstrous' word 'shshshortening' and the identification of the sound 'ch' — which Wolfson characterizes as being symbolized in English by the letters 'sh'.[26] Wolfson neutralizes (while also maintainig) this sound, along with the first 'n', with the Hebrew 'chèmenn', ('oil, fat'); next, he modifies the English 't' via the German 'Schmalz' ('grease'); the 'shor' sound passes through the fictive Russian 'jor' to end up as 'jir' ('fat'); the suffix '-ing' becomes the German '-ung'. As for the second meaning, 'abbreviation', the 'ch' moves into the French 'chétif' ('meagre'), to the German 'schmal' ('slim'), to the Russian 'korotche' or 'kratche' ('shorter'); the 'r' and the 't' become the French 'courte', the German 'kurz', and the Russian 'korotkiy' or 'kratkiy'.[27] At the end of the process, no one solution is offered; rather, all the foreign words, together, disseminated through the narrative, serve to eliminate the one offending English term.

A similar treatment is reserved for whole sentences, where different options are provided for the English words. For instance, the sentence 'Can I please have a sheet of paper?' becomes the following prismatic version: 'kann' (German) 'ich' (German) '(qu'il te) plaise' / 'pojalouysta' (French, Russian) 'haben' / 'avoir' (German, French) 'achad' / 'adîn' (Hebrew, Russian) 'chtchit' / 'Schaltbrett' / 'Schild' / 'Schutzbrett' / 'Schirm' (Russian, German) 'ob' (Russian) 'Papier' (German, French).[28] Despite the intention to maintain the original word order, the foreign words that translate the individual English terms are not presented in the form of a complete sentence. Rather, the languages are broken up into fragments and scattered across a number of pages, alongside other translation choices, linguistic musings, and narrative segments, so that the reader is left with the task of gathering together the foreign words into the composite sentence rendered above.

In this case, the translation of the sentence 'Can I please have a sheet of paper?' begins by generating a string of words based on correspondences between English and German, via a reflection on the transformation of 'v' into 'b' — give, 'geben'; strive, 'streben'; weave, 'weben'; heave, 'heben'; live, 'leben'; love, 'lieben'; shove, 'schieben'; starve, 'sterben'.[29] This list then leads onto a consideration of differences in pronunciation in Spanish between the two consonants 'v' and 'b', through a description of Spanish radio stations and radio programmes; and finally, before returning to the original sentence, the narrative gets sidetracked by the topic of cleaning habits and house chores, due to the double meaning of the term 'sheet' ('paper' and 'bedding'), which leads to the deconstruction of another English sentence, uttered by the protagonist's mother, 'I put a sheet on your bed!'[30]

Despite the fragmentation that each language undergoes in this idiosyncratic practice, Wolfson expresses the hope that his activity will ultimately allow him to reintegrate into a community of English speakers.[31] It is only by experiencing English as what he calls a 'mélange' or a 'pot pourri de divers idiomes'[32] that he envisages being able to use it again — 'il avait, mais peut-être à tort, l'espérance de pouvoir un jour à nouveau employer normalement sa langue maternelle, dont usaient presque exclusivement les gens qui l'environnaient'.[33] But such a statement, and in particular the use of the adverb 'normalement', raises some pressing questions that go beyond the individual's attempts to recompose a fragmented self: what does it mean to speak 'normally'? How is normality defined? And what constitutes the norm into which Wolfson presumably aspires to integrate, from the rejected sidelines of society?

Madness, Illness, and The Perils of Judgment

Wolfson implicitly addresses these questions in relating a conversation that touches upon the issue of his nationality. When asked by his interlocutor where he comes from, given his peculiar way of speaking English, Wolfson exclaims to himself in dismay, 'Moi qui suis né sur cette île! Est-ce que j'oublie vraiment l'anglais ou est-ce plutôt une tare cérébrale?'[34] Here, Wolfson brings together language and illness, as he did in calling himself 'l'étudiant de langues schizophrénique', 'l'étudiant malade mentalement', 'l'étudiant d'idiomes dément'; but, whereas in those definitions illness was associated with language acquisition, here illness is tied to the loss of English.

This change of focus, from acquisition to loss, challenges conventional distinctions between illness and health. If a foreign accent in one's native language may indicate a physiological or psychological imbalance (such as in the case of 'foreign accent syndrome', a rare medical condition characterized by the development of a foreign accent within the native tongue), in Wolfson's case, forgetting how to speak 'normal' English may be a sign of health, given the physical and psychological pain that he experiences in speaking it as a native. On some level, not speaking 'normal' English may allow Wolfson to escape from diagnosis, because his doctors would be hampered in trying to assess his condition, insofar as diagnosing mental illness relies equally on observing symptoms as it does on listening to what the patient says. More precisely, Wolfson's resistance to English is a way of challenging the very status of mental illness and the diagnostic process that reinforces it. Wolfson's text, therefore, moves from describing particular linguistic and translational practices to asking profound questions about how judgments of madness are formed in language and the impact these judgments have on the individual who is subject to them.[35]

This shift reveals a deeper aspect of the significance of the book and, arguably, constitutes the main reason why reading it is so demanding. By implicitly inviting us, as readers, to think about how we relate to our mother tongue (or what we take to be our mother tongue), it encourages us to question how we use that very tongue, in the judgments we make about what is normal and what is not, and in categorizing the world according to those judgments.

This becomes clearer when we examine how Wolfson treats words or expressions that constitute such forms of judgment, insofar as they refer to his so-called madness. Three such words — 'screw-ball', 'mad', 'crazy' — take on special significance in Wolfson's narrative, and constitute the subject matter of the last chapters. The context in which the reflection on these terms develops is a series of conversations between the protagonist and a group of French-speaking labourers, temporarily working on neighbouring houses.

The first conversation takes the form of a largely successful exchange of basic pleasantries (questions such as: Where are you from? Where did you learn French? Do you speak English?). However, upon returning to his study, Wolfson becomes preoccupied with a sentence that he thought he heard the workers whisper to one another, in English, referring to him: 'He's a screw-ball!'[36] While this sentence does not interrupt the conversation, because Wolfson was not entirely sure that it had in fact been uttered, he spends many pages attempting to neutralize the pernicious English words. Following the rules of his self-devised translation practice, Wolfson takes the words through the ringer of his four chosen languages, and produces the following prismatic and splintered translation: 'hou-il' (Hebrew and French) 'est' / 'ist' / 'yest' / 'yèch' (French, German, Russian, Hebrew) 'un' / 'ein' / 'odin' / 'achad' (French, German, Russian, Hebrew) 'écrou' / 'Schraube' / 'Selîl' / 'boRèg' / 'lOUlava' (French, German, Hebrew) 'Ball' (German).[37]

The effects of the expression cut deeper than the pain associated with the fact that the words belong to the English language; the accusation of being abnormal compounds that pain, drawing attention to the judgment that casts him in the position of outsider. In order to dispel this judgment, Wolfson addresses directly the topic of madness in his second conversation with the workers. He informs them that he has been hospitalized on many occasions:

> J'y étais pour alié-lié-na-a-tion, balbutia le jeune homme malade mentalement, et il réussit à ajouter alors quelque vite: 'Je veux dire pour la folie!' cela cependant en pensant toujours qu'il ne disait ni avoir été fou, ni l'être à ce moment-là, qu'il ne disait qu'avoir été dans beaucoup d'hôpitaux *pour* l'aliénation, comme en quelque sorte s'il eût été en prison accusé d'une infraction pénale![38]

Wolfson here stammers out the word 'aliénation', thus presenting his condition as being one of separation from society; not only is this condition expressed through the meaning of the term he uses ('aliénation'), but it is also apparent in the form through which that term is communicated ('alié-lié-na-a-tion'). In talking about his difference, Wolfson is also enacting that very difference. Conversely, he attempts to attenuate his isolation and gestures towards his interlocutors, by adding a clarification to his statement ('je veux dire') and offering a term that may be more readily understood ('folie'). While the more technical term, 'aliénation', is conveyed in a form that maintains the separation that the term implies, the more commonly used word 'folie', communicated by way of an explanation, aims to bridge that very gap.

In so doing, Wolfson interrogates conventional conceptions of what constitutes madness and, at the same time, he reveals how those conceptions are tied to the ways in which language is used. As for the first point, Wolfson goes on to note that madness is not a medical category, but rather it relates to those cultural forms of societal interaction that are philosophy, sociology, religion, and politics — 'les maladies dites psychiques lui semblaient, du moins le plus souvent, relever de la philosophie ou de la sociologie, ou même de la religion ou de la politique, plutôt que de la médecine'.[39] This realization leads to the second point: madness does not refer to a medically diagnosed illness that Wolfson may or may not have; it comes down to judgments that are made by certain members of society who reject him from their community. And, more locally, it comes down to the use of particular words that have a damning effect, leading to exclusion from society and even internment — Wolfson recounts, with a strong dose of dark humour, numerous occasions when his mother would surreptitiously call an ambulance to take him away in a straightjacket, under the watchful eyes of the entire neighbourhood.[40]

The word 'mad' is one of these damaging words and is therefore in need of being subjected to Wolfson's therapeutic translation device. However, the impulse to destroy the term by finding a foreign equivalent comes not from having heard it being said about him by someone else; rather, he involuntarily catches himself thinking it, in the form of the exclamation 'I'm mad!'[41] As such, the expression is particularly upsetting; Wolfson integrates the judgment made by others about him and defines himself in those same terms. Moreover, the translation solution that he finds for the term 'mad', the French term 'malade',[42] capitulates further to society's judgment, because it associates madness with illness, seemingly contradicting his previous comments about madness falling under the remit of culture rather than medicine.

This confusion, between external and internal judgments in the individual's understanding of his own condition, is indicative of the perils of judgment and of the dangers inherent in language use. The term 'schizophrenia' exemplifies such a confusion because, as Wolfson notes, it is an umbrella term that refers to a variety of psychic anomalies — 'ce concept psychiatrique pour un assemblage en quelque sorte arbitraire d'anomalies psychiques diverses'.[43] The slipperiness of the word, which, according to Wolfson, could mean everything and nothing at the same time, reveals the tensions that underlie the individual's understanding of his own condition, as well as the degree to which that self-understanding is dependent upon external judgment.

Judgment is central to Wolfson's reflection on the third word he associates with madness, namely, 'crazy'. This term is described as being particularly painful to him: not only because it is an English term, but also because it carries with it numerous memories of being ostracized by his peers and neighbours, and it is presented, within the narrative, as a term used to define him by singling him out as different. The conversion solution that Wolfson finds for this word is the French word 'crise', which he describes as being 'un mot étranger familier'.[44] The term is, for him, sufficiently similar in sound and shape to the word 'crazy' so as to neutralize the latter's harmful effect as an English word. While unable to modify the word's meaning, according to the self-imposed rules of his translation practice, Wolfson nevertheless manages to distance himself from the word's painful impact, by changing the adjective ('crazy') into a noun ('crise'); as such, the French noun can no longer be used to qualify *him*, as the English adjective has done on so many occasions.

In this conversion, Wolfson draws attention to the etymology of the term 'crisis', the Greek *krisis*, meaning judgment:

> Mentionnons, cependant, que le nom anglais *craze* (*créïz*, *r* sans roulement, et diphtongue tombante [*i* ouvert et fugitif]) veut dire folie; tocade; et que le français *crise* se traduit en anglais par *crisis* (*craïsis*, la diphtongue est tonique et tombante, les deux *i* sont ouverts et plus et moins bref respectivement et les deux *s* sont sourds), tous deux venus du grec *crísis* (la première syllabe d'un haut ton [simplement accentuée en grec moderne], les *i* fermés, et les *s* sourds), signifiant jugement.[45]

The etymological gloss sheds light on Wolfson's translation practice and, by implication, on the ways in which this practice functions therapeutically in relation to his diagnosed schizophrenia. This becomes apparent when we observe that to judge is to discern, to separate, to hierarchize; this is what a translator does when choosing words or expressions with which to translate a given word or sentence; it constitutes the moment of rupture between languages, the gesture that cuts through the murky in-between area in which many possibilities lie, and produces the translated text on the other side of the translational bridge.

Yet, in his prismatic translation practice, Wolfson often does not choose between possible translation options; rather, he leaves in the text multiple translation choices for any given word, showing that it is precisely in their conjunction that they function as effective, that is, therapeutic translations — 'Et tout cela montre sans doute combien nombreuses sont les possibilités de satisfaire une telle compulsion de transformer les mots de sa langue maternelle en mots étrangers si l'on s'y prend méthodiquement'.[46] In so doing, Wolfson gestures towards the possibility of returning to something akin to a pre-verbal state, where he would be in the presence of all languages together, while at the same time being in no one language in particular.

In revealing the limitations of the judgment process, through his own idiosyncratic translation method, Wolfson is ultimately coming to terms with his condition. Taking the act of judgment to its turning point (the crisis), he finds a way of neutralizing his so-called madness (in this instance, the term 'crazy' applied to him by others); or, more precisely, he neutralizes the act of separation (the judgment) which distinguishes between sanity and madness and which decides that the latter is abnormal in relation to the former.

Wolfson's text, in exploring relations between self and language, echoes Antonin Artaud's desire to be done with all forms of judgment, in a bid to liberate existence from schism and fragmentation.[47] The ultimate success of Wolfson's practice remains, however, in question, as he writes towards the end of the book:

> Du reste, il semble, heureusement, qu'au fur et à mesure que le jeune homme aliéné poursuit ses jeux linguistiques basés sur des similitudes à la fois dans le sens et dans le son entre les mots anglais et les mots étrangers, sa langue maternelle, celle de son entourage, lui devienne de plus en plus supportable. Et il y a même de l'espérance qu'après tout, — mais ceci peut bien être seulement quand il serait, entre autres choses, vraiment devenu ennuyé de tels jeux (et il apparaît peu ou prou qu'il le deviendrait), — le jeune homme malade mentalement sera un jour capable, de nouveau, d'employer normalement cette langue, le fameux idiome anglais.[48]

Echoing the hope of recovery he expressed earlier in the book — 'il avait [...] l'espérance'[49] —, Wolfson here employs the impersonal expression 'il y a [...] de l'espérance'. This, along with the claim that he 'seems' to have become more tolerant of English (according to whom?) and the reference to the fact that he supposedly once spoke English 'normally' (seemingly denying the narrative about his learning difficulties), reveals the individual's tenuous grasp of his self and his voice, subject to external pressures, and precariously held together by compulsive 'language games'.

Given the seriousness of the games in question, it is no wonder that the book makes for an unsettling read;[50] it is also no surprise that readers may feel compelled to write about it, because doing so pushes them to think through fundamental questions about what it means to be a language user. But, following Wolfson, it would seem that any response to the book, whether or not it is written down, will always be tinged by a certain degree of pain, because it belongs to the self-enclosed world of criticism (i.e. judgment). Reading and writing about Wolfson's text, then, are unsettling activities because the book reveals to us, readers, writers, and critics alike, the extent to which what we take for granted — the ability to use language — is predicated on a serious, and often painful, 'game'.[51]

Perhaps translating the book might open up a different perspective. If translation, as Wolfson leads us to understand, can be thought of as a way of, counter-intuitively, going back to something that pre-dates the respective crystallization of languages into distinct grammatical and syntactical structures, might it provide a therapy to appease the discomfort associated with reading and writing about Wolfson's text? The question remains open as to whether translating such a book would be possible or even desirable (translating into English would be problematic for obvious reasons), not to mention the translation approach that it would require; and, unsurprisingly, no major attempts to translate the book have been made — Paul Auster describes it as 'une œuvre qui exclut toute possibilité de traduction'.[52] Yet, by raising the question of whether it should be translated, and what the limitations of such a project would be, we come to see translation as more than just a device used within the book to manage a particular mental condition, or indeed, more than merely a relationship between two given languages; rather, translation becomes central to developing an understanding of relatedness, by taking into account verbal and non-verbal dynamics that inform human interactions.

Works Cited

ARTAUD, ANTONIN, Œuvres, ed. by Évelyne Grossman (Paris: Gallimard, 2004)

DELEUZE, GILLES, 'Schizologie', Preface to Louis Wolfson, Le Schizo et les langues (Paris: Gallimard, 1970), pp. 5–23

—— Critique et clinique (Paris: Les Éditions de Minuit, 1993)

LECERCLE, JEAN-JACQUES, 'Louis Wolfson and the Philosophy of Translation', Oxford Literary Review, 11: 1–2 (1989), 103–20

MALLARMÉ, STÉPHANE, Œuvres complètes, vol. II, ed. by Bertrand Marchal (Paris: Gallimard, 2003)

MEHLMAN, JEFFREY, 'Portnoy in Paris', Diacritics, 2: 4 (Winter, 1972), 21–28

PONTALIS, J.-B. and OTHERS, *Dossier Wolfson ou L'affaire du Schizo et les langues* (Paris: Gallimard, 2009)
SCARRY, ELAINE, *The Body in Pain. The Making and Unmaking of the World* (Oxford: Oxford University Press, 1985)
SELZER, RICHARD, 'The Language of Pain', *The Wilson Quarterly*, 18:4 (Autumn, 1994), 28–33
STERN, DANIEL N., *The Interpersonal World of the Infant: A View from Psychoanalysis and Developmental Psychology* (New York: Basic Books, 1985)
REY, ALAIN, 'Le Schizolexe', *Critique*, n. 279–80 (août-septembre 1970), 677–91
WOLFSON, LOUIS, *Le Schizo et les langues* (Paris: Gallimard, 1970)

Notes to Chapter 17

1. J.-B. Pontalis and others, *Dossier Wolfson ou L'affaire du Schizo et les langues* (Paris: Gallimard, 2009), p. 14.
2. Wolfson describes the disjunction between his writing aims and the book's reception: 'Quoique songeant, au commencement, d'écrire quelque chose concernant surtout l'étude des langues, le résultat de son travail est sans doute une monstruosité qui intéresserait les psychiatres avec leurs théories de complexe œdipien, d'instinct de mort...plutôt que les linguistes' (Louis Wolfson, *Le Schizo et les langues* [Paris: Gallimard, 1970], p. 259).
3. Ibid., p. 261.
4. Pontalis et al, *Dossier Wolfson*, p. 20.
5. To name but a few, Queneau, Paulhan, Pontalis, Sartre, Deleuze, Foucault, Pierssens, Dionys Mascolo, Jean-Pierre Faye, Paul Auster, Alain Rey, Le Clézio, Olivier Cadiot, Pierre Alferi, and Judith Revel.
6. Wolfson, *Le Schizo et les langues*, pp. 65–66.
7. Ibid., pp. 117–18.
8. After the death of his mother, Wolfson managed to leave New York, moving first to Montreal in 1984, then to Puerto Rico in 1994.
9. Wolfson, *Le Schizo et les langues*, pp. 62–63.
10. Ibid., p. 63.
11. Elaine Scarry, *The Body in Pain. The Making and Unmaking of the World* (Oxford: Oxford University Press, 1985), p. 5.
12. Ibid., p. 4. The nature of this pre-linguistic state remains in question, as does the possibility of reverting to it after having entered into language. Antonin Artaud's experiments with glossolalia come close to illustrating what happens to the individual when he returns to a state before language; see, in particular, the figure of Artaud le Mômo who 'returns' after the experience of electroshock treatment ('Le Retour d'Artaud, Le Mômo' in *Artaud le Mômo*, in Antonin Artaud, *Œuvres*, ed. by Évelyne Grossman [Paris: Gallimard, 2004], pp. 1123–29).
13. Richard Selzer, 'The Language of Pain', *The Wilson Quarterly*, 18:4 (Autumn, 1994), 28–33, p. 29.
14. Wolfson, *Le Schizo et les langues*, pp. 138–39.
15. Le Clézio speaks of Wolfson's book as enacting 'le drame du passage du langage' and defines it in these terms: 'Nous avions voulu l'oublier: c'est que le monde du langage est un monde total, totalement fermé; il n'admet aucun compromis, aucun partage. Dès l'instant que nous y avons pénétré, il ne nous est plus possible de retourner en arrière — vers cet autre monde, celui du silence' (Pontalis et al, *Dossier Wolfson*, p. 41).
16. The psychoanalyst Daniel N. Stern's work on infants reflects some of these points: 'the advent of language is a very mixed blessing to the child. What begins to be lost (or made latent) is enormous; what begins to be gained is also enormous. The infant gains entrance into a wider cultural membership, but at the risk of losing the force and wholeness of original experience' (Daniel N. Stern, *The Interpersonal World of the Infant: A View from Psychoanalysis and Developmental Psychology* [New York: Basic Books, 1985], p. 177).
17. Wolfson, *Le Schizo et les langues*, p. 34.

18. Significantly, Wolfson's interest in language is directly tied to his perception of his body, and the development of his translation practice is concomitant with the physical rigours to which he subjects himself (specifically in the form of eating disorders). In an added chapter at the end of the book, Wolfson provides more details of how he willfully inflicts pain on his body, by taking cold showers in the winter, burning parts of his body, and choking himself (ibid., pp. 248–56).
19. Ibid., p. 127.
20. Jean-Jacques Lecercle uses the image of bringing languages together in order to describe the 'philosophy of translation' implicit in Wolfson's practice: 'there must be material, even physical contact between the two languages' (Jean-Jacques Lecercle, 'Louis Wolfson and the Philosophy of Translation', *Oxford Literary Review*, 11: 1–2 (1989), 103–20, p. 107); 'The truth about translation which Wolfson's practice spells out and theories of translation commonly deny is that there is no escaping the direct contact with and between words. Or, in other words, that language is both material and maternal' (ibid., p. 112).
21. Wolfson, *Le Schizo et les langues*, p. 29, emphasis in the original.
22. Ibid., p. 33.
23. Gilles Deleuze, 'Schizologie', Preface to Louis Wolfson, *Le Schizo et les langues* (Paris: Gallimard, 1970), pp. 5–23, p. 10.
24. Alain Rey comments, 'En sélectionnant un terme pour chaque emplacement, on obtient la suite terminale d'une grammaire générative *anglaise*, où chaque emplacement lexical est occupé par une unité fonctionnelle (partie du discours) extraite ad libitum d'un corpus polyglotte' (Alain Rey, 'Le Schizolexe', *Critique*, n. 279–80 [août-septembre 1970], 677–91, p. 686, emphasis in the original).
25. As the narrative progresses, Yiddish (the mother tongue of Wolfson's parents) emerges as a composite language poised to replace English as the originary whole that Wolfson seeks; see Lecercle ('Louis Wolfson and the Philosophy of Translation', p. 114). On the topic of an originary language, Jeffrey Mehlman writes, 'at the heart of this mad science is the dream of a primal language' (Jeffrey Mehlman, 'Portnoy in Paris', *Diacritics*, 2:4 [Winter, 1972], 21–28, p. 23); and Dionys Mascolo notes, 'on a le sentiment d'être devant un vrai langage original' (Pontalis et al, *Dossier Wolfson*, p. 26).
26. Wolfson, *Le Schizo et les langues*, p. 54.
27. Ibid., pp. 53–56.
28. Ibid., pp. 168–79.
29. Ibid., p. 170.
30. Ibid., p. 175.
31. Le Clézio notes that the aim of the idiosyncratic practice is to be able to communicate: 'La seule recherche, pour l'étudiant malade mental, sera la recherche de cette possibilité de communication, par d'autres moyens que celui du langage habituel. Parler étranger' (Pontalis et al, *Dossier Wolfson*, pp. 46–47). Lecercle remarks that, while Wolfson's translation may ultimately save communication, it remains unspoken and part of his interior discourse (Lecercle, 'Louis Wolfson and the Philosophy of Translation', p. 105).
32. Wolfson, *Le Schizo et les langues*, p. 246.
33. Ibid., p. 63.
34. Ibid., p. 77.
35. It is important to note that the book came out at a time when, in France, debates were rife among critics, philosophers, and psychoanalysts about the status of madness (Foucault, Derrida, Deleuze, and others). Cusset comments, 'Tout se passe comme si un seul livre inclassable, parfaitement imparfait, écrit dans un français bizarre et selon des procédés curieux, parvenait à lui seul à prolonger l'histoire foucauldienne de la folie occidentale, à défricher en pionnier les mille plateaux deleuzo-guattariens (leur livre paraîtra en 1980), à accomplir tout l'ambitieux programme de l'antipsychiatrie' (Pontalis et al, *Dossier Wolfson*, p. 150).
36. Wolfson, *Le Schizo et les langues*, p. 184.
37. Ibid., pp. 184–88.
38. Ibid., p. 190, emphasis in the original.
39. Ibid., p. 191.

40. Ibid., p. 217.
41. Ibid., p. 214.
42. Ibid., p. 215.
43. Ibid., p. 68.
44. Ibid., p. 218.
45. Ibid., pp. 218–19.
46. Ibid., p. 188.
47. Deleuze points out that judgment cuts up existence: 'Voilà l'essentiel du jugement: l'existence découpée en lots' (Gilles Deleuze, *Critique et clinique* [Paris: Les Éditions de Minuit, 1993], p. 161).
48. Wolfson, *Le Schizo et les langues*, p. 247.
49. Ibid., p. 63.
50. Le Clézio claims that Wolfson's book belongs to the category of works that are not so much read as they are lived: 'Chaque fois qu'un de ces livres paraît, si nouveau, si extraordinairement lui-même, un de ces livres qu'on ne lit pas vraiment, mais qu'on vit; alors il semble que c'est la littérature tout entière qui soit remise en question' (Pontalis et al, *Dossier Wolfson*, p. 39).
51. Stéphane Mallarmé famously described writing as an insane game: 'ce jeu insensé d'écrire' (Stéphane Mallarmé, *Œuvres complètes*, vol.II, ed. by Bertrand Marchal (Paris: Gallimard, 2003), p. 23).
52. Pontalis et al, *Dossier Wolfson*, p. 54.

CHAPTER 18

Less than Paper-Thin: Pseudotranslations, Absent Fathers and Harry Mathews's *Armenian Papers*

Dennis Duncan

This is a chapter about *bad* translations. What does it mean to read a translation and feel — not necessarily all the way through, perhaps only at certain moments — that it is inadequate? I daresay anyone who has worked much with translations has had this feeling, a bristling of the senses, at some time or another. Sometimes the tingling might be aesthetic at root, a series of moments that jar on the ear, pinpricks that build up to a sense of the translator's tone-deafness: inelegant phrasing or odd lexical choices that we find it hard to imagine in a work celebrated in its original language. Maybe we suspect the translator of timidity, of not daring to turn away from their source. Or perhaps our suspicion is an intellectual one, of concepts being misrepresented: ambiguities resolved, the complex being rendered simple, or vice versa? In these instances, a gap has opened up between the text we have in front of us and the one we *expected* to read, and we have adjudged the translator responsible. (This verdict, conveniently, saves us the awkwardness of reassessing a work illustrious enough to have been considered worthy of translation in the first place.)

So far, so familiar. If you're reading this collection, then at some point you'll have encountered a translation that has lost your trust: I'm sure of it. But can we say more? Do we just *recognize* these moments when a translation jars, or do we also experience intimations of what we *should* be reading: what a *better* translator would have done: how *we* would have done it: what the original author *must have meant*? I hope it is not just me that does. But, of course, these are very problematic sentiments. More so if, in fact, it is not just bad translations that we read like this — if, in fact, like Freudian slips, the bum notes in a translation are merely the glitches, the fractures, that allow us to glimpse something larger lurking beneath, something more general about our behaviour as readers. In fact, rather than the Freudian slip, this chapter will introduce another concept from psychotherapy as a metaphor for the way we read translation: the idealization of the absent father. Here, the absent father, the parent who is no longer accessible to the child, becomes an obstacle to the child's ability to accept their reality, as well as a stick with which to beat the mother, who is *not* absent. *If Dad were here, he would have let me do that,* and so on. This is also going to be a chapter about pseudotranslation, translations with no originals, so the absent father in this particular set-up will be obvious. But we can take this further, reading outwards from the specific to the general. The absent father is, after all, *always* a condition of reading translation: the original is always, to some degree, inaccessible, otherwise we wouldn't need the translation in the first place. This will be a chapter about the act, or the phenomenon, of *reading* translation, and it will use a pseudotranslation, the poem sequence *Armenian Papers* by Harry Mathews, to illustrate just how seductive this idea — that we might, somehow, glimpse the original through the translation — can be. Firstly, however, it will recap how pseudotranslation, over the last two decades, has become a critical tool in Translation Studies, a mirror that reflects back at us our attitudes as readers of translation.

Pseudotranslation and its Recent Theorisation

A Borgesian detail: the first and second editions of the *Routledge Encyclopedia of Translation Studies* both feature an article entitled 'Pseudotranslation'. The article in the first edition, however, bears little similarity to the one in the second. The two are by two different authors — Douglas Robinson and Paolo Rambelli — and take different approaches to the subject. What we can infer from this is that in the gap between the two editions — between 1998 and 2009 — pseudotranslation's status within the field of Translation Studies had shifted significantly, necessitating the overhaul of the earlier article. Pseudotranslation had gone from being a minor historical oddity to something with a particular theoretical usefulness, and the object of an emerging microfield.

Writing in the 1970s, Anton Popovič defined pseudotranslation with clarity and economy. He called it simply 'a fictitious translation', and this is how we understand the term today: a text whose claim to be a translation is fictitious.[1] When Paolo Rambelli attempts to pin down the word's history, however, he finds that it hasn't always carried this sense: '[t]he first use of the term "pseudotranslation" dates back to 1823, in a review of Alexis's *Walladmor* for *The Literary Gazette and Journal of the Belle-Lettres, Arts, Sciences*, as a synonym for "free translation"'.[2] In fact, the circumstances surrounding this first instance are considerably more unusual than Rambelli would have it. While the reviewer for the *Literary Gazette* may well have intended the term to mean 'free translation', within a year it would become apparent that *Walladmor* was not a translation at all, but rather a pseudotranslation in the modern sense. Here is the original reference, which appeared as the concluding paragraph of a review of Sir Walter Scott's novel *St Ronan's Well*:

> It is a curiosity of literature, that a *pseudo* German translation of [*St Ronan's Well*] reached London before the original. It is entitled 'Walladmor', and published by Herbij, Berlin. The first Chapter is an account of the explosion and wreck of the Steam-packet *Halcyon*, off Bristol; and details, with some attempt at effect, the struggles of two of the passengers in endeavouring to save their lives on the same cask!! The whole indeed is a Tale of a Tub.[3]

The reviewer, then, supposed the German work *Walladmor* to be a translation of Scott's novel and was surprised, understandably, that its appearance antedated that of its original. The term *pseudo*, as Rambelli says, is there to imply a looseness in the relationship between the two.

Looseness, however, is putting it too mildly by far. In fact, *Walladmor* bears no similarity to *St Ronan's Well* whatsoever. When its first volume appeared in Berlin, towards the end of 1823, the title page declared that it was 'Frei nach dem Englischen des Walter Scott' ['Freely translated from the English of Walter Scott']. However, it makes no mention of *St Ronan's Well* or any other specific work of Scott's. It was probably only the closeness of their publication dates and their contemporary settings (none of Scott's other novels is set in the nineteenth century) that led the *Literary Gazette*'s reviewer to identify *St Ronan's Well* as the source text. Within a few months, the truth was out: *Walladmor* was not a translation at all, but a spoof. Surveying the case at a hundred years' distance, L. H. C. Thomas would write that, in early 1824,

> the third and last volume [appeared], in which the elements of parody were so obvious as to reveal, without any doubt, that the work was neither a Scott novel nor a forgery but a literary hoax. Shortly afterwards it became public knowledge, first in Germany, later in England and the rest of Europe, that the work had been composed by a young writer who used the literary pseudonym of Willibald Alexis.[4]

An English version was quickly prepared, translated by Thomas De Quincey, and given the ironic title, *Walladmor: 'Freely Translated into German from the English of Sir Walter Scott' and Now Freely Translated from the German into English*. (De Quincey also supplied a highly ironic preface in which he threatened to take revenge on the German literati with a hoax based on Kant's works.)[5] Thus, with no direct relationship between itself and any single work by Scott, *Walladmor* is the perfect example of the type of text that concerns us in this chapter.

While *Walladmor* might have a claim to be the first text to be labelled with the term *pseudotranslation*, it was certainly not the first fictitious translation, nor was it the most famous. As Douglas Robinson points out, '[t]he textbook case of pseudotranslation is probably James Macpherson's (1736–1796) "translation" of Ossianic poems'.[6] Macpherson's poems, while they were believed to have been translations from a third-century Gaelic poet, were extremely influential, becoming

> a kind of literary signpost for the movement that would become Romanticism, evidence that literary greatness did not require all the trappings of an advanced civilization, education, sophistication, carefully controlled classical form, but could (and should) arise from the collective imagination of each individual people, from the peasantry or common folk.[7]

Exposed as Macpherson's own work, however, the poems themselves no longer command the literary attention they once did (although the history of their reception remains the subject of academic interest).[8] This, until the turn of the twenty-first century, was the characteristic trajectory for works identified as pseudotranslation.

Their treatment has historically tended to take the form of detective work, focussing on the position of the text within the archive: identifying the hoax, then ironing out the archival rupture by reclassifying the text and reattributing its authorship. As in the case of the Ossian poems, there may be a concomitant banishment from the canon as the text loses its cultural value at the moment its genre is reassigned. In the case of *Walladmor*, where the text was only translated after its *pseudo* status had been discovered, an 'Advertisement' in the front matter of De Quincey's translation announces that

> the good people of Germany, as we are assured, were universally duped. A work, produced to the German public and circulated with success under such assumptions, must naturally excite some curiosity in this country; to gratify which it has been judged proper to translate it.[9]

Thus the work is reduced to a curio. Its value and interest are not intrinsic to the text itself, but are entirely based on its reception among a credulous German readership.[10]

As Emily Apter has noted, this treatment both reinforces and is motivated by a rigid hierarchy between source and target text in translation, or more loosely between original and version:

> Pseudotranslation [...] invites emphasis on the exposure of fraudulent translations, with the critic's efforts concentrated on rectifying mistaken attributions in literary history, on drawing generic distinctions between model and imitation, or on refining criteria used in authenticating the status and value of an original work of literature.[11]

Nevertheless, since the mid 1990s there has been a branch of Translation Studies that has taken a different line, seeking to dismantle the hierarchy of source and target by treating pseudotranslations as worthy of study in their own right and examining the motivations for their creation. Gideon Toury, the principal theoretician of the Descriptive Translation Studies approach argues that

> questions [can] be asked as to why a disguised mode of presentation was selected, to begin with, and why it was this (presumed) language, or textual tradition, that was picked up as a 'source', as well as what it was that made the public fall for it for a longer or a shorter period of time.[12]

Analyses in this vein include Toury's own work on Holz and Schlaf's *Papa Hamlet*, Ian McCall's essay on Andreï Makine, and Şehnaz Tahir-Gürçağlar's research on Turkish Sherlock Holmes pseudotranslations, plus surveys of the field by Brigitte Rath and Tom Toremans and Beatrijs Vanacker.[13]

Furthermore, pseudotranslation has become a provocative subject in fields beyond Translation Studies. Rambelli writes that,

> [a]s a relatively recent discipline, translation studies has often adopted terms and concepts developed in other fields. The concept of pseudotranslation, however, seems to have travelled in the opposite direction, proving extremely productive in cultural studies, particularly in the study of phenomena such as transnationalism and postcolonialism.[14]

He has in mind, perhaps, the case of Araki Yasusada, supposedly a Japanese Hiroshima survivor whose 'translated' poetry was published in the early 1990s. When it was revealed that the poems were, in all likelihood, pseudotranslations by an Illinois college professor named Kent Johnson, the ensuing debate polarized a considerable swathe of the American literary and academic establishment. Summarising the controversy (and others, such as that of the *Lettres portugaises* [*Letters of a Portuguese Nun*]), Eric Hayot portrays it as a struggle between poststructuralism and postcolonialism: 'On the one hand, we need to recognize the poststructuralist critique of epistemology; on the other, we need to make choices in a political landscape that neither recognizes nor corresponds to that critique.'[15]

Marjorie Perloff sees the Yasusada debate as one between a Foucauldian position — 'the continuing predilection for viewing individual poetry as the fruit of [...] cultural construction' — and a 'deep-seated and instinctive [demand] for individual authenticity, for uniqueness, for the Benjaminian aura that comes only in the presence of the Real Thing, not its copies'.[16] Apter too sees Benjaminian aura at the root of readers' anxieties about pseudotranslation, but she does not share Perloff's biological essentialist idea that aura fulfils a deep-seated and instinctive demand in us. For Apter, as for Benjamin, the auratic status of the original belongs to a historical moment which is passing, and pseudotranslations, or rather their study, force us to confront some of the paradoxes of the traditional hierarchy of translation:

> The diminished status of originality (long a fixture of avant-garde doctrine or modernist credos of authorial impersonality), finds a limit case in examples of pseudotranslation in which readers are, in effect, urged to accept the clone of a code as a replacement for the original, or to give up conventional, essentialist notions of what the original 'is'.[17]

It is interesting that Apter notes that modernist literature challenged the concept of the auratic original long before pseudotranslation began to be theorized. Robinson too argues that there is

> a group of literary works, especially novels, that use pseudotranslation as a deliberately transparent extension of the 'found-manuscript' conceit. [...] In this literary tradition, a pseudotranslation is merely a found manuscript that happens (or is claimed) to have been written in a foreign language.[18]

Indeed, Apter's article, 'Translation with No Original', begins with a discussion of Mathews's short story, 'The Dialect of the Tribe', in which she suggests that

> What makes Mathews's story so clever, in the manner, say, of Jorge Luis Borges's short story 'Tlön, Uqbar, Orbis Tertius' [...] is that it reveals the way in which translations are always trying to disguise the impossibility of fidelity to the original tongue.[19]

This is a wonderful formulation, that translations themselves try to cover up their own inalienable contingency. But there is another factor here which we perhaps don't mention enough: our collusion in this as readers, the fact that one of the commonest modes of reading translation is one which denies or suppresses the impossibility of communing with the original. Here, the translation becomes an uncomfortable truth, and sometimes the aura of the original upstages and undermines the translation, authorising a certain licence in our reading behaviour when we read the translated text (This is especially the case if we suspect the translation of being a bad one.) And it is this licence — a rejection of the words on the page in favour of our fantasy of the gleaming but inaccessible original — which Mathews analyses in detail in the poem sequence *Armenian Papers*.

Armenian Papers: Reading Beyond the Original

A quick word about Mathews. An American who spent half of his life living in Paris, from 1973 until his death in 2017, he was a member of the Oulipo, the Parisian literary coterie devoted to exploring the possibilities of constraints in the writing process. As well as a being a novelist and a poet, Mathews worked as a professional translator, translating the work of his friend Georges Perec, along with Bataille and others. And more than almost any writer one might care to think of, Mathews's work returns to translation as its dominant theme. In 'The Dialect of the Tribe', Mathews's narrator declares his conviction that 'translation is the paradigm, the exemplar of all writing', but it is a line that might just as easily have come from one of Mathews's essays or interviews. It is not, then, a mere conceit to assume that carefully unpicking one of Mathews's stories should reveal a wry and sophisticated critique of the way we read translation.

In 1984, Mathews published a work entitled *Armenian Papers*, the main part of which consists of a sequence of thirty-two 'poems'. The foreword, of which more later, tells us that these are poems in translation. With a single exception however, they take the form of short pieces of prose, identified by a Roman numeral. The poems relate the narrator's passive role in the wars of conquest and settlement in an unnamed pre-industrial region, presumably Armenia. In summary, the narrator is an orphan who brews alcohol in secret for his fellow villagers. His village is oppressed by the violent settlers who killed the narrator's father. One day, one of the settlers, Parno, invites the narrator to leave the village and become a brewer on his estate. Parno becomes a father figure to the narrator, overseeing his instruction not only in the brewing process, but also in the mysticism of the settlers. Parno also picks him out a wife, Sirvan, from his own village. The villagers, however, expect Sirvan and the narrator to act as their spies within the settlers' court, and when this does not happen they take their revenge by recapturing and (it is implied) killing Sirvan. Parno too is ultimately killed in the course of further conquest. Poem XXX, in which he dies, is representative of the poems' style and length, as well as the theme of cyclical violence, conquest, settlement and reconquest:

> Parno followed Genna north into the barren valleys, the ones down which I had journeyed from my village (now ours once again, though hardly mine). Our invaders had pushed farther south, raising up rebellion by their reputation as slaughterers, moving fluidly into the breaches of nature and their antagonists, attentive to night paths and fords briefly unwatched. The land that could be ceded to them, land empty or newly settled, would soon be theirs, they would perch on the hills above our plains; and two armies would so kill and be killed

that winning would resemble extinction more than triumph. Parno went forth to rally men armed and unarmed. With Genna he incited the enemy to plunge into indefensible predicaments. With others he made the settlers into spies and messengers, men, women, children, weaving a slow-closing net of loyalty and shrewdness, entangling those forward-minded strangers by their own speed, making them at last look back... He was caught in a dead-end gorge into which his enemies had been driven, trapped by the trapped. At the end, he laughed and swore that no man could lessen the rapture of a living act, even if his last, even death.[20]

The poems which immediately follow this, however — the last two in the series — have a numbering which is discontinuous from the rest. Having run from I to XXX, with a narrative which has been continuous and sequential, we then jump to XXXIX and finally to XLIX. The implication, of course, is that *our* series is not the full one: that there is an *original* series, inaccessible to us, which contains *additional* poems. XLIX has a rather different form from its predecessors — it has a title of its own, 'Saint Gregory's Hymn to Saint Michael', and it is rendered not in prose, but in four quatrains. Furthermore, as a hymn, it has no direct relation to the narrative of the other poems:

> Angel of light,
> at this doom's parting
> gather our smart
> against new soul's night.[21]

We are invited to see to see it as distinct from the others, 'translated' according to different norms, and therefore the last poem not only of our translated sequence, but also of the source. Thus we are left with seventeen missing poems: XXXI–XXXVIII and XL–XLVIII. In addition to the usual binary hierarchies of translation — source versus target; original versus reproduction — Mathews is reminding us that another implicit opposition generally obtains: fullness versus lack. He is reminding us that translation is viewed as a negative function, a necessary evil, and in *Armenian Papers* 'lost in translation' becomes a literal loss. We have followed Apter in applying Benjamin's notion of aura to the original of translation. She attributes to him 'a philosophy of writing that defines translation as a mechanism of textual reproducibility'.[22] Nevertheless, it is perhaps worth tracing a little more clearly how this concept, which Benjamin used to refer to works of art, should become relevant when looking at translation.

Benjamin spells out the hierarchy of translation when he asks, 'is a translation aimed at those readers who do not understand the original? That would seem adequately to account for the differing status of the two in terms of art.'[23] Yet this formula needs some closer examination. It is relevant in our case since not understanding the original and not having access to it (because it is lost or does not exist) amount to essentially the same thing: a reliance on the translation. But that alone should not account for the differing status of original and translation: things don't have a reduced status simply because we rely on them. The key to Benjamin's causal formulation lies in the phrase 'in terms of art'. It is precisely *because* of the inaccessibility of the original and the availability of the translation that the latter has a lower status than the former. Benjamin's essay on translation needs to be understood in the terms of his later article, 'The Work of Art in the Age of Mechanical Reproduction'. Here also he is concerned with the relative statuses of the original artwork and its reproduction. It is here that Benjamin asserts that an original work of art has an aura which is the result of its uniqueness, which includes 'not only the changes it has undergone in its physical structure over the course of time; it also includes the fluctuating conditions of ownership through which it may have passed'.[24] He also notes 'the historical witness that it bears'.[25] But the unique work of art is almost by definition inaccessible. Unlike their reproductions, to hear a symphony or see a famous painting, one must act out a ritual: one must *go* to it. Thus Benjamin can define aura as 'a unique manifestation of remoteness'.[26] Reproduction, on the other hand, is completely without aura — it lacks the uniqueness and history of the original — and yet it is able to 'place the copy of the original in situations beyond the reach of the original itself'.[27]

To return to the quotation from 'The Task of the Translator', we can then say that the text in translation must be seen 'in terms of art', that is to say, it is the *remoteness* of the original in translation — its inaccessibility, its absence — that gives it an aura which is lacking from the reproduction or target text, and the differing status between original and translation is based on this aura. (This formulation throws up an interesting displacement whereby the *reader's* inability to understand ultimately stains the *text* of the translation.) Mathews's poems further dramatize this sense of absence and incompleteness which already adheres to translation *per se* by positing a literal incompleteness in the form of the missing poems. The semantic loss, the loss of meaning — which we expect from translation as a matter of course — is compounded by a narrative loss: What happens to the narrator in the missing sections?

The most notable part of the *Armenian Papers* is its short foreword, entitled 'A Venetian Palimpsest', in which a present day narrator, ostensibly Mathews himself, describes a visit to the Armenian Monastery of San Lazzaro in Venice. While there, the subject of lost manuscripts arises:

> When Padre Gomidas led us into the famous library, already restored from the damages done by the fire of 1976, Professor Kalstone asked him if any manuscripts or incunabula had been lost in that conflagration. None, replied Father Gomidas, that were of the first importance; and in the ensuing discussion he mentioned, as the very type of a truly catastrophic loss, a manuscript of medieval poems that had mysteriously and irrevocably disappeared during the decade preceding the First World War, long before (he sighed) the invention of microfilm or reprography. When, intrigued by the undisguised intensity of his feelings in the matter, we questioned him further, he revealed that, because of indifference and incompetence, no copy had ever been made of the manuscript, whose text was nowhere else to be found.[28]

Of the missing manuscript, barely an intertextual trace remained: 'no description of the work survived it, [...] no gloss, no excerpts in literary histories or anthologies.' Its afterlife was confined to a single document: 'a translation made during the 1870s during a visit to the monastery by the young Arturo Graf, helped most probably by one or several of the Armenian inmates.' Graf's translation is briskly dismantled as being one of 'radical inadequacy'. Graf is described as being under the overwhelming influence of another poet, Giosuè Carducci, and the narrator identifies a line in Graf's translation that is lifted wholesale from Carducci's magnum opus *Odi barbare*:

> *fresche a voi mormoran l'acque pe'l florido clivo scendenti.*[29]
> [to you fresh waters murmur as they run down the flowered cleft]

This is translation as horticulture: Graf is grafting, splicing a line of modern Italian poetry into the ancient Armenian.[30] The narrator, however, leaves us in no doubt that this is not a successful innovation. The Armenian poem (number XXXIX in the sequence) is focused on depicting a landscape empty of human beings and parched by a dessicating wind. The phrases Graf introduces from Carducci — *a voi, l'acque, florido clivo* — are anomalous and absurd, demonstrating only the translator's 'indifference to any kind of fidelity to his original'.

It is easy to lose sight, in this type of discussion, of what is actually fictitious. The line from Carducci is authentic; the translation in which Graf quotes it is not. Mathews's set-up has become a complex, Borgesian blending of the real and the made-up. Graf, Carducci, Father Gomidas: all are genuine figures. Even the fire in the library really happened, as I was assured when I visited the monastery myself. We are being led, subtly, up the garden path. The lost manuscript and its translation are the kinks, the ruptures, in a tissue of verifiable information.

In the set-up of *Armenian Papers* then, the pseudotranslation — Mathews's creation, carefully nestled among so much that is not — is a text which is unique, a single document, and yet, for several reasons, utterly without aura. Firstly, it stands in absolute contrast to its own source (the stolen manuscript), and to some original beyond even that: the complete poem in which all forty-nine poems are present. Secondly, it is a bastard text, reproducing not only ancient Armenian but also Carducci's contemporary Italian. Finally, as the ultimate reminder of its non-auratic status we see it subjected to that tool of mass reproduction, the photocopier: 'Father Gomidas consented to make me, on a modern machine lodged in the rooms of the prestigious, centuries-old press, a copy of Graf's translation.'

That the narrator should explicitly cite a lack of 'fidelity to his original' as the main charge against Graf is deeply ironic, given what is to come. He has become spellbound by the aura of the 'original': 'I have spent many hours contemplating [the photocopied Graf translation], imagining the original poems from which it derives, imagining how those originals, if they existed, might have been Englished.' (*If they existed* is wonderful here — the perfect example of Mathews's wry humour — implying both 'If they hadn't been stolen' and 'If I hadn't just made them up'.) In this richly ironic sentence Mathews encapsulates the mode of reading translation as the idealisation of the absent father: overidentifying with the lost text, developing a set of fantasies which distort his perception of other relationships, the translation he actually has. As P. B. Neubauer puts it, 'when a parent is absent, there is an absence of oedipal reality. The absent parent becomes endowed with magical power either to gratify or to punish.'[31] Contemplating the base, maligned text which is actually present, and which he only ever criticizes, Mathews's narrator chooses mentally to look beyond it, imagining instead the unattainable Ur-text, wishing he might translate *that* and not *this*. It is a situation which is at once ridiculous and maybe recognisable — a joke at the expense of any reader who has perceived something lost in translation and presumed to conjecture how it *should be*, imagined that they might read *past* the translation, achieving a direct communion with the absent original, understanding it even as the text in their hands does not. In the language of fidelity — so often used to hold translators to account — as *readers* it is the original, the auratic Ur-text, which appeals to our faithfulness, even when this means rejecting the translation. But of course, this fidelity is illusory: we cannot reject the translation — at least not for long — as it is only by way of its mediation that the mirage of originary fullness can be perpetuated.

Mathews takes the joke even further. His reader is not content merely to imagine how the poems might have been translated. This is the final, glorious twist in the set up: the *Armenian Papers* — the book we have in our hands: thirty-one prose poems and a hymn — are his retranslations of Graf, the translation of a translation. Yet, in them, he hopes, the traces of the lost original will appear *more* strongly than in his immediate, flawed source:

> The work that eventually issued [...] is in truth less than paper-thin — a shadow cast by some phantasmal thing deduced from the evidence of other shadows. [...] Even less substantial, of course, is the presence of the original author, although my true and even less credible ambition has been to divine his almost but not utterly lost identity — not his name, but his character, and his intentions in writing his poem. Why, above all, did he devote himself to this account of unknown events of an unknown time and place? Was it he who then chose to remain himself unknown? The pages that follow inscribe my guess, my guess of a guess, at answering these remote and ghostly questions.

The narrator of the foreword has actually set out to translate the original, using the reproductions. His intention is not to replicate or to render Graf, but to *deduce*, or (that magnificently ambiguous word) *divine*, what came before. Couched in coyness — 'less than paper-thin', 'a desperate hypothesis', 'my even less credible ambition', 'my guess, my guess of a guess' — is the implication that a sensitive translator can strip away the impasto of the 'false' layer — the imposture of the first translator's own concerns and authorial intentions — and rebuild the original, 'Englished' but purified. Thus, the poem sequence which constitutes the main text of *Armenian Papers* represents the fruits of a fantasy in overinterpretation and overidentification: of an *unmediated* reading *by means of* a spurned *mediating* text.

The Venetian palimpsest of the foreword's title, of course, refers to the missing manuscript itself. But Mathews is far too sly a writer for this to be its sole meaning. The palimpsest is a metaphorical one too. The word, from πάλιν (*again*) and ψηστός from ψῆν (*to rub smooth*), indicates a parchment which has been reused. However, the method of effacement of the earlier text will determine whether it is lost forever or eventually becomes visible again. Where the original writing was *washed* from the parchment using milk or oat bran, it is liable in time to reappear, showing through the wash as a fainter *scriptio inferior*. However, in later palimpsests the manuscript was *scraped* using pumice powder, meaning that the original writing would be lost forever. In the *Armenian Papers*, Mathews's narrator clearly hopes that his Venetian palimpsest is of the former kind, and that the ghostly *scriptio inferior* will show through the wash of age and bad translation; for us as readers, however, the truth really is 'less than paper-thin'. The palimpsest is scraped clean, and nothing appears on it but the projections of the second, delusional translator.

Emily Apter had it just right: long before the academy began to theorize pseudotranslation, Mathews, an avant-gardist and a late modernist, had seen the potential of the form. In the *Armenian Papers*, he has served us up a medley of fictitious translators: Graf, willfully anachronistic, poaching lines from his poetic master; and the narrator, in hock to an uncorroborated vision of medieval Armenia. Both are unfaithful, but it is Graf who is the less deceived. The *Armenian Papers* is a warning for those moments when our Bad Translation senses start to bristle, a reminder not to overreach and make fantasists of ourselves by imagining an impossible communion. In its wry, satirical unfolding *Armenian Papers* shows us just how plausible it can seem to read in thrall to the aura of the original, gleaming like a medallion, but beyond our reach, an absent father who is not coming back.

Works Cited

ALEXIS, WILLIBALD ['Walter Scott'], *Walladmor: 'Freely Translated into German from the English of Sir Walter Scott' and Now Freely Translated from the German into English*, trans. by Thomas De Quincey and Willibald Alexis (London: Taylor and Hessey, 1825)

APTER, EMILY, 'Translation with No Original: Scandals of Textual Reproduction', in *Nation, Language, and the Ethics of Translation*, ed. by Sandra Bermann and Michael Wood (Princeton: Princeton University Press, 2005), pp. 159–74

BENJAMIN, WALTER, 'The Task of the Translator', in *One-way Street and Other Writings*, ed. and trans. by J. A. Underwood (London: Penguin, 2009), pp. 29–45

—— 'The Work of Art in the Age of Mechanical Reproduction', in *One-way Street*, pp. 228–59

CARDUCCI, GIOUSÈ, *Odi barbare*, ed. by Gianni A. Papini (Milan: Mondadori, 1988)

GASKILL, HOWARD (ed.), *The Reception of Ossian in Europe* (London: Thoemmes Continuum, 2004)

DE GROOTE, BRECHT, and TOM TOREMANS, 'From Alexis to Scott and De Quincey: *Walladmor* and the Irony of Pseudotranslation', *Essays in Romanticism*, 21.2 (2014): 107–23

HAYOT, ERIC R. J., 'The Strange Case of Araki Yasusada: Author, Object', *PMLA*, 120.3 (2005): 66–81

MATHEWS, HARRY, 'Armenian Papers', in *Armenian Papers: Poems 1954–1984* (Princeton: Princeton University Press, 1987), pp. 81–117

MCCALL, IAN, 'Translating the Pseudotranslated: Andreï Makine's *La Fille d'un héros de l'Union soviétique*', *Forum for Modern Language Studies*, 42. 3 (2006), 286–97

NEUBAUER, P. B., 'The One-Parent Child and His Oedipal Development', *The Psychoanalytic Study of the Child*, 15 (1960), 286–309

PERLOFF, MARJORIE, 'In Search of the Authentic Other: The Poetry of Araki Yasusada', in *Doubled Flowering: From the Notebooks of Araki Yasusada: Edited and Translated by Tosa Motokiyu, Ojiu Norinaga and Okura Kyojin* (New York: Roof, 1997), pp. 148–68

PLATO, *The Apology, Phaedo and Crito of Plato*, trans. by Benjamin Jowett (New York: Collier, 1909)

Popovič, Anton, *Dictionary for the Analysis of Literary Translation* (Edmonton: University of Alberta Press, 1975)

Rambelli, Paolo, 'Pseudotranslation', in *Routledge Encyclopedia of Translation Studies*, ed. by Mona Baker and Gabriela Saldanha, 2nd edn (London: Routledge, 2009), pp. 208–11

Rath, Brigitte, 'Pseudotranslation', *Futures of Comparative Literature: ACLA State of the Discipline Report*, ed. by Ursula K. Heise et al. (New York: Routledge, 2017), pp. 230–33

Robinson, Douglas, 'Pseudotranslation', in *Routledge Encyclopedia of Translation Studies*, ed. by Mona Baker (London: Routledge, 1998), pp. 183–85

Tahir-Gürçağlar, Şehnaz, 'Sherlock Holmes in the Interculture: Pseudotranslation and Anonymity in Turkish Literature', in *Beyond Descriptive Translation Studies: Investigations in Homage to Gideon Toury*, ed. by Anthony Pym, Miriam Shlesinger and Daniel Simeoni (Amsterdam: Benjamins, 2008), pp. 133–51

Thomas, L. H. C., '*Walladmor*: A Pseudo-Translation of Sir Walter Scott', *Modern Language Review*, 46.2 (1951): 218–31

Toury, Gideon, 'Enhancing Cultural Changes by Means of Fictitious Translations', in *Translation and Cultural Change: Studies in History, Norms, and Image-Projection*, ed. by Eva Hung (Amsterdam: Benjamins, 2005), pp. 3–17

—— *Descriptive Translation Studies and Beyond* (Amsterdam: Benjamins, 1995)

Toremans Tom, and Beatrijs Vanacker, 'Introduction: The Emerging Field of Pseudotranslation', *Canadian Revue of Comparative Literature*, 44. 4 (2017), 629–36

Notes to Chapter 18

1. Anton Popovič, *Dictionary for the Analysis of Literary Translation* (Edmonton: University of Alberta Press, 1975), p. 20.
2. Paolo Rambelli, 'Pseudotranslation', in *Routledge Encyclopedia of Translation Studies*, ed. by Mona Baker and Gabriela Saldanha, 2nd edn (London: Routledge, 2009), pp. 208–11 (p. 209).
3. 'Review: St. Ronan's Well', *The Literary Gazette, and Journal of Belles Lettres, Arts, Sciences, &c.*, 27 December 1823, pp. 817–18 (p. 818).
4. L. H. C. Thomas, '*Walladmor*: A Pseudo-Translation of Sir Walter Scott', *Modern Language Review*, 46.2 (1951): 218–31 (218–19).
5. De Quincey, signing himself as 'Your obedient (but not quite faithful) Translator', dedicates his two-volume translation to Alexis, and writes: 'I am not quite sure but we ought be angry at your taking these sort of hoaxing liberties with our literati; and I don't know but some of us will be making reprisals. What should you say to it in Germany if one of these days for example you were to receive a large parcel by the "*post-wagen*" containing Posthumous Works of Mr. Kant. I won't swear but I shall make up such a parcel myself: and, if I should, I bet you any thing you choose that I hoax the great Bavarian professor [Schelling] with a treatise on the "Categorical Imperative", and "The last words of Mr. Kant on Transcendental Apperception". — Look about you, therefore, my gay fellows in Germany: for, if I live, you shall not have all the hoaxing to yourselves' [Thomas De Quincey, 'Dedication', in Willibald Alexis ['Walter Scott'], *Walladmor: 'Freely Translated into German from the English of Sir Walter Scott' and Now Freely Translated from the German into English*, trans. by Thomas De Quincey and Willibald Alexis (London: Taylor and Hessey, 1825), pp. xi–xxi (p. xix–xx)].
6. Douglas Robinson, 'Pseudotranslation', in *Routledge Encyclopedia of Translation Studies*, ed. by Mona Baker (London: Routledge, 1998), pp. 183–85 (p. 183).
7. Robinson, 'Pseudotranslation', p. 184.
8. See Howard Gaskill (ed.), *The Reception of Ossian in Europe* (London: Thoemmes Continuum, 2004).
9. 'Advertisement', in Alexis, *Walladmor*, trans. by De Quincey, pp. v–ix (p. viii).
10. For more on the *Walladmor* case, see Brecht de Groote and Tom Toremans, 'From Alexis to

Scott and De Quincey: *Walladmor* and the Irony of Pseudotranslation', *Essays in Romanticism*, 21.2 (2014): 107–23.
11. Emily Apter, 'Translation with No Original: Scandals of Textual Reproduction', in *Nation, Language, and the Ethics of Translation*, ed. by Sandra Bermann and Michael Wood (Princeton: Princeton University Press, 2005), pp. 159–74 (p. 161).
12. Gideon Toury, *Descriptive Translation Studies and Beyond* (Amsterdam: Benjamins, 1995), p. 40.
13. Gideon Toury, 'Enhancing Cultural Changes by Means of Fictitious Translations', in *Translation and Cultural Change: Studies in History, Norms, and Image-Projection*, ed. by Eva Hung (Amsterdam: Benjamins, 2005), pp. 3–17; Ian McCall, 'Translating the Pseudotranslated: Andreï Makine's *La Fille d'un héros de l'Union soviétique*', *Forum for Modern Language Studies*, 42.3 (2006), 286–97; Şehnaz Tahir-Gürçağlar, 'Sherlock Holmes in the Interculture: Pseudotranslation and Anonymity in Turkish Literature', in *Beyond Descriptive Translation Studies: Investigations in Homage to Gideon Toury*, ed. by Anthony Pym, Miriam Shlesinger and Daniel Simeoni (Amsterdam: Benjamins, 2008), pp. 133–51; Brigitte Rath, 'Pseudotranslation', *Futures of Comparative Literature: ACLA State of the Discipline Report*, ed. by Ursula K. Heise et al. (New York: Routledge, 2017), pp. 230–33; Tom Toremans and Beatrijs Vanacker, 'Introduction: The Emerging Field of Pseudotranslation', *Canadian Revue of Comparative Literature*, 44.4 (2017): 629–36.
14. Rambelli, 'Pseudotranslation', p. 211.
15. Eric R. J. Hayot, 'The Strange Case of Araki Yasusada: Author, Object', *PMLA*, 120.3 (2005): 66–81 (p. 78).
16. Marjorie Perloff, 'In Search of the Authentic Other: The Poetry of Araki Yasusada', in *Doubled Flowering: From the Notebooks of Araki Yasusada: Edited and Translated by Tosa Motokiyu, Ojiu Norinaga and Okura Kyojin* (New York: Roof, 1997), pp. 148–68 (p. 165).
17. Apter, 'Translation with No Original', pp. 169–70.
18. Robinson, 'Pseudotranslation', p. 184.
19. Apter, 'Translation with No Original', p. 159.
20. Harry Mathews, 'Armenian Papers', in *Armenian Papers: Poems 1954–1984* (Princeton: Princeton University Press, 1987), pp. 81–117 (p. 115).
21. Mathews, 'Armenian Papers', p. 117.
22. Apter, 'Translation with No Original', p. 169.
23. Walter Benjamin, 'The Task of the Translator', in *One-way Street and Other Writings*, ed. and trans. by J. A. Underwood (London: Penguin, 2009), pp. 29–45 (p. 29).
24. Walter Benjamin, 'The Work of Art in the Age of Mechanical Reproduction', in *One-way Street*, pp. 228–59 (pp. 231–32).
25. Benjamin, 'The Work of Art', p. 233.
26. Benjamin, 'The Work of Art', p. 235.
27. Benjamin, 'The Work of Art', p. 232.
28. Mathews, 'Armenian Papers', p. 83.
29. It appears in the poem 'Fuori alla Certosa di Bologna', in Giusè Carducci, *Odi barbare*, ed. by Gianni A. Papini (Milan: Mondadori, 1988), pp. 41–42.
30. For a non-fictional example of this type of sly anachronism, see Jowett's translation of Plato's *Phaedo* in which Socrates quotes Paul's letter to the Corinthians: 'I am very far from admitting that he who contemplates existences through the medium of thought sees them only "through a glass darkly"' [Plato, *The Apology, Phaedo and Crito of Plato*, trans. by Benjamin Jowett, vol. 2 of 2 (New York: Collier, 1909), p. 94].
31. P. B. Neubauer, 'The One-Parent Child and His Oedipal Development', *The Psychoanalytic Study of the Child*, 15 (1960): 286–309 (308).

CHAPTER 19

Original-esque: Diderot and Goethe in Back-Translation

Stefan Willer

In the winter of 1804–05, Johann Wolfgang Goethe translated Denis Diderot's dialogue *Le Neveu de Rameau*. This was the initial incident of a curious episode in literary history which is at the same time an interesting case of prismatic translation: Goethe's translation held the status of an original for some time, for it was actually the German version of the work that served as the basis for the first French publication of the literary dialogue in the 1820s. Diderot himself had not published the French original, and, moreover, the French publishers who wanted to print the text did not even have Diderot's manuscript when they published their version almost forty years after the author's death. With no original to work from, they looked to Goethe's German version and translated it back into French — without, it should be noted, making clear that the text was a back-translation.

The first part of this chapter outlines the text's history with special attention to its extraordinary value in the literary tradition, as it led to numerous elucidations and commentaries and sparked many polemical debates. The second part focuses specifically on the commentaries written by Goethe himself in which he discusses the translation and back-translation history of *Rameau's Nephew*. In these writings, Goethe reflects on what makes something an original and what it means to be 'originalmäßig'. This neologism, used by Goethe in his discussion of the case, signifies 'original-esque' or 'based on the original', but also 'measuring up to the original'. The case is about the subtle relationships that exist between an original, a copy, and a translation, as well as those between originality, authenticity, imitation, and deception — all relationships that are particularly relevant in terms of prismatic translation.

I.

Denis Diderot (1713–1784) wrote *Le Neveu de Rameau* at the beginning of the 1760s, revised it in the 1770s, but then never published it. The dialogue is many things at once: social and literary satire, a treatise on music theory and theories of representation — and all of this in such a self-contradictory, paradoxical manner that *Rameau's Nephew* has often been considered one of the founding texts of modernism. Diderot introduces two speakers: 'Me' and 'Him' ('Moi' and 'Lui'). The 'Him' character is the eponymous nephew of the composer Jean-Philippe Rameau, a historical figure, who probably had little in common with the personality that we encounter in the dialogue. But this is precisely what is at stake in the dialogue: the question of personality and *persona*, of societal masks, deception, and the possibility that there is an authentic self hiding behind all of that. Even before becoming an instance of prismatic translation, *Le Neveu de Rameau* takes up the problem of manufactured originality and fabricated authenticity in diverse and complex ways.

In 1804, twenty years after Diderot's death, Goethe received a copy of the manuscript through complicated channels.[1] He didn't waste any time with the translation, which was published as *Rameaus Neffe* just one year later in 1805, with an appendix written by Goethe, entitled, 'Anmerkungen über Personen und Gegenstände, deren in dem Dialog "Rameaus Neffe" erwähnt wird' ('Commentaries on the People and Objects Alluded to in the Dialogue "Rameau's Nephew"'). This appendix to the translation is the very first in the extensive history of Goethe's commentaries mentioned above. The copy that Goethe used for his translation went missing soon after, and by the end of 1805 was nowhere to be found. Over the course of the nineteenth century various copies of the French manuscript were in circulation, some of which differed significantly from one another. Finally, in 1891 Diderot's signed manuscript was found. In French studies on Diderot, scholars speak with good reason of a 'roman bibliographique'.[2]

The strangest episode in the text's history began in 1818, when a multi-volume edition of Diderot's works was published. The supplementary volume of this edition included a table of contents for *Rameau's Nephew*, based on Goethe's translation, and it also contained two excerpts in French back-translation. In this early instance, they were explicitly labeled as such, rather indicating the absence of the original text than pretending to be its proxy. The translator behind these back-translated passages was Georg Bernhard Depping, a German man of letters living in Paris, to whom Goethe explicitly granted the authority to use his translation. Three years later, in 1821, two other young Parisian men of letters, Joseph-Henri de Saur and Léonce de Saint-Geniès, published the first French edition of *Le Neveu de Rameau* — the complete back-translation. This version, however, was created without Goethe's knowledge, and it was not labeled as a back-translation. De Saur and de Saint-Geniès thus created a new work in French under Diderot's name, but not one written by him.

To demonstrate the deviations at play between the three texts, here is a short sample passage from Diderot's French original, Goethe's German translation, and the French back-translation:[3]

| MOI. Il n'y a personne qui ne pense comme vous, et qui ne fasse le procès à l'ordre qui est; sans s'apercevoir qu'il renonce à sa propre existence.
LUI. Il est vrai. | ICH. Jeder denkt wie Ihr, und doch will jeder an der Ordnung der Dinge, wie sie sind, etwas aussetzen, ohne zu merken, daß er auf sein eigen Dasein Verzicht tut.
ER. Das ist wahr. | MOI. Chacun pense comme vous, et cependant chacun veut critiquer quelque chose à l'ordre de la nature tel qu'il est, sans se douter qu'il renonce par-là à sa propre existence.
LUI. C'est vrai. |

The differences can be described in detail. In this passage, for instance, Goethe translates the double negation ('Il n'y a personne qui ne pense comme vous'), a characteristic grammatical feature of the French language, as a simple affirmation ('Jeder denkt wie ihr'). This is reproduced by de Saur and de Saint-Geniès ('Chacun pense comme vous'), who are faithful to their original — the German translation — while deviating from the unknown French original, and also, to some extent, from idiomatic French. Continuing the sentence, Diderot keeps up the double negative structure ('[Il n'y a personne] qui ne fasse'), whereas Goethe constructs a more complicated follow-up ('und doch will jeder'); so does the back-translation, which turns Goethe's 'doch' into the more circumstantial 'cependant' ('et cependant chacun veut'). It is telling that the back-translation becomes longer than Goethe's translation, which already stretches Diderot's original. Also, in this passage, we find one of many semantic divergences, when Diderot's 'l'ordre qui est' becomes 'Ordnung der Dinge' in Goethe and 'l'ordre de la nature' in the back-translation. But it also needs to be stressed that there is an almost perfect recovery of Diderot's text at the end of the 'Moi'-sentence when 'qu'il renonce à sa propre existence' becomes 'qu'il renonce par-là à sa propre existence' in the back-translation.

A fuller comparison of the three versions is very instructive, as Ulrich Ricken demonstrated forty years ago in his article on this topic.[4] There are substantial differences between the original, the translation, and the back-translation, including passages that Goethe translated freely (and sometimes even incorrectly) as well as many passages that de Saur and de Saint-Geniès simply added themselves. But perhaps even more striking are the similarities between back-translation and original. According to Ricken's argument these points of convergence are due to Goethe's, for the most part, highly accurate translation. The French-German author and translator Georges-Arthur Goldschmidt has even claimed that Goethe's translation was 'presque identique à l'original' ('almost identical with the original'), hence an exemplar of faithful translation, otherwise it could not have been utilized to retrieve the lost original.[5] However, there are several examples that indicate that Goethe was fairly 'liberal' with the original, yet the back-translators were still able to 'retrieve' a more Diderot-esque turn of phrase.[6]

In contemporary debates on translation, e.g. in Friedrich Schleiermacher's 1813 essay 'On the different methods of translation', the ambiguity of faithfulness and freedom was both a technical and an ethical problem, and so was any blurring of the boundaries between original and translation, let alone author and translator.[7] However, in the Goethe/Diderot case, it was this very ambiguity from which the prism of versions, commentaries, and discontinuous continuances began. Two years after the back-translation, in 1823, the same duo, de Saur and de Saint-Geniès, published a French version of Goethe's 'Commentaries' on *Rameau's Nephew* which they entitled, *Des hommes célèbres de France au dix-huitième siècle, et de l'état de la littérature et des arts à la même époque. Par M. Goëthe: traduit de l'allemand par MM. de Saur et de Saint-Geniès*' (*On Famous Frenchmen of the Eighteenth Century and the State of Literature and the Arts during that Same Period. By Monsieur Goëthe: Translated from the German by Messieurs de Saur and de Saint-Geniès*). The French edition not only has a completely different title, but the translators expanded the former appendix to a monograph, four times as long as Goethe's commentaries. In this respect, Goethe's elucidations on the French literary and cultural history of the eighteenth century are nothing more than a façade, behind which the book's true concern reveals itself to be a 'reaction to political and literary life in France during the Restoration period'.[8]

One last part of the text's publication history needs to be mentioned. In 1823 the French publisher J.L.J. Brière completed his edition of Diderot's works with a volume entitled *Œuvres inédites* (*Unpublished Works*), which included *Le Neveu de Rameau* based on a manuscript that Brière had obtained from Diderot's daughter. He changed the printed publication date to 1821, two years prior to its actual publication, in order to mark this edition as predating the back-translation and thus as more authoritative. This set off another controversy in the publishing world. The first publisher, de Saur, admitted to having published a back-translation, but then went on to challenge Brière, claiming that he too had merely produced a translation of Goethe's translation — and a bad one at that. In one of many articles that de Saur wrote at the time, he points out countless stylistic mistakes. In reality, these instances were idiosyncrasies in Diderot's own style; yet according to de Saur, they were proof that the text edited by Brière could not be the penmanship of Diderot. Even if these findings were mainly due to de Saur's polemical intentions, the very idea that an author's text may be dissimilar to what is otherwise perceived as his authorial character, addresses the central issues of self-identity and the nature of authenticity and originality.

2.

Twenty years after commencing his Diderot translation, Goethe returned to the matter in a series of notes and observations, responding to the controversy that erupted in Paris surrounding the back-translation and the authenticity of the different competing editions of Diderot's text. He took up the topic on multiple occasions, repeating the details of the story numerous times. This ongoing involvement was due to his contact with the various parties caught up in the Parisian literary debate. Indeed, as Goethe writes, at the time he had Parisian friends who were following the saga as it unfolded 'Schritt für Schritt' ('step by step').[9] And thus Goethe was able to provide a running commentary during the entire process: from the actual back-translation, to the vastly expanded translation of his 'Commentaries', to the publication of the actual Diderot manuscript, which he knew about beforehand because the French publisher Brière had contacted him. Basically, Goethe was kept up to date, making the most of a French-German network of correspondents and contributing to the bi-national exchange himself.

In their proceeding 'step by step', the commentaries on 'Rameau's Nephew' also evince a complex production history, in terms of both composition and publication, with four published journal articles and one treatise that was left unpublished.[10] A first short note on the back-translation case appeared in Goethe's own journal *Über Kunst und Alterthum* (*On Art and Antiquity*) in 1823. One year later, after Brière had requested a statement of the case from Goethe, he published another note in the same journal, referring back to the former article in the very opening lines:

> As in the aforesaid passage, and on several other occasions, it has been more circuitously stated that I translated the above-mentioned dialogue by Diderot from a copy of the original manuscript, while the publication of the work in French remained to be undertaken — a gap in French literature that did not fail to go unnoticed from time to time, until finally two bold, young minds published a back translation in 1821 that was considered to be the original for quite some time.[11]

Goethe's intense engagement in the case was something of a correspondence with himself, in which he responded to a series of self-commentaries, self-paraphrases, and self-citations. This is also true for another essay, published likewise in *On Art and Antiquity*. It is an expanded edition of one section from the 1805 'Commentaries' on *Rameau's Nephew*, dealing with a satirical play from the 1760s, Palissot's *Les Philosophes*. Diderot had cast Palissot, one of the men of letters discussed in the dialogue, in a very bad light; Goethe tries to do him justice in his commentary. The subject matter is remote and occasional, and this is even stressed in the title of the article: 'On the Occasion of Palissot's Play "The Philosophers"' ('Bei Gelegenheit des Schauspiels "Die Philosophen" von Palissot'). But in fact, the ephemerality of both Diderot's polemic and Goethe's apology is considered worthy of being commemorated and refreshed in the ongoing debate of the 1820s. The reprint contains the following concluding lines: 'Geschrieben und gedruckt im Jahre 1805. Aber und Abermals erprobt 1823.' ('Written and printed in the year 1805. Tried and tested over and again in 1823.'[12]) Obviously, for Goethe, the literary combat in Paris is an occasion to re-evaluate his own work as a translator — and of re-framing it as a mutual exchange between him and Diderot.

'Tried and tested, over and again' is not just some unimportant side note, a commentary on a commentary, but a highly significant phrase in the context of prismatic translations. This series of commentaries is representative of a certain destabilizing questioning of the status of originals, a distancing from the idea that things can truly exist only once. In his later years, Goethe was more and more interested in the possibility of overcoming such notions of singularity — which explains why the supposed scandal produced by the secondary, derivative original of *Rameau's Nephew* (that is, the back-translation) motivated him to write a series of reflections that are far from being scandalized. Consequently, a generous attitude towards the French back-translators de Saur and de Saint-Geniès permeates his responses. He refers to them in a rather fatherly tone as 'muntere junge Köpfe' ('bold, young minds'), who stirred up a bit of 'humoristische Schelmerei' ('humorous tomfoolery').[13]

It is this very same attitude that characterizes another of his supplementary Diderot writings: the actual review of de Saur's and de Saint-Geniès's 1823 book *Des hommes célèbres*. The article was published anonymously in the rather catchpenny *Journal für Literatur, Kunst, Luxus und Mode* (*Journal for Literature, Art, Luxury, and Fashion*). As it was Goethe's 1805 'Commentaries' that served as the basis for *Des hommes célèbres*, the article is partly a self-review. One might expect some critical words about plagiarism, or at least about un-authorized appropriation, since the French writers had considerably altered Goethe's text, not only by expanding it, but also by abandoning the alphabetical order of the entries. Indeed, Goethe notes that due to this change, the 'comparison of the translated with the original is considerably impeded', to the extent of 'blurring what actually belongs to the German and what belongs to the Frenchmen'.[14] But it is precisely due to this equivocal quality of the translational re-writing, that Goethe's review turns out to be unabashedly positive. He dignifies the 'young men with a passionate devotion to German authors'; and although they 'unconsciously attest to divergences between the French and German mindsets', they do so with the goal of finding 'correspondences wherever possible'.[15]

From this perspective, the production of secondary originals still seems a bit cheeky, but not altogether inappropriate or preposterous given that their writings can be integrated into a whole series of literary exchanges. In Goethe's view, at least, de Saur's and de Saint-Geniès's unacknowledged back-translation is not substantially different from Depping's authorized and openly admitted partial back-translation that had been published a few years before the 'tomfoolery'. Even the publisher Brière, with his competing Diderot project, may be seen as a protagonist in the same interplay, although he contacted Goethe to gain his expert testimony in the public debate. Goethe indeed confirmed without a doubt that the Brière edition was identical to Diderot's primary text. And yet, the faithfulness to the original did not matter to Goethe that much — it was not the only criterion for him, nor the most important one. Significantly he keeps on mentioning that he translated Diderot's dialogue not from the original manuscript, but 'from a copy' (701; 705; 706), thus stressing the reproducibility and convertibility of texts. Instead of confirming, or even monumentalizing the one and only original, he is much more interested in the circulation of copies and in translation as a historical process. Back-translation is conceived as just another kind of retranslation.

Here we arrive back at the expression 'original-esque' — 'originalmäßig': something that measures up to the idea of an original. Goethe uses it in the last and most comprehensive of his Diderot supplements, a posthumous memorandum simply entitled 'Rameaus Neffe', arguably not written until 1825 and thus indicating Goethe's long-lasting preoccupation with the matter. In this text, he recapitulates a letter from the publisher, in which Brière, trying to gain Goethe as his ally, said, 'your German translation of this remarkable production is so faithful [...] that it would allow for an original-esque reconstruction of Diderot's work' (or: 'for a reconstruction that could measure up to the original').[16] The expression 'originalmäßig', which praises the translator and the act of translation, is itself a product of translation. This can clearly be seen in Goethe's appendix to his final post-script, where he thinks it advisable to include the original letter of the French publisher. The French expression that Goethe translates as 'originalmäßig' is not 'originalement' nor 'd'une manière orginale', but: 'textuellement'. According to Brière, Goethe's translation was 'so faithful [...] that it would be quite easy to textually reproduce Diderot'.[17]

What does Goethe's choice of 'originalmäßig' for 'textuellement' imply? First of all, it means that 'original' stands for *text* in this case — the absent original (primary) text, the missing *Urtext*, the 'Haupt Original'[18] around which all things revolve and which a fortiori can never be regained as such, but only reconstructed through textual means: in order make it as 'original-esque' as possible. One might even say that in the domain of the textual, in a world which is always made up of circulating copies, duplicate manuscripts, translations, and back-translations, originality is only ever found in the gray area of the 'not-quite-original', in the domain of the 'original-esque'. Thus the Diderot translation, with its commentaries and its wide array of various configurations, establishes a pattern in the poetological thinking of Goethe later in his life that attends to keywords like 'collective authorship' and 'world literature'.[19] These ideas reveal that literature in its worldly relationships — e.g. in the French-German connections discussed in this chapter — is always already translated. And they do so through the munificent language and expressions characteristic of the late Goethe, who did not have to worry so much about the status of his own authorship anymore.

Still, these various statements and formulations cannot, and are not intended to, hide the problems associated with the issue of 'original-esque'. In one of the few comments that are truly critical of the back-translation, Goethe speaks of the 'damage' caused by 'forged, partly or completely made-up writings' that then make it impossible to differentiate 'the mediocre from the excellent, the weak from the strong, the absurd from the sublime'.[20] But even in this critique of forgery and untruthfulness, originality as such is not emphasized. Instead, Goethe only speaks of 'Annäherung an gewisse Originalitäten' ('approximation to certain originalities'). This observation could easily be part of Diderot's dialogue, for it too deals with replicating and mimicking originality, along with the difficulty of separating the mediocre from the excellent and the absurd from the sublime. It is, in fact, one of the central themes that 'Moi' and 'Lui' take up. Their moralistic considerations about what it means to be good and great are constantly interrupted by the nephew's biting comments concerning his subaltern status as a parasite of society. To make matters more complicated, the nephew's forte just happens to be the art of deception — both in his various theatrical impersonations and in other social contexts — which leads to particularly pressing questions, in his case, about the authenticity of one's identity.

It is no accident that in his last and longest memorandum on *Rameau's Nephew* Goethe states that people in France were beginning to doubt whether the famous nephew ever really existed as a historical person. He then introduces a rather long quote from Louis-Sébastien Mercier's *Tableau de Paris*, 'which removes any doubt as to his existence'. It comes as no surprise that Goethe explicitly mentions that the passage is 'rendered here in translation'.[21] Moreover, he quotes Mercier not directly, but from a citation in de Saur's and de Saint-Geniès's *Des hommes célèbres*. On top of it all, the passage by Mercier underscores the overdetermined nature of the question of translation and original, given that the nephew himself, in his idiosyncratic (in-)authenticity, is then referred to as an 'original'.[22] Apparently, there are complex connections between the circumstantial conditions surrounding the translation and transmission that unfolded around this text, and its way of dealing with problems of originality and authenticity. 'Rameau's Nephew' in and out of translation sparked a highly important debate about questions of what it means to be original, originary, and original-esque, and what it means to measure up to an original whose status has itself become questionable.

Works Cited

DENIS DIDEROT, *Le Neveu de Rameau. Dialogue. Ouvrage posthume et inédit* (Paris: Delaunay 1821) [ed. by Joseph-Henri de Saur and Léonce de Saint-Geniès, back-trans. from Goethe's German translation] <https://gallica.bnf.fr/ark:/12148/bpt6k1231405/f1.image.texteImage>

DENIS DIDEROT, *Rameaus Neffe/Le Neveu de Rameau*, French/German, trans. by Johann Wolfgang Goethe, ed. by Horst Günther (Frankfurt a/M: Insel, 1984)

DENIS DIDEROT, *Rameau's Nephew: A Multi-Media Edition*, trans. by Kate E. Turnstall and Caroline Warman, ed. by Marian Hobson (Cambridge: Open Book Publishers, 2014)

JOHANN WOLFGANG GOETHE, 'Nachträgliches zu "Rameaus Neffe"' in Goethe, *Sämtliche Werke nach Epochen seines Schaffens (Münchner Ausgabe)*, vol. 7, ed. by Norbert Miller and John Neubauer (Munich: Hanser, 1991), pp. 693–714

GEORGES-ARTHUR GOLDSCHMIDT, 'Scènes de la vie d'un traducteur', in Goldschmidt, *Un enfant aux cheveux gris: Entretiens avec François Dufay* (Paris: CNRS Éditions, 2008), pp. 73–82

HEINZ HAMM, 'Die französische Übersetzung und Kommentierung von Goethes Anmerkungen zu "Rameaus Neffe" von Diderot', *Weimarer Beiträge*, 29 (1983), 1309–15

DIETER LAMPING, *Die Idee der Weltliteratur: Ein Konzept Goethes und seine Karriere* (Stuttgart: Kröner, 2010)

NORBERT MILLER and JOHN NEUBAUER, 'Einleitung: Rameaus Neffe', in Johann Wolfgang Goethe, *Sämtliche Werke nach Epochen seines Schaffens (Münchner Ausgabe)*, vol. 7, ed. by Miller/Neubauer (Munich: Hanser, 1991), pp. 1064–88

GÜNTER OESTERLE, 'Goethe und Diderot: Camouflage und Zynismus. "Rameaus Neffe" als deutsch-französischer Schlüsseltext', in *Volk — Nation — Europa: Zur Romantisierung und Entromantisierung politischer Begriffe*, ed. by Alexander von Borman (Würzburg: Königshausen & Neumann, 1998), pp. 117–36

ULRICH RICKEN, 'Die französische Rückübersetzung des "Neveu de Rameau" nach der deutschen Übertragung von Goethe', *Beiträge zur Romanischen Philologie*, 15 (1976), 99–116

FRIEDRICH SCHLEIERMACHER, 'Ueber die verschiedenen Methoden des Uebersezens', in *Das Problem des Übersetzens*, ed. by Hans Joachim Störig (Darmstadt: Wissenschaftliche Buchgesellschaft, 1963), pp. 38–70

Notes to Chapter 19

1. Cf. Günter Oesterle, 'Goethe und Diderot: Camouflage und Zynismus. "Rameaus Neffe" als deutsch-französischer Schlüsseltext', in *Volk — Nation — Europa: Zur Romantisierung und Entromantisierung politischer Begriffe*, ed. by Alexander von Borman (Würzburg: Königshausen & Neumann, 1998), pp. 117–36 (p. 121).
2. Cf. Norbert Miller and John Neubauer, 'Einleitung: Rameaus Neffe', in Johann Wolfgang Goethe, *Sämtliche Werke nach Epochen seines Schaffens (Münchner Ausgabe)*, vol. 7, ed. by Miller/Neubauer (Munich: Hanser, 1991), pp. 1064–88 (p. 1068).

3. Left and middle columns: Denis Diderot, *Rameaus Neffe/Le Neveu de Rameau*, French/German, trans. by Johann Wolfgang Goethe, ed. by Horst Günther (Frankfurt a/M: Insel, 1984), pp. 30–31. Right column: Denis Diderot, *Le Neveu de Rameau. Dialogue. Ouvrage posthume et inédit* (Paris: Delaunay 1821) https://gallica.bnf.fr/ark:/12148/bpt6k1231405/f1.image.texteImage, pp. 30–31. Cf. a recent English translation of the same passage: 'ME — There isn't a single person who doesn't think like you, and who doesn't criticize the way things are, without thereby wishing himself out of existence. HIM — True.' Denis Diderot, *Rameau's Nephew: A Multi-Media Edition*, trans. by Kate E. Tunstall and Caroline Warman, ed. by Marian Hobson (Cambridge: Open Book Publishers, 2014), pp. 15–16.
4. Ulrich Ricken, 'Die französische Rückübersetzung des "Neveu de Rameau" nach der deutschen Übertragung von Goethe', *Beiträge zur Romanischen Philologie*, 15 (1976), 99–116.
5. Georges-Arthur Goldschmidt, 'Scènes de la vie d'un traducteur', in Goldschmidt, *Un enfant aux cheveux gris: Entretiens avec François Dufay* (Paris: CNRS Éditions, 2008), pp. 73–82 (p. 77).
6. Ricken, 'Die französische Rückübersetzung', p. 110.
7. Cf. Friedrich Schleiermacher, 'Ueber die verschiedenen Methoden des Uebersezens', in *Das Problem des Übersetzens*, ed. by Hans Joachim Störig (Darmstadt: Wissenschaftliche Buchgesellschaft, 1963), pp. 38–70.
8. Heinz Hamm, 'Die französische Übersetzung und Kommentierung von Goethes Anmerkungen zu "Rameaus Neffe" von Diderot', *Weimarer Beiträge*, 29 (1983), 1309–15 (p. 1310).
9. Johann Wolfgang Goethe, 'Nachträgliches zu "Rameaus Neffe"' in Goethe, *Sämtliche Werke nach Epochen seines Schaffens (Münchner Ausgabe)*, vol. 7, ed. by Norbert Miller and John Neubauer (Munich: Hanser, 1991), pp. 693–714 (p. 695).
10. In the 'Münchner Ausgabe', the editorial heading 'Nachträgliches zu "Rameaus Neffe"' ('Supplement to "Rameau's Nephew"') comprises all five texts.
11. 'An vorbemeldeter Stelle, so wie an manchen andern Orten, ist umständlicher ausgesprochen, daß ich obgenannten Dialog von Diderot aus einer Kopie des Original-Manuskriptes übersetzt, daß die Ausgabe des französischen Werkes aber unterblieben, doch von Zeit zu Zeit diese Lücke in der französischen Literatur bemerkt worden, bis endlich ein paar muntere Köpfe, im Jahre 1821, eine Rückübersetzung unternahmen und sie eine Zeitlang für das Original gelten ließen.' Goethe, 'Nachträgliches zu "Rameaus Neffe"', p. 701.
12. Goethe, 'Nachträgliches zu "Rameaus Neffe"', p. 701.
13. Goethe, 'Nachträgliches zu "Rameaus Neffe"', p. 701 and 695.
14. 'Durch dieses Umstellen jedoch, wird die Vergleichung des Übertragenen mit dem Original sehr erschwert, und es wird nicht deutlich, was eigentlich dem Deutschen und was den Franzosen angehöre.' Goethe, 'Nachträgliches zu "Rameaus Neffe"', p. 697.
15. 'Im Ganzen wird ihm [dem Leser] jedoch höchst merkwürdig und lehrreich erscheinen, wie diese guten jungen Männer, die mit Leidenschaft Deutschen Schriftstellern zugetan sind, oftmals, indem sie manches nach eigenem Sinne vortragen, den Zwiespalt Französischer und Deutscher Denkweise unbewußt aussprechen [...]; doch sucht ihr Urteil überall irgend eine Vermittelung.' Goethe, 'Nachträgliches zu "Rameaus Neffe"', p. 698.
16. 'Ihre deutsche Übersetzung dieser merkwürdigen Produktion ist so treu [...], um darnach Diderots Arbeit originalmäßig wieder herstellen zu können.' Goethe, 'Nachträgliches zu "Rameaus Neffe"', p. 705.
17. 'La traduction allemande que vous avez donnée de cet ouvrage remarquable es si fidèle [...] qu'il serait très-facile de reproduire textuellement Diderot.' Goethe, 'Nachträgliches zu "Rameaus Neffe"', p. 713.
18. Goethe, 'Nachträgliches zu "Rameaus Neffe"', p. 705.
19. Cf. Dieter Lamping, *Die Idee der Weltliteratur: Ein Konzept Goethes und seine Karriere* (Stuttgart: Kröner, 2010).
20. 'Aus Vorstehendem erkennt man den großen und unersetzlichen Schaden, welchen falsche, ganz oder halb erlogene Schriften im Publikum anrichten [...], die durch Annäherung an gewisse Originalitäten gerade das Bessere zu sich herabziehen, so daß das Mittelmäßige vom Vortrefflichen, das Schwache vom Starken, das Absurde vom Erhabenen nicht mehr zu scheiden ist.' Goethe, 'Nachträgliches zu "Rameaus Neffe"', p. 706.

21. 'Glücklicherweise fand man, in Merciers Tableau de Paris, eine Stelle welche sein Dasein außer Zweifel stellt [...]. Auch diese fügen wir übersetzt bei [...].' Goethe, 'Nachträgliches zu "Rameaus Neffe"', p. 709.
22. Goethe, 'Nachträgliches zu "Rameaus Neffe"', p. 712.

INDEX

9/11, 2001: 158, 166

Achilles 31
Aciman, André 41–42, 47
Ács, Bori 329n
Adams, James Noel 71n
Aeneas 31–34, 42
Aeschylus 21–23, 27, 31
Afghanistan 166
Africa 216
Afzal 60
Agassi, Joseph 285n
Aitken, Molly 68n
Akkadian 94n
al-'Aziz, Shah 'Abd 55
Alaol 54–55
Alexis, Willibald 347–48
Alferi, Pierre 343n
Allahabad 54
Allen, James 77–78
al-Jāḥiẓ 80
al-Lakhmi, Ibn Hisham 94n
Alvi, Tanvir Ahmad 70n
Amun 75
Anidjar, Gil 172
Antarctica 156
Antelme, Ruth-Schumann 94n
Anti-Semitism 315, 326
Appiah, Kwame Anthony 207, 216–17
Apple:
    Macintosh 173
    Siri 263
Apter, Emily 47, 114, 180, 243, 349–50, 352, 356
Apuleius 317
Arabia, South 94n
Arabic 52–53, 54, 55, 57, 59, 79–80, 94n, 274, 301
    Andalusian 94n
    Egyptian 94n
    Maghribian 94n
    Poetry 79–80
    Western dialects 94n
    Yemenite 94n
Arab world 9
Arany, János 319
Archer, Carol M. 217
Ariosto, Ludovico 292
Armenia 351, 356

Arndt, Walter 134–36, 139n, 143
Arruzza, Cinzia 204n
Artaud, Antonin 341, 343
Artificial Intelligence 263–64
Ascanius 34
Ashcroft, Bill 220n
Ashkenazim 273–74
Asia 210
    East 52
    South 51–52
    Southeast 65, 124
Assmann, Jan 93n
Attanucci, Timothy 204n
Attar, Fariduddin 57
Attila 251
Auerbach, Erich 328n
Auster, Paul 342
Austin, J. L. 191, 192–94, 197, 199, 203n
Avadh 53
Avadhi 53, 54
Avidan, David 264
Azov, Andrei 138n

Babel 304, 335
Babylon 80
Bacon, Francis 123
Badawi, el-Said 94n
Baer, Brian James 128, 137n
Bailey, Michael 288
Bakardjieva, Maria 285n
Baker, Mona 17n, 154n, 202n, 357n
Baker, Sir Richard 153n
Bakhsh, Ilahi 55
Bakhtin, Mikhail 71n, 176, 313, 315
Ballard, Michel 308n
Balmont, Konstantin 299, 303
Bangha, Imre 70n
Barańczak, Stanisław 153n
Barnstone, Willis 150
Baroque 122, 153n
Barrett, Arthur 71n
Barrett, Douglas 188n
Barthes, Roland 3, 176, 227, 288
Barwin, Gary 146
Bashō, Matsuo 142, 146–47
Bass, Alan 203n
Bassnett, Susan 3, 16n, 68n

Baudelaire, Charles 64, 141, 150, 158–62, 171, 175, 224
Bay of Bengal 54
Bazzanella, Carla 92n
Beaulieu, Derek 146
Beckett, Samuel 112–14
Behl, Aditya 69n
Behn, Aphra 34
Béládi, Miklós 329n
Belfast 36–37, 39, 287, 290
Belgium 253
Belle, Marie-Alice 153n
Belloc, Hilaire 258n
Bellos, David 157, 171
Bengali 54–55
Bengio, Yoshua 269
Benjamin, Walter 11, 35, 106, 108, 144, 176, 182, 224, 251, 350, 352–53
Benkō, Loránd 329n
Benveniste, Emile 197
Bergvall, Caroline 144–48, 154n
Berlant, Lauren 188n
Berlin 347–48
Berlina, Alexandra 188n
Berman, Antoine 12, 17n, 243–44, 246–47, 251, 255
Bermann, Sandra 154n, 358n
Berry, George Ricker 285n
Bervin, Jen 172
Berwick, Robert C. 117n
Bhabha, Homi K. 189–92
Bhakti 59
Bhojpuri 59
Bialik, Chaim Machman 157
Bible 1, 12, 141, 144, 306, 317
    Deuteronomy 279
    Epistles of Paul 358
    Exodus 282
    Genesis 280–81, 318
    Torah / Pentateuch 279–82
    Wycliffite 287
Bielsa, Esperança 16n
Bilgrami, Ghulam Ali Azad 70n
Birkbeck, University of London 288
Black, Jeremy 94n
Blanchot, Maurice 114
Bloom, Harold 45, 187n
Bly, Robert 166, 172
Blyth, Reginald Horace 154n
Boase-Beier, Jean 9, 251
Boethius, Anicius Manlius Severinus 153n
Bohn, William 89
Boileau-Despréaux, Nicolas 126
Bök, Christopher 148
Bolshevik Revolution 128
Bonnefoy, Yves 227, 307, 311n
Borges, Jorge Luis 267, 347, 350, 354
Borkent, Mike 154n

Borman, Alexander von 366
Bougainville, Louis Antoine de 210
Boulanger, Pier-Pascale 258n
Boyce, Bret 328n
bpNichol 143, 146
Bradbury, Steve 181
Brajbhasha 52–53, 55, 59, 61, 62, 64
Bratislava 321
Brecht, Bertolt 149
Breitwieser, Wolfgang 298, 303
Brière, J. L. J. 362
Briggs, Kate 3, 18n, 142
Brillat-Savarin, Jean Anthelme 211
Briseis 31
Bristol 347
British Museum 302
Broda, Martine 260n
Brontë, Charlotte 17n
Brooks, Cleanth 170
Brower, Reuben A. 17n
Brown, Barclay 188n
Brown, Hilary 69n
Brown, William Edward 125–26
Browning, Elizabeth Barrett 4, 10, 21–24, 27–28, 30–31, 35, 42, 45
Browning, Robert 22, 27
Brzostowska-Tereszkiewicz, Tamara 153n
Buddhism 144
    Sutras 1
    Zen 281
Buden, Boris 189–91
Bulgakov, Mikhail 136
Burgess, Anthony 153n
Burke, Michael 222, 228–29
Burton, Tim 251
Busch, Allison 68n, 70n
Butler, Judith 11, 190–200
    Excitable Speech 193–97
    'Restaging the Universal' 195
Byron, Lord George Gordon 129, 302
    Don Juan 129

Cadiot, Olivier 343n
Cage, John 282
Callender, John 94n
Callimachus 325
Calvino, Italo 146, 293n
Cameron, David 143, 158–62, 166, 171
Canada 146, 228
Caracciolo, Antoine 288, 292
Caracciolo, Enriqué 288
Carducci, Giosuè 354
Caro, Annibale 31–33, 46
Carpo, Mario 36
Carroll, Lewis 245–46, 248, 252, 254
Carson, Anne 149, 156, 159, 170, 171

Carson, Ciaran 10, 36–40, 42, 47
Carver, Terrell 203n
Casarino, Cesare 204n
Cassin, Barbara 16n, 243
Catalonia 293
Catholicism 212–13, 318
Cato, Dionysus 153n
Catullus 319
Caucasus 21, 65
Cavell, Stanley 203n
Cazamian, Louis 298, 304
Cesarco, Alejandro 146
Cezanne, Paul 225
Chabouts, L. and F. 220n
Chamberlain, Lori 3
Chambers, Samuel A. 203n
Chan, Sandee 174
Chapelle, Dave 192
Charles V 288
Chaucer, Geoffrey 288
Chauvin, Catherine 47
Chaze, Rai 11, 208–18
Chen, Kai 285n
Chesterman, Andrew 12
Cheung, Martha P. Y. 16n
Cheyfitz, Edward 3, 17n
Chinese (Mandarin) 8, 11, 102, 113, 141, 144, 148, 301, 305
  in relation to English 173–82
  in relation to Japanese 163–65
  Poetry 163
Chomsky, Noam 104–05
Christianity 121, 125, 210, 313, 317–18, 326
Chun, Maureen 204n
Church Slavonic 124–25
Clark, Katerina 128
Clark, T. J. 39, 47, 147
Cliff, William 253
Cobb, Allison 148
Cohen, Sharmilla 143
Cohen, Shirit Avitan 285n
Colchester 287
Cold War 11, 130, 133–35
Coleman, Jen 148–49
Coleridge, Ernest H. 308n
Coleridge, Samuel Taylor 12, 297–307
Coleridge, Sara 299
Colligan, Colette 187n
Collini, Stefan 288
Collins, Martha 140, 149
Collins, Sophie 3
Colne 289
Communism 319
Computational Linguistics 262
Computational Literature 264
Computer Science 262, 265, 274

Congregation of the Sacred Hearts of Jesus and Mary 212
Contardi, Federico 94n
Conte, Gian Biagio 313
Conté, Nicolas-Jacques 210
Cook, James 212–13
Cooper, Lane 310n
Coptic 80
Corriente, Federico 93n–94n
Cort, John D. 54, 68n
Counter Reformation 122
Cowley, Abraham 30, 34
Cowper, William 22
Creasman, Pearce Paul 94n
Creusa 31–34, 42
Critchley, Simon 26, 45
Cronin, Michael 16n, 36, 47, 122
Crook, John 46
Crosby, Harry 163
Csehy, Zoltán 314, 321
Culler, Jonathan 17n
Cusset, François 344n
Czigány, Lóránt 329n
Czuczor, Gergely 329n

Dante Alighieri 8, 37, 47, 130, 141, 142, 144–46
Darras, Jacques 298, 304, 306
David (King) 287
Davidson, Donald 308n
Davis, Lydia 4, 10, 40–42, 47
Davis, Paul 34
Dawn of the Dead 292
d'Hangest, Germain 298, 304
d'Hubert, Thibaut 54–55
de Bruijn, Thomas 69n
de Buck, Adriaan 153n
de Gaulle, Charles 209–10
de Man, Paul 26, 45
De Quincey, Thomas 348–49, 357n
de Saint-Geniès, Léonce 360–65
de Saur, Joseph-Henri 360–65
de Segrais, Jean Regnault 29, 32–33, 46
Dean & Son 245
Dean, Jeffrey 285n
Deane-Cox, Sharon 16n, 18n
Def Comedy Jam 203n
Defoe, Daniel 123
Dehaene, Stanislaus 117n
Dehlawi, Shah Waliullah 55
Delers, Olivier 137n
Deleuze, Gilles 157, 171, 176, 331, 336
Delhi 55, 61
Dembeck, Till 154n
Denham, Sir John 29–30, 34, 46
Depping, Georg Bernhard 360, 364
Derieg, Aileen 202n

Derrida, Jacques 24, 25–28, 35, 36, 45, 46, 97–100, 103, 105, 109, 112, 114, 142, 165, 172, 176, 191–94, 198–99, 203n, 204n, 243, 304
  Acts of Religion 165, 172
  De la grammatologie [*Of Grammatology*] 25–26, 97–98
  Limited Inc 191–94
  L'oreille de l'autre [*The Ear of the Other*] 297
  Marges de la philosophie [*Margins of Philosophy*] 193, 203n
  'Survivre' ['Living On / Border Lines'] 26, 35, 114
Descartes, René 264
Desmet, Mieke 256
Deutsche Guggenheim 145
Deutsches Wörterbuch 16n
Devatine, Flora 219n
Devil, the 135
Devy, Ganesh N. 51–52
Dickens, Charles 127, 288
Dickinson, Emily 143
Diderot, Denis 13, 359–66
Dido 31–33
Dillon, Wentworth, 4th Earl of Roscommon 31
Dodson, Katrina 4
Donne, John 149
Doolittle, Eliza 264
Dostoevsky, Fyodor Mikhailovich 123–24, 127
Dowland, John 287
Doyle, Sir Arthur Conan 187n
Drummond, Clara 45
Drury, Annmarie 5, 243–44
Dryden, John 7, 10, 21, 27, 28–35, 39–40, 46
Du Bellay, Joachim 12, 286–88
Ducasse, Isidore, *see* Lautreamont, Comte de
Ducrot, Oswald 199
Duran, Angelica 16n
Dutch 29, 125, 153n
Dutton, E. P. 134
Dworkin, Craig 153n, 187n

East Anglia, University of 290
East Asia, *see* Asia, East
Eden, Garden of 225
Edmond, Jacob 176
Eco, Umberto 2, 24, 45, 130, 259n
Éditions Gallimard 331
Edwardian era 246
Efroimson, Vladimir Pavlovich 129–30
Egypt 10, 12, 159, 282
  Ancient writing 72–90
  Egyptology 10–11, 81
  Middle Kingdom of 77
Elden, Stuart 188n
Elliot, Allison 162, 171
Ellis, Steve 145
Emberling, Geoff 92n
Emmerich, Karen 7, 10, 24, 45

Engels, Friedrich 128
England 245, 348
English 8, 11, 12, 22–25, 27, 29, 31, 37, 39–40, 52, 63–64, 99, 106–08, 110, 113–14, 121, 123, 125–26, 131, 140–41, 143–45, 149, 168, 209–10, 274, 297, 306, 307
  American English 161, 166, 171
  Belfast English 39
  in relation to Chinese 173–82
  in relation to French 159–62, 245–55, 331–42
  in relation to German 336, 347–49, 354–55
  in relation to Hebrew 262–79
  in relation to Hungarian 322
  in relation to Japanese 163–65
  in relation to Persian 221–22, 228–29
  in relation to Russian 121, 123, 125–26, 131
  Old English 247
  Weblish 175, 180
Enmarch, Roland 94n
Enzensberger, Hans Magnus 153n
Epstein, Mikhail 176
Erman, Adolf 93n
Ernst, Carl W. 68n
Esperanto 36
Essex, University of 286–89, 292–93
Etkind, Efim 129
Eurasia 122
Europe 8–9, 52, 59, 64, 78, 93n, 121–23, 125, 128, 141, 143, 209, 348
  Eastern 128, 318
  Eurocentricity 93n
  Europeanisation 212, 214
  European languages 80
  Europeans 59
  Modernism 142
  Northern 125
  Western 122
European Parliament 1
Evans, Jonathan 47
Evens, Aden 118n
Eyre, Christopher 88

Fales, Frederick M. 94n
Faludy, György 314, 321–26
Fantham, Elaine 328n
Fare Vāna'a 217
Faust, Johann Georg 136
Faye, Jean-Pierre 343n
Feeley, Jennifer 176
Fellini, Federico 321, 325
Felman, Shoshana 199
Ferrante, Elena 24
Ferry, Jules 258n
Fielding, Henry 123
Fink, Thomas 171
Finland 122

Finnish 36
Firth, John Rupert 269
First World War 37, 165, 353
Fischer-Lichte, Erika 199
Flamant, Ludovic 251–54, 260n
Flaubert, Gustave 40–41
Fleissner, Robert F. 310n
Florence, Penny 111–12
Florentine 37
Florida 304
Floring, John 5
Floyd, Kevin 204n
Foer, Jonathan Safran 143
Fogarasi, János 329n
Folkart, Barbara 244
Follain, Jean 36–40
Forster, Anthony 292
Fort, Camille 298, 304
Foucault, Michel 130, 187n, 343n, 344n, 350
Fowler, Roger 17n
France 174, 258n, 344n
Franchi, Stefano 285n
Frederick Warne & Co 245
Freedman, Des 288
French 2, 8, 12, 13, 23–25, 31–32, 36, 40, 99, 110, 113–14, 121, 124, 126, 144, 147, 158–64, 166, 173, 208, 212, 243, 244, 293n, 298–99, 301, 303–04, 306, 310, 315, 317
   in relation to English 159–62, 245–55, 331–42
   in relation to German 359–66
   in relation to Persian 224
   in relation to Russian 121, 124, 126
   Middle French 164, 253
   Modernism 164
   Old French 164
French Polynesia 210–11, 213–14, 219n, 220n
Freud, Sigmund 331, 346–47
Friedberg, Maurice 124
Frogier, Johanne 215, 218
Frost, Robert 157, 221
Frost, William 31

Gabriel (angel) 60
Gabrielli, Aldo 16n
Gábor, Devecseri 320
Gachechiladze, Givi 137n
Gâcon, Gérard 298, 304
Gada, Yusuf 69n
Gaelic 348
Gaiman, Neil 244, 248–52
Galicia, Eastern Europe 165
Gamgohi, ʿAbdul Quddus 57–58
Ganjavi, Nizami 60
Gardiner, Alan 74–75, 85, 87
Gaskill, Howard 357n
Gauguin, Paul 210

Gauvain, Jean-Luc 269
Gehl, Robert W. 285n
Genghis Khan 299
Genoa 301
Gentzler, Edwin 176
Geoffrey of Monmouth 307
George, Andrew 94n
Gerber, Richard 302
German 2, 5, 8, 12, 13, 23–25, 106–08, 110, 123, 125, 146, 165–66, 247, 298–99, 303, 310, 314, 322, 333, 337, 339
   Expressionism 165
   in relation to English 336, 347–49, 354–55
   in relation to French 359–66
   in relation to Russian 121, 123, 125
Germany 348–49
Gibbons, Reginald 227
Giovanardi, Claudio 70n
Gladding, Jody 158, 167–68, 172
Glissant, Édouard 217–18
Gnedich, Tatiana 129
God 57–58, 79, 81, 86, 132, 135, 212, 281–82, 317
Goethe, Johann Wolfgang von 13, 123, 359–66
Goldberg, Leah 157, 170
Goldenberg, G. 94n
Golding, Arthur 5
Goldschmidt, Georges-Arthur 361
Goldsmith, Kenneth 153n, 173
Goldsmith, Oliver 63
Goldstein, Anna 24
Goldwasser, Orly 82
Gomidas [Komitas or Soghomon Soghomonian] 353–54
Gong, Haomin 184
Google 270–73, 275
   News 272–73
   Translate 7, 272
Göranssen, Johannes 4–5, 157, 170
Gorey, Edward 244, 251–55
Gorky, Maxim 128
Gould, Rebecca 93n
Graf, Arturo 353–56
Graham, Joseph F. 172, 310n
Gramling, David 8
Grande Dizionario Italiano 16n
Grapow, Hermann 93n
Grass, Thierry 308n-309n
Grassi, G. F. 94n
Greece 93n
Greek 22–23, 30, 92n, 193, 310n, 340, 355
   Ancient 123, 149, 159, 229, 314, 317, 321–22, 324–25
Greene, Ian 258n
Griffith, Francis 81–82
Griffiths, Gareth 219n
Griggs, Earl Leslie 310n
Grimly, Gris 249
Gródek, Ukraine 165

Groote, Brecht de 357n
Grossman, Évelyne 343n
Gruss, Eyal 271
Guattari, Félix 157, 171
Guérin-Mueller 245
Guest, Jennifer 172
Gussow, Mel 260n
Günther, Horst 367n
Güzeldere, Güven 285n

Hachette Book Group 245
Habermas, Jürgen 190, 191
HBO 203n
Hafez 221
Hagan, Edward 45
Hakluyt, Richard 301
Halliday, Michael 7–8
Halpern, Daniel 142
Hamedani, Ayn al Quzat 222–23
Hamm, Heinz 367
Hammarberg, Gitta 137n
Hammond, Paul 28, 46
Hann, Chris 137n
Hare, David 5
Harman, Gilbert 308n
Harrison, Tony 27
Hart, John 259n
Hartman, Geoffrey 45
Hawkes, David 141
Hawkey, Christian 143, 158, 165–67, 168, 172
Hayes, Julie Candler 28, 46
Hayles, Katherine 187n
Hayot, Eric 350
Heaney, Seamus 145, 288
Hebrew 12, 92n, 156–57, 168, 170, 333, 337, 339
    Biblical 263, 279–82
    in relation to English 262–79
Hegel, Georg Wilhelm Friedrich 193, 195
Heinzelman, Kurt 37, 40, 47
Heise, Ursula K. 358n
Helen of Troy 325
Helgerson, Richard 293n
Henry, William 213
Hercules 317
Hermans, Theo 2, 3, 68n, 153n
Herranz, Arturo Agüero 298, 303
Heseltine, Michael 316
Hess, Linda 70n
Heyerdahl, Thor 210
Hieroglyphs 72–90
Higgins, Dick 72
Hill, John Spencer 308n
Hilton, James 307
Hindavi, 53–55, 57–61
Hindi 53, 59, 60–64
Hinds, Martin 94n

Hiraizumi, Masako 163
Hiro, Henri 208, 213, 214, 218
Hiroshima 350
Hobbs, Jerry R. 279
Hobson, Marian 367n
Hodgson, Marshall 70n
Hofer, Jen 163, 171
Hofmann, Michael 142
Hofmeyr, Isabel 16n
Hofstadter, Douglas R. 16n, 144–46
Holman, Michael 251
Holmes, Sherlock 182, 187n, 349
Holquist, Michael 328n
Holz, Arno 349
Homer 1, 8, 22, 28, 323
Honneth, Axel 203n
Hooker, E. N. 46
Hopkins, David 28–30, 46
Horace 28, 141, 320, 323–24
Horáček, Josef 154n
Horváth, István Károly 314, 319–22, 324–26
Hosington, Brenda M. 153n
Hsia Yü 11, 173–85
Hsieh, Lili, 176
Hudson, Ronald 45
Hughes, Ted 225
Hulbert, James 45
Hung, Eva 358n
Hungarian 12, 312–27
Hungarian Soviet Republic 317, 319
Hungary 313, 319–22, 325
Hurford, James R. 117n

Iamandi, Petru 299, 303
Ibykos 149
Ignatov, Sergei 92n
Illinois 350
India 9, 10, 51–55, 59, 62–63, 65
    Indian languages 51–53, 63
    North India 52–55, 59, 62, 65
Intelligent Personal Assistants 263
Internet 263
Iran 222, 226, 233
Iraq 80, 166
Ireland 287–88, 290
Irish 36–37
Iron Curtain 130
Isaac 281
Islam 59
Israel 156, 273, 279, 280, 282
Issa, Islam 16n
Iswolsky, Helene 329n
Italian 2, 12, 23–25, 31, 32, 37, 130, 299, 301–03, 310n, 317
    in relation to Armenian 354
    Futurism 185

Italy 314, 318

Jackson, Holbrook 258n
Jacobs, Adriana X. 3, 155n
Jahangir 54
Jain, Saskya Iris 204n
Jainism 53, 54
Jakobson, Roman 17n, 221
Jandl, Ernst 146, 143
Janeiro, Pedro António 299, 303
Janse, Mark 71n
Japan 183, 350
Japanese 8, 147, 163–65, 310n
    Haikus 279
    Modernism 163
JavaScript 107, 111, 274–76
Jayasi, Malik Muhammad 69n
Jerusalem Bloomfield Science Museum 265
Jibril 60
John of the Cross 150, 212
Johnson, Kent 350
Johnson, Mark 9
Johnston, David Jhave 176
Jones, William 54, 63
Joosen, Vanessa 258n, 259n
Jost, François 170
Jowett, Benjamin 358n
Judaism 279–80
Juhaz, Ferenc 225
Jullien, Dominique 47
Junge, Friedrich 93n
Juvenal 28, 319, 324

Kagemni 85–86
Kahn, Robert 16n
Kalstone, David 353
Kamuf, Peggy 308n, 310n
Kanji 183
Kant, Immanuel 195, 348, 357n
Kaplan, Robert B. 171
Kappler, Claire 309n
Kar, Parfulla C. 202n
Kara 59
Karamzin, Nikolai 137n
Karatzogianni, Athina 188n
Karl, Rebecca E. 204n
Kaufman, Shirley 156, 170
Kelley, Philip 45
Kellman, Steven G. 176
Kennedy, Stephen 177, 179–80
Key, Alexander 93n
Kilito, Abdelfattah 93n
Kimmel, Jimmy 131
King Jr., Martin Luther 191–92, 202n, 271–72
Kirsanov, Semen 143
Kishangarh 70n

Kleppe, Martin 275
Koch, Roland 92n
Kopacki, Andrzej 153n
Kostionova, Marina 127
Kothari, Rita 71n
Knight, G. Wilson 310n
Kripke, Saul 308n
Krongaus, Maksim 131–32
Kublai Khan 293n, 297–307
Kuntsman, Adi 188n

Lacan, Jacques 130
Lach, Donald F. 309n
Laclau, Ernesto 202n, 203n
Lakoff, George 9
Lal, Vinay 137n
Lamping, Dieter 367n
Lapita-Taiwanese hypothesis 210
La Porta, S. 93n
Lasdun, James 142
Lateef-Jan, Katie 47
Latin 7, 23, 27–29, 32, 34, 121, 125, 153n, 193, 292, 301, 306
    in relation to Hungarian 312–27
Latin America 163
Latium 34
Latour, Bruno 130
Lautreamont, Comte de 180
Lawlor, Leonard 117n
Lear, Edward 244–48, 252
Lebanon 274
Lecercle, Jean-Jacques 258n, 260n, 344n
Le Clézio, Jean-Marie Gustave 343n, 344n, 345n
Lee, Tong King 176
Leese, Simon 55, 68n
Leeteg, Edgar 210
Lefebvre, Henri 188n, 220n
Lefevere, André 128
Legault, Paul 143
Lehto, Leevi 36, 47, 274
Leighton, Lauren 128
Lennon, John 292
Leopardi, Giacomo 150
Lepper, Verena 94n
Leppihalme, Ritva 216
Lermontov, Mikhail 127
Lessing, Lawrence 179
Lestrade, Claude 220n
Lethem, Jonathan 187n
Lévi-Strauss, Claude 97–98, 187n, 204n
Levine, Suzanne Jill 47
Levine-Keating, Helane 41, 47
Levy, Lital 71n
Lewiński, Marcin 93n
Lewis, Philip E. 243
Lewis, Scott 45

Li, Chen 176
Linley, Margaret 187n
Lispector, Clarice 4
Litaudon-Bonnardot, Marie-Pierre 245, 258n, 259n
Liu, Lydia H. 18n, 117n
Lloyd, Moya 203n
Loffredo, Eugenia 16n
Loire 287–88
Lomonosov, Mikhail 126
London 347
London Missionary Society 212
London Underground 149
Loprieno, Antonio 72, 93n
Lowell, Robert 159–60, 171
Lowes, John Livingstone 309n
Loxley, James 203n
Loy, Mina 163
Lucien Stryk Asian Translation Prize 172
Lucretius 28
Luzi, Mario 299, 303

Mac Low, Jackson 143
Macpherson, James 348
Mahe, Ciáran 154n
Maioli, Chiara 187n
Maithili 55
Makdisi, Saree 204n
Makine, Andreï 349
Mallarmé, Stéphane 111, 113, 123, 345n
Mallol, Christophe Serra 212
Malte-Brun, Conrad 309n
Malukdas 59–60
Man, John 309n
Mandeville, John 309n-310n
Manovich, Lev 179
Mā'ohi 208, 212–13, 215, 219n
Marbach, Alfred 330n
Marbury, Herbert Robinson 202n
Marchal, Bertrand 345n
Mari, Syria 94n
Marks, Alfred H. 146
Marot, Clément 144–45
Marquesas Islands 213–14
Mars (god) 292
Marseillaise, La 153n
Martin, Frédéric 260n
Martindale, Charles 6, 27, 38, 45
Martinville 42
Marx, Karl 128
Marxism 129, 319
Mascolo, Dionys 343n, 344n
Masorti Europe 285n
Matheson, William 146
Mathews, Harry 13, 148, 287, 351
  '35 Variations on a Theme from Shakespeare' 148
  Armenian Papers 13, 347, 351–56

Trial Impressions 287
Mathews, Jackson 17n, 171
Mathews, Marthiel 171
Matthiessen, Christian M. I. M. 7, 30
McCaffery, Steve 146
McCall, Ian 349
McDonald, Angela 88
McDonald, Christie V. 308n
McEvoy, Sebastian 204n
McGee, Vern W. 71n
McHugh, Heather 37
McKinsey & Company 286
McKitterick, David 45
McSweeney, Joyelle 156–57, 168, 170
Meads, Joseph 170
Mediterranean 65
Mehlman, Jeffrey 203n, 344n
Meltzer, Edmund 93n
Ménard, Philippe 309n
Mendelssohn, Anna 293
Menippus of Gadara 313
Mercier, Louis-Sébastien 365
Mertner, Edgar 298, 303
Merwin, W. S. 37, 40, 47
Meschonnic, Henri 243–44, 255, 258n, 306
Michael, Saint 352
Midan, Michel 298, 304
Middle Ages 245
Middleton, Christopher 37, 40, 47
Miklashevskii, Ilya 138n
Mikolov, Tomas 270–72
Miller, J. Hillis 199
Miller, Norbert 366
Milohnić, Aldo 203n
Milton, John 310n
Min 183
Miraji 64
Mizrahim 65, 273–74
Moati, Raoul 204n
Močnik, Rastko 203n
Mohammed, Dina 93n
Moncrieff, Scott 41
Mongolia 299, 301–02, 305
Mongolian 301
Montague, Richard 279
Montaigne, Michel de 5
Monti, Enrico 16n
Montreal 343n
Moore, David Chioni 16n
Moore, Gerald 188n
Mor, G. 285n
Mordvintsev, Alexander 285n
More, Thomas 310n
Morin, Frédéric 269
Mormonism 212, 213
Morra, Lucia 92n

Morris, Daniel 187n
Moses 79, 279
Mother Earth 323
Moule, Arthur Christopher 309n
Moure, Erín 4
Mrauk-U 54
Mughal 54, 62
Munday, Jeremy 17n
Muscovite kingdom 125

Nabokov, Vladimir Vladimirovich 11, 133–36
Nádasdy, Ádám 330n
Nagari script 55
Nagaridas (Savant Singh) 61–62
Nagy, Gábor O. 329n
Naiman, Antoly 139n
Najman, Hindy 159, 171
Nakayasu, Sawako 143, 147–48, 158, 163–66, 168–69, 171, 172
   The Collected Poems of Chika Sagawa 168–69, 171
   Mouth: Eats Color: Sagawa Chika Translations, Anti-Translations, and Originals 158, 163–66, 168–69, 171, 172
   'Promenade' 142, 147–48
Nasser, Ramsey 274
Nechvatal, Joseph 177–78, 180, 184
Nepos, Cornelius 314
Netherlands 125
Neubauer, John 366
Neubauer, Peter B. 354
Newton, Isaac 123
New York 174, 343n
New York Review of Books, The 41, 134–35
New Zealand 212, 220n, 274
Niranjana, Tejsawini 3
Nodelman, Perry 249
Normandy 37
North America 9, 166
Northern Ireland 37
Norton, David 16n

Oesterle, Günter 366n
Ogilby, John 31–33, 46
Oittinen, Riitta 249–50
Olah, Christopher 285n
Olson, Jonathan R. 16n
O'Neill, Patrick 16n
Ong, Walter 97, 117n
Ono, Yoko 292
Orcus 317
Orientalism 51, 63
Ortega, Ramón López 298, 303
Orthodoxy, Russian 121, 125
Ortony, Andrew 45
Orwell, George 130
Ottoman Empire 125

Oulipo 162, 254, 258n, 260n, 262, 283, 287, 293n, 351
Ovid 5, 27, 28, 30, 31, 141, 142, 287, 289, 319
Oxford 41, 323
Oxford English Dictionary 16n, 309n
Oxyrhynchus, Egypt 159

Pacific 210, 214, 219n
Palissot (Charles Palissot de Montenoy) 363
Papini, Gianni A. 358n
Paraizs, Júlia 330n
Paris 350, 360, 362, 365
Parisot, Henri 298, 304, 306
Parkinson, Richard 94n
Parry, Amie Elizabeth 179–80
Parsons, T. W. 145
Partridge, A. C. 16n
Pastior, Oskar 143
Paterson, Don 4
Pathak, Shridhar 63–64
Patrick, John M. 310n
Patterson, Cyril 147
Paul the Apostle 358n
Paulhan, Jean 343n
Pauthier, Guillaume 304
Pauwels, Heidi C. 61–62
Paz, Octavio 16n, 163
Peacock, Margaret 135
Pelliot, Paul 309n
Pellò, Stefano 68n, 70n
Penguin Classics *Poets in Translation* 141
Perec, Georges 351
Perloff, Marjorie 148, 350
Perry, Seamus 310n
Persian 12, 52–64, 221–22, 228, 230, 233, 235, 301
Persius 319
Perteghella, Manuela 16n
Pessoa, Fernando António Nogueira 4
Peter I, Tsar 122, 124, 125, 130, 137n
Petrie, William 82
Petronius 12, 313–27
Pharaoh's daughter (wife of Solomon) 287
Phillips, Carl 150
Picasso, Pablo 225
Pierssens, Michel 343n
Pincott, Frederic 71n
Pisan dialect 301
Plato 98, 358n
Playboy 134
Plutarch 28
Polgár, Anikó 329n
Polish 153n, 154n
Polo, Marco 293n, 299–305, 309n
Polynesia 208, 210, 212, 213, 214, 219n, 220n
Pontalis, Jean-Bertrand 331
Pope, Alexander 22
Popovič, Anton 347

Porter, Catherine 154n, 204n
Portuguese 12, 299, 303
Postgate, Nicholas 94n
Potter, Robert 22
Pound, Ezra 27, 143, 174, 282
Poussin, Nicolas 147
Praz, Mario 299, 303–04
Princen, Anne 171
Princeton, New Jersey 235
Prins, Yopie 22–23, 45
Prisse Papyrus 85
Procopi, Nickolas 101–04
Prometheus 21, 289
Protestantism 212–13
Proust, Marcel 40–42, 106, 110, 293
Prufer, Kevin 149
Puerto Rico 343n
Purchas, Samuel 299–302
Pushkin, Alexander 11, 122, 125–26, 127, 134–35, 221
Putin, Vladimir 125, 131
Pym, Anthony 176, 358n

Queneau, Raymond 148, 150, 293n, 343n
Quinn, David B. 309n
Quirke, Stephen 78
Qur'an 55, 57, 58, 79
Qutban 54, 58

Rabelais, François 321
Rachmaninoff, Sergei 154n
Racine, Pierre 309n
Racz, Gregory 5
Rājkunwar 69n
Ram, Harsha 71n
Ramanujan, A. K. 51–52
Ramayana 52
Rambelli, Paolo 154n, 347–49
Rambosson, Yvanhoe 224
Rameau, Jean-Philippe 359–60
Ramusio, Giovanni Battista 301
Rankin, Herbert David 330n
Raslin, Ghulam Nabi 62–63
Rassokina, Elena 138n
Rath, Brigitte 349
Raworth, Tom 293
Récanati, François 308n
Reddy, Michael 24–26, 45
Reid, Christopher 143
Reiss, Katharina 17n
Rekhta 61
Relihan, Joel C. 328n
Renaissance, European 121, 123
Restoration 362
Révay, József 313, 317–20, 324–26
Revel, Judith 343n
Rey, Alain 343n, 344n

Reynolds, Matthew 90, 141, 150, 222, 225, 259n, 287
Ricci, Ronit 71n
Richard, Earl of Lauderdale 32–33, 46
Richards, I. A. 141
Richardson, Samuel 123
Richman, Paula 68n
Ricken, Ulrich 361, 367n
Rimbaud, Arthur 287
Ritchie, David 18n
Ritter, Valerie 70n, 71n
Robinson, Douglas 3, 9, 28, 38, 46, 154n, 347–48, 350
Robinson, Peter 89
Rogers, Carl 264
Rogue Factorial 163, 171
Rollins, Jonathan 176
Romanian 12, 299, 303, 310n
Romanticism 123, 145, 348
Rome 30, 93n, 286–88, 323
Rónay, László 329n
Roscommon's Academy 31
Rosenschein, Stanley J. 285n
Rossini, Stéphane 94n
Roubaud, Jacques 254–55
Rousseau, Jean-Jacques 26
Routledge 245
Rowe, Will 288
Ruaeus, Carolus 32–33, 46
Russia 11, 12, 121–25, 128, 130, 134
Russian 12, 121–33, 221, 299, 303, 310n, 333, 337, 339
Russolo, Luigi 188n
Rustichello da Pisa 301

Sabiron, Céline 16n, 47
Sagawa, Chika 143, 147, 163–65, 168–69, 171, 172
Sakai, Naoki 3, 6–8, 35, 38, 46
Saldanha, Gabriela 154n, 202n, 357n
Samoa 220n
Sanguineti, Edoardo 325
San Lazzaro, Venice 353
Sanskrit 52–53, 55, 62, 63, 64
Sappho 159, 171
Sartre, Jean-Paul 343n
Sato, Hiroaki 16n, 142, 155n
Saura, Bruno 215
Saussure, Ferdinand de 105, 113
Saussy, Haun 89
Scandinavia 122
Scarpa, Federica 18n
Scarry, Elaine 334
Scherr, Barry 138n
Schlaf, Johannes 349
Schlegel, August Wilhelm 5
Schleiermacher, Friedrich 361
Schmeling, Gareth 329n
Schneider, Elisabeth 310n
Schnyder, Peter 16n

Schofield, Katherine Butler 62, 68n
Schwenk, Holger 269
Schwitters, Kurt 174
Scott, Clive 7, 16n, 24, 45, 222–27
Scott, Sir Walter 347–48
Second World War 104
Sedgwick, Eve Kosofsky 199
Selim, Samah 70n
Selzer, Richard 334
Semitic languages 94n
Senécal, Jean-Sébastien 269
Serianni, Luca 70n
Seth, Catriona 16n
Sethe, Kurt 93n, 94n
Sewell, Elizabeth 244
Shackle, C. S. 70n
Shafii Kadkani, Mohammad Reza 12, 221–22, 226–28
Shah, Husain 54
Shakespeare, William 1, 5, 8, 123, 141, 143, 148, 175, 221
    Romeo and Juliet 200
    Sonnets 143, 180
Shangdu 299
Sharmi, Sunil 70n
Sharqi dynasty 54
Shaver, Chester Linn 309n
Shaw, George Bernard 264
Sheikh, Samira 69n, 70n
Sherlock (software) 173–74, 180–84, 187n
Sherwood, Mary Martha 258n
Shi, Hu 176
Shisha-Halevy, Ariel 94n
Shklovsky, Victor 180
Shlesinger, Miriam 358n
Shohat, Ella 93n
Shore, John, 1st Baron Teignmouth 68n
Shortsleeve, Kevin 260n
Short Story of the Father and the Crocodiles, The 76–87
Shulman, D. 93n
Simeoni, Daniel 358n
Simon, Sherry 3, 251
Simoniti, Jure 203n
Sinuhe 74
Sipe, Lawrence R. 259n
Slavic languages 121
Sloman, Albert 292
Small, Margaret 309n
Smalley, William A. 16n
Smith IV, Jack 285n
Smith, Anna Marie 203n
Smith, Helen 153n
Sneferu, Pharaoh 85
Snyder, Edward 310n
Socialist Realist art 129
Socrates 358n
Solomon 287

Somerset 299
South America 210
Soviet Union 122, 125, 128, 129–30, 134
Spanish 12, 298–99, 310n
    Mexican Spanish 247
Spicer, Jack 143
Spitz, Chantal 219n
Spivak, Gayatri Chakravorty 45, 207
Sreenivasan, Ramya 68n, 69n
St André, James 3, 9
St Petersburg 122, 128
St-Pierre, Paul 202n
Stalin, Joseph 129
Stalinism 123
Stalling, Jonathan 176
Stam, Robert 93n
Stančič, Suzana 203n
Steiner, George 255
Stern, Daniel N. 343n
Sterne, Laurence 123
Stevens, Wallace 144
Stevenson, Warren 309n
Stewart, Susan 150
Stewart, Tony K. 69n
Steyerl, Hito 189, 202n
Stiller, Robert 153n
Structuralism 97
Sturge, Kate 202n
Suetonius 314
Sufism 53, 57, 59, 61
Sumarokov, Alexander 124
Sutskever, Ilya 285n
Swain, Simon 71n
Swanwick, Anna 23
Swedenberg, Jr., H. T. 46
Swensen, Cole 150
Swift, Jonathan 293, 307
Sze, Arthur 150
Székely, István 313–16, 326
Szepessy, Tibor 330n
Szymborska, Wisława 150

Tabbi, Joseph 118n
Tahir-Gürçağlar, Şehnaz 349
Tahiti 11, 207–18
    Chinese community in 210, 212–13, 220n
Taipei 174
Taiwan 11, 174–76, 181–83
Taoism 149, 150
Taylor, Astra 203n
Teeter, Emily 73
Tehran 228, 235
Theocritus 28
Thiolier-Méjean, Suzanne 309n
Thirlwell, Adam 16n, 143
Thomas, L. H. C. 348

Thomason, Richmond H. 285n
Thutmose III 75
Tieck, Ludwig 5
Tiffin, Helen 219n
Tigges, Wim 258n, 260n
Tikhomirova, Yulia 137n
Times, The 293
Titunik Irwin R. 139n
Tivari, Bhanupratap 55–56
Tolkien, J. R. R. 307
Tolstoy, Lev Nikolayevich [Leo] 123–24, 127, 292
Tonson, Jacob 31
Toremans, Tom 349
Tourny, Gideon 3, 349
Toyama, Jean 220n
Trakl, Georg 165–67, 172
Translation Studies 2, 3, 9, 27–28, 51, 151, 190, 297, 347–49
Trediakovsky, Vasilii 124, 126
Trésor de la langue française informatisé 16n
Trifone, Pietro 70n
Trivedi, Harish 10, 52–53, 56, 189
Troy 29, 31, 33, 34, 314
Troyes 288
Trump, Donald 131
Truschke, Audrey 68n
Trusk, Willard R. 328n
Tsou, Zona Yi-Ping 175
Tsu, Jing 188n
Turgenev, Ivan 123–24, 127
Turing, Alan 263–64
Turkish 301
Tunstall, Kate E. 367
Tuscan 37, 301
Tyka, Mike 285n
Tymoczko, Maria 3, 220n
Tzara, Tristan 174
Tzu, Chuang 148, 149

Ugly Duckling Presse 158
Ulmer, Gregory L. 117n
Unbelievable Alligator 158
United Kingdom 64, 286–87
    British Army 287
United Nations 1
United States 11, 12, 93n, 122, 131–32, 135, 143, 158, 163, 166, 173, 216, 245, 274, 350
    US English, *see* English, American
Urale, Sima 220n
Urdu 53, 55, 59, 61, 62, 64
Urizen 286

Valles, Alissa 150
Valverde, José María 298, 303
Vanacker, Beatrijs 349
Vas, István 320

Vauthier, Étienne 298, 304
Venice 293n, 299, 353, 355–56
    Venetian dialect 301
Venus (goddess) 210, 325
Venuti, Lawrence 2, 8, 46, 128, 255
Vermeer, Hans J. 17n
Victorian era 244, 246
Vietnam 293
Viitamäki, Mikko 69n
Villon, François 326
Virgil 7, 28–35, 37, 39, 141, 150, 323–24
Virot, Benoît 260n

Wachtel, Andrew 127
Waisman, Sergio Gabriel 285n
Walkowitz, Rebecca 140
Walsh, Peter G. 323
Warman, Caroline 367n
Warner, Marina 288
Warren, Robert Penn 170
Warren, Rosanna 155n
Watson, Ellen Doré 150
Watt, Ian 123, 124
Watt, William C. 93n
Weaver, Warren 184
Webb, Lindsey 172
Weber, Samuel 203n
Webster, Augusta 23
Weeks, Kathi 204n
Wei, Wang 144
Weil, Peggy 264
Weinberger, Eliot 16n, 144–47, 163
Weissbort, Daniel 242n
Weizenbaum, Joseph 263–64
Welles, Orson 304
Weng, A. 175
Wershler, Darren 154n
Whitman, Walt 66
    'To a Stranger' 64
Wieseltier, Meir 156–57, 170
Wikipedia 1
Wilkinson, Richard H. 94n
Williams, Alan 221, 228
Wilson, Edmund 135
Witt, Susanna 137n, 138n
Wolf, Uljana 143
Wolfson, Louis 12, 331–42
Wood, Michael 358n
Woods, Christopher 92n
Woods, Michelle 18n
Word2Dream 269, 271–73, 282–83
Word2Vec 270–73
Wordsworth, William 301
World Literature 128
Worthen, John 310n
Wright, Chantal 142

Wright, James 166, 172
Würtz, Ádám 314

Yang, Xin 184
Yasusada, Araki 350
Yeh, Michelle 176
Yeshurun, Avot 168, 172
Yiddish 344n
Young, Robert 3, 8, 35–36, 47
YouTube 1
Yuan dynasty 301

Zamacona, Carlos Gracia 89
Zappulla, Elio 145
Zapruder, Matthew 156
Zhukovsky, Vasilii 123
Zionism 272
Zipes, Jack 258n
Zipoli, Riccardo 70n
Žižek, Slavoj 202n–203n
Zuhayr, Ka'b ibn 55
Zukofsky, Celia 143
Zukofsky, Louis 143, 282

www.ingramcontent.com/pod-product-compliance
Lightning Source LLC
Chambersburg PA
CBHW080910170426
43201CB00017B/2279